Lecture Notes in Computer Science 3576

Commenced Publication in 1973
Founding and Former Series Editors:
Gerhard Goos, Juris Hartmanis, and Jan van Leeuwe

Kousha Etessami Sriram K. Rajamani (Eds.)

Computer Aided Verification

17th International Conference, CAV 2005
Edinburgh, Scotland, UK, July 6-10, 2005
Proceedings

Springer

Volume Editors

Kousha Etessami
University of Edinburgh
School of Informatics
Laboratory for Foundations of Computer Science
EH9 3JZ, Scotland, UK
E-mail: kousha@inf.ed.ac.uk

Sriram K. Rajamani
Microsoft Research
One Microsoft Way
Redmond, WA 98052, USA
E-mail: sriram@microsoft.com

Library of Congress Control Number: 2005928168

CR Subject Classification (1998): F.3, D.2.4, D.2.2, F.4.1, I.2.3, B.7.2, C.3

ISSN 0302-9743
ISBN-10 3-540-27231-3 Springer Berlin Heidelberg New York
ISBN-13 978-3-540-27231-1 Springer Berlin Heidelberg New York

Springer is a part of Springer Science+Business Media

springeronline.com

Printed in Germany

Typesetting: Camera-ready by author, data conversion by Scientific Publishing Services, Chennai, India
Printed on acid-free paper SPIN: 11513988 06/3142 5 4 3 2 1 0

Preface

This volume contains the proceedings of the International Conference on *Computer Aided Verification* (CAV), held in Edinburgh, Scotland, July 6–10, 2005. CAV 2005 was the seventeenth in a series of conferences dedicated to the advancement of the theory and practice of computer-assisted formal analysis methods for software and hardware systems. The conference covered the spectrum from theoretical results to concrete applications, with an emphasis on practical verification tools and the algorithms and techniques that are needed for their implementation.

We received 123 submissions for regular papers and 32 submissions for tool papers. Of these submissions, the Program Committee selected 32 regular papers and 16 tool papers, which formed the technical program of the conference.

The conference had three invited talks, by Bob Bentley (Intel), Bud Mishra (NYU), and George C. Necula (UC Berkeley). The conference was preceded by a tutorial day, with two tutorials:

- Automated Abstraction Refinement, by Thomas Ball (Microsoft) and Ken McMillan (Cadence); and
- Theory and Practice of Decision Procedures for Combinations of (First-Order) Theories, by Clark Barrett (NYU) and Cesare Tinelli (U Iowa).

CAV 2005 had six affiliated workshops:

- BMC 2005: 3rd Int. Workshop on Bounded Model Checking;
- FATES 2005: 5th Workshop on Formal Approaches to Testing Software;
- GDV 2005: 2nd Workshop on Games in Design and Verification;
- PDPAR 2005: 3rd Workshop on Pragmatics of Decision Procedures in Automated Reasoning;
- RV 2005: 5th Workshop on Runtime Verification; and
- SoftMC 2005: 3rd Workshop on Software Model Checking.

Publications of workshop proceedings were managed by their respective chairs. In addition to the workshops, a special tools competition called "Satisfiability Modulo Theories Competition" was held for tools implementing decision procedures for combinations of theories. A preliminary report on this competition is included in this volume.

The CAV 2005 banquet was dedicated to Prof. Ed Clarke on his 60th birthday.

CAV 2005 was supported by generous sponsorships from IBM, Microsoft, the J. von Neumann Minerva Center for Verification of Reactive Systems at the Weizmann Institute, Intel, Jasper Design Automation, Synopsys and Cadence Design Systems. We are grateful for their support. We would like to thank the Program Committee members and the subreferees for their hard work in evaluating the submissions and the selection of the program. We also thank the Steering Committee and the chairs of CAV 2004 for their help and advice.

For logistical support we are grateful to the staff at the School of Informatics, University of Edinburgh, the National eScience Centre in Edinburgh, and to the support staff of Microsoft Research's Conference Management Toolkit.

July 2005 Kousha Etessami and Sriram K. Rajamani

Organization

Program Committee

Thomas Ball, Microsoft Research
Alessandro Cimatti, Istituto per la Ricerca Scientifica e Tecnologica, Italy
Edmund M. Clarke, Carnegie Mellon University, USA
E. Allen Emerson, University of Texas at Austin, USA
Kousha Etessami, University of Edinburgh, UK (Co-chair)
Patrice Godefroid, Bell Labs, USA
Susanne Graf, Verimag, France
Orna Grumberg, Technion, Israel
Nicolas Halbwachs, Verimag, France
John Hatcliff, Kansas State University, USA
Thomas A. Henzinger, EPFL, Switzerland and U. California at Berkeley, USA
Gerard J. Holzmann, NASA Jet Propulsion Laboratory, USA
Somesh Jha, University of Wisconsin, USA
Robert B. Jones, Intel, USA
Daniel Kroening, Carnegie Mellon University, USA
Orna Kupferman, Hebrew University, Israel
Robert Kurshan, Cadence, USA
Marta Kwiatkowska, University of Birmingham, UK
Rupak Majumdar, University of California at Los Angeles, USA
Sharad Malik, Princeton University, USA
Ken McMillan, Cadence Berkeley Labs, USA
Kedar Namjoshi, Bell Labs, USA
John O'Leary, Intel, USA
P. Madhusudan, University of Illinois at Urbana-Champaign, USA
Doron Peled, University of Warwick, UK
Sriram K. Rajamani, Microsoft Research, USA (Co-chair)
Jakob Rehof, Microsoft Research, USA
Harald Ruess, Stanford Research Institute, USA
Mooly Sagiv, Tel Aviv University, Israel
Stefan Schwoon, University of Stuttgart, Germany
Ofer Strichman, Technion, Israel
Helmut Veith, Technical University of Munich, Germany
Thomas Wilke, Kiel University, Germany
Yaron Wolfsthal, IBM Research, Israel
Yunshan Zhu, Synopsys, USA

Steering Committee

Edmund M. Clarke, Carnegie Mellon University, USA
Mike Gordon, University of Cambridge, UK
Robert Kurshan, Cadence, USA
Amir Pnueli, New York University, USA, and Weizmann Institute, Israel

Sponsors

IBM
Microsoft
John von Neumann Minerva Center for Verification of Reactive Systems, Weizmann Institute
Intel
Jasper Design Automation
Synopsys
Cadence Design Systems

Referees

Nina Amla
Flemming Andersen
Roy Armoni
Tamarah Arons
Eugene Asarin
Ismail Assayad
Mohammad Awedh
Roberto Bagnara
Sharon Barner
C. Bartzis
Eli Bendersky
Sergey Berezin
Mikhail Bernadsky
Piergiorgio Bertoli
Dirk Beyer
Armin Biere
Per Bjesse
Patricia Bouyer
Marius Bozga
Marco Bozzano
Glenn Bruns
Roberto Bruttomesso
Jeremy Casas
Paul Caspi
Krishnendu Chatterjee
Yirng-An Chen
Hana Chockler
Ching-Tsun Chou
Mihai Christodorescu
Michael Codish
Jamieson M. Cobleigh
Byron Cook
Scott Cotton
Leonardo de Moura
Deepak D'Souza
Dennis Dams
Thao Dang
Jyotirmoy Deshmukh
Juergen Dingel
Laurent Doyen
Ashvin Dsouza
Xiaoqun Du
Marie Duflot
Bruno Dutertre
Orit Edelstein
Cindy Eisner
Javier Esparza
Marco Faella
Jean-Claude Fernandez
David Fink
Alain Finkel
Jeff Fischer
Kathi Fisler
Dana Fisman
Cormac Flanagan
Ranan Fraer
Anders Franzen
G. Frehse
Zhaohui Fu
Vinod Ganapathy
Hubert Garavel
Danny Geist
Samir Genaim
Blaise Genest
Roman Gershman
Ziv Glazberg
Benny Godlin
Eugene Goldberg
Denis Gopan
Pascal Gribomont
Alex Groce
Jim Grundy
Sumit Gulwani
Aarti Gupta
Anubhav Gupta

Z. Han
Rene Rydhof Hansen
Steve Haynal
Tamir Heyman
Hkan Hjort
Pei-Hsin Ho
Michael Huth
Nili Ifergan
Radu Iosif
Amatai Irron
Franjo Ivančić
Subramanian Iyer
Christian Jacobi
Radha Jagadeesan
Himanshu Jain
Bertrand Jeannet
Sumit K Jha
Ranjit Jhala
Rajeev Joshi
Georg Jung
Tommi Junttila
Marcin Jurdzinski
Vineet Kahlon
Roope Kaivola
Sara Kalvala
Timothy Kam
Gila Kamhi
Sujatha Kashyap
Stefan Katzenbeisser
Stefan Kiefer
Mike Kishinevsky
Nils Klarlund
Gerwin Klein
Alfred Koelbl
Barbara König
Maya Koifman
Steve Kremer
Moez Krichen
Sava Krstic
Antonín Kučera
Ralf Küsters
Salvatore La Torre
David Lacey
Shuvendu K. Lahiri
Yassine Lakhnech
Ranko Lazic
Flavio Lerda
Tal Lev-Ami
Ninghui Li
Alexey Loginov
Yuan Lu
Yoad Lustig
Michael Luttenberger
Markus Müller-Olm
Stephen Magill
Yogesh Mahajan
Oded Maler
Roman Manevich
Freddy Mang
Shawn Manley
Darko Marinov
Wim Martens
Vaibhav Mehta
Orly Meir
Alice Miller
Antoine Mine
Priyank Mishra
Manav Mital
David Monniaux
In-Ho Moon
Mark Moulin
Laurent Mounier
Matthieu Moy
Madan Musuvathi
Anders Möller
Aleks Nanevski
Ziv Nevo
Robert Nieuwenhuis
Gethin Norman
Dirk Nowotka
Albert Oliveras
Alfredo Olivero
Avigail Orni
Sam Owre
Robert Palmer
Seungjoon Park
Dave Parker
Holger Pfeifer
Nir Piterman
Carl Pixley
Andreas Podelski
Vinayak Prabhu
Shaz Qadeer
Hongyang Qu
Ishai Rabinovitz
C.R. Ramakrishnan
Silvio Ranise
Rajeev K Ranjan
Kavita Ravi
Pascal Raymond
Noam Rinetzky
Robby
Edwin Rodriguez
Marco Roveri
Shai Rubin
Andrey Rybalchenko
Vadim Ryvchin
Hassen Saidi
Ramzi Ben Salah
Christian Schallhart
Karsten Schmidt
Roberto Sebastiani
Simone Semprini
Koushik Sen
Alexander Serebrenik
Sanjit Seshia
Ohad Shacham
Natasha Sharygina
Ilya Shlyakhter
Sharon Shoham
Vigyan Singhal
Nishant Sinha
Anna Slobodova
Fabio Somenzi
Maria Sorea
Jeremy Sproston
Alin Ştefănescu
Ken Stevens
Scott Stoller
Zhendong Su
D. Suwimonteerabuth
Don Syme
Muralidhar Talupur
Daijue Tang
Andrei Tchaltsev

Prasanna Thati
Ashish Tiwari
Richard Trefler
Stavros Tripakis
Ashutosh Trivedi
Oksana Tymchyshyn
Rachel Tzoref
Shmuel Ur
Noppanunt Utamaphethai
Moshe Vardi
Tatyana Veksler
Srikanth Venkateswaran
Mahesh Viswanathan
Thomas Wahl
Dong Wang
Poul Williams
Yaron Wolfsthal
Nicolas Wolovick
Howard Wong-Toi
Avi Yadgar
Eran Yahav
Jin Yang
Karen Yorav
Greta Yorsh
Håkan Younes
Yinlei Yu
Yunshan Zhu

Table of Contents

Invited Talks

Tools Competition

Abstraction and Refinement

Bounded Model Checking

Tool Papers I

Verification of Hardware, Microcode, and Synchronous Systems

Games and Probabilistic Verification

Tool Papers II

Decision Procedures and Applications

Automata and Transition Systems

Tool Papers III

Program Analysis and Verification I

Program Analysis and Verification II

Applications of Learning

Randomized Algorithms for Program Analysis and Verification

George C. Necula and Sumit Gulwani

Department of Electrical Engineering and Computer Science,
University of California, Berkeley
{necula, gulwani}@cs.berkeley.edu

Program analysis and verification are provably hard, and we have learned not to expect perfect results. We are accustomed to pay this cost in terms of incompleteness and algorithm complexity. Recently we have started to investigate what benefits we could expect if we are willing to trade off controlled amounts of soundness. This talk describes a number of randomized program analysis algorithms which are simpler, and in many cases have lower computational complexity, than the corresponding deterministic algorithms. The price paid is that such algorithms may, in rare occasions, infer properties that are not true. We describe both the intuitions and the technical arguments that allow us to evaluate and control the probability that an erroneous result is returned, in terms of various parameters of the algorithm. These arguments will also shed light on the limitations of such randomized algorithms.

The randomized algorithms for program analysis are structured in a manner similar to an interpreter. The key insight is that a concrete interpreter is forced to ignore half of the state space at each branching point in a program. Instead, a random interpreter executes both branches of a conditional and combines the resulting states at the join point using a linear combination with random weights. This function has the property that it preserves all linear invariants between program variables, although it may introduce false linear relationships with low probability. This insight leads to a quadratic (in program size) algorithm for inferring linear relationships among program variables, which is both simpler and faster than the cubic deterministic algorithm due to Karr (1976). This strategy can be extended beyond linear equality invariants, to equality modulo uninterpreted functions, a problem called global value numbering. This results in the first polynomial-time algorithm for global value numbering (randomized or deterministic).

These ideas have application in automated deduction as well. We describe a satisfiability procedure for uninterpreted functions and linear arithmetic. Somewhat surprisingly, it is possible to extend the randomized satisfiability procedure to produce satisfying models for the satisfiable problems, and proofs for the unsatisfiable problems. This allows us to detect by proof checking all instances when the randomized algorithm runs unsoundly.

We will also show that it is possible to integrate symbolic and randomized techniques to produce algorithms for more complex problems. We show that in this manner we can extend in a natural way randomized algorithms to interprocedural analyses.

K. Etessami and S.K. Rajamani (Eds.): CAV 2005, LNCS 3576, p. 1, 2005.

Validating a Modern Microprocessor
Extended Abstract

Bob Bentley

2111 N.E. 25th Avenue, Hillsboro, Oregon 97124, U.S.A.
bob.bentley@intel.com

1 Introduction

The microprocessor presents one of the most challenging design problems known to modern engineering. The number of transistors in each new process generation continues to follow the growth curve outlined by Gordon Moore 40 years ago. Microarchitecture complexity has increased immeasurably since the introduction of out-of-order speculative execution designs in the mid-90s; and subsequent enhancements such as Hyper-Threading (HT) Technology, Extended Memory 64 Technology and ever-deeper pipelining indicate that there are no signs of a slowdown any time soon. Power has become a first-order concern thanks to a 20x increase in operating frequencies in the past decade and leakier transistors at smaller geometries, and the various schemes for managing and reducing power while retaining peak performance have added their own dimensions of complexity.

2 Microprocessor Design

Microprocessor design teams vary widely in size and organizational structure. Within Intel, implementing a new microarchitecture for the IA-32 product family typically requires a peak of more than 500 design engineers across a wide range of disciplines - logic and circuit design, physical design, validation and verification, design automation, etc. – and takes upwards of 2 years from the start of RTL coding to initial tape-out. Many of the same engineers, plus specialists in post-silicon debug, test, product engineering, etc. are needed to get from first silicon to production, which typically takes between 9 and 12 months. The product then has to be ramped into high-volume manufacturing, at a run rate of tens of millions of units per quarter, and sustained until end of life. The overall cycle is significantly longer than the time (roughly 24 months) between successive semiconductor process generations.

3 Microprocessor Validation

Microprocessor validation starts early in the design cycle – these days, even before the start of RTL coding. Validation engineers are involved in microarchitecture definition, helping to prevent architectural bugs and produce a more validatable design. On our most recent design, we have for the first time deployed formal tools and methods – built around Lamport's TLA - during the microarchitecture definition phase.

K. Etessami and S.K. Rajamani (Eds.): CAV 2005, LNCS 3576, pp. 2–4, 2005.

Most validation starts with the first release of RTL code. For a new microprocessor, code is typically created and released in a number of carefully planned phases, over the course of approximately one year. We rely heavily on Cluster Test Environments (CTEs) to allow us to do microarchitecture validation on logically related subsets of the design, which provides for a much greater degree of controllability than full chip and also decouples each cluster from the others. Even after a full chip model is available, we continue to focus much of our dynamic validation effort and cycles at the cluster level, since controllability in the later pipeline stages of an out-of-order machine will always be a significant issue. During the RTL development phase of the project, we have also started to deploy SAT checking as bug-finding tool.

4 Formal Verification

The Pentium® 4 processor was the first project of its kind at Intel where we deployed Formal Property Verification (FPV) as a mainstream validation technique during CPU development. Hitherto, FPV had only been applied retroactively, as was done for the FP divider of the Pentium® Pro processor. We focused on the areas of the design where we believed that FV could make a significant contribution – in particular, the floating-point execution units and the instruction decode logic. Bugs in these areas had escaped detection on previous designs, so this allowed us to apply FPV to some real problems with real payback.

A major challenge for the FPV team was to develop the tools and methodology needed to handle a large number of proofs in a highly dynamic environment. The RTL model is constantly changing due to feature additions or modifications, bug fixes, timing-induced changes, etc. By the time we taped out we had over 10,000 proofs in our proof database, each of which had to be maintained and regressed as the RTL changed over the life of the project.

Though our primary emphasis was on proving correctness rather than bug hunting, FPV had found close to 200 logic bugs by the time we taped out. This was not a large number in the overall scheme of things (we found almost 8000 bugs total), but about 20 of them were "high quality" bugs that we do not believe would had been found by any other of our pre-silicon validation activities. Two of these bugs were classic floating-point data space problems:

- The FADD instruction had a bug where, for a specific combination of source operands, the 72-bit FP adder was setting the carryout bit to 1 when there was no actual carryout
- The FMUL instruction had a bug where, when the rounding mode was set to "round up", the sticky bit was not set correctly for certain combinations of source operand mantissa values, specifically:
  src1[67:0] := X*2(i+15) + 1*2i
  src2[67:0] := Y*2(j+15) + 1*2j
  where i+j = 54, and {X,Y} are any integers that fit in the 68-bit range

These bugs could easily have gone undetected, not just in the pre-silicon environment but in post-silicon testing also.

5 Future Challenges

Validating the next generation of microprocessors is going to be a real challenge. One area that we are exploring is the development of a more abstract level of microarchitectural specification to help us in this task - both to slow the rate of growth for bugs from its historical trend line and to enable us to find bugs earlier in the design cycle. We are already applying formal methods at a higher level of abstraction during the microarchitecture definition phase of the project.

We are also looking to increase the contribution of formal verification to the overall validation effort. We are developing combined FPV and dynamic verification plans whose implementation will be coordinated so that we apply the best approach to the problem at hand. We are counting on the next generation of FPV tools like gSTE to provide greater capacity, thus reducing the effort needed to decompose problems into a tractable form. In addition, we are applying SAT solver technology for bug hunting (falsification), especially in combination with dynamic verification.

References

1. Lamport, L: The Temporal Logic of Actions. ACM Transactions on Programming Languages and Systems 16, 3, May 1994.
2. Colwell, R.P. and Brennan, R: Intel's Formal Verification Experience on the Willamette Development. Proceedings of the 13th International Conference on Theorem Proving in Higher Order Logics, August 2000.
3. Bentley, B: Validating the Intel® Pentium® 4 Microprocessor. Proceedings of the International Conference on Dependable Systems and Networks, June-July 2001.
4. Burns, D.: Pre-Silicon Validation of Hyper-Threading Technology. Intel Technology Journal, Volume 6, Issue 1, February 2002.
5. Kaivola, R and Narasimhan, N: Verification of Pentium®4 Multiplier with Symbolic Simulation & Theorem Proving. Proceedings of the Design, Automation and Test in Europe Conference, March 2002
6. Bentley, B: High Level Validation of Next-Generation Microprocessors. Seventh Annual IEEE International Workshop on High Level Design, Validation and Test, October 2002.
7. Schubert, T: High Level Formal Verification of Next-Generation Microprocessors. Proceedings of the 40th Design Automation Conference, June 2003.

Algorithmic Algebraic Model Checking I: Challenges from Systems Biology*

C. Piazza[1], M. Antoniotti[2], V. Mysore[2], A. Policriti[1], F. Winkler[4], and B. Mishra[2,3]

[1] Dept. of Mathematics and Computer Science, University of Udine, Udine, Italy
[2] Courant Institute of Mathematical Sciences, NYU, New York, NY, U.S.A.
[3] Dept. of cell Biology, School of Medicine, NYU, New York, NY, U.S.A.
[4] Research Inst. for Symbolic Computation, J. Kepler University, Linz, Austria
{piazza, policriti}@dimi.uniud.it, winkler@risc.uni-linz.ac.at,
{marcoxa, vm40, mishra}@nyu.edu

Abstract. In this paper, we suggest a possible confluence of the theory of hybrid automata and the techniques of algorithmic algebra to create a computational basis for systems biology. We describe a method to compute bounded reachability by combining Taylor polynomials and cylindric algebraic decomposition algorithms. We discuss the power and limitations of the framework we propose and we suggest several possible extensions. We briefly show an application to the study of the Delta-Notch protein signaling system in biology.

1 Prologue

Presently, there is no clear way to determine if the current body of biological facts is sufficient to explain phenomenology. In the biological community, it is not uncommon to assume certain biological problems to have achieved a cognitive finality without rigorous justification. In these particular cases, rigorous mathematical models with automated tools for reasoning, simulation, and computation can be of enormous help to uncover cognitive flaws, qualitative simplification or overly generalized assumptions. Some ideal candidates for such study would include: prion hypothesis, cell cycle machinery (DNA replication and repair, chromosome segregation, cell-cycle period control, spindle pole duplication,

* The work reported in this paper was supported by grants from NSF's Qubic program, NSF's ITR program, Defense Advanced Research Projects Agency (DARPA), Howard Hughes Medical Institute (HHMI) biomedical support research grant, the US Department of Energy (DOE), the US Air Force (AFRL), National Institutes of Health (NIH) and New York State Office of Science, Technology & Academic Research (NYSTAR). F.W. was partially supported by the Austrian Science Foundation (FWF) under the research project DET (P16357-N04). C.P. was partially supported by MIUR FIRB grant RBAU018RCZ and the MIUR PRIN'04 grant 2004013015.

K. Etessami and S.K. Rajamani (Eds.): CAV 2005, LNCS 3576, pp. 5–19, 2005.

etc.), muscle contractility, processes involved in cancer (cell cycle regulation, angiogenesis, DNA repair, apoptosis, cellular senescence, tissue space modeling enzymes, etc.), signal transduction pathways, circadian rhythms (especially the effect of small molecular concentration on its robustness), and many others.

Fortunately, similar issues had been tackled in the past by other disciplines: verification of VLSI circuits, hybrid supervisory controllers, robotics, etc. Yet, biology poses new challenges. The most interesting biology combines unimaginable diversity with an understanding of molecular events in minute detail. A single base-pair change can influence the folding of a protein, and alter the femtosecond dynamics of any of a tangle of interacting macromolecules. Of course, a system of millions of ordinary differential equations (ODEs) and their accurate simulation via numerical integration will not have much effect on uncovering the key biological insights. What sort of natural computational abstractions of biological systems can then be most effective? Can we understand biology by "simulating the biologist, and not biology"?

1.1 Biological Models

The central dogma of biology is a good starting point for understanding a mathematical formalism for biochemical processes involved in gene regulation. This principle states that biochemical information flow in cells is unidirectional—DNA molecules code information that gets transcribed into RNA, and RNA then gets translated into proteins. To model a regulatory system for genes, we must also include an important subclass of proteins (transcription activators), which also affects and modulates the transcription processes itself, thus completing the cycle. We can write down *kinetic mass-action* equations for the time variation of the concentrations of these species, in the form of a system of *ODEs* [10, 14, 23]. In particular, the transcription process can be described by equations of the *Hill* type, with its Hill coefficient n depending on the *cooperativity* among the transcription binding sites. If the concentrations of DNA and RNA are denoted by x_M, y_M, etc., and those of proteins by x_P, y_P, etc., then the relevant equations are of the form:

$$\dot{x}_M = -k_1 x_M + k_3 \frac{1 + \theta y_P^n}{1 + y_P^n} \tag{1}$$

$$\dot{x}_P = -k_2 x_P + k_4 x_M \tag{2}$$

where the superscripted dots denote the time-derivatives.

Each equation above is an algebraic differential equation consisting of two algebraic terms, a positive term representing synthesis and a negative term representing degradation. For both RNA and DNA, the degradation is represented by a linear function; for RNA, synthesis through transcription is a highly nonlinear but a rational Hill-type function; and for proteins, synthesis through translation is a linear function of the RNA concentration. In the equation for transcription, when $n = 1$, the equations are called *Michaelis-Menten* equations; y_P denotes the concentration of proteins involved in the transcription initiation of the DNA, k_1 and k_2 are the forward rate constants of the degradation of RNA and proteins respectively, k_3 and k_4 are the rate constants for RNA and protein synthesis and θ models the saturation effects in transcription.

If one knew all the species x_i involved in any one pathway, the mass-action equations for the system could be expressed in the following form

$$\dot{x}_i = f_i(x_1, x_2, \ldots, x_n), \qquad i = 1, 2, \ldots, n$$

When the number of species becomes large, the complexity of the system of differential equations grows rapidly. The integrability of the system of equations, for example, depends on the algebraic properties of appropriate bracket operations [19, 18]. But, we can approximately describe the behavior of such a system using a *hybrid automaton* [2, 21]. The "flow", "invariant", "guard", and "reset" conditions can be approximated by algebraic systems and the decision procedures for determining various properties of these biological systems can be developed using the methods of symbolic algorithmic algebra.

1.2 Intercellular Communication

Communication between adjacent cells are used by biological systems in coordinating the roles, which can be ultimately assigned to any individual cell. For instance, in both vertebrates as well as invertebrates, lateral inhibition through the Delta-Notch signaling pathway leads to cells, starting initially in uniform distribution, to differentiate into "salt-and-pepper" regular-spaced patterns. In a communication mechanism employing lateral inhibition, two adjacent cells interact by having one cell adopt a particular fate, which in turn inhibits its immediate neighbors from doing likewise. In flies, worms and vertebrates, the transmembrane proteins Notch and Delta (or homologs) mediate the reaction, with Notch playing a receptor with its ligand being a Delta protein on a neighboring cell.

Thus, imagine that one has a description of this system in terms of a state-space, its dynamics (i.e. rules for flows and state transitions), and the subregion of its state space corresponding to a desired property (e.g., fine-grained patterning of cells in a neighborhood). The *first* interesting question would be whether the model adequately predicts that, when started in a biologically reasonable initial state with all the model parameters assuming some known values, this system actually evolves into the subregion encoding the desired properties. If it does, the *second* question to ask would be whether one can completely and succinctly characterize all possible regions ("backward-reachable region") from which the system also evolves into the desired subregion. The volume of such a region, its symmetry and other invariants may tell us quite a lot about those properties of the underlying biological system, which may have attributed to its selective advantages. Furthermore, the model is now amenable to verification by wet-lab experimentation involving the creation and analysis of mutants (in the genes/proteins of relevance), some of which may "live" inside the reachable region and others outside. To answer the first question, a good numerical simulation tool suffices. However, it is less clear how best the second problem should be solved computationally.

In a simplified continuous time model, the changes to the normalized levels of Notch $n_{P,X}$ and Delta $d_{P,X}$ activity in a cell X can be expressed as the ODEs $\dot{n}_{P,X} = \mu[f(\bar{d}_{P,X}) - n_{P,X}]$ and $\dot{d}_{P,X} = \rho[g(n_{P,X}) - d_{P,X}]$, where

$$\bar{d}_{P,X} = \frac{1}{\#\mathcal{N}(X)} \sum_{X' \in \mathcal{N}(X)} d_{P,X'}, \; f(x) = \frac{x^k}{a + x^k}, \; g(x) = \frac{b}{b + x^h},$$

with $\mathcal{N}(X)$ being the set of neighboring cells of the cell X and μ, ρ, a, $b > 0$, k, $h \geq 1$. Note that f monotonically increases from 0 to 1 and g monotonically decreases from 1 to 0 as x takes increasing value from 0 to ∞ (see Collier et al. [9] for details of the model). Collier et al. concluded that the feedback loop was adequate for generating spatial patterns from random stochastic fluctuations in a population of initially equivalent cells, *provided that feedback is strong enough*. Though they also observed that the model does not account for the longer-range patterns.

In a related computational analysis, Ghosh et al. [11] proposed a piecewise linear approximation to the continuous time model to generate a hybrid automaton. On this automaton, they conducted a symbolic reachability analysis using SAL - a heuristic symbolic decision procedure, to characterize the reachable region by numerical constraints, further sharpening the observations of [9]. Our model described below, shows that the reachable set computed by Ghosh et al. lacks a completeness in description.

2 Technical Preliminaries

2.1 Semi-algebraic Hybrid Automata: Syntax

The notion of *hybrid automata* was first introduced as a model and specification language for systems with both continuous and discrete dynamics, i.e., for systems consisting of a discrete program within a continuously changing environment. A useful restriction is through the notion of *semi-algebraic hybrid automata* whose defining conditions are built out of polynomials over the reals, and reflect the algebraic nature of the DAEs (differential algebraic equations) appearing in kinetic mass-action models of regulatory, metabolic and signal transduction processes.

Definition 1. Semi-algebraic Hybrid Automata. *A k-dimensional* hybrid automaton *is a 7-tuple, $H = (Z, V, E, Init, Inv, Flow, Jump)$, consisting of the following components:*

- *$Z = \{Z_1, \ldots, Z_k\}$ a finite set of variables ranging over the reals $\mathbb{R}$; $\dot{Z} = \{\dot{Z}_1, \ldots, \dot{Z}_k\}$ denotes the first derivatives with respect to the time $t \in \mathbb{R}$ during continuous change; $Z' = \{Z'_1, \ldots, Z'_k\}$ denotes the set of values at the end of a discrete change;*
- *(V, E) is a directed graph; the vertices of V are called* control modes, *the edges of E are called* control switches;

- *Each vertex $v \in V$ is labeled by "initial", "invariant" and "flow" labels: $Init(v)$, $Inv(v)$, and $Flow(v)$; the labels $Init(v)$ and $Inv(v)$ are constraints whose free variables are in Z; the label $Flow(v)$ is a constraint whose free variables are in $Z \cup \dot{Z}$;*
- *Each edge $e \in E$ is labeled by "jump" conditions: $Jump(e)$, which is a constraint whose free variables are in $Z \cup Z'$.*

We say that H is semi-algebraic *if the constraints in Init, Inv, Flow, and Jump are unquantified first-order formulæ over the reals (i.e., over $(\mathbb{R}, +, \times, =, <)$). We say that H is* in explicit form *if each $Flow(v)$ is of the form $\bigwedge_{i=1}^{k} \dot{Z}_i = f_i(Z_1, \ldots, Z_k)$.* □

In this paper we consider only semi-algebraic hybrid automata in explicit form. Notice that although, as defined, semi-algebraic hybrid automata in explicit form apply only to the cases where the f_i's of the flow conditions are all polynomials, the definitions can be immediately extended to deal with rational functions instead without significant changes to the basic approach.

Example 1. Consider the following semi-algebraic automaton in explicit form.

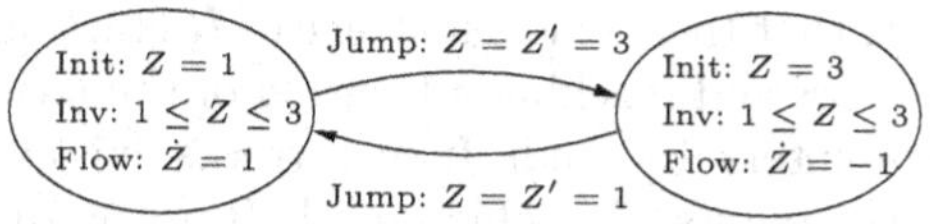

The initial mode of this hybrid automaton is shown on the left, where from the starting value of $Z = 1$, Z grows with a constant rate of 1. At time $t = 2$, when the automaton reaches a value of $Z = 3$, it jumps to the other mode on the right. In this second mode, Z wanes with a constant rate of -1 and upon reaching the value of $Z = 1$, it jumps back to the initial mode. □

2.2 Hybrid Automata: Semantics

Let H be a hybrid automaton of dimension k. For any given control mode $v \in V$, we denote with $\Phi(v)$ the set of functions from $\mathbb{R}^+$ to $\mathbb{R}^k$ satisfying the constraints in $Flow(v)$. In addition, for any given $r \in \mathbb{R}^k$, we use $Init(v)(r)$ ($Inv(v)(r)$ and $Flow(v)(r)$) to denote the Boolean value obtained by pairwise substitution of r with Z in $Init(v)$ ($Inv(v)$ and $Flow(v)$, respectively). Similarly, for any given r, $s \in \mathbb{R}^k$, we use $Jump(e)(r, s)$ to denote the boolean value obtained by pairwise substitution of r with Z and s with Z' in $Jump(e)$. The semantics of hybrid automata can now be given in terms of execution traces as in the definition below.

Definition 2. Semantics of Hybrid Automata. *Let $H = (Z, V, E, Init, Inv, Flow, Jump)$ be a hybrid automaton of dimension k.*

A location *ℓ of H is a pair $\langle v, r \rangle$, where $v \in V$ is a state and $r \in \mathbb{R}^k$ is an assignment of values to the variables of Z. A location $\langle v, r \rangle$ is said to be* admissible *if $Inv(v)(r)$ is satisfied.*

The continuous reachability transition relation, $\rightarrow_C$, *between admissible locations is defined as follows:*

$$\langle v, r\rangle \rightarrow_C \langle v, s\rangle$$
$$\textit{iff} \quad \exists t > 0, f \in \Phi(v)\Big(f(0) = r \ \wedge \ f(t) = s \ \wedge \ \forall t' \in [0,t](Inv(v)(f(t')))\Big).$$

The discrete reachability transition relation, $\rightarrow_D$, *between admissible locations is defined as follows:*

$$\langle v, r\rangle \rightarrow_D \langle u, s\rangle \qquad \textit{iff} \qquad \langle v, u\rangle \in E \ \wedge \ Jump(\langle v, u\rangle)(r, s)$$

A trace *of H is a sequence ℓ_0,ℓ_1, ..., ℓ_n, ... of admissible locations such that*

$\forall i \geq 0 \ \ \ell_i \rightarrow_C \ell_{i+1} \ \vee \ \ell_i \rightarrow_D \ell_{i+1}$. □

2.3 The Bounded Reachability Problem

Let H be a semi-algebraic k-dimensional hybrid automaton in explicit form, $S \subseteq \mathbb{R}^k$ be a set of "start states", characterized by the first order formula $\mathbb{S}(Z)$, and $B \subseteq \mathbb{R}^k$ be a set of "bad states", characterized by the first order formula $\mathbb{B}(Z)$. We wish to check that there exists no trace of H starting from a location of the form $\langle v,\ s\rangle$ with $s \in S$ and reaching a location of the form $\langle u,\ b\rangle$ with $b \in B$ within a specified time interval $[0, \mathsf{end}]$. If such traces exist we are interested in a characterization of the points of S which reach B in the time interval $[0, \mathsf{end}]$.

Note that for our applications of interest, it suffices to place an upper-bound on the time interval.

3 Our Approach

In this paper, we explore solutions to the bounded-reachability problem through symbolic computation methods, applied to the descriptions of the traces of the hybrid automaton. Because the description of the automaton is through semi-algebraic sets, the evolution of the automaton can be described even in cases where system parameters and initial conditions are unspecified. Nonetheless, semialgebraic decision procedures provide a succinct description of algebraic constraints over the initial values and parameters for which proper behavior of the system can be expected. In addition, by keeping track of conservation principles (e.g., of mass and energy) in terms of constraint or invariant manifolds on which the system must evolve, we avoid many of the obvious pitfalls of numerical approaches.

Note also that the "algorithmic algebraic model checking approach" that we propose here naturally generalizes many of the basic ideas inherent to BDD-based symbolic model checking or even the more recent SAT-based approaches.

Nonetheless, our method has an inherent incompleteness: we proceed on the traces using a time step δ which implies that our answer is relative to a limited time interval. Furthermore, when the solutions of the differential equations cannot be computed we approximate them using the first few terms of the corresponding Taylor polynomials, hence the error we accumulate depends on δ.

We start by presenting how our method applies to the case of a system of differential equations, i.e., a hybrid automaton with only just one mode and no *Init*, *Inv*, and *Jump* conditions.

3.1 The Basic Case

Consider a system of differential equations of the form $\dot{Z} = f(Z)$, where $\dot{Z}$ and Z are vectors of length k and f is a function that operates on them.

Let S, $B \subseteq \mathbb{R}^k$ be characterized by the formulæ $\mathbb{S}(Z)$ and $\mathbb{B}(Z)$, respectively. As before, let $[0, \mathsf{end}]$ be a time interval and $0 < \delta \leq \mathsf{end}$ be a time step.

We use $pj(Z0, \delta)$ to denote the Taylor polynomial of degree j relative to the solution $Z(t)$ centered in $Z0$ with a step size of δ. For instance, $p1(Z0, \delta)$ is the vector expression $Z0 + f(Z0) \cdot \delta$.

Consider the following first-order formula over the reals

$$\mathbb{F}_\delta(Z0, Z) \equiv \mathbb{S}(Z0) \ \wedge\ \exists \delta' \Big(Z = pj(Z0, \delta') \ \wedge\ 0 \leq \delta' \leq \delta \Big).$$

The points reachable from S in the time interval $[0, \delta]$ can be approximated with the set of points satisfying the formula $\exists Z0(\mathbb{F}_\delta(Z0, Z))$. Hence, the points in B and reachable from S in $[0, \delta]$ can be approximated by the formula

$$\exists Z0(\mathbb{F}_\delta(Z0, Z)) \ \wedge\ \mathbb{B}(Z).$$

Symbolic algebraic techniques can be applied in order to both simplify (e.g., eliminate quantifiers) and decide the satisfiability of this formula. If the formula is satisfiable, then the values of Z for which the formula is true represent the portion of B that can be reached in time $\delta' \leq \delta$. Similarly, the points in S which reach any point in B within the time interval $[0, \delta]$ can be characterized by the formula $\exists Z(\mathbb{F}_\delta(Z0, Z) \ \wedge\ \mathbb{B}(Z))$. If these formulæ are not satisfiable then we can proceed with a second step, getting the formula

$$\mathbb{F}_{2\delta}(Z0, Z) \equiv \mathbb{S}(Z0) \wedge \exists Z1, \delta'(Z1 = pj(Z0, \delta) \ \wedge\ Z = pj(Z1, \delta') \ \wedge\ 0 \leq \delta' \leq \delta).$$

The above reasoning can now be applied to $\mathbb{F}_{2\delta}(Z0, Z)$, i.e., use $\mathbb{F}_{2\delta}(Z0, Z)$ instead of $\mathbb{F}_\delta(Z0, Z)$, to check if S reaches B within the time interval $[0, 2\delta]$, etc. Notice that the new variable $Z1$ which occurs in $\mathbb{F}_{2\delta}(Z0, Z)$ can be eliminated by applying substitutions. If after time end all the formulæ we generate are unsatisfiable, then S cannot reach B within the time interval $[0, \mathsf{end}]$.

It is important to notice that: (1) The only approximation we have introduced is due to the use of the Taylor polynomials; (2) We have only used existential quantified formulæ; (3) The degree of the Taylor polynomial together with the degrees of the f_i's influence the complexity of the first-order formulæ we create and the number of steps needed to get a sufficient precision. As far as the approximation issues are concerned, when the derivative of order $j+1$ of f is bounded we can use the Lagrange Remainder Theorem to both under and over approximate the set of points reachable within the time interval $[0, \mathsf{end}]$ and to estimate the error. It is easy to see that our method can be generalized to the case in which the f_i's are rational functions, i.e., ratios of polynomial functions. In fact, in this case we only have to preprocess the formulæ by computing the LCMs of the denominators and using them to get formulæ over polynomial functions.

When we terminate, we are left with deciding the satisfiability of a semialgebraic formula involving $n = 2 + k \cdot \lceil \mathsf{end}/\delta \rceil + N(\mathbb{S}) + N(\mathbb{B})$ variables in degree $d = \max[j + \deg(f), \deg(\mathbb{S}), \deg(\mathbb{B})]$, where N and deg denote the number of variables and total degree, respectively used in the semialgebraic description of $\mathbb{S}$ and $\mathbb{B}$. In addition, if we assume that the coefficients of the polynomials can be stored with at most L bits, then the total time complexity (bit-complexity) [17, 20, 24] of the decision procedure is $(L \log L \log\log L)d^{O(n)}$. We note that even with low degree polynomials, this exponential complexity in the number of variables makes it impractical to test for bounded-reachability even when the specified time interval is relatively short. Here we focus on rather simple examples where the complexity is rather manageable, and is achieved by approximating polynomial and rational functions by piecewise linear functions.

Example 2. Next, examine the following toy example. The following system of differential equations describes the dynamics $\dot{Z} = 2Z^2 + Z$, with S and B characterized by $\mathbb{S} \equiv Z > 4$ and $\mathbb{B} \equiv Z^2 < 4$. Now, consider the time interval $[0, 0.5]$ and time step 0.5. After time 0.5, using an approximation with Taylor polynomial of degree 2, we derive the formula

$$\exists Z0, \delta' \Big(Z0 > 4 \wedge Z = Z0 + (2Z0^2 + Z0) \cdot \delta' + (8Z0^3 + 6Z0^2 + Z0) \cdot (\delta')^2/2 \\ \wedge\, 0 \leq \delta' \leq 0.5 \wedge Z^2 < 4 \Big).$$

This formula is unsatisfiable, thus implying that the dynamical system reaches no bad states in the specified time interval $[0, 0.5]$. □

The formulæ involved in our method can be easily simplified, if we introduce further approximations. For instance, we may approximate reachability by first evaluating the maxima and the minima of the j-th Taylor polynomial $pj(Z, \delta')$s over S and $[0, \delta]$, and then using them as upper and lower bounds.

Example 3. Next, consider the differential equation $\dot{Z} = 2Z$, with S and B characterized by $\mathbb{S} \equiv 2 \leq Z \leq 4$ and $\mathbb{B} \equiv 3 < Z < 5$.

The Taylor polynomial of degree 1 with $\delta = 0.5$ is $Z + 2Z \cdot \delta'$, i.e., $2Z$. Note that since the maximum and the minimum in S are 8 and 4, respectively, and since the interval $[4, 8]$ intersects $(3, 5)$, S reaches B in time 0.5. □

3.2 The General Case

We are ready to deal with the general case, where we have a polynomial k-dimensional hybrid automaton H in explicit form.

Given a mode v of H, we use the notation $pj_v(Z, \delta)$ to denote the Taylor polynomial of degree j in the mode v centered in Z. The first-order formula

$$\mathbb{F}[v, \mathbb{S}](Z0, Z) \equiv \mathbb{S}(Z0) \wedge \exists \delta' \Big(Z = pj_v(Z0, \delta') \wedge 0 \leq \delta' \leq \delta \\ \wedge \forall \delta''(0 \leq \delta'' \leq \delta' \rightarrow Inv(v)(pj_v(Z0, \delta''))) \Big)$$

characterizes the points reached within time δ in the mode v, under the approximation implied by the use of the Taylor polynomial. Notice that, if we assume that the invariant regions are convex and we use the Taylor polynomial of degree 1, we can avoid the universal quantification. As before, the formula

$$\exists Z0(\mathbb{F}[v, \mathbb{S}](Z0, Z)) \wedge \mathbb{B}(Z)$$

is satisfiable if and only if the set B can be reached from S without leaving mode v within the time step δ. In this case, the points of S which reach B are characterized by $\exists Z(\mathbb{F}[v, \mathbb{S}](Z0, Z) \wedge \mathbb{B}(Z))$. If the preceding formula is not satisfiable, we have to consider all possible alternative situations: that is, either we continue to evolve within the mode v or we discretely jump to another mode, $u \in V$. We define the formula $\mathbb{S}_\delta^{vu}$

$$\mathbb{S}_\delta^{vu}(Z) \equiv \begin{cases} \exists Z0(\mathbb{F}_\delta^v(Z0, Z), & \text{if } u = v; \\ \exists Z0, Z1(\mathbb{F}_\delta^v(Z0, Z1) \wedge Jump(\langle v, u \rangle)(Z1, Z)), & \text{otherwise.} \end{cases}$$

representing the states reached within time δ in the mode u. In this way, in the worst case we generate $|E|$ satisfiable formulæ on which we have to iterate the method, treating them as we treated $\mathbb{S}(Z)$ in the first step. In practice, many of these formulæ would be unsatisfiable, and hence at each iteration, the number of formulæ we have to consider will remain considerably low. We may also use an optimized traversal over the graph to reduce the number of generated formulæ.

Let end be the total amount of time during which we examine the hybrid system's evolution in terms of at most $m = \lceil \mathsf{end}/\delta \rceil$ time steps: the number $m \in \mathbb{N}$ is such that $(m-1)\delta < \mathsf{end} \leq m\delta$. Since at each iteration the jumps can occur before δ instants of time have passed, just iterating the method for m steps does not ensure that we have indeed covered the entire time interval $[0, \mathsf{end}]$. In particular, if there are Zeno paths starting from S, i.e., paths in which the time does not pass since only the jumps are used, our method will fail to converge in a finite number of steps. For these reasons, at each step, we must check the minimum elapsed time before a jump can be taken. Let $\mathbb{M}(Z) \equiv \mathbb{S}^{v,u \ldots, w}(Z)$ be one of the formulæ obtained after some number of iterations. Suppose now that we intend to jump from this mode w to the next mode z. We will then need to check whether the minimum amount of time has passed before the jump can be taken. Consider the formula:

$$\mathbb{T}(w, z, \mathbb{M})(T) \equiv \exists Z0, Z1, Z \Big(\mathbb{M}(Z0) \wedge Z1 = pj_w(Z0, T) \wedge 0 \leq T \leq \delta \\ \wedge \forall T'(0 \leq T' \leq T \rightarrow Inv(v)(pj_v(Z0, T'))) \wedge Jump(\langle w, z \rangle)(Z1, Z) \Big).$$

The minimum amount of time can now be computed as solution of the formula

$$Min(w,z,\mathbb{M})(T) \equiv \mathbb{T}(w,z,\mathbb{M})(T) \wedge \forall T'\Big(T' < T \rightarrow \neg\mathbb{T}(w,z,\mathbb{M})(T')\Big).$$

To avoid Zeno paths we could eliminate the paths in which the minimum is 0. Along each generated path we have to iterate until the sum of the minimum amounts reaches end. If all the paths accumulate a total amount of time greater than end and B is never reached we can be sure that B cannot be reached from S in the time interval $[0, \mathsf{end}]$. If B is reached, i.e., one of the formulæ involving $\mathbb{B}$ is satisfiable before m iterations, then we can be sure that B is reachable from S in the time interval $[0, \mathsf{end}]$. If B is reached after the first m iterations, then B is reachable from S but we are not sure about the elapsed time, since we keep together flows of different length. It is possible that some paths do not accumulate a total time greater than end, e.g., the sequence of the minimum times converges rapidly to 0. In this case our method could not converge. Notice that even in this general case, we can extend the method to rational flows.

Notice that if at each step the derivatives of order $j+1$ of the involved flows are bounded on the set of points satisfying the invariant conditions, we can again exploit the Lagrange Remainder Theorem to both under and over approximate the set of reachable points and to estimate errors (see [15]).

In order to provide a time-complexity, assume the special situation where no path accrues more than M discrete jumps (i.e., our method has converged). When we terminate, we are left with deciding the satisfiability of a quantified semialgebraic formula with $O(M)$ alternations and involving $n = k \cdot [\lceil \mathsf{end}/\delta \rceil + O(M)] + N(\mathbb{S}) + N(\mathbb{B})$ variables in degree $d = \max[j + \deg(Init,\ Inv,\ Jump),\ \deg(\mathbb{S}),\ \deg(\mathbb{B})]$, where N and deg denote the number of variables and total degree, respectively as before. Assume that the coefficients of the polynomials can be stored with at most L bits. Then the total time complexity (bit-complexity) [17, 20, 24] of the decision procedure is $(L \log L \log\log L) d^{2^{O(n)}}$, i.e., double-exponential in the number of variables.

3.3 Rectangular Regions

When the formulæ $Init(v)$s, $Inv(v)$s, $Jump(e)$s, $\mathbb{S}$, and $\mathbb{B}$ identify rectangular (closed) regions (e.g., product of intervals) we can rely on other approaches from symbolic computations, while achieving further simplifications along the way.

Given a mode v of H, the region obtained from the intersection of $Inv(v)$ and $\mathbb{S}$ is of the form $\mathbb{R}(v) \equiv a(v) \leq Z \leq b(v)$. We can symbolically determine the maximum $max(v)$ and the minimum $min(v)$ of $pj_v(Z, \delta')$ over $\mathbb{R}(v) \times [0, \delta]$. We can use the following formula to over-approximate the points reached within the time interval $[0, \delta]$:

$$\mathbb{O}v(Z) \equiv \min(v) \leq Z \leq max(v) \wedge Inv(v)(Z).$$

The formulæ $\mathbb{O}v(Z) \wedge \mathbb{B}(Z)$ and $\mathbb{O}v(Z1) \wedge Jump(\langle v,u\rangle)(Z1, Z)$, can be used to check if the set B is reached or if it is possible to jump to another mode. Since these formulæ identify rectangular regions, we can iterate the method.

4 A Case Study: the Delta-Notch Protein Signaling

Let us now return to the Delta-Notch protein signaling system that we had introduced earlier. The mathematical model for the Delta-Notch signaling presented in [9] can be approximated by piecewise linear functions and results in a rectangular hybrid automaton that can be analyzed symbolically.

For instance, in [11] a rather simple piecewise linear hybrid automaton model was created, and was extensively studied through the predicate abstraction method of [22]. The piecewise affine hybrid automaton of [11] is defined by: (1) A set of *global invariant conditions* which must be always true; (2) A finite number of modes; (3) Each mode is characterized by a set of *local invariant conditions* and a set of *differential equations* determining the flow of the variables.

The automaton modeling the evolution of a one-cell system has been described using the SAL language [7] in [11]. In this description, all the fluxes have been reversed in order to determine the set of initial conditions from which a particular steady-state is reached (by solving a forward reachability problem). The automata relative to the two and four cell systems have also been similarly studied. Here we consider the two-cell piecewise affine hybrid automaton and apply our method to the forward reachability problem. For a complete description of the automaton we refer the reader to [11].

The system representing the evolution of two cells presented in [11] has the following set of invariant conditions

$$\begin{aligned} &0 \le d_1, d_2 \le R_D/\lambda_D \ \wedge \ 0 \le n_1, n_2 \le R_N/\lambda_N \\ \wedge \ &-R_N/\lambda_N \le h_D \le 0 \ \wedge \ 0 \le h_N \le R_D/\lambda_D. \end{aligned}$$

The variables d_1 and d_2 represent the concentration of the Delta protein in the first and in the second cell, respectively. The variables n_1 and n_2 represent the concentration of the Notch protein in the first and in the second cell, respectively. R_D and R_N are constants representing the Delta and Notch production rates, respectively. λ_D and λ_N are the Delta and Notch protein decay constants, respectively. h_D is an unknown switching threshold which determines the Delta protein production. h_N, similar to h_D, is an unknown switching threshold which determines the Notch protein production.

A possible equilibrium for the system is given by the point $d_1^* = 0$, $n_1^* = R_N/\lambda_N$, $d_2^* = R_D/\lambda_D$, $n_2^* = 0$, which belongs to the mode v characterized by the following invariant and flow conditions

$$\begin{gathered} 0 \le d_1 \le h_N \ \wedge \ -h_D \le n_1 \le R_N/\lambda_N \ \wedge \ h_N \le d_2 \le R_D/\lambda_D \ \wedge \ 0 \le n_2 \le -h_D, \\ \dot{d}_1 = \lambda_D d_1 \wedge \dot{n}_1 = -R_N + \lambda_N n_1 \wedge \dot{d}_2 = -R_D + \lambda_D d_2 \wedge \dot{n}_2 = \lambda_N n_2. \end{gathered}$$

We apply our method to the analysis of the admissible locations reachable from v. In particular, in this case we can apply the simplifications described in Section 3.3. Even if we limit our attention to one possible evolution with relatively few iterations, this suffices to compute a somewhat different result from what is presented in [11].

The formula $\mathbb{O}v(\langle d_1, n_1, d_2, n_2\rangle)$ representing the points reached in the time interval $[0, \delta]$ is

$$0 \leq d_1 \leq h_N + \lambda_D \cdot h_N \cdot \delta \ \wedge \ -h_D - R_N \cdot \delta - \lambda_N \cdot h_D \cdot \delta \leq n_1 \leq R_N/\lambda_N \ \wedge \\ h_N - R_D \cdot \delta + \lambda_D \cdot h_N \cdot \delta \leq d_2 \leq R_D/\lambda_D \ \wedge \ 0 \leq n_2 \leq -h_D - \lambda_N \cdot h_D \cdot \delta.$$

Consider a mode u characterized by the following invariant conditions

$$h_N \leq d_1 \leq R_D/\lambda_D \wedge -h_D \leq n_1 \leq R_N/\lambda_N \wedge h_N \leq d_2 \leq R_D/\lambda_D \wedge 0 \leq n_2 \leq -h_D.$$

Since the formula $\mathbb{O}(v) \ \wedge \ Inv(u)$ is satisfiable we can jump to the mode u. In particular, assuming that δ is so chosen that $h_N + \lambda_D \cdot h_N \cdot \delta \leq R_D/\lambda_D$, in the interval $[0, \delta]$, we can reach the points satisfying

$$h_N \leq d_1 \leq h_N + \lambda_D \cdot h_N \cdot \delta \ \wedge \ -h_D \leq n_1 \leq R_N/\lambda_N \\ \wedge \ h_N \leq d_2 \leq R_D/\lambda_D \ \wedge \ 0 \leq n_2 \leq -h_D.$$

This formula in conjunction with $d_1 < d_2$ is easily seen to be satisfiable. For instance, one can prove that with $R_N = R_D = \lambda_N = \lambda_D = 1.0$ and $-h_D = h_N = 0.5$ and starting from v with values $\langle 0.5, 0.89, 0.68, 0.42\rangle$, at time 0.5, we can reach $\langle 0.84, 0.81, 0.47, 0.04\rangle$. In [11], it was proven that all the points satisfying $d_1 < d_2 \wedge n_1 > n_2$ are reachable from the stable equilibrium state belonging to v. Our observation, which does not contradict this result of [11], nonetheless proves that our method can be combined with that of [11] to obtain better approximations of the region reachable from the equilibrium in v.

5 Related Literature, Future Work and Conclusions

To place the results described here in the context of a large existing and continually growing literature, we mention a few related results.

In [4] symbolic computation over $(\mathbb{R}, +, <, =)$ is used to compute preconditions on automata with linear flow conditions. Avoiding multiplication ensures good performance, but the class of automata on which the result can be applied is quite restricted, and of limited descriptive power.

In the d/dt tool (see [6]), a method involving several successive time steps is applied. Since the flow conditions (differential equations) are linear, the exact solution after a time step dt is used to compute the set of points that can be reached in that time. In another similar tool CheckMate (see [8]), a more sophisticated method involving time steps is introduced for the case of regions defined by polyhedra and solvable flow differential equations.

In a much closer related result of [22], predicate abstraction was introduced to map a hybrid automaton into a discrete one. The states of the discrete automaton represent sets of values which are indistinguishable with respect to a fixed set of predicates over the reals. Symbolic computation is used to determine the edges of the discrete automaton. In [11], the method was applied on piecewise linear hybrid automata to study the Delta-Notch signaling process. In a sequel, we will explain connections and differences between these and our methods.

Recently in [3], predicate abstraction is combined with symbolic computations over the reals and with the use of time steps. The symbolic computation is used to determine the transitions between the abstract states, but the differential equations are kept linear so that the exact solutions are used in the symbolic computation. In particular, abstract states are forced to evolve at a given time step and symbolic computation is used to draw transitions by determining if intersections between (abstract) states are non empty. The main differences with respect to our methods are as follows: (1) We do not use predicate abstraction; (2) We can apply our method in the case of non-linear differential equations as well, through the use of Taylor polynomials.

The approach outlined here provides a general framework, but still lacks the needed degree of applicability, especially in the context of biological questions. We enumerate these issues: (1) Can one deal with unbounded time interval? (2) Can one deal with different and adaptively chosen time steps? This is particularly important if one is dealing with slow reactions as well as reactions that are relatively fast. (3) Can one conclude about the limiting situations when the time step sizes approach zero in the limit? (4) Is there a purely differential algebraic approach (e.g., Ritt algebra) for studying reachability?

In the other directions, one can ask similar questions about how to extend these constructs for reachability to cases involving various modal operators (e.g., next). Beyond these questions, the other remaining problems are of algorithmic nature dealing with approximability, complexity, and probabilistic computations.

Our plan is to address these problems in a sequence of papers that will form sequels to the current paper: "Algorithmic Algebraic Model Checking (AAMC) series." An incomplete, and evolving list of topics that will be addressed are as follows: generalization to the dense time logic TCTL [1, 12]; decidability issues in this context and under various reasonable models of computation [16]; state-space discretization and predicate abstractions; "quasi-static simulation," combining flux-balanced analysis with slow dynamics; a topological characterization of bio-chemical processes, etc.

The present status of this project is as described below: There is a preliminary implementation of the algorithms in *C/C++*: part of the software system Tolque, the algebraic model checker for semi-algebraic hybrid automata. As it gets integrated with our *Lisp*-based Systems Biology tool Simpathica[5], it will allow biochemical networks to be easily represented, stored and analyzed. The resulting technology is hoped to provide a simple framework for biologists to think about biology and computer scientists to think about how biologists think about biology.

References

1. R. Alur, C. Courcoubetis, and D. Dill. Model-Checking for Real-Time Systems. In *International Symposium on Logic in Computer Science*, 5, pages 414–425. IEEE Computer Press, 1990.

2. R. Alur, C. Courcoubetis, N. Halbwachs, T. A. Henzinger, P.-H. Ho, X. Nicollin, A. Olivero, J. Sifakis, and S. Yovine. The Algorithmic Analysis of Hybrid Systems. *Theoretical Computer Science*, 138:3–34, 1995.
3. R. Alur, T. Dang, and F. Ivancic. Progress on Reachability Analysis of Hybrid Systems Using Predicate Abstraction. In O. Maler and A. Pnueli, editors, *Hybrid Systems: Computation and Control*, volume 2623 of *LNCS*, pages 4–19. Springer, 2003.
4. R. Alur, T. A. Henzinger, and Pei-Hsin Ho. Automatic Symbolic Verification of Embedded Systems. In *IEEE Real-Time Systems Symposium*, pages 2–11. IEEE Press, 1993.
5. M. Antoniotti, A. Policriti, N. Ugel, and B. Mishra. Reasoning about Biochemical Processes. *Cell Biochemistry and Biophysics*, 38:271–286, 2003.
6. E. Asarin, T. Dang, O. Maler, and O. Bournez. Approximate Reachability Analysis of Piecewise-Linear Dynamical Systems. In B. Krogh and N. Lynch, editors, *Hybrid Systems: Computation and Control*, volume 1790 of *LNCS*, pages 20–31. Springer, 2000.
7. S. Bensalem, V. Ganesh, Y. Lakhnech, C. Muñoz, S. Owre, H. Rueß, J. Rushby, V. Rusu, H. Saïdi, N. Shankar, E. Singerman, and A. Tiwari. An overview of SAL. In C. M. Holloway, editor, *NASA Langley Formal Methods Workshop*, pages 187–196, 2000.
8. L.Blum, F. Cucker, M. Shub, and S. Smale. *Complexity and Real Computation.* Springer-Verlag, 1997.
9. A. Chutinan and B. Krogh. Verification of Polyhedral-Invariant Hybrid Automata Using Polygonal Flow Pipe Approximations. In F. W. Vaandrager and J. H. van Schuppen, editors, *Hybrid Systems: Computation and Control*, volume 1569 of *LNCS*, pages 76–90. Springer, 1999.
10. J. R. Collier, N. A. M. Monk, P. K. Maini, and J. H. Lewis. Pattern Formation by Lateral Inhibition with Feedback: a Mathematical Model of Delta-Notch Intercellular Signalling. *Journal of Theor. Biology*, 183:429–446, 1996.
11. A. Cornish-Bowden. *Fundamentals of Enzyme Kinetics (3rd edn.).* Portland Press, London, 2004.
12. R. Ghosh, A. Tiwari, and C. Tomlin. Automated Symbolic Reachability Analysis; with Application to Delta-Notch Signaling Automata. In O. Maler and A. Pnueli, editors, *Hybrid Systems: Computation and Control*, volume 2623 of *LNCS*, pages 233–248. Springer, 2003.
13. T. A. Henzinger, X. Nicollin, J. Sifakis, and S. Yovine. Symbolic Model Checking for Real-time Systems. In *7th Annual IEEE Symposium on Logic in Computer Science*, pages 394–406. IEEE, IEEE Computer Society Press, June 1992.
14. H. Hong. Quantifier elimination in elementary algebra and geometry by partial cylindrical algebraic decomposition, version 13. *WWW site* `www.eecis.udel.edu/~saclib`, 1995.
15. J.P. Keener and J. Sneyd. *Mathematical Physiology.* Springer-Verlag, New York, 1998.
16. R. Lanotte and S.Tini. Taylor Approximation for Hybrid Systems. In M. Morari and L. Thiele, editors, *Hybrid Systems: Computation and Control (HSCC'05)*, volume 3414 of *LNCS*, pages 402–416. Springer, 2005.
17. B. Mishra. *Algorithmic Algebra.* Springer-Verlag, New York, 1993.
18. B. Mishra. *Computational Differential Algebra*, pages 111–145. World-Scientific, Singapore, 2000.

19. B. Mishra. A Symbolic Approach to Modeling Cellular Behavior. In S. Sahni, V. K. Prasanna, and U. Shukla, editors, *High Performance Computing*, volume 2552 of *LNCS*, pages 725–732. Springer, 2002.
20. B. Mishra. *Computational Real Algebraic Geometry*, pages 740–764. CRC Press, Boca Raton, FL, 2004.
21. A. Nerode and W. Kohn. Hybrid Systems and Constraint Logic Programming. In D. S. Warren, editor, *International Conference on Logic Programming (ICLP'93)*, pages 18–24. MIT Press, 1993.
22. A. Tiwari and G. Khanna. Series of Abstraction for Hybrid Automata. In C. J. Tomlin and M. Greenstreet, editors, *Hybrid Systems: Computation and Control*, volume 2289 of *LNCS*, pages 465–478. Springer, 2002.
23. E. O. Voit. *Computational Analysis of Biochemical Systems. A Pratical Guide for Biochemists and Molecular Biologists.* Cambridge University Press, 2000.
24. F. Winkler. *Polynomial Algorithms in Computer Algebra.* Springer-Verlag, Wien, New York, 1996.

SMT-COMP: Satisfiability Modulo Theories Competition

Clark Barrett[1], Leonardo de Moura[2], and Aaron Stump[3]

[1] Department of Computer Science, New York University
[2] Computer Science Laboratory, SRI International
[3] Department of Computer Science and Engineering, Washington University in St. Louis

1 Introduction

Decision procedures for checking satisfiability of logical formulas are crucial for many verification applications (e.g., [2, 6, 3]). Of particular recent interest are solvers for Satisfiability Modulo Theories (SMT). SMT solvers decide logical satisfiability (or dually, validity) with respect to a background theory in classical first-order logic with equality. Background theories useful for verification are supported, like equality and uninterpreted functions (EUF), real or integer arithmetic, and theories of bitvectors and arrays. Input formulas are often syntactically restricted; for example, to be quantifier-free or to involve only *difference constraints*. Some solvers support a combination of theories, or quantifiers.

The Satisfiability Modulo Theories Competition (SMT-COMP) is intended to spark further advances in the SMT field, especially for applications in verification. Public competitions are a well-known means of stimulating advancement in automated reasoning. Examples include the CASC Competition for first-order reasoning, the SAT Competition for propositional reasoning, and the Termination Competition for checking termination of term rewriting systems [4, 1, 7]. Significant improvements in tool capabilities are reported from year to year, which anecdotal evidence suggests the competitions play a strong role in fueling. The primary goals of SMT-COMP at CAV 2005 are:

- To spur development of SMT solver implementations.
- To collect benchmarks in a common format, namely the SMT-LIB format [5].
- To jump start definition of SMT theories, again using the proposed SMT-LIB format.
- To connect implementors of SMT solvers with potential users in the verification community.

The idea of holding SMT-COMP came out of discussions of the SMT-LIB initiative at the 2nd International Workshop on Pragmatics of Decision Procedures in Automated Reasoning (PDPAR) at IJCAR 2004. SMT-LIB is an initiative of the SMT community to build a library of SMT benchmarks in a proposed standard format. SMT-COMP aims to serve this goal by contributing collected benchmark formulas used for the competition to the library, and by providing an incentive for implementors of SMT solvers to support the SMT-LIB format.

K. Etessami and S.K. Rajamani (Eds.): CAV 2005, LNCS 3576, pp. 20–23, 2005.

Evaluation of SMT solvers entered in SMT-COMP takes place July 6-10, while CAV 2005 is meeting, in the style of CASC [4]. Intermediate results are posted periodically as SMT-COMP proceeds, and final results are announced on the last day of CAV. The local organizers have arranged for SMT-COMP to have exclusive access to a group of GNU Linux machines, which are used to run the competition.

The SMT organizers wish to thank Cesare Tinelli and Silvio Renise for developing the SMT-LIB format and theory specifications for SMT-COMP. Also to be thanked are Sriram Rajamani and Kousha Etessami for helping make SMT-COMP possible at CAV 2005. Finally, thanks go to everyone contributing benchmarks or entering solvers to SMT-COMP, and the entire SMT community for supporting the competition.

2 Rules and Competition Format

This Section presents a summary of the rules and competition format for SMT-COMP. These draw substantially on ideas from the design and organization of CASC [4]. More detailed information can be found on the SMT-COMP web site: `http://www.csl.sri.com/users/demoura/smt-comp/`

2.1 Entrants

An entrant to SMT-COMP is an SMT solver submitted in either source code or binary format to the organizers. The organizers reserve the right to submit their own systems, or other systems of interest, to the competition. For solvers submitted in source code form, the organizers take reasonable precautions to ensure that the source code is not viewed by anyone other than the organizers. Submitters of an SMT-COMP entrant are encouraged to be physically present at SMT-COMP, but are not required to be so to participate or win. The organizers commit to making reasonable efforts to install each system, but they reserve the right to reject an entrant if its installation process proves overly difficult. Finally, an entrant to SMT-COMP must include a short (1-2 pages) description of the system.

2.2 Execution of Solvers

Each SMT-COMP entrant, when executed, must read a single input formula presented on its standard input channel. All formulas are given in the concrete syntax of the SMT-LIB format, version 1.1 [5]. For its given input formula, each SMT-COMP entrant is expected to report on its standard output channel whether the formula is satisfiable or unsatisfiable. An entrant may also report "`unknown`" to indicate that it cannot determine satisfiability of the formula. Each SMT-COMP solver is executed on an unloaded competition machine for each given formula, up to a fixed time limit. This limit is yet to be determined, but expected to be at least 5 minutes.

2.3 Judging and Scoring

Scoring is done using the system of points and penalties in Figure 1. In recognition of the greater difficulty of achieving completeness than soundness in SMT systems, smaller penalties are assessed for incompleteness than for unsoundness. The organizers take responsibility for determining in advance whether formulas are satisfiable or not. In the event of a tie in total number of points, the solver with the lower average CPU time on formulas for which it did not timeout is considered the winner.

Reported	Points for correct response	Penalty for incorrect response
`unsat`	+1	-8
`sat`	+1	-4
`unknown`	0	0
timeout	0	0

Fig. 1. Points and Penalties

2.4 Problem Divisions

Each SMT-COMP problem division consists of well-sorted formulas in SMT-LIB format version 1.1. Divisions and the corresponding theories are defined in SMT-LIB format on the SMT-LIB web page (linked from SMT-COMP's page). The divisions contain a range of problems from relatively easy to difficult. Benchmark formulas for the divisions have been collected by the organizers from other researchers in the field, mostly from verification applications. The organizers reserve the right to cancel a division if there are too few solvers entered or benchmarks collected. For more detailed information on the divisions, see the SMT-COMP web page. The prefix "QF_" below means the formulas in the division are quantifier-free, and in some cases there are pairs of divisions for integers and reals, respectively.

- QF_UF: uninterpreted functions
- QF_IDL (QF_RDL): integer (real) difference logic
- QF_UFIDL: integer difference logic with uninterpreted functions
- QF_LIA (QF_LRA): linear integer (real) arithmetic
- QF_UFLIA (QF_UFLRA): linear integer (real) arithmetic with uninterpreted functions
- QF_A: non-extensional arrays
- QF_AUFLIA: linear integer arithmetic with uninterpreted functions, arrays
- AUFLIA: linear integer arithmetic with uninterpreted functions, arrays, quantifiers

2.5 Proofs and Models

SMT-COMP recognizes entrants which produce suitable evidence for the results they report. Entrants which can produce proofs for unsatisfiable formulas are recognized as proof-producing, and entrants which can produce models for satisfiable formulas are recognized as model-generating. No award other than this recognition is given on the basis of such capabilities, and such capabilities are strictly optional for SMT-COMP entrants.

References

1. D. Le Berre and L. Simon. The essentials of the SAT 2003 competition. In *Sixth International Conference on Theory and Applications of Satisfiability Testing*, volume 2919 of *LNCS*, pages 452–467. Springer-Verlag, 2003.
2. H. Jin, H. Han, and F. Somenzi. Efficient Conflict Analysis for Finding All Satisfying Assignments of a Boolean Circuit. In L. Zuck and N. Halbwachs, editors, *11th International Conference on Tools and Algorithms for the Construction and Analysis of Systems*, 2005.
3. S. Lerner, T. Millstein, and C. Chambers. Automatically Proving the Correctness of Compiler Optimizations. In R. Gupta, editor, *In ACM SIGPLAN Conference on Programming Language Design and Implementation*, 2003. received best paper award.
4. F.J. Pelletier, G. Sutcliffe, and C.B. Suttner. The Development of CASC. *AI Communications*, 15(2-3):79–90, 2002.
5. Silvio Ranise and Cesare Tinelli. The SMT-LIB standard, version 1.1, 2005. Available from the "Documents" section of http://combination.cs.uiowa.edu/smtlib.
6. M. Velev and R. Bryant. Effective Use of Boolean Satisfiability Procedures in the Formal Verification of Superscalar and VLIW Microprocessors. *Journal of Symbolic Computation*, 35(2):73–106, February 2003.
7. H. Zantema, 2005. personal communication.

Predicate Abstraction via Symbolic Decision Procedures

Shuvendu K. Lahiri, Thomas Ball, and Byron Cook

Microsoft Research
{shuvendu, tball, bycook}@microsoft.com

Abstract. We present a new approach for performing predicate abstraction based on *symbolic decision procedures*. A symbolic decision procedure for a theory T (SDP_T) takes sets of predicates G and E and symbolically executes a decision procedure for T on $G' \cup \{\neg e \mid e \in E\}$, for all the subsets G' of G. The result of SDP_T is a shared expression (represented by a directed acyclic graph) that implicitly represents the answer to a predicate abstraction query.

We present symbolic decision procedures for the logic of Equality and Uninterpreted Functions(EUF) and Difference logic (DIF) and show that these procedures run in pseudo-polynomial (rather than exponential) time. We then provide a method to construct *SDP*'s for simple mixed theories (including EUF + DIF) using an extension of the Nelson-Oppen combination method. We present preliminary evaluation of our procedure on predicate abstraction benchmarks from device driver verification in SLAM.

1 Introduction

Predicate abstraction is a technique for automatically creating finite abstract models of finite and infinite state systems [10]. The method has been widely used in abstracting finite-state models of programs in SLAM [2] and numerous other software verification projects [11, 4]. It has also been used for synthesizing loop invariants [9] and verifying distributed protocols [8, 13].

The fundamental operation in predicate abstraction can be summarized as follows: Given a set of predicates P describing some set of properties of the system state, and a formula e, compute the weakest Boolean formula $\mathcal{F}_P(e)$ over the predicates P that implies e[1]. Most implementations of predicate abstraction [10, 2] construct $\mathcal{F}_P(e)$ by collecting the set of cubes (a conjunction of the predicates or their negations) over P that imply e. The implication is checked using a first-order theorem prover. This method may require making a very large ($2^{|P|}$ in the worst case) number of calls to a theorem prover and can be expensive.

[1] The dual of this problem, which is to compute the strongest Boolean formula $\mathcal{G}_P(e)$ that is implied by e, can be expressed as $\neg\mathcal{F}_P(\neg e)$.

K. Etessami and S.K. Rajamani (Eds.): CAV 2005, LNCS 3576, pp. 24–38, 2005.

Several techniques have been suggested to improve the performance of predicate abstraction. Some techniques enumerate the cubes over P in an increasing order of size [8, 9, 18]. However, these techniques still require an exponential number of theorem prover calls in the worst case, and demonstrate worst case behavior in practice. Other techniques sacrifice precision to gain efficiency, by only considering cubes of some fixed length [2].

Alternately, predicate abstraction can be formulated as a quantifier elimination problem. Lahiri et al. [13] and Clarke et al. [5] perform predicate abstraction by reducing the problem to Boolean quantifier elimination. The former method first transforms a first-order quantifier elimination problem into Boolean quantifier elimination by encoding first-order formulas into Boolean formulas; the latter assumes a finite representation of integers. The method in [13] first converts the quantifier-free first-order formula to a Boolean formula such that the translation preserves the set of satisfying assignments of the Boolean variables in the original variable. Both these techniques use incremental Boolean Satisfiability (SAT) techniques [5, 14] to perform the Boolean quantifier elimination. Namjoshi and Kurshan [15] also proposed using quantifier elimination for first-order logic directly to perform predicate abstraction — however many theories (such as the theory of Equality with Uninterpreted Functions) do not admit quantifier elimination.

Most of the above approaches use decision procedures or SAT solvers as "black boxes", at best in an incremental fashion, to perform predicate abstraction. We believe that having a customized procedure for predicate abstraction can help improve the efficiency of predicate abstraction on large problems.

We propose a new way to perform predicate abstraction based on *symbolic decision procedures*. A symbolic decision procedure for a theory T (SDP_T) takes sets of predicates G and E and symbolically executes a decision procedure for T on $G' \cup \{\neg e \mid e \in E\}$, for all the subsets G' of G. The output of $SDP_T(G, E)$ is a shared expression (an expression where common subexpressions can be shared) representing those subsets $G' \subseteq G$, for which $G' \cup \{\neg e \mid e \in E\}$ is unsatisfiable. We show that such a procedure can be used to compute $\mathcal{F}_P(e)$ for performing predicate abstraction.

We present symbolic decision procedures for the logic of Equality and Uninterpreted Functions(EUF) and Difference logic (DIF) and show that these procedures run in polynomial and pseudo-polynomial time respectively, and therefore produce compact shared expressions. We provide a method to construct SDP for a combination of two simple theories $T_1 \cup T_2$ (including EUF + DIF), by using an extension of the Nelson-Oppen combination method. We use Binary Decision Diagrams (BDDs) [3] to construct $\mathcal{F}_P(e)$ from the shared representations efficiently in practice. The proofs for the theorems and lemmas can be found in a detailed technical report [12].

We present a preliminary evaluation of our procedure on predicate abstraction benchmarks from device driver verification in SLAM, and show that our method outperforms existing methods for doing predicate abstraction.

2 Setup

Figure 1 defines the syntax of a quantifier-free fragment of first-order logic. An expression in the logic can either be a *term* or a *formula*. A *term* can either be a variable or an application of a function symbol to a list of terms. A *formula* can be the constants `true` or `false` or an atomic formula or Boolean combination of other formulas. Atomic formulas can be formed by an equality between terms or by an application of a predicate symbol to a list of terms.

$$\begin{aligned}
\mathit{term} &::= \mathit{variable} \mid \mathit{function\text{-}symbol}(\mathit{term}, \ldots, \mathit{term}) \\
\mathit{formula} &::= \texttt{true} \mid \texttt{false} \mid \mathit{atomic\text{-}formula} \\
&\mid \quad \mathit{formula} \wedge \mathit{formula} \mid \mathit{formula} \vee \mathit{formula} \mid \neg \mathit{formula} \\
\mathit{atomic\text{-}formula} &::= \mathit{term} = \mathit{term} \mid \mathit{predicate\text{-}symbol}(\mathit{term}, \ldots, \mathit{term})
\end{aligned}$$

Fig. 1. Syntax of a quantifier-free fragment of first-order logic

The function and predicate symbols can either be *uninterpreted* or can be defined by a particular theory. For instance, the theory of integer linear arithmetic defines the function-symbol "+" to be the addition function over integers and "<" to be the comparison predicate over integers. If an expression involves function or predicate symbols from multiple theories, then it is said to be an expression over *mixed* theories.

A formula F is said to be *satisfiable* if it is possible to assign values to the various symbols in the formula from the domains associated with the theories to make the formula `true`. A formula is *valid* if $\neg F$ is not satisfiable (or unsatisfiable). We say a formula A *implies* a formula B ($A \Rightarrow B$) if and only if $(\neg A) \vee B$ is valid.

We define a *shared expression* to be a Directed Acyclic Graph (DAG) representation of an expression where common subexpressions can be shared, by using names to refer to common subexpressions. For example, the intermediate variable t refers to the expression e_1 in the shared expression "**let** $t = e_1$ **in** $(e_2 \wedge t) \vee (e_3 \wedge \neg t)$".

2.1 Predicate Abstraction

A *predicate* is an atomic formula or its negation[2]. If G is a set of predicates, then we define $\widetilde{G} \doteq \{\neg g \mid g \in G\}$, to be the set containing the negations of the predicates in G. We use the term "predicate" in a general sense to refer to any atomic formula or its negation and should not be confused to only mean the set of predicates that are used in predicate abstraction.

Definition 1. *For a set of predicates P, a literal l_i over P is either a predicate p_i or $\neg p_i$, where $p_i \in P$. A cube c over P is a conjunction of literals. A clause*

[2] We always use the term "predicate symbol" (and not "predicate") to refer to symbols like "<".

cl over P is a disjunction of literals. Finally, a minterm over P is a cube with $|P|$ literals, and exactly one of p_i or $\neg p_i$ is present in the cube.

Given a set of predicates $P \doteq \{p_1, \ldots, p_n\}$ and a formula e, the main operation in predicate abstraction involves constructing the *weakest* Boolean formula $\mathcal{F}_P(e)$ over P such that $\mathcal{F}_P(e) \Rightarrow e$. The expression $\mathcal{F}_P(e)$ can be expressed as the set of all the minterms over P that imply e:

$$\mathcal{F}_P(e) = \bigvee\{c \mid c \text{ is a minterm over } P \text{ and } c \text{ implies } e\} \tag{1}$$

Proposition 1. *For a set of predicates P and a formula e, (i) $\mathcal{F}_P(\neg e) \Rightarrow \neg\mathcal{F}_P(e)$, (ii) $\mathcal{F}_P(e_1 \wedge e_2) \Leftrightarrow \mathcal{F}_P(e_1) \wedge \mathcal{F}_P(e_2)$, and (iii) $\mathcal{F}_P(e_1) \vee \mathcal{F}_P(e_2) \Rightarrow \mathcal{F}_P(e_1 \vee e_2)$ (refer to [12] for proofs).*

The operation $\mathcal{F}_P(e)$ does not distribute over disjunctions. Consider the example where $P \doteq \{x \neq 5\}$ and $e \doteq x < 5 \vee x > 5$. In this case, $\mathcal{F}_P(e) = x \neq 5$. However $\mathcal{F}_P(x < 5) = \texttt{false}$ and $\mathcal{F}_P(x > 5) = \texttt{false}$ and thus $(\mathcal{F}_P(x < 5) \vee \mathcal{F}_P(x > 5))$ is not the same as $\mathcal{F}_P(e)$.

The above properties suggest that one can adopt a two-tier approach to compute $\mathcal{F}_P(e)$ for any formula e:

1. Convert e into an equivalent Conjunctive Normal Form (CNF), which comprises of a conjunction of clauses, i.e., $e \equiv (\bigwedge_i cl_i)$.
2. For each clause $cl_i \doteq (e^i_1 \vee e^i_2 \ldots \vee e^i_m)$, compute $r_i \doteq \mathcal{F}_P(cl_i)$ and return $\mathcal{F}_P(e) \doteq \bigwedge_i r_i$.

We focus here on computing $\mathcal{F}_P(\bigvee_{e_i \in E} e_i)$ when e_i is a predicate. Unless specified otherwise, we always use e to denote $(\bigvee_{e_i \in E} e_i)$, a disjunction of predicates in the set E in the sequel. For converting a formula to an equivalent CNF efficiently, we can use the method proposed by McMillan [14].

3 Symbolic Decision Procedures (SDP)

We now show how to perform predicate abstraction using symbolic decision procedures. We start by describing a saturation-based decision procedure for a theory T and then use it to describe the meaning of a symbolic decision procedure for the theory T. Finally, we show how a symbolic decision procedure can yield a shared expression of $\mathcal{F}_P(e)$ for predicate abstraction.

$$\frac{X = Y}{Y = X} \qquad \frac{X = Y \quad X \neq Y}{\bot}$$

$$\frac{X = Y \quad Y = Z}{X = Z} \qquad \frac{X_1 = Y_1 \quad \cdots \quad X_n = Y_n}{f(X_1, \cdots, X_n) = f(Y_1, \cdots, Y_n)}$$

Fig. 2. Inference rules for theory of equality and uninterpreted functions

A set of predicates G (over theory T) is unsatisfiable if the formula $(\bigwedge_{g \in G} g)$ is unsatisfiable. For a given theory T, the decision procedure for T takes a set of predicates G in the theory and checks if G is unsatisfiable. A theory is defined by a set of *inference rules*. An inference rule R is of the form:

$$\frac{A_1 \quad A_2 \quad \ldots \quad A_n}{A} \qquad (R)$$

which denotes that the predicate A can be derived from predicates $A_1, \ldots, A_n$ in one step. Each theory has least one inference rule for deriving *contradiction* ($\perp$). We also use $g :- g_1, \ldots, g_k$ to denote that the predicate g (or $\perp$, where $g = \perp$) can be derived from the predicates $g_1, \ldots, g_k$ using one of the inference rules in a single step. Figure 2 describes the inference rules for the theory of Equality and Uninterpreted Functions.

3.1 Saturation Based Decision Procedures

Consider a simple saturation-based procedure DP_T shown in Figure 3, that takes a set of predicates G as input and returns SATISFIABLE or UNSATISFIABLE.

The algorithm maintains two sets: (i) W is the set of predicates derived from G up to (and including) the current iteration of the loop in step (2); (ii) W' is the set of all predicates derived before the current iteration. These sets are initialized in step (1). During each iteration of step (2), if a new predicate g can be derived from a set of predicates $\{g_1, \ldots, g_k\} \subseteq W'$, then g is added to W. The loop terminates after a bound $derivDepth_T(G)$. In step (3), we check if *any* subset of facts in W can derive contradiction. If such a subset exists, the algorithm returns UNSATISFIABLE, otherwise it returns SATISFIABLE.

The parameter $d \doteq derivDepth_T(G)$ is a bound (that is determined solely by the set G for the theory T) such that if the loop in step (2) is repeated for at least d steps, then $DP_T(G)$ returns UNSATISFIABLE if and only if G is unsatisfiable. If such a bound exists for any set of predicates G in the theory, then DP_T procedure implements a decision procedure for T.

Definition 2. *A theory T is called a saturation theory, if the procedure DP_T described in Figure 3 implements a decision procedure for T.*

In the rest of the paper, we only consider saturation theories. To show that a theory T is a saturation theory, it suffices to consider a decision procedure algorithm for T (say A_T) and show that DP_T implements A_T. This can be shown by deriving a bound on $derivDepth_T(G)$ for any set G in the theory.

3.2 Symbolic Decision Procedure

For a (saturation) theory T, a symbolic decision procedure for T (SDP_T) takes sets of predicates G and E as inputs, and symbolically simulates DP_T on $G' \cup \widetilde{E}$, for every subset $G' \subseteq G$. The output of $SDP_T(G, E)$ is a symbolic expression representing those subsets $G' \subseteq G$, such that $G' \cup \widetilde{E}$ is unsatisfiable. Thus with $|G| = n$, a single run of SDP_T symbolically executes 2^n runs of DP_T.

1. Initialize $W \leftarrow G$. $W' \leftarrow \{\}$.
2. For $i = 1$ to $derivDepth_T(G)$:
   (a) Let $W' \leftarrow W$.
   (b) For every fact $g \notin W'$, if $(g :- g_1, \ldots, g_k)$ and $g_m \in W'$ for all $m \in [1, k]$:
      - $W \leftarrow W \cup \{g\}$.
3. If $(\bot :- g_1, \ldots, g_k)$ and $g_m \in W$ for all $m \in [1, k]$:
   - return UNSATISFIABLE
4. else return SATISFIABLE

Fig. 3. $DP_T(G)$: A simple saturation-based procedure for theory T

We introduce a set of Boolean variables $B_G \doteq \{b_g \mid g \in G\}$, one for each predicate in G. An assignment $\sigma : B_G \to \{\mathtt{true}, \mathtt{false}\}$ over B_G uniquely represents a subset $G' \doteq \{g \mid \sigma(b_g) = \mathtt{true}\}$ of G.

Figure 4 presents the symbolic decision procedure for a theory T, which symbolically executes the saturation based decision procedure DP_T on all possible subsets of the input component G. Just like the DP_T algorithm, this procedure also has three main components: *initialization*, *saturation* and *contradiction* detection. The algorithm also maintains sets W and W', as the DP_T algorithm does.

Since $SDP(G, E)$ has to execute $DP_T(G' \cup \widetilde{E})$ on all $G' \subseteq G$, the number of steps to iterate the saturation loop equals the maximum $derivDepth_T(G' \cup \widetilde{E})$ for any $G' \subseteq G$. For a set of predicates S, we define the bound $maxDerivDepth_T(S)$ as follows:

$$maxDerivDepth_T(S) \doteq max\{derivDepth_T(S') \mid S' \subseteq S\}$$

During the execution, the algorithm constructs a set of shared expressions with the variables over B_G as the leaves and temporary variables $t[\cdot]$ to name intermediate expressions. We use $t[(g, i)]$ to denote the expression for the predicate g *after* the iteration i of the loop in step (2) of the algorithm. We use $t[(g, \top)]$ to denote the top-most expression for g in the shared expression. Below, we briefly describe each of the phases of SDP_T:

Initialization [Step (1)]. The set W is initialized to $G \cup \widetilde{E}$ and W' to $\{\}$. The leaves of the shared expression symbolically encode each subset $G' \cup \widetilde{E}$, for every $G' \subseteq G$. For each $g \in G$, the leaf $t[(g, 0)]$ is set to b_g. For any $e_i \in E$, since $\neg e_i$ is present in all possible subset $G' \cup \widetilde{E}$, we replace the leaf for $\neg e_i$ with true.

Saturation [Step (2)]. For each predicate g, $S(g)$ is the set of derivations of g from predicates in W' during any iteration. For any predicate g, we first add all the ways to derive g until the previous steps by adding $t[(g, i-1)]$ to $S(g)$. Every time g can be derived from some set of facts $g_1, \ldots, g_k$ such that each g_j is in W', we add this derivation to $S(g)$ in Equation 2. At the end of the iteration i, $t[(g, i)]$ and $t[(g, \top)]$ are updated with the set of derivations in $S(g)$. The loop is executed $maxDerivDepth_T(G \cup \widetilde{E})$ times.

Contradiction [Steps (3,4)]. We know that if $G' \cup \widetilde{E}$ is unsatisfiable, then G' implies e (recall, e stands for $\bigvee_{e_i \in E} e_i$). Therefore, each derivation of $\bot$

1. Initialization
   (a) $W \leftarrow G \cup \widetilde{E}$ and $W' \leftarrow \{\}$.
   (b) For each $g \in G$, $t[(g, 0)] \leftarrow b_g$.
   (c) For each $e_i \in E$, $t[(\neg e_i, 0)] \leftarrow$ `true`.
2. For $i = 1$ to $maxDerivDepth_T(G \cup \widetilde{E})$ do:
   (a) $W' \leftarrow W$.
   (b) Initialize $S(g) = \{\}$, for any predicate g.
   (c) For every $g \in W'$, $S(g) \leftarrow S(g) \cup \{t[(g, i-1)]\}$.
   (d) For every g, if $(g :- g_1, \ldots, g_k)$ and $g_m \in W'$ for all $m \in [1, k]$:
      i. Update the set of derivations of g at this level:
$$S(g) \leftarrow S(g) \cup \{\left(\bigwedge_{m \in [1,k]} t[(g_m, i-1)]\right)\} \tag{2}$$
      ii. $W \leftarrow W \cup \{g\}$.
   (e) For each $g \in W$: $t[(g, i)] \leftarrow \bigvee_{d \in S(g)} d$
   (f) For each $g \in W$, $t[(g, \top)] \leftarrow t[(g, i)]$
3. Check for contradiction:
   (a) Initialize $S(e) = \{\}$.
   (b) For every $\{g_1, \ldots, g_k\} \subseteq W$, if $(\perp :- g_1, \ldots, g_k)$ then
$$S(e) \leftarrow S(e) \cup \{\left(\bigwedge_{m \in [1,k]} t[(g_m, \top)]\right)\} \tag{3}$$
   (c) Create the derivations for the goal e as $t[e] \leftarrow \left(\bigvee_{d \in S(e)} d\right)$
4. Return the shared expression for $t[e]$.

Fig. 4. Symbolic decision procedure $SDP_T(G, E)$ for theory T. The expression e stands for $\bigvee_{e_i \in E} e_i$.

from predicates in W gives a new derivation of e. The set $S(e)$ collects these derivations and constructs the final expression $t[e]$, which is returned in step (4).

The output of the procedure is the shared expression $t[e]$. The leaves of the expression are the variables in B_G. The only operations in $t[e]$ are conjunction and disjunction; $t[e]$ is thus a Boolean expression over B_G. We now define the evaluation of a (shared) expression with respect to a subset $G' \subseteq G$.

Definition 3. *For any expression $t[x]$ whose leaves are in set B_G, and a set $G' \subseteq G$, we define $eval(t[x], G')$ as the evaluation of $t[x]$, after replacing each leaf b_g of $t[x]$ with* `true` *if $g \in G'$ and with* `false` *otherwise.*

The following theorem explains the correctness of the symbolic decision procedure.

Theorem 1. *If $t[e] \doteq SDP_T(G, E)$, then for any set of predicates $G' \subseteq G$, $eval(t[e], G') =$* `true` *if and only if $DP_T(G' \cup \widetilde{E})$ returns* UNSATISFIABLE.

Corollary 1. *For a set of predicates P, if $t[e] \doteq SDP_T(P \cup \widetilde{P}, E)$, then for any $P' \subseteq (P \cup \widetilde{P})$ representing a minterm over P (i.e. $p_i \in P'$ iff $\neg p_i \notin P'$), $eval(t[e], P') = eval(\mathcal{F}_P(e), P')$.*

Hence $t[e]$ is a shared expression for $\mathcal{F}_P(e)$, where e denotes $\bigvee_{e_i \in E} e_i$. An explicit representation of $\mathcal{F}_P(e)$ can be obtained by first computing $t[e] \doteq SDP_T(P \cup \widetilde{P}, E)$ and then enumerating the cubes over P that make $t[e]$ **true**.

In the following sections, we will instantiate T to be the EUF and DIF theories and show that SDP_T exists for such theories. For each theory, we only need to determine the value of $maxDerivDepth_T(G)$ for any set of predicates G.

Remark 1. It may be tempting to terminate the loop in step (2) of $SDP_T(G, E)$ once the set of predicates in W does not change across two iterations. However, this would lead to an incomplete procedure and the following example demonstrates this.

Example 1. Consider an example where G contains a set of predicates that denotes an "almost" fully connected graph over vertices $x_1, \ldots, x_n$. G contains an equality predicate between every pair of variables except the edge between x_1 and x_n. Let $E \doteq \{x_1 = x_n\}$.

After one iteration of the SDP_T algorithm on this example, W will contain an equality between every pair of variables including x_1 and x_n since $x_1 = x_n$ can be derived from $x_1 = x_i, x_i = x_n$, for every $1 < i < n$. Therefore, if the SDP_T algorithm terminates once the set of predicates in W terminates, the procedure will terminate after two steps.

Now, consider the subset $G' = \{x_1 = x_2, x_2 = x_3, \ldots, x_i = x_{i+1}, \ldots, x_{n-1} = x_n\}$ of G. For this subset of G, $DP_T(G' \cup \widetilde{E})$ requires $lg(n) > 1$ (for $n > 2$) steps to derive the fact $x_1 = x_n$. Therefore $SDP_T(G, E)$ does not simulate the action of $DP_T(G' \cup \widetilde{E})$. More formally, we can show that $eval(t[e], G') =$ **false**, but $G' \cup \widetilde{E}$ is unsatisfiable.

3.3 *SDP* for Equality and Uninterpreted Functions

The terms in this logic can either be variables or application of an uninterpreted function symbol to a list of terms. A predicate in this theory is $t_1 \sim t_2$, where t_i is a term and $\sim \in \{=, \neq\}$. For a set G of EUF predicates, $G_=$ and $G_{\neq}$ denote the set of equality and disequality predicates in G, respectively. Figure 2 describes the inference rules for this theory.

Let $terms(\phi)$ denote the set of syntactically distinct terms in an expression (a term or a formula) ϕ. For example, $terms(f(h(x)))$ is $\{x, h(x), f(h(x))\}$. For a set of predicates G, $terms(G)$ denotes the union of the set of terms in any $g \in G$.

A decision procedure for EUF can be obtained by the *congruence closure* algorithm [17], described in Figure 5.

For a set of predicates G, let $m = |terms(G)|$. We can show that if we iterate the loop in step (2) of $DP_T(G)$ (shown in Figure 3) for at least $3m$ steps, then DP_T can implement the congruence closure algorithm. More precisely, for two

1. Partition the set of terms in *terms*(G) into equivalence classes using the $G_=$ predicates. At any point in the algorithm, let $EC(t)$ denote the equivalence class for any term $t \in terms(G)$.
   (a) Initially, each term belongs to its own distinct equivalence class.
   (b) We define a procedure $merge(t_1, t_2)$ that takes two terms as inputs. The procedure first merges the equivalence classes of t_1 and t_2. If there are two terms $s_1 \doteq f(u_1, \ldots, u_n)$ and $s_2 \doteq f(v_1, \ldots, v_n)$ such that $EC(u_i) = EC(v_i)$, for every $1 \leq i \leq n$, then it recursively calls $merge(s_1, s_2)$.
   (c) For each $t_1 = t_2 \in G_=$, call $merge(t_1, t_2)$.
2. If there exists a predicate $t_1 \neq t_2$ in $G_{\neq}$, such that $EC(t_1) = EC(t_2)$, then return UNSATISFIABLE; else SATISFIABLE.

Fig. 5. Simple description of the congruence closure algorithm

terms t_1 and t_2 in *terms*(G), the predicate $t_1 = t_2$ will be derived within $3m$ iterations of the loop in step 2 of $DP_T(G)$ if and only if $EC(t_1) = EC(t_2)$ after step (1) of the congruence closure algorithm (the proof can be found in [12]).

Proposition 2. *For a set of EUF predicates G, if $m \doteq |terms(G)|$, then the value of $maxDerivDepth_T(G)$ for the theory is bound by $3m$.*

Complexity of SDP_T. The run time and size of expression generated by SDP_T depend both on $maxDerivDepth_T(G)$ for the theory and also on the maximum number of predicates in W at any point during the algorithm. The maximum number of predicates in W can be at most $m(m-1)/2$, considering equality between every pair of term. The disequalities are never used except for generating contradictions. It is also easy to verify that the size of $S(g)$ (used in step (2) of SDP_T) is polynomial in the size of input.Hence the run time of SDP_T for EUF and the size of the shared expression returned by the procedure is polynomial in the size of the input.

3.4 *SDP* for Difference Logic

Difference logic is a simple yet useful fragment of linear arithmetic, where predicates are of the form $x \bowtie y + c$, where x, y are variables, $\bowtie \in \{<, \leq\}$ and c is a real constant. Any equality $x = y + c$ is represented as a conjunction of $x \leq y + c$ and $y \leq x - c$. The variables x and y are interpreted over real numbers. The function symbol "+" and the predicate symbols $\{<, \leq\}$ are the interpreted symbols of this theory. Figure 6 presents the inference rules for this theory[3].

Given a set G of difference logic predicates, we can construct a graph where the vertices of the graph are the variables in G and there is a directed edge in the graph from x to y, labeled with $(\bowtie, c)$ if $x \bowtie y + c \in G$. We will use a predicate and an edge interchangeably in this section.

Definition 4. *A simple cycle $x_1 \bowtie x_2 + c_1, x_2 \bowtie x_3 + c_2, \ldots, x_n \bowtie x_1 + c_n$ (where each x_i is distinct) is "illegal" if the sum of the edges is $d = \Sigma_{i \in [1,n]} c_i$*

[3] Constraints like $x \bowtie c$ are handled by adding a special variable x_0 to denote the constant 0, and rewriting the constraint as $x \bowtie x_0 + c$ [19].

and either (i) all the edges in the cycle are $\leq$ *edges and* $d < 0$, *or (ii) at least one edge is an* $<$ *edge and* $d \leq 0$.

It is well known [6] that a set of difference predicates G is unsatisfiable if and only the graph constructed from the predicates has a simple illegal cycle. Alternately, if we add an edge $(\bowtie, c)$ between x and y for every simple path from x to y of weight c ($\bowtie$ determined by the labels of the edges in the path), then we only need to check for simple cycles of length two in the resultant graph. This corresponds to the rules (C) and (D) in Figure 6.

$$\frac{X \leq Z + C \qquad Z \bowtie Y + D}{X \bowtie Y + (C + D)} \text{ (A)}$$

$$\frac{X < Z + C \qquad Z \bowtie Y + D}{X < Y + (C + D)} \text{ (B)}$$

$$\frac{X < Y + C \qquad Y \bowtie X + D \qquad C + D \leq 0}{\bot} \text{ (C)}$$

$$\frac{X \leq Y + C \qquad Y \leq X + D \qquad C + D < 0}{\bot} \text{ (D)}$$

$$\frac{X \leq Y \qquad Y \leq X}{X = Y} \text{ (E)}$$

Fig. 6. Inference rules for Difference logic

For a set of predicates G, a predicate corresponding to a simple path in the graph of G can be derived within $lg(m)$ iterations of step (2) of DP_T procedure, where m is the number of variables in G (the proof is in [12]).

Proposition 3. *For a set of DIF predicates* G, *if* m *is the number of variables in* G, *then* $maxDerivDepth_T(G)$ *for the DIF theory is bound by* $lg(m)$.

Complexity of SDP_T**.** Let c_{max} be the absolute value of the largest constant in the set G. We can ignore any derived predicate in of the form $x \bowtie y + C$ from the set W where the absolute value of C is greater than $(m-1) * c_{max}$. This is because the maximum weight of any simple path between x and y can be at most $(m-1) * c_{max}$. Again, let *const(g)* be the absolute value of the constant in a predicate g. The maximum weight on any simple path has to be a combination of these weights. Thus, the absolute value of the constant is bound by:

$$C \leq min\{(m-1) * c_{max}, \Sigma_{g \in G} const(g)\}$$

The maximum number of derived predicates in W can be $2 * m^2 * (2 * C + 1)$, where a predicate can be either $\leq$ or $<$, with m^2 possible variable pairs and the absolute value of the constant is bound by C. This is a *pseudo polynomial* bound as it depends on the value of the constants in the input.

However, many program verification queries use a subset of difference logic where each predicate is of the form $x \bowtie y$ or $x \bowtie c$. For this case, the maximum number of predicates generated can be $2 * m * (m - 1 + k)$, where k is the number of different constants in the input.

4 Combining *SDP* for Saturation Theories

In this section, we provide a method to construct a symbolic decision procedure for the combination of saturation theories T_1 and T_2, given *SDP* for T_1 and T_2. The combination is based on an extension of the Nelson-Oppen (N-O) framework [16] that constructs a decision procedure for the theory $T_1 \cup T_2$ using the decision procedures of T_1 and T_2.

We assume that the theories T_1 and T_2 have disjoint signatures (i.e., they do not share any function symbol), and each theory T_i is *convex* and *stably infinite*[4]. Let us briefly explain the N-O method for combining decision procedures before explaining the method for combining *SDP*.

4.1 Nelson-Oppen Method for Combining Decision Procedures

Given two theories T_1 and T_2, and the decision procedures DP_{T_1} and DP_{T_2}, the N-O framework constructs the decision procedure for $T_1 \cup T_2$, denoted as $DP_{T_1 \cup T_2}$.

To decide an input set G, the first step in the procedure is to *purify* G into sets G_1 and G_2 such that G_i only contains symbols from theory T_i and G is satisfiable if and only if $G_1 \cup G_2$ is satisfiable. Consider a predicate $g \doteq p(t_1, \ldots, t_n)$ in G, where p is a theory T_1 symbol. The predicate g is purified to g' by replacing each subterm t_j whose top-level symbol does not belong to T_1 with a fresh variable w_j. The expression t_j is then purified to t'_j recursively. We add g' to G_1 and the *binding predicate* $w_j = t'_j$ to the set G_2. We denote the latter as binding predicate because it binds the fresh variable w_j to a term t'_j.

Let V_{sh} be the set of *shared* variables that appear in $G_1 \cap G_2$. A set of equalities Δ over variables in V_{sh} is maintained; Δ records the set of equalities implied by the facts from either theory. Initially, $\Delta = \{\}$.

Each theory T_i then alternately decides if $DP_{T_i}(G_i \cup \Delta)$ is unsatisfiable. If any theory reports UNSATISFIABLE, the algorithm returns UNSATISFIABLE; otherwise, the theory T_i generates the new set of equalities over V_{sh} that are implied by $G_i \cup \Delta$[5]. These equalities are added to Δ and are communicated to the other theory. This process is continued until the set Δ does not change. In this case, the method returns SATISFIABLE. Let us denote this algorithm as $DP_{T_1 \cup T_2}$.

Theorem 2 ([16]). *For convex, stably infinite and signature-disjoint theories T_1 and T_2, $DP_{T_1 \cup T_2}$ is a decision procedure for $T_1 \cup T_2$.*

There can be at most $|V_{sh}|$ irredundant equalities over V_{sh}, therefore the N-O loop terminates after $|V_{sh}|$ iterations for any input.

4.2 Combining *SDP* Using Nelson-Oppen Method

We will briefly describe a method to construct the $SDP_{T_1 \cup T_2}$ by combining SDP_{T_1} and SDP_{T_2}. As before, the input to the method is the pair (G, E) and

[4] We need these restrictions only to exploit the N-O combination result. The definition of convexity and stably infiniteness can be found in [16].

[5] We assume that each theory has an inference rule for deriving equality between variables in the theory, and DP_T also returns a set of equality over variables.

the output is an expression $t[e]$. The facts in E are also purified into sets E_1 and E_2 and the new binding predicates are added to either G_1 or G_2.

Our goal is to symbolically encode the runs of the N-O procedure for $G' \cup \widetilde{E}$, for every $G' \subseteq G$. For any equality predicate δ over V_{sh}, we maintain an expression ψ_δ that records all the different ways to derive δ (initialized to `false`). We also maintain an expression ψ_e to record all the derivations of e (initialized to `false`).

The N-O loop operates just like the case for constructing $DP_{T_1 \cup T_2}$. The SDP_{T_i} for each theory T_i now takes $(G_i \cup \Delta, E_i)$ as input, where Δ is the set of equalities over V_{sh} derived so far. In addition to computing the (shared) expression $t[e]$ as before, SDP_{T_i} also returns the expression $t[(\delta, \top)]$, for each equality δ over V_{sh} that can be derived in step (2) of the SDP_T algorithm.

The leaves of the expressions $t[e]$ and $t[(\delta, \top)]$ are $G_i \cup \Delta$ (since leaves for $\widetilde{E_i}$ are replaced with `true`). We substitute the leaves for any $\delta \in \Delta$ with the expression ψ_δ, to incorporate the derivations of δ until this point. We also update $\psi_\delta \leftarrow (\psi_\delta \vee t[(\delta, \top)])$ to add the new derivations of δ. Similarly, we update $\psi_e \leftarrow (\psi_e \vee t[e])$ with the new derivations.

The N-O loop iterates $|V_{sh}|$ number of times to ensure that it has seen every derivation of a shared equality over V_{sh} from any set $G'_1 \cup G'_2 \cup \widetilde{E_1} \cup \widetilde{E_2}$, where $G'_i \subseteq G_i$.

After the N-O iteration terminates, ψ_e contains all the derivations of e from G. However, at this point, there are two kind of predicates in the leaves of ψ_e; the purified predicates and the binding predicates. If g' was the purified form of a predicate $g \in G$, we replace the leaf for g' with b_g. The leaves of the binding predicates are replaced with `true`, as the fresh variables in these predicates are really names for subterms in any predicate, and thus their presence does not affect the satisfiability of a formula. Let $t[e]$ denote the final expression for ψ_e that is returned by $SDP_{T_1 \cup T_2}$. Observe that the leaves of $t[e]$ are variables in B_G.

Theorem 3. *For two convex, stably-infinite and signature-disjoint theories T_1 and T_2, if $t[e] \doteq SDP_{T_1 \cup T_2}(G, E)$, then for any set of predicates $G' \subseteq G$, $eval(t[e], G') =$ `true` if and only if $DP_{T_1 \cup T_2}(G' \cup \widetilde{E})$ returns* UNSATISFIABLE.

Since the theory of EUF and DIF satisfy all the restrictions of the theories of this section, we can construct an *SDP* for the combined theory that still runs in pseudo-polynomial time.

5 Implementation and Results

We have implemented a prototype of the symbolic decision procedure for the combination of EUF and DIF theories. To construct $\mathcal{F}_P(e)$, we first build a BDD (using the CUDD [7] BDD package) for the expression $t[e]$ (returned by $SDP_T(P \cup \widetilde{P}, E)$) and then enumerate the cubes from the BDD.

Creating the BDD for the shared expression $t[e]$ and enumerating the cubes from the BDD can have exponential complexity in the worst case. This is because

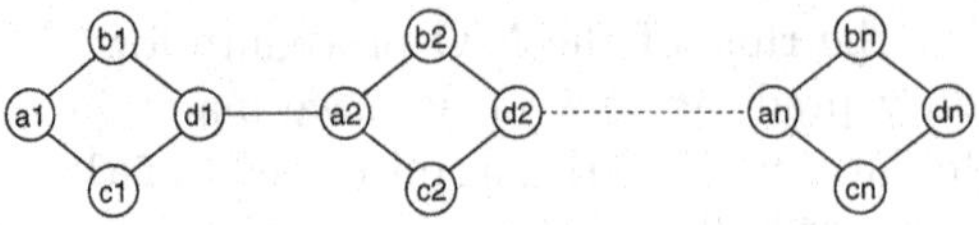

n	$\|P\|$	SDP_T time (s)	UCLID time (s)
3	14	0.20	19.37
4	19	0.43	656
5	24	0.65	-
10	49	5.81	-
12	59	12.28	-

Fig. 7. Result on diamond examples with increasing number of diamonds. The expression e is $(a1 = dn)$. A "-" denotes a timeout of 1000 seconds

the expression for $\mathcal{F}_P(e)$ can involve an exponential number of cubes (e.g. the example in Fig 7). However, most problems in practice have a few cubes in $\mathcal{F}_P(e)$. Secondly, as the number of leaves of $t[e]$ (alternately, number of BDD variables) is bound by $|P|$, the size of the overall BDD is usually small, and is computed efficiently in practice. Finally, by generating only the *prime implicants*[6] of $\mathcal{F}_P(e)$ from the BDD, we obtain a compact representation of $\mathcal{F}_P(e)$.

We report preliminary results evaluating our symbolic decision procedure based predicate abstraction method on a set of software verification benchmarks. The benchmarks are generated from the predicate abstraction step for constructing Boolean Programs from C programs of Microsoft Windows device drivers in SLAM [2].

We compare our method with two other methods for performing predicate abstraction: (i) DP-based: This method uses the decision procedure ZAPATO [1] to enumerate the set of cubes that imply e. Various optimizations (e.g. considering cubes in increasing order of size) are used to prevent enumerating exponential number of cubes in practice. (ii) UCLID-based: This method performs quantifier-elimination using incremental SAT-based methods [13].

To compare with the DP-based method, we generated 665 predicate abstraction queries from the verification of device-driver programs. Most of these queries had between 5 and 14 predicates in them and are fairly representative of queries in SLAM. The run time of DP-based method was 27904 seconds on a 3 GHz. machine with 1GB memory. The run time of *SDP*-based method was 273 seconds. This gives a little more than 100X speedup on these examples, demonstrating that our approach can scale much better than decision procedure based methods. We have not been able to run UCLID-based method on SLAM benchmarks at the point of submitting this paper.

To compare with UCLID-based approach, we generated different instances of a problem (see Figure 7 for the example) where P is a set of equality predicates representing n diamonds connected in a chain and e is an equality $a1 = dn$. We generated different problem instances by varying the size of n. For an instance

[6] For any Boolean formula ϕ over variables in V, prime implicants of ϕ is a set of cubes $C \doteq \{c_1, \ldots, c_m\}$ over V such that $\phi \Leftrightarrow \bigvee_{c \in C} c$ and two or more cubes from C can't be combined to form a larger cube.

with n diamonds, there are $5n - 1$ predicates in P and 2^n cubes in $\mathcal{F}_P(e)$ to denote all the paths from $a1$ to dn. Figure 7 shows the result comparing both the methods. We should note that UCLID method was run on a slightly slower 2GHz machine. The results illustrate that our method scales much better than the SAT-based enumeration used in UCLID for this example. Intuitively, UCLID-based approach grows exponentially with the number of predicates ($2^{|P|}$), whereas our approach only grows exponentially with the number of diamonds (2^n) in the result.

References

1. T. Ball, B. Cook, S. K. Lahiri, and L. Zhang. Zapato: Automatic Theorem Proving for Software Predicate Abstraction Refinement. In *Computer Aided Verification (CAV '04)*, LNCS 3114. Springer-Verlag, 2004.
2. T. Ball, R. Majumdar, T. Millstein, and S. K. Rajamani. Automatic predicate abstraction of C programs. In *Programming Language Design and Implementation (PLDI '01)*, Snowbird, Utah, June, 2001. *SIGPLAN Notices,* 36(5), May 2001.
3. R. E. Bryant. Graph-based algorithms for Boolean function manipulation. *IEEE Transactions on Computers*, C-35(8), August 1986.
4. S. Chaki, E. M. Clarke, A. Groce, S. Jha, and H. Veith. Modular Verification of Software Components in C. *IEEE Transactions on Software Engineering*, 30(6), June 2004.
5. E. Clarke, D. Kroening, N. Sharygina, and K. Yorav. Predicate abstraction of ANSI–C programs using SAT. *Formal Methods in System Design (FMSD)*, 25, 2004.
6. T. H. Cormen, C. E. Leiserson, and R. L. Rivest. *Introduction to Algorithms.* MIT Press, 1990.
7. CUDD:CU Decision Diagram Package. Available at `http://vlsi.colorado.edu/ fabio/CUDD/cuddIntro.html`.
8. S. Das, D. Dill, and S. Park. Experience with predicate abstraction. In *Computer-Aided Verification (CAV '99)*, LNCS 1633. Springer-Verlag, July 1999.
9. C. Flanagan and S. Qadeer. Predicate abstraction for software verification. In *Symposium on Principles of programming languages (POPL '02)*. ACM Press, 2002.
10. S. Graf and H. Saïdi. Construction of abstract state graphs with PVS. In *Computer-Aided Verification (CAV '97)*, LNCS 1254. Springer-Verlag, June 1997.
11. T. A. Henzinger, R. Jhala, R. Majumdar, and G. Sutre. Lazy Abstraction. In *Symposium on Principles of programming languages (POPL '02)*. ACM Press, 2002.
12. S. K. Lahiri, T. Ball, and B. Cook. Predicate abstraction via symbolic decision procedures. Technical Report MSR-TR-2005-53, Microsoft Research, April 2005.
13. S. K. Lahiri, R. E. Bryant, and B. Cook. A symbolic approach to predicate abstraction. In *Computer-Aided Verification (CAV 2003)*, LNCS 2725. Springer-Verlag, 2003.
14. K. McMillan. Applying SAT Methods in Unbounded Symbolic Model Checking. In *Proc. Computer-Aided Verification (CAV'02)*, LNCS 2404, July 2002.
15. K. S. Namjoshi and R. P. Kurshan. Syntactic program transformations for automatic abstraction. In *Computer Aided Verification*, LNCS 1855, 2000.
16. G. Nelson and D. C. Oppen. Simplification by cooperating decision procedures. *ACM Transactions on Programming Languages and Systems (TOPLAS)*, 2(1), 1979.

17. G. Nelson and D. C. Oppen. Fast decision procedures based on the congruence closure. *Journal of the ACM*, 27(2), 1980.
18. H. Saïdi and N. Shankar. Abstract and model check while you prove. In *Computer-Aided Verification*, volume 1633 of *LNCS*. Springer-Verlag, July 1999.
19. O. Strichman, S. A. Seshia, and R. E. Bryant. Deciding Separation Formulas with SAT. In *Proc. Computer-Aided Verification (CAV'02)*, LNCS 2404, July 2002.

Interpolant-Based Transition Relation Approximation

Ranjit Jhala[1] and K.L. McMillan[2]

[1] University of California, San Diego
[2] Cadence Berkeley Labs

Abstract. In predicate abstraction, exact image computation is problematic, requiring in the worst case an exponential number of calls to a decision procedure. For this reason, software model checkers typically use a weak approximation of the image. This can result in a failure to prove a property, even given an adequate set of predicates. We present an interpolant-based method for strengthening the abstract transition relation in case of such failures. This approach guarantees convergence given an adequate set of predicates, without requiring an exact image computation. We show empirically that the method converges more rapidly than an earlier method based on counterexample analysis.

1 Introduction

Predicate abstraction [15] is a technique commonly used in software model checking in which an infinite-state system is represented abstractly by a finite-state system whose states are the truth valuations of a chosen set of predicates. The reachable state set of the abstract system corresponds to the strongest inductive invariant of the infinite-state system expressible as a Boolean combination of the given predicates.

The primary computational difficulty of predicate abstraction is the *abstract image* computation. That is, given a set of predicate states (perhaps represented symbolically) we wish to compute the set of predicate states reachable from this set in one step of the abstract system. This can be done by enumerating the predicate states, using a suitable decision procedure to determine whether each state is reachable in one step. However, since the number of decision procedure calls is exponential in the number of predicates, this approach is practical only for small predicates sets. For this reason, software model checkers, such as SLAM [2] and BLAST [16] typically use weak approximations of the abstract image. For example, the Cartesian image approximation is the strongest cube over the predicates that is implied at the next time. This approximation loses all information about predicates that are neither deterministically true nor deterministically false at the next time. Perhaps surprisingly, some properties of large programs, such as operating system device drivers, can be verified with this weak approximation [2, 7]. Unfortunately, as we will observe, this approach

K. Etessami and S.K. Rajamani (Eds.): CAV 2005, LNCS 3576, pp. 39–51, 2005.

fails to verify properties of even very simple programs, if the properties relate to data stored in arrays.

This paper introduces an approach to approximating the transition relation of a system using Craig interpolants derived from proofs of bounded model checking instances. These interpolants are formulas that capture the information about the transition relation of the system that was deduced in proving the property in a bounded sense. Thus, the transition relation approximation we obtain is tailored to the property we are trying to prove. Moreover, it is a formula over only state-holding variables. Hence, for abstract models produced by predicate abstraction, the approximate transition relation is a purely propositional formula, even though the original transition relation is characterized by a first-order formula. Thus, we can apply well-developed Boolean image computation methods to the approximate system, eliminating the need for a decision procedure in the image computation. By iteratively refining the approximate transition relation we can guarantee convergence, in the sense that whenever the chosen predicates are adequate to prove the property, the approximate transition relation is eventually strong enough to prove the property.[1]

Related work. The most closely related method is that of Das and Dill [6]. This method analyzes abstract counterexamples (sequences of predicate states), refining the transition relation approximation in such a way as to rule out infeasible transitions. This method is effective, but has the disadvantage that it uses a specific counterexample and does not consider the property being verified. Thus it can easily generate refinements not relevant to the property. The interpolation-based method does not use abstract counterexamples. Rather, it generates facts relevant to proving the given property in a bounded sense. Thus, it tends to generate more relevant refinements, and as a result converges more rapidly.

In [7], interpolants are used to choose new predicates to refine a predicate abstraction. Here, we use interpolants to refine an approximation of the abstract transition relation for a given set of predicates.

The chief alternative to iterative approximation is to produce an exact propositional characterization of the abstract transition relation. For example the method of [9] uses small-domain techniques to translate a first-order transition formula into a propositional one that is equisatisfiable over the state-holding predicates. However, this translation introduces a large number of auxiliary

[1] The reader should bear in mind that there are two kinds of abstraction occurring here. The first is *predicate abstraction*, which produces an abstract transition system whose state-holding variables are propositional. The second is *transition relation approximation*, which weakens the abstract transition formula, yielding a purely propositional approximate transition formula. To avoid confusion, we will always refer to the former as *abstraction*, and the latter as *approximation*. The techniques presented here produce an exact reachability result *for the abstract model*. However, we may still fail to prove unreachability if an inadequate set of predicates is chosen for the abstraction.

Boolean variables, making it impractical to use BDD-based methods for image computation. Though SAT-base Boolean quantifier elimination methods can be used, the effect is still essentially to enumerate the states in the image. By contrast, the interpolation-based method produces an approximate transition relation with no auxiliary Boolean variables, allowing efficient use of BDD-based methods.

Outline. In the next section, we introduce some notations and definitions related to modeling infinite-state systems symbolically, and briefly describe the method of deriving interpolants from proofs. Then in section 3, we introduce the basic method of transition relation approximation using interpolants. In the following section, we discuss a number of optimizations of this basic method that are particular to software verification. Section 6 then presents an experimental comparison of the interpolation method with the Das and Dill method.

2 Preliminaries

Let S be a first-order signature, consisting of individual variables and uninterpreted n-ary functional and propositional constants. A *state formula* is a first-order formula over S, (which may include various interpreted symbols, such as $=$ and $+$). We can think of a state formula ϕ as representing a set of states, namely, the set of first-order models of ϕ. We will express the proposition that an interpretation σ over S models ϕ by $\phi[\sigma]$.

We also assume a first-order signature S', disjoint from S, and containing for every symbol $s \in S$, a unique symbol s' of the same type. For any formula or term ϕ over S, we will use ϕ' to represent the result of replacing every occurrence of a symbol s in ϕ with s'. Similarly, for any interpretation σ over S, we will denote by σ' the interpretation over S' such that $\sigma' s' = \sigma s$. A *transition formula* is a first-order formula over $S \cup S'$. We think of a transition formula T as representing a set of state pairs, namely the set of pairs (σ_1, σ_2), such that $\sigma_1 \cup \sigma_2'$ models T. Will will express the proposition that $\sigma_1 \cup \sigma_2'$ models T by $T[\sigma_1, \sigma_2]$.

The *strongest postcondition* of a state formula ϕ with respect to transition formula T, denoted $\mathrm{sp}_T(\phi)$, is the strongest proposition ψ such that $\phi \wedge T$ implies ψ'. We will also refer to this as the *image* of ϕ with respect to T. Similarly, the *weakest precondition* of a state formula ϕ with respect to transition formula T, denoted $\mathrm{wp}_T(\phi)$ is the weakest proposition ψ such that $\psi \wedge T$ implies ϕ'.

A *transition system* is a pair (I, T), where I is a state formula and T is a transition formula. Given a state formula ψ, we will say that ψ is k*-reachable* in (I, T) when there exists a sequence of states $\sigma_0, \ldots, \sigma_k$, such that $I[\sigma_0]$ and for all $0 \leq i < k$, $T[\sigma_i, \sigma_{i+1}]$, and $\psi[\sigma_k]$. Further, ψ is *reachable* in (I, T) if it is k-reachable for some k. We will say that ϕ is an *invariant* of (I, T) when $\neg\phi$ is not reachable in (I, T). A state formula ϕ is an *inductive invariant* of (I, T) when I implies ϕ and $\mathrm{sp}_T(\phi)$ implies ϕ (note that an inductive invariant is trivially an invariant).

Bounded Model Checking. The fact that ψ is k-reachable in (I,T) can be expressed symbolically. For any symbol s, and natural number i, we will use the notation $s^{\langle i\rangle}$ to represent the symbol s with i primes added. Thus, $s^{\langle 3\rangle}$ is s'''. A symbol with i primes will be used to represent the value of that symbol at time i. We also extend this notation to formulas. Thus, the formula $\phi^{\langle i\rangle}$ is the result of adding i primes to every uninterpreted symbol in ϕ.

Now, assuming T is total, the state formula ψ is k-reachable in (I,T) exactly when this formula is consistent:

$$I^{\langle 0\rangle} \wedge T^{\langle 0\rangle} \wedge \cdots T^{\langle k-1\rangle} \wedge \psi^{\langle k\rangle}$$

We will refer to this as a *bounded model checking* formula [3], since by testing satisfiability of such formulas, we can determine the reachability of a given condition within a bounded number of steps.

Interpolants From Proofs. Given a pair of formulas (A,B), such that $A \wedge B$ is inconsistent, an *interpolant* for (A,B) is a formula $\hat{A}$ with the following properties:

- A implies $\hat{A}$,
- $\hat{A} \wedge B$ is unsatisfiable, and
- $\hat{A}$ refers only to the common symbols of A and B.

Here, "symbols" excludes symbols such as $\wedge$ and $=$ that are part of the logic itself. Craig showed that for first-order formulas, an interpolant always exists for inconsistent formulas [5]. Of more practical interest is that, for certain proof systems, an interpolant can be derived from a refutation of $A \wedge B$ in linear time. For example, a purely propositional refutation of $A \wedge B$ using the resolution rule can be translated to an interpolant in the form of a Boolean circuit having the same structure as the proof [8, 13].

In [11] it is shown that linear-size interpolants can be derived from refutations in a first-order theory with uninterpreted function symbols and linear arithmetic. This translation has the property that whenever A and B are quantifier-free, the derived interpolant $\hat{A}$ is also quantifier-free.[2] We will exploit this property in the sequel.

Heuristically, the chief advantage of interpolants derived from refutations is that they capture the facts that the prover derived about A in showing that A is inconsistent with B. Thus, if the prover tends to ignore irrelevant facts and focus on relevant ones, we can think of interpolation as a way of filtering out irrelevant information from A.

For the purposes of this paper, we must extend the notion of interpolant slightly. That is, given an indexed set of formulas $A = \{a_1, \ldots, a_n\}$ such that $\bigwedge A$ is inconsistent, a *symmetric interpolant* for A is an indexed set of formulas

[2] Note that the Craig theorem does not guarantee the existence of quantifier-free interpolants. In general this depends on the choice of interpreted symbols in the logic.

$\hat{A} = \{\hat{a}_1, \ldots, \hat{a}_n\}$ such that each a_i implies $\hat{a}_i$, and $\bigwedge \hat{A}$ is inconsistent, and each $\hat{a}_i$ is over the symbols common to a_i and $A \setminus a_i$. We can construct a symmetric interpolant for A from a refutation of $\bigwedge A$ by simply letting $\hat{a}_i$ be the interpolant derived from the given refutation for the pair $(a_i, \bigwedge A \setminus a_i)$. As long as all the individual interpolants are derived *from the same proof*, we are guaranteed that their conjunction is inconsistent. In the sequel, if $\hat{A}$ is a symmetric interpolant for A, and the elements of A are not explicitly indexed, we will use the notation $\hat{A}(a_i)$ to refer to $\hat{a}_i$.

3 Transition Relation Approximation

Because of the expense of image computation in symbolic model checking, it is often beneficial to abstract the transition relation before model checking, removing information that is not relevant to the property to be proved. Some examples of techniques for this purpose are [4, 12].

In this paper, we introduce a method of approximating the transition relation using bounded model checking and symmetric interpolation. Given a transition system (I, T) and a state formula ψ that we wish to prove unreachable, we will use interpolation to refine an approximation $\hat{T}$ of the transition relation T, such that T implies $\hat{T}$. The initial approximation is just $\hat{T} = \text{TRUE}$.

$\hat{T} \leftarrow \text{TRUE}$
repeat
  if ψ unreachable in $(I, \hat{T})$, return "unreachable"
  else, if ψ reachable in k steps in $(I, \hat{T})$
    $A \leftarrow \{I^{\langle 0 \rangle}, T^{\langle 0 \rangle}, \ldots, T^{\langle k-1 \rangle}, \psi^{\langle k \rangle}\}$
    if $\bigwedge A$ satisfiable, return "reachable in k steps"
    else
      $\hat{A} \leftarrow \text{ITP}(A)$
      $\hat{T} \leftarrow \hat{T} \wedge \bigwedge_{i=0}^{k-1} (\hat{A}(T^{\langle i \rangle}))^{\langle -i \rangle}$
end repeat

Fig. 1. Interpolation-based transition approximation loop. Here, ITP is a function that computes a symmetric interpolant for a set of formulas

We begin the refinement loop by attempting to verify the unreachabilty of ψ in the approximate system $(I, \hat{T})$, using an appropriate model checking algorithm. If ψ is found to be unreachable in $(I, \hat{T})$, we know it is unreachable in the stronger system (I, T). Suppose, on the other hand that ψ is found to be k-reachable in $(I, \hat{T})$. It may be that in fact ψ is k-reachable in (I, T), or it may be that $\hat{T}$ is simply too weak an approximation to refute this. To find out, we will use bounded model checking.

That is, we construct the following set of formulas:

$$A \doteq \{I^{\langle 0\rangle}, T^{\langle 0\rangle}, \ldots, T^{\langle k-1\rangle}, \psi^{\langle k\rangle}\}$$

Note that $\bigwedge A$ is exactly the bounded model checking formula that characterizes k-reachability of ψ in (I, T). We use a decision procedure to determine satisfiability of $\bigwedge A$. If it is satisfiable, ψ is reachable and we are done. If not, we obtain from the decision procedure a refutation of $\bigwedge A$. From this, we extract a symmetric interpolant $\hat{A}$. Notice that for each i in $0 \ldots k-1$, $\hat{A}(T^{\langle i\rangle})$ is a formula implied by $T^{\langle i\rangle}$, the transition formula shifted to time i. Let us shift these formulas back to time 0, thus converting them to transition formulas. That is, for $i = 0 \ldots k-1$, let:

$$\hat{T}_i \doteq (\hat{A}(T^{\langle i\rangle}))^{\langle -i\rangle}$$

where we use $\phi^{\langle -i\rangle}$ to denote removal of i primes from ϕ, when feasible. We will call these formulas the *transition interpolants*. From the properties of symmetric interpolants, we know the bounded model checking formula

$$I_0 \wedge \hat{T}_0^{\langle 0\rangle} \wedge \cdots \hat{T}_{k-1}^{\langle k-1\rangle} \wedge \psi_k$$

is unsatisfiable. Thus we know that the conjunction of the transition interpolants $\bigwedge_i \hat{T}_i$ admits no path of k steps from I to ψ. We now compute a refined approximation $\dot{T} \doteq \hat{T} \wedge \bigwedge_i \hat{T}_i$. This becomes our approximation $\hat{T}$ in the next iteration of the loop. This procedure is summarized in Figure 1. Notice that at each iteration, the refined approximation $\dot{T}$ is strictly stronger than $\hat{T}$, since $\hat{T}$ allows a counterexample of k steps, but $\dot{T}$ does not. Thus, for finite-state systems, the loop must terminate. This is simply because we cannot strengthen a formula with a finite number of models infinitely.

The approximate transition formula $\hat{T}$ has two principle advantages over T. First, it contains only facts about the transition relation that were derived by the prover in resolving the bounded model checking problem. Thus it is in some sense an abstraction of T relative to ψ. Second, $\hat{T}$ contains only state-holding symbols. We will say that a symbol $s \in S$ is *state-holding* in (I, T) when s occurs in I, or s' occurs in T. In the bounded model checking formula, the only symbols in common between $T^{\langle i\rangle}$ and the remainder of the formula are of the form $s^{\langle i\rangle}$ or $s^{\langle i+1\rangle}$, where s is state-holding. Thus, the transition interpolants $\hat{T}_i$ contain only state-holding symbols and their primed versions.

The elimination of the non-state-holding symbols by interpolation has two potential benefits. First, in hardware verification there are usually many non-state-holding symbols representing inputs of the system. These symbols contribute substantially to the cost of the image computation in symbolic model checking. Second, for this paper, the chief benefit is in the case when the state-holding symbols are all propositional (*i.e.*, they are propositional constants). In this case, even if the transition relation T is a first-order formula, the approximation $\hat{T}$ is a propositional formula. The individual variables and function symbols are eliminated by interpolation. Thus we can apply well-developed Boolean methods for symbolic model checking to the approximate system. In the next section, we will apply this approach to predicate abstraction.

4 Application to Predicate Abstraction

Predicate abstraction [15] is a technique commonly used in software model checking in which the state of an infinite-state system is represented abstractly by the truth values of a chosen set of predicates P. The method computes the strongest inductive invariant of the system expressible as a Boolean combination of these predicates.

Let us fix a concrete transition system (I, T) and a finite set of state formulas P that we will refer to simply as "the predicates". We assume a finite set $V \subset S$ of uninterpreted propositional symbols not occurring in I or T. The set V consists of a symbol v_p for every predicate $p \in P$. We will construct an abstract transition system $(\bar{I}, \bar{T})$ whose states are the minterms over V. To relate the abstract and concrete systems, we define a concretization function γ. Given a formula over V, γ replaces every occurrence of a symbol v_p with the corresponding predicate p. Thus, if ϕ is a Boolean combination over V, $\gamma(\phi)$ is the same combination of the corresponding predicates in P.

For the sake of simplicity, we assume that the initial condition I is a Boolean combination of the predicates. Thus we choose $\bar{I}$ so that $\gamma(\bar{I}) = I$. We define the abstract transition relation $\bar{T}$ such that, for any two minterms $s, t \in 2^V$, we have $\bar{T}[s, t]$ exactly when $\gamma(s) \wedge T \wedge \gamma(t)'$ is consistent. In other words, there is a transition from abstract state s to abstract state t exactly when there is a transition from a concrete state satisfying $\gamma(s)$ to a concrete state satisfying $\gamma(t)$.

We can easily show by induction on the number of steps that if a formula ψ over V is unreachable in $(\bar{I}, \bar{T})$ then $\gamma(\psi)$ is unreachable in (I, T) (though the converse does not hold). To allow us to check whether a given ψ is in fact reachable in the abstract system, we can express the abstract transition relation symbolically [9]. The abstract transition relation can be expressed as

$$\bar{T} \doteq \left(\left(\bigwedge_{p \in P}(v_p \iff p)\right) \wedge T \wedge \left(\bigwedge_{p \in P}(p' \iff v_p')\right)\right) \downarrow (V \cup V')$$

where $Q \downarrow W$ denotes the "hiding" of non-W symbols in Q by renaming them to fresh symbols in S. Hiding the concrete symbols in this way takes the place of existential quantification. Notice that, under this definition, the state-holding symbols of $(\bar{I}, \bar{T})$ are exactly V. Moreover, for any two minterms $s, t \in 2^V$, the formula $s \wedge \bar{T} \wedge t'$ is consistent exactly when $\gamma(s) \wedge T \wedge \gamma(t)'$ is consistent. Thus, $\bar{T}$ characterizes exactly the transitions of our abstract system.

To determine whether ψ is reachable in this system using the standard "symbolic" approach, we would compute the reachable states R of the system as the limit of the following recurrence:

$$R_0 \doteq \bar{I}$$
$$R_{i+1} \doteq R_i \vee \mathrm{sp}_{\bar{T}}(R_i)$$

The difficulty here is to compute the image $\mathrm{sp}_{\bar{T}}$. We cannot apply standard propositional methods for image computation, since the transition formula $\bar{T}$ is not propositional. We can compute $\mathrm{sp}_{\bar{T}}(\phi)$ as the disjunction of all the minterms

$s \in 2^V$ such that $\phi \wedge \bar{T} \wedge s'$ is consistent. However, this is quite expensive in practice, since it requires an exponential number of calls to a theorem prover. In [9], this is avoided by translating $\bar{T}$ into a propositional formula that is equisatisfiable with $\bar{T}$ over $V \cup V'$. This makes it possible to use well developed Boolean image computation methods to compute the abstract strongest postcondition. Nonetheless, because the translation introduces a large number of free propositional variables, the standard approaches to image computation using Binary Decision Diagrams (BDD's) were found to be inefficient. Alternative methods based on enumerating the satisfiable assignments using a SAT solver were found to be more effective, at least for small numbers of predicates. However, this method is still essentially enumerative. Its primary advantage is that information learned by the solver during the generation of one satisfying assignment can be reused in the next iteration.

Here, rather than attempting to compute images exactly in the abstract system, we will simply observe that state-holding symbols of the abstraction $(\bar{I}, \bar{T})$ are all propositional. Thus, the interpolation-based transition relation approximation method of the previous section reduces the transition relation to a purely propositional formula. Moreover, it does this without introducing extraneous Boolean variables. Thus, we can apply standard BDD-based model checking methods to the approximated system $(I, \hat{T})$ without concern that non-state-holding Boolean variables will cause a combinatorial explosion. Finally, termination of the approximation loop is guaranteed because the abstract state space is finite.

5 Software Model Checking

In model checking sequential deterministic programs, we can make some significant optimizations in the above method.

Path-Based Approximation. The first optimization is to treat the program counter explicitly, rather than modeling it as a symbolic variable. The main advantage of this is that it will allow us to apply bounded model checking only to particular program paths (*i.e.*, sequences of program locations) rather than to the program as a whole.

We will say that a *program* Π is a pair (L, R), where L is a finite set of *locations*, and R is a finite set of *operations*. An operation is a triple (l, T, l') where T is a transition formula,. $l \in L$ is the entry location of the statement, and $l' \in L$ is the exit location of the statement.

A *path* of program Π from location $l_0 \in L$ to location $l_k \in L$ is a sequence $\pi \in R^{k-1}$, of the form $(l_0, T_0, l_1)(l_1, T_1, l_2) \cdots (l_{k-1}, T_{k-1}, l_k)$. We say that the path is *feasible* when there exists a sequence of states $\sigma_0 \cdots \sigma_k$ such that, for all $0 \leq i < k$, we have $T_i[\sigma_i, \sigma_{i+1}]$. The reachability problem is to determine whether program Π has a feasible path from a given initial location l_0 to a given final location l_f.

As in the previous section, we assume a fixed set of predicates P, and a corresponding set of uninterpreted propositional symbols V. Using these, we construct an abstract program $\bar{\Pi} = (L, \bar{R})$. For any operation $r = (l, T, l')$, let the abstract operation $\bar{r}$ be $(l, \bar{T}, l')$, where, as before

$$\bar{T} \doteq \left(\left(\bigwedge_{p \in P}(v_p \iff p)\right) \wedge T \wedge \left(\bigwedge_{p \in P}(p' \iff v'_p)\right)\right) \downarrow (V \cup V')$$

The abstract operation set $\bar{R}$ is then $\{\bar{r} \mid r \in R\}$. We can easily show that if a path $r_0 \cdots r_{k-1}$ is feasible, then the corresponding abstract path $\bar{r}_0 \cdots \bar{r}_{k-1}$ is also feasible. Thus if a given location l_f is unreachable from l_0 in the abstract program, it is unreachable from l_0 in the concrete program.

Now we can apply the interpolation-based approximation approach to programs. We will build an approximate program $\hat{\Pi} = (L, \hat{R})$, where $\hat{R}$ consists of an operation $\hat{r} = (l, \hat{T}, l')$ for every $\bar{r} = (l, \bar{T}, l')$ in $\bar{R}$, such that $\bar{T}$ implies $\hat{T}$, and $\hat{T}$ is over $V \cup V'$. Initially, every $\hat{T}$ is just TRUE.

At every step of the iteration, we use standard model checking methods to determine whether the approximation $\hat{\Pi}$ has a feasible path from l_0 to l_f. We can do this because the transition formulas $\hat{T}$ are all propositional. If there is no such path, then l_f is not reachable in the concrete program and we are done. Suppose on the other hand that there is such a path $\hat{\pi} = \hat{\pi}_0 \cdots \hat{\pi}_{k-1}$. Let $\bar{\pi} = \bar{\pi}_0 \cdots \bar{\pi}_{k-1}$ be the corresponding path of $\bar{\Pi}$. We can construct a bounded model checking formula to determine the feasibility of this path. Using the notation $T(r)$ to denote the T component of an operation r, let

$$A \doteq \{T(\bar{\pi}_i)^{\langle i \rangle} \mid i \in 0 \ldots k-1\}$$

The conjunction $\bigwedge A$ is consistent exactly when the abstract path $\bar{\pi}$ is feasible. Thus, if $\bigwedge A$ is consistent, the abstraction does not prove unreachability of l_f and we are done. If it is inconsistent, we construct a symmetric interpolant $\hat{A}$ for A. We extract transition interpolants as follows:

$$\hat{T}_i \doteq (\hat{A}(T(\bar{\pi}_i)^{\langle i \rangle}))^{\langle -i \rangle}$$

Each of these is implied by the $T(\bar{\pi}_i)$, the transition formula of the corresponding abstract operation. We now strengthen our approximate program $\hat{\Pi}$ using these transition interpolants. That is, for each abstract operation $\bar{r} \in \bar{R}$, the refined approximation is $\dot{r} = (l, T(\dot{r}), l')$ where

$$T(\dot{r}) \doteq T(\hat{r}) \wedge \left(\bigwedge\{\hat{T}_i \mid \bar{\pi}_i = \bar{r},\ i \in 0 \ldots k-1\}\right)$$

In other words, we constrain each approximate operation $\hat{r}$ by the set of transition interpolants for the occurrences of $\bar{r}$ in the abstract path $\bar{\pi}$. The refined approximate program is thus $(L, \dot{R})$, where $\dot{R} = \{\dot{r} \mid \bar{r} \in \bar{R}\}$. From the interpolant properties, we can easily show that the refined approximate program does not admit a feasible path corresponding to $\bar{\pi}$.

We continue in this manner until either the model checker determines that the approximate program $\hat{\Pi}$ has no feasible path from l_0 to l_f, or until bounded

statement	transition interpolant
$a[x] \leftarrow y$	$(x = z)' \Rightarrow (a[z] = y)'$
$y \leftarrow y + 1$	$(a[z] = y \Rightarrow (a[z] = y - 1)') \wedge ((x = z)' \Rightarrow x = z)$
assume $z = x$	$(a[z] = y - 1 \Rightarrow (a[z] = y - 1)') \wedge x = z$
assume $a[z] \neq y - 1$	$a[z] \neq y - 1$

Fig. 2. An infeasible program path, with transition interpolants. The statement "assume ϕ" is a guard. It aborts when ϕ is false. In the transition interpolants, we have replaced v_p with p for clarity, but in fact these formulas are over $V \cup V'$

model checking determines that the abstract program $\bar{\Pi}$ does have such a feasible path. This process must terminate, since at each step $\hat{\Pi}$ is strengthened, and we cannot strengthen a finite set of propositional formulas infinitely.

The advantage of this approach, relative to that of section 3, is that the bounded model checking formula $\bigwedge A$ only relates to a single program path. In practice, the refutation of a single path using a decision procedure is considerably less costly than the refutation of all possible paths of a given length.

As an example of using interpolation to compute an approximate program, Figure 2 shows a small program with one path, which happens to be infeasible. The method of [7] chooses the predicates $x = z$, $a[z] = y$ and $a[z] = y - 1$ to represent the abstract state space. Next to each operation in the path is shown the transition interpolant $\hat{T}_i$ that was obtained for that operation. Note that each transition interpolant is implied by the semantics of the corresponding statement, and that collectively the transition interpolants rule out the program path (the reader might wish to verify this). Moreover, the transition interpolant for the first statement, $a[x] \leftarrow y$, is $x = z \Rightarrow a[z] = y$. This is a disjunction and therefore cannot be inferred by predicate image techniques that use the Cartesian or Boolean programs approximations. In fact, the BLAST model checker cannot rule out this program path. However, using transition interpolants, we obtain a transition relation approximation that proves the program has no feasible path from beginning to end.

Modeling with Weakest Precondition. A further optimization that we can use in the case of deterministic programs is that we can express the abstract transition formulas $\bar{T}$ in terms of the weakest precondition operator. That is, if T is deterministic, the abstract transition formula $\bar{T}$ is satisfiability equivalent over $V \cup V'$ to:

$$\left(\bigwedge_{p \in P}(v_p \iff p)\right) \wedge \neg \mathrm{wp}_T(\mathrm{FALSE}) \wedge \left(\bigwedge_{p \in P}(v'_p \iff \mathrm{wp}_T(p))\right)$$

Thus, if we can symbolically compute the weakest precondition operator for the operations in our programming language, we can use this formula in place of $\bar{T}$ as the abstract transition formula. In this way, the abstract transition formula is localized to just those program variables that are related in some way to predicates P. In particular, if π is an assignment to a program variable not occurring in P, then we will have $v'_p \iff p$, for every predicate in P.

Interpolant Strengthening. In preliminary tests of the method, we found that transition interpolants derived from proofs by the method of [10] were often unnecessarily weak. For example, we might obtain $(p \wedge q) \Rightarrow (p' \wedge q')$ when the stronger $(p \Rightarrow p') \wedge (q \Rightarrow q')$ could be proved. This slowed convergence substantially. For this reason, we use here a modified version of the method of [10] that produces stronger interpolants. Space prohibits a description of this method here, but a discussion can be found in a full version of this paper [1]. The full version also discusses a hybrid between the Cartesian approximation and the interpolation-based approximation.

6 Experiments

We now experimentally compare the method of the previous section with a method due to Das and Dill [6]. This method refines an approximate transition relation by analyzing counterexamples from the approximate system to infer a refinement that rules out each counterexample. More precisely, a *counterexample* of the approximate program $(L, \hat{R})$ is an alternating sequence $\pi = \sigma_0 \hat{r}_0 \sigma_1 \cdots \hat{r}_{k-1} \sigma_k$, where each σ_i is a minterm over V, each $\hat{r}_i$ is an operation in $\hat{R}$, $l(r_0) = l_0$, $l'(r_{k-1}) = l_f$, and for all $0 \leq i < k$, we have $T(\hat{r}_i)[\sigma_i, \sigma_{i+1}]$. This induces a set of *transition minterms*, $t_i = \sigma_i \wedge \sigma'_{i+1}$, for $0 \leq i < k$. Note that each t_i is by definition consistent with $T(\hat{r}_i)$.

To refine the approximate program, we test each t_i for consistency with the corresponding abstract transition formula $T(\bar{r}_i)$. If it is inconsistent, the counterexample is false (due to over-approximation). Using an incremental decision procedure, we then greedily remove literals from t_i that can be removed while retaining inconsistency with $T(\bar{r}_i)$. The result is a minimal (but not minimum) cube that is inconsistent with $T(\bar{r}_i)$. The negation of this cube is implied by $T(\bar{r}_i)$, so we use it to strengthen corresponding approximate transition formula $T(\hat{r}_i)$. Since more than one transition minterm may be inconsistent, we may refine several approximate operations in this way (however if none are inconsistent, we have found a true counterexample of the abstraction).

Both approximation refinement procedures are embedded as subroutines of the BLAST software model checker. Whenever the model checker finds a path from an initial state to a failure state in the approximate program, it calls the refinement procedure. If refinement fails because the abstraction does not prove the property, the procedure of [7] is used to add predicates to the abstraction. Since both refinement methods are embedded in the same model checking procedure and use the same decision procedure, we can obtain a fairly direct comparison.

Our benchmarks are a set of C programs with assertions embedded to test properties relating to the contents of arrays.[3] Some of these programs were written expressly as tests. Others were obtained by adding assertions to a sample device driver for the Linux operating system from a textbook [14]. Most of the

[3] Available at `http://www-cad.eecs.berkeley.edu/~kenmcmil/cav05data.tar.gz`

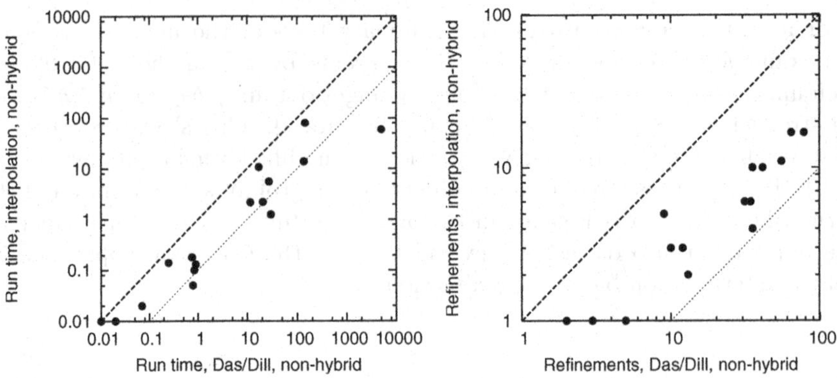

Fig. 3. Comparison of the Das/Dill and interpolation-based methods as to run time and number of refinement steps

properties are true. None of the properties can be verified or refuted by BLAST without using a refinement procedure, due to its use of the Cartesian image.

Figure 3 shows a comparison in terms of run time (on a 3GHz Intel Xeon processor) and number of refinement steps. The latter includes refinement steps that fail, causing predicates to be added. Run time includes model checking, refinement, and predicate selection. Each point represents a single benchmark problem. The X axis represents the Das/Dill method and the Y axis the interpolation-based method. Points below the heavy diagonal represent wins for the interpolation method, while points below the light diagonal represent improvements of an order of magnitude (note in one case a run-time improvement of two orders of magnitude is obtained).

The lower number of refinement steps required by interpolation method is easily explained. The Das/Dill method uses a specific counterexample and does not consider the property being verified. Thus it can easily generate refinements not relevant to proving the property. The interpolation procedure considers only the program path, and generates facts relevant to proving the property for that path. Thus, it tends to generate more relevant refinements, and as a result it converges in fewer refinements.

7 Conclusions

We have described a method that combines bounded model checking and interpolation to approximate the transition relation of a system with respect to a given safety property. The method is extensible to liveness properties of finite-state systems, in the same manner as the method of [12]. When used with predicate abstraction, the method eliminates the individual variables and function symbols from the approximate transition formula, leaving it in a propositional form. Unlike the method of [9], it does this without introducing extraneous Boolean variables. Thus, we can apply standard symbolic model checking methods to the approximate system.

For a set of benchmark programs, the method was found to converge more rapidly that the counterexample-based method of Das and Dill, primarily due to the prover's ability to focus the proof, and therefore the refinements, on facts relevant to the property. The benchmark programs used here are small (the largest being a sample device driver from a textbook), and the benchmark set contains only 19 problems. Thus we cannot draw broad conclusions about the applicability of the method. However, the experiments do show a potential to speed the convergence of transition relation refinement for real programs. Our hope is that this will make it easier to model check data-oriented rather than control-oriented properties of software.

References

1. http://www-cad.eecs.berkeley.edu/~kenmcmil/papers/cav05full.pdf.
2. Thomas Ball and Sriram K. Rajamani. The SLAM project: debugging system software via static analysis. In *POPL*, pages 1–3, 2002.
3. A. Biere, A. Cimatti, E. M. Clarke, and Y. Zhu. Symbolic model checking without BDDs. In *TACAS*, pages 193–207, 1999.
4. E. M. Clarke, O. Grumberg, S. Jha, Y. Lu, and H. Veith. Counterexample-guided abstraction refinement. In *CAV*, pages 154–169, 2000.
5. W. Craig. Three uses of the Herbrand-Gentzen theorem in relating model theory and proof theory. *J. Symbolic Logic*, 22(3):269–285, 1957.
6. S. Das and D. L. Dill. Successive approximation of abstract transition relations. In *LICS*, pages 51–60, 2001.
7. T. A. Henzinger, R. Jhala, R. Majumdar, and K. L. McMillan. Abstractions from proofs. In *POPL*, pages 232–244, 2004.
8. J. Krajíček. Interpolation theorems, lower bounds for proof systems, and independence results for bounded arithmetic. *J. Symbolic Logic*, 62(2):457–486, June 1997.
9. S. K. Lahiri, R. E. Bryant, and B. Cook. A symbolic approach to predicate abstraction. In *CAV*, pages 141–153, 2003.
10. K. L. McMillan. Interpolation and sat-based model checking. In *CAV*, pages 1–13, 2003.
11. K. L. McMillan. An interpolating prover. *Theoretical Computer Science*, 2005. To appear.
12. K. L. McMillan and N. Amla. Automatic abstraction without counterexamples. In *TACAS*, pages 2–17, 2003.
13. P. Pudlák. Lower bounds for resolution and cutting plane proofs and monotone computations. *J. Symbolic Logic*, 62(2):981–998, June 1997.
14. A. Rubini and J. Corbet. *Linux Device Drivers*. O'Reilly, 2001.
15. H. Saïdi and S. Graf. Construction of abstract state graphs with PVS. In *CAV*, pages 72–83, 1997.
16. R. Majumdar T. A. Henzinger, R. Jhala and G. Sutre. Lazy abstraction. In *POPL*, pages 58–70, 2002.

Concrete Model Checking with Abstract Matching and Refinement

Corina S. Păsăreanu[1], Radek Pelánek[2,*], and Willem Visser[3]

[1] Kestrel Technology/QSS, NASA Ames, Moffett Field, CA 94035, USA
[2] Masaryk University Brno, Czech Republic
[3] RIACS/USRA, NASA Ames, Moffett Field, CA 94035, USA

Abstract. We propose an abstraction-based model checking method which relies on refinement of an under-approximation of the feasible behaviors of the system under analysis. The method preserves errors to safety properties, since all analyzed behaviors are feasible by definition. The method does not require an abstract transition relation to be generated, but instead executes the concrete transitions while storing abstract versions of the concrete states, as specified by a set of abstraction predicates. For each explored transition the method checks, with the help of a theorem prover, whether there is any loss of precision introduced by abstraction. The results of these checks are used to decide termination or to refine the abstraction by generating new abstraction predicates. If the (possibly infinite) concrete system under analysis has a finite bisimulation quotient, then the method is guaranteed to eventually explore an equivalent finite bisimilar structure. We illustrate the application of the approach for checking concurrent programs. We also show how a lightweight variant can be used for efficient software testing.

1 Introduction

Over the last few years, model checking based on abstraction-refinement has become a popular technique for the analysis of software. In particular the abstraction technique of choice is a property preserving over-approximation called predicate abstraction [13] and the refinement removes spurious behavior based on automatically analyzing abstract counter-examples. This approach is often referred to as CEGAR (counter-example guided automated refinement) and forms the basis of some of the most popular software model checkers [2, 3, 17]. Furthermore, a strength of model checking is its ability to automate the detection of subtle errors and to produce traces that exhibit those errors. However, over-approximation based abstraction techniques are not particularly well suited for this, since the detected defects may be spurious due to the over-approximation — hence the need for refinement. We propose an alternative approach based

* Partially supported by the Grant Agency of Czech Republic grant No. 201/03/0509 and by the Academy of Sciences of Czech Republic grant No. 1ET408050503.

K. Etessami and S.K. Rajamani (Eds.): CAV 2005, LNCS 3576, pp. 52–66, 2005.

on refinement of under-approximations, which effectively preserves the defect detection ability of model checking in the presence of aggressive abstractions.

The technique uses a novel combination of (explicit state) model checking, predicate abstraction and automated refinement to efficiently analyze increasing portions of the feasible behavior of a system. At each step, either an error is found, we are guaranteed no error exists, or the abstraction is refined. More precisely, the proposed model checking technique traverses the concrete transitions of the system and for each explored concrete state, it stores an abstract version of the state. The abstract state, computed by predicate abstraction, is used to determine whether the model checker's search should continue or backtrack (if the abstract state has been visited before). This effectively explores an under-approximation of the feasible behavior of the analyzed system. Hence all counter-examples to safety properties are preserved.

Refinement uses weakest precondition calculations to check, with the help of a theorem prover, whether the abstraction introduces any loss of precision with respect to each explored transition. If there is no loss of precision due to abstraction (we say that the abstraction is *exact*) the search stops and we conclude that the property holds. Otherwise, the results from the failed checks are used to refine the abstraction and the whole verification process is repeated anew. In general, the iterative refinement may not terminate. However, if a finite bisimulation quotient [19] exists for the system under analysis, then the proposed approach is guaranteed to eventually explore a finite structure that is bisimilar to the original system.

The technique can also be used in a lightweight manner, without a theorem prover, i.e. the refinement guided by the exactness checks is replaced with refinement based on syntactic substitutions [21] or heuristic refinement. The proposed technique can be used for systematic testing, as it examines increasing portions of the system under analysis. In fact, our method extends existing approaches to testing that use abstraction mappings [14, 28], by adding support for automated abstraction refinement.

To the best of our knowledge, the presented approach is the first predicate abstraction based analysis which focuses on automated refinement of under-approximations with the goal of efficient error detection. We illustrate the application of the approach for checking safety properties in concurrent programs and for testing container implementations.

Comparison with Related Work. The most closely related work to ours is that of Grumberg et al. [15] where a refinement of an under-approximation is used to improve analysis of multi-process systems. The procedure in [15] checks models with an increasing set of allowed interleavings of the given processes, starting from a single interleaving. It uses SAT-based bounded model checking for analysis and refinement, whereas here we focus on explicit model checking and predicate abstraction, and we use weakest precondition calculations for abstraction refinement.

Our approach can be contrasted with the work on predicate abstraction for modal transition systems [12, 24], used in the verification and refutation of branching time temporal logic properties. An abstract model for such logics distinguishes between *may* transitions, which over-approximate transitions of the concrete model, and *must* transitions, which under-approximate the concrete transitions (see also [1, 6, 7]). The method presented here explores and generates a structure which is *more precise* (contains more feasible behaviors) than the model defined by the *must* transitions, for the same abstraction predicates. The reason is that the model checker explores transitions that correspond not only to *must* transitions, but also to *may* transitions that are feasible (see Section 2).

Moreover, unlike [12, 24] and over-approximation based abstraction techniques [2, 3], the under-approximation and refinement approach does not require the a priori construction of the abstract transition relation, which involves exponentially many theorem prover calls (in the number of predicates), regardless of the size of (the reachable portion of) the analyzed system. In our case, the model checker executes concrete transitions and a theorem prover is only used during refinement, to determine whether the abstraction is exact with respect to each executed transition. Every such calculation makes at most two theorem prover calls, and it involves only the *reachable* state space of the system under analysis. Another difference with previous abstraction techniques is that the refinement process is not guided by the spurious counter-examples, since no spurious behavior is explored. Instead, the refinement is guided by the failed exactness checks for the explored transitions.

In previous work [22], we developed a technique for finding guaranteed feasible counter-examples in abstracted programs. The technique essentially explores an under-approximation defined by the *must* abstract transitions (although the presentation is not formalized in these terms). The work presented here explores an under-approximation which is more precise than the abstract system defined by the *must* transitions. Hence it has a better chance of finding bugs while enabling more aggressive abstraction and therefore more state space reduction.

Model-driven software verification [18] advocates the use of abstraction mappings during concrete model checking in a way similar to what we present here. The CMC model checking tool [20] also attempts to store state information in memory using aggressive compressing techniques (which can be seen as a form of abstraction), while the detailed state information is kept on the stack. These techniques allow the detection of subtle bugs which can not be discovered by classical model checking, using e.g. breadth first search. or by state-less model checking [11]. While these techniques use abstractions in an ad-hoc manner, our work contributes the automated generation and refinement of abstractions.

Dataflow and type-based analyzes have been used to check safety properties of software (e.g. [25]). Unlike our work, these techniques analyze over-approximations of system behavior and may generate false positive results due to infeasible paths.

Layout. The rest of the paper is organized as follows. Section 2 shows an example illustrating our approach. Section 3 gives background information. Section 4 describes the main algorithm for performing concrete model checking with abstract matching and refinement. Section 5 discusses correctness and termination for the algorithm. Section 6 proposes extensions to the main algorithm. Section 7 illustrates applications of the approach and Section 8 concludes the paper.

2 Example

The example in Fig. 1 illustrates some of the main characteristics of our approach. Fig. 1 **(a)** shows the state space of a concrete system that has only one variable x; states are labelled with the program counter (e.g. A, B, C ...) and the concrete value of x. Fig. 1 **(b)** shows the abstract system induced by the *may* transitions for predicate $p = x < 2$. Fig. 1 **(c)** shows the abstract system induced by the *must* transitions for predicate p.

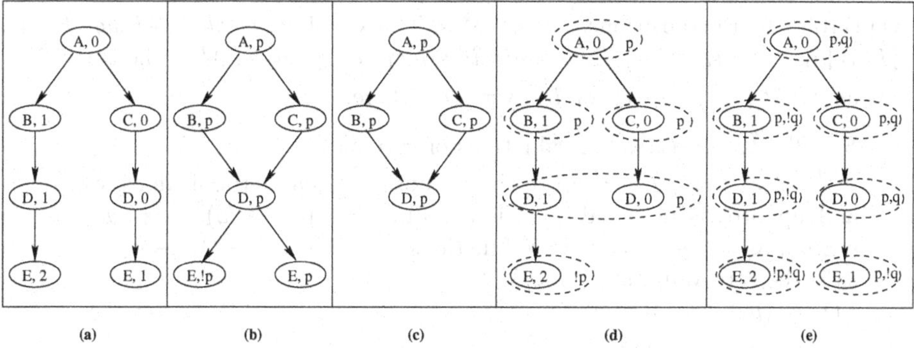

Fig. 1. **(a)** Concrete system **(b)** *May* abstraction using predicate $p = x < 2$ **(c)** *Must* abstraction using p **(d)** Concrete search with abstract matching using p **(e)** Concrete search with abstract matching using predicates p and $q = x < 1$

Fig. 1 **(d)** shows the state space explored using our proposed approach, for an abstraction specified by predicate p. Dotted circles denote the abstract states which are stored, and used for matching, during the concrete execution of the system. The approach explores only the *feasible* behavior of the concrete system, following transitions that correspond to both *may* and *must* transitions, but it might miss behavior due to abstract matching. For example, state $(E, 1)$ is not explored, assuming a breadth-first search, since $(D, 0)$ was matched with $(D, 1)$ - both have the same program counter and both satisfy p. Notice that, with respect to reachable states, the produced structure is a better under-approximation than the *must* abstraction. Fig. 1 **(e)** illustrates concrete execution with abstract matching, after a refinement step, which introduced a new predicate $q = x < 1$. The resulting structure is an exact abstraction of the concrete system.

3 Background

Program Model. To make the presentation simple, we use as a specification language a guarded commands language over integer variables. Most of the results extend directly to more sophisticated programming languages. Let V be a finite set of integer variables. Expressions over V are defined using standard boolean $(=,<,>)$ and binary $(+,-,\cdot,...)$ operations. A *model* is a tuple $M = (V,T)$. $T = \{t_1,\ldots,t_k\}$ is a finite set of transitions, where $t_i = (g_i(\boldsymbol{x}) \longmapsto \boldsymbol{x} := e_i(\boldsymbol{x}))$. $g_i(\boldsymbol{x})$ is a guard and $e_i(\boldsymbol{x})$ are assignments to the variables represented by tuple $\boldsymbol{x}$; throughout the paper, we write this as a sequence of assignments.

Semantics. As a semantics of a model we use transition systems. A *transition system* over a finite set of atomic propositions AP is a tuple (S,R,s_0,L) where S is a (possibly infinite) set of states, $R = \{\xrightarrow{i}\}$ is a finite set of deterministic transition relations: $\xrightarrow{i}\subseteq S \times S$, s_0 is an initial state, and $L : S \to 2^{AP}$ is a labelling function. State s is *reachable* if it is reachable from the initial state via zero or more transitions, i.e. $s_0 \to^* s$. The set of *reachable labellings* RL is $\{L(s) \mid \exists s \in S : s_0 \to^* s\}$. The *concrete semantics* of model M is the transition system $C(M) = (S,\{\xrightarrow{i}\},s_0,L)$ over AP, where:

- $S = 2^{V \to \mathbb{Z}}$, i.e. states are valuations of variables,
- $s \xrightarrow{i} s' \Leftrightarrow s \models g_i \wedge s' = u_i(s)$; the semantics of guards (boolean expressions) and updates is as usual; guards are functions $(V \to \mathbb{Z}) \to \{\mathit{true},\mathit{false}\}$, written as $s \models g_i$; updates are functions $u_i : (V \to \mathbb{Z}) \to (V \to \mathbb{Z})$,
- s_0 is the zero valuation $(\forall v \in V : s_0(v) = 0)$,
- $L(s) = \{p \in AP \mid s \models p\}$.

Weakest Precondition. The *weakest precondition* of a set of states X with respect to transition i is $wp(X,i) = \{s \mid s \xrightarrow{i} s' \Rightarrow s' \in X\}$. If the set of states X is characterized by a predicate ϕ, then the weakest precondition with respect to transition i can be expressed as $wp(\phi,i) = (g_i \Rightarrow \phi[e_i(\boldsymbol{x})/\boldsymbol{x}])$.

Predicate Abstraction. Predicate abstraction is a special instance of the framework of abstract interpretation [5] that maps a (potentially infinite state) transition system into a finite state transition system via a set of predicates $\Phi = \{\phi_1,\ldots,\phi_n\}$ over the program variables. Let $\mathbb{B}_n$ be a set of bitvectors of length n. We define abstraction function $\alpha_\Phi : S \to \mathbb{B}_n$, such that $\alpha_\Phi(s)$ is a bitvector $b_1 b_2 \ldots b_n$ such that $b_i = 1 \Leftrightarrow s \models \phi_i$. Let Φ_s be the set of all abstraction predicates that evaluate to *true* for a given state s, i.e. $\Phi_s = \{\phi \in \Phi \mid s \models \phi\}$. For succinctness we sometimes write $\alpha_\Phi(s)$ (or just $\alpha(s)$) to denote $\bigwedge_{\phi \in \Phi_s} \phi \wedge \bigwedge_{\phi \notin \Phi_s} \neg\phi$.

We also give here the definitions of *may* and *must* abstract transitions. Although not necessary for formalizing our algorithm, these definitions clarify the comparison with related work. For two abstract states (bitvectors) a_1 and a_2:

- $\longrightarrow_{must}$: $a_1 \xrightarrow{i}_{must} a_2$ iff for all concrete states s_1 such that $\alpha(s_1) = a_1$, there exists concrete state s_2 such that $\alpha(s_2) = a_2$ and $s_1 \xrightarrow{i} s_2$,
- $\longrightarrow_{may}$: $a_1 \xrightarrow{i}_{may} a_2$ iff there exists concrete state s_1 such that $\alpha(s_1) = a_1$ and there exists concrete state s_2 such that $\alpha(s_2) = a_2$, such that $s_1 \xrightarrow{i} s_2$.

Algorithms for computing abstractions using over-approximation based predicate abstraction are given in e.g. [2, 13] (they compute *may* abstract transitions automatically, with the help of a theorem prover). In the worst case, these algorithms make $2^n \times n \times 2$ calls to the theorem prover for each program transition. Note that our approach does not require the computation of abstract transitions, since it executes the concrete transitions directly.

Bisimulation. A symmetric relation $R \subseteq S \times S$ is a bisimulation relation iff for all $(s, s') \in R$:

- $L(s) = L(s')$
- For every $s' \xrightarrow{i} s'_1$ there exists $s \xrightarrow{i} s_1$ such that $R(s_1, s'_1)$

The bisimulation is the largest bisimulation relation, denoted $\sim$. Two transition systems are bisimilar if their initial states are bisimilar. As $\sim$ is an equivalence relation, it induces a *quotient* transition system whose states are equivalence classes with respect to $\sim$ and there is a transition between two equivalence classes A and B if $\exists s_1 \in A$ and $\exists s_2 \in B$ such that $s_1 \xrightarrow{i} s_2$.

4 Concrete Model Checking with Abstract Matching

Algorithm. Fig. 2 shows the reachability procedure that performs model checking with abstract matching (αSEARCH). It is basically concrete state space exploration with matching on abstract states; the main modification with respect to classical state space search is that we store $\alpha(s)$ instead of s. The procedure uses the following data structures:

- *States* is a set of abstract states visited so far,
- *Transitions* is a set of abstract transitions visited so far,
- *Wait* is a set of concrete states to be explored.

The procedure performs validity checking, using a theorem prover, to determine whether the abstraction is *exact* with respect to each explored transition — see discussion below. The set Φ_{new} maintains the list of abstraction predicates. The procedure returns the computed structure and a set of new predicates that are used for refinement.

Fig. 3 gives the iterative refinement algorithm for checking whether M can reach an error state described by φ. At each iteration of the loop, the algorithm invokes procedure αSEARCH to analyze an under-approximation of the system, which either violates the property, it is proved to be correct (if the abstraction is found to be exact with respect to all transitions), or it needs to be refined. Counterexamples are generated as usual (with depth-first search order using the stack, with breadth-first search order using parent pointers).

Checking for Exact Abstraction and Refinement. We say that an abstraction function α is *exact* with respect to transition $s \xrightarrow{i} s'$ iff for all s_1 such

```
proc αSEARCH(M, Φ)
  Φ_new = Φ; add s_0 to Wait; add α_Φ(s_0) to States
  while Wait ≠ ∅ do
        get s from Wait
        L(α_Φ(s)) = {a ∈ AP | s ⊨ a}
        foreach i from 1 to n do
          if s ⊨ g_i then
                    if α_Φ(s) ⇒ g_i is not valid
                      then add g_i to Φ_new fi
                    s' = u_i(s)
                    if α_Φ(s) ⇒ α_Φ(s')[e_i(x)/x] is not valid
                      then add predicates in α_Φ(s')[e_i(x)/x] to Φ_new fi
                    if α_Φ(s') ∉ States then
                                add s' to Wait
                                add α_Φ(s') to States
                    fi
                    add (α_Φ(s), i, α_Φ(s')) to Transitions
                else
                    if α_Φ(s) ⇒ ¬g_i is not valid
                      then add g_i to Φ_new fi
          fi
        od
  od
  A = (States, Transitions, α_Φ(s_0), L)
  return (A, Φ_new)
end
```

Fig. 2. Search procedure with checking for exact abstraction

```
proc REFINEMENTSEARCH(M, φ)
  i = 1; Φ_i = ∅
  while true do
        (A_i, Φ_{i+1}) = αSEARCH(M, Φ_i)
        if φ is reachable in A_i then return counter-example fi
        if Φ_{i+1} = Φ_i then return unreachable fi
        i = i + 1
  od
end
```

Fig. 3. Iterative refinement algorithm

that $\alpha(s) = \alpha(s_1)$ there exists s_1' such that $\alpha(s_1') = \alpha(s')$ and $s_1 \xrightarrow{i} s_1'$. In other words, α is *exact* with respect to $s \xrightarrow{i} s'$ iff $\alpha(s) \xrightarrow{i}_{must} \alpha(s')$. This definition is also related to the notion of *completeness* in abstract interpretation (see e.g. [10]), which states that no loss of precision is introduced by the abstraction.

Checking that the abstraction is *exact* with respect to concrete transition $s \xrightarrow{i} s'$ is equivalent to checking that $\alpha_\Phi(s) \Rightarrow wp(\alpha_\Phi(s'), i)$ is valid. This formula is equivalent to $\alpha_\Phi(s) \Rightarrow \alpha_\Phi(s')[e_i(\boldsymbol{x})/\boldsymbol{x}]$ when $s \models g_i$. Checking the validity for these formulas is in general undecidable. As is customary, if the theorem prover can not decide the validity of a formula, we assume that it is not valid. This may cause some unnecessary refinement, but it keeps the correctness of the approach. If the abstraction can not be proved to be exact with respect to some transition, then the new predicates from the failed formula are added to the set of abstraction predicates. Intuitively, these predicates will be useful for proving exactness in the next iteration.

5 Correctness and Termination

In this section we discuss the properties of the refinement algorithm. We state only the main theorems, technical lemmas and proofs are given in [23] (due to space limitations). First, we show that the set $RL(\alpha\text{SEARCH}(M, \Phi))$ of reachable labellings computed by the algorithm REFINEMENTSEARCH is a subset of the reachable labellings of the system under analysis. Note that sometimes we let $\alpha\text{SEARCH}(M, \Phi)$ denote just the structure A computed by the algorithm and not the tuple (A, Φ_{new}).

Theorem 1. *Let* $AP \subseteq \Phi$. *Then* $RL(\alpha\text{SEARCH}(M, \Phi)) \subseteq RL(C(M))$.

Moreover, it holds that $RL(\alpha\text{SEARCH}(M, \Phi))$ is a superset of the reachable labellings in the *must* abstraction (see Lemma 1 in [23]), hence it is (potentially) a better approximation.

We now show that, if the iterative algorithm terminates then the result is correct and moreover, if the error state is unreachable, the output structure is bisimilar to the system under analysis:

Theorem 2. *If* REFINEMENTSEARCH(M, φ) *terminates then:*

- *If it returns a counter-example, then it is a real error.*
- *If it returns 'unreachable', then the error state is indeed unreachable in* M *and moreover the computed structure is bisimilar to* $C(M)$.

In general, the proposed algorithm might not terminate (because of the halting problem). However, the algorithm is guaranteed to eventually find all the reachable labellings of the concrete program, although it might not be able to detect that (to decide termination). Moreover, if the (reachable part of the) system under analysis has a finite bisimulation quotient, then the algorithm will eventually produce a finite bisimilar structure.

Theorem 3. *Let the* αSEARCH *use breadth-first search order and let* A_1, A_2 ... *be a sequence of transition systems generated during iterative refinement performed by* REFINEMENTSEARCH(M, φ). *Then*

- *There exits* i *such that* $RL(A_i) = RL(C(M))$.
- *If the reachable part of the bisimulation quotient is finite, then there exists* i *such that* $A_i \sim C(M)$.

The basic idea of the proof is that any two states that are in different bisimulation classes ($s \not\sim s'$) will eventually be distinguished by the abstraction function ($\alpha_{\Phi_i}(s) \neq \alpha_{\Phi_i}(s')$). Moreover, each bisimulation class will eventually be visited by RefinementSearch and the (finite set) of reachable labellings will emerge.

Discussion. The search order used in αSearch (depth-first or breadth-first) influences the size of the generated structure, the newly computed predicates, and even the number of iterations of the main algorithm. If there are two states s_1 and s_2 such that $\alpha_\Phi(s_1) = \alpha_\Phi(s_2)$ but $s_1 \not\sim s_2$ then, depending on whether s_1 or s_2 is visited first, different parts of the transition system will be explored.

Also note that the refinement algorithm is non-monotone, i.e. a labelling which is reachable in one iteration may not be reachable in the next iteration. A similar problem occurs in the context of *must* abstractions: the set of *must* transitions is not generally monotonically increasing when predicates are added to refine an abstract system [12, 24]. However, we should note that the algorithm is guaranteed to converge to the correct answer.

We should also note that the proposed iterative algorithm is not guaranteed to terminate even for a finite state program. This situation is illustrated by the following example (the property we are checking is that $pc = 2$ is unreachable).

$$\begin{aligned} &pc = 0 \longmapsto x := 0, y := 0, pc := 1 \\ &pc = 1 \wedge y \geq 0 \longmapsto y := y + x \\ &pc = 1 \wedge y < 0 \longmapsto pc := 2 \end{aligned}$$

Although the program is finite state (and therefore the problem can be easily solved with classical explicit model checking), it is quite difficult to solve using abstraction refinement techniques. The iterative algorithm will not terminate on this example: it will keep adding predicates $y \geq 0, y + x \geq 0, y + 2x \geq 0, \ldots$. Note that, in accordance with Theorem 3, it will eventually produce a bisimilar structure. However, the algorithm will not be able to detect termination, and it will keep refining indefinitely. The reason is that the algorithm keeps adding predicates that refine the unreachable part of the system under analysis. Also note that the same problem will occur with over-approximation based abstraction techniques that use refinement based on weakest precondition calculations [3, 21]. Those techniques will introduce the same predicates.

To solve this problem, we propose to use the following heuristic. If there is a transition for which we cannot prove that the abstraction is exact in several subsequent iterations of the algorithm, then we add predicates describing the concrete state; i.e. in our example we would add predicates $x = 0$; $y = 0$. The abstraction will eventually become exact with respect to each transition. And since the number of reachable transitions is finite, the algorithm must terminate.

Corollary 1. *If $C(M)$ is finite state then the modified algorithm terminates.*

6 Extensions

Lightweight Approach. As mentioned, the under-approximation and refinement approach can be used in a lightweight but systematic manner, without using a theorem prover for validity checking. Specifically, for each explored transition t_i refinement adds the new predicates from $\alpha_\Phi(s')[e_i(\boldsymbol{x})/\boldsymbol{x}]$, regardless of the fact that the abstraction is exact with respect to transition t_i. This approach may result in unnecessary refinement. A similar refinement procedure was used in [21] for automated over-approximation predicate abstraction.

We are also considering several heuristics for generating new abstraction predicates. For example, it is customary to add the predicates that appear in the guards and in the property to be checked. One could also add predicates generated dynamically, using tools like Daikon [9], or predicates from known invariants of the system (generated using static analysis techniques).

In order to extend the applicability of the proposed technique to the analysis of full-fledged programming languages, we are investigating abstractions that record information about the shape of the program heap, to be used in conjunction with the abstraction predicates. Section 7 shows an example use of such abstractions for the analysis of Java programs.

Transition Dependent Predicates. The predicates that are generated after the validity check for one transition are used 'globally' at the next iteration. This may cause unnecessary refinement — the new predicates may distinguish states which do not need to be distinguished. To avoid this, we could use 'transition dependent' predicates. The idea is to associate the abstraction predicates with the program counter corresponding to the transition that generated them. New predicates are then added only to the set of the respective program counter. However, with this approach, it may take longer before predicates are 'propagated' to all the locations where they are needed, i.e. more iterations are needed before an error is detected or an exact abstraction is found. We need to further investigate these issues. Similar ideas are presented in [4, 16], in the context of over-approximation based predicate abstraction.

7 Applications

We have implemented our approach for the guarded command language. Our implementation is done in the language Ocaml and it uses the Simplify theorem prover [8]. The implementation uses several optimizations for checking only necessary queries. When updating Φ_{new} for refinement, we add only those conjuncts of $\alpha_\Phi(s')[e_i(\boldsymbol{x})/\boldsymbol{x}]$ for which we cannot prove validity. Moreover, we cache queries to ensure that the theorem prover is not called twice for the same query.

We discuss the application of our implementation for two concurrent programs: property verification for the Bakery mutual exclusion protocol and error detection in RAX (Remote Agent Experiment), a component extracted from an embedded spacecraft-control application.

These preliminary experiments show the merits of our approach. Of course, much more experimentation is necessary to really assess the practical benefits of the proposed technique and a lot more engineering is required to apply it to real programming languages. We are currently doing an implementation in the Java PathFinder (JPF) model checking framework [26] for the analysis of Java

(Process 1)	(Process 2)
$pc_1 = 0 \longmapsto x := y, pc_1 := 1$	$pc_2 = 0 \longmapsto y := x, pc_2 := 1$
$pc_1 = 1 \longmapsto x := x + 1, pc_1 := 2$	$pc_2 = 1 \longmapsto y := y + 1, pc_2 := 2$
$pc_1 = 2 \wedge x \leq y \longmapsto pc_1 := 3$	$pc_2 = 2 \wedge y < x \longmapsto pc_2 := 3$
$pc_1 = 3 \longmapsto pc_1 := 0$	$pc_2 = 3 \longmapsto pc_2 := 0$

Fig. 4. Bakery example

Iteration	Concrete states	Abstract states	New predicates
1	17	11	$x \leq y$
2	18	12	$x + 1 \leq y, x \leq y + 1, y \geq 0$
3	26	19	$x + 2 \leq y, y \geq 1, x \leq 1$
4	44	32	$y \leq 1, x \leq 0, y \geq 2$
5	48	36	-

Fig. 5. Bakery example: intermediate results of the refinement algorithm

programs. We briefly discuss at the end of this section the use of our approach for test-case generation for Java container implementations.

The Bakery Mutual Exclusion Protocol. We have analyzed several versions of the Bakery mutual exclusion protocol (for two and more processes). These versions are infinite state but they have a finite bisimulation quotient. The guarded command representation for a simplified version of the protocol is given in Fig. 4.

The mutual exclusion property is encoded as "$pc_1 = 3 \wedge pc_2 = 3$ is unreachable". We used our tool to successfully prove that the property holds. Fig. 5 gives the intermediate results of the analysis. For each iteration, we report the number of generated concrete states, the number of stored abstract states and the newly generated predicates. Note that we never abstract the program counter. The reported results are for the breadth-first search order. For the depth-first search order the algorithm requires only 4 iterations (see the discussion in Section 5). The algorithm proceeds in similar way for the full version of the protocol.

RAX. The RAX example (illustrated in Fig. 6) is derived from the software used within the NASA Deep Space 1 Remote Agent experiment, which deadlocked during flight [27]. We encoded the deadlock check as "$pc_1 = 4 \wedge pc_2 = 5 \wedge w_1 = 1 \wedge w_2 = 1$ is unreachable". The error is found after one iteration, for breadth-first search order; the reported counter-example has 8 steps. For depth-first search order, the algorithm needs one more iteration to find the error, using the predicates that appear in the guards $c_1 = e_1$ and $c_2 = e_2$.

Note that the state space of the program is unbounded, as the program keeps incrementing the counters e_1 and e_2, when $pc_2 = 2$ and $pc_1 = 6$, respectively. We also ran our algorithm to see if it converges to a finite bisimulation quotient. Interestingly, the algorithm does not terminate for the RAX example, although it has a finite bisimulation quotient. The results are shown in Fig. 7 (breadth-first search order). However, if we assume that the counters in the program are non-negative, i.e. we introduce two new predicates, $e1 \geq 0$, $e2 \geq 0$, then the algorithm terminates after three iterations.

The application of over-approximation based predicate abstraction to a Java version of RAX is described in detail in [27]. In that work, four different predicates were used to produce an abstract model that is bisimilar to the original program. In contrast, the work presented here allowed more aggressive abstraction to recover feasible counter-examples.

In general, we believe that the technique presented here is complementary to over-approximation abstraction methods and it can be used in conjunction with such methods, as an efficient way of discovering feasible counter-examples. We view the integration of the two approaches as an interesting topic for future research. Our technique explores transitions that are guaranteed to be feasible in the state space bounded by the abstraction predicates. In contrast, the over-approximation based methods may also explore transitions that are spurious and therefore could require additional refinement before reporting a real counter-example. Hence, our technique can potentially finish in fewer iterations and it can use fewer predicates (which enable more state space reduction), while retaining the model checker's capability of finding real bugs.

(Process 1)	(Process 2)
$pc_1 = 1 \longmapsto c_1 := 0, pc_1 := 2$	$pc_2 = 1 \longmapsto c_2 := 0, pc_2 := 2$
$pc_1 = 2 \wedge c_1 = e_1 \longmapsto pc_1 := 3$	$pc_2 = 2 \longmapsto e_1 := e_1 + 1, w_1 := 0, pc_2 := 3$
$pc_1 = 3 \longmapsto w_1 := 1, pc_1 := 4$	$pc_2 = 3 \wedge c2 = e2 \longmapsto pc_2 := 4$
$pc_1 = 4 \wedge w_1 = 0 \longmapsto pc_1 := 5$	$pc_2 = 4 \longmapsto w_2 := 1, pc_2 := 5$
$pc_1 = 2 \wedge c_1 \neq e_1 \longmapsto pc_1 := 5$	$pc_2 = 5 \wedge w_2 = 0 \longmapsto pc_2 := 6$
$pc_1 = 5 \longmapsto c_1 := e_1, pc_1 := 6$	$pc_2 = 3 \wedge c_2 \neq e_2 \longmapsto pc_2 := 6$
$pc_1 = 6 \longmapsto e_2 := e_2 + 1, w_2 := 0, pc_1 := 2$	$pc_2 = 6 \longmapsto c_2 := e_2, pc_2 := 2$

Fig. 6. RAX example

Iteration	Concrete states	Abstract states	New predicates
1	56	35	$c_1 = e_1, c_2 = e_2$
2	68	44	$e_1 = 0, e_2 = 0$
3	100	65	$e_1 = -1, e_2 = -1$
4	100	65	$e_1 = -2, e_2 = -2$
5	100	65	...

Fig. 7. RAX example: intermediate results of the refinement algorithm

Testing. We have used our preliminary implementation in the JPF model checker to perform test case generation to achieve code coverage for Java container classes (tree-map, linked-list, fibonacci-heap). Test cases are sequences of API calls, i.e. method calls that *add* and *remove* elements in a container, to obtain for example, branch coverage. The model checker analyzes all sequences of API calls up to a predefined sequence size and generates paths that are witnesses to testing coverage criteria encoded as reachability properties. Abstraction is used to match states between API calls and to avoid the generation of redundant tests.

We used an abstraction recording the (concrete) shape of the containers augmented with different predicate abstractions on the data fields from each container element — two states are matched if they represent containers that have the same shape and valuation for the abstraction predicates. The behavioral coverage obtained in this fashion is highly dependent on the different abstractions that are used. Therefore we believe that the capability of generating and refining the abstractions automatically is crucial for achieving good coverage. Although the work presented here is only a first step towards this goal (the JPF implementation does not yet allow automated refinement), we obtained better behavioral coverage than with exhaustive model checking. In fact, for some of the examples, exhaustive analysis runs out of memory even before generating tests that cover all the reachable branches in the code.

8 Conclusions and Future Work

We presented a novel model checking algorithm based on refinement of under-approximations, which effectively preserves the defect detection ability of model checking in the presence of powerful abstractions. The under-approximation is obtained by traversing the concrete transition system and performing the state matching on abstract states computed by predicate abstraction. The refinement is done by checking exactness of abstractions with the use of a theorem prover. We illustrated the application of the algorithm for checking safety properties of concurrent programs and for testing container implementations. In the future, we plan to extend the algorithm to checking liveness properties. We also plan to do an extensive evaluation of our approach on real systems.

References

1. T. Ball. A theory of predicate-complete test coverage and generation. *Technical Report MSR-TR-2004-28, Microsoft Research*, 2004.
2. T. Ball, A. Podelski, and S. Rajamani. Boolean and cartesian abstractions for model checking C programs. In *Proc. Tools and Algorithms for the Construction and Analysis of Systems (TACAS'01)*, volume 2031 of *LNCS*, 2001.
3. S. Chaki, E. Clarke, A. Groce, S. Jha, and H. Veith. Modular verification of software components in C. *ACM Trans. Computer Systems*, 30(6):388–402, 2004.
4. S. Chaki, E. Clarke, A. Groce, and O. Strichman. Predicate abstraction with minimum predicates. In *Proc. 12th CHARME*, volume 2860 of *LNCS*, 2003.
5. P. Cousot and R. Cousot. Abstract interpretation frameworks. *Journal of Logic and Computation*, 4(2):511–547, August 1992.

6. D. Dams and K. S. Namjoshi. The existence of finite abstractions for branching time model checking. In *Proc. 19th Symposium on Logic in Computer Science (LICS'04)*, 2004.
7. L. de Alfaro, P. Godefroid, and R. Jagadeesan. Three-valued abstractions of games: Uncertainty, but with precision. In *Proc. 19th Symposium on Logic in Computer Science (LICS'04)*, 2004.
8. D. L. Detlefs, K. R. M. Leino, G. Nelson, and J. B. Saxe. Extended static checking. *Research Report 159, Compaq Systems Research Center*, 1998.
9. M. D. Ernst, A. Czeisler, W. G. Griswold, and D. Notkin. Quickly detecting relevant program invariants. In *Proc. 22nd International Conference on Software Engineering (ICSE'00)*, 2000.
10. R. Giacobazzi and E. Quintarelli. Incompleteness, counterexamples and refinements in abstract model checking. In *Proc. 8th Static Analysis Symposium (SAS'01)*, volume 2126 of *LNCS*, 2001.
11. P. Godefroid. Software Model Checking: the Verisoft Approach. *Formal Methods in Systems Design (to appear)*.
12. P. Godefroid, M. Huth, and R. Jagadeesan. Abstraction-based model checking using modal transition systems. In *Proc. CONCUR 2001 - Concurrency Theory*, volume 2154 of *LNCS*, 2001.
13. S. Graf and H. Saidi. Construction of abstract state graphs with PVS. In *Proc. Computer Aided Verification (CAV'97)*, volume 1254 of *LNCS*, 1997.
14. W. Grieskamp, Y. Gurevich, W. Schulte, and M. Veanes. Generating finite state machines from abstract state machines. In *Proc. International Symposium on Software Testing and Analysis (ISSTA'04)*, July 2002.
15. O. Grumberg, F. Lerda, O. Strichman, and M. Theobald. Proof-guided underapproximation-widening for multi-process systems. In *Proc. 32nd Symposium on Principles of Programming Languages (POPL'05)*, 2005.
16. T. A. Henzinger, R. Jhala, R. Majumdar, and K. McMillan. Abstractions from proofs. In *Proc. 31st Symposium on Principles of Programming Languages (POPL'04)*, 2004.
17. T. A. Henzinger, R. Jhala, R. Majumdar, and Gregoire Sutre. Lazy abstraction. In *Proc. 29th Symposium on Principles of Programming Languages*, 2002.
18. G. J. Holzmann and R. Joshi. Model-driven software verification. In *Proc. 11th SPIN Workshop*, volume 2989 of *LNCS*, Barcelona, Spain, 2004.
19. D. Lee and M. Yannakakis. Online minimization of transition systems. In *Proc. 24th ACM Symposium on Theory of Computing*, 1992.
20. M. Musuvathi, D. Y. W. Park, A. Chou, D. R. Engler, and D. L. Dill. CMC: A pragmatic approach to model checking real code. In *Proc. 5th Symposium on Operating Systems Design and Implementation (OSDI'02)*, 2002.
21. K. S. Namjoshi and R. P. Kurshan. Syntactic program transformations for automatic abstraction. In *Proc. Computer Aided Verification (CAV'00)*, volume 1855 of *LNCS*, 2000.
22. C. S. Păsăreanu, M. B. Dwyer, and W. Visser. Finding feasible abstract counterexamples. *STTT*, 5(1):34–48, November 2003.
23. C. S. Păsăreanu, R. Pelánek, and W. Visser. Concrete model checking with abstract matching and refinement (extended version). *RIACS Technical Report*, 05.04, 2005.
24. S. Shoham and O. Grumberg. Monotonic abstraction-refinement for CTL. In *Proc. Tools and Algorithms for the Construction and Analysis of Systems (TACAS'04)*, volume 2988 of *LNCS*, Barcelona, Spain, 2004.

25. A. Venet and G. Brat. Precise and efficient static array bound checking for large embedded C programs. In *Proc. Programming Language Design and Implementation (PLDI'04)*, 2004.
26. W. Visser, K. Havelund, G. Brat, S. J. Park, and F. Lerda. Model checking programs. *Automated Software Engineering Journal*, 10(2), April 2003.
27. W. Visser, S. Park, and J. Penix. Applying predicate abstraction to model check object-oriented programs. In *3rd ACM SIGSOFT Workshop on Formal Methods in Software Practice*, 2000.
28. T. Xie, D. Marinov, and D. Notkin. Rostra: A framework for detecting redundant object-oriented unit tests. In *Proc. 19th Automated Software Engineering*, 2004.

Abstraction for Falsification

Thomas Ball[1], Orna Kupferman[2], and Greta Yorsh[3]

[1] Microsoft Research, Redmond, WA, USA
tball@microsoft.com
www.research.microsoft.com/~tball

[2] Hebrew University, School of Eng. and Comp. Sci., Jerusalem 91904, Israel
orna@cs.huji.ac.il
www.cs.huji.ac.il/~orna

[3] Tel-Aviv University, School of Comp. Sci., Tel-Aviv 69978, Israel
gretay@post.tau.ac.il
www.math.tau.ac.il/~gretay

Abstract. Abstraction is traditionally used in the process of *verification*. There, an abstraction of a concrete system is sound if properties of the abstract system also hold in the concrete system. Specifically, if an abstract state a satisfies a property ψ then *all* the concrete states that correspond to a satisfy ψ too. Since the ideal goal of proving a system correct involves many obstacles, the primary use of formal methods nowadays is *falsification*. There, as in *testing*, the goal is to detect errors, rather than to prove correctness. In the falsification setting, we can say that an abstraction is sound if errors of the abstract system exist also in the concrete system. Specifically, if an abstract state a violates a property ψ, then *there exists* a concrete state that corresponds to a and violates ψ too.

An abstraction that is sound for falsification need not be sound for verification. This suggests that existing frameworks for abstraction for verification may be too restrictive when used for falsification, and that a new framework is needed in order to take advantage of the weaker definition of soundness in the falsification setting.

We present such a framework, show that it is indeed stronger (than other abstraction frameworks designed for verification), demonstrate that it can be made even stronger by parameterizing its transitions by predicates, and describe how it can be used for falsification of branching-time and linear-time temporal properties, as well as for generating testing goals for a concrete system by reasoning about its abstraction.

1 Introduction

Automated abstraction is a powerful technique for reasoning about systems. An abstraction framework [CC77] consists of a concrete system with (large, possibly infinite) state space C, an abstract system with (smaller, often finite) state space A, and an abstraction function $\rho: C \to A$ that relates concrete and abstract states. An abstraction framework is sound with respect to a logic L if all properties specified in L that hold in an abstract state a also hold in all the concrete states that correspond to a. Formally, for all $a \in A$ and $\varphi \in L$, if a satisfies φ then for all $c \in C$ with $\rho(c, a)$, we have that c satisfies φ.

K. Etessami and S.K. Rajamani (Eds.): CAV 2005, LNCS 3576, pp. 67–81, 2005.

The soundness of the abstraction framework enables the user to verify properties of the abstract system using techniques such as model checking [CE81, QS81] and conclude their validity in the concrete system.

While the ultimate goal of formal verification is to prove that a system satisfies some specification, there are many obstacles to achieving this ideal in practice. Thus, the primary use of formal methods nowadays is *falsification*, where the goal is to detect errors rather than to provide a proof of correctness. This is reflected in the extensive research done on bounded model checking (c.f., [FKZ+00]), runtime verification (c.f., [Sip99]), etc. In the falsification setting, we can say that an abstraction is sound with respect to a logic L if all errors specified in L that hold in an abstract state a also hold in some concrete state that corresponds to a. Formally, for all $a \in A$ and $\varphi \in L$, if a satisfies φ then there is $c \in C$ such that $\rho(c, a)$ and c satisfies φ. [1] Since every abstract state corresponds to at least one concrete state, the soundness condition in the falsification setting is weaker than the soundness condition in the verification setting. To see that this weaker definition is sufficiently strong for falsification, note that the concrete state c that satisfies φ witnesses that the concrete system is erroneous (we note that in the falsification setting φ is a "bad" property that we don't wish the system to have, while in the verifications setting φ is a "good" property that we wish the system to have).

We develop a new abstraction framework to take advantage of the weaker definition of soundness in the falsification setting. Our framework is based on *modal transition systems* (MTS) [LT88]. Traditional MTS have two types of transitions: may (over-approximating transitions) and $must$ (under-approximating transitions). The use of $must$ transitions in the falsification setting was explored in [PDV01, GLST05], with different motivations. Our framework contains, in addition, a new type of transition, which can be viewed as the reverse version of $must$ transitions [Bal04]. Accordingly, we refer to transitions of this type as $must^-$ transitions and refer to the traditional $must$ transitions as $must^+$ transitions. While a $must^+$ transition from an abstract state a to an abstract state a' implies that for all concrete states c with $\rho(c, a)$ there is a successor concrete state c' with $\rho(c', a')$, a $must^-$ transition from a to a' implies that for all concrete states c' with $\rho(c', a')$ there is a concrete predecessor state c with $\rho(c, a)$. The $must^-$ transitions correspond to the weaker soundness requirement in the falsification setting and are incomparable to $must^+$ transitions.

Consider, for example, a simple concrete system consisting of the assignment statement `x:=x-3`. Suppose that the abstract system is formed via predicate abstraction using the predicate $x > 6$. Consider the abstract transition $\{x > 6\}$ `x:=x-3` $\{x > 6\}$. This transition is not a $must$ transition, as there are pre-states satisfying $x > 6$ (namely $x = 7$, $x = 8$, and $x = 9$) for which the assignment statement results in a post-state that does not satisfy $x > 6$. Therefore, in a traditional MTS this transition is a

[1] Note that the falsification setting is different than the problem of *generalized model checking* [GJ02]. There, the existential quantifier ranges over all possible concrete systems and the problem is one of satisfiability (does there exist a concrete system with the same property as the abstract system?). Here, the concrete system is given and we only replace the universal quantification on concrete states that correspond to a by an existential quantification on them.

may transition. However, in an MTS with $must^-$ transitions, the above transition is a $must^-$ transition, as for every post-state c' satisfying $x > 6$ there is a pre-state c satisfying $x > 6$ such that the execution of `x:=x-3` from c yields c'. It is impossible to make this inference in a traditional MTS, even those augmented with hyper-must transitions [LX90, SG04]. As we shall see below, the observation that the abstract transition is a $must^-$ transition rather than a *may* transition enables better reasoning about the concrete system.

We study MTS with these three types of transitions, which we refer to as *ternary modal transition systems* (TMTS)[2]. We first show that the TMTS model is indeed stronger than the MTS model: while MTS with only *may* and $must^+$ transitions are logically characterized by a 3-valued modal logic with the AX and EX (for all successors/exists a successor) operators, TMTS are logically characterized by a strictly more expressive modal logic which has, in addition, the AY and EY (for all predecessors/exists a predecessor) past operators. We then show that by replacing $must^+$ transitions by $must^-$ transitions, existing work on abstraction/refinement for verification [GHJ01, SG03, BG04, SG04, DN05] can be lifted to abstraction/refinement for falsification.

In particular, this immediately provides a framework for falsification of CTL and μ-calculus specifications. Going back to our example, by letting existential quantification range over $must^-$ transitions, we can conclude from the fact that the abstract system satisfies the property $EXx > 6$ (there is a successor in which $x > 6$ is valid) that some concrete state also satisfies $EXx > 6$. Note that such reasoning cannot be done in a traditional MTS, as there the $must^-$ transition is overapproximated by a *may* transition, which is not helpful for reasoning about existential properties. Thus, there are cases where evaluation of a formula on a traditional MTS returns $\perp$ (nothing can be concluded for the concrete system, and refinement is needed) and its evaluation on a TMTS returns an *existential* **true** or *existential* **false**. Formally, we describe a *6-valued falsification semantics* for TMTS. In addition to the **T** (all corresponding concrete states satisfy the formula), **F** (all corresponding concrete states violate the formula), and $\perp$ truth values that the 3-valued semantics for MTS has, the falsification semantics also has the $\mathbf{T}_\exists$ (there is a corresponding concrete state that satisfies the formula), $\mathbf{F}_\exists$ (there is a corresponding concrete state that violates the formula), and M (mixed – both $\mathbf{T}_\exists$ and $\mathbf{F}_\exists$ hold) truth values.

The combination of $must^+$ and $must^-$ transitions turn out to be especially powerful when reasoning about *weak reachability*, which is useful for abstraction-guided test generation [Bal04] and falsification of linear-time properties. As discussed in [Bal04], if there is a sequence of $must^-$ transitions from a_0 to a_j followed by a sequence of $must^+$ transitions from a_j to a_k, then there are guaranteed to be concrete states c_0 and c_k (corresponding to a_0 and a_k) such that c_k is reachable from c_0 in the concrete system (in which case we say that a_k is weakly reachable from a_0). In this case, we can conclude that it is possible to cover the abstract state a_k via testing. When the abstraction is the product of an abstract system with a nondeterministic Büchi automaton accepting all the faults of the system, weak reachability can be used in order to de-

[2] Not to be confused with the three-valued logic sometimes used in these systems.

tect faults in the concrete system. We focus on abstractions obtained from programs by predicate abstraction, and study the problem of composing transitions in an TMTS in a way that guarantees weak reachability. We suggest a method where $must^+$ and $must^-$ transitions are parameterized with predicates, automatically induced by the weakest preconditions and the strongest postconditions of the statements in the program[3].

The paper is organized as follows. Section 2 formally presents ternary modal transition systems (TMTS), how they abstract concrete systems (as well as each other) and characterizes their abstraction pre-order via the full propositional modal logic (full-PML). Section 2.3 presents the 6-valued falsification semantics for TMTS and demonstrates that TMTS are more precise for falsification than traditional MTS. We also show that falsification can be lifted to the μ-calculus as well as linear-time logics. Section 3 shows that weak reachability can be made more precise by parameterizing both $must^+$ and $must^-$ transitions via predicates. Section 4 describes describes applications of TMTS to abstraction-guided testing and to model checking. Section 5 concludes the paper.

Due to a lack of space, this version does not contain proofs and contains only a partial discussion of the results. For a full version, the reader is referred to the authors' URLs and our technical report [BKY05].

2 The Abstraction Framework

In this section we describe our abstraction framework. We define TMTS — ternary modal transition systems, which extend modal transition systems by a third type of transition, and study their theoretical aspects.

2.1 Ternary Modal Transition Systems

A *concrete transition system* is a tuple $C = \langle AP, S_C, I_C, \longrightarrow_C, L_C \rangle$, where AP is a finite set of atomic propositions, S_C is a (possibly infinite) set of states, $I_C \subseteq S_C$ is a set of initial states, $\longrightarrow_C \subseteq S_C \times S_C$ is a transition relation and $L_C \colon S_C \times AP \mapsto \{\mathbf{T}, \mathbf{F}\}$ is a labeling function that maps each state and atomic proposition to the truth value of the proposition in the state.[4]

An abstraction of C is a partially defined system. Incompleteness involves both the value of the atomic propositions, which can now take the value $\perp$ (unknown), and the transition relation, which is approximated by over- and/or under-approximating transitions. Several frameworks are defined in the literature (c.f. [LT88, BG99, HJS01]). We define here a new framework, which consists of *ternary transition systems* (TMTS, for short). Unlike the traditional MTS, our TMTS has two types of under-approximating transitions. Formally, we have the following.

[3] We note (see the remark at the end of Section 3 for a detailed discussion) that our approach is different than refining the TMTS as the predicates we use are local to the transitions.

[4] We use **T** and **F** to denote the truth values **true** and **false** of the standard (verification) semantics, and introduce additional truth values in Section 2.3.

A TMTS is a tuple $A = \langle AP, S_A, I_A, \xrightarrow{may}_A, \xrightarrow{must^+}_A, \xrightarrow{must^-}_A, L_A\rangle$, where AP is a finite set of atomic propositions, S_A is a finite set of abstract states, $I_A \subseteq S_A$ is a set of initial states, the transition relations $\xrightarrow{may}_A$, $\xrightarrow{must^+}_A$, and $\xrightarrow{must^-}_A$ are subsets of $S_A \times S_A$ satisfying $\xrightarrow{must^+}_A \subseteq \xrightarrow{may}_A$ and $\xrightarrow{must^-}_A \subseteq \xrightarrow{may}_A$, and $L_A \colon S_A \times AP \to \{\mathbf{T}, \mathbf{F}, \bot\}$ is a labeling function that maps each state and atomic proposition to the truth value (possibly unknown) of the proposition in the state. When A is clear from the context we sometimes use $may(a, a')$, $must^+(a, a')$, and $must^-(a, a')$ instead of $a \xrightarrow{may}_A a$, $a \xrightarrow{must^+}_A a'$, and $a \xrightarrow{must^-}_A a'$, respectively.

The elements of $\{\mathbf{T}, \mathbf{F}, \bot\}$ can be arranged in an "information lattice" [Kle87] in which $\bot \sqsubseteq \mathbf{T}$ and $\bot \sqsubseteq \mathbf{F}$. We say that a concrete state c *satisfies* an abstract state a if for all $p \in AP$, we have $L_A(a,p) \sqsubseteq L_C(c,p)$ (equivalently, if $L_A(a,p) \neq \bot$ then $L_C(c,p) = L_A(a,p)$).

Let $C = \langle AP, S_C, I_C, \longrightarrow_C, L_C\rangle$ be a concrete transition system. A TMTS $A = \langle AP, S_A, I_A, \xrightarrow{may}_A, \xrightarrow{must^+}_A, \xrightarrow{must^-}_A, L_A\rangle$ is an *abstraction* of C if there exists a total and onto function $\rho \colon S_C \to S_A$ such that (i) for all $c \in S_C$, we have that c satisfies $\rho(c)$, and (ii) the transition relations $\xrightarrow{may}_A$, $\xrightarrow{must^+}_A$, and $\xrightarrow{must^-}_A$ satisfy the following:

- $a \xrightarrow{may}_A a'$ if there is a concrete state c with $\rho(c) = a$, there is a concrete state c' with $\rho(c') = a'$, and $c \longrightarrow_C c'$.
- $a \xrightarrow{must^+}_A a'$ only if for every concrete state c with $\rho(c) = a$, there is a concrete state c' with $\rho(c') = a'$ and $c \longrightarrow_C c'$.
- $a \xrightarrow{must^-}_A a'$ only if for every concrete state c' with $\rho(c') = a'$, there is a concrete state c with $\rho(c) = a$ and $c \longrightarrow_C c'$.

Note that may transitions over-approximate the concrete transitions. In particular, the abstract system can contain may transitions for which there is no corresponding concrete transition. Dually, $must^-$ and $must^+$ transitions under-approximate the concrete transitions. Thus, the concrete transition relation can contain transitions for which there are no corresponding $must$ transitions. Since ρ is onto, each abstract state corresponds to at least one concrete state, and so $\xrightarrow{must^+}_A \subseteq \xrightarrow{may}_A$ and $\xrightarrow{must^-}_A \subseteq \xrightarrow{may}_A$. On the other hand, $\xrightarrow{must^+}_A$ and $\xrightarrow{must^-}_A$ are incomparable. Finally, note that by letting $must$-transitions become may-transitions, and by adding superfluous may-transitions, we can have several abstractions of the same concrete system.

A *precision preorder* on TMTS defines when one TMTS is more abstract than another. For two TMTS $A = \langle AP, S_A, I_A, \xrightarrow{may}_A, \xrightarrow{must^+}_A, \xrightarrow{must^-}_A, L_A\rangle$ and $B = \langle AP, S_B, I_B, \xrightarrow{may}_B, \xrightarrow{must^+}_B, \xrightarrow{must^-}_B, L_B\rangle$, the precision preorder is the greatest relation $\mathcal{H} \subseteq S_A \times S_B$ such that if $\mathcal{H}(a,b)$ then

C0. for all $p \in AP$, we have $L_A(a,p) \sqsubseteq L_B(b,p)$,
C1. if $b \xrightarrow{may}_B b'$, then there is $a' \in S_A$ such that $\mathcal{H}(a', b')$ and $a \xrightarrow{may}_A a'$,
C2. if $b' \xrightarrow{may}_B b$, then there is $a' \in S_A$ such that $\mathcal{H}(a', b')$ and $a' \xrightarrow{may}_A a$,

C3. if $a \xrightarrow{must^+}_A a'$, then there is $b' \in S_B$ such that $\mathcal{H}(a', b')$ and $b \xrightarrow{must^+}_B b'$, and

C4. if $a' \xrightarrow{must^-}_A a$, then there is $b' \in S_B$ such that $\mathcal{H}(a', b')$ and $b' \xrightarrow{must^-}_B b$.

When $\mathcal{H}(a, b)$, we write $(A, a) \preceq (B, b)$, which indicates that A is more abstract (less defined) than B.

By viewing a concrete system as an abstract system whose may, $must^+$, and $must^-$ transition relations are equivalent to the transition relation of the concrete system, we can use the precision preorder to relate a concrete system and its abstraction. Formally, the precision preorder $\mathcal{H} \subseteq S_C \times S_A$ (also known as *mixed simulation* [DGG97, GJ02]) is such that $\mathcal{H}(c, a)$ iff $\rho(c) = a$.

2.2 A Logical Characterization

The logic *full-PML* is a propositional logic extended with the modal operators AX ("for all immediate successors") and AY ("for all immediate predecessors"). Thus, full-PML extends PML [Ben91] by the past-time operator AY. The syntax of full-PML is given by the rules $\theta ::= p \mid \neg\theta \mid \theta \wedge \theta \mid AX\theta \mid AY\theta$, for $p \in AP$.

We define a 3-*valued semantics* of full-PML formulas with respect to TMTS. The value of a formula θ in a state a of a TMTS $A = \langle S_A, I_A, \xrightarrow{may}_A, \xrightarrow{must^+}_A, \xrightarrow{must^-}_A, L_A\rangle$, denoted $[(A, a) \models \theta]$, is defined as follows:

$$[(A,a) \models p] = L_A(a,p).$$

$$[(A,a) \models \neg\theta] = \begin{cases} \mathbf{T} & \text{if } [(A,a) \models \theta] = \mathbf{F}. \\ \mathbf{F} & \text{if } [(A,a) \models \theta] = \mathbf{T}. \\ \bot & \text{otherwise.} \end{cases}$$

$$[(A,a) \models \theta_1 \wedge \theta_2] = \begin{cases} \mathbf{T} & \text{if } [(A,a) \models \theta_1] = \mathbf{T} \text{ and } [(A,a) \models \theta_2] = \mathbf{T}. \\ \mathbf{F} & \text{if } [(A,a) \models \theta_1] = \mathbf{F} \text{ or } [(A,a) \models \theta_2] = \mathbf{F}. \\ \bot & \text{otherwise.} \end{cases}$$

$$[(A,a) \models AX\theta] = \begin{cases} \mathbf{T} & \text{if for all } a', \text{ if } may(a,a') \text{ then } [(A,a') \models \theta] = \mathbf{T}. \\ \mathbf{F} & \text{if exists } a' \text{ s.t. } must^+(a,a') \text{ and } [(A,a') \models \theta] = \mathbf{F}. \\ \bot & \text{otherwise.} \end{cases}$$

$$[(A,a) \models AY\theta] = \begin{cases} \mathbf{T} & \text{if for all } a', \text{ if } may(a',a) \text{ then } [(A,a') \models \theta] = \mathbf{T}. \\ \mathbf{F} & \text{if exists } a' \text{ s.t. } must^-(a',a) \text{ and } [(A,a') \models \theta] = \mathbf{F}. \\ \bot & \text{otherwise.} \end{cases}$$

While PML logically characterizes the precision preorder on MTS [GJ02], full-PML characterizes the precision preorder on TMTS. It follows that the TMTS model is indeed stronger than the MTS model, because TMTS are logically characterized by a strictly more expressive modal logic which has the past operators AY and EY, in addition to AX and EX operators. Formally, we have the following.

Theorem 1. *Let* $A = \langle AP, S_A, I_A, \xrightarrow{may}_A, \xrightarrow{must^+}_A, \xrightarrow{must^-}_A, L_A\rangle$ *and* $B = \langle AP, S_B, I_B, \xrightarrow{may}_B, \xrightarrow{must^+}_B, \xrightarrow{must^-}_B, L_B\rangle$ *be two TMTS. For every two states* $a \in S_A$ *and* $b \in S_B$, *we have that* $(A, a) \preceq (B, b)$ *iff* $[(A, a) \models \theta] \sqsubseteq [(B, b) \models \theta]$ *for all full-PML formulas* θ.

2.3 Falsification Using TMTS

As shown in Section 2.2, the backwards nature of $must^-$ transitions makes them suitable for reasoning about the past. Thus, TMTS can be helpful in the verification setting for reasoning about specifications in full μ-calculus and other specification formalisms that contain past operators. We view this as a minor advantage of TMTS. In this section we study their significant advantage: reasoning about specifications in a falsification setting[5].

In addition to the truth values **T**, **F**, and $\bot$, we now allow formulas to have the values $\mathbf{T}_\exists$ (existential **true**), $\mathbf{F}_\exists$ (existential **false**), and **M** ("mixed" – both **T** and **F**). Intuitively, the values $\mathbf{T}_\exists$, $\mathbf{F}_\exists$, and **M** refine the value $\bot$, and are helpful for falsification and testing, as they indicate that the abstract state corresponds to at least one concrete state that satisfies the property ($\mathbf{T}_\exists$), at least one concrete state that violates the property ($\mathbf{F}_\exists$), and at least one pair of concrete states in which one state satisfies the property, and the other state violates it (**M**).

As shown in the figure on the next page, the six values $\mathcal{L}_6 = \{\mathbf{T}, \mathbf{F}, \mathbf{M}, \mathbf{T}_\exists, \mathbf{F}_\exists, \bot\}$ can be ordered in the information lattice depicted on the left. The values can also be ordered in the "truth lattice" depicted on the right:

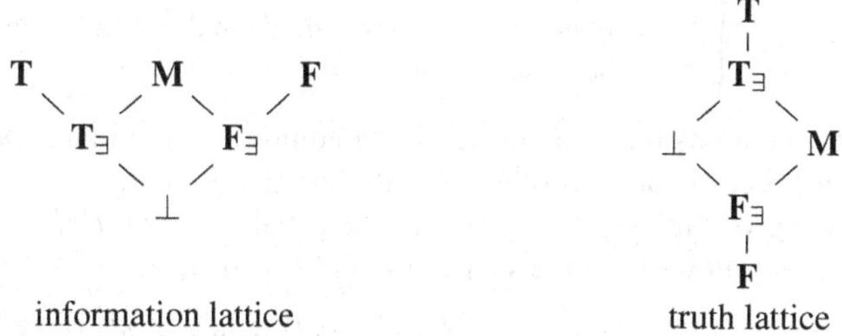

information lattice truth lattice

We allow the truth values of the (abstract) labeling function L_A to range over the six truth values.

A TMTS $A = \langle AP, S_A, I_A, \xrightarrow{may}_A, \xrightarrow{must^+}_A, \xrightarrow{must^-}_A, L_A\rangle$ is an abstraction of a concrete transition system $C = \langle AP, S_C, I_C, \longrightarrow_C, L_C\rangle$ if there exists a total and onto function $\rho\colon S_C \to S_A$ such that for all $a \in S_A$ and $p \in AP$:

- $L_A(a,p) = \mathbf{T}$ only if for all $c \in S_C$ such that $\rho(c) = a$, $L_C(c,p) = \mathbf{T}$;
- $L_A(a,p) = \mathbf{F}$ only if for all $c \in S_C$ such that $\rho(c) = a$, $L_C(c,p) = \mathbf{F}$;
- $L_A(a,p) = \mathbf{T}_\exists$ only if there exists $c \in S_C$ such that $\rho(c) = a$ and $L_C(c,p) = \mathbf{T}$;
- $L_A(a,p) = \mathbf{F}_\exists$ only if there exists $c \in S_C$ such that $\rho(c) = a$ and $L_C(c,p) = \mathbf{F}$;
- $L_A(a,p) = \mathbf{M}$ only if there exist $c, c' \in S_C$ such that $\rho(c) = \rho(c') = a$, $L_C(c,p) = \mathbf{T}$, and $L_C(c',p) = \mathbf{F}$.

In addition, ρ satisfies the requirement (ii) defined in Section 2.1.

[5] The specifications may contain both future and past operators. For simplicity, we describe the framework here for the μ-calculus, which does not contain past modalities. By letting the AY modality range over $must^+$ transitions, the framework can be used for falsification of full μ-calculus specifications.

The complementation ($\neg: \mathcal{L}_6 \to \mathcal{L}_6$) and the conjunction ($\wedge: \mathcal{L}_6 \times \mathcal{L}_6 \to \mathcal{L}_6$) operations are defined as follows:

	$\neg$
$\mathbf{F}$	$\mathbf{T}$
$\mathbf{F}_\exists$	$\mathbf{T}_\exists$
$\mathbf{M}$	$\mathbf{M}$
$\mathbf{T}_\exists$	$\mathbf{F}_\exists$
$\mathbf{T}$	$\mathbf{F}$
$\perp$	$\perp$

$\wedge$	$\mathbf{F}$	$\mathbf{F}_\exists$	$\mathbf{M}$	$\mathbf{T}_\exists$	$\mathbf{T}$	$\perp$
$\mathbf{F}$	$\mathbf{F}$	$\mathbf{F}$	$\mathbf{F}$	$\mathbf{F}$	$\mathbf{F}$	$\mathbf{F}$
$\mathbf{F}_\exists$	$\mathbf{F}$	$\mathbf{F}_\exists$	$\mathbf{F}_\exists$	$\mathbf{F}_\exists$	$\mathbf{F}_\exists$	$\mathbf{F}_\exists$
$\mathbf{M}$	$\mathbf{F}$	$\mathbf{F}_\exists$	$\mathbf{F}_\exists$	$\mathbf{F}_\exists$	$\mathbf{M}$	$\mathbf{F}_\exists$
$\mathbf{T}_\exists$	$\mathbf{F}$	$\mathbf{F}_\exists$	$\mathbf{F}_\exists$	$\perp$	$\mathbf{T}_\exists$	$\perp$
$\mathbf{T}$	$\mathbf{F}$	$\mathbf{F}_\exists$	$\mathbf{M}$	$\mathbf{T}_\exists$	$\mathbf{T}$	$\perp$
$\perp$	$\mathbf{F}$	$\mathbf{F}_\exists$	$\mathbf{F}_\exists$	$\perp$	$\perp$	$\perp$

We define a 6-*valued falsification semantics* of PML formulas with respect to TMTS. The value of a formula θ in a state a of a TMTS $A = \langle AP, S_A, I_A, \xrightarrow{may}_A, \xrightarrow{must^+}_A, \xrightarrow{must^-}_A, L_A\rangle$, denoted $[(A, a) \models \theta]$, is defined as follows:

$$[(A,a) \models p] = L_A(a,p).$$
$$[(A,a) \models \neg\theta] = \neg([(A,a) \models \theta])$$
$$[(A,a) \models \theta_1 \wedge \theta_2] = \wedge([(A,a') \models \theta_1], [(A,a') \models \theta_1])$$

$$[(A,a) \models AX\theta] = \begin{cases} \mathbf{T} & \text{if for all } a', \text{ if } may(a,a') \text{ then } [(A,a') \models \theta] = \mathbf{T}. \\ \mathbf{F} & \text{if exists } a' \text{ s.t. } must^+(a,a') \text{ and } [(A,a') \models \theta] = \mathbf{F}. \\ \mathbf{F}_\exists & \text{if exists } a' \text{ s.t. } must^-(a,a') \text{ and } [(A,a') \models \theta] \sqsupseteq \mathbf{F}_\exists. \\ \perp & \text{otherwise.} \end{cases}$$

Note that the conditions for the **F** and the $\mathbf{F}_\exists$ conditions are not mutually exclusive. If both conditions hold, we take the value to be the stronger **F** value.

For clarity, we give the semantics for the existential operator EX explicitly (an equivalent definition follows from the semantics of AX and $\neg$):

$$[(A,a) \models EX\theta] = \begin{cases} \mathbf{F} & \text{if for all } a', \text{ if } may(a,a') \text{ then } [(A,a') \models \theta] = \mathbf{F}. \\ \mathbf{T} & \text{if exists } a' \text{ s.t. } must^+(a,a') \text{ and } [(A,a') \models \theta] = \mathbf{T}. \\ \mathbf{T}_\exists & \text{if exists } a' \text{ s.t. } must^-(a,a') \text{ and } [(A,a') \models \theta] \sqsupseteq \mathbf{T}_\exists. \\ \perp & \text{otherwise.} \end{cases}$$

Thus, the semantics of the next-time operators follows both $must^-$ and $must^+$ transitions (that is, a' is such that $must^-(a,a')$ or $must^+(a,a')$). To understand why $must^-$ transitions are suitable for falsification, let us explain the positive falsification semantics for the EX modality. The other cases are similar. Consider a concrete transition system $C = \langle AP, S_C, I_C, \longrightarrow_C, L_C\rangle$, and an abstraction for it $A = \langle AP, S_A, I_A, \xrightarrow{may}_A, \xrightarrow{must^+}_A, \xrightarrow{must^-}_A, L_A\rangle$. Let $\rho: S_C \to S_A$ be the witness function for the abstraction.

We argue that if $[(A,a) \models EXp] = \mathbf{T}_\exists$, then there is a concrete state c such that $\rho(c) = a$ and $c \models EXp$. By the semantics of the EX operator, $[(A,a) \models EXp] = \mathbf{T}_\exists$ implies that there is $a' \in S_A$ such that $must^-(a,a')$ and $L_A(a',p) \sqsupseteq \mathbf{T}_\exists$. Let $\hat{c}$ be a concrete state with $\rho(\hat{c}) = a'$ and $L_C(\hat{c},p) = \mathbf{T}$ (by the definition of abstraction, at least one such $\hat{c}$ exists). Since $must^-(a,a')$, then for every concrete state c' such that $\rho(c') = a'$ there is a concrete state c such that $\rho(c) = a$ and $c \longrightarrow_C c'$. In particular, there is a concrete state c such that $\rho(c) = a$ and $c \longrightarrow_C \hat{c}$. Thus, $c \models EXp$ and we are done.

Let a and a' be abstract states. The (reflexive) transitive closure of $must^-$, denoted $[must^-]^*$ is defined in the expected manner as follows: $[must^-]^*(a, a'')$ if either $a = a''$ or there is an abstract state a' such that $[must^-]^*(a, a')$ and $must^-(a', a'')$. We say that an abstract state a' is *onto reachable* from an abstract state a if for every concrete state c' that satisfies a', there is a concrete state c that satisfies a and c' is reachable from c. Dually, we can define the transitive closure of $must^+$ transitions, denoted $[must^+]^*$, and *total reachability*. The transitive closure of $must^+$ and $must^-$ transitions retain the reachability properties for a single transition: $[must^-]^*(a, a')$ only if a' is onto reachable from a, and $[must^+]^*(a, a')$ only if a' is total reachable from a [Bal04].

By extending PML by fixed-point operators, one gets the logic μ-calculus [Koz83], which subsumes the branching temporal logics CTL and CTL*. The 3-valued semantics of PML can be extended to the μ-calculus [BG04]. Note that in the special case of CTL and CTL* formulas, this amounts to letting path formulas range over may and $must^+$ paths [SG03]. The fact that the "onto" nature of $must^-$ transitions is retained under transition closure enables us to extend the soundness argument for the 6-valued falsification semantics described above for a single EX or AX modality to nesting of such modalities and thus, to PML and the μ-calculus, as shown in our technical report [BKY05].

3 Weak Reachability

When reasoning about paths in the abstract system, one can often manage with an even weaker type of reachability (than transitive closure over $must^-$ transitions): we say that an abstract state a' is *weakly reachable* from an abstract state a if there is a concrete state c' that satisfies a', there is a concrete state c that satisfies a, and c' is reachable from c. The combination of $must^+$ and $must^-$ transitions turn out to be especially powerful when reasoning about weak reachability.

If there are three abstract states a_1, a_2, and a_3 such that a_2 is onto reachable from a_1 and a_3 is total reachable from a_2, then a_3 is weakly reachable from a_1. Hence, weak reachability can be concluded from the existence of a sequence of $must^-$ transitions followed immediately by a sequence of $must^+$ transitions:

Theorem 2. [Bal04] *If* $[must^-]^*(a_1, a_2)$ *and* $[must^+]^*(a_2, a_3)$, *then* a_3 *is weakly reachable from* a_1.

3.1 Weak Reachability in Predicate Abstraction

We now focus on the case where the concrete system is a program, and its abstraction is obtained by predicate abstraction. We then show that weak reachability can be made tighter by parameterizing the abstract transitions by predicates. The predicates used in these transitions may be (and usually are) different from the predicates used for predicate abstraction.

Consider a program P. Let X be the set of variables appearing in the program and variables that encode the program location, and let D be the domain of all variables (for technical simplicity, we assume that all variables are over the same domain). We model P by a concrete transition system in which each state is labeled by a valuation in D^X.

```
L0  if x < 6 then
L1      x := x + 3;
L2      if x > 7 then
L3          x := x − 3;
L4  end
```

Fig. 1. The program P

Let $\Phi = \{\phi_1, \phi_2, \ldots, \phi_n\}$ be a set of predicates (quantifier-free formulas of first-order logic) on X. For a set $a \subseteq \Phi$ and an assignment $c \in D^X$, we say that c *satisfies* a iff c satisfies all the predicates in a. The satisfaction relation induces a total and onto function $\rho : D^X \to 2^{\Phi}$, where $\rho(c) = a$ for the unique a for which c satisfies a. An abstraction of the program P that is based on Φ is a TMTS with state space 2^{Φ}, thus each state is associated (and is labeled by) the set of predicates that hold in it. For a detailed description of predicate abstraction see [GS97].

Note that all the transitions of the concrete system in which only the variables that encode the program location are changed (all transitions associated with statements that are not assignments, c.f., conditional branches, skip, etc.) are both $must^+$ and $must^-$ transitions, assuming that Φ includes all conditional expressions in the program. We call such transitions *silent* transitions. The identification of silent transitions makes our reasoning tighter: if $a \xrightarrow{silent}_A a'$ we can replace the transition from a to a' with transitions from a's predecessors to a'. The type of a new transition is the same as the type of the transitions leading to a. [6] Such elimination of silent transitions result in an abstract system in which each transition is associated with an assignment statement.

For simplicity of exposition, we present a toy example.[7] Consider the program P appearing in Figure 1.

When describing an abstract system, it is convenient to describe an abstract state in S_A as a pair of program location and a Boolean vector describing which of the program predicates in Φ hold. Let $\phi_1 = (x < 6)$ and $\phi_2 = (x > 7)$. The abstraction of P that corresponds to the two predicates is described in the left-hand side of Figure 2. In the right-hand side, we eliminate the silent transitions.

We now turn to study weak reachability in the abstract system. By Theorem 2, if $[must^-]^*(a_1, a_2)$ and $[must^+]^*(a_2, a_3)$, then a_3 is weakly reachable from a_1. While Theorem 2 is sound, it is not complete, in the sense that it is possible to have two abstract states a and a' such that a' is weakly reachable from a and still no sequence of transitions as specified in Theorem 2 exists in the abstract system. As an example, consider the abstract states $a = (\mathrm{L1} : \mathrm{TF})$ and $a' = (\mathrm{L4} : \mathrm{TF})$. While a' is weakly reachable from a; c.f., c' =(L4:$x = 5$) is reachable from c =(L0:$x = 5$), the only path from a to a' in the abstraction contains two may transitions, so Theorem 2 cannot be

[6] A transition from a' may also be silent, in which case we continue until the chain of silent transitions either reaches an end state or reaches an assignment statement. If the chain reaches an end state, we can make a an end state.

[7] Our ideas have proven useful also in real examples, as described in our technical report [BKY05].

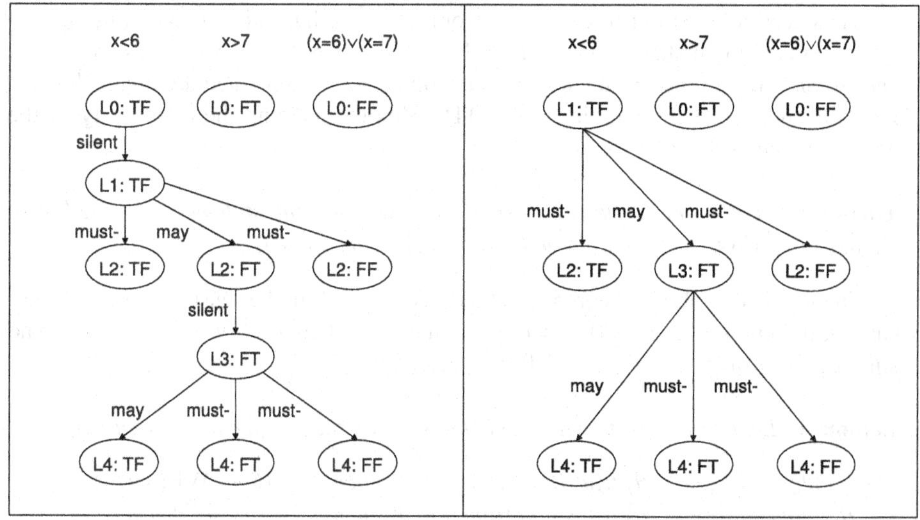

Fig. 2. The abstract transition system of the program P from Figure 1

applied. In fact, the status of the abstract states (L4:FT) and (L4:FF) also is not clear, as the paths from a to these states do not follow the sequence specified in Theorem 2. Accordingly, Theorem 2 does not help us determining whether there is an input $x < 6$ to P such that the execution of P on x would reach location L4 with x that is strictly bigger than 7 or with x that is equal to 6 or 7. Our goal is to tighten Theorem 2, so that we end up with fewer such undetermined cases.

3.2 Parameterized Must Transitions

Recall that each abstract state is associated with a location of the program, and thus it is also associated with a statement. For a statement s and a predicate e over X, the *weakest precondition* $\mathrm{WP}(s, e)$ and the *strongest postcondition* $\mathrm{SP}(s, e)$ are defined as follows [Dij76]:

- The execution of s from every state that satisfies $\mathrm{WP}(s, e)$ results in a state that satisfies e, and $\mathrm{WP}(s, e)$ is the weakest predicate for which the above holds.
- The execution of s from a state that satisfies e results in a state that satisfies $\mathrm{SP}(s, e)$, and $\mathrm{SP}(s, e)$ is the strongest predicate for which the above holds.

For example, in the program P, we have $\mathrm{WP}(x := x + 3, x > 7) = x > 4$, $\mathrm{SP}(x := x + 3, x < 6) = x < 9$, $\mathrm{WP}(x := x - 3, x < 6) = x < 9$, and $\mathrm{SP}(x := x - 3, x > 7) = x > 4$.

Let θ be a predicate over X. We parameterize $must^{+}$ and $must^{-}$ transitions by θ as follows:

- $must^{+}(\theta)(a, a')$ only if for every concrete state c that satisfies $a \wedge \theta$, there is a concrete state c' that satisfies a' and $c \longrightarrow_C c'$.
- $must^{-}(\theta)(a, a')$ only if for every concrete state c' that satisfies $a' \wedge \theta$, there is a concrete state c that satisfies a and $c \longrightarrow_C c'$.

Thus, a $must^+(\theta)$ transition is total from all states that satisfy θ, and a $must^-(\theta)$ transition is onto all states that satisfy θ. Note that when $\theta = \mathbf{T}$, we get usual $must^+$ and $must^-$ transitions. Parameterized transitions can be generated automatically (using WP and SP) while building the TMTS without changing the complexity of the abstraction algorithm.

Theorem 3. *Let a and a' be two abstract states, and s the statement executed in a. Then, $must^+(\mathrm{WP}(s, a'))(a, a')$ and $must^-(\mathrm{SP}(s, a))(a, a')$.*

The good news about Theorem 3 is that it is complete in the sense that for all predicates θ, if there is a $must^+(\theta)$ transition from a to a', then $a \rightarrow (\theta \rightarrow \mathrm{WP}(s, a'))$, and similarly for $must^-$ transitions, as formalized below.

Lemma 1. *Let a and a' be two abstract states, and s the statement executed in a.*

- *If there is a $must^+(\theta)$ transition from a to a', then $a \rightarrow (\theta \rightarrow \mathrm{WP}(s, a'))$.*
- *If there is a $must^-(\theta)$ transition from a to a', then $a' \rightarrow (\theta \rightarrow \mathrm{SP}(s, a))$.*

Thus, the pre and post conditions, which can be generated automatically, are the strongest predicates that can be used. Note that using Theorem 3, it is possible to replace all may transitions by parameterized $must^-$ and $must^+$ transitions.

It is easy to see how parameterized transitions can help when we consider weak reachability. Indeed, if $must^-(\theta_1)(a, a')$, $must^+(\theta_2)(a', a'')$, and $\theta_1 \wedge \theta_2 \wedge a'$ is satisfiable, then a'' is weakly reachable from a, as formalized by the following lemma.

Lemma 2. *If $must^-(\theta_1)(a, a')$, $must^+(\theta_2)(a', a'')$, and $\theta_1 \wedge \theta_2 \wedge a'$ is satisfiable, then there are concrete states c and c'' such that $a(c)$, $a''(c'')$, and c'' is reachable from c.*

The completeness of Theorem 3 implies that when a' is weakly reachable from a via two transitions, this always can be detected by taking $\theta_1 = \mathrm{SP}(s, a)$ and $\theta_2 = \mathrm{WP}(s', a')$, where s and s' are the statements executed in the two transitions.

In our example, we have seen that the transitions from (L1:TF) to (L3:FT) and from (L3:FT) to (L4:TF) are both may transitions, and thus Theorem 2 cannot be applied. However, the fact that the first transition also is a $must^-(x < 9)$ transition and the second also is a $must^+(x < 9)$, together with the fact that $x > 7 \wedge x < 9$ is satisfiable, guarantee that there is a concrete state that corresponds to (L1:TF) and from which a concrete state that corresponds to (L4:TF) is reachable. Indeed, as we noted earlier, (L4:$x = 5$) is reachable from (L0:$x = 5$).

When a and a' are of distance greater than two transitions, parameterization is useful for composing the sequence of $must^-$ transitions with the sequence of $must^+$ transitions:

Theorem 4. *If $[must^-]^*(a_1, a_2)$, $must^-(\theta_1)(a_2, a_3)$, $must^+(\theta_2)(a_3, a_4)$, $[must^+]^*(a_4, a_5)$, and $a_3 \wedge \theta_1 \wedge \theta_2$ is satisfiable, then a_5 is weakly reachable from a_1.*

Again, the predicates θ_1 and θ_2 are induced by the pre and postconditions of the statement leading to the abstract state in which the two sequences are composed.

The transitive closure of the parameterized *must* transitions does not retain the reachability properties of a single transition and requires reasoning in an assume-guarantee fashion, where two predicates are associated with each transition. Our technical report [BKY05] presents such an extension and shows how to use it to extend the set of reachable states further.

4 Applications

This section describes application of weak reachability for linear-time falsification and for abstraction-guided test generation.

In *linear-time model checking*, we check whether all the computations of a given program P satisfy a specification ψ, say an LTL formula. In the automata-theoretic approach to model checking, one constructs an automaton $\mathcal{A}_{\neg\psi}$ for the negation of ψ. The automaton $\mathcal{A}_{\neg\psi}$ is usually a nondeterministic Büchi automaton, where a run is accepting iff it visits a set of designated states infinitely often. The program P is faulty with respect to ψ if the product of $\mathcal{A}_{\neg\psi}$ with the program contains a fair path – one that visits the set of designated states infinitely often. The product of $\mathcal{A}_{\neg\psi}$ with an abstraction of P may contain fair paths that do not correspond to computations of P, thus again there is a need to check for weak reachability.

When reasoning about concrete systems, emptiness of the product automaton can be reduced to a search for an accepting state that is reachable from both an initial state and itself. In the context of abstraction, we should make sure that the path from the accepting state to itself can be repeated, thus weak reachability is too weak here[8], and instead we need the following.

Theorem 5. *If, in the product automaton of P with respect to LTL formula ψ, there is an initial abstract state a_{init} and an accepting state a_{acc} such that a_{acc} is onto reachable from a_{init} and from itself, or a_{acc} is weakly reachable from a_{init} and total reachable from itself, then P violates ψ.*

Falsification methods are related to *testing*, where the system is actually executed. The infeasible task of executing the system with respect to all inputs is replaced by checking a test suite consisting of a finite subset of inputs. It is very important to measure the exhaustiveness of the test suite, and indeed, there has been an extensive research in the testing community on *coverage metrics*, which provide such a measure.

Some coverage metrics are defined with respect to an abstraction of the system. For example, in *predicate-complete testing* [Bal04], the goal is to cover all the reachable observable states (evaluation of the system's predicates under all reachable states), and reachability is studied in an abstract system whose state space consists of an overapproximation of the reachable observable states. The observable states we want our test suite to cover are abstract states that are weakly reachable.

The fundamental question in this setting is how to determine which abstract states are weakly reachable. As we have seen, TMTS provide a sufficient condition for deter-

[8] When ψ is a safety property, $\mathcal{A}_{\neg\psi}$ is an automaton accepting finite bad prefixes [KV01], and weak reachability is sufficient.

mining weak reachability (via a sequence of $must^-$ transitions followed by a sequence of $must^+$ transitions). The parameterization method makes this condition tighter.

5 Conclusion

We have described an abstraction framework that contains $must^-$ transitions, the backwards version of $must$ transitions, and showed how $must^-$ transitions enable reasoning about past-time modalities as well as future-time modalities in a falsification semantics. We showed that the falsification setting allows for a stronger type of abstraction and described applications in falsification of temporal properties and testing.

A general idea in our work is that by replacing $must^+$ by $must^-$ transitions, abstraction frameworks that are sound for verification become abstraction frameworks that are sound (and more precise) for falsification. We demonstrated it with model checking and refinement, and we believe that several other ideas in verification can be lifted to falsification in the same way. This includes generalized model checking [GJ02], making the framework complete [DN05], and its augmentation with hyper-transitions [LX90, SG04].

Another interesting direction is to use $must^-$ transitions in order to strengthen abstractions in the verification setting: the ability to move both forward and backwards across the transition relation has proven helpful in the concrete setting. Using $must^-$ transitions, this also can be done in the abstraction setting.

References

[Bal04] T. Ball. A theory of predicate-complete test coverage and generation. In *3rd International Symposium on Formal Methods for Components and Objects*, 2004.

[Ben91] J. Benthem. Languages in actions: categories, lambdas and dynamic logic. *Studies in Logic*, 130, 1991.

[BG99] G. Bruns and P. Godefroid. Model checking partial state spaces with 3-valued temporal logics. In *Computer Aided Verification*, pages 274–287, 1999.

[BG04] G. Bruns and P. Godefroid. Model checking with 3-valued temporal logics. In *31st International Colloquium on Automata, Languages and Programming*, volume 3142 of *Lecture Notes in Computer Science*, pages 281–293, 2004.

[BKY05] T. Ball, O. Kupferman, and G. Yorsh. Abstraction for falsification. Technical Report MSR-TR-2005-50, Microsoft Research, 2005.

[CC77] P. Cousot and R. Cousot. Abstract interpretation: a unified lattice model for the static analysis of programs by construction or approximation of fixpoints. In *POPL 77: Principles of Programming Languages*, pages 238–252. ACM, 1977.

[CE81] E.M. Clarke and E.A. Emerson. Design and synthesis of synchronization skeletons using branching time temporal logic. In *Proc. Workshop on Logic of Programs*, volume 131 of *Lecture Notes in Computer Science*, pages 52–71. Springer-Verlag, 1981.

[DGG97] D. Dams, R. Gerth, and O. Grumberg. Abstract interpretation of reactive systems. *ACM Trans. Program. Lang. Syst.*, 19(2):253–291, 1997.

[Dij76] E.W. Dijksta. *A Discipline of Programming*. Prentice-Hall, 1976.

[DN05] D. Dams and K. S. Namjoshi. Automata as abstractions. In *VMCAI 2005*, Paris, 2005. to appear, LNCS, Springer-Verlag.

[FKZ+00] R. Fraer, G. Kamhi, B. Ziv, M. Vardi, and L. Fix. Prioritized traversal: efficient reachability analysis for verication and falsification. In *Proc. 12th Conference on Computer Aided Verication*, volume 1855 of *Lecture Notes in Computer Science*, pages 389–402, Chicago, IL, USA, July 2000. Springer-Verlag.

[GHJ01] P. Godefroid, M. Huth, and R. Jagadeesan. Abstraction-based model checking using modal transition systems. In *Proceedings of CONCUR'2001 (12th International Conference on Concurrency Theory)*, volume 2154 of *Lecture Notes in Computer Science*, pages 426–440. Springer-Verlag, 2001.

[GJ02] P. Godefroid and R. Jagadeesan. Automatic abstraction using generalized model checking. In *Computer Aided Verification*, pages 137–150, 2002.

[GLST05] O. Grumberg, F. Lerda, O. Strichman, and M. Theobald. Proof-guided underapproximation-widening for multi-process systems. In *POPL*, pages 122–131, 2005.

[GS97] S. Graf and H. Saidi. Construction of abstract state graphs with PVS. In *CAV 97: Computer-aided Verification*, LNCS 1254, pages 72–83. Springer-Verlag, 1997.

[HJS01] M. Huth, R. Jagadeesan, and D. Schmidt. Model checking partial state spaces with 3-valued temporal logics. In *ESOP*, pages 155–169, 2001.

[Kle87] S. C. Kleene. *Introduction to Metamathematics*. North Holland, 1987.

[Koz83] D. Kozen. Results on the propositional μ-calculus. *Theoretical Computer Science*, 27:333–354, 1983.

[KV01] O. Kupferman and M.Y. Vardi. Model checking of safety properties. *Formal methods in System Design*, 19(3):291–314, November 2001.

[LT88] K.G. Larsen and G.B. Thomsen. A modal process logic. In *Proc. 3th Symp. on Logic in Computer Science*, Edinburgh, 1988.

[LX90] K. G. Larsen and L. Xinxin. Equation solving using modal transition systems. In *LICS*, pages 108–117, 1990.

[PDV01] C. S. Pasareanu, M. B. Dwyer, and W. Visser. Finding feasible counter-examples when model checking abstracted java programs. In *TACAS*, pages 284–298, 2001.

[QS81] J.P. Queille and J. Sifakis. Specification and verification of concurrent systems in Cesar. In *Proc. 5th International Symp. on Programming*, volume 137 of *Lecture Notes in Computer Science*, pages 337–351. Springer-Verlag, 1981.

[SG03] S. Shoham and O. Grumberg. A game-based framework for CTL counterexamples and 3-valued abstraction-refinement. In *Computer Aided Verification*, pages 275–287, 2003.

[SG04] S. Shoham and O. Grumberg. Monotonic abstraction-refinement for CTL. In *Tools and Algorithms for Construction and Analysis of Systems (TACAS)*, volume 2988 of *Lecture Notes in Computer Science*, pages 546–560. Springer-Verlag, 2004.

[Sip99] H.B. Sipma. *Diagram-based Verification of Discrete, Real-time and Hybrid Systems*. PhD thesis, Stanford University, Stanford, California, 1999.

Bounded Model Checking of Concurrent Programs

Ishai Rabinovitz[1,2] and Orna Grumberg[1]

[1] Technion - Israel Institute of Technology
[2] IBM Haifa Research Laboratory, Haifa, Israel
ishai@il.ibm.com, orna@cs.technion.ac.il

Abstract. We propose a SAT-based bounded verification technique, called TCBMC, for threaded C programs. Our work is based on CBMC, which models sequential C programs in which the number of executions for each loop and the depth of recursion are bounded.

The novelty of our approach is in bounding the number of context switches allowed among threads. Thus, we obtain an efficient modeling that can be sent to a SAT solver for property checking. We also suggest a novel technique for modeling mutexes and Pthread conditions in concurrent programs. Using this bounded technique, we can detect bugs that invalidate safety properties. These include races and deadlocks, the detection for which is crucial for concurrent programs.

1 Introduction

In recent years there have been two main trends in formal verification. The first is that SAT-based Bounded Model Checking (BMC) [2] has become the leading technique for model checking of hardware. BMC constructs a propositional formula describing all possible executions of the system of length k, for some bound k. This formula, conjuncted with the negation of the specification, is fed into a SAT solver. If the formula is satisfied, the specification is violated.

The second trend is that software verification using formal methods has become an active research area. Special attention is given to verification of concurrent programs, in which testing tools often fail to find bugs that are revealed only with very specific inputs or timing windows.

However, adopting the BMC technique for software causes a severe problem. This technique is sensitive to the length of the error trace, i.e., the number of execution steps until an error state is reached. In software, error traces are typically quite long, and therefore a large bound k is needed. This, in turn, may result in a propositional formula that is too large to be handled by a SAT solver. Ivancic et al. [6] try to shorten the trace length by compressing multiple statements within one basic block into one complex statement. However, the resulting traces may still be too long.

C-Bounded Model Checking (CBMC) [4] presents a different approach to utilizing a SAT solver in order to verify software. CBMC translates a program

K. Etessami and S.K. Rajamani (Eds.): CAV 2005, LNCS 3576, pp. 82–97, 2005.

with no loops and no function calls into *single assignment form* (SSA form). In this form, variables are renamed so that each variable is assigned only once. As a result there is no need for a notion of state. Such a program can be viewed as a set of constraints and solved using a SAT solver. This technique is less sensitive to the length of a trace.

CBMC can also deal with pointers, arrays, and real size integers rather than just their restricted abstractions. This distinguishes it from other model checkers, which use abstractions in order to cope with size problems. Still, most if not all interesting programs include functions and loops. CBMC handles this by bounding the number of times each loop may be executed and unwinding the loop to this bound. It is then possible to inline function calls and even handle recursion (after bounding its depth as well). As in ordinary Bounded Model Checking, the bounds over the loops can be increased iteratively until a bug is found or the SAT solver explodes.

Each variable in a bounded program has a bounded number of assignments that can be indexed statically in an increasing order. CBMC translates the program in such a way that each indexed assignment is to a fresh variable, yielding a program in SSA form. This is very simple for sequential programs and was proven effective for some real-life examples [7].

However, it is not straightforward to extend this approach to concurrent programs. This is because it is not possible to index assignments to global variables statically. When there are assignments in two different threads to the same global variable, we cannot determine the order in which they will be executed.

In this paper we propose an extension of CBMC to concurrent C programs, called TCBMC (Threaded-C Bounded Model Checking). Concurrent C programs have shared memory and several threads that run concurrently. Each thread has its own local variables, whereas global variables are shared. Only one thread is executed at any given time, until, after an unknown period, a *context switch* occurs and another thread resumes its execution (see Figure 2). A set of consecutive lines of code executed with no intervening context switch is called a *context switch block*.

To obtain a bounded concurrent C program, TCBMC bounds the number of allowed context switches. This strategy is reasonable since most bug patterns have only a few context switches [5]. For each context switch block i and each global variable x, TCBMC adds a new variable val_x_i, which represents the value of x at the end of block i. It then models the concurrent program in SSA form, where the value of x in block $i + 1$ is initialized to val_x_i.

The technique of bounding the number of context switches was independently suggested in [8], However [8] uses this idea on Boolean programs using pushdown automata.

Next we show how synchronization primitives such as mutexes and conditions can be modeled efficiently within TCBMC. We present a novel approach which, instead of modeling the internal behavior of a mutex, eliminates all executions in which a thread has waited for a mutex to unlock. We show that any bug which can be found in the naive model will also be found in our reduced model.

Our approach to modeling synchronization primitives is general, and as such, it is applicable to explicit and BDD-based symbolic model checkers as well. There, it decreases the number of interleavings and hence gains efficiency.

We next suggest how the TCBMC model can be altered to detect synchronization bugs such as races and deadlocks. Different extensions to the model are needed for each one. Thus, it will be more efficient to apply TCBMC three times: for detecting "regular" bugs, races, and deadlocks.

We implemented a preliminary version of TCBMC. This version supports only two threads. It supports mutexes and conditions, but it cannot detect deadlocks. Preliminary experiments show that TCBMC can handle a real representation of integers and that it performs well for data-dependent bugs.

The rest of this paper is organized as follows. The next section presents the preliminaries and explains CBMC. Section 3 presents TCBMC. Section 4 extends TCBMC to model mutexes and conditions. Section 5 describes another extension of TCBMC that allows for detection of races and deadlocks. Section 6 presents our experiments with TCBMC, and Section 7 outlines future work.

2 Preliminaries

A statement *uses* a variable when it reads its value, and it *defines* a variable when it writes a value to it. A statement *accesses* a variable when it either uses it or defines it.

In this paper we consider a *concurrent program* to be a program with several threads that share global variables. An *execution* of such a program starts to execute statements from a certain thread, after which it performs a context switch and continues to execute statements from another thread. It keeps track of the last statement executed in each thread and, when performing a context switch back to this thread, it continues the execution from the next statement.

A statement is *visible* if it accesses a global variable[1], and it is *invisible* otherwise. A *visible block* is a block of consecutive lines in which only the first statement is visible. A statement is *atomic* if no context switch is allowed during its execution. A sequence of consecutive statements is atomic if each statement is atomic and no context switch is allowed between them.

The *assert* function receives a Boolean predicate that should evaluate to True in all executions. Evaluation of assert to False indicates a bug in the program.

In this paper x and x_i are global variables, and y, y_i, w, w_i, z and z_i are local variables.

2.1 CBMC: C-Bounded Model Checking

CBMC [4] is a tool that gets a C program and an integer bound. It translates the program into a bounded program by unrolling each loop to the given

[1] A local variable that can be pointed by a global pointer is considered to be global for this definition.

bound, inlining functions (bounding also the number of recursion calls with the given bound). CBMC then takes the bounded C program and generates a set of constraints. There is a one-to-one mapping from the possible executions of the bounded program to the satisfying assignments of the set of constraints.

CBMC automatically generates cleanness specifications such as no access to dangling pointers, no access out of array bounds, and no assert violations. It adds a constraint which requires that one of these specifications be violated. It then activates a SAT solver over these constraints. If it finds a satisfying assignment to all the constraints, then it follows that there exists a valid execution that violates one of the specifications.

CBMC generates the constraints by translating the code to SSA form, in which each variable is assigned no more than once. To this aim CBMC generates several copies of each variable, indexed from zero to the number of assignments to this variable.

Each statement in a C program is executed only if all the "if" conditions that lead to it are evaluated to True. In order to reflect this in the generated constraint, CBMC also has several guard variables. Each guard variable is associated with the conjunction of all the conditions in the "if"s that lead to a certain statement in the code (If the statement is in the "else" clause of an "if" condition, the negation of the condition is used). Note that several statements may have the same guard.

CBMC is best understood by example. Assume CBMC gets the following C program with bound two.

```
x = 3;
while  (x > 1){
        if (x%2 == 0)  x = x/2;
        else           x = 3 * x + 1;
}
```

It first unrolls the loop, resulting in the program in Figure 1(a). It also adds an assert that ensures sufficient unrolling (This assert will fail in our example). Figure 1(b) presents the constraints representing this bounded code. Consider Constraint (3). It describes the behavior of Line (4) in the bounded code. This is the second assignment to x and therefore the constraint is on x_1. This statement is executed only if the two "if"s leading to it are True, i.e, $guard_2$ is True. The constraint presents the following behavior: if $guard_2$ is True, then $x_1 = x_0/2$; otherwise (the statement is not executed) $x_1 = x_0$ (x does not change).

As mentioned previously, CBMC supports the assert function and detects bugs in which an assert is violated. CBMC also supports the assume function. This function informs CBMC that all legal executions of the program must satisfy a certain constraint. Assume is the opposite of assert in the sense that when the constraint does not hold in a certain execution, CBMC ignores this execution without complaining.

```
x = 3;
if (x > 1){
    if (x%2 == 0)
        x = x/2;
    else x = 3 * x + 1;
    if(x > 1){
        if (x%2 == 0)
            x = x/2;
        else x = 3 * x + 1;
        assert(x <= 1);
    }
}
```

(a) Bounded C code

(0) $x_0 = 3$
(1) $guard_1 = x_0 > 1$
(2) $guard_2 = guard_1 \ \& \ x_0\%2 == 0$
(3) $x_1 = (guard_2 ? x_0/2 : x_0)$
(4) $guard_3 = guard_1 \ \& \ !(x_0\%2 == 0)$
(5) $x_2 = (guard_3 ? 3 * x_1 + 1 : x_1)$
(6) $guard_4 = guard_1 \ \& \ x_2 > 1$
(7) $guard_5 = guard_4 \ \& \ x_2\%2 == 0$
(8) $x_3 = (guard_5 ? x_2/2 : x_2)$
(9) $guard_6 = guard_4 \ \& \ !(x_2\%2 == 0)$
(10) $x_4 = (guard_6 ? 3 * x_3 + 1 : x_3)$
Specification: $!(x_4 <= 1)$

(b) Constraints

Fig. 1. Translation from bounded code to constraints

Pointers and Arrays. In CBMC, every assignment to a dereference of a pointer is actually instantiated to several assignments, one for each possible value of the pointer. The instantiations are limited to values that the pointer might have gotten in the previous assignments. Here is the code for the statement $*p_1 = 3$; where the indexes are for a possible program in which this statement appears.

$$x_{12} = (p == \&x) ? 3 : x_{11};$$
$$y_7 = (p == \&y) ? 3 : y_6;$$
$$z_4 = (p == \&z) ? 3 : z_3;$$
...

Every assignment to an array cell is treated similarly, by instantiating it for each possible value of the array index. Statements that include the use of a dereference of a pointer or of an array cell are treated in a similar manner.

Since the program is bounded, the number of malloc calls is bounded as well. CBMC treats each allocated memory as a regular global variable. CBMC also supports pointer arithmetic inside array bounds.

3 Bounded Model Checking for Concurrent C Programs

In this section we describe how a concurrent program can be efficiently translated to a set of constraints.

The main idea is to bound the number of context switches in the run while allowing them to be anywhere in the code. We denote this bound by n. This strategy is reasonable since most bug patterns have only a few context switches [5]. This strategy is also consistent with the main idea of CBMC. We first present our method for programs with two threads. Later, we describe the required changes for more than two threads.

We note that it is possible to limit the places in which a context switch can occur. There is no advantage in allowing a context switch before an invisible statement [3]; allowing context switches only before visible statements decreases the number of possible executions.

Similarly to CBMC, our goal is to translate concurrent C programs into a set of constraints. As in CBMC, these constraints will be conjuncted with those representing the negation of the specification, and checked for satisfiability.

The translation process consists of three stages.

Stage 1 - Preprocessing. A C statement is not always executed as an atomic statement. Consider the code generated by a compiler for a C statement of the form $x_1 = x_2 + x_3$. The generated assembly code is: $r_a \leftarrow x_2;\ r_b \leftarrow x_3;\ r_c \leftarrow r_a + r_b;\ x_1 \leftarrow r_c;$ (Where each r is a register). A context switch may occur between these instructions. Statements that involve at most one global variable are not affected by this. To allow such context switches in statements that access more than one global variable we need to break statements just as a compiler does. For example, the statement $x_1 = x_2 + x_3$; (in which each x_i is a global variable) is translated to the following code (in which each y_i is a new temporary local variable): $y_1 = x_2;\ \ y_2 = x_3;\ \ x_1 = y_1 + y_2;$ "if" and loop statements, in which the condition accesses more than one global variable, are treated similarly. Note that the order of execution of an expression is not guaranteed under C semantics. Since we assume that this order is consistent for a compiler, we can configure CBMC for compatibility with any given compiler. This preprocessing can also be avoided if we are not interested in examining such interleavings.

Stage 2 - Applying CBMC Separately on Each Thread. In this stage the first phase of CBMC is applied on each thread, and a list of constraints is obtained for each. We refer to this set of constraints as a *template.* In this template each variable has several copies, and each copy appears only once on the left-hand side of a constraint.

We can think of this template as either a list of constraints or as a program in which each constraint is an assignment and each variable is assigned only once. In the rest of this section we use the latter interpretation, and refer to the template as being executed.

As a result of the preprocessing, this template has four types of statements:

1. An assignment of an expression defined over local variables to a local variable, e.g., $w_k = (guard_r ? y_c * 2 : w_{k-1})$
2. An assignment of an expression defined over local variables to a global variable, e.g., $x_k = (guard_r ? y_c * 2 : x_{k-1})$
3. An assignment of a global variable to a local variable, e.g., $y_c = (guard_r ? x_k : y_{c-1})$
4. An assignment to a guard variable. The guard is local and there may be at most one copy of a global variable on the right-hand side, e.g., $guard_r = guard_{r-1} \&\& x_k > y_c$

After CBMC is applied, each variable has several copies, one for each assignment, where x_j refers to the j-th assignment to x.

We will denote by m the number of constraints in this template and enumerate them from 0 to $m-1$. We will use the notation l_{x_j} to refer to the number of the constraint in which x_j is assigned.

Each thread may have its own code and therefore its own template. We translate each thread into a set of constraints. In the following description we will refer to thread t. To avoid name collision, we add the prefix $thread_t$ to each variable.

Stage 3 - Generating Constraints for Concurrency. The main idea of this stage is to associate with each line l in the template a variable $thread_t\_cs(l)$. The value of this variable indicates the number of context switches that occurred before this line was executed.

We induce the following constraints on the values of the $thread_t\_cs(l)$ variables:

- **Monotonicity:** The value of $thread_t\_cs$ must increase monotonically: $\forall_{0 \leq l < m-1}\ thread_t\_cs(l) \leq thread_t\_cs(l+1)$. [2]
- **Interleaving bound:** There is a bound on the number of context switches. If the bound is n, then the maximum value of $thread_t\_cs$ is n. This is described as follows: $thread_t\_cs(m-1) \leq n$
- **Parity:** Each context switch changes the thread that runs. Having only two threads (see extension at the end of Section 3), the values of $thread_t\_cs(l)$ can be restricted to be even for $t = 0$ and odd for $t = 1$. This is described as follows: $\forall_{0 \leq l < m-1}\ (thread_t\_cs(l) mod\ 2) = t$.

Any assignment to the $thread_t\_cs(l)$ variables determines a concurrent execution over the thread templates: first the block of lines for which $thread_0\_cs(l) = 0$ is executed, then those that have $thread_1\_cs(l) = 1$, then those that have $thread_0\_cs(l) = 2$, and so on. Figure 2 illustrates such an execution.

It will be useful to extend the definition of $thread_t\_cs$ in the following manner: $thread_t\_cs(v_j) = thread_t\_cs(l_{v_j})$. This definition maps a copy of a variable to the value of $thread_t\_cs(l_{v_j})$, where l_{v_j} is the line in which v_j was assigned. Thus $thread_t\_cs(v_j)$ is the context switch block number in which v_j gets its value.

Up to this point we added the $thread_t\_cs(l)$ variables that determine where the context switches occurs. We still need to generate constraints for the values of global variables. Because the global variables are shared among the threads, their behavior is not fully covered by the constraints in the templates.

In order to correctly model the global variables in a concurrent program, we define n new variables x_val_i for each global variable x, and $0 \leq i < n$. Variable x_val_i is the value of variable x at the end of the i-th context switch block. We

---

[2] Our implementation of the tool is more efficient: When two lines are in the same visible block (the assignment in line $l+1$ is invisible), the constraint can be $thread_t\_cs(l) = thread_t\_cs(l+1)$. As a result, these two variables can become one. In this paper we disregard this improvement for better readability.

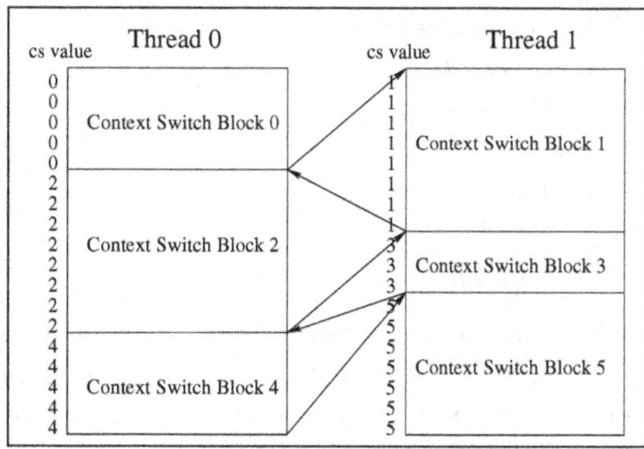

Fig. 2. Context Switch Blocks

can think of x_val_i as the thread interface. This is because in our model, threads can influence each other only through these variables.

Before we define the constraint over x_val_i, we remind the reader that x has several copies in a template, one for each assignment. These assignments are numbered from 0 to $p-1$ (assuming p is the number of assignments to x). The assignment to x_j is in context switch block $thread_t\_cs(x_j)$. Note that the template of thread zero sets x_val_i for even values of i, and the template of thread one sets x_val_i for odd values of i.

Variable x_val_i should get its value according to the last assignment that was made to x in the i-th context switch block. If x was assigned in the i-th context switch block, x_val_i will be equal to x_j, the last assignment to x in this block. Otherwise, if there were no assignments to x in the i-th context switch block, then x_val_i preserves the value it had at the end of the previous block.

$$
\begin{array}{l}
\forall_{i \ s.t. \ i \ mod \ 2=t} \\
\quad x\_val_i = \text{for } \ 0 \leq j < p \\
\qquad\qquad\qquad \text{if } \ (thread_t\_cs(x_j) == i) \wedge (i < thread_t\_cs(x_{j+1}))) \\
\qquad\qquad\qquad\quad thread_t\_x_j \\
\qquad\qquad\quad \text{if } \ (\forall_{0 \leq j < p} \, thread_t\_cs(x_j) \neq i) \\
\qquad\qquad\qquad x\_val_{i-1}
\end{array}
$$

For simplicity we define: $x\_val_{(-1)} = init\_value(x)$, $thread_t\_cs(x_p) = n+1$.

After introducing the additional variables needed for concurrent programs and their constraints, we are now ready to translate each statement in the template into a constraint. We present the translation for each of the four statement types in the template:

1. For regular statements, which do not access global variables (e.g. $y_j = (guard_r?(f(z_k, w_c), y_{j-1})$, we simply add the thread prefix: $thread_t\_y_j = (thread_t\_guard_r?f(thread_t\_z_k, thread_t\_w_c) : thread_t\_y_{j-1})$
2. For statements of the form $y_j = (guard_r?x_k : y_{j-1})$, where y is a local variable and x is a global variable, there are two options:
   - If the assignment to x_k is in the same context switch block as the assignment to y_j, the thread prefix can simply be added.
   - Otherwise, the x_val of the previous context switch block should be used.

$$
\begin{aligned}
thread_t\_y_j = \text{if } & (thread_t\_guard_r) \\
& \text{if } (thread_t\_cs(y_j) == thread_t\_cs(x_k)) \\
& \quad thread_t\_x_k \\
& \text{else} \\
& \quad x\_val_{(thread_t\_cs(y_j)-1)} \\
\text{else} & \\
& thread_t\_y_{(j-1)}
\end{aligned}
$$

3. For statements that have a global variable in their left-hand side and in the else clause of their right-hand side (e.g., $x_j = (guard_r?f(y_k, w_c) : x_{j-1})$, special treatment is required for the else clause. This treatment is similar to that given in the previous item.

$$
\begin{aligned}
thread_t\_x_j = \text{if } & (thread_t\_guard_r) \\
& f(thread_t\_y_k, thread_t\_w_c); \\
\text{else} & \\
& \text{if } (thread_t\_cs(x_j) == thread_t\_cs(x_{j-1})) \\
& \quad thread_t\_x_{j-1}; \\
& \text{else} \\
& \quad x\_val_{(thread_t\_cs(x_j)-1)};
\end{aligned}
$$

4. For an assignment to a guard that does not access a global variable, we simply add the correct prefixes (as in the first item). An assignment to a guard that uses a global variable is treated as in the second item.

Pointers and Arrays. No special treatment is required to support assignments to a pointer dereference or to a cell in an array. Such an assignment is already instantiated into several assignments, one for each possible value, when executing CBMC in Stage 2. Note that for concurrent programs there are more potential values for a global pointer (or a global index of an array), since it may get its value in another thread.

However, we do need to handle dereference of a pointer that may point to a global variable (or a use of a global array cell). These are handled in the preprocessing stage. Their handling is similar to that of expressions with more than one global variable: we break the statement in two. In the first statement, the value of the dereference of the pointer is assigned to a new local variable, y. The second statement is a copy of the original statement, in which the value of the dereference is replaced with y. For example, the statement $v_1 = *p + v_2$; (in which each p may point to a global variable, and each v_i is a local variable) is translated to the following code: $y = *p; \quad v_1 = y + v_2;$

More Than Two Threads. There are two options for extending this algorithm to T threads where $T > 2$: The first is to enforce a round robin among the threads (thread 0 runs first, then thread 1, 2, ..., T-1, and then 0 again and so on). Note that a thread might not perform any statement while running, but the number of context switches still increases. The changes to the constraints are quite trivial. In particular, we change the parity constraint and use *mod* T instead of *mod* 2. This will often require a larger bound over the number of context switches.

Another option for extending TCBMC to T threads is to add a new set of variables: run_i for $0 \leq i < n$, where run_i is the ID of the thread that runs in the i-th context switch block. The value of run_i is set by the SAT solver, and determines the order in which the threads run. There are some changes in the constraints, which we explain in the full version of this paper. We suggest two methods for extending TCBMC because neither one is better than the other for all input programs.

Note that, when threads are dynamically generated, T can be increased iteratively until a bug is found or the SAT solver explodes.

4 Modeling Synchronization Primitives

Until this point the model we present enables the threads to communicate with each other only via global variables. Concurrent programs usually use synchronization primitives as well. In this section we will describe how we can efficiently model mutexes and the Pthread condition (i.e., the *wait/signal* mechanism). The modeling presented in this section interferes with deadlock detection, and will be revisited in subsection 5.2 where deadlocks are handled. We will present the modeling of the synchronization primitives via transformation to C code. It is possible and sometimes even more efficient to directly create the model without changing the C code first. In fact, our implementation actually constructs the model directly from the original code. However, we find the current presentation more readable and easy to understand.

4.1 Modeling Atomic Sections

The first primitive we model is the atomic section, which is not a real programming primitive but is used to model other primitives. Atomic sections are also useful in the verification process. If TCBMC users do not wish to allow context switch along certain sections, they can mark these sections as atomic. This will yield a shorter formula, which will result in a better performance of the SAT solver.

Modeling an atomic section is very simple. We just add constraints that force the $thread_t\_cs$ values of the lines in an atomic section to be identical. Thus, no context switch is allowed along this section.

4.2 Modeling Mutexes

Mutex is the mechanism for implementing mutual exclusion between threads. A mutex has two states, L (locked) and U (unlocked), and at least two basic operations: lock and unlock. Lock waits until the mutex is in U and then changes its state to L. Unlock is applied to a mutex in state L and changes its state to U. There are two common ways to implement the lock operation: The first is to wait until the mutex is in state U. This is done by means of a busy wait. The second is to move the thread to the operating system's sleep state. The thread will return to a ready state when the mutex returns to state U.

A naive approach may model mutexes by including one of these implementations explicitly. The result is a complicated model. In fact, this is not necessary. Our goal is not to verify that the mutex implementation is correct; we assume it is correct. Rather we aim at verifying the programs that use mutexes. We also manage to avoid the main difficulty in modeling mutexes: the modeling of lock operations when the mutex is in state L.

Before explaining how we model mutexes, we present two definitions and a lemma that help us to explain the idea behind our method.

Two executions of a concurrent program are *mutex-free-equivalent* iff they have the same states when ignoring the internal implementation of mutexes (We consider only the state of the mutex U or L). We use the notation $\pi \approx_w \pi'$ to indicate that π and π' are mutex-free-equivalent.

We define *redundant-attempt* as an attempt to lock a mutex that is already in state L. A *wait-free execution* is an execution that has no redundant-attempts.

Lemma 1. *Let P be a concurrent program. For every non-wait-free execution π of P there is a wait-free execution π' that satisfies $\pi \approx_w \pi'$.*

In our modeling all executions are wait-free. If a thread tries to lock a mutex, it either succeeds (the mutex is in state U) or this execution is eliminated. Furthermore, all errors other than deadlock that appear in a non-wait-free execution appear also in a mutex-free equivalent wait-free execution. Thus it is possible to find all the errors.

We model a mutex by implementing special C functions for the lock and unlock primitives, and translate it using CBMC. The lock function uses the assume function. Figure 3 presents the modeling of lock and unlock. Only 1 bit is used for each mutex. In order to improve performance, we maximize the atomic sections in the modeling of lock. We will continue to maximize the atomic sections in other modelings as well.

locking_trd_id can be added to the mutex modeling to ensure that the thread that performs the unlock operation is the same one that locked it earlier. A bounded counter of the number of locks can also be added to support recursive mutexes.

```
atomic{
  assume(*mutex == U);
  *mutex = L;
}
```

(a) lock(mutex)

```
atomic{
  assert(*mutex == L);
  *mutex = U;
}
```

(b) unlock(mutex)

Fig. 3. Modeling of lock and unlock in C

4.3 Modeling Conditions

A condition has 3 primitives: *wait*, *signal* and *broadcast*. *wait*(*cond*, *mutex*) stops the run of the thread until it is awakened by another thread's call to signal or broadcast. *Signal*(*cond*) awakens one of the threads that are waiting for this condition. There is no guarantee as to which of the waiting threads will be awakened. Broadcast awakens all the threads that are waiting for this condition. If a signal is sent and there is no thread waiting for it, then the signal is lost; there is no accumulation of signals. *wait* also receives mutex as parameter. It needs to unlock it before stopping and lock it again before continuing (after the thread has been awakened).

Here we model each condition *cond* using a vector of flags, one for each thread. To model a wait in thread i we raise the $cond[i]$ flag, allow context switch, and then assume that the $cond[i]$ is down. The idea is similar to the one we used for mutexes; we actually eliminate all the interleavings in which this thread resumes running before it should. To model *signal*, we nondeterministically choose one raised flag and lower it. *Broadcast* is modeled by simply lowering all the flags.

In order to understand why this modeling is similar to that of mutexes, recall that the *wait* operation can be divided into four stages:

1. Raise a flag indicating that this thread is waiting.
2. *Unlock* the mutex.
3. Wait for this flag to reset.
4. *Lock* the mutex again.

We model only wait-free executions: wait operations that do not wait in the third stage.

Figure 4 presents the modeling of wait and signal. broadcast(cond) is simply modeled by lowering all the flags.

```
atomic{
  cond[current thread] = 1;
  unlock(mutex);
}
assume(cond[current thread] == 0);
lock(mutex);
```

(a) *wait(cond, mutex)*

```
atomic{
  i = rand(number of threads);
  assume(cond[i] == 1||cond == 0);
  cond[i] = 0;
}
```

(b) *signal(cond)*

Fig. 4. Modeling of *wait* and *signal* in C

5 Verifying Race Conditions and Deadlocks

When verifying concurrent programs it is important to detect race conditions and deadlocks. This section presents the changes in the model for each of them.

5.1 Detecting Races

A *race condition* is a state in which the next instructions of different threads access the same memory location and at least one of them is a write.

We can identify races by adding to each global variable x a new global bit variable x_write_flag. x_write_flag is raised whenever x is defined (i.e., assigned to) and lowered in the next instruction. There can be a context switch between these two instructions. In addition, on every access to x we assert that its x_write_flag is low. Figure 5 presents an example of such translation.

Pointers and Arrays. Special treatment is required for pointers and arrays. When there is an assignment to a dereference of a pointer p that points to x, we should change x_write_flag. We have to consider all possible variables which p might point to (see example in subsection 2.1). For each one, we change the corresponding flag while changing the variable itself. Arrays are handled similarly.

```
atomic{
  assert(x_write_flag == 0);
  x = 3;
  x_write_flag = 1;
}
x_write_flag = 0;
```

(a) Translation of $x = 3$

```
assert(x_write_flag == 0);
y = x;
```

(b) Translation of $y = x$

Fig. 5. Detecting races

5.2 Finding Deadlocks

Deadlock detection is one of the most interesting issues in concurrent programs. We divide deadlocks into two kinds: a global deadlock is a deadlock in which all the threads are waiting for a mutex or a condition, and a local deadlock is a deadlock in which some of the threads form a waiting cycle (e.g., thread 1 is waiting for mutex m_a which is held by thread 2 which is waiting for mutex m_b which is held by thread 1). In this section we present the extension to TCBMC that allows for detection of global deadlocks. In the full version of this paper we present the extension of TCBMC that allows for detection of local deadlocks [3].

When modeling the code to detect deadlocks, we ignore the existence of other errors. As mentioned before, we encourage TCBMC users to perform three runs: for detecting "regular" errors, for detecting races, and for detecting deadlocks.

In the model we presented in Section 4 we eliminated non-wait-free executions. But this could result in missing global deadlocks because these occur when all threads are in a waiting state. Therefore, we must change the modeling of $lock(m)$, and $wait(cond, mutex)$: We add a new global counter called $trds\_in\_wait$. This counter counts the number of threads in a wait state. When modeling $lock(m)$, if mutex m is already in state L, we increase $trds\_in\_wait$, allow context switch, and then assert that $trds\_in\_wait < T$. If the assertion fails, a global deadlock was detected; otherwise we eliminate this execution, as in the original mutex modeling. When modeling $wait(cond, mutex)$, we increase

[3] We are able to find local deadlocks that involve only mutexes. It is not always possible to find deadlocks that involve conditions when bounding the program.

trds_in_wait after raising the *cond*[*current thread*] flag, allow context switch, and then assert that *trds_in_wait* $< T$. If the assertion fails, a deadlock was detected; otherwise we decrease *trds_in_wait* and continue as in the original modeling of *wait*(*cond*, *mutex*) by assuming that the flag is down.

We also add a global Boolean flag named *dd*(deadlock detected), This flag is raised when a deadlock is found. Once a deadlock has been detected, we know that a bug has been found, and so we can ignore later uses of *lock* and *wait*. More details can be found in the full version.

Figure 6 present the modeling of *lock*(*m*) and *wait*(*cond*, *mutex*).

```
if (!dd){
  atomic{
    unlocked = (*m == U);
    if (unlocked) *m = L
    else          trds_in_wait + +;
  }
  atomic{
    if (!unlocked){
       dd = (trds_in_wait == T);
       assert(!dd);
       assume(dd);
    }
  }
}
```

(a) *lock*(*m*)

```
if  (!dd){
  atomic{
    cond[current thread] = 1;
    unlock(mutex);
    trds_in_wait + +;
  }
  atomic{
    dd = (trds_in_wait == T);
    assert(!dd);
    assume(dd ∨ cond[current thread] == 0);
    trds_in_wait − −;
  }
  lock(mutex);
}
```

(b) *wait*(*cond*, *mutex*)

Fig. 6. Modeling of lock and unlock in C when looking for deadlocks

6 Experimental Results

We implemented an initial version of TCBMC that works with two threads and supports mutexes and conditions. Future extensions will support more than two threads, as well as detect deadlocks using the described algorithms. We performed preliminary experiments that checked TCBMC on a naive concurrent implementation of bubble sort. We executed TCBMC over several array sizes, for different values of n (i.e., the number of allowed context switches), and for different integer widths. We used a sufficient loop unwinding bound. The bug in this implementation was dependent on both data and the interleaving.

We also compared it with Microsoft's Zing [1], a state-of-the-art explicit model checker for software that uses various reductions including partial order resuctions. Note that Zing and TCBMC were executed on different platforms [4]. The results are summarized in Table 1.

[4] Zing was executed on the Windows operating system on a Pentium4 1.8Ghz with 1GB memory. TCBMC was executed on the Linux operating system on a Pentium4 2Ghz with 250MB memory.

Table 1. Run time comparison of Zing and TCBMC

array size	Zing		TCBMC					
	8 bit	12 bit	8 bit		16 bit		32 bit	
			n=6	n=10	n=6	n=10	n=6	n=10
3	330.0s	> 1h	0.4s	0.2s	3.6s	4.0s	20.3s	48.3s
4	831.0s	> 1h	11.5s	1.3s	14.6s	58.7s	135.2s	323.0s
5	1496.0s	> 1h	71.0s	94.1s	125.7s	3013.0s	1124.0s	> 1h

From this preliminary experiment we can deduce the following:

– It seems that TCBMC scales better with respect to integer widths. Zing ran for more than an hour for 12 bits, while TCBMC managed to get results even for 32 bits.
– Although tested on different platforms, it seems that TCBMC performs better than Zing for detecting bugs dependent on both data and interleavings.
– Increasing the number of allowed context switches (n) sometimes improves the performance (e.g., array size of 4, and 8 bits). This unexpected behavior can be explained by the fact that for larger n, TCBMC generates a larger formula, but with more satisfying assignments.

7 Conclusions and Future Work

This paper presented an extension of CBMC for concurrent C programs. It explained how to model synchronization primitives and how to detect races and deadlocks. We should complete our implementation to support all of the above.

We also consider changing the template translation into constraints: rather than defining for each line a variable indicating in which context switch block it is executed, we can define, for each context switch block, a variable indicating in which line it begins. This will result in a completely different formula which may be handled better by the SAT solver.

Acknowledgments. We thank Sharon Barner, Ziv Glazberg and Daniel Kroening for many helpful discussions.

References

1. T. Andrews, S. Qadeer, S. K. Rajamani, J. Rehof, and Y. Xie. Zing: Exploiting program structure for model checking concurrent software. In *CONCUR*, 2004.
2. A. Biere, A. Cimatti, E. Clarke, and Y. Zhu. Symbolic model checking without BDDs. In *Proc. 5th International Conference on Tools and Algorithms for the Construction and Analysis of Systems (TACAS)*, LNCS 1579. Springer-Verlag, 1999.
3. E. Clarke, O. Grumberg, and D. Peled. *Model Checking*. MIT Press, 1999.

4. E. Clarke, D. Kroening, and F. Lerda. A tool for checking ANSI-C programs. In *TACAS 2004*, pages 168–176. Springer, 2004.
5. E. Farchi, Y. Nir, and S. Ur. Concurrent Bug Patterns and How to Test them. Workshop on Parallel and Distributed Systems: Testing and Debugging, 2003.
6. F. Ivancic, Z. Yang, A. Gupta, M. K. Ganai, and P. Ashar. Efficient SAT-based bounded model checking for software verification, ISoLA, 2004.
7. D. Kroening, E. Clarke, and K. Yorav. Behavioral consistency of C and Verilog programs using bounded model checking. In *DAC*, 2003.
8. S. Qadeer and J. Rehof. Context-bounded model checking of concurrent software. In *TACAS*, 2005.

Abstraction Refinement for Bounded Model Checking

Anubhav Gupta[1] and Ofer Strichman[2]

[1] School of Computer Science, Carnegie Mellon University, USA
anubhav@cs.cmu.edu
[2] Information Systems Engineering, Technion, Israel
ofers@ie.technion.ac.il

Abstract. Counterexample-Guided Abstraction Refinement (CEGAR) techniques have been very successful in model checking large systems. While most previous work has focused on model checking, this paper presents a Counterexample-Guided abstraction refinement technique for Bounded Model Checking (BMC). Our technique makes BMC much faster, as indicated by our experiments. BMC is also used for generating refinements in the Proof-Based Refinement (PBR) framework. We show that our technique unifies PBR and CEGAR into an abstraction-refinement framework that can balance the model checking and refinement efforts.

1 Introduction

One of the most successful techniques for combating the infamous state-explosion problem in model checking is abstraction combined with automatic refinement. Starting from Kurshan's *localization reduction* [Kur94] in the 80's and later on a long list of symbolic techniques based at least partially on BDDs [CGKS02] [BGA02] [CCK+02] [GKMH+03], this framework proves to be highly efficient in solving model checking problems, many of which simply cannot be solved without it. The reason abstraction works, is that sometimes the checked property can be proved or refuted with only partial information about the model. Algorithms following the abstraction-refinement framework try to identify small subsets of the original model that on the one hand contain enough information to get the correct answer, and on the other hand are small enough to be handled by a model checker.

Abstraction techniques are mostly *conservative*: they preserve all the behaviors of the original model, but may introduce additional behaviors in the abstract model. This means that the model checker can produce *spurious counterexamples*, i.e. traces that are only possible in the abstract model, and not in the original model. In such cases we need to *refine* the abstraction in order to remove the spurious behavior. If the refinement is done based on an analysis of the spurious counterexample, which is the typical case, it is known as *Counterexample-Guided Abstraction Refinement* (CEGAR).

In this paper, we present a *Counterexample-Guided* abstraction-refinement technique for *Bounded Model Checking*, called CG-BMC. SAT-based Bounded

K. Etessami and S.K. Rajamani (Eds.): CAV 2005, LNCS 3576, pp. 112–124, 2005.

Model Checking (BMC) [BCCZ99] has gained wide acceptance in industry in the last few years, as a technique for refuting properties with shallow counterexamples, if they exist. Given a model M, a property φ and a positive integer k representing the depth of the search, a Bounded Model Checker generates a propositional formula that is satisfiable if and only if there is a counterexample of length k or less to φ, in M. BMC iteratively deepens the search for counterexamples until either a bug is found or the problem becomes too hard to solve in a given time limit. The motivation for making this technique more powerful, i.e. to enable it to go deeper in a given time limit, is clear.

The guiding principle behind CG-BMC is similar to that of any good CEGAR technique: attempt to eliminate spurious behavior in few iterations, while keeping the abstract model small enough to be solved easily. CG-BMC therefore focuses on eliminating those spurious transitions that may lead to an error state.

Our abstraction makes parts of the model non-deterministic as in [Kur94], i.e. the defining logic of some variables (those that are known in literature as *invisible variables*) is replaced with a nondeterministic value. This abstraction works well with a SAT-solver since it corresponds to choosing a set of 'important' clauses as the abstract model. Our initial abstraction is simply the empty set of clauses, and in each refinement step we add clauses from the original, concrete model.

We start the CG-BMC loop with search depth $k = 1$. In each iteration of the loop, we first try to find a counterexample of length k in the current abstract model, with a standard BMC formulation and a SAT-solver. If the abstract model has no counterexamples of length k, the property holds at depth k and we move to depth $k+1$. Otherwise, if a counterexample is detected in the abstract model, we check the validity of the counterexample on the original model. More specifically, we formulate a standard BMC instance with length k, and restrict the values of the visible variables (those that participate in the abstract model) to their values in the counterexample. If the counterexample is real, we report a bug and exit. If the counterexample is spurious, the abstract model is refined by adding to it gates that participated in the proof of unsatisfiability. This refinement strategy has been previously used by Chauhan et al.[CGKS02] in the context of model checking. We chose this technique because for our purposes, it provides a good balance between the effort of computing the refinement and the quality of the refinement, i.e. how fast it leads to convergence and how hard it makes the abstract model to solve.

An alternative to our two-stage heuristic, corresponding to checking the abstract and concrete models, is to try to emulate this process within a SAT-solver by controlling the decision heuristic (focusing first on the parts of the model corresponding to the abstract model). Wang et al. [WJHS04] went in this direction: they use the unsatisfiable cores from previous cycles to guide the search of the SAT-solver when searching for a bug in the current cycle. Guidance is done by changing the variable selection heuristic to first decide on the variables that participated in the previous unsatisfiable cores. Furthermore, McMillan observed in [McM03] that modern SAT-solvers internally behave like abstraction-refinement engines by themselves: their variable selection heuristics move variables involved in recent conflicts up in the decision order. However, a major drawback of this approach is that while operating on a BMC instance, they propagate values to variables that are not part of the abstract model that we wish to concentrate on, and this can lead to long phases in which the SAT-solver attempts to solve *local conflicts* that are irrelevant to proving the property. In other words, this approach allows irrelevant clauses to be pulled into the proof through propagation and cause conflicts. This is also the drawback of [WJHS04], as we will prove by experiments. Our approach solves this problem by forcing the SAT-solver to first find a complete abstract trace before attempting to refute it. We achieve this by isolating the important clauses from the rest of the formula in a separate SAT instance.

Another relevant work is by Gupta et al. [GGYA03], that presents a top-down abstraction framework where proof analysis is applied iteratively to generate successively smaller abstract models. Their work is related because they also suggest using the abstract models to perform deeper searches with BMC. However, their overall approach is very different from ours. They focus on the top-down iterative abstraction, and refinement is used only when they cannot go deeper with BMC.

We take the CG-BMC approach one step further in Section 5.2, by considering a new abstraction-refinement framework, in which CG-BMC unifies CEGAR and Proof-Based Refinement (PBR) [MA03, GGYA03]. PBR eliminates all counterexamples of a given length in a single refinement step. The PBR refinement uses the unsatisfiable core of the (unrestricted) BMC instance to generate a refinement. Amla et al. showed in [AM04] that CEGAR and PBR are two extreme approaches: CEGAR burdens the model checker by increasing the number of refinement iterations while PBR burdens the refinement step because the BMC unfolding without the counterexample constraints is harder to refute. They also present a hybrid approach that tries to balance between the two, which results in a more robust overall behavior. We show that by replacing BMC with a more efficient CG-BMC as the refinement engine inside PBR, we also get a hybrid abstraction-refinement framework that can balance the model checking and refinement efforts.

In the next section we briefly describe the relevant issues in BMC, unsatisfiable cores produced by SAT-solvers, and the CEGAR loop. In Section 3 we describe our CG-BMC algorithm, which applies CEGAR to BMC. We also describe a variant of this algorithm, called CG-BMC-T, which uses timeouts in one stage of the algorithm to avoid cases in which solving the abstract model becomes too hard. In Section 4 we describe our experiments with these two techniques and compare them to both standard BMC and [WJHS04]. Our implementation of CG-BMC on top of zChaff [MMZ+01] achieved significant speed-ups comparing to the other two techniques. In Section 5, we describe how this approach can very naturally be integrated in a hybrid approach, which benefits from the advantages of both CEGAR and PBR. We conclude in Section 6 by giving some directions for future work.

2 Preliminaries

2.1 Bounded Model Checking

SAT-based Bounded Model Checking [BCCZ99] is a rather powerful technique for refuting properties. Given a model M, a property φ and a positive integer k representing the depth of the search, a Bounded Model Checker generates a propositional formula that is satisfiable if and only if there is a counterexample of length k or less to φ, in M. In this case we write $M \not\models_k \varphi$. The idea is to iteratively deepen the search for counterexamples until either a bug is found or the problem becomes too hard to solve in a given time limit. The extreme efficiency of modern SAT-solvers make it possible to check properties typically up to a depth of a few hundred cycles. More importantly, there is a very weak correlation, if any, between what is hard for standard BDD-based model checking, and BMC. It is many times possible to refute properties with the latter that cannot be handled at all by the former. It should be clear, then, that every attempt to make this technique work faster, and hence enable to check larger circuits and in deeper cycles, is worth while.

2.2 Unsatisfiable Cores Generated by SAT-Solvers

While a satisfying assignment is a checkable proof that a given propositional formula is satisfiable, until recently SAT-solvers produced no equivalent evidence when the formula is unsatisfiable. The notion of generating resolution proofs from a SAT-solver was introduced in [MA03]. From this resolution proof, one may also extract the *unsatisfiable core*, which is the set of clauses from the original CNF formula that participate in the proof. Topologically, these are the roots of the resolution graph. The importance of the unsatisfiable core is that it represents a subset, hopefully a small one, of the original set of clauses that is unsatisfiable by itself. This information can be valuable in an abstraction-refinement process as well as in other techniques, because it can point to the reasons for unsatisfiability. In the case of abstraction-refinement, it can guide the refinement process, since it points to the reasons for why a given spurious counterexample cannot be satisfied together with the concrete model.

2.3 Counterexample-Guided Abstraction-Refinement

Given a model M and an ACTL property φ, the abstraction-refinement framework encapsulates various automatic algorithms for finding an abstract model $\hat{M}$ with the following two properties:

- $\hat{M}$ over-approximates M, and therefore $\hat{M} \models \varphi \rightarrow M \models \varphi$;
- $\hat{M}$ is smaller than M, so checking whether $\hat{M} \models \varphi$ can be done more efficiently than checking the original model M.

This framework is an important tool for tackling the state-explosion problem in model checking. Algorithm 1 describes a particular implementation of the Counterexample-Guided Abstraction-Refinement (CEGAR) loop. We denote by

$BMC(M, \varphi, k)$ the process of generating the length k BMC unfolding for model M and solving it, according to the standard BMC framework as explained in Section 2.1. The loop simulates the counterexample on the concrete model using a SAT-solver (line 4), and uses the unsatisfiable core produced by the SAT-solver to refine the abstract model (lines 5,6). This refinement strategy was proposed by Chauhan et al.[CGKS02].

Algorithm 1 Counterexample-Guided Abstraction-Refinement

CEGAR (M, φ)

1: $\hat{M} = \{\}$;
2: **if** $MC(\hat{M}, \varphi) = TRUE$ **then return** 'TRUE';
3: **else** let C be the length k counterexample produced by the model checker;
4: **if** $BMC(M, k, \varphi) \wedge C = SAT$ **then return** 'bug found in cycle k';
5: **else** let U be the set of gates in the unsatisfiable core produced by the SAT-solver;
6: $\hat{M} = \hat{M} \cup U$;
7: **goto** line 2;

3 Abstraction-Refinement for Bounded Model Checking

The underlying principles behind the CEGAR framework are the following:

- The information that was used to eliminate previous counterexamples, which is captured by the abstract model, is relevant for proving the property.
- If the abstract model does not prove the property, then the counterexamples in the abstract model can guide the search for a refinement.

We apply these principles to guide the SAT-solver, thereby making BMC faster.

3.1 The CG-BMC Algorithm

The pseudo-code of our Counterexample-Guided Bounded Model Checking algorithm is shown in Algorithm 2. We start with an empty initial abstraction and an initial search depth $k = 1$. In each iteration of the CG-BMC loop, we first try to find a counterexample in the abstract model (line 3). If there is no counterexample in the abstract model, the property holds at cycle k and the abstract model now contains the gates in the unsatisfiable core generated by the SAT-solver (lines 4,5). Otherwise, if a counterexample is found, we simulate the counterexample on the concrete model (line 8). If the counterexample can be concretized, we report a real bug. If the counterexample is spurious, the abstract model is refined by adding the gates in the unsatisfiable core (line 10). Like standard BMC, CG-BMC either finds an error or continues until it becomes too complex to solve within a given time limit.

3.2 Inside a SAT-Solver

Most modern SAT-solvers are based on the DPLL search procedure [DP60]. The search for a satisfying assignment in the DPLL framework is organized as a binary search tree in which at each level a *decision* is made on the variable to split

Algorithm 2 Counterexample-Guided Bounded Model Checking

```
CG-BMC (M, φ)
k = 0; M̂ = {};
k = k + 1;
if BMC(M̂, k, φ) = UNSAT then
    Let U be the set of gates in the unsatisfiable core produced by the SAT-solver;
    M̂ = U;
    goto line 2;
else let C be the satisfying assignment produced by the SAT-solver;
if BMC(M, k, φ) ∧ C = SAT then return 'bug found in cycle k';
else let U be the set of gates in the unsatisfiable core produced by the SAT-solver;
M̂ = M̂ ∪ U;
goto line 3;
```

on, and the first branch to be explored (each of the two branches corresponds to a different Boolean assignment to the chosen variable). After each decision, Boolean Constrain Propagation (BCP) is invoked, a process that finds the implications of the last decision by iteratively applying the *unit-clause rule* (the unit-clause rule simply says that if in an l-length clause $l-1$ literals are unsatisfied, then the last literal must be satisfied in order to satisfy the formula). Most of the computation time inside a SAT-solver is spent on BCP. If BCP leads to a conflict (an empty clause), the SAT-solver backtracks and changes some previous decision.

The performance of a SAT-solver is determined by the choice of the decision variables. Typically SAT-solvers compute a score function for each undecided variable that prioritizes the decision options. Many branching heuristics have been proposed in the literature: see, for example, [Sil99]. The basic idea behind many of these heuristics is to increase the score of variables that are involved in conflicts, thereby moving them up in the decision order. This can be viewed as a form of refinement [McM03].

An obvious question that comes to mind is why do we need an abstraction-refinement framework for BMC when a SAT-solver internally behaves like an abstraction-refinement engine. A major drawback of the branching heuristics in a SAT-solver is that they have no global perspective of the structure of the problem. While operating on a BMC instance, they tend to get 'distracted' by local conflicts that are not relevant to the property at hand. CG-BMC avoids this problem by forcing the SAT-solver to find a satisfying assignment to the abstract model, which contains only the relevant part of the concrete model. It involves the other variables and gates only if it is not able to prove unsatisfiability with the current abstract model.

The method suggested by Wang et al. [WJHS04] that we mentioned in the introduction, tries to achieve a similar effect by modifying the branching heuristics. They perform BMC on the concrete model, while changing the score function of the SAT-solver so it gives higher priority to the variables in the abstract model (they do not explicitly refer to an abstract model, rather to the unsatisfiable core of the previous iteration, which is what we refer to as the abstract model). Since their SAT-solver operates on a much larger concrete model, it spends a lot more time doing BCP. Moreover, many of the variables in the abstract model are also present in clauses that are not part of the abstract model and their method often encounters conflicts on these clauses. CG-BMC, on the other hand, *isolates* the abstract model and solves it separately, in order to avoid this problem.

3.3 The CG-BMC-T Algorithm

The following is an implicit assumption in the CG-BMC algorithm: Given two unsatisfiable sets of clauses C_1 and C_2 such that $C_1 \subset C_2$, solving C_1 is faster than solving C_2. While this is a reasonable assumption and mostly holds in practice, it is not always true. It is possible that the set of clauses C_2 is *over-constrained*, so that the SAT-solver can prove its unsatisfiability with a small search tree. Removing clauses from C_2, on the other hand, could produce a set of clauses C_1 that is *critically-constrained* and proving the unsatisfiability of C_1 could take much more time [CA93].

We observed this phenomenon in some of our benchmarks. As an example, consider circuit *PJ05* in Table 1 (see Section 4). The CG-BMC algorithm takes much longer than BMC to prove the property on *PJ05*. This is not because of the overhead of the refinement iterations: the abstract model has enough clauses to prove the property after an unfolding length of 9. The reason for this is that BMC on the small abstract model takes more time than BMC on the original model.

In order to deal with such situations, we propose a modified CG-BMC algorithm, called CG-BMC-T (T stands for Timeout). The intuition behind this algorithm is the following: if the SAT-solver is taking a long time on the abstract model, it is possible that it is stuck in a critically-constrained search region, and therefore we check if it can quickly prune away this search region by adding some constraints from the concrete model. The algorithm is described in Algorithm 3. In each iteration of the CG-BMC-T loop, we set a timeout T for the SAT-solver (line 4) and try to find a counterexample in the abstract model (line 5). If the SAT-solver completes, the loop proceeds like CG-BMC. However, if the SAT-solver times-out, we simulate the partial assignment on the concrete model with a smaller timeout ($T \times \beta$, $\beta < 1$) (lines 14,16). If the concrete model is able to concretize the partial assignment, we report a bug (line 17). If the concrete model refutes the partial assignment, we add the unsatisfiable core generated by the SAT-solver to the abstract model, thereby eliminating the partial assignment (line 21). If the concrete solver also times-out, we go back to the abstract solver. However, for this next iteration, we increase the timeout with a factor of α (line 14). The CG-BMC-T algorithm is more robust, as indicated by our experiments.

4 Experiments

We implemented our techniques on top of the SAT-solver zChaff [MMZ$^+$01]. Some modifications were made to zChaff to produce unsatisfiable cores while adding and deleting clauses incrementally. Our experiments were conducted on

Algorithm 3 CG-BMC with Timeouts

CG-BMC-T (M, φ)
1: $k = 0$; $\hat{M} = \{\}$;
2: $k = k + 1$;
3: $T = T_{init}$;
4: $Set\_Timeout(T)$;
5: $Res = BMC(\hat{M}, k, \varphi)$;
6: **if** $Res = UNSAT$ **then**
7:     Let U be the set of gates in the unsatisfiable core produced by the SAT-solver;
8:     $\hat{M} = U$;
9:     **goto** line 2;
10: **else**
11:     **if** $Res = SAT$ **then**
12:         Let C be the satisfying assignment produced by the SAT-solver;
13:     **else**
14:         $T = T \times \alpha$; $Set\_Timeout(T \times \beta)$;
15:         Let C be the partial assignment produced by the SAT-solver;
16: $Res = BMC(M, k, \varphi) \wedge C$;
17: **if** $Res = SAT$ **then return** 'bug found in cycle k';
18: **else**
19:     **if** $Res = UNSAT$ **then**
20:         Let U be the set of gates in the unsat core produced by the SAT-solver;
21:         $\hat{M} = \hat{M} \cup U$;
22: **goto** line 4;

a set of benchmarks that were derived during the formal verification of an open source Sun PicoJava II microprocessor [MA03]. All experiments were performed on a 1.5GHz Dual Athlon machine with 3Gb RAM. We set a timeout of 2 hours and a maximum BMC search depth of 60.

We use the incremental feature of zChaff to optimize the CG-BMC loop as follows. We maintain two incremental SAT-instances: *solver-Abs* contains the BMC unfolding of the abstract model while *solver-Conc* contains the BMC unfolding of the concrete model. The counterexample generated by *solver-Abs* is simulated on *solver-Conc* by adding unit clauses. The unsatisfiable core generated by *solver-Conc* is added to *solver-Abs*. Our algorithm can in principle be implemented inside a SAT-solver although this requires fundamental changes in the way it works, and it is not clear if it will actually perform better or worse. We discuss this option further in Section 6.

Table 1 compares our techniques with standard BMC. For each circuit, we report the depth that was completed by all techniques, the runtime in seconds, and the number of backtracks (for CG-BMC/CG-BMC-T we report the backtracks on both abstract and concrete models). We see a significant overall reduction in runtime. This reduction is due to a decrease in the total number of backtracks, and the fact that most of the backtracks (and BCP) are performed on a much smaller abstract model. We also observe a more robust behavior with CG-BMC-T ($T_{init} = 10\text{s}, \alpha = 1.5, \beta = 0.2$).

Table 2 compares our technique with the approach based on modifying the SAT-solver's branching heuristics, as described in Wang et al. [WJHS04]. We re-

Table 1. Comparison of CG-BMC/CG-BMC-T with standard BMC.

Circuit	Depth	Time(s)			Backtracks				
		BMC	CG-BMC	CG-BMC-T	BMC	CG-BMC		CG-BMC-T	
						Abs	Conc	Abs	Conc
PJ00	35	7020	48	48	139104	378	27	378	27
PJ01	60	273	99	99	169	187	9	187	9
PJ02	39	6817	51	51	79531	807	5	807	5
PJ03	39	6847	51	51	79531	807	5	807	5
PJ04	60	125	99	98	169	184	7	184	7
PJ05	25	751	2812	296	12476	582069	59	64846	445
PJ06	33	2287	2421	364	23110	346150	92	82734	137
PJ07	60	1837	789	449	34064	197843	86	111775	132
PJ08	60	5061	201	201	43564	44468	124	44468	124
PJ09	60	1092	110	110	22858	32453	57	32453	57
PJ10	50	6696	47	46	76153	3285	67	3285	67
PJ11	33	6142	69	70	120158	1484	95	1484	95
PJ12	24	5266	28	28	117420	2029	91	2029	91
PJ13	60	327	103	102	1005	4019	4	4019	4
PJ14	60	5086	295	316	103217	64392	84	62944	93
PJ15	34	6461	117	115	86567	16105	111	16105	111
PJ16	56	4303	172	173	37843	30528	56	30528	56
PJ17	20	7039	815	1153	81326	68728	548	72202	2530
PJ18	43	7197	719	992	170988	102186	1615	126155	1904
PJ19	9	5105	2224	2555	544941	522702	2534	522460	34324

port results for both *static* (Ord-Sta) and *dynamic* (Ord-Dyn) ordering methods. The *static* ordering method gives preference to variables in the abstract model throughout the SAT-solving process. The *dynamic* ordering method switches to the SAT-solver's default heuristic after a threshold number of decisions. Our approach performs better than these methods.

5 A Hybrid Approach to Refinement

5.1 Proof-Based Refinement and a Hybrid Approach

We described the CEGAR loop in Section 2.3. An alternative approach, called Proof-Based Refinement (PBR), was proposed by McMillan et al. [MA03] (and independently by Gupta et al.[GGYA03]). The pseudo-code for this approach is shown in Algorithm 4. In each refinement iteration, PBR performs BMC on the concrete model (line 4) and uses the unsatisfiable core as the abstract model for the next iteration (line 6). As opposed to CEGAR that eliminates one counterexample, PBR eliminates all counterexamples of a given length in a single refinement step.

Amla et. al. [AM04] performed an industrial evaluation of the two approaches and concluded that PBR and CEGAR are extreme approaches. PBR has a more ex-

Table 2. Comparison of CG-BMC/CG-BMC-T with Wang et al. [WJHS04]

Circuit	Depth	Time(s)			
		Ord-Sta	Ord-Dyn	CG-BMC	CG-BMC-T
PJ00	60	961	942	104	104
PJ01	60	729	711	99	99
PJ02	60	694	678	101	101
PJ03	60	693	679	101	100
PJ04	60	656	641	99	98
PJ05	25	219	205	2812	296
PJ06	20	4786	1192	148	154
PJ07	25	4761	124	40	41
PJ08	60	703	712	201	201
PJ09	60	494	483	110	110
PJ10	54	827	6493	54	69
PJ11	60	816	796	135	111
PJ12	60	1229	973	101	101
PJ13	60	673	657	103	102
PJ14	60	3101	2746	295	316
PJ15	60	3488	3456	296	371
PJ16	60	3022	3021	198	199
PJ17	21	3132	6114	1069	1570
PJ18	38	6850	4846	556	721
PJ19	5	5623	176	113	116

Algorithm 4 Proof-Based Refinement

PBR(M, φ)
1: $\hat{M} = \{\}$;
2: **if** $MC(\hat{M}, \varphi) = TRUE$ **then return** 'TRUE';
3: **else** let k be the length of the counterexample produced by the model checker;
4: **if** $BMC(M, k, \varphi) = SAT$ **then return** 'bug found in cycle k';
5: **else** let U be the set of gates in the unsatisfiable core produced by the SAT-solver.
6: $\hat{M} = U$;
7: **goto** line 2;

pensive refinement step than CEGAR, since PBR performs unrestricted BMC while CEGAR restricts BMC to the counterexample produced by the model checker. CEGAR, on the other hand, has a larger number of refinement iterations since it only eliminates one counterexample per refinement iteration, thereby putting more burden on the model checker. To balance the two, they propose a hybrid of the two approaches.

Their hybrid approach also performs BMC on the concrete model after given a counterexample from the abstract model. However, they use the counterexample only to provide the initial decisions to the SAT-solver. They also set a time limit to the SAT-solver. If the SAT-solver completes before the time-out with an Unsat answer, the hybrid approach behaves like PBR. On the other hand if the

SAT-solver times-out, they rerun a BMC instance conjoined with constraints on some of the variables in the counterexample (but not all). From this instance they extract an unsatisfiable core, thereby refuting a much larger space of counterexamples (note that this instance has to be unsatisfiable if enough time was given to the first instance due to the initial decisions). Their experiments show that the hybrid approach is more robust than PBR and CEGAR.

5.2 A Hybrid Approach Based on CG-BMC

Since the CG-BMC algorithm outperforms BMC, it can be used as a replacement for BMC in the refinement step of PBR. For example, in our experiments on *PJ17* (see Section 4), CG-BMC proved the property up to a depth of 29, and model checking could prove the correctness of the property on the generated abstract model. BMC could only finish upto depth of 20, and the resulting abstract model had a spurious counterexample of length 21.

CG-BMC is also a better choice than BMC because it provides an elegant way of balancing the effort between model checking and refinement. Algorithm 5 shows the pseudo code of our HYBRID algorithm, that we obtained after replacing BMC with CG-BMC inside the refinement step of PBR, and adding a choice function (line 2). At each iteration, HYBRID chooses either the model checker (line 3) or a SAT-solver (line 8) to find a counterexample to the current abstract model. The model checker returns 'TRUE' if the property holds for all cycles (line 3). If the SAT-solver returns UNSAT, the property holds at the current depth and the unsatisfiable core is used to refine the current abstraction. If a counterexample is produced by either the model checker or the SAT-solver, it is simulated on the concrete model (line 13). If the counterexample is spurious, the unsatisfiable core generated by the SAT-solver is added to the abstract model (line 15).

At a first glance, the HYBRID algorithm looks like a CEGAR loop, with the additional option of using a SAT-solver instead of a model checker for verifying the abstract model. However, the HYBRID algorithm captures both the CEGAR and the PBR approaches. If the choice function always chooses the model checker (line 3), it corresponds to the standard CEGAR algorithm. Now consider a strategy that chooses the model checker every time there is an increase in k at line 10, but chooses the SAT-solver (line 8) in all other cases. This is exactly the PBR loop that uses CG-BMC instead of BMC. Other choice functions correspond to a hybrid approach. There can be many strategies to make this choice, some of which are: 1) Use previous run-time statistics to decide which engine is likely to perform better on the next model, and occasionally switch to give the other engine a chance; 2) Measure the *stability* of the abstract model, i.e., whether in the last few iterations (increases of k) there was a need for refinement. Only if not - send it to a model checker; and, 3) Run the two engines in parallel.

6 Conclusions and Future Work

We presented CG-BMC, a Counterexample-Guided Abstraction Refinement algorithm for BMC. Our approach makes BMC faster, as indicated by our experiments.

Algorithm 5 Hybrid of CEGAR and PBR

HYBRID (M, φ)

1: $k = 1$; $\hat{M} = \{\}$;
2: **goto** line 3 *OR* **goto** line 8;
3: **if** $MC(\hat{M}, \varphi) = TRUE$ **then return** 'TRUE';
4: **else**
5:     Let C be the length r counterexample produced by the model checker;
6:     $k = r$;
7:     **goto** line 13;
8: **if** $BMC(\hat{M}, k, \varphi) = UNSAT$ **then**
9:     Let U be the set of gates in the unsatisfiable core produced by the SAT-solver;
10:     $\hat{M} = U$; $k = k + 1$;
11:     **goto** line 2;
12: **else** let C be the satisfying assignment produced by the SAT-solver;
13: **if** $BMC(M, k, \varphi) \wedge C = SAT$ **then return** 'bug found in cycle k';
14: **else** let U be the set of gates in the unsatisfiable core produced by the SAT-solver;
15: $\hat{M} = \hat{M} \cup U$;
16: **goto** line 2;

There are many directions in which this research can go further. First, the HYBRID algorithm should be evaluated empirically, and appropriate choice functions should be devised. The three options we listed in the previous section are probably still naive. Based on the experiments of Amla et al. reported in [AM04] in hybrid approaches, it seems that this can provide a better balance between the efforts spent in model checking and refinement, and also enjoy the benefit of CG-BMC. Second, it is interesting to check whether implementing CG-BMC inside a SAT-solver can make it work faster. This requires significant changes in various fundamental routines in the SAT-solver. In particular, this requires some mechanism for clustering the clauses inside the SAT-solver into abstraction levels, and postponing BCP on the clauses in the lower levels until all the higher levels are satisfied. Refinement would correspond to moving clauses up (and down) across levels, possibly based on their involvements in conflicts. We are currently working on this implementation. A third direction for future research is to explore the application of CG-BMC to other theories and decision procedures, like bit-vector arithmetic.

Acknowledgements. The first author would like to thank Ken McMillan for useful discussions.

References

[AM04] N. Amla and K. L. McMillan. A hybrid of counterexample-based and proof-based abstraction. In *Formal Methods in Computer-Aided Design, 5th International Confrence, FMCAD 2004*, pages 260–274, 2004.

[BCCZ99] A. Biere, A. Cimatti, E. Clarke, and Y. Zhu. Symbolic model checking without BDDs. In *In Tools and Algorithms for the Construction and Analysis of Systems (TACAS'99)*, LNCS, 1999.

[BGA02] S. Barner, D. Geist, and A.Gringauze. Symbolic localization reduction with reconstruction layering and backtracking. In *Proc. of Conference on Computer-Aided Verification (CAV)*, Copenhagen, Denmark, July 2002.

[CA93] J. M. Crawford and L. D. Anton. Experimental results on the crossover point in satisfiability problems. In *Proceedings of the Eleventh National Conference on Artificial Intelligence*, pages 21–27. AAAI Press, 1993.

[CCK+02] P. Chauhan, E. Clarke, J. Kukula, S. Sapra, H. Veith, and D. Wang. Automated abstraction refinement for model checking large state spaces using SAT based conflict analysis. In *Fourth International Conference on Formal Methods in Computer-Aided Design (FMCAD'02)*, LNCS, 2002.

[CGKS02] E. Clarke, A. Gupta, J. Kukula, and O. Strichman. SAT based abstraction-refinement using ILP and machine learning techniques. In *Proc. 14th Intl. Conference on Computer Aided Verification (CAV'02)*, LNCS, pages 265–279. Springer-Verlag, 2002.

[DP60] M. Davis and H. Putnam. A computing procedure for quantification theory. *J. ACM*, 7:201–215, 1960.

[GGYA03] A. Gupta, M. K. Ganai, Z. Yang, and P. Ashar. Iterative abstraction using SAT-based bmc with proof analysis. In *ICCAD*, pages 416–423, 2003.

[GKMH+03] M. Glusman, G. Kamhi, S. Mador-Haim, R. Fraer, and M. Y. Vardi. Multiple-counterexample guided iterative abstraction refinement: An industrial evaluation. In *Tools and Algorithms for the Construction and Analysis of Systems, TACAS 2003,*, LNCS, pages 176–191, 2003.

[Kur94] R. Kurshan. *Computer aided verification of coordinating processes.* Princeton University Press, 1994.

[MA03] K. McMillan and N. Amla. Automatic abstraction without counterexamples. In *9th Intl. Conf. on Tools And Algorithms For The Construction And Analysis Of Systems (TACAS'03)*, volume 2619 of *LNCS*, 2003.

[McM03] Ken McMillan. From bounded to unbounded model checking, 2003.

[MMZ+01] M. Moskewicz, C. Madigan, Y. Zhao, L. Zhang, and S. Malik. Chaff: Engineering an efficient SAT solver. In *Proc. Design Automation Conference 2001 (DAC'01)*, 2001.

[Sil99] J. P. M. Silva. The impact of branching heuristics in propositional satisfiability algorithms. In *9th Portuguese Conference on Artificial Intelligence (EPIA)*, 1999.

[WJHS04] C. Wang, H. Jin, G. D. Hachtel, and F. Somenzi. Refining the SAT decision ordering for bounded model checking. In *ACM/IEEE 41th Design Automation Conference (DAC'04)*, pages 535–538, 2004.

Symmetry Reduction in SAT-Based Model Checking

Daijue Tang*, Sharad Malik*, Aarti Gupta†, and C. Norris Ip‡

* Princeton University, Princeton, NJ 08540, USA
{dtang, sharad}@princeton.edu
† NEC Laboratories America, Princeton, NJ 08540, USA
agupta@nec-labs.com
‡ Jasper Design Automation, Mountain View, CA 94041, USA
ip@jasper-da.com

Abstract. The major challenge facing model checking is the state explosion problem. One technique to alleviate this is to apply symmetry reduction; this exploits the fact that many sequential systems consist of interchangeable components, and thus it may suffice to search a reduced version of the symmetric state space. Symmetry reduction has been shown to be an effective technique in both explicit and symbolic model checking with Binary Decision Diagrams (BDDs). In recent years, SAT-based model checking has been shown to be a promising alternative to BDD-based model checking. In this paper, we describe a symmetry reduction algorithm for SAT-based unbounded model checking (UMC) using circuit cofactoring. Our method differs from the previous efforts in using symmetry mainly in that we do not require converting any set of states to its representative or orbit set of states except for the set of initial states. This leads to significant simplicity in the implementation of symmetry reduction in model checking. Experimental results show that using our symmetry reduction approach improves the performance of SAT-based UMC due to both the reduced state space and simplification in the resulting SAT problems.

1 Introduction

Model checking [1] is an important technique for verifying sequential systems. The use of BDDs in symbolic model checking [2] has led to the successful verification of many industrial designs that could not be verified previously. However, BDD-based model checking does not scale well and suffers from a potential state space explosion problem. In order to alleviate this problem, symmetry reduction techniques have been explored in both explicit and BDD-based symbolic model checking [3, 4, 5, 6, 7, 8, 9]. In recent years, SAT-based model checking [10, 11, 12, 13] has been shown to be a promising alternative to BDD-based model checking. However, symmetry reduction techniques specific to SAT-based model checking have not been developed thus far. This paper aims to fill this gap.

The existence of more than one instance of the same component indicates the possible existence of symmetry in the design. Such high level symmetric descriptions imply symmetries in the underlying Kripke structure. The basic idea behind most of the existing work on symmetry reduction is to partition the state space into equivalence

K. Etessami and S.K. Rajamani (Eds.): CAV 2005, LNCS 3576, pp. 125–138, 2005.

classes and choose one or more representatives from each equivalence class during model checking. Previous work has demonstrated reductions in both memory and time consumption when symmetries are exploited in model checking. Therefore, it is worthwhile exploring the possibility of using symmetry reduction in SAT-based model checking. However, due to their different approaches of computing and representing state sets, symmetry reduction techniques in explicit and BDD-based symbolic model checking cannot be applied directly in SAT-based model checking.

In this paper, we describe a symmetry reduction approach based on the SAT-based model checking algorithm recently proposed by Ganai *et al.* [13]. We show that adding symmetry reduction in SAT-based model checking using circuit cofactoring gives uniform speedups on all the instances that we have tried. Further, our symmetry reduction can be easily applied to those systems where symmetry exists in only part of the system. To verify properties for the whole system, we do not need to scale down the symmetric part, or reason about it separately as a (meta-)theorem. Rather, we can simply incorporate the symmetry reduction into the verification of the whole system, where the reduction will automatically ensure that only the representative states from the symmetric part are explored.

2 SAT-Based Model Checking: A Review

Solutions of SAT instances have been used in two scenarios in model checking: Bounded Model Checking (BMC) [10] and Unbounded Model Checking (UMC) [11, 12, 13, 14, 15]. BMC unrolls the transition relation and uses a SAT solver to search for counterexamples of certain length. BMC tends to be robust and quick for finding bugs, which are reported as counterexamples. However, if no counterexample exists, verification is incomplete unless a completeness threshold is reached. SAT-based UMC is complete and provides the capability to prove properties that are true. Image and pre-image computations are the key operations of UMC. In the interpolation-based method [12], the refutation produced by a SAT solver is used to get an over-approximated image, while for other SAT-based UMC methods, quantifier elimination is at the core of image and pre-image computations. SAT-based existential quantification is done by enumerating satisfying solutions. Repeated enumerations of the same satisfying solutions are prevented by adding blocking constraints which are negations of the previously enumerated solutions [11, 13]. Suppose we want to compute $g(X) = \exists Y f(X,Y)$, where X and Y are sets of Boolean variables and $f(X,Y)$ is a propositional formula. A partial assignment, also called a cube, of the X variables can be derived each time a satisfying solution of $f(X,Y)$ is returned by a SAT solver. The blocking constraints are conjuncted with $f(X,Y)$ until the resulting propositional formula is unsatisfiable. $g(X)$ is the disjunction of all the enumerated cubes of the X variables. Many approaches [11, 14, 15] use this cube enumeration method to do existential quantification. A variation uses a SAT-based decision procedure to disjunctively accumulate sets of solutions computed using BDD-based quantification methods [16]. Alternately, a recently proposed method [13] does existential quantification by enumerating the cofactors [1] with respect to complete

[1] A cofactor of a function $f(X,Y)$ with respect to an assignment $Y = a$ is the function $f(X,a)$.

assignments (minterms) of the Y variables, and adding the negations of these cofactors (represented as circuits) as blocking constraints. $g(X)$ is the disjunction of all the enumerated cofactors. It is demonstrated in [13] that the cofactor enumeration method captures a larger set of satisfying assignments with each enumeration than the cube enumeration method, thus giving much better performance when utilized in SAT-based UMC. We use the algorithms proposed in [13] to do our pre-image and fixed-point computations and add symmetry reduction to this framework.

It is generally known (though not documented!) that image computation using SAT results in an explicit enumeration of the state set, while pre-image computation allows avoiding this problem by state enlargement techniques. Thus, we focus on backward reachability using pre-image computation for our implementations of model checking.

3 Symmetry Reduction: A Review

3.1 Preliminaries

For a sequential system that contains k identical components, usually a unique integer index is assigned to each component in the description of the system. Informally, two components are identical to each other if exchanging their indices does not affect the behavior of the system. This means that permuting the indices of symmetric components does not change the state transition relation of the system.

If the set of component indices is denoted as I, the set of all permutations acting on I forms a group, denoted as G_I, under the composition operation. Permuting the component indices induces corresponding changes of the evaluation of the state variables. For a Kripke structure $M = (S, S_0, \Delta, L)$, where S is the state space, S_0 is the set of initial states, Δ is the transition relation and L is the labeling function, a component index permutation α is a symmetry if and only if the following condition holds: $\forall s, t \in S((s,t) \in \Delta \rightarrow (\alpha s, \alpha t) \in \Delta)$. G_I is a symmetry group of M iff for each $\alpha \in G_I$, α is a symmetry of M. Given a group G, the orbit of a state s is defined as the set of states $\theta(s) = \{s' | \exists \alpha \in G, \alpha s = s'\}$. Two states are symmetric if and only if they are in the same orbit. We require that all states in an orbit have the same labeling function, i.e. $\forall t \in \theta(s), L(s) = L(t)$. The orbit of a set of states S is defined as $\theta(S) = \cup_{s \in S} \theta(s)$. The orbit relation is $\Theta = \{(s,t) | s,t \in S; t \in \theta(s)\}$. The set of representative states S_R is obtained by choosing one or more representatives in each orbit. The representative relation is defined as $\Gamma = \{(s,r) | s \in S; r \in S_R; \exists \alpha \in G_I, (\alpha s = r)\}$. The selection of representative states is described in section 4.3. When each state has a single representative, the representative relation is a function denoted by $\gamma(s) = \{t | t \in S_R, t \in \theta(s)\}$. The representative set of a set of states S is defined as $\gamma(S) = \cup_{s \in S} \gamma(s)$. A symmetry group G_I of M is an invariance group for an atomic proposition p if $\forall \alpha \in G_I \forall s \in S(p(s) \Leftrightarrow p(\alpha s))$. The quotient model of the model $M = (S, S_0, \Delta, L)$ is defined as $M_R = (S_R, S_{R0}, \Delta_R, L_R)$, where $S_R = \gamma(S)$, $S_{R0} = \gamma(S_0)$, $\Delta_R = \{(r, r') | r, r' \in S_R; \exists \alpha_1, \alpha_2 \in G_I, (\alpha_1 r, \alpha_2 r') \in \Delta\}$ and $L_R(\gamma(s)) = L(s)$. It has been shown that given a formula f and the condition that G_I is an invariance group for every atomic proposition in f, f holds in M if and only if it holds in M_R[4, 5]. Therefore, model checking over M can be reduced to model checking over M_R.

3.2 Symmetry Reduction in Model Checking: Previous Work

Symmetry reduction is beneficial for explicit state model checking due to the reduction of the state space [3, 4]. Many research efforts have considered combining symmetry reduction with BDD-based symbolic model checking [5, 8, 9]. To compute the set of representative states for a given set of states represented by a BDD, an orbit relation is needed if a unique representative is chosen for each orbit [5]. Although computing the orbit relation is of exponential complexity in general, it can be done in polynomial time for certain practical symmetric systems [6]. It has also been proposed to allow multiple representatives for each orbit [5, 6]. Although choosing multiple representatives gives less savings in terms of the state space reduction, it has been pointed out that computing the orbit relation can be avoided in this case and better overall performance obtained. On-the-fly representatives have also been proposed [8], where at any iteration of the fixed-point computation, states whose symmetric states are not encountered in the previous iterations are chosen to be the representative states of their respective orbits. Thus, it is possible to have multiple representatives for each orbit. Another way to exploit symmetry is to first translate the description of the symmetric system into a generic form, where the local state variables of the symmetric components are substituted by global counter variables, then translate the generic representation into corresponding BDDs [9]. Such translations require modifications to the front-end of the verification tool that cannot be done easily.

3.3 Symmetry Reduction in SAT: Previous Work

There has been some work done in exploiting symmetry in solving SAT instances. Symmetry breaking predicates can be added to a SAT instance in conjunctive normal form (CNF) to prune the search of SAT solvers by restricting the satisfying assignments to contain only one representative member of a symmetric set [17, 18]. These works consider symmetries in the CNF formula only and cannot be directly applied for using symmetry reduction in model checking. When high level descriptions are translated into Boolean functions and further encoded as SAT instances, most of the high level symmetries are lost. Specifically, automorphisms of the state transition graph do not necessarily translate to automorphisms of the corresponding Boolean next state functions and their CNF formulations. Moreover, symmetry breaking for a SAT problem only ensures that its satisfiability does not change. It blocks some of the satisfying solutions of the original formula. This is not acceptable for our use of SAT in model checking, as the solutions corresponding to representative states should not be blocked. Therefore, breaking symmetries in the Boolean formula cannot guarantee the correctness of the model checking algorithms. Symmetries in the state transition sequences have also been explored in prior work [19]. Symmetry breaking constraints that allow only one transition sequence in a symmetric set are added to the Boolean representation of the transition systems. Although this approach can be beneficial for BMC, it is not clear how to use it in SAT-based UMC.

4 Symmetry Reduction in SAT-Based Model Checking

4.1 Overview of the Algorithm

We add our symmetry reduction scheme to the pre-image computation and fixed-point computation algorithms using SAT-based circuit cofactoring[13]. The algorithm for checking the CTL [20] AG property, enhanced by symmetry reduction, is shown in algorithm 1. The major differences between this algorithm and the one without symmetry reduction are in lines 2, 5 and 11. The characteristic function for the set of representative states $Rep(X)$ are determined before the CHECK_AG procedure. We will describe in section 4.3 how $Rep(X)$ is derived. In line 2, the orbit $I_{orb}(X)$ of the set of initial states $I(X)$ is computed. Computing the orbit of a set of states is discussed in section 4.4. The set of representative states $R(X)$ that can reach a bad state are calculated iteratively in the while loop. In the ith iteration, $f_i(X, W)$ is an unrolling of the transition relation for i time frames with the last state constrained by the predicate B. Let $W_j (j = 1, \cdots, i)$ denote the set of primary input variables for the jth time frame. A cofactor of $f_i(X, W)$ with respect to the primary input sequence $W = W_1 W_2 \cdots W_i$ yields a circuit C_W that has only the X variables as inputs. In the ith iteration, the predicate B ensures that every state in C_W can reach a bad state in i steps. The predicates $\neg R$ and Rep, also depending on only the X variables, respectively ensure that every state in C_W has never been reached in previous iterations and is a representative state. The frontier representative set $F(X)$ is the disjunction of all the enumerated C_W. It is worth emphasizing that to compute $F(X)$ in the SAT-based UMC approach proposed in [13], no state set at any intermediate time frame of $f_i(X, W)$ needs to be computed because an unrolling implicitly represents such intermediate state sets at the price of quantifying out more variables. Note also that these intermediate states are not restricted to be representative states, only the states at the ith time frame (expressed in terms of the X variables) are restricted to be representative states. Furthermore, in our setting, the SAT-based existential quantification using circuit cofactoring is performed directly on the circuit with the constraint $\neg R(X) \wedge Rep(X)$. Thus, non-representative states as well as previously reached states of the X variables are never enumerated. If the set $F(X)$ overlaps with $I_{orb}(X)$ in any iteration, the property p is false (line 13). On the other hand, if $R(X)$ has no intersection with $I_{orb}(X)$, $AG(p)$ must hold (line 16).

Note that in the existential quantification step (line 11), only representative states are enumerated as the input formula has the conjunct $Rep(X)$, All other states, even though they might be backward reachable from the set of bad states, are blocked. For the correctness of this algorithm, we need to make sure that for every backward reachable state, its representative state is also backward reachable.

Lemma 1. *Given a Kripke structure* $M = (S, S_0, \Delta, L)$ *and a symmetry group* G *of* M*, if* S_q *is the orbit of a set of states, then the set of pre-image states* S_p *of* S_q *is also an orbit of a set of states.*

Proof: We prove this by contradiction. Assume S_p is not an orbit of a set of states. Then there must exists two states s and t such that they are in the same orbit and $s \in S_p$ and $t \notin S_p$. Let s' and t' be the image states of s and t respectively. Since $s \in S_p$ and S_q

is the image state set of S_p, $s' \in S_q$. Since s and t are in the same orbit, $\exists \alpha \in G$ such that $s = \alpha t$. Since G is a symmetry group of M, α is a symmetry of M. This means that $s' = \alpha t'$. Therefore, s' and t' are in the same orbit. Because S_q is an orbit of a set of states and $s' \in S_q$, we must have $t' \in S_q$. Thus $t \in S_p$ as S_p is the pre-image of S_q. This contradicts the assumption. Therefore, S_p is an orbit of a set of states. □

Using Lemma 1, we can prove the following theorem.

Algorithm 1 Algorithm for computing AG with symmetry reduction

```
1: procedure CHECK_AG(p)
2:     I_orb(X) ← COMPUTE_ORBIT(I(X))                ▷ X is the present state variables
3:     i ← 0
4:     R(X) ← ∅
5:     B(X) ← COMPUTE_ORBIT(¬p(X))
                 ▷ This line is for sanity check, it should be equivalent to B(X) ← ¬p(X)
6:     F(X) ← B(X) ∧ Rep(X)
7:     while F(X) ≠ ∅ do
8:         R(X) ← R(X) ∨ F(X)
9:         i ← i + 1
10:        f_i(X, W) ← Unroll(B(X), i)
11:        F(X) ← ∃W(f_i(X, W) ∧ ¬R(X) ∧ Rep(X))
                 ▷ SAT-based existential quantification using circuit cofactoring
12:        if (F(X) ∧ I_orb(X)) ≠ ∅ then
13:            return false
14:        end if
15:    end while
16:    return true
17: end procedure
```

Theorem 1. *Let B be the set of bad states from which we want to compute the set of backward reachable states R. If B is an orbit of a set of states, then the representative state of every state in R is also in R.*

Proof: As B is an orbit of a set of states, from Lemma 1, we know that the pre-image state set at every iteration is an orbit of a set of states. Thus every backward reachable state and its representative are reached at the same iteration. □

Note that algorithm 1 uses the fact that the symmetry group G_I of M is an invariance group of p. This implies that states belonging to the same orbit either all satisfy p or all violate p. Thus p and $\neg p$ are both characteristic functions of an orbit set of states. As the orbit of an orbit set is the set itself, line 5 of algorithm 1 can simply be $B(X) \leftarrow \neg p(X)$. Thus COMPUTE_ORBIT($\neg p(X)$) provides a mechanism to check whether p is truly an invariance with respect to G_I. Although only the algorithm for checking the *AG* property is given here, similar ideas can be applied to derive algorithms for computing other CTL modalities by using *Rep*(X) appropriately in pre-image computations to restrict enumerations to representative states only.

4.2 Discussion and Comparison to Related Work

In previous work, representative states are obtained by either converting the reached states to their representatives [5] or picking the first reached states in each orbit as representatives for that orbit [8]. Figure 1(a) illustrates previous approaches for symmetry reduction in backward reachability analysis with BDDs. B is the set of bad states for backward reachability analysis. $F_i (i = 0, 1, \cdots, n)$ is the set of frontier representative states at iteration i. $S_i (i = 1, \cdots, n)$ is the pre-image set of F_{i-1}. A dotted line in the figure maps a set of states to its frontier representative set. The solid line indicates the process of pre-image computation. Converting a set of states to their representatives can be done symbolically by image computation where the representative relation is treated as the transition relation. Although this conversion can be done using BDDs once the representative relation is known, it is hard for SAT as SAT-based image computation explicitly enumerates the image states. The on-the-fly scheme for choosing the representatives [8] in this context essentially lets every state be the representative, unless the approximations of state sets that are not orbits are used. This is because, by Lemma 1 and the fact that B is the orbit of a set of states, states symmetric to each other are reached at the same iteration. Figure 1(b) illustrates our approach for obtaining the representatives. The dashed lines indicate the pre-image computation, denoted as $Preimage_i$, with the transition relation unrolled i times. In general, our algorithm for symmetry reduction differs from the symmetry reduction techniques used in previous BDD-based model checking [5, 8] in the following two ways:

1. Our approach does not require either the orbit relation or the representative relation. Except for the initial states, we do not convert any state to its orbit. States that are not representatives are blocked during the existential quantification, and thus are never enumerated as intermediate data. This implies that our algorithm searches for solutions over the smaller representative state space without the more complicated re-encoding of the original model as a quotient model.
2. Except during the initialization step where the orbit of the bad states and the initial states are computed, we do not need to expand any state to its orbit. In practice, the orbit calculation during the initialization step for the bad states and the initial states is often simpler than on-the-fly orbit/representative calculations for the intermediate sets of backward reachable states.

Note that if there is no symmetry reduction in algorithm 1, most of the computation is in the existential quantification step. Therefore, accelerating existential quantification is key to improving the performance of SAT-based model checking. Our approach for symmetry reduction is likely to speed up the SAT-based existential quantification due to the following two reasons:

1. Doing existential quantification using SAT requires multiple calls to the SAT procedure. As described in section 2, SAT-based existential quantification is done by enumerating cofactors of the variables to be eliminated. Constraining the input of the existential quantification procedure by adding the conjunct *Rep* reduces the number of satisfying solutions of the input propositional formula. Therefore, it is possible to have fewer cofactor enumerations and thus fewer calls to the expensive SAT procedure.

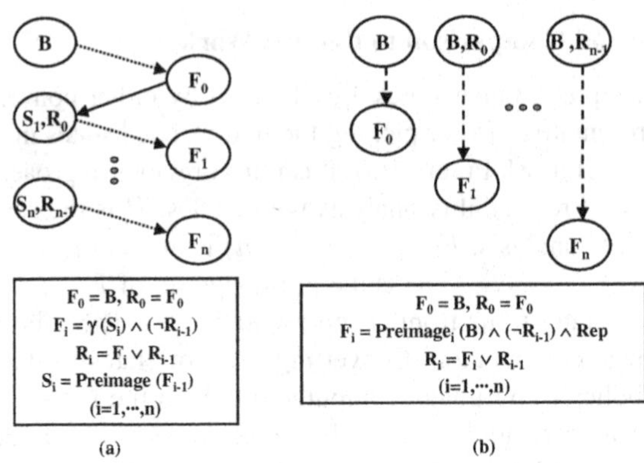

Fig. 1. Backward reachability analysis with symmetry reduction

2. It has been shown that adding symmetry breaking predicates to SAT instances gives significant speed-ups [17, 18]. This is because the search space of the SAT solver is confined to only non-symmetric regions. *Rep* is a high-level symmetry breaking constraint that often cannot be extracted from low-level representations like CNF. Thus, *Rep* can also confine the search space of the SAT solver which results in reduced SAT runtime.

4.3 Using the Representative Predicate as a Symmetry Breaking Constraint

As stated in section 3.1, the symmetry considered in this paper is that between isomorphic components of the same sequential system. Similar to the shared variable model of computation[4, 6], the state of the system is described by the local state $l_i(i = 1, ..., k)$ of each component and the assignment to the global state variables. There are two types of global state variables: those that are not relevant to any symmetric component and those that are relevant to one or more symmetric components. For example, in a shared-memory multiprocessor system, state variables indicating the status of the memory are the first type of global state variables; state variables describing which processor has write access to the shared-memory are the second type of global state variables. Permuting the indices of the symmetric components implies permuting the local states and remapping the values of the second type of global state variables. The assignments to the first type of global state variables remains the same. Let us illustrate this by using the example of a shared-memory multiprocessor system whose components indices are $1, 2, ..., k$. Suppose after index permutation operation α, the new sequence of indices are $i_1, i_2, ..., i_k$. α can also be viewed as renaming the symmetric components. If before the index permutation, the local states are $l_1, l_2, ..., l_k$, then after renaming, the local states become $l_{i_1}, l_{i_2}, ..., l_{i_k}$. If the state variable W_{idx} stores the index of the component that has write access to the shared memory and the value of W_{idx} is j before the index permutation, then the new value of W_{idx} after permuting the indices is i_j. Two states s and t are symmetric if there exists an index permutation α of the symmetric components such that s can be transformed to t by the state mapping illustrated above.

The set of representative states are those states that satisfy the symmetry breaking constraint *Rep*. *Rep* must make sure that there exists a representative for every state.

In another words, each orbit has at least one representative. Representatives can be chosen by imposing a certain order on the components. For example, we can order the components by sorting the binary encodings of the local states. In this case, $Rep = (l_1 \leq l_2 \leq \cdots \leq l_n)$. Note that we use $\leq$ instead of $<$ in this formula. This is because for a state where two components with indices i and j are in the same local states, i.e. $l_i = l_j$, its representative state, which must satisfy *Rep*, also has two components with indices i' and j' that satisfy $l_{i'} = l_{j'}$. We can also select the representative states as those that have the value of some global variables fixed. For example, the index of the processor that has the write access to the shared memory of the multiprocessor system is fixed to be 1. In this case, $Rep = (W_{idx} == 1)$. To ensure the presence of at least one representative for each orbit, *Rep* should not be over constrained. For instance, $Rep = (W_{idx} == 1) \wedge (l_1 \leq l_2 \leq ... \leq l_n)$ is over constrained, while $Rep = (W_{idx} == 1) \wedge (l_2 \leq ... \leq l_n)$ is a valid constraint. In general, a more constrained symmetry breaking predicate means fewer representatives, thus more reductions in the state space. Currently, the symmetry breaking constraints are provided manually. Since symmetry breaking constraints are essentially characteristic functions for representative states, their correctness can be checked by checking whether the orbit of the states satisfying *Rep* is equivalent to the state space of the original model.

4.4 Computing Orbits

In this section, we describe two approaches to compute the orbit of a set of states given the characteristic function of an arbitrary set of states.

The first approach is essentially a pre-image computation. In section 4.3, we described how a state can be mapped to its symmetric state by permuting the local states of the symmetric components and re-assigning the global state variables given a permutation α of the component indices. If all possible α in the symmetric group G_I of the system to be verified are applied on a state, then we can get the orbit of this state. In this way, the orbit of an arbitrary state set can be obtained by applying every α in G_I on the state set. Based on this, we construct a combinational circuit $O_c(Id, S, T)$ where Id and S are sets of input variables and T is the set of output variables for this circuit. For a k component symmetric system, Id is an array of k integers: $id_1, id_2, \cdots, id_k$. The values of Id are all permutations of $1, 2, ..., k$, where each permutation is interpreted as a permutation of the component indices. It maps the states S into their symmetric states T. Let A denote the set of states whose orbit needs to be computed. Let $Perm$ denote all possible assignments to Id resulting from permuting $1, 2, ..., k$. Then $Perm(Id) = (\bigwedge_{i=1,\cdots,k}(1 \leq id_i \leq k)) \wedge (\bigwedge_{i \neq j}(id_i \neq id_j))$. The orbit of A is denoted as Orb. It is easy to see that $Orb(T) = \exists Id, S.\, O_c(Id, S, T) \wedge Perm(Id) \wedge A(S)$ and $Orb(S) = \exists Id, T.\, O_c(Id, S, T) \wedge Perm(Id) \wedge A(T)$. The above two equations compute the same set of states in terms of state variables T and S respectively. If O_c is viewed as the transition relation from S to T, then computing $Orb(T)$ and $Orb(S)$ correspond to image and pre-image computations respectively. As mentioned earlier, it is not efficient to do SAT-based existential quantification for image computation. Therefore, we use the pre-image computation for $Orb(S)$ to compute orbits.

The second method to compute orbits uses generators of G_I. Let $g_1, g_2, ..., g_m$ be the generators of G_I. If A is a set of states and Orb is the orbit of A, then Orb is the least fix-point of the equation $f(x) \equiv x \vee (g_1x \vee g_2x \vee ... \vee g_mx)$ where $x = A$ initially. This is similar to the approach used in [8], although [8] does not require that a fixed-point is obtained.

The first method of computing orbits requires eliminating the Id variables through existential quantification. Since the existential quantification is done by multiple calls to SAT, this method of computing orbits may be slow. Although the second method of computing orbits does not require quantification, it needs to run many iterations before reaching a fixed-point. Each iteration conjuncts m state sets, which usually results in a large circuit representation of the state sets even when circuit simplification techniques are used. This large representation of state sets tends to slow down the subsequent pre-image computation. Moreover, the fixed-point has to be checked using SAT solvers. Such SAT problems become harder as the circuit representation gets larger. Both of the above methods to compute orbits are computationally expensive. Luckily, we only need to invoke orbit computation for the initial states. This makes our approach different from past efforts. Computing the orbit of an orbit of a set of states returns the same set, thus it can be used to check whether a state set is an orbit.

5 Experimental Results

We implemented the SAT-based framework using circuit cofactoring as described in [13]. This is then augmented with the symmetry reduction techniques described in section 4. We chose four examples to conduct our experiments. One is a handmade example called swap described in [11]. The state variables of swap are an array of k integers. The state transition is swapping the neighboring integers. The property that we verified was that for all $1 \le i \le k$, the ith integer at time t is different from the $((i + k/2) \bmod k)^{th}$ integer at time $(t + k/2 - 1)$, i.e. you cannot move a value by $k/2$ positions in $(k/2 - 1)$ steps. The other three examples all come from the VIS package [21]. All of the four examples consist of symmetric components and the number of components can be increased. All experiments were run on a workstation with Intel Pentium IV 2.8 GHz Processor and 1GB physical memory running Linux Fedora Core 1. We imposed a five hour time limit on each property checking run.

We compared the performance of SAT-based model checking with and without symmetry reductions. The results are shown in table 1. Column 2 shows whether a safety property of the instance in column 1 is true or false. Column 3 shows the number of components that are symmetric to each other. The number of state variables for each instance is indicated in column 4. Columns 5-8 show the number of pre-image iterations finished within the time limit and the CPU time needed to finish these iterations with and without symmetry reduction respectively. The results demonstrate the effectiveness of our symmetry reduction technique. Our approach can either compute more pre-images within the time limit or finish the same number of pre-image computations in less time. To obtain a more detailed analysis of the impact of symmetry reduction on the number of cofactor enumerations and the difficulty of the SAT problems, we compare the results at each step of the fixed-point computation for the gigamax example and the swap example, both with 8 components. The results are shown in table 2. Column 1 shows the depth of the fixed-point computation, columns 2-9 show the number of cofactor enumerations and the time used at the corresponding depth with and without symmetry reduction. In general, using symmetry reduction reduces the number of cofactor enumerations as shown in the gigamax example. The time spent on these enumerations is reduced with symmetry reduction because of two reasons: one is that the time spent on the extra enumerations is omitted by exploiting symmetry; the other is that the SAT problems become easier when the symmetry breaking constraints are added. The latter of the two reasons can be demonstrated by the swap example. Here, the number of cofactor enumerations remains the same even when symmetry is exploited, but there is significant reduction in runtime.

Table 3 shows the effect of symmetry reduction with increased number of components. The label of each column has the same meaning as that of table 1 and 2. The last column shows the time used to check the correctness of the representative predicate. We can see from table 3 that greater benefit from symmetry reduction can be obtained with increased number of components. This can be expected since the ratio of the original number of states to the number of representative states increases when the number of symmetric components increases. In general, checking the correctness of the representative predicate by computing its orbit requires $n!$ SAT solution enumerations since all possible permutations of component indices may need to be enumerated. This scales poorly with increased number of components as shown in table 3. However, the representative predicate is usually a parametric description in terms of the number of replicated components. Thus, once it is known that the representative predicate for smaller n is correct, this can be used to infer that the representative predicate for larger n is also correct.

Although we do not have a BDD-based model checker with symmetry reduction to compare our symmetry reduction approach against, we implemented previous symmetry-based techniques in our SAT-based model checker. Specifically, the standard iterative procedure (as shown in figure 1(a)) using pre-image computations, where each intermediate state set is converted to a set of representatives, is adapted for SAT-based UMC. Representative computation is done by first computing the orbit set and then conjoining the orbit set with the representative predicate. The experimental data for this approach are shown in table 4. The pre-image and representative computation time for each iteration are shown in columns 2-9 for different instances. The number inside the parenthesis besides the instance name is the number of components for that instance. From the data which shows larger runtime for representative computation than pre-image computation, it can be seen that previous symmetry reduction techniques used in BDD-based model checking do not work well with SAT-based UMC. This is mainly due to the inefficiency of converting a set of states to its representative set using the SAT-based method. Moreover, this method of symmetry reduction needs to use the result of pre-image and representative computation for the next iteration, thereby losing the possible benefit of compact state set representation introduced by unrolling.

Most model checkers will generate a debugging trace when a testcase does not satisfy a certain property. Due to the use of a representative predicate, the trace returned by our algorithm may be the result of permuting the component indices of a real trace. As an alternative to the process of getting the actual trace by permuting back the component indices on the counter-example returned by our algorithm, we use BMC method

Table 1. Performance summary

Testcase	T/F	#Comp	#Var	w/o symm		w/ symm	
				#Iter	Time(s)	#Iter	Time(s)
swap	T	8	24	3	>5Hr	4	0.54*
coherence	T	3	43	6	>5Hr	8	>5Hr
needham(buggy)	F	3	54	8	8142.28*	8	3948.53*
needham(fixed)	T	3	57	8	6542.73*	8	1853.49*
gigamax	T	8	41	5	>5Hr	11	17844.70*

* indicates either a bug is found or fixed-point is reached

Table 2. Detailed comparison of performance

Iter#	swap w/o symm		swap w/ symm		gigamax w/o symm		gigamax w/ symm	
	#Enum	Time(s)	#Enum	Time(s)	#Enum	Time(s)	#Enum	Time(s)
1	8	0.01	8	0.03	7	0.03	2	0.02
2	21	0.32	21	0.32	18	0.31	5	0.07
3	18	10.86	18	0.06	152	14.37	32	0.89
4	0	>5Hr	0	0.07*	461	586.11	46	12.72
5	-	-	-	-	1091	9838.08	119	54.01
6	-	-	-	-	0	>5Hr	85	316.76
7-11	-	-	-	-	-	-	109	17196.35*

* indicates either a bug is found or fixed-point is reached

Table 3. Performance with increased number of components

#Comp	#Var	gigamax w/o symm			gigamax w/ symm			Check Rep
		#Iter	#Enum	Time(s)	#Iter	#Enum	Time(s)	Time(s)
4	21	9	114	167.21*	9	77	61.84*	0
5	26	11	421	8845.18*	11	157	1183.48*	0.01
6	31	7	901	>5Hr	11	243	3259.92*	0.22
7	36	6	1555	>5Hr	11	272	6343.68*	11.64
8	41	5	1729	>5Hr	11	398	17844.70*	392.87

* indicates either a bug is found or fixed-point is reached

Table 4. Performance of SAT-based procedure using standard pre-image computations

Iter#	swap(8) time(s)		coherence(3) time(s)		needham(buggy)(3) time(s)		gigamax(8) time(s)	
	Pre-image	Rep	Pre-image	Rep	Pre-image	Rep	Pre-image	Rep
1	1.98	>5Hr	0.02	0.06	0.03	0.10	2.13	377.34
2	-	-	0.14	0.68	1.28	128.85	65.80	7568.49
3	-	-	5.83	46.66	73.84	5349.00	16.48	>5Hr
4	-	-	1041.63	>5Hr	1192.04	>5Hr	-	-

to generate the counter-example once its length is known from our algorithm. BMC for this length is likely to be much simpler than UMC using the cofactoring technique used here. For example, for the buggy version of the needham example, we know that there is a counter-example with length 8. A counter-example was generated using BMC under one second.

6 Conclusions and Future Work

Significant research has been done on exploiting symmetry reduction techniques in explicit and BDD-based symbolic model checking with some demonstrated benefits of the proposed approaches. Compared to BDD-based UMC, SAT-based UMC offers possibly better behavior with respect to memory utilization and is therefore gaining interest in the verification community. We propose a symmetry reduction algorithm for model checking using SAT-based methods. Our symmetry reduction approach is not a natural extension of the previous works. It takes advantage of the structure of the algorithm for SAT-based UMC using circuit cofactoring. Experimental results show the effectiveness of our approach, especially when the number of components gets large. An interesting future direction is to see how our symmetry reduction method can be extended to checking fairness properties, as has been done in explicit model checking [22, 23]. It is also worth investigating the application of symmetry reduction in SAT-based UMC using interpolation[12].

References

1. Clarke, E.M., Grumberg, O., Peled, D.: Model Checking. MIT Press (1999)
2. McMillan, K.L.: Symbolic Model Checking: An Approach to the State Explosion Problem. Kluwer Academic Publishers (1993)
3. Ip, C.N., Dill, D.L.: Better verification through symmetry. Formal Methods in System Design (1996) 41–75
4. Emerson, E.A., Sistla, A.P.: Symmetry and model checking. Formal Methods in System Design **9** (1996) 105–131
5. Clarke, E.M., Enders, R., Filkorn, T., Jha, S.: Exploiting symmetry in temporal logic model checking. Formal Methods in System Design **9** (1996) 77–104
6. Clarke, E.M., Emerson, E.A., Jha, S., Sistla, A.P.: Symmetry reductions in model checking. In: International Conference on Computer Aided Verification (CAV). (1998)
7. Jha, S.: Symmetry and Induction in Model Checking. PhD thesis, School of Computer Science, Carnegie Mellon University (1996)
8. Barner, S., Grumberg, O.: Combining symmetry reduction and under-approximation for symbolic model checking. In: International Conference on Computer-Aided Verification (CAV). (2002)
9. Emerson, E.A., Wahl, T.: On combining symmetry reduction and symbolic representation for efficient model checking. In: Conference on Correct Hardware Design and Verification Methods (CHARME). (2003)
10. Biere, A., Cimatti, A., Clarke, E.M., Fujita, M., Zhu, Y.: Symbolic model checking using SAT procedures instead of BDDs. In: Design Automation Conference (DAC). (1999)

11. McMillan, K.L.: Applying SAT methods in unbounded symbolic model checking. In: International Conference on Computer-Aided Verification (CAV). (2002)
12. McMillan, K.L.: Interpolation and SAT-based model checking. In: International Conference on Computer-Aided Verification (CAV). (2003)
13. Ganai, M., Gupta, A., Ashar, P.: Efficient SAT-based unbounded symbolic model checking using circuit cofactoring. In: International Conference on Computer-Aided Design (ICCAD). (2004)
14. Kang, H.J., Park, I.C.: SAT-based unbounded symbolic model checking. In: Design Automation Conference(DAC). (2003)
15. Sheng, S., Hsiao, M.: Efficient pre-image computation using a novel success-driven ATPG. In: Design, Automation and Test in Europe Conference (DATE). (2003)
16. Gupta, A., Yang, Z., Ashar, P., Gupta, A.: SAT-based image computation with application in reachability analysis. In: International Conference Formal Methods in Computer-Aided Design (FMCAD). (2000)
17. Crawford, J.M., Ginsberg, M., Luks, E., Roy, A.: Symmetry breaking predicate for search problems. In: International Conference on Principles of Knowledge Representation and Reasoning (KR). (1996)
18. Aloul, F.A., Ramani, A., Markov, I.L., Sakallah, K.A.: Solving difficult instances of Boolean satisfiability in the presence of symmetry. IEEE Transactions on CAD **22** (2003) 1117–1137
19. Rintanen, J.: Symmetry reduction for SAT representation of transition systems. In: International Conference on Automated Planning and Scheduling. (2003)
20. Clarke, E.M., Emerson, E.A.: Synthesis of synchronization skeletons from branching time temporal logic. In: Workshop on Logics of Programs. (1982)
21. VIS: The VIS Home Page. In: http://www-cad.eecs.berkeley.edu/Respep/Research/vis/. (1996)
22. Emerson, E.A., Sistla, A.P.: Utilizing symmetry when model-checking under fairness assumptions: an automata-theoretic approach. ACM Trans. Program. Lang. Syst. **19** (1997) 617–638
23. Gyuris, V., Sistla, A.P.: On-the-fly model checking under fairness that exploits symmetry. Formal Methods in System Design **15** (1999) 217–238

Saturn: A SAT-Based Tool for Bug Detection*

Yichen Xie and Alex Aiken

Computer Science Department
Stanford University
{yxie, aiken}cs.stanford.edu

1 Introduction

SATURN is a boolean satisfiability (SAT) based framework for static bug detection. It targets software written in C and is designed to support a wide range of property checkers.

The goal of the SATURN project is to realize SAT's potential for precise checking on very large software systems. Intraprocedurally, SATURN uses a bit-level representation to faithfully model common program constructs. Interprocedurally, it employs a summary-based modular analysis to infer and simulate function behavior. In practice, this design provides great precision where needed, while maintaining observed linear scaling behavior to arbitrarily large software code bases. We have demonstrated the effectiveness of our approach by building a lock analyzer for Linux, which found hundreds of previously unknown errors with a lower false positive rate than previous efforts [16].

The rest of the paper is organized as follows. Section 2 gives an overview of the SATURN analysis framework. Section 3 describes the modeling of common program constructs in SATURN. Section 4 describes the lock checker for Linux. We discuss related work in Section 5 and our conclusions in Section 6.

2 Overview

The SATURN framework consists of four components: 1) a low-level SATURN *Intermediate Language* (SIL) that models common program constructs such as integers, pointers, records, and conditional branches, 2) a CIL-based [14] *frontend* that parses C code and transforms it into SIL, 3) a SAT-based *transformer* that translates SIL statements and expressions into boolean formulas, and 4) property *checkers* that infer and check program behavior with respect to a specific property.

A SATURN analysis proceeds as follows:

- First, we use the frontend to parse C source files and transform them into SIL. The resulting abstract syntax trees are stored in a database indexed by file and function names.

* Supported by NSF grant CCF-0430378.

K. Etessami and S.K. Rajamani (Eds.): CAV 2005, LNCS 3576, pp. 139–143, 2005.

- Second, we construct the static call graph of the program. The call graph is then sorted in topological order (callee first). Strongly connected components (SCC) in the call graph are collapsed into supernodes that represent the collection of functions in the SCC.
- Third, the property checker retrieves and analyzes each function in the codebase in topological order. (Property checkers determine how call graph cycles are handled; currently our analyses simply break such cycles arbitrarily.) It infers and checks function behavior with respect to the current property by issuing SAT-queries constructed from the boolean constraints generated by the transformer. The inferred behavior is then summarized in a concise representation and stored in the summary database, to be used later in the analysis of the function's callers.
- Finally, violations of the property discovered in the previous step are compiled into bug reports. The summary database is also exported as documentation of the inferred behavior of each function, which is immensely helpful during bug confirmation.

3 The Saturn Intermediate Language

In this section, we briefly highlight the program constructs supported by the SATURN Intermediate Language (SIL). The formal definition of SIL and the details of its translation to the boolean representation are described in [16].

Integers. SATURN models n-bit signed and unsigned integers by using bit-vector representations. Signed integers are expressed using the 2's complement representation and common operations such as addition, subtraction, comparison, negation, and bitwise operations are modeled faithfully by constructing boolean formulas that carry out the computation (e.g., a ripple carry adder). More complex operations such as division and remainder are modeled approximately.

Pointers. SATURN supports pointers in C-like languages with two operations: *load* and *store*. We use a novel representation called *guarded location sets* (GLS), defined as a set of pairs (g, l) where g is a boolean guard and l is an abstract location. GLS track the set of locations that a pointer can point to and the condition under which the points-to relationship holds. This approach provides a precise and easily accessible representation for the checker to obtain information about the shape and content of a program's heap.

Records. Records (i.e., `structs` in C) in SATURN are modeled as a collection of component objects. Supported operations include field selection (e.g. `x.state`), dereference (e.g. `p->data.value`) and taking an address through pointers (e.g. `&curr->next`).

Control flow. SATURN supports programs with reducible control flow graphs.[1] Loops are modeled by unrolling a predetermined number of times and discarding the backedges. The rationale of our approach is based on the observation that

[1] Non-reducible control flow are rare (0.05% in the Linux kernel), and can be transformed into reducible ones by node-splitting [1].

many errors have simple counterexamples, and therefore should surface within the first few iterations of the loop; this approach is essentially an instance of the *small scope hypothesis* [12]. Compared to abstraction based techniques, unrolling trades off soundness for precision in modeling the initial iterations of the loop. Our experiments have shown that for the properties we have checked, unrolling contributes to the low false positive rate while missing few errors compared to sound tools.

Function calls. We adopt a modular approach to modeling function calls. SATURN analyzes one function at a time, inferring and summarizing function behavior using SAT queries and expressing the behavior in a concise representation. Each call site of the function is then replaced by instrumentation that simulates the function's behavior based on the summary. This approach exploits the natural abstraction boundary at function calls and allows SATURN to scale to arbitrarily large code bases.[2] The summary definition is checker specific; we give a concrete example in the following section.

4 Case Study: A Lock Checker for Linux

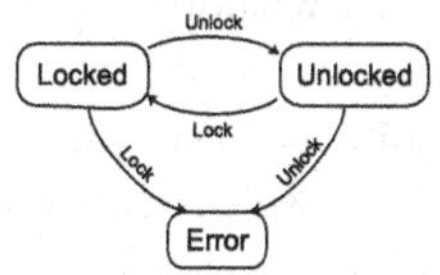

Fig. 1. FSM for locks

To experimentally validate our approach, we have developed a checker using the SATURN framework that infers and checks locking behavior in Linux. Locks are a classic example of a temporal safety property and have been the focus of several previous studies [8, 7, 3]. Locking behavior for a single lock in a single thread is described by the finite state machine (FSM) shown in Figure 1. Re-locking an already locked object may result in a system hang, and releasing an unlocked object also leads to unspecified behavior. Our checker targets such violations.

We model locks using SIL constructs. We use integer constants to represent the three states `locked`, `unlocked`, and `error`, and we attach a special `state` field to each lock object to keep track of its current state. State transitions on a lock object are modeled using conditional assignments. We show an example of this instrumentation below:

```
void lock_wrapper(lock_t *l) {         ⇒     void lock_wrapper(lock_t *l) {
  lock(l);                                      if (l->state == UNLOCKED)
}                                                 l->state = LOCKED;
                                                else
                                                  l->state = ERROR;
                                              }
```

For the `lock` operation above, we first ensure the current state is `unlocked`. If so, the new state is `locked`; otherwise, the new state is `error`. Every call to `lock` is replaced by this instrumentation. The instrumentation for `unlock` is similar.

Using this instrumentation for locks, we infer the locking behavior of a function `f` by issuing SAT queries for each possible pair of start and finish states

[2] The lock checker we describe in Section 4 averages 67LOC/s over nearly 5M lines of Linux.

of each lock `f` uses. If the query is satisfiable, then there is a possible transition between that pair of states across the function. In the example above, the satisfiable pairs are `unlocked` → `locked` and `locked` → `error`. We record the set of possible transitions in the summary database and use it later when we analyze the callers of the function. To check a function's locking behavior, we check that there is at least one legal transition (i.e. one that does not end in the `ERROR` state) through the function.

We have run the lock checker over Linux, which contains roughly 5 million lines of code. Our analysis finished in about 20 hours and issued 300 warnings, 179 of which are believed to be real errors by manual inspection.

5 Related Work

Jackson and Vaziri were apparently the first to consider finding bugs via reducing program source to boolean formulas [12]. Subsequently there has been significant work on a similar approach called *bounded model checking* [13, 4, 11]. While there are algorithmic differences between SATURN and these other systems, the primary conceptual difference is our emphasis on scalability (e.g., function summaries) and focus on fully automated checking of properties without separate programmer-written specifications.

Static analysis tools commonly rely on abstraction techniques to simplify the analysis of program properties. SLAM [3] and BLAST [10, 9] use predicate abstraction techniques to transform C code into boolean programs. ESP [5] and MC [8, 6] use the finite state machine (FSM) abstraction and employ interprocedural dataflow analyses to check FSM properties. CQual [7, 2] is a type-based checking tool that uses flow-sensitive type qualifiers to check similar properties. In contrast, a SAT-based approach naturally adapts to a variety of abstractions, and therefore should be more flexible in checking a wide range of properties with precision.

Several other systems have investigated encoding C pointers using boolean formulas. CBMC [13] uses uninterpreted functions. SpC [15] uses static points-to sets derived from an alias analysis. There, the problem is much simplified since the points-to relationship is concretized at runtime and integer tags (instead of boolean formulas) can be used to guard the points-to relationships. F-Soft [11] models pointers by introducing extra equivalence constraints for all objects reachable from a pointer, which is inefficient in the presence of frequent pointer assignments.

6 Conclusion

We have presented SATURN, a scalable and precise error detection framework based on boolean satisfiability. Our system has a novel combination of features: it models all values, including those in the heap, path sensitively down to the bit level, it computes function summaries automatically, and it scales to millions of lines of code. We demonstrate the utility of the tool with a lock checker for Linux, finding in the process 179 unique locking errors in the Linux kernel.

References

1. A. V. Aho, R. Sethi, and J. D. Ullman. *Compilers: Principles, Techniques, and Tools.* Addison-Wesley, Reading, Massachusetts, 1986.
2. A. Aiken, J. S. Foster, J. Kodumal, and T. Terauchi. Checking and inferring local non-aliasing. In *Proceedings of the ACM SIGPLAN 2003 Conference on Programming Language Design and Implementation*, pages 129–140, June 2003.
3. T. Ball and S. K. Rajamani. Automatically validating temporal safety properties of interfaces. In *Proceedings of SPIN 2001 Workshop on Model Checking of Software*, pages 103–122, May 2001. LNCS 2057.
4. E. Clarke, D. Kroening, and F. Lerda. A tool for checking ANSI-C programs. In K. Jensen and A. Podelski, editors, *Tools and Algorithms for the Construction and Analysis of Systems (TACAS)*, volume 2988 of *Lecture Notes in Computer Science*, pages 168–176. Springer, 2004.
5. M. Das, S. Lerner, and M. Seigle. Path-sensitive program verification in polynomial time. In *Proceedings of the ACM SIGPLAN 2002 Conference on Programming Language Design and Implementation*, Berlin, Germany, June 2002.
6. D. Engler, B. Chelf, A. Chou, and S. Hallem. Checking system rules using system-specific, programmer-written compiler extensions. In *Proceedings of Operating Systems Design and Implementation (OSDI)*, Sept. 2000.
7. J. S. Foster, T. Terauchi, and A. Aiken. Flow-sensitive type qualifiers. In *Proceedings of the ACM SIGPLAN 2002 Conference on Programming Language Design and Implementation*, pages 1–12, June 2002.
8. S. Hallem, B. Chelf, Y. Xie, and D. Engler. A system and language for building system-specific, static analyses. In *Proceedings of the ACM SIGPLAN 2002 Conference on Programming Language Design and Implementation*, Berlin, Germany, June 2002.
9. T. A. Henzinger, R. Jhala, and R. Majumdar. Lazy abstraction. In *Proceedings of the 29th Annual Symposium on Principles of Programming Languages (POPL)*, January 2002.
10. T. A. Henzinger, R. Jhala, R. Majumdar, and G. Sutre. Software verification with Blast. In *Proceedings of the SPIN 2003 Workshop on Model Checking Software*, pages 235–239, May 2003. LNCS 2648.
11. F. Ivancic, Z. Yang, M. Ganai, A. Gupta, and P. Ashar. Efficient SAT-based bounded model checking for software verification. In *Proceedings of 1st International Symposium on Leveraging Applications of Formal Methods (ISoLA)*, 2004.
12. D. Jackson and M. Vaziri. Finding bugs with a constraint solver. In *Proceedings of the 2000 ACM SIGSOFT International Symposium on Software Testing and Analysis*, 2000.
13. D. Kroening, E. Clarke, and K. Yorav. Behavioral consistency of C and Verilog programs using bounded model checking. In *Proceedings of the 40th Design Automation Conference*, 2003.
14. G. Necula, S. McPeak, S. Rahul, and W. Weimer. CIL: Intermediate language and tools for analysis and transformation of C programs. In *Proceedings of the 11th International Conference on Compiler Construction*, Mar. 2002.
15. L. Semeria and G. D. Micheli. SpC: synthesis of pointers in C, application of pointer analysis to the behavioral synthesis from C. In *Proceedings of 21st IEEE/ACM International Conference on Computer Aided Design (ICCAD)*, 1998.
16. Y. Xie and A. Aiken. Scalable error detection using boolean satisfiability. In *Proceedings of the 32th Annual Symposium on Principles of Programming Languages (POPL)*, January 2005.

JVer: A Java Verifier

Ajay Chander[1], David Espinosa[1], Nayeem Islam[1],
Peter Lee[2], and George Necula[3]

[1] DoCoMo Labs USA, San Jose, CA
{chander, espinosa, islam}@docomolabs-usa.com
[2] Carnegie Mellon University, Pittsburgh, PA
Peter.Lee@cs.cmu.edu
[3] University of California, Berkeley, CA
necula@eecs.berkeley.edu
fax 408-573-1090

1 Introduction

We describe JVer, a tool for verifying Java bytecode programs annotated with pre and post conditions in the style of Hoare and Dijkstra. JVer is similar to ESC/Java [1], except that: (1) it produces verification conditions for Java bytecode, not Java source; (2) it is sound, because it makes conservative assumptions about aliasing and heap modification; (3) it produces verification conditions directly using symbolic simulation, without an intermediate guarded-command language; (4) by restricting predicates to conjunctions of relations between integers, it produces verification conditions that are more efficient to verify than general first-order formulae; (5) it generates independently verifiable proofs using the Kettle proof-generating theorem prover [2].

We initially designed JVer as a tool for verifying that downloaded Java bytecode programs do not abuse the computational resources available on a cell phone [3]. These resources include physical resources such as CPU, memory, storage, and network bandwidth, and virtual resources such as handles and threads. However, since JVer uses standard pre and post conditions, it has many uses not limited to resource certification, such as bug finding and security hole detection. We describe JVer's implementation, as well as an experiment using it to limit the resources consumed by a cell phone version of `tetris`.

2 Verifier

Figure 1 shows our annotation language, which is a subset of JML. It includes the usual Hoare-style pre and post conditions, global invariants, loop invariants, and side-effect annotations. The `exsures` annotation means that the method terminates with an exception of the given class.

Predicates are conjunctions of literals. Literals are of the form $e_0 \geq e_1$ or $e_0 = e_1$. Expressions include only the usual Java operators, without method calls. Expressions can refer to class fields and instance fields. Expressions in post conditions can include the keyword `result` to refer to the method's return value (in `ensures`) or thrown exception (in `exsures`).

K. Etessami and S.K. Rajamani (Eds.): CAV 2005, LNCS 3576, pp. 144–147, 2005.

JVER uses `true` as the default loop invariant. If necessary for verification, the user must supply a stronger invariant, which is located by program counter value. In this respect, JVer differs from ESC/Java, which unrolls loops a fixed number of times and is therefore unsound.

```
annotation ::=
   invariant      pred        |
   ghost          class.field |
   static ghost   class.field |
   type class.method (type argument, ...)
     method-annotation*

method-annotation ::=
   requires         pred        |
   ensures          pred        |
   exsures          class pred  |
   loop_invariant   pc, pred

pred ::= literal ∧ ··· ∧ literal

literal ::= exp relop exp

exp ::= int | argument | class.field | exp.field |
   exp binop exp | \old(exp) | \result

relop ::= = | != | < | <= | > | >=

binop ::= + | - | * | / | % | << | >> | >>> | & | | | ^
```

Fig. 1. Annotation definition

To verify Java bytecode, we use a standard verification condition generator (VCG) based on weakest pre conditions. The verifier begins at the start of a method and at each loop invariant and traces all paths through the code. Each path must terminate either at the end of the method, or at a loop invariant. If a path loops back on itself without encountering a loop invariant, the verifier raises an error and fails to verify the program.

Along each path, the verifier begins with a abstract symbolic state containing logical variables for the method's arguments and for all class fields. It simulates the bytecode using a stack of expressions. At the end of the path, it produces the VC that if the pre condition (or initial loop invariant) holds of the initial state, and all of the conditionals hold at their respective intermediate states, then the post condition (or final loop invariant) holds of the final state.

The VC for the program is the conjunction of the VCs for the methods. The VC for the method is the conjunction of the VCs for the execution paths. The VC for each path is an implication between conjunctions of literals, of the form

$$a_1 \wedge \cdots \wedge a_m \Rightarrow b_1 \wedge \cdots \wedge b_n$$

where the a_i and b_i are literals. This implication is valid if and only if

$$a_1 \wedge \cdots \wedge a_m \wedge \neg b_i$$

is unsatisfiable for each b_i, which we check with a decision procedure for satisfiability of conjuncts of literals. In essence, we check the original formula for validity by converting it to CNF [4].

2.1 Java Features

Java includes several features that make it more difficult to verify than a hypothetical "simple imperative language": concurrency, exceptions, inheritance, and the object heap. We address these issues in turn.

Concurrency. Since most cell phone applets are single-threaded, JVER does not handle concurrency. In particular, we assume that each method has exclusive access to shared data for the duration of its execution. In contrast, ESC/Java detects unprotected shared variable access and discovers race conditions using a user-declared partial order.

Exceptions. Java has three sources of exceptions: explicit `throw` instructions, instructions that raise various exceptional conditions, such as `NullPointer` or `ArrayIndexOutOfBounds`, and calling methods that themselves raise exceptions. Since our control flow analyzer produces a *set* of possible next instructions, it handles exceptions without difficulty. In essence, an exception is a form of multi-way branch, like the usual conditionals, or the JVM instructions `tableswitch` and `lookupswitch`. ESC/Java provides essentially the same support for exceptions.

Inheritance. If class `B` extends class `A`, then when invoking method `m` on an object of class `A`, we may actually execute `B.m` instead of `A.m`. Thus, the pre condition for `B.m` must be weaker than the pre condition for `A.m`, while the post condition for `B.m` must be *stronger* than the post condition for `A.m`. Thus, when we compute the post condition for `B.m`, we conjoin the post condition for `A.m`. And when we compute the pre condition for `A.m`, we conjoin the pre condition for `B.m`. Thus, we inherit post conditions *downwards* and pre conditions *upwards.* On the other hand, if class `B` defines method `m`, but class `A` does not, then we do not inherit pre or post conditions in either direction.

Inheritance of pre and post conditions is convenient, because we can state them just once, and JVer propagates them as necessary. However, to determine the specification for a method, we need the specification for the methods related to it by inheritance, both up *and* down. However, once we know its specification, we can verify each method in isolation. ESC/Java inherits pre conditions *downwards*, which is unsound in the presence of multiple inheritance via interfaces.

Object Heap. At the moment, we use Java's type system to automatically over-estimate the set of heap locations that each method modifies. That is, we assume that the assignment `a.x = e` modifies the `x` field of all objects whose type is compatible with `a`. We also determine automatically which static class variables each method modifies. In the future, we plan to experiment with more precise alias analysis algorithms. If the user requires more precise modification information, he can declare explicitly in the post condition that `x = \old(x)`. ESC/Java requires the user to state explicitly which heap locations each method modifies, but since it does not verify this information, its heap model is unsound.

3 Applications

We are using JVer to enforce resource bounds on downloaded cell phone applets using proof-carrying code [3]. Thus, we need a prover that can generate proofs and a small, fast verifier that can check them on the handset.

Our resource-verification technique uses a static ghost variable `pool` to ensure that the applet dynamically allocates the resources that it uses. Allocations increment `pool`, while uses decrease it. We use JVer to check the invariant that `pool` remains non-negative.

In an experiment, we verified the security of a Tetris game / News display cell phone applet running on DoCoMo's DoJa Java library. The security policy limited the applet's use of the network, persistent storage, and backlight. The 1850-line applet required 111 lines of annotation and verified in less than one second. By checking network use once per download of the news feed rather than once per byte, we reduced the number of dynamic checks by a factor of roughly 5000.

4 Conclusion

Unlike ESC/Java, JVer is sound, simple, efficient, and produces independently-verifiable proofs from Java bytecode, not source. It accomplishes these goals by restricting the properties that it checks and by requiring more user-supplied annotations. We have found in practice that JVer is a useful and efficient tool for verifying properties of cell phone applets.

References

1. Flanagan, C., Leino, R., Lilibridge, M., Nelson, G., Saxe, J., Stata, R.: Extended static checking for Java. In: Programming Language Design and Implementation, Berlin, Germany (2002)
2. Necula, G.C., Lee, P.: Efficient representation and validation of proofs. In: Logic in Computer Science, Indianapolis, Indiana (1998)
3. Chander, A., Espinosa, D., Islam, N., Lee, P., Necula, G.: Enforcing resource bounds via static verification of dynamic checks. In: European Symposium on Programming, Edinburgh, Scotland (2005)
4. Paulson, L.: ML for the Working Programmer. Cambridge University Press (1996)

Building Your Own Software Model Checker Using the Bogor Extensible Model Checking Framework*

Matthew B. Dwyer[1], John Hatcliff[2], Matthew Hoosier[2], and Robby[2]

[1] University of Nebraska,
Lincoln, NE 68588, USA
dwyer@cse.unl.edu
[2] Kansas State University,
Manhattan, KS 66506, USA
{hatcliff, matt, robby}@cis.ksu.edu

Abstract. Model checking has proven to be an effective technology for verification and debugging in hardware and more recently in software domains. We believe that recent trends in both the requirements for software systems and the processes by which systems are developed suggest that domain-specific model checking engines may be more effective than general purpose model checking tools. To overcome limitations of existing tools which tend to be monolithic and non-extensible, we have developed an extensible and customizable model checking framework called Bogor. In this tool paper, we summarize (a) Bogor's direct support for modeling object-oriented designs and implementations, (b) its facilities for extending and customizing its modeling language and algorithms to create domain-specific model checking engines, and (c) pedagogical materials that we have developed to describe the construction of model checking tools built on top of the Bogor infrastructure.

Motivation

Temporal logic model checking [CGP00] is a powerful framework for reasoning about the behavior of finite-state system descriptions and it has been applied, in various forms, to reasoning about a wide-variety of software artifacts. The effectiveness of these efforts has in most cases relied on detailed knowledge of the model checking framework being applied. In some cases, a *new* framework was developed targeted to the semantics of a family of artifacts [BHPV00], while in other cases it was necessary to study an *existing* model checking framework in detail in order to customize it [CAB+01]. Unfortunately, the level of knowledge and effort required to do this kind of work currently prevents many *domain* experts, who are not necessarily experts in model-checking, from successfully

* This work was supported in part by a 2004 IBM Eclipse Innovation Grant, by the U.S. Army Research Office (DAAD190110564), by DARPA/IXO's PCES program (AFRL Contract F33615-00-C-3044), and by NSF (CCR-0306607, CCF-0429149, CCF-04444167).

K. Etessami and S.K. Rajamani (Eds.): CAV 2005, LNCS 3576, pp. 148–152, 2005.

applying model checking to systems and software analysis problems. Our broad goal is to allow these experts to apply model checking without the need to build their own model-checker or to pour over the details of an existing model-checker implementation while carrying out substantial modifications.

The Bogor Extensible Software Model Checking Framework

To meet the challenges of using model checking in the context of current trends in software development, we have constructed an extensible and highly modular explicit-state model checking framework called Bogor [RDH03, SAnToS03]. Using Bogor, we seek to enable more effective incorporation of domain knowledge into verification models and associated model checking algorithms and optimizations, by focusing on the following principles.

Software-oriented Modeling Language: In contrast to most existing model checkers, Bogor's modeling language (BIR) provides constructs commonly found in modern programming languages including dynamic creation of objects and threads, garbage collection, virtual dispatch and exceptions. This rich language has enabled model checking relatively large featureful concurrent Java programs by translating them to Bogor using the next generation of the Bandera tool set.

Software-oriented State Representations and Reduction Algorithms: To support effective checking of BIR software models, we have adapted and extended well-known optimization/reduction strategies such as collapse compression [Hol97], data and thread symmetry [BDH02], and partial-order reductions to support models of object-oriented software by providing sophisticated heap representations [RDHI03], partial-order reduction strategies that leverage static and dynamic escape and locking analyses [DHRR04], and thread and heap symmetry strategies[Ios02, RDHI03].

Extensible Modeling Language: Bogor's modeling language can be extended with new primitive types, expressions, and commands associated with a particular domain (e.g, multi-agent systems, avionics, security protocols, etc.) and a particular level of abstraction (e.g., design models, source code, byte code, etc.)

Open Modular Architecture: Bogor's well-organized module facility allows new algorithms (e.g., for state-space exploration, state storage, etc) and new optimizations (e.g., heuristic search strategies, domain-specific scheduling, etc.) to be easily swapped in to replace Bogor's default model checking algorithms.

Robust Feature-rich Graphical Interface: Bogor is written in Java and comes wrapped as a plug-in for *Eclipse* – an open source and extensible universal tool platform from IBM. This user interface provides mechanisms for collecting and naming different Bogor configurations, specification property collections, and a variety of visualization and navigation facilities.

Design for Encapulation: Bogor provides an open architecture with well-defined APIs and intermediate data formats that enable it (and customized versions of it) to be easily encapsulated within larger development/verification environments for specific domains.

Courseware and Pedagogical Materials: Even with a tool like Bogor that is designed for extensibility, creating customizations requires a significant amount of knowledge about the internal Bogor architecture. To communicate this knowledge, we have developed an extensive collection of tutorial materials and examples. Moreover, we believe that Bogor is an excellent pedagogical vehicle for teaching foundations and applications of model checking because it allows students to see clean implementations of basic model checking algorithms and to easily enhance and extend these algorithms in course projects. Accordingly, we have developed a comprehensive collection of course materials [SAnToS04] that have already been used in graduate level courses on model checking at several institutions.

In short, Bogor aims to be not only a robust and feature-rich software model checking tool that handles the language constructs found in modern large-scale software system designs and implementations, it also aims to be a model checking *framework* that enables researchers and engineers to create families of domain-specific model checking engines.

Experience Using Bogor

In the past ten months, Bogor has been downloaded more than 800 times by individuals in 22 countries. We know that many of those individuals are using Bogor in interesting ways. To date, we are aware of more than 28 substantive extensions to Bogor that have been built by 18 people, only one of whom was the primary Bogor developer.

It is difficult to quantify the effort required to build a high-quality extension in Bogor. As with all software framework there is a learning curve. In the case of Bogor, which is a non-trivial system consisting more than 22 APIs, we find that reasonably experienced Java developers get up to speed in a couple of weeks. At that point extensions are generally require only a few hundred lines of code and often they can be modeled closely after already existing extensions. To give a sense of the variety of extensions built with Bogor we list a sampling of those extensions and indicate, in parentheses, the number of non-comment source statement lines of Java code used to implement the extension.

Partial-order Reduction (POR) Extensions: Multiple variations on POR techniques have been implemented in Bogor including: sleep sets (298), conditional stubborn sets (618), and ample sets (306) approaches. Multiple variations of the notion of dependence have been incorporated into these techniques that increase the size of the independence relation by exploiting : read-only data (515), patterns of locking (73), patterns of object ownership (69), and escape information (216). These latter reductions, while modest in size and complexity to implement, have resulted in more than four orders of magnitude reduction in model checking concurrent Java programs [DHRR04].

State-encoding and Search Extensions: Bogor is factored into separate modules that can be treated independently to help lower the cost of learning the framework's APIs. For example, extensions to the state-encoding and management APIs have yielded implementations of collapse compression (483), heap and thread symmetry (317), and symmetric collection data structures (589). Extensions to Bogor's searcher APIs have enabled the POR extensions above in addition to ones supporting stateless search (14) and heuristic selective search (641).

Property Extensions: Supporting different property languages is just as important as supporting flexibility in modeling languages. Bogor's property APIs have allowed multiple checker extensions to be implemented including : regular expression/finite-state automata (1083), an automata-theoretic Linear Temporal Logic (1011) checker, and a Computation-tree Logic (1418) checker based on alternating tree automata. We have also implemented a checker extension for the Java Modeling Language [RRDH04] (3721).

Problem Domain Extensions: A main objective of Bogor was to bring sophisticated state-space analyses to a range of systems and software engineering domains. Several extensions have been built that target specific issues in reasoning about multi-threaded Java programs, for example, treating dynamic class loading (425), reasoning about event-handler behavior in program written using the Swing framework [DRTV04], and reasoning about properties of method atomicity (359) [HRD04].

Departing from the software domain somewhat, in our work on the Cadena development environment [HDD+03] for designing component-based avionics systems, we have extended Bogor's modeling language to include APIs associated with the CORBA component model and an underlying real-time CORBA event service (2593). [DDH+02, DRDH03]. For checking avionics system designs in Cadena, we have customized Bogor's scheduling strategy to reflect the scheduling strategy of the real-time CORBA event channel (439), and created a customized parallel state-space exploration algorithm that takes advantage of properties of periodic processing in avionics systems (516). These customizations for Bandera and Cadena have resulted in space and time improvements of over three orders of magnitude compared to our earlier approaches.

We are currently building extensions of Bogor for checking highly dynamic multi-agent systems. Researchers outside of our group are extending Bogor to support checking of programs constructed using AspectJ, and UML designs. Bogor is targetted as a framework for explicit state checking, and its current architecture is not necessarily amenable for incorporating symbolic techniques. We are working with researchers at Brigham Young University to refactor the framework (or develop an alternate set of APIs) to facilitate the use of symbolic techniques.

References

[BDH02] D. Bosnacki, D. Dams, and L. Holenderski. Symmetric SPIN. *International Journal on Software Tools for Technology Transfer*, 4(1):92–106, 2002.

[BHPV00] G. Brat, K. Havelund, S. Park, and W. Visser. Java PathFinder – a second generation of a Java model-checker. In *Proceedings of the Workshop on Advances in Verification*, July 2000.

[CAB+01] W. Chan, R. J. Anderson, P. Beame, D. Notkin, D. H. Jones, and William E. Warner. Optimizing symbolic model checking for statecharts. *IEEE Transactions on Software Engineering*, 27(2):170–190, 2001.

[CGP00] E. Clarke, O. Grumberg, and D. Peled. *Model Checking.* MIT Press, 2000.

[DDH+02] W. Deng, M. Dwyer, J. Hatcliff, G. Jung, and Robby. Model-checking middleware-based event-driven real-time embedded software. In *Proceedings of the 1st Internatiuonal Symposium on Formal Methods for Component and Objects*, pages 154–181, 2002.

[DHRR04] M. B. Dwyer, J. Hatcliff, Robby, and V. R.Prasad. Exploiting object escape and locking information in partial order reduction for concurrent object-oriented programs. *Formal Methods in System Design*, 25(2-3):199–240, 2004.

[DRDH03] M. B. Dwyer, Robby, X. Deng, and J. Hatcliff. Space reductions for model checking quasi-cyclic systems. In *Proceedings of the Third International Conference on Embedded Software*, pages 173–189, 2003.

[DRTV04] M. B. Dwyer, Robby, O. Tkachuk, and W. Visser. Analyzing interaction orderings with model checking. In *Proceedings of the 19th IEEE Conference on Automated Software Engineering*, pages 154–163, 2004.

[HDD+03] J. Hatcliff, W. Deng, M. Dwyer, G. Jung, and V. Prasad. Cadena: An integrated development, analysis, and verification environment for component-based systems. In *Proceedings of the 25th International Conference on Software Engineering*, pages 160–173, 2003.

[Hol97] G. J. Holzmann. The model checker SPIN. *IEEE Transactions on Software Engineering*, 23(5):279–294, May 1997.

[HRD04] J. Hatcliff, Robby, and M. B. Dwyer. Verifying atomicity specifications for concurrent object-oriented software using model checking. In M. Young, editor, *Proceedings of the Fifth International Conference on Verification, Model Checking, and Abstract Interpretation (VMCAI 2004)*, volume 2937 of *Lecture Notes In Computer Science*, pages 175–190, Jan 2004.

[Ios02] R. Iosif. Symmetry reduction criteria for software model checking. In *Proceedings of Ninth International SPIN Workshop*, volume 2318 of *Lecture Notes in Computer Science*, pages 22–41. Springer-Verlag, April 2002.

[SAnToS03] SAnToS Laboratory. Bogor website. `http://bogor.projects.cis.ksu.edu`, 2003.

[SAnToS04] SAnToS Laboratory. Software Model Checking course materials website. `http://model-checking.courses.projects.cis.ksu.edu`, 2004.

[RDH03] Robby, M. B. Dwyer, and J. Hatcliff. Bogor: An extensible and highly-modular model checking framework. In *Proceedings of the 9th European Software Engineering Conference held jointly with the 11th ACM SIGSOFT Symposium on the Foundations of Software Engineering*, pages 267–276, 2003.

[RDHI03] Robby, M. B. Dwyer, J. Hatcliff, and R. Iosif. Space-reduction strategies for model checking dynamic software. In *Proceedings of the 2nd Workshop on Software Model Chekcing*, volume 89(3) of *Electronic Notes in Theoritical Computer Science*, 2003.

[RRDH04] Robby, E. Rodríguez, M. B. Dwyer, and J. Hatcliff. Checking strong specifications using an extensible software model checking framework. In *Proceedings of the 10th International Conference on Tools and Algorithms for the Construction and Analysis of Systems*, volume 2988 of *Lecture Notes in Computer Science*, pages 404–420, March 2004.

Wolf - Bug Hunter for Concurrent Software Using Formal Methods

Sharon Barner, Ziv Glazberg, and Ishai Rabinovitz

IBM Haifa Research Lab, Haifa, Israel
{sharon, glazberg, ishai}@il.ibm.com

Abstract. Wolf is a "push-button" model checker for concurrent C programs developed in IBM Haifa. It automatically generates both the model and the specification directly from the C code. Currently, Wolf uses BDD-based symbolic methods integrated with a guided search framework. According to our experiments, these methods complement explicit exploration methods of software model checking.

1 Introduction

Wolf is a software bug hunter that uses formal methods in order to discover bugs in a concurrent C program. Concurrency related bugs may depend on a specific rare interleaving of the program, and are likely to be missed by standard testing tools. In addition, even when the presence of a bug is known, it is hard to reproduce it, or locate its source. When using formal methods, we can explore all possible interleavings; hence, detecting the presence of a bug. In addition, we can generate the trace that led to the bug.

Wolf is a "push-button" bug hunter, that is, it does not require intervention by the user. Unlike with hardware verification, users need not be experts in verification. Users who are familiar with verification can use their knowledge of the software to tune the model or verify additional specification. Wolf operates the IBM model checker RuleBase PE [4] using special software algorithms [3] on an automatic generated model and cleanness properties. Cleanness properties are those that every program should obey. For example, a dangling pointer should never be dereferenced, there should never be a deadlock situation, and no assert should fail. Programmers can validate functional properties of a program using the assert mechanism with which they are already familiar.

Wolf displays the bug trace in a debugger-like GUI named Vet. Vet translates the trace into an easy-to-understand graphical display which is intuitive for the average programmer.

We believe that there is no ultimate software model checking algorithm. Each different kind of software and bug has a different winning algorithm. We designed Wolf as an easy to upgrade framework, which enables us to add different algorithms in the future.

There are a number of explicit model checkers for software, among them are ZING [1], SPIN [10] and JPF [9]. Explicit model checkers handle the dereferenc-

K. Etessami and S.K. Rajamani (Eds.): CAV 2005, LNCS 3576, pp. 153–157, 2005.

ing of pointers and the dynamic allocation of resources well. Using various reductions such as partial order reductions [6] enables them to find bugs in concurrent software as well. However, they have a hard time coping with non-deterministic behaviors that result from non-deterministic inputs.

Other software model checkers use SAT-based methods, in these methods a formula that represents bounded length executions is generated and being fed to a SAT-solver. SAT-solver does not cope well with long formulas, and therefore SAT-based tools try to compact the formula. NEC [11] tries to compact each basic blocks into one transition, and CBMC [7] changes the code to a single assignment form. Neither [11] nor [7] supports concurrent programs. A new approach, taken by [12], tries to extend this approach for such programs.

Currently, we are exploring symbolic algorithms. In contrast to Bebop [2] and JPF [9], which combine symbolic and explicit methods, Wolf uses a pure symbolic exploration. BDD-based symbolic methods are less bounded than SAT-based methods and, unlike explicit methods symbolic methods, support non-deterministic choices naturally. In this sense, BDD-based symbolic algorithms complement SAT-based and explicit algorithms.

Wolf's symbolic BDD algorithm uses partial disjunctive partitions [3]. This method uses the software property of a few changes in each "cycle" to enhance the speed of image computation by several orders of magnitude.

We acknowledge the fact that the verification of concurrent software is a hard task, due to the enormous number of possible states. This can cause state explosion to occur when dealing with big and complex models. In order to avoid this problem and find a bug prior to explosion, we use automatically generated "hints" and "guides" to manipulate the model checker into examining "interesting" states. This way, we enter bug-pattern knowledge [8] into Wolf and allow it to search for specific occurrences of these patterns.

Section 2 describes the internal modules within Wolf. Section 3 presents our experimental results, and in section 4, we discuss possible future directions.

2 Structure of Wolf

Wolf is composed of three modules: a C-to-model translator, software verification algorithms integrated into RuleBase PE, and Vet.

Translator: The translator receives a concurrent C program and generates a finite model. This translation, described in [3], is not trivial. We model software concurrent control using two variables: TC (thread chooser) and PC (program counter vector). These signals point to the next command to be executed. In each cycle, only TC, PC, and one additional variable may change their values in order to allow the use of disjunctive partitions [3]. Moreover, the translator models the synchronization primitives [1]. Similarly to the method described in [12], the modeling of these primitives removes some unnecessary interleavings from the

[1] Currently, we support concurrent programs that use Pthread libraries.

model without changing its behavior. The translator also bounds the number of threads, the size of the heap, of the stack, and of all data types, making the problem decidable. In addition to that, it generates cleanness properties such as assert never fails, no use of/set to dangling pointer, no deadlock occur, no livelock, no data race, etc. The translator also generates hints and guides that will guide the software model checker toward the bug. These hints and guides are generated according to the program and the user's preferences.

Software Model Checker: Wolf uses a specialized version of RuleBase PE [4] as its underlying model checker. As mentioned, we are currently focusing on symbolic model checking using a BDD based model checker. Our algorithm uses disjunctive partitions [3], which enable faster image computation for software models. We implemented a dynamic BDD reordering algorithm especially designed to reduce the reordering time of software disjunctive BDDs.

Since we are using guided search, we implemented two different ways to divert the model checker to examine interesting states: hints and guides. In [5], the hints method was presented: in each step, the image computation is intersected with the current hint. When a fixed point is reached, the hint is replaced with the next hint. When all hints are used, another search is done from the reachable states of the last iteration without any constraints. We implemented this method with one change: our hints are cyclic, when the last hint results in a fixed-point, the first hint is rechecked and so forth. Only when all hints do not discover a new state, the final search is performed. Our hints are usually used to force a

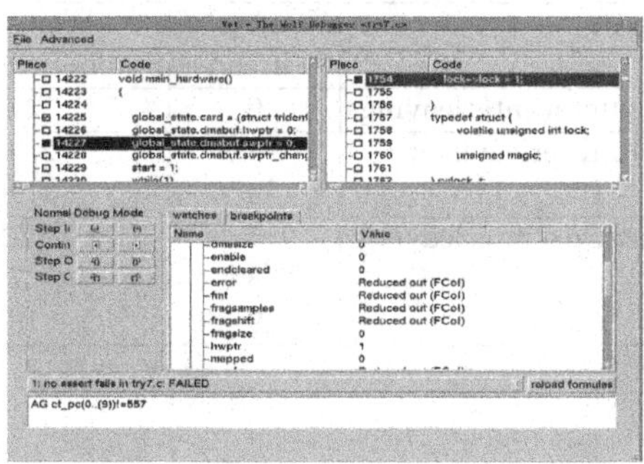

Fig. 1. Vet - wolf's debugger

round-robin execution of the threads: when the i-th hint is active, we intersect the image with $TC = i$. We observed that using such hints kept the BDDs relatively small.

Guides are another method to direct the model checker toward a bug. After each K iterations, the model checker finds the highest priority guide that is satisfied in the frontier[2], and continues to step forward only from the states in

[2] A frontier is the set of new states which were discovered in the last iteration.

the frontier that satisfy this guide. If no bug is found after one round-robin, the model checker backtracks and explores other states. For example, when looking for a deadlock, a guide may be *one thread is locked* and a higher priority guide may be *two threads are locked.*

Vet: Wolf's debugger: Finally, Vet displays the trace in a debugger-like GUI, highlighting the code line that caused the bug [3]. Vet allows the user to traverse the trace forward and backward. Also, the user can display watches over the variables. Since the trace is of concurrent software, Vet is designed in such a way that all the threads are displayed side-by-side, and the next line to be executed in each thread is marked. Figure 1 shows a trace as it is presented by Vet.

3 Experimental Results

We ran Wolf on two Linux drivers and synchronization code taken from an IBM's software group. We detected access violation bugs, data races, and deadlocks. In addition, we tried to estimate the potential that symbolic model checking for software has with respect to explicit model checking. We compared Wolf with Zing [1] on three different types of programs. This comparison is problematic because it could be done only on different platforms. However, it can be seen in Table 1 that symbolic model checking for software scales better when bugs occur only in rare interleavings, when the program has nondeterministic inputs.

Table 1. Comparison between Wolf and Zing with of different types of programs

Example	Number of Threads	Wolf Symbolic MC	Zing Explicit MC
Deterministic input common interleavings	6	2100s	374s
Deterministic input rare interleavings	8	21907s	614s
	9	31200s	> 10h
Non-deterministic input rare interleavings	7	724s	360s
	8	794s	> 10h
	9	1373s	> 10h

4 Future Work

We are now working on new guides and hints based on known bug-patterns [8]. We believe that bug-hunting for hard to detect bugs is worthwhile for our costumers. Simple bug-patterns, such as lock one thread then lock other thread on the same mutex, are already implemented in Wolf and show great promise. In addition, we are interested in introducing other model checking algorithms to the Wolf platform such as explicit and SAT-based model checking.

[3] The model checker exports information about the specific state that led to the property failure. Vet translates this into a specific code line.

References

1. T. Andrews, S. Qadeer, S. K. Rajamani, J. Rehof, and Y. Xie. Zing: A model checker for concurrent software. In *CAV*, pages 484–487, 2004.
2. T. Ball and S. K. Rajamani. Bebop: A symbolic model checker for boolean programs. In *Proc. 7th International SPIN Workshop*, 2000.
3. S. Barner and I. Rabinovitz. Effcient symbolic model checking of software using partial disjunctive partitioning. In *CHARME*, pages 35–50, 2003.
4. I. Beer, S. Ben-David, C. Eisner, and A. Landver. RuleBase: An industry-oriented formal verification tool. In *Design Automation Conference*, pages 655–660, 1996.
5. R. Bloem, K. Ravi, and F. Somenzi. Symbolic guided search for CTL model checking. In *Design Automation Conference*, pages 29–34, June 2000.
6. E. Clarke, O. Grumberg, and D. Peled. *Model Checking*. MIT press, 1999.
7. E. M. Clarke, D. Kroening, and F. Lerda. A tool for checking ansi-c programs. In *TACAS*, pages 168–176, 2004.
8. E. Farchi, Y. Nir, and S. Ur. Concurrent bug patterns and how to test them. In *IPDPS*, page 286, 2003.
9. K. Havelund and T. Pressburger. Model checking JAVA programs using JAVA pathfinder. *STTT*, 2(4):366–381, 2000.
10. G. Holzmann. On the fly, LTL model checking with SPIN: Simple Spin manual. At http://cm.bell-labs.com/cm/cs/what/spin/Man/Manual.html.
11. F. Ivancic, Z. Yang, A. Gupta, M. K. Ganai, and P. Ashar. Efficient SAT-based bounded model checking for software verification, ISoLA, 2004.
12. I. Rabinovitz and O. Grumberg. Bounded model checking of concurrent programs. In *CAV*, 2005.

Model Checking x86 Executables with CodeSurfer/x86 and WPDS++

G. Balakrishnan[1], T. Reps[1,2], N. Kidd[1], A. Lal[1], J. Lim[1],
D. Melski[2], R. Gruian[2], S. Yong[2], C.-H. Chen, and T. Teitelbaum[2]

[1] Comp. Sci. Dept., University of Wisconsin
{bgogul, reps, kidd, akash, junghee}@cs.wisc.edu
[2] GrammaTech, Inc.
{melski, radu, suan, chi-hua, tt}@grammatech.com

Abstract. This paper presents a toolset for model checking x86 executables. The members of the toolset are *CodeSurfer/x86*, *WPDS++*, and the *Path Inspector*. CodeSurfer/x86 is used to extract a model from an executable in the form of a *weighted pushdown system*. WPDS++ is a library for answering generalized reachability queries on weighted pushdown systems. The Path Inspector is a software model checker built on top of CodeSurfer and WPDS++ that supports safety queries about the program's possible control configurations.

1 Introduction

This paper presents a toolset for model checking x86 executables. The toolset builds on (i) recent advances in static analysis of program executables [1], and (ii) new techniques for software model checking and dataflow analysis [14, 10]. In our approach, CodeSurfer/x86 is used to extract a model from an x86 executable, and the reachability algorithms of the WPDS++ library [9] are used to check properties of the model. The Path Inspector is a software model checker that automates this process for safety queries involving the program's possible control configurations (but not the data state). The tools are capable of answering more queries than are currently supported by the Path Inspector (and involve data state); we illustrate this by describing two custom analyses that analyze an executable's use of the run-time stack.

Our work has three distinguishing features:

- The program model is extracted from the executable code that is run on the machine. This means that it automatically takes into account platform-specific aspects of the code, such as memory-layout details (i.e., offsets of variables in the run-time stack's activation records and padding between fields of a struct), register usage, execution order, optimizations, and artifacts of compiler bugs. Such information is hidden from tools that work on intermediate representations (IRs) that are built directly from the source code.
- The entire program is analyzed—including libraries that are linked to the program.
- The IR-construction and model-extraction processes do not assume that they have access to symbol-table or debugging information.

K. Etessami and S.K. Rajamani (Eds.): CAV 2005, LNCS 3576, pp. 158–163, 2005.

Because of the first two properties, our approach provides a "higher fidelity" tool than most software model checkers that analyze source code. This can be important for certain kinds of analysis; for instance, many security exploits depend on platform-specific features, such as the structure of activation records. Vulnerabilities can escape notice when a tool does not have information about adjacency relationships among variables.

Although the present toolset is targeted to x86 executables, the techniques used [1, 14, 10] are language-independent and could be applied to other types of executables.

The remainder of the paper is organized as follows: §2 sketches the methods used in CodeSurfer/x86 for IR recovery. §3 gives an overview of the model-checking facilities that the toolset provides. §4 discusses related work.

2 Recovering Intermediate Representations from x86 Executables

To recover IRs from x86 executables, CodeSurfer/x86 makes use of both IDAPro [8], a disassembly toolkit, and GrammaTech's CodeSurfer system [4], a toolkit for building program-analysis and inspection tools. Fig. 1 shows the various components of CodeSurfer/x86.

An x86 executable is first disassembled using IDAPro. In addition to the disassembly listing, IDAPro also provides access to the following information: (1) procedure boundaries, (2) calls to library functions using an algorithm called the Fast Library Identification and Recognition Technology (FLIRT) [6], and (3) statically known memory addresses and offsets. IDAPro provides access to its internal resources via an API that allows users to create plug-ins to be executed by IDAPro. We created a plug-in to IDAPro, called the Connector, that creates data structures to represent the information that it obtains from IDAPro. The IDAPro/Connector combination is also able to create the same data structures for dynamically linked libraries, and to link them into the data structures that represent the program itself. This infrastructure permits whole-program analysis to be carried out—including analysis of the code for all library functions that are called.

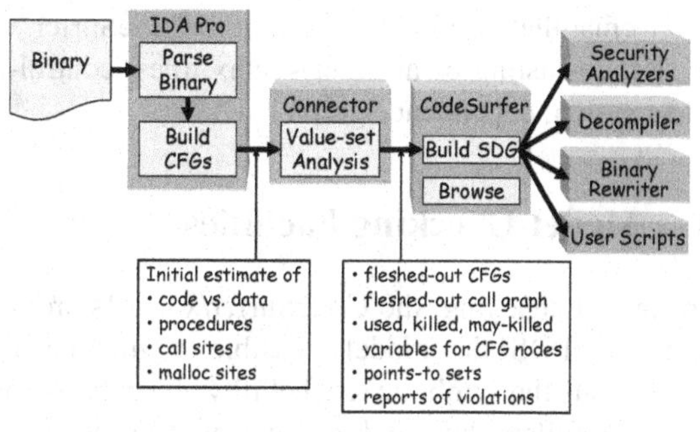

Fig. 1. Organization of CodeSurfer/x86

Using the data structures in the Connector, we implemented a static-analysis algorithm called *value-set analysis* (VSA) [1]. VSA does not assume the presence of symbol-table or debugging information. Hence, as a first step, a set of data objects called a-locs (for "abstract locations") is determined based on the static memory addresses and offsets provided by IDAPro. VSA is a combined numeric and pointer-analysis algorithm that determines an over-approximation of the set of numeric values and addresses (or *value-set*) that each a-loc holds at each program point. A key feature of VSA is that it tracks integer-valued and address-valued quantities simultaneously. This is crucial for analyzing executables because numeric values and addresses are indistinguishable at execution time.

IDAPro does not identify the targets of all indirect jumps and indirect calls, and therefore the call graph and control-flow graphs that it constructs are not complete. However, the information computed during VSA can be used to augment the call graph and control-flow graphs on-the-fly to account for indirect jumps and indirect calls.

VSA also checks whether the executable conforms to a "standard" compilation model—i.e., a runtime stack is maintained; activation records (ARs) are pushed onto the stack on procedure entry and popped from the stack on procedure exit; a procedure does not modify the return address on stack; the program's instructions occupy a fixed area of memory, are not self-modifying, and are separate from the program's data. If it cannot be confirmed that the executable conforms to the model, then the IR is possibly incorrect. For example, the call-graph can be incorrect if a procedure modifies the return address on the stack. Consequently, VSA issues an error report whenever it finds a possible violation of the standard compilation model; these represent possible memory-safety violations. The analyst can go over these reports and determine whether they are false alarms or real violations.

Once VSA completes, the value-sets for the a-locs at each program point are used to determine each point's sets of used, killed, and possibly-killed a-locs; these are emitted in a format that is suitable for input to CodeSurfer. CodeSurfer then builds a collection of IRs, consisting of abstract-syntax trees, control-flow graphs (CFGs), a call graph, and a system dependence graph (SDG).

3 Model-Checking Facilities

For model checking, the CodeSurfer/x86 IRs are used to build a weighted pushdown system (WPDS) that models possible program behaviors. WPDS++ [9] is a library that implements the symbolic reachability algorithms from [14] on *weighted pushdown systems*. We follow the standard convention of using a pushdown system (PDS) to model the interprocedural control-flow graph (one of CodeSurfer/x86's IRs). The stack symbols correspond to program locations; there is only a single PDS state; and PDS rules encode control flow as follows:

Rule	Control flow modeled
$q\langle u\rangle \hookrightarrow q\langle v\rangle$	Intraprocedural CFG edge $u \rightarrow v$
$q\langle c\rangle \hookrightarrow q\langle entry_P\ r\rangle$	Call to P from c that returns to r
$q\langle x\rangle \hookrightarrow q\langle\rangle$	Return from a procedure at exit node x

Given a configuration of the PDS, the top stack symbol corresponds to the current program location, and the rest of the stack holds return-site locations—much like a standard run-time execution stack.

This encoding of the interprocedural CFG as a pushdown system is sufficient for answering queries about reachable control states (as the Path Inspector does; see §3.2): the reachability algorithms of WPDS++ can determine if an undesirable PDS configuration is reachable [2]. However, WPDS++ also supports *weighted* PDSs. These are

PDSs in which each rule is weighted with an element of a (user-defined) semiring. The use of weights allows WPDS++ to perform interprocedural dataflow analysis by using the semiring's *extend* operator to compute weights for sequences of rule firings and using the semiring's *combine* operator to take the meet of weights generated by different paths. (When the weights on rules are conservative abstract data transformers, an over-approximation to the set of reachable concrete configurations is obtained, which means that counterexamples reported by WPDS++ may actually be infeasible.)

3.1 Stack-Qualified Dataflow Queries

The CodeSurfer/x86 IRs are a rich source of opportunities to check properties of interest using WPDS++. For instance, WPDS++ has been used to implement an illegal-stack-manipulation check: for each node n in procedure P, this checks whether the net change in stack height is the same along all paths from $entry_P$ to n that have perfectly matched calls and returns (i.e., along "same-level valid paths"). In this analysis, a weight is a function that represents a stack-height change. For instance, `push ecx` and `sub esp,4` both have the weight $\lambda height.height - 4$. Extend is (the reversal of) function composition; combine performs a meet of stack-height-change functions. (The analysis is similar to linear constant propagation [15].) When a memory access performed relative to r's activation record (AR) is out-of-bounds, stack-height-change values can be used to identify which a-locs could be accessed in ARs of other procedures.

VSA is an interprocedural dataflow-analysis algorithm that uses the "call-strings" approach [16] to obtain a degree of context sensitivity. Each dataflow fact is tagged with a call-stack suffix (or *call-string*) to form (call-string, dataflow-fact) pairs; the call-string is used at the exit node of each procedure to determine to which call site a (call-string, dataflow-fact) pair should be propagated. The call-strings that arise at a given node n provide an opportunity to perform stack-qualified dataflow queries [14] using WPDS++. CodeSurfer/x86 identifies induction-variable relationships by using the affine-relation domain of Müller-Olm and Seidl [12] as a weight domain. A *post** query builds an automaton that is then used to find the affine relations that hold in a given calling context—given by call-string *cs*—by querying the *post**-automaton with respect to a regular language constructed from *cs* and the program's call graph.

3.2 The Path Inspector

The Path Inspector provides a user interface for automating safety queries that are only concerned with the possible control configurations that an executable can reach. It uses an automaton-based approach to model checking: the query is specified as a finite automaton that captures forbidden sequences of program locations. This "query automaton" is combined with the program model (a WPDS) using a cross-product construction, and the reachability algorithms of WPDS++ are used to determine if an error configuration is reachable. If an error configuration is reachable, then *witnesses* (see [14]) can be used to produce a program path that drives the query automaton to an error state.

The Path Inspector includes a GUI for instantiating many common reachability queries [5], and for displaying counterexample paths in the disassembly listing.[1] In the current implementation, transitions in the query automaton are triggered by program points that the user specifies either manually, or using result sets from CodeSurfer queries. Future versions of the Path Inspector will support more sophisticated queries in which transitions are triggered by matching an AST pattern against a program location, and query states can be instantiated based on pattern bindings. Future versions will also eliminate (many) infeasible counterexamples by using transition weights to represent abstract data transformers (similar to those used for interprocedural dataflow analysis).

4 Related Work

Several others have proposed techniques to obtain information from executables by means of static analysis (see [1] for references). However, previous techniques deal with memory accesses very conservatively; e.g., if a register is assigned a value from memory, it is assumed to take on any value. VSA does a much better job than previous work because it tracks the integer-valued and address-valued quantities that the program's data objects can hold; in particular, VSA tracks the values of data objects *other than just the hardware registers*, and thus is not forced to give up all precision when a load from memory is encountered. This is a fundamental issue; the absence of such information places severe limitations on what previously developed tools can be applied to.

Christodorescu and Jha used model-checking techniques to detect malicious code variants [3]. Given a sample of malicious code, they extract a parameterized state machine that will accept variants of the code. They use CodeSurfer/x86 to extract a model of each procedure of the program, and determine potential matches between the program's code and fragments of the malicious code. Their technique is intraprocedural, and does not analyze data state.

Other groups have used run-time program monitoring and checkpointing to perform a systematic search of a program's dynamic state space [7, 11, 13]. Like our approach, this allows for model checking properties of the low-level code that is actually run on the machine. However, because the dynamic state space can be unbounded, these approaches cannot perform an exhaustive search. In contrast, we use static analysis to perform a (conservative) exhaustive search of an abstract state space.

References

1. G. Balakrishnan and T. Reps. Analyzing memory accesses in x86 executables. In *Comp. Construct.*, Lec. Notes in Comp. Sci., pages 5–23. Springer-Verlag, 2004.
2. H. Chen, D. Dean, and D. Wagner. Model checking one million lines of C code. In *Symp. on Network and Distributed Systems Security*, 2004.

[1] We assume that source code is not available, but the techniques extend naturally if it is: one can treat the executable code as just another IR in the collection of IRs obtainable from source code. The mapping of information back to the source code is similar to what C source-code tools already have to perform because of the use of the C preprocessor.

3. M. Christodorescu and S. Jha. Static analysis of executables to detect malicious patterns. In *USENIX Security Symposium,*, 2003.
4. CodeSurfer, GrammaTech, Inc., http://www.grammatech.com/products/codesurfer/.
5. M. Dwyer, G. Avrunin, and J. Corbett. Patterns in property specifications for finite-state verification. In *Int. Conf. on Softw. Eng.*, 1999.
6. Fast library identification and recognition technology, DataRescue sa/nv, Liège, Belgium, http://www.datarescue.com/idabase/flirt.htm.
7. P. Godefroid. Model checking for programming languages using VeriSoft. In ACM, editor, *Princ. of Prog. Lang.*, pages 174–186. ACM Press, 1997.
8. IDAPro disassembler, http://www.datarescue.com/idabase/.
9. N. Kidd, T. Reps, D. Melski, and A. Lal. WPDS++: A C++ library for weighted pushdown systems. Univ. of Wisconsin, 2004.
10. A. Lal, T. Reps, and G. Balakrishnan. Extended weighted pushdown systems. In *Computer Aided Verif.*, 2005.
11. P. Leven, T. Mehler, and S. Edelkamp. Directed error detection in C++ with the assembly-level model checker StEAM. In *Spin Workshop*, 2004.
12. M. Müller-Olm and H. Seidl. Analysis of modular arithmetic. In *ESOP*, 2005.
13. M. Musuvathi, D. Park, A. Chou, D. Engler, and D. Dill. CMC: A pragmatic approach to model checking real code. In *Op. Syst. Design and Impl.*, 2002.
14. T. Reps, S. Schwoon, S. Jha, and D. Melski. Weighted pushdown systems and their application to interprocedural dataflow analysis. *Sci. of Comp. Prog.*, 2005. To appear.
15. M. Sagiv, T. Reps, and S. Horwitz. Precise interprocedural dataflow analysis with applications to constant propagation. *Theor. Comp. Sci.*, 167:131–170, 1996.
16. M. Sharir and A. Pnueli. Two approaches to interprocedural data flow analysis. In *Program Flow Analysis: Theory and Applications*. Prentice-Hall, Englewood Cliffs, NJ, 1981.

The ComFoRT Reasoning Framework

Sagar Chaki, James Ivers, Natasha Sharygina, and Kurt Wallnau

Software Engineering Institute, Carnegie Mellon University

1 Introduction

Model checking is a promising technology for verifying critical behavior of software. However, software model checking is hamstrung by scalability issues and is difficult for software engineers to use directly. The second challenge arises from the gap between model checking concepts and notations, and those used by engineers to develop large-scale systems. ComFoRT [15] addresses both of these challenges. It provides a model checker, Copper, that implements a suite of complementary complexity management techniques to address state space explosion. But ComFoRT is more than a model checker. The ComFoRT *reasoning framework* includes additional support for building systems in a particular component-based idiom. This addresses transition issues.

2 The Containerized Component Idiom

In the containerized component idiom, custom software is *deployed* into prefabricated containers. A component is a container and its custom code. Containers restrict visibility of custom code to its external environment (other components and a standard runtime environment), and vice versa. Components exhibit reactive behavior, characterized by how stimuli received through the container interface lead to responses emitted via the container interface. A runtime environment provides component coordination mechanisms (or "connectors") and implements other resource management policies (scheduling, synchronization, etc.). We define a component technology as an implementation of this design idiom [17], and many such implementations are possible [19]. Our approach has much in common with [12], although we give full behavioral models for components (UML statecharts and action language) and, subsequently, can generate full implementations of components and assemblies.

We formalize this idiom in the construction and composition language (CCL) [18]. The structural aspects of CCL (e.g., interfaces, hierarchy, topology) are similar to those found in a typical architecture description language [1]. The behavioral aspects of CCL use a subset of UML statecharts. Our formalization retains the statechart semantics already familiar to software engineers while refining it to precisely define those semantics intentionally left open in the standard. In formalizing both aspects of CCL, we exploit our connection with a specific component technology, which we use as the oracle for our choice of semantics.

K. Etessami and S.K. Rajamani (Eds.): CAV 2005, LNCS 3576, pp. 164–169, 2005.

ComFoRT exploits this design idiom and its formalization in several ways. Threading information in CCL specifications is exploited to generate concurrent state machines that more closely approximate actual concurrency than might otherwise be the case if threading were not considered [16]. The factoring of component-based systems into custom code and prefabricated containers and connectors presents opportunities for exploiting compositional reasoning. Models of containers and connectors can also be pre-fabricated; therefore, developers need only model their custom code to use the model checker. Moreover, as explained in Section 3, verification properties are specified using a formalism adapted to easily describe patterns of interaction among stateful components.

Because CCL is a design language, model checking can be used to verify early design decisions. However, model checking of software implementations is also possible because the model checker also processes a restricted form of ANSI-C source code (even though it is unsound with respect to pointers). The cumulative result is to make model checking more accessible to the practicing software engineer by using familiar notations, supporting verification throughout the development process, and providing automation to hide complexity.

3 Overview of the Model Checking Engine

Combined State Space Reduction. The ComFoRT model checker, Copper, is built on the top of the MAGIC tool [14]. Copper implements a number of state space reduction techniques, including 1) automated predicate abstraction, 2) counterexample-guided abstraction refinement (also known as a CEGAR loop), and 3) compositional reasoning. These techniques are widely used by the majority of software model checking tools (such as SLAM [2], BLAST [13], CBMC [9]). The advantage of Copper is that it combines *all* three of them in a complementary way to combat the state space explosion of software verification. For example, it enables compositional abstraction/refinement loop where each step of the CEGAR loop can be performed *one* concurrent unit at a time. Moreover, Copper integrates a number of complementary state space reduction techniques. An example is a *two-level abstraction approach* [3] where predicate abstraction for data is augmented by action-guided abstraction for events. Another key feature of the Copper approach is that if a property can be proved to hold or not based on a given finite set of predicates P, the predicate refinement procedure used in Copper automatically detects a minimal subset of P that is sufficient for the proof. This, along with the explicit use of compositionality, delays the onset of state-space explosion for as long as possible.

State/Event-based Verification. The Copper model checker provides formal models for software verification that leverage the distinction between data (states) and communication structures (events). Most formal models are either state-based (e.g., the Kripke structures used in model checking) or event-based (e.g., process algebras), but Copper provides models that incorporate both [7]. Semantically, this does not increase expressive power, since one can encode states as events or events as state changes, but providing both directly in the model fits more natural to software modeling and property specification. It is, indeed, essential in supporting the containerized component idiom. As importantly, it allows *more efficient verification* [7]. COPPER models such systems as *Labeled Kripke Structures* and provides both state/event-LTL [7] and ACTL formalisms [5]. Both versions of temporal logic are sufficiently expressive, yet allow a tractable implementation for model checking. The COPPER model checking algorithms support verification of both *safety* and *liveness* properties of state/event systems. Another feature of the state/event-based framework is a *compositional deadlock detection* technique [6] that not only efficiently detects deadlocks but also acts as an additional space reduction procedure.

Verification of Evolving Systems. The COPPER model checker also provides features that enable it to *automatically* verify *evolving software.* These features simplify verification throughout the development process—and through the extended life-cycle of a software system—by reducing the cost of re-verification when changes are made. We define verification of evolving systems as a component substitutability problem: (i) previously established properties must remain valid for the new version of a system, and (ii) the updated portion of the system must continue to provide all (and possibly more) services offered by its earlier counterpart. COPPER uses a completely automated procedure based on learning techniques for regular sets to solve the substitutability problem in the context of verifying individual component upgrades [4]. Furthermore, COPPER also supports analysis of component substitutability in the presence of *simultaneous upgrades of multiple components* [8]. COPPER uses *dynamic* assume-guarantee reasoning, where previously generated assumptions are reused and altered on-the-fly to prove or disprove the global safety properties on the updated system.

4 Tool Support

COMFORT consists of two sets of tools: those for generating the state machines to be verified and those that perform the actual model checking. The first set deals with the topics discussed in Section 2, parsing and performing semantic analysis of design specifications (in CCL) and the generation of the state machines in the input language of COPPER. COPPER, as discussed in Section 3, is the model checker at the core of COMFORT. COPPER was built on top of MAGIC, portions of which we developed together with collaborators from Carnegie Mellon's School of Computer Science specifically to support COMFORT[1]. COPPER has since evolved beyond the MAGIC v.1.0 code base, and a brief overview of some of the key features of COPPER and their lineage in terms of various tool releases is found in Figure 1. COMFORT is available at http://www.sei.cmu.edu/pacc/comfort.html.

[1] The reader, therefore, should not be confused by the fact that results of this collaboration have been presented in the contexts of both projects.

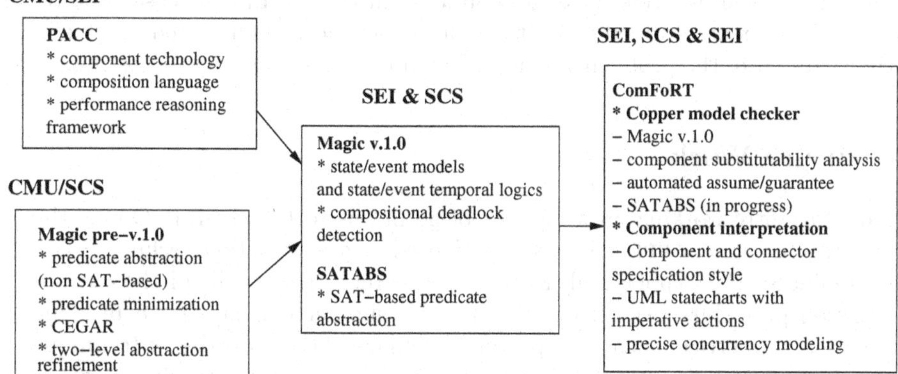

Fig. 1. Evolution of the MAGIC and ComFoRT projects

5 Results

We have used ComFoRT to analyze several industrial benchmarks. Our first benchmark was derived from the OpenSSL-0.9.6c implementation of SSL. Specifically, we verified the implementation of the handshake between a client (2500 LOC) and a server (2500 LOC) attempting to establish a secure connection with respect to several properties derived from the SSL specification. Figure 2 shows verification results of two properties, each of which was expressed using only states (`ss` suffix) and both states and events (`se` suffix). Note that the models depend on the property - and hence are different for the pure-state and state/event versions, even though they are constructed from the same source code. As shown in Figure 2, verification of the state/event properties outperforms the corresponding pure-state properties.

Name	St(B)	Tr(B)	St(Mdl)	T(BA)	T(Mdl)	T(Ver)	T(Total)	Mem
ssl-1-ss	25	47	25119360	1187	69969	*	*	324
ssl-1-se	20	45	13839168	848	37681	113704	153356	165
ssl-2-ss	25	47	33199244	1199	67419	3545288	3615016	216
ssl-2-se	18	40	16246624	814	38080	298601	338601	172

Fig. 2. **St(B)** and **Tr(B)** = number of Büchi states and transitions; **St(Mdl)** = number of model states; **T(Mdl)** = model construction time; **T(BA)** = Büchi construction time; **T(Ver)** = model checking time; **T(Total)** = total verification time. Times are in milliseconds. **Mem** = memory in MB. A * ≡ model checking aborted after 2 hours

Two other benchmarks we have used are Micro-C OS and the interprocess-communication library of an industrial robot controller. With Micro-C OS, verification of source code revealed a locking protocol violation. With the communication library, verification of CCL models derived from the implementation revealed a problem wherein messages could be misrouted. In both cases, the respective developers informed us that the problems had been detected and fixed; in the latter case, the problem was undetected during seven years of testing.

6 Future Work

We are currently working on a number of additions to ComFoRT. One is the incorporation into Copper a SAT-based predicate abstraction technique [10] that eliminates the exponential number of theorem prover calls of the current abstraction procedure. Another is the use of a simpler language for expressing verification properties, such as a pattern language [11]. A third is a technique for confirming that design-level (i.e., CCL designs) verification results are satisfied by eventual component implementations by proving a conformance relation between the model and its implementation.

References

1. F. Achermann, M. Lumpe, J. Schneider, and O. Nierstrasz. Piccola – a Small Composition Language. In *Formal Methods for Distributed Processing–A Survey of Object-Oriented Approaches*. 2002.
2. T. Ball and S. Rajamani. Boolean programs: A model and process for software analysis. Technical Report 2000-14, Microsoft Research, February 2000.
3. S. Chaki, E. Clarke, A. Groce, J. Ouaknine, O. Strichman, and K. Yorav. Efficient verification of sequential and concurrent C programs. *FMSD*, 25(2), 2004.
4. S. Chaki, N. Sharygina, and N. Sinha. Verification of evolving software. In *SAVCBS'04: Worksh. on Specification and Verification of Component-based Systems*, 2004.
5. E. Clarke, S. Chaki, O. Grumberg, T. Touili, J. Ouaknine, N. Sharygina, and H. Veith. An expressive verification framework for state/event systems. Technical Report CS-2004-145, CMU, 2004.
6. E. Clarke, S. Chaki, J. Ouaknine, and N. Sharygina. Automated, compositional and iterative deadlock detection. In *2nd ACM-IEEE MEMOCODE 04*, 2004.
7. E. Clarke, S. Chaki, J. Ouaknine, N. Sharygina, and N. Sinha. State/event-based software model checking. In *IFM 04: Integrated Formal Methods*, LNCS 2999, 2004.
8. E. Clarke, S. Chaki, N. Sharygina, and N. Sinha. Dynamic component substitutability analysis. In *FM 2005: Formal Methods, to appear*. LNCS, 2005.
9. E. Clarke, D. Kroening, and F. Lerda. A tool for checking ANSI-C programs. In *TACAS*, volume 2988 of *LNCS*, pages 168–176. Springer, 2004.
10. E. Clarke, D. Kroening, N. Sharygina, and K. Yorav. Predicate abstraction of ANSI-C programs using SAT. *Formal Methods in System Design*, 25(2), 2004.
11. M. Dwyer, G. Avrunin, and J. Corbett. Patterns in property specifications for finite-state verification. In *Proceedings of the 21st ICSE*, 1999.
12. J. Hatcliff, X. Deng, M. B. Dwyer, G. Jung, and V. P. Ranganath. Cadena: An integrated development, analysis, and verification environment for component-based systems. In *ICSE*, pages 160–173, 2003.
13. T. A. Henzinger, R. Jhala, R. Majumdar, and G. Sutre. Lazy abstraction. In *Principles of Programming Languages 02*.

14. http://www.cs.cmu.edu/chaki/magic. Magic tool.
15. J. Ivers and N. Sharygina. Overview of ComFoRT: A Model Checking Reasoning Framework. Technical Report CMU/SEI-2004-TN-018, SEI, CMU, 2004.
16. J. Ivers and K. Wallnau. Preserving real concurrency. In *Correctness of model-based software composition Workshop*, July 2003.
17. K. Wallnau. Vol III: A Technology for Predictable Assembly from Certifiable Components (PACC). Technical Report CMU/SEI-2003-TR-009, SEI,CMU, 2003.
18. K. Wallnau and J. Ivers. Snapshot of CCL: A Language for Predictable Assembly. Technical Report CMU/SEI-2002-TR-031, SEI, CMU, 2002.
19. N. Ward-Dutton. Containers: A sign components are growing up. *Application Development Trends*, pages 41–44,46, January 2000.

Formal Verification of Pentium®4 Components with Symbolic Simulation and Inductive Invariants

Roope Kaivola

Intel Corporation, JF4-451, 2111 NE 25th Avenue, Hillsboro, OR 97124, USA

Abstract. We describe a practical methodology for large-scale formal verification of control-intensive industrial circuits. It combines symbolic simulation with human-generated inductive invariants, and a proof tool for verifying implications between constraint lists. The approach has emerged from extensive experiences in the formal verification of key parts of the Intel IA-32 Pentium®4 microprocessor designs. We discuss it the context of two case studies: Pentium 4 register renaming mechanism and BUS recycle logic.

1 Introduction

It is easy to explain why formal verification of microprocessors is hard. A state-of-the-art microprocessor may have millions of state elements, whereas a state-of-the-art formal verification engine providing complete coverage can usually handle a few hundred significant state elements. This basic technology problem stems from the computational complexity of many of the algorithms used for formal verification. At the same time, the strong guarantees of correctness given by verification would be particularly valuable in the domain of microprocessors. The products are used in circumstances where their reliability is crucial, and just the financial cost of correcting problems can be very high.

In an industrial product development project formal verification is a tool, one among others, and it has to compete with other validation methods such as traditional testing and simulation. We believe quite strongly that in this setting the greatest value of formal verification comes from its ability to provide complete coverage, finding subtle design problems that testing may have missed, and yielding strong evidence about the absence of any further problems. This is naturally not the only usage model for formal methods: more lightweight approaches providing partial coverage such as partial model exploration, bounded model checking, capturing design intent by assertions etc. can also provide value to a project. Nevertheless, systematic testing and simulation often provide reasonable partial coverage already, and in our opinion the most compelling argument for the adoption of formal verification is that it can provide guarantees of correctness that testing cannot.

Formal verification has been pursued in various forms for roughly a decade now in Intel [19]. Usually the goal of a verification effort is to relate a detailed register transfer level circuit model to a clear and abstract specification. In some areas, most notably in arithmetic hardware, verification methods have reached sufficient maturity that they can now be routinely applied (for discussion see [14]). The work still requires a great deal of human expertise, but tasks that used to take months can be carried out in days, and the work can be planned ahead with reasonable confidence. In other areas the track record

K. Etessami and S.K. Rajamani (Eds.): CAV 2005, LNCS 3576, pp. 170–184, 2005.

is mixed. Traditional temporal logic model checkers perform well for local properties, but quickly run out of steam when the size of the sub-circuit relevant for the property grows. Decompositions and assume-guarantee reasoning can alleviate this problem, but the help they provide tends to gradually diminish as the circuits grow larger, as well.

Large control intensive circuits have proved to be particularly resistant to formal verification. They contain enough state elements that even after applying common reduction strategies, such as data independence or symmetry reductions, the system is far too large for traditional model-checking. The state elements tend to be tightly interconnected, and natural decompositions often do not exist, or lead to a replication of the circuit structure in the specification. Circuit optimizations often take advantage of various restrictions that are expected to hold throughout the execution of the circuit, and in order to prove correct behaviour, one needs to first establish the validity of these restrictions. If a restriction depends on the correct behaviour of the circuit in a global level, local low level properties become contingent on correctness in a global level. In effect, either everything in the circuit works, or nothing does.

In the current paper we discuss a methodology that has allowed us to tackle these large verification problems with far greater success than before. Our starting point is a simple, concrete and computationally undemanding approach: We try to mechanically verify inductive invariants written by a human verifier, and conformance to a non-deterministic high-level model. The approach avoids any explicit automated computation of a fixed point. The concreteness of the computation steps in the approach allows a user to locate and analyze computational problems and devise a strategy around them when a tool fails because of capacity issues. This is a very common scenario in practice, and in our experience one of the key issues regarding the practical usability of a verification tool. On a philosophical level, we approach verification in much the same way as program construction, by emphasizing the role of the human verifier over automation.

Our methodology has gradually emerged over several years of work on large verification tasks. In the current paper we report on two cases: BUS recycle logic and a register renaming mechanism, both from a Pentium® 4 design. The BUS recycle mechanism contains about 3000 state elements, and with the methods presented here, the verification is a fairly straightforward task. The logic covered in the verification of the register renaming mechanism involves about 15000 state elements in the circuit and an environment model. The case is to our knowledge one of the largest and most complex circuit verification efforts in the field to date.

We consider the main contributions of the current paper to be the empirical observation that the methodology is an efficient strategy for practical verification, and the collection of heuristics and technical innovations used in our implication verification tool. The methodology scales smoothly to circuits with tens of thousands of state elements, and allows us to relate low-level RTL circuit models to algorithmically clear and concise high-level descriptions. Building the verification method on the intuitively very tangible idea of an invariant allows us to communicate the work easily to designers, and to draw on their insights in the work. A somewhat surprising observation in the work was just how difficult the computational task still is. Encountering this kind of complexity in a verification strategy that is heavily user guided leads us to believe that the chances of success for fully automatic methods on similar tasks are negligible.

2 Methodology Overview

2.1 Background

Let us assume that we have a circuit *ckt* and want to verify that a simple safety property I_{spec} holds throughout the execution of the circuit, under some external assumptions I_{ext}. The circuit models we use are effectively gate-level descriptions of the circuit functionality. They are mechanically translated from the RTL code used in the development project, linked to the actual silicon via schematics.

Let us write *Nodes* for the set of node or signal names of the circuit, and define the *signature Sig* and the set of *valuations Val* of the circuit by $Sig \equiv_{df} Nodes \times int$ and $Val \equiv_{df} Sig \rightarrow bool$. We call the elements of *Sig timed signals*. Intuitively they are references to circuit nodes at specific times. The combinational logic and the state elements of the circuit naturally generate a set of *runs* of the circuit, $Runs \subseteq Val$, the definition of which we do not formalize here. Our circuit models do not have distinguished initial states, which means that the set *Runs* is closed under suffixes. A circuit can be powered up in any state, and we use an explicit initialization sequence to drive it to a sufficiently well-defined state. The initialization sequence can be described by a collection of timed signals, a valuation assigning values to elements of these signals, and an initialization end time t_{init}. We write *Iruns* for the set of all initialized runs of the circuit.

We formulate the specification I_{spec} and the external assumptions I_{ext} as implicitly conjuncted sets of *constraints*. Intuitively a constraint is a property characterizing a set of runs of the circuit, and formally we define the set of constraints *Constr* by $Constr \equiv_{df} Val \rightarrow bool$. If $C \subseteq Constr$ and $v \in Val$, we define $C(v) \equiv_{df} \bigwedge_{c \in C} c(v)$. We also define a *next step* operation $\mathtt{N}$ for timed signals $(s,t) \in Sig$ by $\mathtt{N}(s,t) \equiv_{df} (s,t+1)$ and the notion extends naturally to signatures, valuations, constraints and constraint sets. We consider an invariant property I_{spec} to be valid over a circuit iff it is valid for all time points after the end of the initialization sequence for all initialized runs of the circuit.

More generally, we want to verify the conformance of the circuit behaviour against a non-deterministic high-level model (HLM). In this case, a specification consists of an HLM and a relation between RTL states and HLM states. The components of an HLM state form its signature Sig_{HLM}. We write Val_{HLM} for the set of valuations mapping each $s \in Sig_{HLM}$ to an element of an appropriate type, and describe the behaviour of the HLM by a set of initial state predicates $init_{HLM} \subseteq Val_{HLM} \rightarrow bool$ and a set of transition predicates $trans_{HLM} \subseteq Val_{HLM} \times Val_{HLM} \rightarrow bool$. Both sets are considered implicitly conjuncted. The relation between RTL and HLM states is described by an abstraction map $abs \in Val \rightarrow Val_{HLM}$. We consider the circuit behaviour to conform to the HLM iff for all initialized runs $v \in Iruns$,

- the RTL state at the end of the initialization sequence maps to an HLM state satisfying all the all the initial state predicates in $init_{HLM}$, and
- for all points n after the end of the initialization sequence, the RTL transition from point n to $n+1$ maps to an HLM transition satisfying all the HLM transition predicates in $trans_{HLM}$.

2.2 Symbolic Simulation

Symbolic simulation is based on traditional notions of digital circuit simulation. In conventional symbolic simulation, the value of a signal is either a constant (T or F) or a symbolic expression representing the conditions under which the signal is T. To perform symbolic simulation on circuit RTL models, we use the technique of *symbolic trajectory evaluation (STE)* [20]. Trajectory evaluation extends the normal Boolean logic to a quaternary logic, with the value X denoting lack of information, i.e. the signal could be either T or F, and the value $\top$ denoting contradictory information, and carries out circuit simulation with quaternary values. In the current work we use STE to symbolically simulate the circuit and trace the values of relevant signals. In this context we can view STE as a routine that is given a circuit *ckt*, an antecedent signature and valuation $sig_{ant} \subseteq Sig$, $v_{ant} \in Val$, and a signature of interest $sig_{intr} \subseteq Sig$, and which produces a valuation $v_{STE} \in Val$ such that:

$$\forall v \in Runs.(\forall s \in sig_{ant}.v(s) = v_{ant}(s)) \Rightarrow (\forall s \in sig_{intr}.v(s) = v_{STE}(s)) \tag{1}$$

Technically our verification work is carried out in the Forte verification framework, built on top of the Voss system [10]. The interface language to Forte is FL, a strongly-typed functional language in the ML family [18]. It includes binary decision diagrams as first-class objects and symbolic trajectory evaluation as a built-in function. In writing the specification constraints I_{spec} and I_{ext}, we use all the facilities of the programming language FL. When describing an HLM, we use an abstract record-like FL data-type to characterize its signature and the intended types of the state components.

2.3 Inductive Verification

A simple way to verify the safety property I_{spec} is to strengthen it to an inductive invariant I_{ind}. Using a symbolic circuit simulator, the base and inductive steps can then be carried out as follows:

- symbolically simulate the circuit model from an unconstrained state, driving the circuit initialization sequence on the inputs of the circuit, and check that I_{ind} holds in the state after circuit initialization,
- symbolically simulate the circuit model from an unconstrained state for a single cycle, and check that if I_{ind} holds in the start state of the simulation, then it also holds in the end state, assuming that I_{ext} holds

In more detail, this approach involves the following verification steps:

A Determine the sub-circuit of interest, i.e. determine signatures sig_{inv} and sig_{ext} so that sig_{inv} contains all the timed signals referenced in I_{spec} and *abs*, and for every $s' \in \mathtt{N}(sig_{inv})$, the value of s' in the circuit simulation is a function of timed signals in sig_{inv} and sig_{ext}. Define the signature of interest for all subsequent STE runs as the union of the two sets.

B Determine a set of constraints $I_{ind} \subseteq Constr$ such that $I_{spec} \subseteq I_{ind}$.

C Symbolically simulate the circuit with STE using the initialization signature and valuation as antecedent. Write $v_{STEinit}$ for the valuation valuation computed by STE after the initialization sequence.

D Verify that after initialization, the inductive invariant I_{ind} holds, and the circuit state maps to an initial HLM state, i.e. that $I_{ind}(v_{STEinit})$ and $init_{HLM}(abs(v_{STEinit}))$ hold

E Symbolically simulate the circuit with STE using antecedent signature sig_{intr} and an antecedent valuation function that assigns a fresh symbolic variable to every element of sig_{intr}. Write v_{STE} for the valuation computed by STE.

F Verify that the inductive invariant remains true, and the circuit transition maps to a legal HLM transition:

$$(I_{ind} \cup I_{ext})(v_{STE}) \Rightarrow \mathtt{N}(I_{ind})(v_{STE}) \tag{2}$$

$$(I_{ind} \cup I_{ext})(v_{STE}) \Rightarrow trans_{HLM}(abs(v_{STE}), abs(\mathtt{N}(v_{STE}))) \tag{3}$$

Much of step A can be automated by causal fan-in analysis of signals, but human intuition is needed to determine which signals to include in the inductive set sig_{inv} and which to consider external inputs sig_{ext} in the scope of the proof. Step B is obviously the most labour-intensive task, and requires great ingenuity and detailed understanding of the circuit's behaviour. Typically a verifier builds I_{ind} incrementally by adding constraints to I_{spec} until the resulting set is inductive. Steps C and E are carried out automatically by STE, with a moderate amount of user intervention required to create a reasonable BDD variable ordering and to avoid simulating unnecessary parts of the circuit. Step D is usually trivial. Step F is the most computation intensive one. It is carried out with the implication verification tool discussed next. It is easy to see from equation 1 and the disjointness of the symbolic variables used in step E, that the verification goals for invariant and HLM conformance verification follow from the steps above. It is also easy to see that the method is complete in a theoretical sense: Since circuits are finite, one can in principle write down a constraint characterizing its reachable state space, and verify every valid I_{spec} with the help of this constraint.

3 Implication Verification

In verification of the inductive step, we need to determine the implication between two sets of constraints: Given $A, G \subseteq Constr$ and a valuation $v \in Val$, determine whether $A(v) \Rightarrow G(v)$, i.e. whether $\bigwedge_{a \in A} a(v) \Rightarrow \bigwedge_{g \in G} g(v)$. The problem is non-trivial, given that for some of our cases the sets have tens of thousands of elements, and the timed signals map to relatively complex BDD's in the right side of the implication.

For small instances, one can solve the problem by just computing $\mathcal{A} = \bigwedge_{a \in A} a(v)$, $\mathcal{G} = \bigwedge_{g \in G} g(v)$, and the implication $\mathcal{A} \Rightarrow \mathcal{G}$. In our setting, the naive solution is feasible only when the constraint sets have less than fifty elements. A simple improvement is to consider each goal separately, to compute $\mathcal{A} \Rightarrow g(v)$ for each $g \in G$. In our experience this strategy works when the constraint sets have up to a few hundred elements. To move forward we developed techniques which improve the obvious strategy primarily along two axes. First, instead of using all the assumptions $a \in A$, we can pick a selection of them and use the selected constraints incrementally in a particular order. Secondly, we can avoid the computation of complex BDD's by considering an exhaustive collection of special cases instead of a single general case, and by applying parametric substitutions.

Let us discuss assumption selection first. It is quite likely that some assumptions in A are more useful than others for verifying a goal $g(v)$. In practice we have found that a simple and useful strategy is to look for overlap in the support of BDD variables, and to pick assumptions sharing at least one variable with the goal. This heuristic is incomplete, but in our experience two or three iterations of assumption selection using the rule, each followed by the application of the selected assumptions to the goal, are very likely to pick all relevant assumptions. If we are unable to verify the goal at this stage, it is better to give up and give the user an opportunity to analyze the problem, rather than continue applying more assumptions, which will quickly cause a BDD blowup.

In which order should assumptions be applied? A heuristic we have found consistently useful is to look for assumptions that are as specific to the goal as possible. For example, if a goal talks about a particular data element in a table, assumptions about the same data element are preferable to assumptions about some other data element. To automate the heuristic, we statically classify BDD variables into a number of increasingly specific buckets, for example to reset/control/pointer/data variables, and prioritize assumptions based on the bucket the variables shared with the goal belong to. The more specific the bucket with the shared variables, the earlier the assumption should be used.

Selection, ordering and other similar heuristics can be fully automated, and they allow verification of many goals without user intervention. Nevertheless, the larger the assumption set is, the easier it is for a mechanism to pick useless assumptions, leading to BDD blow-ups. The verifier also often knows roughly what assumptions would be likely to contribute to a goal. After all, the verifier has written the constraints and typically has a reason for believing why they hold. Therefore it is beneficial to allow the verifier to customize a strategy for a goal. The degree of customization may vary. In some instances, the user may just want to guide the heuristics. In others, the user may want to completely control the strategy down to the level of an individual assumption.

Our second area for complexity reduction, i.e. case splitting and parametric substitutions, are needed because we encounter goals for which BDD's are incomputable within the limits of the current machines. For example, the BDD for a goal about table elements in a range determined by control bits and pointers reflects both the circuit logic for all the relevant entities and the calculation of the constraint itself. Case splitting also allows us to use different verification strategies for different cases. For example, the reason an invariant holds might depend on an operating mode, and one would like to write different verification strategies for different modes.

Parametric substitutions are a well-understood technique [13] with direct library support in Forte. The essence of the parametric representation is to encode a Boolean predicate P as a vector of Boolean functions whose range is exactly the set of truth assignments satisfying P. Then, if one wants to verify a statement of the type $P \Rightarrow Q$, one can instead verify the statement Q' obtained from Q by replacing all occurrences of variables of P in Q by the corresponding parametric representations. This allow us to evaluate a goal and required assumptions only in scenarios where the parameterized restriction holds, never evaluating the constrains in full generality.

To apply the various heuristics and human-guided techniques, a user needs a flexible way to direct the verification of a goal. We formulate the task as a specialized tableau system refining sequents $A \vdash_v G$, intuitively "A implies goal G under valuation v", where

concr $$\frac{A \vdash_v g}{A \vdash_v [] \rhd g(v)}$$

choose(*sel*) $$\frac{A \vdash_v [] \rhd g}{A \setminus elems(A_s) \vdash_v A_s \rhd g} \quad \text{where } A_s = sel(A, v, g) \text{ and } elems(A_s) \subseteq A$$

apply $$\frac{A \vdash_v [a_1, a_2, \ldots a_n] \rhd g}{A \vdash_v [a_2, \ldots a_n] \rhd (a_1(v) \Rightarrow g)}$$

split(*S*) $$\frac{A \vdash_v g}{A \cup \{c_1\} \vdash_v g \;\ldots\; A \cup \{c_n\} \vdash_v g \quad A \vdash_v (c_1 \vee' \ldots \vee' c_n)} \quad \text{where } \{c_1, \ldots c_n\} = S \subseteq Constr$$

psplit(*S*) $$\frac{A \vdash_v g}{A \vdash_{v1} g \;\ldots\; A \vdash_{vn} g \quad A \vdash_v (c_1 \vee' \ldots \vee' c_n)} \quad \text{where } \{c_1, \ldots c_n\} = S \subseteq Constr \text{ and } vi = \lambda x.param(c_i(v))(v(x))$$

where $[]$ is the empty list, $sel(A, v, g)$ is a function returning a list of constraints in A, $elems(A)$ the set of elements of list A, $a \vee' b \equiv_{df} \lambda x.a(x) \vee b(x)$, and $param(c, b)$ for a function that computes a parametric substitution corresponding to $c \in bool$ and applies the substitution to $b \in bool$.

Fig. 1. Implication verification tableau rules

$A \subseteq Constr$ and $v \in Val$, and the right side G is either an uninstantiated goal $g \in Constr$, or an instantiated goal $[a_1, \ldots a_n] \rhd g$, where $a_1, \ldots a_n \in Constr$ and $g \in bool$. The tableau rules are listed in Figure 1. We consider a leaf of a tableau *good*, if it is an instantiated sequent where the goal is true, i.e. of the type $A \vdash_v As \rhd T$. It is easy to see that if there exists a tableau with root $A \vdash_v g$ and only good leaves, then $\bigwedge_{a \in A} a(v) \Rightarrow g(v)$.

To verify a goal, the user describes a strategy for building a tableau. Basic strategy steps describe case splits and selection functions for the *choose* rule. They can be combined with looping, sequencing and stop constructs. Trusted code then builds a tableau on the basis of the strategy, using the *apply* and *concr* rules automatically. The process provides constant feedback: which strategies are used, which assumptions are applied, what the BDD sizes are, etc. This allows the user to quickly focus on a problem, when one occurs. The code also stores aside intermediate results to facilitate counterexample analysis later on. In our experience, this approach to user interaction leads to a good combination of human guidance and automation. Many goals can be verified completely automatically with a heuristic default strategy, and user guidance can be added incrementally to overcome complexity barriers in more complex goals.

The tableau rules have evolved during a significant amount of practical work, and although they may look peculiar at first sight, they reflect key empirical learnings from that work. For example, we consciously keep the *choose* and *apply* rules separate, although a more elegant system could be obtained by replacing them with a single rule picking an assumption from A and applying it. The reason for this is that the selection process usually involves iteration over elements of A, which becomes a bottleneck if done too often, and so in practice it is better to select and order a collection of assumptions at once. Similarly, distinguishing uninstantiated and instantiated goals reflects the need to postpone the time when BDD evaluation happens.

4 BUS Recycle Logic

Recycle logic forms a key component of the Bus cluster in Pentium 4, the logical portion of the processor enabling communication with other components of a computer system (for an overview of Pentium 4 micro-architecture, see [11]). The Bus cluster communicates with the processor's Memory Execution cluster, which processes data loads and stores and instruction requests from the execution units, and passes requests to the Bus cluster as needed. The Bus cluster includes the Bus sequencing unit (BSU) which is the centralized transaction manager to handle all the transactions that communicate between the core and the External Bus Controller (EBC). The BSU consists of an arbiter unit and two queues: the Bus L1 Queue (BSL1Q) to track requests through the Level 1 cache pipelines and the Bus Sequencing Queue (BSQ) to manage transactions that need to go to the EBC or the Programmable Interrupt Controller.

All requests travel through the arbiter unit. If a request is granted, Level 1 Cache and the BSL1Q both receive it. If the Level 1 Cache satisfies the request, BSL1Q can drop the request after allocating it. Otherwise the request stays in the BSL1Q for some time and then moves to the BSQ when the BSQ has all the resources to accept it. For every granted cacheable request, the BUS recycle logic initiates an address match against all outstanding requests residing in the BSL1Q and the BSQ queues. If the incoming request has a conflict with an existing request in the queues or in the pipeline ahead of it, it is recycled and the issuing agent will need to reissue the request. For simplicity we can assume that there are two types of requests: READ and WRITE requests.

The recycle logic is intended to guarantee that no two requests with conflicts should reside in the BSL1Q or the BSQ. This is essential to avoid data corruption and to maintain the cache coherency. One such conflict is between two cacheable READ requests: no two cacheable READ requests with the same address should reside in the BSL1Q and BSQ. Let v_i, r_i and $addr_i$ stand for the signals containing the valid bit, cacheable read bit and the address vector in BSQ. We consider all the signals at the same moment, without relative timing offsets, and write just v_i for the timed signal $(v_i, 0)$. Let i and j be indices pointing to different entries in the BSQ, and define the constraint $R(i, j)$ as the function mapping a valuation v to:

$$v(v_i) \wedge v(r_i) \wedge v(v_j) \wedge v(r_j) \Rightarrow v(A_i) \neq v(A_j)$$

The specification I_{spec} consists of constraints $R(i, j)$ over all pairs of different entries in BSQ, similar constraints comparing all pairs of different BSL1Q entries, and a set of constraints comparing pairs with one element in BSQ and the other in BSL1Q.

Showing that I_{spec} is satisfied in the base case, after a global reset, is trivial, as reset clears all the valid bits. However, in general we have found it valuable to run the base case step early, since it is usually a computationally cheap and quick sanity check.

The inductive step fails immediately for I_{spec} for several reasons:

- I_{spec} does not contain any information on what needs to happen when a new request comes into the pipeline and its address matches with the addresses of existing entries in the BSL1Q and the BSQ.
- The recycle logic powers down when there is no request in the pipeline and no valid entry in the Bus queues, but I_{spec} contains no information about the power-up logic.

- I_{spec} does not capture any conditions involving requests moving from BSL1Q to BSQ. It also does not contain any information on the request-acknowledgement protocol between BSL1Q and BSQ.
- Address match computation is done over several cycles, and I_{spec} does not capture the relation of already computed partial information to the actual addresses.

We strengthened I_{spec} by adding constraints which capture the conditions mentioned above along with several others, and arrived at I_{ind}. This was an iterative process and required low level circuit knowledge. At each step of the iteration, new BDD variables were introduced and placed in the existing variable ordering based on the knowledge of the circuit. For example, variables related to the power-up logic were placed highest, those related to control logic next, and variables related to the address bits were interleaved and placed at the bottom. This provided a good initial order which was occasionally fine tuned. We reached an inductive I_{ind} after some fifty iterations of adding new constraints based on debugging the failure of the previous attempt.

The logic we verified consists of about 3000 state elements and is clearly beyond the capacity of model-checkers which compute reachable states of the circuit. The entire verification task took about three person months. The BDD complexity was not very high, peaking at about 10M BDD nodes, and the peak memory consumption during the entire verification session did not exceed 1M. The recycle logic had undergone intensive simulation-based validation and our verification did not uncover new bugs. However, we artificially introduced some high quality bugs found earlier into the design and were able to reproduce them with ease.

5 Register Renaming

The Intel NetBurst® micro-architecture of the Pentium 4 processor contains an out-of-order execution engine. Before reaching the engine, architecturally visible instructions have been translated to micro-operations (μops) in the Front End of the processor, and these μops have been sent to the out-of-order engine by the Micro-Sequencer (MS). The out-of-order engine consists of the Allocation, Renaming, and Scheduling functions. This part of the machine re-orders μops to allow them to execute as quickly as their input operands are ready. It can have up to 126 μops in flight at a time.

The register renaming logic renames the logical IA-32 registers such as EAX onto the processors 128-entry physical register file. This allows the small, 8-entry, architecturally defined IA-32 register file to be dynamically expanded to use the 128 physical registers in the Register File (RF) to remove false conflicts between μops. The renaming logic remembers the most current version of each register in the Register Alias Table (RAT) so that a new μop coming down the pipeline can translate its logical sources (lsrcs) to physical sources (psrcs).

The Allocator logic allocates many of the machine resources needed by each μop, and sends μops to scheduling and execution. During allocation, a sequence number is assigned to each μop, indicating its relative age. The sequence number points to an entry in the Reorder Buffer (ROB) array, which tracks the the completion status of the μop. The Allocator allocates one of the 128 physical registers for the physical destination data (pdst) of the μop. The Register File (RF) entry is allocated from a separate list of available registers, known as the Trash Heap (TH), not sequentially like the ROB entries. The Allocator maintains a data structure called the Allocation Free List (ALF), effectively a patch list that keeps track of the binding of logical to physical destinations done at μop allocation. Both ROB and ALF have 126 entries. The lists are filled in a round-robin fashion, with head and tail pointers. The head pointer points to the index of next μop to be allocated, and the tail pointer to the index of the next μop to be retired.

When the Allocator receives a new μop with logical sources and destination, it grabs a free physical register from the Trash Heap (TH), updating TH in the process, associates the new pdst with the ldst of the μop in RAT, stores the ldst and old and new pdst in ALF at head pointer location, moves head pointer to next location, and sends the μop to scheduling with the psrcs and pdst. The μops are retired in-order by the ROB. When a μop retires, the Allocator returns the old pdst of the retired μop into Trash Heap.

Events are also detected and signalled by ROB at μop retirement. When an event occurs, we need to restore RAT back to where it was when the eventing μop was allocated. This is done on the basis of the information in the ALF: effectively one needs to undo the changes to RAT recorded in ALF, and to return the new pdsts of all the younger μops to the Trash Heap. In the same way, when a branch misprediction occurs, the RAT needs to be restored to the state where it was when the mispredicting μop was allocated. For branch misprediction recovery, the Allocator interacts with the Jump Execution Unit (JEU) and the Checker-Replay unit (CRU), and maintains a data structure called Branch Tracking Buffer (BTB) keeping track of all branch μops in the machine, and whether they are correctly resolved.

The renaming protocol has several sources of complexity. For example, up to three μops are allocated or retired at a time, there can be multiple active branch mispredictions in different stages at the same time, and after a misprediction recovery, allocation starts without waiting for all the previous μops to retire. The RTL implementation of the protocol is highly optimized and consists of several tens of thousands of code lines. It also has a number of implementation-specific complications. For example, instead of one ALF head pointer, there are eight different versions of it, all with their own control logic, and in total, there are over forty pointers to ALF. Many one-step state updates of the abstract level also spread over multiple cycles in the implementation.

It is easy to come up with various expected properties of the protocol, e.g. that two logical registers should never be mapped to the same physical register in the RAT. However, to understand precisely what is expected of the register renaming logic and how it interacts with scheduling and retirement, we wanted to describe the out-of-order mechanism as a whole. We formalized a simple in-order execution model, a non-deterministic high-level model (HLM) of the out-of-order engine with register renaming, and sketched down an argument showing that the out-of-order model should produce the same results as the simple model, when one considers the stream of retiring μops. While both models were written down precisely, the argument connecting the two was not done with full rigour. The primary goal was to guarantee that our specification of the renaming protocol was based on a complete picture.

The actual target of our verification effort was to establish that the behaviours produced by the Allocator, including ALF, TH, BTB and RAT, are consistent with a high level model of the rename logic. The HLM has about 200 lines of code describing the

```
lettype mhs_t =
      MARBLE_HLM_STATE
        { h :: bv_widx_t }                   // ALF head pointer
        { btb :: ( int -> bool ) }           // BTB array
        { brgoodv :: ( int -> bool ) }       // input from CRU:: brgood valid
        { brgood :: ( int -> bv_widx_t ) } // input from CRU:: brgood uop
        ...
let head_trans_cond ( s, s') =
    ( do_alloc s ) => ( s':>h = s:>h +% 3 ) | ( s':>h = s:>h )
    ;
let do_good_idx i s =
    Exists_list [ gi | CHANNELS ] .
      ( s:>brgoodv gi ) AND ( widx2idx ( s:>brgood gi ) '= i )
    ;
let btb_trans_cond i ( s, s') =
    s':>btb i =
    ( ( do_alloc_idx i s )
      => ( s:>uopjmp ( idx2bank i ) )
       | ( ( do_good_idx i s ) => F | ( s:>btb i ) )
    );
...
```

Fig. 2. Parts of register renaming HLM

```
let btb_abs n2v t i =
    let alloc213        = n2v allocateokm213h t in
    let hr              = wrow2row ( head_th_old_wrow TH0 n2v t ) in
    let alloc213_i      = alloc213 AND ( hr '= idx2row i ) in
    let goodbrseq271 c = ptr2idx_bv ( V n2v ( goodbrseqnumCm271h c ) t ) in
    let goodbr271_i c  = ( n2v ( crcgoodbrCm271h c ) t ) AND ( goodbrseq271 c '= i ) in
    // Is there a stage 213 write to this index?
    alloc213_i
    => // If so, the real values are waiting to be written into the FLM
        ( btb_alloc_213 n2v t i )
     | ( // Is there a stage 271 clear to this index?
         // If so, the real value is F, else the real values are in the BTB
         ( Exists_list [ c | CHANNELS ] . goodbr271_i c )
         => F | ( btb_raw n2v t i )
       );
...
```

Fig. 3. Parts of RTL-to-HLM abstraction mapping

```
let head_consistent_213_cond n2v t =
    let aok = n2v allocateokm213h t         in
    let uopv u = n2v ( aluopvUm213h u ) t in
    aok = ( Exists_list [ u | UOPS ] . uopv u )
    ;
let mpred_m_iqjeseq_btb_cons_cond ch d idx n2v t =
    let mbrclear = mjmp_clear_ch_d ch d n2v t in
    let iqjeseq = widx2idx ( iqjeseq_widx ( JUMP_BRCLEAR_DELAY + d ) ch n2v t ) in
    let btb_bit = btb_entry idx TH0 n2v t in
    ( mbrclear AND ( iqjeseq '= idx ) )
    ==>
    ( btb_bit = T );
...
```

Fig. 4. Some consistency invariants

transition relation. The HLM state is defined as an FL abstract data-type. Parts of the HLM are shown in Figure 2. They specify that the head pointer either stays put or moves by three steps, based on whether new μops are allocated, and that the BTB bit is set for branch μops at allocation and cleared based on an indication from CRU. In the verification, the HLM is compared against a full circuit model, combined with an abstract environment circuit. Figure 3 shows a part of the RTL-to-HLM abstraction mapping for a BTB entry. Since the RTL takes multiple cycles for a single-step HLM update, the abstraction function looks at intermediate values when the RTL is in the middle of an update.

We started the verification by determining the sets of timed signals for the invariant sig_{inv} and the proof input boundary sig_{ext}. Together the sets have about 15000 signals. We determined them initially manually, later with automated circuit traversal routines. The advantage of the manual process is that it forces the user to gain a detailed understanding of the RTL behaviour early. The work took several months. After the determination of signals, the simulation steps were quite easy and could be done in a matter of days. We used a relatively coarse static BDD ordering, with reset signals on top, followed by other control signals, interleaved pointer signal vectors and interleaved data signal vectors. The largest individual BDD's in STE simulation have only about 30k nodes, and the complete simulation uses less than 10M BDD nodes.

By far the hardest part of the verification was the determination of a strong enough inductive invariant I_{ind}. In the end, the invariant contains just over 20000 constraints, instantiated from 390 templates. The primary method for deriving the invariant was counterexample analysis. Constraints were added incrementally to prevent circuit behaviour that either failed to conform with the HLM or violated parts of the invariant introduced earlier. The precise content of the added constraints was based on human understanding of the intended circuit behaviour, aided by design annotations and by observing simulation behaviour. During the work, the verifier would typically add a collection of interdependent invariants related to some particular aspect of circuit functionality, e.g. allocation logic, at a time. In the intermediate stages of the work the tentative invariant would have quite accurate description of some functional aspects of circuit behaviour, but leave the yet uncovered aspects unconstrained. Figure 4 contains a few example constraints: a simple relation between some allocation control signals, and a requirement that the BTB bit corresponding to a mispredicted branch μop must be set. The hardest systematic problem in the invariant determination was that some basic properties depend on complex global protocols, which makes it hard to build the invariants incrementally from bottom up. Another common theme is the don't-care space for an invariant. Typically it is easy to see that a certain relation is needed, but determining precisely when it is needed and when it holds can be challenging. The large majority of the invariants are quite natural. Exceptions are constraints that are needed for proper behaviour but hold unintentionally, such as implicit synchronization between different parts of design. In the process of invariant determination, the capability for rapid experimentation and the quick feedback provided by the Forte toolset were highly valuable.

For verification of the invariants we used the full arsenal of techniques discussed in Section 3. Most control invariants were verified automatically, and combinations of user-guided and heuristic strategies were used for pointer and data invariants. Case splitting with parametric substitutions was particularly useful for invariants that relate a pointer and the data it points to, as it allowed us to consider each possible value in the pointer range separately. The largest individual BDD's in the verification had about 20M nodes, and the total usage peaked at about 100M nodes.

The verification took about two person-years of work, part of which was attributable to methodology development. Prior to the current effort, several person-years of work had gone into an attempt to verify the protocol using traditional temporal logic model checking and assume-guarantee reasoning. While achieving partial results, the effort looked unlikely to converge, which led to the adoption of the current approach. During the work we found two subtle bugs in the design. They had escaped dynamic testing and found their way into silicon, but did not cause functional failures in the current design as they were masked in the context of the whole processor. However, they constituted 'time bombs' that could have gone off on future proliferation products.

6 Conclusion

We have discussed a practical methodology which has allowed us to extend the scope of full formal verification to systems that are several magnitudes beyond the limits of current tools based on traditional temporal logic model checking [8]. In our experience the approach is widely applicable. In addition to the cases here, we have used it e.g. to verify bypass and cache behaviour. The approach is based on well-known techniques: BDD's [5] and STE [10]. In a sense, in building our strategy on human-produced invariants, we are going back to basics in verification methods [6, 9, 17].

The verification is computationally manageable, but requires a great deal of human guidance, and a detailed understanding of the design. On the other hand, in our experience any formal verification on a large design requires both of these, so the current approach is no different. Furthermore, the approach does automate a large portion of the task. We believe that completely user-guided verification, such as pure theorem proving, would be infeasible on designs of the size we are dealing with.

Another approach to induction-based verification is to use SAT instead of BDD's [21]. We carried out some experiments, and for many goals, the implication verification could be done automatically with common SAT engines, but for others, the engines failed to reach a conclusion. This leads us to believe that replacing BDD's with SAT is a plausible, maybe in some respects superior approach, but it will also require the creation of a methodology and a tool interface to allow a human to flexibly guide the tool around computational problems, analogous to the role of BDD tableaux used here. Fully automated SAT-checking can of course be used very effectively as a model exploration method on large designs [3, 7], but used in this way, it does not provide the kind of full coverage that in our opinion is one of the compelling advantages of formal verification.

There is a large body of work examining automated discovery of invariants [1, 2, 4, 12, 22]. Here we have concentrated on a simpler, nearly orthogonal task: given a collection of invariants, how to verify them. An automatic method for invariant discovery can of course help and is compatible with our approach, but does not remove the need for verification. Our work also has a number of similarities with formal equivalence verification [15, 16], but the distance between RTL and HLM is larger here.

Finally, given the amount of human effort required for full formal verification, does it make sense to pursue it at all? We believe it does for two reasons. First, full formal verification can provide far higher guarantees of correctness than any competing method. Secondly, it has been our experience that once a robust, practical solution to a verification problem has been found, the effort needed for similar future verification tasks falls dramatically.

Acknowledgements. I would like to thank Khurram Sajid for joint work on the BUS protocol, the numerous participants of the earlier register renaming verification efforts and Robert Jones for many useful discussions, and Tom Schubert for the opportunity to carry out this work.

References

1. S. Bensalem and Y. Lakhnech. Automatic generation of invariants. *Form. Methods Syst. Des.*, 15(1):75–92, 1999.
2. S. Bensalem, Y. Lakhnech, and S. Owre. InVeST: A tool for the verification of invariants. In *CAV '98, Proceedings*, pages 505–510. Springer-Verlag, 1998.
3. P. Bjesse, T. Leonard, and A. Mokkedem. Finding bugs in an alpha microprocessor using satisfiability solvers. In *CAV '01, Proceedings*, pages 454–464. Springer-Verlag, 2001.
4. N. Bjørner, A. Browne, and Z. Manna. Automatic generation of invariants and intermediate assertions. *Theor. Comput. Sci.*, 173(1):49–87, 1997.
5. R. E. Bryant. Graph-based algorithms for boolean function manipulation. *IEEE Trans. on Comp.*, C-35(8):677–691, Aug. 1986.
6. R. Burstall. Program proving as hand simulation with a little induction. In *Information Processing*, pages 308 – 312. North Holland Publishing Company, aug 1974.
7. F. Copty, L. Fix, R. Fraer, E. Giunchiglia, G. Kamhi, A. Tacchella, and M. Y. Vardi. Benefits of bounded model checking at an industrial setting. In *CAV '01*, pages 436–453. Springer.
8. J. Edmund M. Clarke, O. Grumberg, and D. A. Peled. *Model checking.* MIT Press, 1999.
9. R. W. Floyd. Assigning meaning to programs. In *Proceedings of Symposium in Applied Mathematics*, volume 19, pages 19–32. American Mathematical Society, 1967.
10. S. Hazelhurst and C.-J. H. Seger. Symbolic trajectory evaluation. In T. Kropf, editor, *Formal Hardware Verification*, chapter 1, pages 3–78. Springer Verlag; New York, 1997.
11. Hinton, G., Sager, D., Upton, M., Boggs, D., Carmean, D, Kyker, A. and Roussel, P. The microarchitecture of the Pentium 4 processor. *Intel Technology Journal*, Q1, Feb. 2001.
12. R. Jeffords and C. Heitmeyer. Automatic generation of state invariants from requirements specifications. In *SIGSOFT '98/FSE-6, Proceedings*, pages 56–69. ACM Press, 1998.
13. R. B. Jones. *Symbolic Simulation Methods for Industrial Formal Verification.* Kluwer Academic Publishers, 2002.
14. R. Kaivola and K. Kohatsu. Proof engineering in the large: formal verification of Pentium 4 floating-point divider. *Int'l J. on Software Tools for Technology Transfer*, 4:323–334, 2003.
15. Z. Khasidashvili, J. Moondanos, D. Kaiss, and Z. Hanna. An enhanced cut-points algorithm in formal equivalence verification. In *HLDVT '01*, page 171. IEEE, 2001.
16. H. H. Kwak, I.-H. Moon, J. H. Kukula, and T. R. Shiple. Combinational equivalence checking through function transformation. In *ICCAD '02*, pages 526–533. ACM, 2002.
17. Z. Manna and A. Pnueli. *Temporal verification of reactive systems: safety.* Springer-Verlag New York, Inc., 1995.
18. L. Paulson. *ML for the Working Programmer,.* Cambridge University Press, 1996.

19. T. Schubert. High level formal verification of next-generation microprocessors. In *DAC '03: Proceedings of the 40th conference on Design automation*, pages 1–6. ACM Press, 2003.
20. C.-J. H. Seger and R. E. Bryant. Formal verification by symbolic evaluation of partially-ordered trajectories. *Formal Methods in System Design*, 6(2):147–189, Mar. 1995.
21. M. Sheeran, S. Singh, and G. Stålmarck. Checking safety properties using induction and a sat-solver. In *FMCAD '00*, pages 108–125. Springer-Verlag, 2000.
22. A. Tiwari, H. Rueß, H. Saïdi, and N. Shankar. A technique for invariant generation. In *TACAS 2001*, pages 113–127. Springer-Verlag, 2001.

Formal Verification of Backward Compatibility of Microcode*

Tamarah Arons[1], Elad Elster[2], Limor Fix[1], Sela Mador-Haim[3], Michael Mishaeli[2], Jonathan Shalev[1], Eli Singerman[1], Andreas Tiemeyer[1], Moshe Y. Vardi[4], and Lenore D. Zuck[5]

[1] Design Technology, Intel Corporation
firstname.lastname@intel.com
[2] Mobile Micro-processor Group, Intel Corp.
firstname.lastname@intel.com
[3] Technion, Israel
selam@cs.technion.ac.il
[4] Rice University
vardi@cs.rice.edu
[5] University of Illinois at Chicago
lenore@cs.uic.edu

Abstract. Microcode is used to facilitate new technologies in Intel CPU designs. A critical requirement is that new designs be backwardly compatible with legacy code when new functionalities are disabled. Several features distinguish microcode from other software systems, such as: interaction with the external environment, sensitivity to exceptions, and the complexity of instructions. This work describes the ideas behind MICROFORMAL, a technology for fully automated formal verification of functional backward compatibility of microcode.

1 Introduction

The performance and functionality requirements from current CISC (Complex Instruction Set Computing) CPUs mandate a dual-layer design. While the external (architectural) appearance is that of a CISC CPU, the internal mechanisms employ RISC (Reduced Instruction Set Computing) methodologies. A microcode layer captures the architectural intent of the processor and translates between the architecture and the hardware layer, which contains the microarchitectural implementation details [Sta02].

Improvements in successive generations of CPU designs are measured not only in terms of performance improvements, but also in functional enhancements, such as security (e.g., LaGrande technology), hardware virtualization (e.g., Vanderpool technology), and the like. A significant portion of the implementation of such new functionalities is done in microcode. Thus, a mature architecture such as the IA32 is accompanied by a large base of microcode, which is essentially very low-level software.

* This research was supported in part by SRC grant 2004-TJ-1256, NSF grants CCF-0456163, CCR-9988322, CCR-0124077, CCR-0311326, IIS-9908435, IIS-9978135, EIA-0086264, ANI-0216467, BSF grant 9800096, and by Texas ATP grant 003604-0058-2003.

K. Etessami and S.K. Rajamani (Eds.): CAV 2005, LNCS 3576, pp. 185–198, 2005.

When adding new functionality to an existing CPU design, the validation team faces a major verification challenge of ensuring backward functional compatibility, to guarantee that legacy software in the marketplace works without changes on the new CPU. Since functionality enhancement is often implemented in microcode, this verification challenge has to be met at the microcode level.

In this paper we describe MICROFORMAL, design technology being developed at Intel to automatically and formally verify the functional backward compatibility of microcode.

There is scant work on formal verification at the microcode level. Several papers describe efforts to prove that the microarchitectural level of a microprocessor implements correctly the instruction-set architecture [Cyr93, SM96, SH02]. The approach of these works is that of computer-aided deduction, while we are seeking a more automated solution. Furthermore, our focus is on functional compatibility between successive generations of microcode, which we refer to as *source* and *target*. Closer to our work is the automated equivalence verification approach, as applied, for example, in [CHRF00, HUK00, FH02, CKY03]. These works aim to prove equivalence of low-level code with higher-level code, using symbolic execution and automated decision procedures. (We note that while equivalence verification is a common verification technique nowadays [HC98], its industrial application is generally limited to hardware.)

Automated equivalence verification has also been successfully applied to *translation validation*, which is an automated verification technique for showing that target code, generated by an automatic translator (e.g., an optimizing compiler) accurately translates source code. Rather than proving the correctness of the *translator* itself, the translation-validation approach attempts to prove the correctness of each *translation* separately, by proving the equivalence of the source and target codes, using symbolic execution and automated decision procedures [PSS98, Nec00, ZPFG03].

Our work differs from these works in several aspects. The first difference is that our focus is not on equivalence, but rather on backward compatibility. Nevertheless, we show that equivalence verification techniques are applicable here. We define *backward compatibility of target with source* as equivalence under restrictions that disable the new functionalities. We view this as an important conceptual contribution, as the problem of backward compatibility under functionality enhancements is quite common. For example, when adding features to the telephony systems, users who do not subscribe to the new features or have instruments that do not support the new features, should notice no change when the system is upgraded.

A second, and more challenging difference is our focus on microcode. While microcode is software, it is extremely "machine aware", as execution of microcode is heavily dependent on the microarchitectural state. Previous applications of equivalence verification to software, for example, in translation validation, typically consider *closed systems* that do not interact with their environment (except for initial and final I/O). In order to make this approach applicable to microcode, we have to make the dependence of the microcode on the microarchitectural state, as well as the effect that the microcode has on this state, explicit. Furthermore, we assume that the microarchitectural state does not essentially change during the execution of the microcode, unless explicitly modified by the microcode. This assumption matches the intuition of microcode designers. (An alternative approach would be to consider microcode as a *reactive system* [HP85]. This would make the verification task considerably harder, as defining equivalence of programs in fully open environments is rather nontrivial [AHKV98].)

In addition to considering interactions with the environment, at the microcode level, executions leading to exceptions are considered normal and can terminate in many different states. Thus, in our framework, we need to deal with exceptions in a rather elaborate way and define equivalence to mean that the rich exception structure is preserved. In contrast, prior works did not report on handling exceptions, cf. [Nec00]. The need to model interactions with the environment and executions that terminate in exceptions poses a nontrivial challenge to the application of automated equivalence verification to the problem of microcode backward compatibility. Furthermore, the need to apply the technique to industrial problems of today's scale and complexity poses another formidable challenge.

Our approach is also considerably different from recent approaches to formal property verification of software, where both theory and practice have been gaining momentum. Recent tools include SLAM [BR02], BLAST [HJMS03] and others. A common feature of these works is the focus on abstracting data away as much as possible. In microcode, the data types are simpler than those in higher-level software, but control flow and data flow are tightly integrated, so standard abstraction techniques, such as predicate abstraction, are not easily applicable.

One challenge in developing generic tools for microcode verification is the complexity and variability of the instruction sets of modern microprocessor designs. Rather than work directly with microcode, our tool uses an intermediate representation language (IRL) that is general and is suitable for a wide family of low-level languages. The translation between the actual code and IRL is accomplished by means of *templates*, where each template consists of IRL code that is operationally equivalent to a microinstruction. IRL can also be used to provide microcode with formal semantics and drive microcode emulators.

Once both source and target are translated into IRL, they are processed by MICROFORMAL, which constructs the verification conditions (VCs). The VCs are checked by a validity checker. Their validity establishes that the target is backwardly compatible with the source. Failure to establish validity produces a counterexample in the form of input values that causes the behaviors of source and target to diverge.

A major obstacle to the success of our methodology is the complexity of checking the VCs. Since we are dealing with low-level code, the correctness is expressed in terms of bit vectors. Unfortunately, to date, there are no efficient validity checkers that handle bit vectors, and we are forced to reduce bit vectors to bit level and use a propositional validity checker (i.e., a SAT solver). Another problem is the size of the VCs: even for relatively small microprograms (several hundred lines), the size of the VCs is often prohibitively large, i.e., beyond the capacity of most validity checkers. We use various simplification techniques, such as decomposition and symbolic pruning, to make verification practically feasible.

2 Modeling Microcode

Microprograms are essentially low-level, machine-oriented programs with a sequential control flow. The basic, atomic statements of microprograms are microinstructions. These are implemented in hardware and executed by various units of the CPU. The basic data types of microprograms are registers (architectural, control and temporary). A microinstruction can be thought of as a function that (typically) gets two register arguments, performs some computation and assigns the result to a third register.

The control flow of microprograms is facilitated by `jump-to-label` instructions, where the labels appear in the program or indicate a call to an external procedure. It is possible to have indirect jumps, in which case the target label resides in a register and is known only at run time.

The semantics of microinstructions involves both the variables that appear in the instructions and several other auxiliary variables that reflect the status of the hardware. In addition to the explicit effect of microprograms on their hardware environment via microinstructions, microprograms also have implicit interaction with hardware by reading/setting various shared machine-state variables (e.g., memory, special control bits for signaling microarchitectural events, etc.). The latter is used for governing the microarchitectural state and is mostly modeled as side-effects (not visible in the microprogram source code) of specific microinstructions.

The first challenge in applying formal verification to microcode is defining a suitable intermediate representation. We need a way to fully capture the functional behavior of microprograms, including the microinstructions they employ. To that end we have introduced a new modeling language, which we call IRL– Intermediate Representation Language. IRL is expressive enough to describe the behavior of microprograms and their interaction with the hardware environment at the "right" abstraction level, yet its sequential semantics is simple enough to reason about with formal tools.

IRL is a simple programming language that has bits and bit vectors as its basic data types. IRL basic statements are conditional assignments and `gotos`. Vector expressions in IRL are generated by applying a rich set of bit-vector operations (e.g. logical, arithmetic, shift, concatenation and sub-vector extraction operations) to bit-vector arguments. IRL has the following characteristics:

1. Simple, easy to read and understand with a well-defined semantics;
2. Generic, extendible, and maintainable. It is a formalism that is not tied up to the microcode language of a specific CPU;
3. Explicit. That is, all operations of a microprogram can be explicitly represented, with no implicit side effects;
4. Can be the target of a compiler from native microcode.

To make it convenient to (automatically) translate microprograms to IRL and to bridge the gap between native microcode and IRL, we coupled IRL with a *template* mechanism by which each microinstruction has a corresponding IRL template. The template signature represents the formal arguments of a microinstruction and its body is a sequence of (plain) IRL statements that compute the effect of the microinstruction and store the result in the designated argument. In addition, each template's body also reflects the side effects of a microinstruction computation by updating the relevant auxiliary variables.

The template language includes convenient abstract data types, such as structures and enumeration, and coding aids such as *if-then-else* and case statements. These constructs make the code easier to read and maintain. During translation these constructs are transformed into basic IRL.

Fig. 1 presents a small microcode-like example that illustrates some basic features of microcode. There, a value is read from a location in memory determined by the `memory_read` parameters (address and offset) and the result added to another value. Registers, as used in the example, are bitvectors of width 64. The memory is an array `array[32][64] memory`. That is, an address space of 32 bits is mapped to entries of 64 bits. The `zeroFlag` variable is a a single bit zero flag.

```
BEGIN_FLOW(example) {
  reg1 := memory_read(reg2, reg3);
  reg4 := add(reg1, reg5);
};
```

Fig. 1. A simple program

Each of the two operations are defined by a template. The `add` template is described in Fig. 2. The template has three formal parameters, corresponding to the two input registers and the target register of the microinstruction (Fig. 1). The first parameter of a template is the target variable, which is instantiated with the variable on the left-hand side of the assignment (`reg4` in our case). Note that a side effect of the add microinstruction— setting `zeroFlag`— is specified explicitly in the template. (For simplicity, we ignore the possibility of add overflow.)

```
template uop_add(register result,
 register src1, register src2) {
 result := src1 + src2;
 zeroFlag := (result = 0);
};
```

Fig. 2. A template for `add`

The `memory_read` microinstruction (Fig. 3) is somewhat more complex and includes a possible exception. The address is calculated as `tmp_address + offset`. If this is out of the memory address range of 32 bits, then an `address_overflow` exception is signalled. Exceptions are a normal part of microprograms, and are modeled as executions at the end of which various parameters are checked. If no exception occurs, the memory contents at this address are placed in register result and the system bit `found_valid_address` is set to true. Such "side-effects" are typical of microinstructions – an intrinsic part of their functionality is that they read and set global system bits. In this example the microcode is translated to the (basic) IRL program of Fig. 4.

```
exception address_overflow(bit[32]);
template uop_memory_read(register result,
                register tmp_address, register offset) {
  TMP0 := tmp_address + offset;
  if (TMP0 > 0xFFFFFFFF)
     exit address_overflow(TMP0[63:32]);
  result := memory[TMP0[31:0]];
  zeroFlag := (result = 0);
  found_valid_address := 1;
};
```

Fig. 3. Simple memory_read template

```
1. entry (reg1, reg2, reg3, reg4, reg5, memory, pc);
2. TMP0 := reg2 + reg3;
3. (TMP0 > 0xFFFFFFFF) ? exit address_overflow(TMP0[63:32]);
4. reg1 := memory[TMP0[31:0]];
5. zeroFlag := (reg1 = 0);
6. found_valid_address := 1;
7. reg4 := reg1 + reg5;
8. zeroFlag := (reg4 = 0);
9. exit end (found_valid_address, reg1, reg2, memory);
```

Fig. 4. Basic IRL for the original program: Numbered statements

Note that the address_overflow exit has a parameter of type bit[32]. In general, an exit has parameters defining the *observables* at this exit. Similarly, observables have to be defined also for the entry and for the end exit. When defining backward compatibility we need to ensure that, when run under the same conditions, the source and target microprograms would reach the same type of exit with the same observable values. In contrast, there are variables whose values are ignored or lost at the program exit and we have no interest in comparing them, e.g. temporary registers. Furthermore, different expressions may be relevant at different exits – in our example the value of TMP0 is relevant at the address_overflow exit, but not at the end exit, where its "temporary" value is discarded. Defining the correct observables for the various exits is not a trivial exercise – too few observables may result in real mismatches being missed, too many observables may result in false negatives when comparing expressions which need not be equal. In practice, the observability expressions are built and stabilized over time; starting with the microcode validator's first approximation, the expressions

```
BEGIN_FLOW(example) {
 reg1 := memory_read(reg2, reg3, reg6);
 reg4 := add(reg1, reg5);
};
```

Fig. 5. Microcode example II: An extended version

```
template uop_memory_read(register result,
    register tmp_address, register base, register offset) {
  TMP0 := tmp_address + offset;
  TMP0 := TMP0 + base;
  if (TMP0 > 0xFFFFFFFF)
     exit address_overflow(TMP0[63:32]);
  result := memory[TMP0[31:0]];
  zeroFlag := (result = 0);
  found_valid_address := 1;
};
```

Fig. 6. A `memory_read` for the extended version

```
1.  entry (reg1, reg2, reg3, reg4, reg5, reg6, memory, pc);
2   TMP0 := reg2 + reg3;
3.  TMP0 := TMP0 + reg6;
4.  (TMP0 > 0xFFFFFFFF) ? exit address_overflow(TMP0[63:32]);
5.  reg1 := memory[TMP0[31:0]];
6.  zeroFlag := (reg1 = 0);
7.  found_valid_address := 1;
8.  reg4 := reg1 + reg5;
9.  zeroFlag := (reg4 = 0);
10. exit end (found_valid_address, reg1, reg2, memory);
```

Fig. 7. Basic IRL for the updated program: Numbered statements

are tuned during several iterations of false negatives and false positives. Doing so requires a deep understanding of the microcode, and may involve consultation with the the microcode designers.

We now consider an extended version of this system in which memory addresses can also include bases (Fig. 5). The extended `memory_read` microinstruction takes an extra base parameter, and is described in Fig. 6. The IRL corresponding to the microcode of Fig. 5, using the extended read, is in Fig. 7.

3 The Formal Model

In this section we introduce our formal model of computation, *exit-differentiated transitions systems*, which defines the semantics of IRL programs similar to the way transition systems are used to give semantics to "Simple Programming Language" (SPL) in [MP95]. We then give a formal definition to the notion of restricted equivalence, termed *compatibility*, of two IRL programs. We use the program of Fig. 4 as a running example.

A microprogram usually allows for several types of exits, such as the `end` exit and the `address_overflow` exit in our example. At each exit type we may be interested in different observables. For example, at the `address_overflow` exit we care only about the values of the overflow bits, while at the `end` exit we care about the values of found_valid_address, reg1 and reg4. When comparing two microprograms for equivalence or backward compatibility, we would expect that when the two terminate at corresponding exits, the values of the corresponding observables would match. Similarly, when comparing the two microprograms, we make some assumptions about their entry conditions, such as that registers have the same initial values. We refer to the entry and exit points as *doors*. Two microprograms are termed equivalent if whenever their entry values match, they exit through the same doors with matching exit values.

By "matching values" we usually mean that two variables have the same value. However, it is sometimes the case that a comparison between variables is insufficient, and a more involved comparison must be made e.g., a sub-vector or a conditional expression like "if (cond) then $a[7:0]$ else $b[9:2]$". We therefore compare values that are defined by *well-typed observation functions* over the system variables.

In order to capture the formal semantics of equivalence with respect to doors, we define *exit-differentiated transition systems*, EDTS, an extension of the symbolic transition systems of [MP95] to systems with differentiated exit types. An EDTS $S = \langle V, \Delta, \Theta, \rho \rangle$ consists of:

- V: A finite set of typed *system variables*. The set V always includes the program counter pc. A V-*state* is a type-consistent interpretation of V. We denote the symbolic value of variable v in state s by $s.v$;
- Δ: A finite set of *doors*. Each door is associated with an an observation tuple $\mathcal{O}_\delta$ of well-typed observation functions over V. In addition, we have a partial function ν from pc to Δ, where $\nu(\text{pc}) = \delta$ if pc is associated with door δ and $\perp$ if it is associated with no door. The final state of every computation is associated with some door. There is a single distinguished entry door, entry, all other doors are exit doors;
- Θ: An *initial condition* characterizing the initial states of the system. For every state s, $\Theta(s) \longrightarrow \nu(s.\text{pc}) = \texttt{entry}$;
- $\rho(V, V')$: A *transition relation* relating a state to its possible successors;

The semantics of IRL programs is defined in terms of EDTS in a straightforward way (cf. semantics of SPL in terms of symbolic transition systems [MP95]). For example, the EDTS associated with the IRL of Fig. 4 is:

$$V = \{\texttt{pc}, \texttt{TMP0}, \texttt{reg1}, \ldots, \texttt{reg5}, \texttt{found\_valid\_address}, \texttt{memory}\}$$

$$\rho = \bigvee_{\ell=1..7} \rho_\ell$$

$$\Theta = (\text{pc} = 1)$$

$\Delta = \{\texttt{entry}, \texttt{address\_overflow}, \texttt{end}\}$ with associated observation tuples

$$\mathcal{O}_{\texttt{entry}} : (\texttt{reg1}, \ldots, \texttt{reg5}, \texttt{memory})$$
$$\mathcal{O}_{\texttt{address\_overflow}} : (\texttt{TMP0}[63:32]),$$
$$\mathcal{O}_{\texttt{end}} : (\texttt{found\_valid\_address}, \texttt{reg1}, \texttt{reg4}, \texttt{memory})$$

where each ρ_ℓ describes the transition associated with $\text{pc} = \ell$.

As discussed earlier, execution of microcode is heavily dependent on the microarchitectural state. The translation of microcode to IRL makes this dependence fully explicit. While microcode has invisible side effects, these are fully exposed in the IRL.

This, together with the assumption that the microarchitectural state does not change during the execution of the microcode unless explicitly modified by the microcode, makes our IRL programs deterministic; given an initial assignment to the variables, behavior is completely determined. Making microcode dependence on the microarchitectural state fully explicit enables us also to handle *busy-waiting loops*. In such loops, the microcode waits for the hardware to provide a certain readiness signal. Since loops pose a challange to symbolic simulators, we abstract busy-waiting loops, which are quite common, by adding an auxiliary bit for each such loop. This bit "predicts" whether the readiness signal will be provided. When this bit is on, the loop is entered and immediately exited, and when the bit is off, the loop is entered but not exited.

A computation of an EDTS is a maximal sequence of states $\sigma : s_0, s_1, \ldots$ starting with a state that satisfies the initial condition, such that every two consecutive states are related by the transition relation. For $j = 1, 2$, let $P^j = \langle V^j, \Theta^j, \rho^j, \Delta^j \rangle$ be an EDTS. We say that P^1 and P^2 are *comparable* if for every $\delta \in \Delta^1 \cap \Delta^2$, the corresponding observation tuples in both programs are of the same arity and type.

We are interested in notions of compatibility. Often we find that a new system has the same functionality as the old system, plus new functionality. We use *restrictions* to constrain the set of initial values and thus compare only the legacy functionality of the new system. We define systems P^1 and P^2 to be $\mathcal{R}$*-compatible* with respect to a restriction $\mathcal{R}$, if they are comparable and, and under the restriction of $\mathcal{R}$, every execution in the same environment (with matching entry observables) ends in the same exit state, with matching exit observables. Restrictions are defined as predicates over $V^1 \cup V^2$. Our main focus is on terminating computations; the only non-terminating computations that we consider are those resulting from getting stuck in infinite busy-wait loops, for which we verify that both source and target microprograms diverge under the same conditions.

To illustrate the notion of compatibility, consider again our example codes. Let P^1 be the EDTS of the "source" program of Fig. 4, and let P^2 be the EDTS of the "target" program of Fig. 7. The two systems are clearly comparable. It is easy to see that these two flows do not reach the same exit under all conditions. For example, if initially $\texttt{reg2} + \texttt{reg3} = \texttt{0xFFFFFFFF}$, P^1 exits at `end`. If, in addition, `reg6` is initially non-zero, P^2 exits at `address_overflow`. Under the restriction that in system P^2 `reg6` is initially zero (since `reg6` is not among P^1's variables, there is no danger of restricting P^1's behavior by this restriction), the two are compatible. This is a typical example of a restriction in the new system that disables the new functionality to ensure backward compatibility.

4 Simulation and Verification

We use symbolic simulation to compute the effect of the program on a symbolic initial state. As defined in Sec. 3, a state is a type-consistent interpretation of the variables. Variable values are symbolic expressions over the set of initial values and constants that appear in the program. In our example, in the initial state s_0, before any statements have executed, all variables have symbolic values. After statement 2 is simulated, the value of `TMP0` is the expression $s_0.\texttt{reg2} + s_0.\texttt{reg3}$ over these symbolic values.

If microprograms were merely lists of assignments, this would suffice. However, they also include conditional and jump statements. Since the state is symbolic, it is at times impossible to determine the evaluation of a condition. For example, at statement 3, the program either exits or continues according to the evaluation of the test (TMP0 $>$ 0xFFFFFFFF), which is equivalent to evaluating whether s_0.reg2 + s_0.reg3 $>$ 0xFFFFFFFF; it is easy to find assignments to s_0.reg2 and s_0.reg3 under which the condition is true, and assignments under which it is false. Both are feasible, under different initial conditions.

We use *symbolic paths* to store, for every control-distinct (as opposed to data-distinct) path the current symbolic variable values, the path condition, and the exit door, once it has been found. Formally, a symbolic path π is a triple (c, s, δ), where c is the condition ensuring that this path is taken, s is a state containing the relevant symbolic values of variables, and δ is an exit door if such is reached, $\perp$ otherwise. The path conditions of a program are exhaustive (their disjuntion is one) and mutually exclusive (no two path conditions can be satisfied simultaneously).

For example, after statement 2 has executed, there is a single symbolic path (TRUE, s_2, $\perp$) where the value of TMP0 in s_2 is s_0.reg2 + s_0.reg3. When statement 3 is executed, the symbolic path is split into two:

$$(s_0.\mathtt{reg2} + s_0.\mathtt{reg3} > \mathtt{0xFFFFFFFF}, s_2, \mathtt{address\_overflow})$$

and

$$(s_0.\mathtt{reg2} + s_0.\mathtt{reg3} \leq \mathtt{0xFFFFFFFF}, s_2, \perp).$$

Statement 3 does not effect the values of variables in the state, but rather the path condition. The symbolic path conditions are always mutually exclusive, and their disjunction is TRUE. We note that some of the symbolic paths will be *non-viable*, that is, their condition evaluates to FALSE. The remainder represent runs of the EDTS.

Symbolic paths fully capture the possible behavior of non-iterative programs. Handling loops (other than busy-waiting loops) requires the identification of loop invariants and is currently beyond the capability of MICROFORMAL. Also, handling indirect jumps is quite challending and cannot always be handled by MICROFORMAL.

4.1 Verification

We recall that systems P^1 and P^2 are $\mathcal{R}$-compatible if every execution in the same environment (matching entry observables) satisfying $\mathcal{R}$ will, under the same conditions, ends in the same exit door, with matching observables. For $j = 1, 2$, Let $\pi^j = (c^j, s^j, \delta^j)$ be a symbolic path in P^j, and s_0^j be the symbolic initial state of P^j. We require that

$$\mathcal{O}_{\mathtt{entry}}(s_0^1) = \mathcal{O}_{\mathtt{entry}}(s_0^2) \wedge \Theta^1(s_0^1) \wedge \Theta^2(s_0^2) \wedge c^1 \wedge c^2 \wedge \mathcal{R}(s_0^1, s_0^2) \longrightarrow \delta^1 = \delta^2 \wedge \mathcal{O}_{\delta^1}(s^1) = \mathcal{O}_{\delta^1}(s^2) \quad (1)$$

We recall that a computation is a path whose initial state satisfies Θ and that our equivalence definition refers to paths starting with matching entry observables. The path conditions, too, are conditions over the symbolic initial values. This formula is thus equivalent to requiring that any two computations π^1 and π^2 starting at matching initial states ($\mathcal{O}_{\texttt{entry}}(s_0^1) = \mathcal{O}_{\texttt{entry}}(s_0^2)$) reach the same door with matching observables, provided that the relevant restrictions $\mathcal{R}$ hold. We note that if $c^1 \wedge c^2$ is unsatifiable, then the formula is trivially true. However, since the path conditions are exhaustive, some instances of this formula are non-trivial.

Returning to our example, P^1 has two symbolic paths,

$$\pi_1^1 = (s_0^1.\texttt{reg2} + s_0^1.\texttt{reg3} > \texttt{0xFFFFFFFF},\ s_2^1,\ \texttt{address\_overflow})$$
$$\pi_2^1 = (s_0^1.\texttt{reg2} + s_0^1.\texttt{reg3} \leq \texttt{0xFFFFFFFF},\ s_9^1,\ \texttt{end})$$

where s_2^1 is s_0^1 with [TMP0= s_0^1.reg2 + s_0^1.reg3], and s_9^1 is the final state after executing instruction 8.

Similarly, the two symbolic paths of P^2 are

$$\pi_1^2 = (s_0^2.\texttt{reg2} + s_0^2.\texttt{reg3} + s_0^2.\texttt{reg6} > \texttt{0xFFFFFFFF},\ s_3^2,\ \texttt{address\_overflow})$$
$$\pi_2^2 = (s_0^2.\texttt{reg2} + s_0^2.\texttt{reg3} + s_0^2.\texttt{reg6} \leq \texttt{0xFFFFFFFF},\ s_{10}^2,\ \texttt{end})$$

where s_3^2 is s_0^2 with [TMP0= s_0^2.reg2+s_0^2.reg3+ s_0^2.reg6].

Applying (1) to π_2^1 and π_1^2 is easy:

$$\begin{array}{ll}
(a) & s_0^1.\texttt{reg1} = s_0^2.\texttt{reg1} \wedge \ldots \wedge s_0^1.\texttt{reg5} = s_0^2.\texttt{reg5} \wedge s_0^1.\texttt{memory} = s_0^2.\texttt{memory} \\
(b) & \wedge\ s_0^1.\texttt{pc} = 1 \wedge s_0^2.\texttt{pc} = 1 \\
(c) & \wedge\ (s_0^1.\texttt{reg2} + s_0^1.\texttt{reg3} < \texttt{0xFFFFFFFF}) \\
 & \qquad \wedge (s_0^2.\texttt{reg2} + s_0^2.\texttt{reg3} + s_0^2.\texttt{reg6} \geq \texttt{0xFFFFFFFF}) \\
(d) & \wedge\ s_0^2.\texttt{reg6} = 0 \longrightarrow \\
(e) & \qquad \texttt{end} = \texttt{address_overflow} \wedge (1 = s_0^2.\texttt{found_valid_address} \wedge \ldots)
\end{array}$$

where (a) is an instantiation of $\mathcal{O}_{\texttt{entry}}(s_0^1) = \mathcal{O}_{\texttt{entry}}(s_0^2)$, (b) of $\Theta^1(s_0^1) \wedge \Theta^2(s_0^2)$, (c) of $c^1 \wedge c^2$, (d) of $\mathcal{R}$, and (e) of $\delta^1 = \delta^2 \wedge \mathcal{O}_{\delta^1}(s^1) = \mathcal{O}_{\delta^1}(s^2)$. Note that without the restriction that $s_0^2.\texttt{reg6} = 0$, the antecedent would be satisfiable, generating a counterexample in which the two flows reach different exits. With the restriction the antecedent evaluates to FALSE, and the formula is valid.

4.2 Optimizations

Instead of verifying (1) for every pair of symbolic paths, we find it more more efficient to merge the symbolic paths of each system reaching the same exit before verification. The merged condition is simply a disjunction of all the conditions of symbolic paths reaching the door. The merged state is built by generating a case statement for each variable, with its value depending on the path condition. The verification condition has to be adapted for the merging of symbolic paths.

Symbolic pruning allows us to evaluate some of the conditional statements that appear in the target code according to the restrictions, and prunes branches of execution, thus reducing the number of non-viable paths generated, and the size of the verification conditions. In the microprograms we experimented with, as is often the case with incremental design, the new functionality is localized in some branches that are led to by tests explicitly referring to the restrictions. Indeed, empirical results establish that often symbolic pruning, combined with simple Boolean reductions, reduces prohibitively large VCs into manageable ones.

5 Results and Future Directions

The MICROFORMAL system has been under intensive research (in collaboration with academia) and development at Intel since the summer of 2003. We currently have a first version providing core functionality. The system is fully automated and requires almost no manual intervention. As inputs it gets:

1. Files containing IRL modeling of microinstructions of current and next generation CPUs.
2. Source and target microprograms to be compared.
3. A set of restrictions under which to verify compatibility.

The output can be either *PASS*, or *FAIL*. In the latter case, a full counter-example – demonstrating the mismatch by concrete execution paths of the two microprograms being compared – is provided.

So far, MICROFORMAL has been used by microcode validators to formally verify backward compatibility for 80 microprograms. In these verification sessions, microcode of next-generation CPU is compared against that of current-generation CPU. The microprograms being verified, selected by microcode experts, are quite complex CISC flows that involve both memory interaction, and multiple sanity and permission checks that can result in exceptions. To date, MICROFORMAL has found three new unknown microcode bugs and redetected four known ones. The novel technology provided by MICROFORMAL has been recognized as one that can significantly improve the quality of microcode.

Some performance data we collected from our regression is presented in the table below.

Microprogram	Paths	Statements on longest path	Time (Seconds)
Program1	156	8497	32851
Program2	112	4323	1759
Program3	72	2346	10967
Program4	50	1988	924
Program5	39	1395	671

There are several interesting future directions that are currently being explored. The first natural extension is verifying compliance with hardware *assumptions*. Microcode and hardware interact through a complicated set of protocols. These protocols are currently expressed as a set of global microcode assumptions. A violation of these protocols by microcode could result in a multitude of undesired results - deadlocks, incorrect results, etc. Another kind of assumptions is local ones, or microcode assertions; some of the assumptions made by designers are formalized as inline assertions. These assertions are written inside the code, and are applicable only locally, at the point where they are written. Both kinds of assumptions (global and local) are validated using standard simulation, but their coverage is minimal. Most of these can be expressed as state predicates relating various environment variables. One way to formally verify assumptions is to use symbolic simulation for computing verification conditions, establishing that the required predicate holds at desired locations starting from an arbitrary initial state.

A more challenging direction is formal verification of new functionality (currently, this is validated only via standard simulation). New architectural functionality is coded both in microcode and in an architectural reference model. For formal verification of new functionality, the architects will be able to code the intended functionality of new microprograms in IRL. MICROFORMAL will then compare the architectural specification against the actual microcode. This comparison should be able to detect discrepancies, providing complete data-path coverage and reducing the need to exercise the code in standard simulation.

Acknowledgements. We wish to thank Ittai Anati for his help in clarifying some of the micro-architectural aspects that are relevant for formally modeling microcode, Amir Pnueli for ideas on modeling and verifying memory interaction, and Jim Grundy for his constructive comments on an earlier version of this paper.

References

[AHKV98] R. Alur, T.A. Henzinger, O. Kupferman, and M.Y. Vardi. Alternating refinement relations. In *CONCUR'98*:163–178, 1998.

[BR02] T. Ball and S.K. Rajamani. The SLAM project: debugging system software via static analysis. In *POPL'02*:1–3, 2002.

[CHRF00] D.W. Currie, A.J. Hu, S. Rajan, and M. Fujita. Automatic formal verification of DSP software. In *DAC'00*: 130–135, 2000.

[CKY03] E.M. Clarke, D. Kroening, and K. Yorav. Behavioral consistency of C and Verilog programs using bounded model checking. In *DAC'03*: 368–371, 2003.

[Cyr93] D. Cyrluk. Microprocessor Verification in PVS: A Methodology and Simple Example. Technical Report SRI-CSL-93-12, Menlo Park, CA, 1993.

[FH02] X. Feng and A.J. Hu. Automatic formal verification for scheduled VLIW code. In *ACM SIGPLAN Joint Conference: Languages, Compilers, and Tools for Embedded Systems, and Software and Compilers for Embedded Systems*, pages 85–92, 2002.

[HC98] S.Y. Huang and K.T. Cheng. *Formal Equivalence Checking and Design Debugging*. Kluwer, 1998.

[HJMS03] T.A. Henzinger, R. Jhala, R. Majumdar, and G. Sutre. Software verification with Blast. In *SPIN'03*:235–239, 2003.

[HP85] D. Harel and A. Pnueli. On the development of reactive systems. In *Logics and Models of Concurrent Systems*, volume F-13 of *NATO ASI Series*, pages 477–498, 1985.

[HUK00] K. Hamaguchi, H. Urushihara, and T. Kashiwabara. Symbolic checking of signal-transition consistency for verifying high-level designs. In *FMCAD'00*:445–469, 2000.

[MP95] Z. Manna and A. Pnueli. *Temporal Verification of Reactive Systems: Safety*. Springer-Verlag, New York, 1995.

[Nec00] G. Necula. Translation validation of an optimizing compiler. In *PLDI'00*: 83–94, 2000.

[PSS98] A. Pnueli, M. Siegel, and E. Singerman. Translation validation. In *TACAS'98*:151–161, 1998.

[SH02] J. Sawada and W.A. Hunt. Verification of FM9801: An out-of-order microprocessor model with speculative execution, exceptions, and program-modifying capability. *J. on Formal Methods in System Design*, 20(2):187–222, 2002.

[SM96] M. Srivas and S. Miller. Applying formal verification to the AAMP5 microprocessor: A case study in the industrial use of formal methods. *J. on Formal Methods in System Design*, 8:153–188, 1996.

[Sta02] W. Stallings. *Computer Organization and Architecture, 6th ed.* Prentice Hall, 2002.

[ZPFG03] L. Zuck, A. Pnueli, Y. Fang, and B. Goldberg. Voc: A translation validator for optimizing compilers. *J. of Universal Computer Science*, 9(2), 2003.

Compositional Analysis of Floating-Point Linear Numerical Filters

David Monniaux

CNRS / Laboratoire d'informatique de l'École normale supérieure
David.Monniaux@ens.fr

Abstract. Digital linear filters are used in a variety of applications (sound treatment, control/command, etc.), implemented in software, in hardware, or a combination thereof. For safety-critical applications, it is necessary to bound all variables and outputs of all filters.

We give a compositional, effective abstraction for digital linear filters expressed as block diagrams, yielding sound, precise bounds for fixed-point or floating-point implementations of the filters.

1 Introduction

Discrete-time digital filters are used in fields as diverse as sound processing, avionic and automotive applications. In many of these applications, episodic arithmetic overflow, often handled through saturated arithmetics, is tolerable — but in safety-critical applications, it may lead to dramatic failures (e.g. disaster of the maiden flight of the Ariane 5 rocket). Our experience with the Astrée static analyzer [3] is that precise analysis of the numerical behavior of such filters is necessary for proving the safety of control-command systems using them.

We provide a method for efficiently computing bounds on all variables and outputs of any digital causal linear filter with finite buffer memory (the most common kind of digital filter). These bounds are sound with respect to fixed- or floating-point arithmetics, and may be used to statically check for arithmetic overflow, or to dimension fixed-point registers, inside the filter, or in computations using its results.

In many cases, filters are specified as diagrams in stream languages such as Simulink, SAO, Scade/Lustre, which are later compiled into lower-level languages. Our method targets such specifications, modularly and compositionally: the analysis results of sub-filters are used when analyzing a complex filter.

Our analysis results are valid for whatever range of the inputs. They can thus be used to simplify the analysis of a more complex, nonlinear filter comprising a linear sub-filter: the linear sub-filter can be replaced by its sound approximation.

In §3, we shall explain our mathematical model for the filters. In §4 we give a compositional semantics for ideal filters working on real numbers. In §5 we explain how to extract bound from this semantics. In §7, we recall some basic properties of floating-point computation. In §8 we enrich our semantics to deal with floating-point inaccuracies and other nonlinear behaviors. In §9, we consider numerical methods and implementation issues.

K. Etessami and S.K. Rajamani (Eds.): CAV 2005, LNCS 3576, pp. 199–212, 2005.

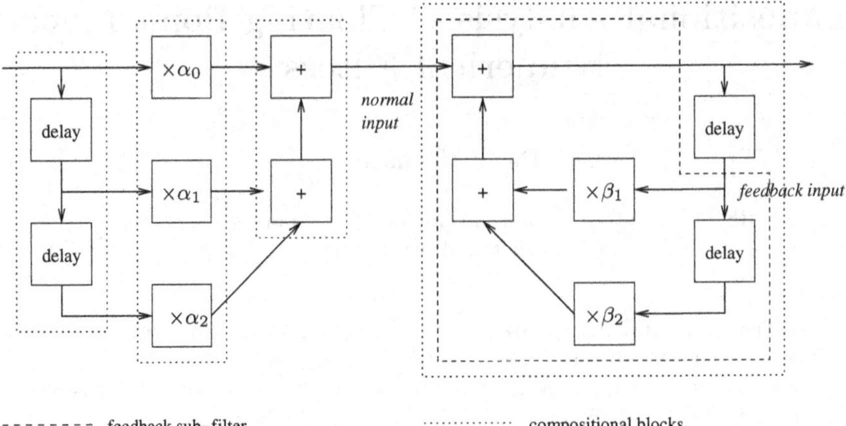

Fig. 1. Decomposition of the TF2 filter $S_n = \alpha_0 E_n + \alpha_1 E_{n-1} + \alpha_2 E_{n-2} + \beta_1 S_{n-1} + \beta_2 S_{n-2}$ into elementary blocks. The compositional blocks are chained by serial composition. Inside each compositional on the left, elementary gates are composed in parallel. On the right hand side, a feedback loop is used

2 Introduction to Linear Filters and Z-Transforms

Let us consider the following piece of C code, which we will use as a running example (called "TF2"):

```
Y = A0*I + A1*Ibuf[1] + A2*Ibuf[2];
O = Y + B1*Obuf[1] + B2*Obuf[2];
Ibuf[2]=Ibuf[1]; Ibuf[1]=I;
Obuf[2]=Obuf[1]; Obuf[1]=O;
```

All variables are assumed to be real numbers (we shall explain in later sections how to deal with fixed- and floating-point values with full generality and soundness). The program takes `I` as an input and outputs `O`; `A0` etc. are constant coefficients. This piece of code is wrapped inside a (reactive) loop; the *time* is the number of iterations of that loop. Equivalently, this filter can be represented by the block diagram in Fig. 1.

Let us note a_0 etc. the values of the constants and i_n (resp. y_n, o_n) the value of `I` (resp. `Y`, `O`) at time n. Then, assuming $o_k = 0$ for $k < 0$, we can develop the recurrence: $o_n = y_n + b_1.o_{n-1} + b_2.o_{n-2} = y_n + b_1.(y_{n-1} + b_1.o_{n-2} + b_2.o_{n-3}) + b_2.(y_{n-2} + b_1.o_{n-3} + b_2.o_{n-4}) = y_n + b_1.y_{n-1} + (b_2 + b_1^2 b_0).y_{n-2} + \ldots$ where ... depends solely on y_k with $k < n-2$. More generally: there exist coefficients c_0, $c_1 \ldots$ such that for all n, $o_n = \sum_{k=0} c_k y_{n-k}$. These coefficients solely depend on the b_k; we shall see later some general formulas for computing them.

But, itself, $y_n = a_0.i_n + a_1.i_{n-1} + a_2.i_{n-2}$. It follows that there exist coefficients c'_n (depending on the a_k and the b_k) such that $o_n = \sum_{k=0} c'_k i_{n-k}$. We again find a similar shape of formula, known as a *convolution product*. The c'_k sequence is called a *convolution kernel*, mapping i to o.

Let us now suppose that we know a bound M_I on the input: for all n, $|i_n| \leq M_I$; we wish to derive a bound M_O on the output. By the triangle inequality, $|O_n| \leq \sum_{k=0} |c'_k|.M_I$. The quantity $\sum_{k=0} |c'_k|$ is called the $l1$-norm of the convolution kernel c'.

What our method does is as follows: from the description of a complex linear filter, it compositionally computes compact, finite representations of convolution kernels mapping the inputs to the outputs of the sub-blocks of the filter, and accurately computes the norms of these kernels (or rather, a close upper bound thereof). As a result, one can obtain bounds on any variable in the system from a bound on the input.

3 Linear Filters: Formalism and Behavior

In this section, we give a rough outline of the class of filters that we analyze and how their basic properties allow them to be analyzed.

3.1 Linear Filters

We deal with numerical filters that take as inputs and output some (unbounded) discrete streams of floating-point numbers, with *causality*; that is, the output of the filter at time t depends on the past and present inputs (times 0 to t), but not on the future inputs. [1] In practice, they are implemented with state variables (in the TF2 example, the `Ibuf[]` and `Obuf[]` arrays), and the output at time t is a function of the input at time t and the internal state (resulting from time $t-1$), which is then updated. In software, this is typically one piece of a synchronous reactive loop:

```
while(true) { ...
  (state, output) = filter(state, input);
... }
```

We are particular interested in filters of the following form (or compounds thereof): if (s_k) and (e_k) are respectively the input and output streams of the filter, there exist real coefficients α_0, α_1, $\ldots \alpha_n$ and β_1, $\ldots \beta_m$ such that for all time t, s_t (the output at time t) is defined as: $s_t = \sum_{k=0}^{n} \alpha_k e_{t-k} + \sum_{k=1}^{m} \beta_k s_{t-k}$. In TF2, $n = m = 2$.

Consider the reaction (s_k) of the system to a unit impulse ($e_0 = 1$ and $\forall k > 0 \; e_k = 0$). If the β are all null, the filter has necessarily *finite impulse response* (FIR): $\exists N \; \forall k \geq N, s_k = 0$. Otherwise, it may have *infinite impulse response* (IIR): s_k decays exponentially if the filter is *stable*; a badly designed IIR filter may be *unstable*, and the response then amplifies with time.

It is possible to design filters that should be stable, assuming the use of real numbers in computation, but that exhibit gross numerical distortions due to the use of floating-point numbers in the implementation.

[1] There exist non-causal numerical filtering schemes; such as Matlab's `filtfilt` function. However, they require buffering the data and thus cannot be used in real time.

3.2 Formal Power Series and Rational Functions

The output streams of a linear filter, as an element of $\mathbb{R}^{\mathbb{N}}$, are linear functions of the inputs and the initial values of the state variables.

Neglecting the floating-point errors and assuming that state variables are initialized to 0, the output O is the *convolution product*, denoted $C \star I$ of the input I by some *convolution kernel* C: there exists a sequence $(q_n)_{n\in\mathbb{N}}$ of reals such that for any n, $o_n = \sum_{k=0}^{n} c_k i_{n-k}$. The filter is FIR if this convolution kernel is null except for the first few values, and IIR otherwise.

Consider two sequences of real numbers $A : (a_k)_{k\in\mathbb{N}}$ and $B : (b_k)_{k\in\mathbb{N}}$. We can equivalently note them as some "infinite polynomials" $\sum_{k=0}^{i} nfty a_k z^k$ and $\sum_{k=0}^{i} nfty b_k z^k$; such "infinite polynomials", just another notation for sequences of reals, are known as *formal power series*. This "Z-transform" notation is justified as follows: the sum $C = A + B$ of two sequences is defined by $c_n = a_n + b_n$, which is the same as the coefficient n of the sum of two polynomials $\sum_k a_k z^k$ and $\sum b_k z^k$; the convolution product $C = A \star B$ of two sequences is defined by $c_n = \sum_k a_k b_{n-k}$, the same as the coefficient n of the product of two polynomials $\sum_k a_k z^k$ and $\sum b_k z^k$.

Consider now some "ordinary" (finite) polynomials in one variable $P(z)$ and $Q(z)$; we define, as usual, the *rational function* P/Q. We shall be particularly interested in the set $\mathbb{R}[z]_{(z)}$ of such rational functions where the 0-degree coefficient of Q is 1 (note that, up to equivalence by multiplication of the numerator and the denominator by the same quantity, this is the same as requesting that the 0-degree coefficient of Q is non-zero). Any sum or product of such fractions is also of the same form. For fraction in $\mathbb{R}[z]_{(z)}$, we can compute its Taylor expansion around 0 to any arbitrary order: $P(z)/Q(z) = c_0 + c_1 z + c_2 z^2 + \ldots + c_n z^n + o(z^n)$. By doing so to any arbitrary n, we define another formal power series $\sum_{k=0}^{\infty} c_k$. We shall identify such rational fraction with the power series that it defines.

We shall see more formally in §4 that the Z-transform of the convolution kernel(s) of any finite-memory, causal linear filter is a rational function

$$\frac{\alpha_0 + \alpha_1 z + \cdots + \alpha_n z^n}{1 - \beta_1 z - \cdots - \beta_m z^m} \tag{1}$$

The above fraction is the Z-transform for a filter implementing $s_n = \sum_{k=0}^{n} \alpha_k . e_{n-k} + \sum_{k=0}^{m} \beta . s_{n-k}$, and thus *any* ideal causal finite-memory linear filter with 1 input and 1 output is equivalent to such a filter.[2]

3.3 Bounding the Response

Let $I : (i_k)_{n\in\mathbb{N}}$ be a sequence of real or complex numbers. We call l_∞*-norm* of I, if finite, and denote by $\|I\|_\infty$ the quantity $\sup_{k\in\mathbb{N}} |i_k|$. Because of the

[2] Though all designs with the same Z-transform compute the same on real numbers, they may differ when implemented in fixed- or floating- point arithmetics. Precision and implementation constraints determine the choice of the design.

isomorphism between sequences and formal power series, we shall likewise note $\|\sum_k i_k z^k\|_\infty = \sup_k |i_k|$. For a sequence (or formal series) A, we denote by $\|A\|_1$ the quantity $\sum_{k=0}^{\infty} |a_k|$, called its l_1-*norm*, if finite.

We then have the following crucial and well-known results: [7, §11.3]:

Lemma 1. *For any I, $\|I \star C\|_\infty \leq \|I\|_\infty.\|C\|_1$. Furthermore, $\|C\|_1 = \infty$, for any $M > 0$ there exists a sequence I_M such that $\|I_M \star C\|_\infty > M$.*

In terms of filters:

- If $\|C\|_1$ is finite, we can easily bound the output of the filter. Our system will thus compute (or, rather, over-approximate very closely) C for any filter.
- If $\|C\|_1 = \infty$, then the filter is *unstable*: it is possible to obtain outputs of arbitrary size by feeding appropriate sequences into the filter.

If C is the power series expansion of a rational fraction P/Q (which will be the case for all the filters we consider, see below), then we have the following stability condition:

Lemma 2. *$\|P/Q\|_1$ is finite if and only if for all $z \in \mathbb{C}$ such that $Q(z) = 0$, then $|z| > 1$.*

Unsurprisingly, our algorithms will involve some approximation of the complex roots of polynomials.

4 Compositional Semantics: Real Field

In this section, we give a compositional abstract semantics of compound filters on the real numbers, exact with respect to input/output behavior.

4.1 Formalism

A filter or filter element has

- n_i inputs $I_1, \ldots, I_{n_i}$ (collectively, vector I), each of which is a *stream* of real numbers;
- n_r reset state values $r_1, \ldots, r_{n_r}$ (collectively, vector R), which are the initial values of the state of the internal state variables of the filter;
- n_o output streams $O_1, \ldots, O_{n_o}$ (collectively, vector O).

In TF2, $n_i = n_o = 1$, and $n_r = 4$.

If M is a matrix (resp. vector) of rational functions, or series, let $N_x(M)$ denote the coordinate-wise application of the norm $\|\cdot\|_x$ to each rational function, or series, thereby providing a vector (resp. matrix) of nonnegative reals. We note $m_{i,j}$ the element in M at line i and column j.

When computed upon the real field, a filter F is characterized by:

- a matrix $T^F \in \mathcal{M}_{n_o,n_i}(\mathbb{R}[z]_{(z)})$ such that $t_{i,j}$ characterizes the linear response of output stream i with respect to input stream j;

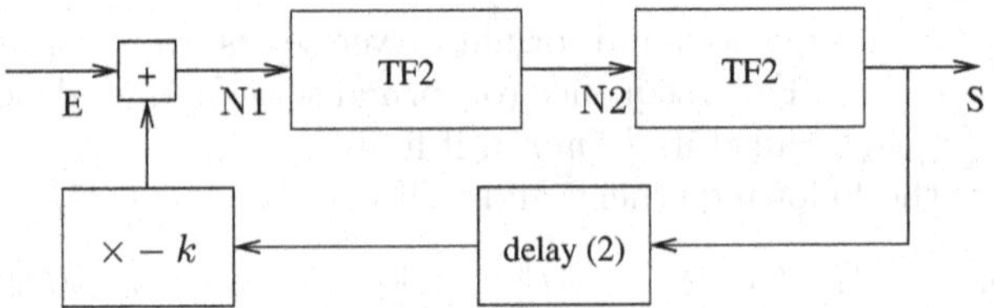

Fig. 2. A compound filter consisting of two second order filters and a feedback loop

- a matrix $D^F \in \mathcal{M}_{n_o,n_r}(\mathbb{R}[z]_{(z)})$ such that $d_{i,j}$ characterizes the (decaying) linear response of output stream i with respect to reset value j.

We note $F(I,R)$ the vector of output streams of filter F over the reals, on the vector of input streams I and the vector of reset values R. $F(I,R) = T^F.I + D^F.R$, and thus $N_\infty(F(I,R)) \leq N_1(T^F).N_\infty(I) + N_1(D^F.R)$, which bounds the output according to the input.

When the number of inputs and outputs is one, and initial values are assumed to be zero, the characterization of the filter is much simpler — all matrices and vectors are scalars (reals, formal power series or rational functions), and D^F is null.

For most gates (addition, reorganization of wires, multiplication by a scalar, generation of a constant...), the interpretation in terms of linear application over power series, or a matrix of rational functions, is straightforward. The only difficulty is the feedback construct: given a circuit C with n_i inputs and $n_o < n_i$ outputs, feed back the outputs into some of the inputs through a unit delay; it can be shown that such systems have a unique solution, obtained by linear algebra over rational functions.

4.2 Examples

The TF2 filter of Fig. 1 is expressed by $S = \alpha_0.E + \alpha_1.\text{delay}_2(E) + \alpha_2.\text{delay}_2(E) + \beta_1.\text{delay}_1(S) + \beta_2.\text{delay}_2(S)$. This yields an equation $S = (\alpha_0 + \alpha_1 z + \alpha_2 z^2)E + (\beta_1 z + \beta_2 z^2)S$. This equation is easily solved into $S = (\alpha_0 + \alpha_1 z + \alpha_2 z^2)(1 - \beta_1 z - \beta_2 z^2)^{-1}.E$.

In Fig. 2, we first analyze the two internal second order IIR filters separately and obtain $Q_1 = \frac{\alpha_0 + \alpha_1 z + \alpha_2 z^2}{1 - \beta_1 z - \beta_2 z^2}$ and $Q_2 = \frac{a_0 + a_1 z + a_2 z^2}{1 - b_1 z - b_2 z^2}$. We then analyze the feedback loop and obtain for the whole filter a rational function with a 6th degree dominator: $S = \frac{Q_1.Q_2}{1 + kz^2.Q_1.Q_2}.E$ where Q_1 and Q_2 are the transfer function of the TF2 filters (form $(\alpha_0 + \alpha_1 z + \alpha_2 z^2)(1 - \beta_1 z - \beta_2 z^2)^{-1}$), which we computed earlier.

4.3 Practical Computations

To avoid problems during matrix inversion, we perform all our computations over the ring $\mathbb{Q}[z]_{(z)}$ of rational functions over the rational numbers. In §8.2 we explain how to use controlled approximation to reduce the size of the rationals and thus ensure good computation speed even with complex filters.

An alternative, at least for the filters on real numbers, is to perform all computations in $\mathbb{Q}(\alpha_1, \ldots, \alpha_n)[z]_{(z)}$: all the coefficients of the rational functions are themselves rational functions whose variables represent the various constant coefficients inside the filter. This makes it possible to perform one computation with one particular shape of filter (i.e. class of equivalence of filters up to difference of coefficients), then use the results for concrete filters, replacing the variables by the values of the coefficients.

5 Bounding the l_∞ and l_1-Norms of Rational Functions

In §3.3 and 4.1, we used l_1-norms of expansions of rational functions to bound the gain of filters. In this section, we explain how to over-approximate these.

Let $P(z)/Q(z) \in \mathbb{R}[z]_{(z)}$ be a rational function representing a power series by its development $(u_n)_{n\in\mathbb{N}}$ around 0. We wish to bound $\|u\|_1$, which we shall note $\|P/Q\|_1$. As we said before, most of the mass of the development of P/Q lies in its initial terms, whereas the "tail" of the series is negligible (but must be accounted for for reasons of soundness). We thus split P/Q into an initial development of N terms and a tail, and use $\|P/Q\|_1 = \|P/Q\|_1^{<N} + \|P/Q\|_1^{\geq N}$. $\|P/Q\|_1^{<N}$ is computed by computing explicitly the N first terms of the development of P/Q. We shall see in Sect. 9.2 the difficulties involved in performing such a computation soundly using interval arithmetics.

Let d_Q be the degree of Q. The development D of P/Q yields an equation $P(z) = D(z).Q(z) + R(z).z^N$. We have $P(z)/Q(z) = D(z) + R(z)/Q(z).z^N$, thus $\|P/Q\|_1^{\geq N} = \|R/Q\|_1 \leq \|R\|_1.\|1/Q\|_1$.

There exist a variety of methods for bounding $\|1/Q\|_1$ using the zeroes of $Q(z)$. One uses the following lemma:

Lemma 3. *If $P(z)/Q(z)$ is a rational function such that $Q(0) \neq 0$ and Q is monic (leading coefficient equal to 1), with roots (counted with their multiplicity) $\xi_1, \ldots, \xi_n$, then $\|P/Q\|_1 \leq \|P\|_1.(|\xi_1| - 1)^{-1} \ldots (|\xi_n| - 1)^{-1}$.*

$\|R\|_\infty$ is bounded by explicit computation of R using interval arithmetics; as we shall see (§9.2), we compute D until the sign of the terms is unknown — that is, when the norm of the developed signal is on the same order of magnitude as the numerical error on it, which happens, experimentally, when the terms are very small in absolute values. Therefore, $\|R\|_\infty$ is small, and thus the roughness of the approximation used for $\|1/Q\|_1$ does not matter much in practice.

The same method way be used for bounding the l_∞-norm: explicit computation of the norm over a finite development, and bounding of the (negligible) tail, if necessary by $\|R\|_\infty \leq \|R\|_1$.

6 Complex Nonlinear Iterated Filter

We now consider a nonlinear, iterated filter due to Roozbehani et al. [11][§5]. We first analyze separately `filter1()` (2nd-order linear filter) and `filter2()`

(2nd-order affine filter). So as to simplify matters, we do not give the transfer functions using matrices, matrices inverses etc. but as the solution of a system of linear equations over polynomials in z. We obtain that system very simply from the program: whenever we see an assignment $x := e$, we turn it into an equation $x = e$ (we assume without loss of generalities that variables are only assigned once in a single iteration step), where e is the original expression where a variable v that has not yet been assigned in the current iteration is replaced by $i_v + z.v$, i_v standing for the initialization value of v.

```
void filter1 () {
  static float E[2], S[2];
  if (INIT1) {
    S[0] = X; P = X;
    E[0] = X; E[1]=0; S[1]=0;
  } else {
    P =0.5*X-0.7*E[0] +0.4*E[1]
      +1.5*S[0]-S[1]*0.7;
    E[1] = E[0];
    E[0] = X;
    S[1] = S[0];
    S[0] = P;
    X=P/6+S[1]/5;
  }
}
```

$$\begin{aligned} p &= 0.5e - 0.7(i_{e_0} + z.e_0) \\ &\quad +0.4(i_{e_1} + z.e_1) + 1.5(i_{s_0} + z.s_0) - 0.7(i_{s_1} + z.s_1) \\ e_1 &= i_{e_0} + z.e_0 \\ e_0 &= e \\ s_1 &= i_{s_1} + z.e_1 \\ s_0 &= p \\ x &= p/6 + s_1/5 \end{aligned}$$

We call e the input value for `X`. We solve the system and obtain $x = Q.e + Q_{i_{e_0}}.i_{e_0} + Q_{i_{e_1}}.i_{e_1} + Q_{i_{s_0}}.i_{s_0} + Q_{i_{s_1}}.i_{s_1}$. The common denominator of the Q fractions is $10 - 15z + 7z^2$, which has complex conjugate roots z such that $|z| \simeq 1.2$. $i_{e_1} = i_{s_1} = 0$ and $i_{e_0} = i_{s_0} = \iota$ (the last value for input e such that `INIT1` is true), thus $\|x\|_\infty \leq \|Q\|_1.\|e\|_\infty + \|Q_{i_{e_0}} + Q_{i_{s_0}}\|_\infty.\|\iota\|$. With a precondition $\|e\|_\infty \leq 400$, this yields $\|x\|_\infty < 339$. If we take the coarser inequality $\|x\|_\infty \leq \|Q\|_1.\|e\|_\infty + (\|Q_{i_{e_0}}\|_\infty + \|Q_{i_{s_0}}\|_\infty).\|\iota\|$ we get $\|x\|_\infty < 528$. Roozbehani et al. find a bound $\simeq 531$.

```
void filter2 () {
  static float E2[2], S2[2];
  if (INIT2) {
    S2[0] =0.5*X; P = X;
    E2[0] = 0.8*X; E2[1]=0; S2[1]=0;
  } else {
    P =0.3*X-E2[0]*0.2+E2[1]*1.4
      +S2[0]*0.5-S2[1]*1.7;
    E2[1] = 0.5*E2[0];
    E2[0] = 2*X;
    S2[1] = S2[0]+10;
    S2[0] = P/2+S2[1]/3;
    X=P/8+S2[1]/10;
  }
}
```

$$\begin{aligned} p &= 0.3e - 0.2(i_{e_0} + z.e_0) \\ &\quad +1.4(i_{e_1} + z.e_1) + 0.5(i_{s_0} + z.s_0) + 1.7(i_{s_1} + z.s_1) \\ e_1 &= 0.5(i_{e_0} + z.e_0) \\ e_0 &= 2e \\ s_1 &= i_{s_0} + z.s_0 + \tau \\ s_0 &= p/2 + s_1/3 \\ x &= p/8 + s_1/10 \end{aligned}$$

We proceed similarily (with the introduction of $\tau = 10/(1-z)$ and obtain $x = Q.e + Q_{i_{e_0}}.i_{e0} + Q_{i_{e_1}}.i_{e1} + Q_{i_{s_0}}.i_{s0} + Q_{i_{s_1}}.i_{s1} + Q_c$. The common denominator of the Q is $60 + 35z + 51z^2$, with complex conjugate roots z such that $|z| \simeq 1.08$. Then $\|x\|_\infty \leq \|Q\|_1.\|e\|_\infty + \|0.8Q_{i_{e_0}} + 0.5Q_{i_{s_0}}\|_\infty.\|\iota\| + \|Q_c\|_\infty$. This yields $\|x\|_\infty \leq 1105$.

The two linear filters are combined into an iterated nonlinear filter. `filter1()` (resp. `filter2()`) is run with a pre-condition of `X` $\in [-400, 400]$ (resp. $[-800, 800]$). We replace the call to the filter by its postcondition `X` $\in [-339, 339]$ (resp. `X` $\in [-1105, 1105]$).

The program then can be abstracted into:

```
while (TRUE) {
  X = 0.98 * X + 85;
  maybe choose X in [−1155,1055]; }
```

We obtain `X` $\in [-1155, 4250.02]$ by running Astrée with a large number of narrowing iterations, whereas Astrée cannot analyze the original program precisely and cannot bound `X`. In this case, the exact solution $[-1155, 4250]$ ($x = 0.98x + 85$ has for unique solution $x = 4250$) could have been computed algebraically, but in more complex filters this would not have been the case. Roozbehani et al. have a bound of 4560.

```
void main () {
  X = 0;
  INIT1 = TRUE; INIT2=TRUE;
  while (TRUE) {
    X = 0.98 * X + 85;
    if (abs(X)<= 400) {
      filter1 ();
      X=X+100;
      INIT1=FALSE;
    } else
    if (abs(X)<=800) {
      filter2();
      X=X-50;
      INIT2=FALSE;
    }
}}
```

Note that the non-abstracted program converges to a value $\simeq 205$, with `X` $\in [0, 209]$. However, this very simple program illustrates our methodology for compositional analysis: finding the optimal solution is possible here because the program is simple, but would not be possible in practice if we had added more nonlinear behavior and nondeterministic inputs, as in real-life reactive code; whereas by analyzing precisely each linear filter and plugging the results back into a generic analyzer, we get reasonable results.

7 Precision Properties of Fixed- or Floating-Point Operations

Most types of numerical arithmetics, including the widely used IEEE-754 floating-point arithmetic, implemented in hardware in all current microcomputers, define the result of elementary operations as follows: if f is the ideal operation (addition, subtraction, multiplication, division etc.) over the real numbers and $\tilde{f}$ is the corresponding floating-point operation, then $\tilde{f} = r \circ f$ where r is a *roundoff* function, depending on the current rounding mode.

In this description, we leave out the possible generation of special values such as infinities ($+\infty$ and $-\infty$) and *not-a-number* (NaN). We assume as a precondition to the numerical filters that we analyze that they are not fed infinities or NaNs.

Our framework provides constructive methods for bounding *any* floating-point quantity x inside the filters as $\|x\|_\infty \leq c_0 + \sum_{k=1}^{n} c_k.\|e_k\|_\infty$ where the e_k are the input streams of the system; it is quite easy to check that the system does not overflow ($\|x\| < M$); one can even easily provide some very wide sufficient conditions on the input ($\|e_k\|_\infty \leq (M - c_0)/(\sum_{k=1}^{n} c_k)$). We will not include such conditions in our description, for the sake of simplicity.

For any arithmetic operation, the discrepancy between the ideal result x and the floating-point result $\tilde{x}$ is bounded, in absolute value, by $\max(\varepsilon_{\text{rel}}|x|, \varepsilon_{\text{abs}})$ where ε_{abs} is the *absolute error* (the least positive floating-point number)[3] and ε_{rel} is the *relative error* incurred. ε_{abs} and ε_{rel} depend on the floating-point type used and possible rounding modes. We actually take the coarser inequality $|x - \tilde{x}| \leq \varepsilon_{\text{rel}}|x| + \varepsilon_{\text{abs}}$. See [1] for more details on floating-point numbers and [9] for more about the affine bound on the error.

In the case of fixed-point arithmetics, we have $\varepsilon_{\text{rel}} = 0$ and $\varepsilon_{\text{abs}} = \delta$ (δ is the smallest positive fixed-point number) if the rounding mode is unknown (round to $+\infty$, $-\infty$ etc.) and $\delta/2$ is it is the rounding mode is known to be round-to-nearest.

8 Compositional Semantics: Fixed- and Floating-Point

8.1 Constraint on the Errors

We now enrich our compositional abstract semantics to reflect numerical errors. Our enriched semantics characterizes a fixed- or floating-point filter $\tilde{F}$ by the exact semantics of the associated filter F over the real numbers and a bound on the discrepancy $\Delta(I) = \tilde{F}(I) - F(I)$ between the ideal and floating-point filters.

Assuming for the sake of simplicity a single input and a single output and no initialization conditions, we obtain an *affine*, *almost linear* constraint on $\|\Delta(I)\|\infty$: $\|\Delta(I)\|_\infty \leq \varepsilon_{\text{rel}}^F \|I\|_\infty + \varepsilon_{\text{abs}}^F$. In short: since the filter is linear, the magnitude of the error is (almost) linear. We generalize this idea to the case of multiple inputs and outputs. The abstract semantics characterizing Δ is given by matrices $\varepsilon_{\text{rel},T}^F \in \mathcal{M}_{n_o,n_i}(\mathbb{R}_+)$ and $\varepsilon_{\text{rel},D}^F \in \mathcal{M}_{n_o,n_r}(\mathbb{R}_+)$ and a vector $\varepsilon_{\text{abs}}^F \in \mathbb{R}_+^{n_o}$ such that $\|F(I,R) - \tilde{F}(I,R)\|_\infty \leq \varepsilon_{\text{rel},T}^F.N_\infty(I) + \varepsilon_{\text{rel},D}^F.N_\infty(R) + \varepsilon_{\text{abs}}$. where $\tilde{F}(I,R)$ is the output on the stream computed upon the *floating-point* numbers on input streams I and initial values I. As before, the matrices for a complex filter may be computed compositionally from the matrices for the sub-filters.

Let us for instance consider the instruction `t = (x + y) + z` where all variables are from the same fixed- or floating-point type (say, IEEE double precision). We shall note $\oplus$ (resp. $\otimes$) the machine operation corresponding to the ideal $+$ (resp $\times$) on reals. Then $x \oplus y = x + y + \varepsilon_1$, with $\varepsilon_1 \leq \varepsilon_{\text{rel}}.|x+y| + \varepsilon_{\text{abs}}$

[3] The absolute error results from the *underflow* condition: a number close to 0 is rounded to 0. Contrary to overflow (which generates infinities, or is configured to issue an exception), underflow is generally a benign condition. However, it precludes merely relying on relative error bounds if one wants to be sound.

$\leq \varepsilon_{\text{rel}}.|x| + \varepsilon_{\text{rel}}.|y| + \varepsilon_{\text{abs}}$. Also, $(x \oplus y) \oplus z = (x \oplus y) + z + \varepsilon_2$, with $\varepsilon_2 \leq \varepsilon_{\text{rel}}.|(x \oplus y) + z| + \varepsilon_{\text{abs}} \leq \varepsilon_{\text{rel}}.|x + y + z + \varepsilon_1| + \varepsilon_{\text{abs}} \leq \varepsilon_{\text{rel}}.(1 + \varepsilon_{\text{rel}}).|x| + \varepsilon_{\text{rel}}.(1 + \varepsilon_{\text{rel}}).|y| + \varepsilon_{\text{rel}}.|z| + \varepsilon_{\text{abs}}.(1 + \varepsilon_{\text{rel}})$. Then $(x \oplus y) \oplus z = x + y + z + (\varepsilon_1 + \varepsilon_2)$ with $|\varepsilon_1 + \varepsilon_2| \leq \varepsilon_{\text{rel}}.(2 + \varepsilon_{\text{rel}}).|x| + \varepsilon_{\text{rel}}.(2 + \varepsilon_{\text{rel}}).|y| + \varepsilon_{\text{rel}}.|z| + \varepsilon_{\text{abs}}.(2 + \varepsilon_{\text{rel}})$.

8.2 Trading Accuracy for Speed; Nonlinear Elements

We have split the behavior of the filter into the sum of the convolution of the input signal by the power development of a rational function, representing the exact behavior, and some error term. If we compute the rational functions exactly over $\mathbb{Q}[z]_{(z)}$, then the rational coefficients might grow expensively large. We can actually take shorter approximations of these coefficients and absorb the error that we introduce into the error term.

An ideal filter of Z-transform P/Q with no initialization condition, $P(z) = \sum_{k=0}^{k} \alpha_k z^k$ and $Q(z) = \sum_{k=0}^{k} \beta_k z^k$ is equivalent to a filter as described in §3.1. Such a filter may be soundly approximated by a non-ideal feedback filter $F^\sharp$ with $T_I^{F^\sharp} = P^\sharp$, $T_O^{F^\sharp} = Q^\sharp$, $\varepsilon_{\text{rel},I} = \|P^\sharp - P\|_1$, $\varepsilon_{\text{rel},O} = \|Q^\sharp - Q\|_1$, $\varepsilon_{\text{abs}} = 0$.

More generally: a filter F (Z-transform P/Q) may be approximated by a filter $F^\sharp$ $(P^\sharp/Q^\sharp)$ with transfer function $T^{F^\sharp} = T^G$, $\varepsilon_{\text{rel},T}^{F^\sharp} = \varepsilon_{\text{rel},T}^{F} + \varepsilon_{\text{rel},T}^{G}$, $\varepsilon_{\text{rel},D}^{F^\sharp} = \varepsilon_{\text{rel},D}^{F} + \varepsilon_{\text{rel},D}^{G}$, $\varepsilon_{\text{abs}}^{F^\sharp} = \varepsilon_{\text{abs}}^{F}$ where G is the feedback filter whose internal filter H is given by $T_I^H = P^\sharp$, $T_O^H = Q^\sharp$, $\varepsilon_{\text{rel},I}^{H} = \|P^\sharp - P\|_1$, $\varepsilon_{\text{rel},I}^{H} = \|Q^\sharp - Q\|_1$, $\varepsilon_{\text{abs}}^{H} = 0$. In this way, a nonlinear sub-filter can be approximated by a linear part and a nonlinear part, the latter being constrained by ε_{rel} and ε_{abs}.

9 Numerical Considerations and Implementation

We have so far given many mathematical formulas that are exact in the *real* field. In this section, we explain how to obtain sound abstractions for these formulas using floating-point arithmetics.

We implemented the algorithms described here. As an example, the serial composition of the filter in Fig. 1 and another TF2 filter, all with realistic coefficients, is analyzed in about 0.04 s on a recent PC; the analyzer finds that $\|S\| \leq g\|E\|$ with $g \simeq 2$, with $\varepsilon_{\text{rel}} \simeq 10^{-12}$ and $\varepsilon_{\text{abs}} \simeq 10^{-305}$.

For filters implemented over the real numbers, the computation of the rational fractions representing the convolution kernels can be performed using arbitrary precision arithmetics; no loss of precision is entailed. When computing the formal development and its sum, one can use floating-point numbers in round-to-$+\infty$ and round-to-$-\infty$ modes and obtain lower and upper bounds, thus also deriving a bound on the computation error; similar bounds may be obtained for the estimate of the norm of the tail. We applied the method to filters extracted from industrial codes; in all cases, the error bounds were small. In practice, outside of artificial cases, floating-point arithmetics does not add significantly to the bounds.

9.1 Interval Arithmetics

IEEE floating-point arithmetics [1] and good extended precision libraries such as MPFR[4] provide functions computing *upward rounded* (or *rounded-to-*$+\infty$) and *downward rounded* (or *rounded-to-*$-\infty$) results: that is, if $f(x_1, \ldots, x_n)$ is the exact operation on real numbers and $\tilde{f}^-$ and $\tilde{f}^+$ are the associated floating-point downward and upward operations, then $f(x_1, \ldots, x_n)$ is guaranteed to be in the interval $[\tilde{f}^-(x_1, \ldots, x_n), \tilde{f}^+(x_1, \ldots, x_n)]$, which will guarantee the *soundness* of our approach. Furthermore, for many operations, $\tilde{f}^-(x_1, \ldots, x_n)$ and $\tilde{f}^+(x_1, \ldots, x_n)$ are guaranteed to be optimal; that is, no better bounds can be provided within the desired floating-point format; this will guarantee local *optimality* of certain of our elementary operations.

9.2 Computation of Developments

When bounding the norm $\|P/Q\|_1$ of a series quotient of two polynomials, we split the series into its N initial terms of development, which we compute explicitly, and a tail whose norm we bound. The first idea is to compute the N first terms of the series by quotienting the series, as explained in Sect. 3.2 or, equivalently, by running the filter for N iterations on the Dirac input $1, 0, 0, \ldots$. In order to provide a sound result, one would work using interval arithmetics over floating-point numbers. However, as already noted by Feret, after some number of iterations the sign of the terms becomes unknown and then the magnitude of the terms increase fast; it is therefore indicated to compute the development until the first term of unknown sign is reached, and assign N accordingly (one may still also enforce a maximal number of iterations $N_{\max}$). In order to be able to develop the quotient further with good precision, one can use a library of extended-precision floating-point computations.

9.3 Bounding the Roots

In order to bound $\|P/Q\|_1$, we have to get lower bounds of the absolute values of the roots of Q. For this, we want to obtain discs $D(x_j, \rho_j)$ such that $|x_j - \xi_j| \leq \rho_j$ where the ξ_j are the roots of Q counted with their multiplicities.

Our polynomial coefficients turned into floating-point intervals $[l_k, h_k]$; it is expected that the $h_k - l_k$ are small. This suggests to us a two-step method for obtaining the desired bounds:

1. Use an efficient and, in practice, very accurate algorithm to obtain *approximations* x_j to the roots of $\sum_{k=1}^{n} \frac{l_k + h_k}{2} z^k$ (the "midpoint polynomial"). We used `gsl_poly_complex_solve` of the GNU Scientific Library [5], which is based on an eigenvalue decomposition of the companion matrix.
2. From those approximations, obtain bounds on the radius of the error committed. There exist a variety of bounding methods [12] which take a polynomial and approximate roots as an input and output error radii; these methods

[4] http://www.mpfr.org

may be performed using interval arithmetics. We implemented the simplest and roughest one [12, Th. 3.1]: ξ_j is in a closed disc of center $x_j - \rho_j$ and radius $|\rho_j|$ where $\rho_j = (nP(x_j))/(2p_n \prod_{k \neq j} x_j - x_k)$.

10 Related Works and Applications

In the field of digital signal processing, some sizable literature has been devoted to the study of the effects of fixed-point and floating-point errors on numerical filters. While the fact that the l_1-norm of the convolution kernel is what matters for judging overflow, it is argued that this norm is "overly pessimistic" [7, §11.3] [6, eq 13], not to mention the difficulties in estimating it. In practice, filter designers have preferred criteria that indicate no saturation for most "commonplace" inputs, excluding pathological inputs. As a consequence, most studies model the errors as random sources of known distribution, independent of each other and with no temporal correlation [2, 10]. This allows estimating the energy spectrum (l_2-norm) of the *typical* numeric noise; however, this does not work for our purpose, which is to provide sound bounds valid in all circumstances.

J. Feret has proposed an abstract domain for analyzing programs comprising digital linear filters [4]. He provides effective bounds for first and second degree filters. In comparison, we consider more complex filter networks, in a compositional fashion; but we analyze specifications, and not C code (which is usually compiled from those specifications, with considerable loss of structure). Another difference is that we do not perform abstract iterations. Feret's method currently considers only second-order filters (i.e. TF2), though it may be possible to adapt it to higher-order filters. On second-order filters, the bounds computed by Feret's method and the method in this paper are very close (since both are based on a development of the convolution kernel, though they use different methods of tail estimation).

Lamb et al. [8] have proposed effective methods, based on linear algebra, for computing equivalent filters for DSP optimization. They do not compute bounds, nor do they study floating-point errors.

Roozbehani et al. [11] find program invariants by Lagrangian relaxation and semidefinite programming, with quadratic invariants. In order to make problems tractable, they too apply a blockwise abstraction. The class of programs that they may analyze directly is potentially larger, but the results are less precise than our method on some linear filters. They do not handle floating-point imprecisions (though this can perhaps be added to their framework).

One possible application of our method would be to integrate it as a pre-analysis pass of a tool such as Astrée [3]. Astrée computes bounds on all floating-point variables inside the analyzed program, in order to prove the absence of errors such as overflow. In order to do so, it needs to compute reasonably accurate bounds on the behavior of linear filters. A typical fly-by-wire controller contains dozens of TF2 filters, some of which may be integrated into more complex feedback loops; in some cases, separate analysis of the filters may yield too coarse bounds.

11 Conclusions and Future Works

We have proposed effective methods for providing sound bounds on the outcome of complex linear filters from their flow-diagram specifications, as found in many applications. Computation times are modest; furthermore, the nature of the results of the analysis may be used for modular analyses — the analysis results of a sub-filter can be stored and never be recomputed until the sub-filter changes.

In the future, we plan to provide abstract domains suitable for the analysis of source code as written in an imperative language such as C, in order to extract the filter specification and arithmetic errors from the source.

References

1. *IEEE Standard for Binary Floating-Point Arithmetic.* IEEE 754.
2. Bruce W. Bomar et al. Roundoff noise analysis of state-space digital filters implemented on floating-point digital signal processors. *IEEE Trans. on Circuits and Systems II*, 44(11):952–955, 1997.
3. P. Cousot et al. The ASTRÉE analyzer. In *ESOP*, number 3444 in LNCS, pages 21–30, 2005.
4. Jérôme Feret. Static analysis of digital filters. In *ESOP '04*, number 2986 in Lecture Notes in Computer Science. Springer-Verlag, 2004.
5. Free Software Foundation. *GSL — GNU scientific library*, 2004.
6. Leland B. Jackson. On the interaction of roundoff noise and dynamic range in digital filters. *The Bell System Technical J.*, 49(2):159–184, February 1970.
7. Leland B. Jackson. *Digital Filters and Signal Processing.* Kluwer, 1989.
8. Andrew A. Lamb, William Thies, and Saman Amarasinghe. Linear analysis and optimization of stream programs. In *PLDI '03*, pages 12–25. ACM, 2003.
9. A. Miné. Relational abstract domains for the detection of floating-point run-time errors. In *ESOP'04*, volume 2986 of *LNCS*, pages 3–17. Springer, 2004.
10. Bhaskar D. Rao. Floating point arithmetic and digital filters. *IEEE Trans. on Signal Processing*, 40(1):85–95, January 1992.
11. M. Roozbehani, E. Feron, and A. Megretski. Modeling, optimization and computation for software verification. In *HSCC*, number 3414 in Lecture Notes in Computer Science, page 606. Springer Verlag, 2005.
12. Siegfried M. Rump. Ten methods to bound multiple roots of polynomials. *J. of Computational and Applied Math.*, 156(2):403–432, 2003.

Syntax-Driven Reachable State Space Construction of Synchronous Reactive Programs

Eric Vecchié and Robert de Simone

INRIA Sophia-Antipolis, France

Abstract. We consider in the current paper the issue of exploiting the structural form of ESTEREL programs [BG92] to partition the algorithmic RSS (reachable state space) fix-point construction used in model-checking techniques [CGP99]. The basic idea sounds utterly simple, as seen on the case of sequential composition: in $P; Q$, first compute *entirely* the states reached in P, and then only carry on to Q, each time using only the relevant local transition relation part. Here a brute-force symbolic breadth-first search would have mixed the exploration of P and Q instead. The introduction of parallel (state product) operators, as well as loop iterators and local synchronizing signals make the problem more difficult (and more interesting). We propose techniques to partition statically ("at compile time") the program body, so as to obtain a good trade-off between locality and multiplicity of steps.

1 Introduction

In the last decade the advent of BDD-based implicit state-space representation [Bry86] allowed to scale up various analysis techniques to large realistic synchronous reactive system designs. But BDDs alone cannot be relied upon to cope with all the complexity of the reachable state space construction. Specifically, while the BDD encoding of the final reachable state space may often be very compact, the transition relation and the intermediate steps of next-state computations can be exceedingly larger. Several clever techniques for partitioning the application of transition functions have been proposed, which partially solve the problem [BCL91,BCL+94,HD93,ISS+03]. In the context of ESTEREL we propose to use the structural syntactic nature of the design to apply transition relations piecewise, only when it may provide further states. Intuitively in a sequential composition $P; Q$ one clearly wants to compute *all* reachable states in P first, then progress to states in Q. While this may seem a trivial idea at first (after all, reachable state space construction can be seen as exhaustive symbolic simulation of all behaviors), care has to be taken, specially in presence of parallel components and internal signal communications, so that the approach retains some of the advantages of symbolic approach, namely that all individual behaviors are not enumerated (or not even nearly so). This is a typical time/space trade-off. Still, using the algorithmic structure of ESTEREL programs to guide (symbolic, exhaustive, breadth-first search) state space construction is a clear, simple idea that was never tried out before to the best of our knowledge. Other

K. Etessami and S.K. Rajamani (Eds.): CAV 2005, LNCS 3576, pp. 213–225, 2005.

works with similar concern usually attempt to precede the symbolic breadth-first search with partial explicit depth-first search simulations that identify new initial configurations "ahead" in the potential behaviors [GB94,PP03].

In essence our refined algorithm proceeds as follows : initially a very restricted transition relation is applied, with many locations of (internal or external) signal receptions "blocked". Then those signal reception occurrences are progressively "re-allowed", in a heuristically ordered fashion. Some transitions can be blocked again in order to deal with loop constructs but in the general case, as the new extensions are always applied to "most recent" states, the old and already largely searched parts get "cleaned up" by some simplification properties of the `TiGeR` BDD package [CMT93], which "cofactors" out the transition parts found to lay outside the domain of states they are applied to. This operation simplifies drastically the support (i.e, the set of variables that the relation effectively depends upon), and thus the computations. Heuristics for ordering the "reception allowances" are based on a graph structure extracted from the structural syntax, so that it is compliant with the natural precedence that may exist (for instance, when a reception on S causes the emission on T otherwise also expected, it is obviously better to release S before T).

The paper is organized as follows : first we give a brief summary of (a restricted micro-subset of) ESTEREL, as well as technical elements of symbolic model-checking. We focus on how the `TiGeR` BDD package [CBM89] performs transition partitioning and "transition cofactoring" in order to decrease the size of data structures (and optimize the variables support) when applying the next-state computation. These techniques will come handy later on to understand ours. Then we provide a description of our approach with the actual algorithm and its BDD implementation, relying on the already mentioned features of `TiGeR`. We justify the correctness of our partitioned approach to build the full RSS. We close with the description of our prototype implementation and performance benchmarks.

2 Context

ESTEREL is an imperative *synchronous reactive language*. We shall only consider here a simple version, where data variables and data-handling are discarded, as often in model-checking. We shall thus only use *Signals* as (identifier) types. A full program consists of a header (where an interface of *input* and *output* signals are defined), followed by a body. Syntax of program statements is provided by the following simple grammar :

P ::= `pause`	| P || P	| `present` S `then` P `else` P `end`
| P ; P	| `emit` S	| `abort` P `when` S
| `loop` P `end`	| `signal` S `in` P `end`	

with S ranging over signals.

Naive semantics of ESTEREL goes as follows : programs behaviors are discretely divided between instants. Control threads are executed until reaching a

pause statement, which is the main statement which cuts behaviors into atomic instants. We call "reaction" the full behavior performed during a given instant. In a reaction *cycle*, input signals are read/sampled, and internal computation takes place until output signals are emitted in answer, and the program state is progressed. Instants are based on a *common* logical clock, which paces all parallel threads. This (the fact that all components proceed with the same atomic steps of instants) is why we call the model "*synchronous*". Of course in a reaction various parallel threads do **not** run independently, as they may synchronize and affect one another causally (hardware people would say "combinationally"). When control reaches a `present S` test statement, it may have to postpone execution until a consistent definitive value (present or absent) is obtained for the signal inside the current reaction (either because it is emitted somewhere in parallel, or because other threads of execution provably progressed to a point where provably *all* potential emissions were discarded).
While being a high-level imperative language, Esterel enjoys a semantic-preserving translation to hardware RTL level (net-lists) where causality issue can be more readily dealt with, and a second level of interpretation into Mealy FSMs (again semantically sound). This second level actually looses information on fine causality issues, but makes explicit the actual reachable state space, and thus can be the definitional background for model-checking analysis techniques. Of course the purpose of implicit (or symbolic) BDD-based model-checking is to apply these analysis at the circuit level. In our case we try to lift them some more by exploiting high-level structuring information from the source syntax.

Symbolic next-state operation. Starting from the initial state ι, the basic breadth-first search Reachable State Space algorithm can be written:

Algorithm 1.1. Breadth-first search algorithm

```
reachable ← ι
new ← ι
while ( new ≠ ∅ ) do
    new ← Image_Δ(new) ∖ reachable
    reachable ← reachable ∪ new
end while
```

The set of states reached at the nth iteration is built from the set of states reached at the $(n-1)^{\text{th}}$ iteration and the set of valid inputs of the program, by computing the image under a transition relation Δ. The algorithm stops when no new state can be found. Each state of the program is a valuation of the set R of boolean registers of the circuit and each input of the program is a valuation of the set I of input signals. The unique global transition relation Δ let us compute the new states of the program with respect to the value of I and R :

$$\Delta : \mathbb{B}^m \times \mathbb{B}^p \rightarrow \mathbb{B}^p$$
$$(I, R) \rightarrow R' = \Delta(I, R)$$

where $\mathbb{B} = \{0, 1\}$, m is the number of input signals and p is the number of registers of the circuit. In fact Δ can be "partitioned" and decomposed into a vector of functions δ_i, where each δ_i concerns a different image register, and depends only on a subset of the source registers and of the input signals :

$$\begin{aligned} \delta_i : \quad & \mathbb{B}^{m_i} \times \mathbb{B}^{p_i} \to \mathbb{B} \\ & (I_i, R_i) \to r'_i = \delta_i(I_i, R_i) \end{aligned}$$

Vectors I_i and R_i are called the support of these transition functions. m_i and p_i are respectively the number of input signals and the number of registers of this support. Such a partitioning scheme is used to speed up applications of BDDs representing the individual δ_i [BCL91].

Extended cofactoring methods. We shall extensively use some well-known BDD transformations, known in general as *extended cofactoring techniques* [Cou91]. In essence the principle is that, if the value of the BDD is only relevant on a subset of the possible valuations of its variables, then this restricted domain of definition can be used to simplify the expression of the BDD (possibly changing its value outside of it). Generally the domain is itself provided as a BDD. We note $f_{\downarrow S}$ the cofactoring of f by the set S :

$$f_{\downarrow S}(X) = \lambda X \to \begin{cases} f(X) & \text{if } X \in S \\ ? & \text{if } X \notin S \end{cases}$$

The value of $f_{\downarrow S}$ out of S is not used and can be anything. It is set in order to minimize the size of the BDD representing $f_{\downarrow S}$. In our algorithm, this operator is used in the **Image** function. It lets us handle smaller BDDs during the image computation since the transition relation is reduced with respect to the domain it is applied on. More precisely, given a register r, if the activation condition of r (the set of states for which $r = 1$) and the domain of the transition relation are disjoint, then the transition function of r can be reduced to a very simple expression $\lambda X \to \neg r$. In other words, the BDD encoding the transition function of registers that will not be activated in the next instant is very small.

3 Partitioned Algorithm

Our partitioned algorithm consists in performing each step of the reachable states exploration in a reduced number of program blocks. State search will be performed inside each block until stabilization, before moving to the next one ; this algorithm is an adaptation of the algorithm 1.1. The BDD area represents the set of all states (reachable or not) lying inside the program blocs we are focusing. At each step of the algorithm, the cofactored image computation is performed only on the pending reachable states lying inside area (line 8). At the end of each step, the new-found states are stored in the pending set (line 9). area is left unchanged as long as new states are found inside it (lines 5, 6, 7).

This algorithm does not describe the evolution of area (this will be developed in section 4).

Algorithm 1.2. Partitioned algorithm

```
reachable ← ι
pending ← ι
area ← area0        /* area0 : see algorithm 1.3 */
while ( pending ≠ ∅ ) do
    if ( (pending ∩ area) = ∅ ) then
        area ← area'        /* area' : see algorithm 1.4 */
    end if
    new ← Image_Δ(pending ∩ area) ∖ reachable
    pending ← (pending ∖ area) ∪ new
    reachable ← reachable ∪ new
end while
```

Partitioning into "macro-states" according to syntax. At the heart of the method is the division of the program body into blocks (or macro-states) of proper granularity. To disallow search in given blocks, one needs only to remove the part of the transition relation where all registers of these blocks are inactive. The bloc division of course relies heavily on the structural syntax, and mostly on signal receptions (as in `abort P when S`) and, to a lesser extent, on signal emissions. We use a control flow graph data structure to help us with this task. We shall stick to the classical translation from ESTEREL to circuits described in [Ber99], which generates exactly one boolean register for each `pause` statement. In the sequel we shall consider an abstract syntax tree version for ESTEREL programs where `pause` constructs are explicitly labeled by the corresponding register names, providing the necessary association. In fact, we want to recognize each instance of instruction that we identify here with a unique label mentioned as exponent. Each node of the tree is typed with respect to the instruction it represents. Thus, the tree node of an instruction of type **instruction** and labeled by L is written :

$$(\textbf{instruction}^L \ \textit{subtree}_1{}^{l_1} \ \ldots \ \textit{subtree}_n{}^{l_n})$$

The control flow graph of a given syntax tree T is defined as follows : $\mathsf{G}(\mathsf{T}) = (\mathrm{I}, \mathsf{O}, \mathsf{N}, \mathsf{E}, \mathsf{F})$ where N is the set of the nodes of the graph. These nodes are the same as those of the syntax tree. I and O are subsets of N and represent respectively the start and final nodes of the graph. The edges of our graph (written $i \mapsto j$) are divided into two categories : E contains "normal" edges and F contains the edges used as frontiers. By construction, the set $\mathsf{E} \cap \mathsf{F}$ is empty. Thus, edges corresponding to `present` and `abort` statements are settled in F. Such edges are called "frontier" edges. Other edges are settled in E.

We describe here the way we build our control flow graph for each ESTEREL instruction. This description uses labels of the syntax tree which are a lighter way to identify the nodes. The usual operator " $\times$ " allows us to join each element of a set $I = \{I_1, \ldots I_m\}$ to each element of a set $J = \{J_1, \ldots J_n\}$.

In this section, we suppose that an instruction I produces a graph $\mathsf{G}(I) = (\mathsf{I}, \mathsf{O}, \mathsf{N}, \mathsf{E}, \mathsf{F})$. As well, for $i \in [1, 2]$ we have $\mathsf{G}(I_i) = (\mathsf{I}_i, \mathsf{O}_i, \mathsf{N}_i, \mathsf{E}_i, \mathsf{F}_i)$. Atomic instructions produce graphs containing a single node and no edge :

$$\mathsf{G}(\mathbf{emit}^L\ s) = (\{L\}, \{L\}, \{L\}, \varnothing, \varnothing)$$
$$\mathsf{G}(\mathbf{pause}^L\ r) = (\{L\}, \{L\}, \{L\}, \varnothing, \varnothing)$$

In our graph, we can abstract the beginnings and the ends of the scope. The graph of a local signal declaration is thus the same as for I :

$$\mathsf{G}(\mathbf{signal}^L\ s\ I\ \mathbf{end}^{L'}) = \mathsf{G}(I)$$

Choice operator. Consider a `present S then` P `else` Q `end` statement. If the reachable state space is computed in a breadth-first search manner on a global transition relation, then states in P and Q will be considered at the same time. In this case the intermediate symbolic description is likely to be larger than the final one, if one grants that intermediate forms of partially reached state spaces are more irregular than final ones. Moreover, the sequentially partitioned state space search here allows to use only the relevant part of the transition relation when dealing with each component (P, then Q). Frontiers are thus placed before and after the "then" branch and the "else" branch.

$$\mathsf{G}(\mathbf{present}^L\ s\ I_1\ I_2\ \mathbf{end}^{L'}) = (\{L\}, \{L'\}, \mathsf{N}_1 \cup \mathsf{N}_2 \cup \{L, L'\}, \mathsf{E}_1 \cup \mathsf{E}_2, \mathsf{F}')$$
$$\text{where} \quad \mathsf{F}' = \mathsf{F}_1 \cup \mathsf{F}_2 \cup (\{L\} \times (\mathsf{I}_1 \cup \mathsf{I}_2)) \cup ((\mathsf{O}_1 \cup \mathsf{O}_2) \times \{L'\})$$

Preemption. An `abort` P `when S` statement allows to add abortive transitions to the natural terminations of P. Our partitioning technique will aim at exploring fully P before exploring the next program blocks activated by P's terminations (of course this will have the effect of blocking also the potential emissions causing the abort, that would figure in the same global transition). Therefore, we want to consider each transition exiting P as frontier. Each `pause` instruction may lead to the end of the `abort` instruction that encloses it. Thus :

$$\mathsf{G}(\mathbf{abort}^L\ s\ I\ \mathbf{end}^{L'}) = (\mathsf{I}, \{L'\}, \mathsf{N} \cup \{L'\}, \mathsf{E}, \mathsf{F} \cup \mathsf{F}')$$
$$\text{where} \quad \mathsf{F}' = (\mathsf{O} \cup \{l \ / \ (\mathbf{pause}^l\ r) \in \mathsf{N}\}) \times \{L'\}$$

Sequence statement. Partitioning a $P;Q$ sequence statement is a waste of energy. If P is a constant-length program like `pause;pause` then the partitioning of $P;Q$ is naturally performed by the breadth-first search algorithm. Variable-length programs are already partitioned since containing `present` or `abort` statements.

$$\mathsf{G}(\mathbf{seq}^L\ I_1\ I_2\ \mathbf{end}^{L'}) = (\mathsf{I}_1, \mathsf{O}_2, \mathsf{N}_1 \cup \mathsf{N}_2, \mathsf{E}', \mathsf{F}_1 \cup \mathsf{F}_2)$$
$$\text{where} \quad \mathsf{E}' = \mathsf{E}_1 \cup \mathsf{E}_2 \cup (\mathsf{O}_1 \times \mathsf{I}_2)$$

Parallel networks and signal synchronizations. The problem here is to establish which blocks put in parallel can be active in parallel, so that the global search can be divided with matching progressions. This is shown in figure 1. The

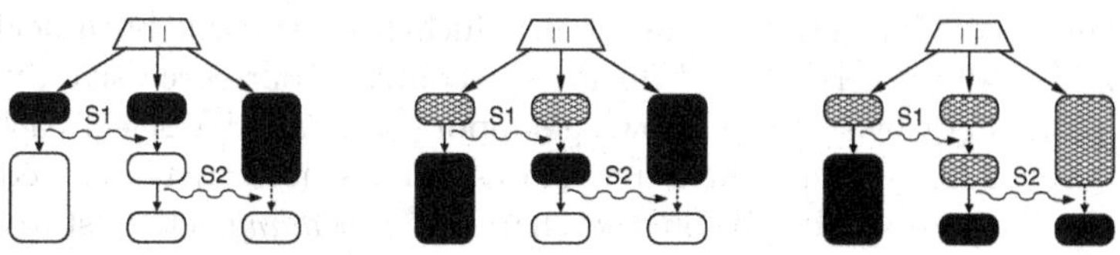

Fig. 1. *Partitioning method for a parallel component. There are two signals synchronizing three parallel components. Our technique aims at partitioning according to the black-colored blocks. Hatched blocks should be removed by cofactoring methods*

only syntactic element at our disposal here to indicate synchronization will of course be signal reception. These receptions must be matched by corresponding emissions when signals are local (otherwise receptions of input signals can occur anytime, but each parallel component must perceive it consistently). Nevertheless it should be noted that, in the synchronous reactive framework, *it is possible* that a local signal emission causes no reception, if none are "actively watching" at the time. So, while we shall use signal receptions to generate frontier transitions, these will automatically generate simultaneous frontiers at *emit* side **when they are enabled**, and otherwise emissions can be passed and go unsynchronized. To clarify further, consider the following simple example : P_1; `emit S;` P_2 `||` Q_1; `await S;` Q_2. If the design of this program is so that any emission of `S` is received by the `await S` statement, then P_2 can not be active if Q_2 is not. Thus partitioning according to Q_1 and Q_2 will partition the first branch according to P_1 and P_2 as well. If some emissions of `S` are not received, then partitioning according to Q_1 and Q_2 will have no precise effect on the first branch. In all case there is a real benefit in partitioning this way. In the best case, the reachable state space computation will concern P_1 and Q_1 first and then, P_2 and Q_2. In the worst case, it will concern P_1, P_2 and Q_1 and then, P_2 and Q_2.

$$\begin{aligned}\mathsf{G}(\mathbf{par}^L\ I_1\ I_2\ \mathbf{end}^{L'}) = (\{L\}, \mathsf{O}_1 \cup \mathsf{O}_2, \mathsf{N}_1 \cup \mathsf{N}_2 \cup \{L\}, \mathsf{E}', \mathsf{F}_1 \cup \mathsf{F}_2)\\ \text{where}\quad \mathsf{E}' = \mathsf{E}_1 \cup \mathsf{E}_2 \cup (\{L\} \times (\mathrm{I}_1 \cup \mathrm{I}_2))\end{aligned}$$

Loops. In loop constructs a new difficulty arises : whether blocks can be truly concurrent is in general only known dynamically (this is in a large part why RSS construction can be so hard). Loops are the only constructs in which we want to lock frontiers during state space exploration. In ESTEREL programs, registers which are not running in parallel cannot be active at the same time. We can use this static information in order to deactivate registers in loop constructs. Thus, each time a register r is activated we shall deactivate the set of registers incompatible with r and belonging to the same loop as r. We call *Lock* (r) such a set which of course can be refined at will. The graph of a loop statement is the following :

$$\mathsf{G}(\mathbf{loop}^L\ I\ \mathbf{end}^{L'}) = (\mathrm{I}, \varnothing, \mathsf{N}, \mathsf{E} \cup \mathsf{E}', \mathsf{F}) \quad \text{where}\quad \mathsf{E}' = \mathsf{O} \times \mathrm{I}$$

Frontier ordering. Currently, the order in which frontiers will be unlocked is defined dynamically, "at run time" during the course of our successive fix-point iterations searching new states in growing support domains. We select each time a frontier that is likely to produce new states, and is not strictly preceded by another one. This relies deeply on the shape of a *pending* set of states that are incompletely processed, and can generate configurations beyond the current frontiers. Details shall be provided in section 4.

This partial order is statically refined according to the syntax of the programs. This static order written "$\prec$" is a guarantee that frontiers will not be opened prematurely. The statement "a frontier x should be opened before a frontier y" is written $x \prec y$. In fact, defining a static order between frontiers consists in defining an order between the target nodes of the frontiers. Thus, if u and v are two nodes, $u \prec v$ means that any frontier leading to u should be opened before any frontier leading to v :

$$u \prec v \Longleftrightarrow (x \mapsto u) \prec (y \mapsto v) \quad \forall x, \forall y$$

The definition of "$\prec$" is purely syntactic. In a sequence ($\mathbf{seq}^L\ I_1\ I_2\ \mathbf{end}^{L'}$), one wants to open frontiers in I_1 before frontiers in I_2. Thus we have $N_1 \prec N_2$.

In an ($\mathbf{abort}^L\ s\ I\ \mathbf{end}^{L'}$) statement, one wants to open frontiers inside I before frontiers leading outside I. This can be written $N \prec L'$.

4 The Precise Algorithm and Its BDD Implementation

We shall introduce useful notations. Given a set $\mathcal{R} = \{r_1, \ldots r_n\}$ of BDD variables, we introduce the operator :

$$NOr(\mathcal{R}) = \lambda X \rightarrow \neg(r_1 \vee \ldots \vee r_n)$$

If $r_1, \ldots r_n$ are variables representing boolean registers $R_1, \ldots R_n$ then $NOr(\mathcal{R})$ represents the set of states in which all registers R_i are inactive for all $i \in [1..n]$. We notice that $Or(\mathcal{R}) = \overline{NOr(\mathcal{R})}$ represents the set of states in which at least one register R_i is active for $i \in [1..n]$. Given a set X of graph nodes, we introduce the operator *Register* (X) which returns the set of register BDD variables in X :

$$Register\,(X) = \{r \mid (\mathbf{pause}\ r) \in X\}$$

This operator will help us to make the link between our control flow graph and the symbolic BDD-based computations. Source and target node of an edge $u \mapsto v$ are written :

$$Src(u \mapsto v) = u \quad \text{and} \quad Dest(u \mapsto v) = v$$

Given a "classical" directed graph (N , E), we write :

$$Succ_{(N,E)}(X) = \{j \in N \mid i \in X \wedge i \mapsto j \in E\}$$

the set of target nodes of edges of E whose source belongs to X and we write :

$$Out_{(\mathsf{N},\mathsf{E})}(\mathsf{X}) = \{i \mapsto j \in \mathsf{E} \mid i \in \mathsf{X}\}$$

the set of edges of E whose source belongs to X. The operator :

$$Closure_{(\mathsf{N},\mathsf{E})}(\mathsf{Y}) = \mu(\lambda \mathsf{X} \to \mathsf{Y} \cup Succ_{(\mathsf{N},\mathsf{E})}(\mathsf{X}))$$

represents the set of nodes reachable from Y through edges in E. The following operator computes the "surface" of a program block. Given a set $\mathsf{Y} \subseteq \mathsf{N}$ of nodes (corresponding to a set of active registers), the surface is the set of edges that can be crossed in the immediate instant following the activation of one or more registers in Y. If P is the set of nodes of type "pause", then :

$$Surface_{(\mathsf{N},\mathsf{E})}(\mathsf{Y}) = \mu(\lambda \mathsf{X} \to \mathsf{Y} \cup (Succ_{(\mathsf{N},\mathsf{E})}(\mathsf{X}) \setminus \mathsf{P}))$$

Given a set $\mathcal{R} = \{r_1, \dots r_n\}$ of registers, we write :

$$Lock\,(\mathcal{R}) = Lock\,(r_1) \cap \dots \cap Lock\,(r_n)$$

the set of registers which we want to deactivate when all $r_1, \dots r_n$ are activated.

4.1 Graph-Guided Algorithm

In this section, we describe the evolution of the set area in the algorithm 1.2 with respect to the control flow graph. We assume that the syntax tree of the analyzed program is given in T.

Control flow graph and restricted area initializations. The initialization process consists in building the graph to obtain an initial set of locked edges and then build the set area_0 with respect to these initial conditions.

Algorithm 1.3. Initialization of area_0

1 $(\mathrm{I}, \mathsf{O}, \mathsf{N}, \mathsf{E}, \mathsf{F}) \leftarrow \mathsf{G}(\mathsf{T})$
2 $\mathtt{inner} \leftarrow Closure_{(\mathsf{N},\mathsf{E})}(\mathrm{I})$
3 $\mathfrak{R} \leftarrow Register\,(\mathsf{N}),\ \mathfrak{R}^+ \leftarrow Register\,(\mathtt{inner})$
4 $\mathsf{area}_0 \leftarrow NOr(\mathfrak{R} \setminus \mathfrak{R}^+)$

The first step consists in building the graph (line 1). Then, we need to know the set $\mathfrak{R}^+$ of registers which are allowed to be active (line 3). Finally, area is defined as the set of states such that no register but those in $\mathfrak{R}^+$ is active (line 4).

Restricted area enlargement. When area is required to be enlarged, we want to unlock "good" edges. We only want to unlock edges which allow us to include some pending states inside the growing area set. Such edges can only be found in the surface of inner (line 1) and are sorted according to "$\prec$" (line 2). Furthermore, more than one edge may be required to be unlocked. This is the typical case where two parallel branches are awaiting the same signal. Thus, while no pending state lies inside area, a new edge is analyzed in order to decide whether it should be unlocked or not.

Algorithm 1.4. Enlargement of area′

```
surface ← Surface_(N,E∪F) (inner)
frontier ← Sort_≺(Out_(N,F)(surface))
i ← 1
while ( (pending ∩ area) = ∅ ) do
    f ← frontier[i]
    /* check if f should be opened, see algorithm 1.5 */
    if ( open? ) then
        /* open f, see algorithm 1.6 */
        /* close some frontiers, see algorithm 1.7 */
    end if
    i ← i + 1
end while
```

Edge crossing. To determine whether an edge should be unlocked, one has to focus on the new active registers in the set pending.

Algorithm 1.5. Crossing a frontier

```
1 inner^new ← Closure_(N,E) (Dest(f))
2 ℜ^new ← Register (inner^new) ∖ ℜ^+
3 open? ← false
4 if ( ℜ^new = ∅ ) then
5     open? ← true
6 else if ( pending ∩ Or(ℜ^new) ≠ ∅ ) then
7     open? ← true
8 end if
```

First, we compute the set of nodes in the graph that would be reached if the edge f was unlocked. We just need to know the new-found registers which are stored in $\mathfrak{R}^{new}$ at line 2. If f leads to no register, it can be unlocked but this will have no effect on the set area (line 4, 5). If $\mathfrak{R}^{new}$ is not empty, we check if there are some states in pending that have activated one or more new registers contained in $\mathfrak{R}^{new}$ (line 6, 7). In this case, the edge can be unlocked.

Unlocking an edge. Once an edge has been decided to be unlocked, we just have to perform the following updates : first, the unlocked edge is moved from F to E. Then, the set area is enlarged.

Algorithm 1.6. Opening a frontier

```
E ← E ∪ {f}, F ← F ∖ {f}
inner ← inner ∪ inner^new, ℜ^+ ← ℜ^+ ∪ ℜ^new
area′ ← NOr(ℜ ∖ ℜ^+)
```

Locking some edges. Finally we close some edges to deal with loop constructs. In this algorithm, graph updates have been discarded.

Algorithm 1.7. Closing frontiers

$\mathfrak{R}^+ \leftarrow \mathfrak{R}^+ \setminus \mathit{Lock}\,(\mathfrak{R}^{new})$
...

4.2 Correctness Arguments (Hints)

Formally, one should prove that our new partitioned technique computes the same RSS as the global one. But the correctness assumption relies on a simple argument, that we shall state only informally.

In the last iteration of the algorithm's main loop, the (ever-growing) transition relation will be the global one, as used in the classical single iteration breadth-first search. But it is only applied to a selection of new initial states (those taken from the temporary `pending` sets), and thus will reach only *all states* reachable from there. But older states were only discarded from the `pending` potential new state generators when all theirs successors were produced (because they could be so in a more restricted transition relation form. So it is harmless not to consider them any longer.

5 Experimental Results

The results presented here have been obtained by executing our program on a Bi-Pentium III - 550 MHz with 1 GByte of memory and running under the Linux operating system. The memory was limited to 900 MBytes in order to avoid the use of disk swap. These results have been obtained without closing frontiers in loop constructs.

We implemented our method with the help of the `TiGeR` BDD package and we tested it on numerous ESTEREL designs. Still, many were small programs which primarily helped us validate our implementation. Results here are not so significant since memory consumption is not an issue, as intermediate BDDs blow-ups are very limited. Figure 2 presents experimental results obtained on pretty big ESTEREL designs. Concerning computation time, our method was slower on the `sequencer` example as expected since more iterations are required to reach RSS completion. But, surprisingly it appeared to win on bigger designs (`mmid`, `sat`). This is so since each iteration step works on much smaller objects (BDD DAGs). We still need more experiments to be fully conclusive on our findings.

6 Conclusion

To the best of or knowledge our method is the only partitioning method based on syntactic {*sequential/alternative/parallel/synchronized*} structural information drawn from (synchronous) programs. Our method tends to mimic the behavioral progression of control through time, but in a context where all paths

Program		Steps	Found states	Crossed states	Memory	Time
globalopt	def.	3	342 858 276 099	583 065 603	$> 900M$	$34m40s$
598 regs.	part.	80	**705 085 932 547**	**5 542 740 483**	$> 900M$	$26h45m32s$
site	def.	3	232 705 179	1 049 601	$> 900M$	$22m51s$
308 regs.	part.	91	**2 380 837 289**	**452 110 875**	$> 900M$	$9h58m45s$
cabin	def.	3	13 321	534	$> 900M$	$14m22s$
919 regs.	part.	147	**719 031 955**	**484 744 348**	$> 900M$	$18h54m29s$
sequencer	def.	18	122 597	all	$40\,359K$	$\mathbf{3m47,22s}$
154 regs.	part.	145	122 597	all	$\mathbf{17\,022K}$	$8m56,59s$
mmid	def.	13	10 308 357	all	$205\,214K$	$45m59s$
111 regs.	part.	113	10 308 357	all	$\mathbf{42\,368K}$	$\mathbf{19m38}$
chorusBin	def.	6	16 928 480	441 417	$> 900M$	$5h39m35s$
92 regs.	part.	79	**136 329 824**	**all**	$851\,369K$	$238h10m45s$
cdtmica	def.	10	12 538 388 785	10 651 674 353	$> 900M$	$15h24m46s$
208 regs.	part.	185	**23 384 736 769**	**all**	$748\,971K$	$36h31m23s$
steam	def.	3	3 865 747 524	396 566 399	$> 900M$	$48m36s$
128 regs.	part.	101	**41 774 141 026**	**all**	$762\,153K$	$25h30m21s$
sat	def.	17	43 487 202 056	17 566 150 006	$> 900M$	$6h42m50s$
192 regs.	part.	339	**35 740 420 392 968**	**all**	$\mathbf{77\,797K}$	$\mathbf{3h00m56s}$

Fig. 2. *Comparison between the default and the partitioned method : the first column* (Steps) *is the number of computation steps achieved with success, the second column* (Found states) *is the number of found states, the third column* (Crossed states) *is the number of states whose image has been successfully computed, the forth column* (Memory) *shows the memory required and the fifth column* (Time) *shows the computation times.*

have to be followed (exhaustive search, as opposed to single path simulation). We presented a solution to partition the RSS computation, primarily according to signal receptions, and then order the evaluation of blocks according to progression of control. This latter information is drawn from a control-flow graph, itself directly extracted from the abstract syntax tree. The graph is also used to actually build the precise transition relation selected at any given macro-step, by including the parts where registers enclosed inside proper frontiers are found. Frontiers are progressively expanded, in a hopefully "sensible" order, so that all reachable states can be captured. Sometimes, frontiers are closed in order to deal with loop constructs as if they were "unrolled". This method provides good experimental results showing the relevance of the approach.

References

[BCL91] J. R. Burch, E. M. Clarke, and D. E. Long. Symbolic model checking with partitioned transition relations. In A. Halaas and P.B. Denyer, editors, *International Conference on Very Large Scale Integration*, pages 49–58, Edinburgh, Scotland, August 1991. IFIP Transactions, North-Holland.

[BCL+94] J. R. Burch, E. M. Clarke, D. E. Long, K. L. McMillan, and D. L. Dill. Symbolic model checking for sequential circuit verification. *IEEE Transactions on Computer-Aided Design of Integrated Circuits and Systems*, 13(4):401–424, April 1994.

[Ber99] Grard Berry. *The Constructive Semantics of Pure Esterel.* INRIA, 1999. http://www-sop.inria.fr/esterel.org/.

[BG92] Grard Berry and Georges Gonthier. The Esterel synchronous programming language: Design, semantics, implementation. *Sci. of Comput. Program.*, 19(2):87–152, 1992.

[Bry86] Randal E. Bryant. Graph-based algorithms for Boolean function manipulation. *IEEE Transactions on Computers*, C-35(8):677–691, August 1986.

[CBM89] O. Coudert, C. Berthet, and J. C. Madre. Verification of synchronous sequential machines using symbolic execution. In *Proceedings of the International Workshop on Automatic Verification Methods for Finite State Systems*, volume 407 of *Lecture Notes in Computer Science*, pages 365–373, Grenoble, France, June 1989. Springer-Verlag.

[CGP99] Edmund M. Clarke, Orna Grumberg, and Doron Peled. *Model Checking.* The MIT Press, Cambridge, Massachusetts, 1999.

[CMT93] Olivier Coudert, Jean-Christophe Madre, and Herv Touati. TIGER *Version 1.0 User Guide.* Digital Paris Research Lab, December 1993.

[Cou91] Olivier Coudert. *SIAM: Une Boite Outils Pour la Preuve Formelle de Systmes Squentiels.* PhD thesis, Ecole Nationale Suprieure des Tlcommunications, Octobre 1991.

[GB94] D. Geist and I. Beer. Efficient model checking by automated ordering of transition relation partitions. In *Proc. 6th International Computer Aided Verification Conference*, volume 818, pages 299–310, 1994.

[HD93] Alan J. Hu and David L. Dill. Reducing BDD size by exploiting functional dependencies. In *Design Automation Conference*, pages 266–271, 1993.

[ISS+03] S. Iyer, D. Sahoo, Ch. Stangier, A. Narayan, and J. Jain. Improved symbolic verification using partitioned techniques. In *Proceedings CHARME'03*, pages 410–424. LNCS 2860, 2003.

[PP03] E. Pastor and M.A. Peña. Combining Simulation and Guided Traversal for the Verification of Concurrent Systems. In *Proceedings of DATE'03*. IEEE publisher, 2003.

Program Repair as a Game*

Barbara Jobstmann, Andreas Griesmayer, and Roderick Bloem

Graz University of Technology

Abstract. We present a conservative method to automatically fix faults in a finite state program by considering the repair problem as a game. The game consists of the product of a modified version of the program and an automaton representing the LTL specification. Every winning finite state strategy for the game corresponds to a repair. The opposite does not hold, but we show conditions under which the existence of a winning strategy is guaranteed. A finite state strategy corresponds to a repair that adds variables to the program, which we argue is undesirable. To avoid extra state, we need a memoryless strategy. We show that the problem of finding a memoryless strategy is NP-complete and present a heuristic. We have implemented the approach symbolically and present initial evidence of its usefulness.

1 Introduction

Model checking formally proves whether a program adheres to its specifications. If not, the user is typically presented with a counterexample showing an execution of the program that violates the specification. The user needs to find and correct the fault in the program, which is a nontrivial task.

The problem of locating a fault in a misbehaving program has been the attention of recent research [SW96, JRS02, BNR03, GV03, Gro04]. Given a suspicion of the fault location, it may still not be easy to repair the program. There may be multiple suggestions, only one of which is the actual fault and knowing the fault is not the same as knowing a fix.

The work presented here goes one step beyond fault localization. Given a set of *suspect statements*, it looks for a modification of the program that satisfies its specifications. It can be used to find the actual fault among the suggestions of a fault localization tool and a correction, while avoiding the tedious debugging that would normally ensue.

The repair problem is closely related to the synthesis problem [PR89]. In order to automatically synthesize a program, a complete specification is needed, which is a heavy burden on the user. For the repair problem, on the other hand, we only need as much of the specification as is necessary to decide the correct repair, just as for model checking we do not need a full specification to detect a fault. (This has the obvious drawback that an automatic repair may violate an unstated property and needs to be reviewed by a designer.) A further benefit is that the modification is limited to a small portion of the program. The structure and logic of the program are left untouched, which makes it amenable to further modification by the user. Automatically synthesized programs may be hard to understand.

* This work was supported in part by the European Union under contract 507219 (PROSYD).

K. Etessami and S.K. Rajamani (Eds.): CAV 2005, LNCS 3576, pp. 226–238, 2005.

We give the necessary definitions in Section 2. We assume that the specification is given in linear time logic (LTL). The program game is an LTL game that captures the possible repairs of the program, by making some value "unknown" (Section 3.1). We focus on finite-state programs and our fault model assumes that either an expression or the left-hand side of an assignment is incorrect. We can thus make an expression or a left-hand side variable "unknown". We have chosen this fault model for the purpose of illustration, and our method applies equally well to other fault models or even to circuits instead of programs.

The game is played between the environment, which provides the inputs, and the system, which provides the correct value for the unknown expression. The game is won if for any input sequence the system can provide a sequence of values for the unknown expression such that the specification is satisfied. A winning strategy fixes the proper values for the unknown expression and thus corresponds to a repair.

In order to find a strategy, we construct a Büchi game that is the product of the program game and the standard nondeterministic automaton for the specification. If the product game is won, so is the program game, but because of the nondeterminism in the automaton, the converse does not hold. In many cases, however, we can find a winning finite state strategy anyway, and the nondeterministic automaton may be exponentially smaller than a deterministic equivalent (Section 3.2).

To implement the repair corresponding to a finite state strategy, we may need to add state to the program, mirroring the specification automaton. Such a repair is unlikely to please the developer as it may significantly alter the program, inserting new variables and new assignments throughout the code. Instead, we look for a memoryless strategy, which corresponds to a repair that changes only the suspected lines and does not introduce new variables. In Section 3.3 we show that deciding whether such a strategy exists is NP-complete, so in Section 3.4 we develop a heuristic to find one.

We obtain a conservative algorithm that yields valid repairs and is complete for invariants. It may, however, fail to find a memoryless repair for other types of properties, either because of nondeterminism in the automaton or because of the heuristic that constructs a memoryless strategy. In Section 3.5 we describe a symbolic method to extract a repair from the strategy. We have implemented the algorithm in VIS and we present initial experiences with the algorithm in Section 4.

Our work is related to controller synthesis [RW89], which studies the problem of synthesizing a "controller" for a "plant". The controller synthesis problem, however, does not assume that the plant is malfunctioning, and our repair application is novel. Also, we study the problem finding a memoryless repair, which corresponds to a controller that is "integrated" in the plant. Buccafurri et al. [BEGL99] consider the repair problem for CTL as an abductive reasoning problem and present an approach that is based on calling the model checker once for every possible repair to see if it is successful. Our approach needs to consider the problem only once, considering all possible repairs at the same time, and is likely to be more efficient. Model-based diagnosis can also be used to suggest repairs for broken programs by incorporating proper fault models into the diagnosis problem. Stumptner and Wotawa [SW96] discuss this approach for functional programs. The approach appears to be able to handle only a small amount of possible repairs, and bases its conclusions on a few failed test cases (typically one) instead of the specification.

2 Preliminaries

In this section, we describe the necessary theoretical background for our work. We assume basic knowledge of the μ-calculus, LTL, and the translation of LTL to Büchi automata. We refer to [CGP99] for an introduction.

A *game* G over *AP* is a tuple $(S, s_0, I, C, \delta, \lambda, F)$, where S is a finite set of states, $s_0 \in S$ is the initial state, I and C are finite sets of environment inputs and system choices, $\delta : S \times I \times C \rightharpoonup S$ is the partial transition function, $\lambda : S \to 2^{AP}$ is the labeling function, and $F \subseteq S^\omega$ is the winning condition, a set of infinite sequences of states. With the exception of this section and Section 3.4, we will assume that δ is a complete function. Intuitively, a game is an incompletely specified finite state machine together with a specification. The environment inputs are as usual, and the system choices C represent the freedom of implementation. The challenge is to find proper values for C such that F is satisfied.

Given a game $G = (S, s_0, I, C, \delta, \lambda, F)$, a *(finite state) strategy* is a tuple $\sigma = (Q, q_0, \mu)$, where Q is a finite set of states, $q_0 \in Q$ is the initial state, and $\mu : Q \times S \times I \to 2^{C \times Q}$ is the *move function*. Intuitively, a strategy automaton fixes a set of possible responses to an environment input, and its response may depend on a finite memory of the past. Note that strategies are nondeterministic. We need nondeterminism in the following in order to have maximal freedom when we attempt to convert a finite state strategy to a memoryless strategy. For the strategy to be winning, a winning play has to ensue for any nondeterministic choices of the strategy.

A *play* on G according to σ is a finite or infinite sequence $\pi = q_0 s_0 \xrightarrow{i_0 c_0} q_1 s_1 \xrightarrow{i_1 c_1} \dots$ such that $(c_i, q_{i+1}) \in \mu(q_i, s_i, i_i)$, $s_{i+1} = \delta(s_i, i_i, c_i)$, and either the play is infinite, or there is an n such that $\mu(q_n, s_n, i_n) = \emptyset$ or $\delta(s_n, i_n, c_n)$ is not defined, which means that the play is finite. A play is *winning* if it is infinite and $s_0 s_1 \cdots \in F$. (If $\mu(q_n, s_n, i_n) = \emptyset$, the strategy does not suggest a proper system choice and the game is lost.) A strategy σ is *winning* on G if all plays according to σ on G are winning.

A *memoryless strategy* is a finite state strategy with only one state. We will write a memoryless strategy as a function $\sigma : Q \times I \to 2^C$ and a play of a memoryless strategy as a sequence $s_0 \xrightarrow{i_0 c_0} s_1 \xrightarrow{i_1 c_1} \dots$, leaving out the state of strategy automaton.

We extend the labeling function λ to plays: the *output word* is $\lambda(\pi) = \lambda(s_0)\lambda(s_1)\dots$ Likewise, the *input word* is $\iota(\pi) = i_0 i_1 \dots$, the sequence of system inputs. The *output language (input language)* $L(G)$ $(I(G))$ of a game is the set of all $\lambda(\pi)$ $(\iota(\pi))$ with π winning.

A *safety game* has the condition $F = \{s_0 s_1 \cdots \mid \forall i : s_i \in A\}$ for some $A \subseteq S$. The winning condition of an *LTL game* is the set of sequences satisfying an LTL formula φ. In this case, we will write φ for F. *Büchi games* are defined by a set $B \subseteq Q$, and require that a play visit the Büchi constraint B infinitely often. For such games, we will write B for F.

We can convert an LTL formula φ over the set of atomic propositions *AP* to a Büchi game $A = (Q, q_0, 2^{AP}, C, \delta, \lambda, B)$ such that $I(A)$ is the set of words satisfying φ. The system choice models the nondeterminism of the automaton. Following the construction proposed in [SB00] we get a *generalized Büchi game*, which has more than one Büchi constraint. Our approach works with such games as well but for simplicity we explain it for games with a single constraint. Besides, we can easily get rid of multiple Büchi constraints with help of the well-known counting construction. The size of the resulting automaton is exponential in the length of the formula in the worst case.

In order to solve games, we introduce some notation. For a set $A \subseteq S$, the set $\mathsf{MX}\,A = \{s \mid \forall i \in I\, \exists c \in C\, s' \in A : (s,i,c,s') \in \delta\}$ is the set of states from which the system can force a visit to a state in A in one step. The set $\mathsf{M}A\,\mathsf{U}\,B$ is defined by the μ-calculus formula $\mu Y.\, B \cup \mathsf{MX}\,(A \cap Y)$. It defines the set of states from which the system can force a visit to B without leaving A. The *iterates* of this computation are $Y_0 = B$ and $Y_{j+1} = Y_j \cup (A \cap \mathsf{MX}\,Y_{j-1})$ for $j > 0$. From Y_j the system can force a visit to B in at most j steps. Note that there are only finitely many distinct iterates.

We define $\mathsf{MG}\,A = \nu Z.A \cap \mathsf{MX}\,Z$, the set of states from which the system can avoid leaving A. For a Büchi game, we define $W = \nu Z.\mathsf{MX}\,\mathsf{M}ZU(Z \cap B)$. The set W is the set of states from which the system can win the Büchi game. Note that these fixpoints are similar to the ones used in model checking of fair CTL and are easily implemented symbolically.

Using these characterizations, we can compute memoryless strategies for safety and Büchi games [Tho95]. For a safety game with condition A, the strategy $\sigma(s,i) = \{c \in C \mid \exists s' \in \mathsf{MG}\,A : (s,i,c,s') \in \delta\}$ is winning if and only if $s_0 \in \mathsf{MG}\,A$. For a Büchi game, let $W = \nu Z.\mathsf{MX}\,\mathsf{M}Z\,\mathsf{U}(Z \cap B)$. Let Y_1 through Y_n be the set of distinct iterates of $\mathsf{M}W\,\mathsf{U}(W \cap B) = W$. We defi ne the *attractor strategy* for B to be

$$\begin{aligned}\sigma(s,i) = {} & \{c \in C \mid \exists j,k < j, s' \in Y_k : s \in Y_j \setminus Y_{j-1}, (s,i,c,s') \in \delta\} \cup \\ & \{c \in C \mid s \in Y_0, \exists s' \in W, \exists i \in I : (s,i,c,s') \in \delta\}.\end{aligned}$$

The attractor strategy brings the system ever closer to B, and then brings it back to a state from which it can force another visit to B.

3 Program Repair

This section contains our main contributions. In 3.1, we describe how to obtain a program game from a program and a suspicion of a fault. The product of the program game and the automaton for the LTL formula is a Büchi game. If the product game is winning, it has a memoryless winning strategy. In 3.2 we show how to construct a finite state strategy for the program game from the strategy for the product game and we discuss under which conditions we can guarantee that the product game is winning. A finite state strategy for the program game corresponds to a repair that adds states to the program. Since we want a repair that is as close as possible to the original program, we search for a memoryless strategy. In 3.3, we show that it is NP-complete to decide whether a memoryless strategy exists, and in 3.4, we present a heuristic to construct a memoryless strategy. This heuristic may fail to find a valid memoryless strategy even if one exists. Finally, we show how to extract a repair from a memoryless strategy.

3.1 Constructing a Game

Suppose that we are given a program that does not fulfill its LTL specification φ. Suppose furthermore that we have an idea which variables or lines may be responsible for the failure, for instance, from a diagnosis tool.

A program corresponds to an LTL game $K = (S, s_0, I, \{c\}, \delta, \lambda, \varphi)$. The set of system choices is a singleton (the game models a deterministic system) and the acceptance condition is the specification. Given an expression e in which the right-hand side (RHS) may be incorrect, we turn K into a *program game* G by *freeing* the value of this expression. That is, if Ω is the domain of the expression e, we change the system choice to $C' = C \times \Omega$ and let the second component of the system choices define the value of the expression. If we can find a winning memoryless strategy for G, we have determined a function from the state of the program to the proper value of the RHS, i.e., a repair.

We can generalize the fault model by including the left-hand side (LHS). Thus, we convert the program to a game by adding a system choice that determines whether the LHS or the RHS should be changed and depending on that choice, which variable is used as the LHS or which expression replaces the RHS. Then we compute the choice that makes the program correct.

We do not consider other fault models, but these can be easily added. The experimental results show that we may find good repairs even for programs with faults that we do not model.

3.2 Finite State Strategies

Given two games $G = (S, s_0, I_G, C_G, \delta_G, \lambda_G, F_G)$ and $A = (Q, q_0, 2^{AP}, C_A, \delta_A, \lambda_A, F_A)$, let the *product game* be $G \rhd A = (S \times Q, (s_0, q_0), I_G, C_G \times C_A, \delta, \lambda, F)$, where $\delta((s,q), i_G, (c_G, c_A)) = (\delta_G(s, i_G, c_G), \delta_A(q, \lambda_G(s), c_A))$, $\lambda(s,q) = \lambda_G(s)$, and $F = \{(s_0, q_0), (s_1, q_1), \cdots \mid s_0, s_1, \cdots \in F_G \text{ and } q_0, q_1, \cdots \in F_A\}$. Intuitively, the output of G is fed to the input of A, and the winning conditions are conjoined. Therefore, the output language of the product is the intersection of the output language of the first game and the input language of the second.

Lemma 1. *For games G, A, $L(G \rhd A) = L(G) \cap I(A)$.*

Lemma 2. *Let G and A be games. If a memoryless winning strategy for $G \rhd A$ exists, then there is a finite state winning strategy σ for G such that for all plays π of G according to σ, $\lambda(\pi) \in L(G)$ and $\lambda(\pi) \in I(A)$.*

The finite state strategy σ is the product of A and the memoryless (single state) strategy for $G \rhd A$. If $F_G = S^\omega$, then σ is the winning strategy for the game G with the winning condition defined by A. The following result (an example of *game simulation*, cf. [Tho95]) follows from Lemma 2.

Theorem 1. *Let $G = (S, s_0, I, C, \delta, \lambda, \varphi)$ be an LTL game, let G' be as G but with the winning condition S^ω, and let A be a Büchi game with $I(A) = L(G)$. If there is a memoryless winning strategy for the Büchi game $G' \rhd A$ then there is a finite state winning strategy for G.*

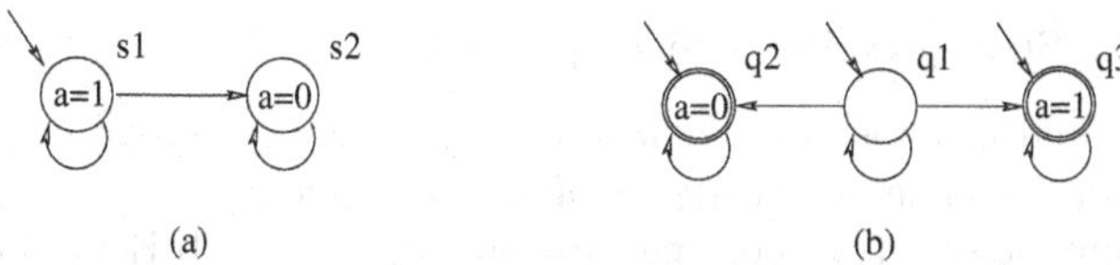

Fig. 1. (a) Game in which the environment can assign the value for variable a. (b) automaton for $\mathsf{F}\,\mathsf{G}(a = 1) \vee \mathsf{F}\,\mathsf{G}(a = 0)$

Note that the converse of the theorem does not hold. In fact, Harding [Har05] shows that we are guarantee to find a winning strategy iff the game fulfills the property and the automaton is *trivially determinizable*, i.e., we can make it deterministic by removing edges without changing the language.

For example, there is no winning strategy for the game shown in Fig. 1. If the automaton for the property $\mathsf{F}\,\mathsf{G}(a = 1) \vee \mathsf{F}\,\mathsf{G}(a = 0))$ moves to the state q_3, the environment can decide to move to s_2 (set $a = 0$), a move that the automaton cannot match. If, on the other hand, the automaton waits for the environment to move to s_2, the environment can stay in s_1 forever and thus force a non-accepting run. Hence, although the game fulfills the formula, we cannot give a strategy. Note that this problem depends not only on the structure of the automaton, but also on the structure of the game. For instance, if we remove the edge from s_1 to s_2, we can give a strategy for the product.

In general, the translation of an LTL formula to a deterministic automaton requires a doubly exponential blowup and the best known upper bound for deciding whether a translation is possible is EXPSPACE [KV98]. To prevent this blowup, we can either use heuristics to reduce the number of nondeterministic states in the automaton [ST03], or we can use a restricted subset of LTL. Maidl [Mai00] shows that translations in the style of [GPVW95] (of which we use a variant [SB00]) yield deterministic automata for the formulas in the set $\mathrm{LTL}^{\mathrm{det}}$, which is defined as follows: If $\varphi_1$and φ_2 are $\mathrm{LTL}^{\mathrm{det}}$ formulas, and p is a predicate, then p, $\varphi_1 \wedge \varphi_2$, $\mathsf{X}\,\varphi_1$, $(p \wedge \varphi_1) \vee (\neg p \wedge \varphi_2)$, $(p \wedge \varphi_1)\,\mathsf{U}(\neg p \wedge \varphi_2)$ and $(p \wedge \varphi_1)\,\mathsf{W}(\neg p \wedge \varphi_2)$ are LTL^{det} formulas. Note that this set includes invariants ($\mathsf{G}\,p$) and $\neg p\,\mathsf{U}\,p = \mathsf{F}\,p$. $\mathrm{LTL}^{\mathrm{det}}$ describes the intersection of LTL and CTL. In fact, deterministic Büchi automata describe exactly the properties expressibly in the alternation-free μ-calculus, a superset of CTL [KV98].

Alur and La Torre [AL01] define a set of LTL fragments for which we can compute deterministic automata using a different tableau construction. They are classified by means of the operators used in their subformulas. (On the top level, negation and other Boolean connectives are always allowed.) Alur and La Torre give appropriate constructions for the classes $\mathrm{LTL}(\mathsf{F}, \wedge)$ and $\mathrm{LTL}(\mathsf{F}, \mathsf{X}, \wedge)$. In contrast, for $\mathrm{LTL}(\mathsf{F}, \vee, \wedge)$ and $\mathrm{LTL}(\mathsf{G}, \mathsf{F})$ they show that the size of a corresponding deterministic automaton is necessarily doubly exponential in the size of the formula. Since trivially deterministic automata can be made deterministic by removing edges, they can be no smaller than the smallest possible deterministic automaton and thus there are no exponential-size trivially deterministic automata for the latter two groups.

3.3 Memoryless Strategies Are NP-Complete

As argued in the introduction, a finite state strategy may correspond to an awkward repair and therefore we wish to construct a memoryless strategy.

It follows from the results of Fortune, Hopcroft, and Wyllie [FHW80] that given a directed graph G and two nodes v and w, it is NP-complete to compute whether there are node-disjoint paths from v to w and back. Assume that we build a game G' based on the graph G. The acceptance condition is that v and w are visited infinitely often, which can easily be expressed by a Büchi automaton. Since the existence of a memoryless strategy for G' implies the existence of two node-disjoint paths from v to w and back, we can deduce the following theorem.

Theorem 2. *Deciding whether a game with a winning condition defined by a Büchi automaton has a memoryless winning strategy is NP-complete.*

It follows that for LTL games there is no algorithm to decide whether there is a memoryless winning strategy that runs in time polynomial in the size of the underlying graph, unless P = NP, even if a finite state strategy is given.

3.4 Heuristics for Memoryless Strategies

Since we cannot compute a memoryless strategy in polynomial time, we use a heuristic. Given a memoryless strategy for the product game, we construct a strategy that is common to all states of the automaton, which is our candidate for a memoryless strategy on the program game. Then, we compute whether the candidate is a winning strategy, which is not necessarily the case. Note that invariants have an automaton consisting of one state and thus the memoryless strategy for the product game is a memoryless strategy for the program game.

Recall that the product game is $G \rhd A = (S \times Q, (s_0, q_0), I_G, C_G \times C_A, \delta, \lambda, B)$. Let $\sigma : (S \times Q) \times I_G \to 2^{C_G \times C_A}$ be the attractor strategy for condition B. Note that the strategy is immaterial on nodes that are either not reachable (under any choice of the system) or not winning (and thus will be avoided by the system). Let R be the set of reachable states of the product game, and let W be the set of winning states. We define

$$\tau'(s, i_G) = \big\{c_G \;\big|\; \forall q \in Q : \big((s,q) \notin R \cap W \text{ or } \exists c_A \in C_A : (c_G, c_A) \in \sigma((s,q), i_G)\big)\big\}.$$

Intuitively, we obtain τ' by taking the moves common to all reachable, winning states of the strategy automaton.[1]

If τ' is winning, then so is σ, but the converse does not hold. To check whether τ' is winning, we construct a game G' from G by restricting the transition relation to adhere to τ': $\delta' = \{(s, i, c, s') \in \delta \mid c \in \tau'(s, i)\}$. This may introduce states without a successor. We see whether we can avoid such states by computing $W' = \mathsf{MG}\, S$. If we find that $s_0 \notin W'$, we cannot avoid visiting a dead-end state, and we give up trying to find a repair. If, on the other hand, $s_0 \in W'$, we get our final memoryless strategy τ by restricting τ' to W', which ensures that a play that starts in W' remains there and never visits a dead-end. We thus reach our main conclusion in the following theorem.

[1] We may treat multiple Büchi constraints, if present, in the same manner. This is equivalent to using the counting construction.

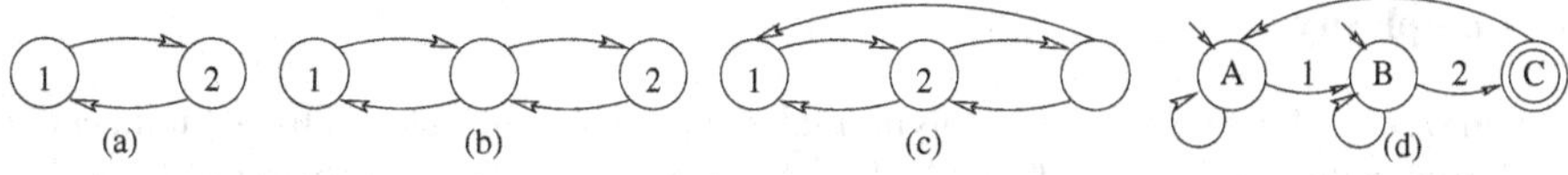

Fig. 2. Fig. a, b, c show three games with the winning condition that states 1 and 2 are both visited infinitely often. Multiple outgoing arcs from a state model a system choice. The winning condition is defined by the Büchi automaton shown in Fig. d. For Fig. a, the strategies for States A, B, and C coincide, and a memoryless strategy exists. For Fig. b, no memoryless strategy exists, and for Fig. c, a memoryless strategy exists, but it is not equal to the intersection of all the strategies for states A, B, and C. (The strategies are contradictory for the state on the right.)

Theorem 3. *If $s_0 \in W'$ then τ is a winning strategy of G.*

3.5 Extracting a Repair

This section shows a symbolic method to extract a repair statement from a memoryless strategy. We determinize the strategy by finding proper assignments to the system choices that can be used in the suspect locations. For any given state of the program, the given strategy may allow for multiple assignments, which gives us room for optimization.

We may not want the repair to depend on certain variables of the program, for example, because they are out of the scope of the component that is being repaired. In that case, we can universally quantify these variables from the strategy and its winning region and check that the strategy still supplies a valid response for all combinations of state and input.

For each assignment to the system choice variables, we calculate a set $P_j \subseteq S \times I$ for which the assignment is a part of the given strategy. We can use these sets P_j to suggest the repair "`if P0 then assign0 else if P1 then ...`", in which `Pj` is an expression that represents the set P_j. The expression `Pj`, however, can be quite complex: even for small examples it can take over a hundred lines, which would make the suggested repair inscrutable.

We exploit the fact that the sets P_j can overlap to construct new sets A_j that are easier to express. We have to ensure that we still cover all winning and reachable states using the sets A_j. Therefore, A_j is obtained from P_j by adding or removing states outside of a *care set*. The care set consists of all states that cannot be covered by A_j because they are not in P_j and all states that must be covered by A_j because they are neither covered by an A_k with $k < j$, nor by a P_k with $k > j$. We then replace `Pj` with an expression for A_j to get our repair suggestion.

For simultaneous assignment to many variables, we may consider generating repairs for each variable seperately, in order to avoid enumerating the domain. For example, we could assign the variables one by one instead of simultaneously.

Extracting a simple repair is similar to multi-level logic synthesis in the presence of satisfiability don't cares and we may be able to apply multi-level minimization techniques [HS96]; the problem of finding the smallest expression for a given relation is NP-hard by reduction from 3SAT. One optimization we may attempt is to vary the order of the `Aj`s, but in our experience, the suggested repairs are typically quite readable.

3.6 Complexity

The complexity of the algorithm is polynomial in the number of states of the system, and exponential in the length of the formula, like the complexity of model checking. A symbolic implementation needs a quadratic number of preimage computations to compute the winning region of a Büchi game, the most expensive operation, like the Emerson-Lei algorithm typically used for model checking [RBS00]. For invariants, model checking and repair both need a linear number of preimage computations. Although the combination of universal and existential quantification makes preimage computations more expensive and we have to do additional work to extract the repair, we expect that repair is feasible for a large class of designs for which model checking is possible.

In our current implementation, we build the strategy as a monolithic BDD, which may use a lot of memory. We are still researching ways to compute the strategy in a partitioned way.

4 Examples

In this section we present initial experimental results supporting the applicability of our approach on real (though small) examples.

We have implemented our repair approach in the VIS model checker [B+96] as an extension of the algorithm of [JRS02]. The examples below are finite state programs given in pseudo code. They are translated to Verilog before we feed them to the repair algorithm. Suspect expressions are freed and a new system choice is added with the same domain as the expression. Assertions are replaced by `if(...) error=1` and the property $\mathsf{G}(\mathrm{error} = 0)$. In the current version, this translation and the code augmentation are done manually.

4.1 Locking Example

We start with the abstract program shown in Fig. 3 [GV03]. This programs abstracts a class of concrete programs with different if and while conditions, all of which perform simple lock request/release operations. The method `lock()` checks that the lock is available and requests it. Vice versa, `unlock()` checks that the lock is held and releases it. The `if(*)` in the first line causes the lock to be requested nondeterministically, and the `while(*)` causes the loop to be executed an arbitrary number of times. The variable `got_lock` is used to keep track of the status of the lock (Lines 4 and 5). The assertions in Lines 11 and 21 constitute a safety property that is violated, e.g., if the loop is executed twice without requesting the lock. The fault is that the statement `got_lock--` should be placed within the scope of the preceding `if`.

Model-based diagnosis can be used to find a candidate for the repair [MSW00]. A diagnosis of the given example was performed in [CKW05] and localizes the fault in Lines 1, 6, or 7. We reject the possibility of changing Line 1 or 7 because we want the repair to work regardless of the if and while conditions in the concrete program. Instead, we look for a faulty assignment to `got_lock`. Thus, we free the RHS in Lines 3 and 6. The algorithm suggests a correct repair, `got_lock=1` for Line 3 and `got_lock=0`

```
   int got_lock = 0;
   do{
1    if (*) {
2      lock();
3      got_lock++; }
4    if (got_lock != 0) {
5      unlock();}
6    got_lock--;
7  } while(*)

   void lock() {
11   assert(L = 0);
12   L = 1; }

   void unlock(){
21   assert(L = 1);
22   L = 0; }
```

Fig. 3. Locking Example

```
1  int least = input1;
2  int most = input1;
3  if(most < input2){
4     most = input2; }
5  if(most < input3){
6     most = input3;}
7  if(least > input2){
8     most = input2; }
9  if(least > input3){
10    least = input3;}
11 assert (least <= most);
```

Fig. 4. MinMax Example

for Line 6. Note that we repair the program using a different fault model than the one which caused it, i.e., after the repair the program is correct, even though we did not suggest to move `got_lock--` inside the scope of the `if`.

4.2 MinMax

To present a more general fault model we show a simple program which assigns the minimal and maximal values out of three input values to `least` and `most`, resp. [Gro04].

The fault is located in Line 8 of Fig. 4, where `input2` is assigned to `most` (instead of `least`), which was one of five single fault diagnoses found by a model based debugger based on [MSW00]. To find the correct repair, we replace the assignments in lines 4, 6, 8, and 10 with switch-statements over the system choice that selects whether to assign to `least`, to `most`, or to replace the RHS. The algorithm correctly suggests to assign to variable `most` in Lines 4 and 6, and to `least` in Lines 8 and 10.

4.3 Critical Sections

Fig. 5 demonstrates how to cope with problems when testing properties that have no deterministic automaton (see Section 3.2). The example from [BEGL99] depicts two processes that share `flag` and `turn` variables, which are used to avoid concurrent access to the variables `x` and `y`. The process contains an arbiter (not shown) that nondeterministically yields control to either Process A or B, and records its choice in the variable `arbiter`. The fault is that `turn1B` is set to `false` in Line 2 of Process A. The correct value is `true`. This can cause both a deadlock and a violation of the critical region of `x`.

Process A

```
1  flag1A = true;
2  turn1B = false;
3  while(flag1B && turn1B);
4  x = x && y;
5  flag1A = false;
6  if(turn1B){
7    flag2A = true;
8    turn2B = true;
9    while(flag2B && turn2B);
10   y = false;
11   flag2A = false;}
12 goto 1;
```

Process B

```
1  flag1B = true;
2  turn1B = false;
3  while(flag1A && !turn1B);
4  x = x && y;
5  flag2B = true;
6  turn2B = false;
7  while(flag2A && !turn2B);
8  y = !y;
9  x = x || y;
10 flag2B = false;
11 flag1B = false;
12 goto 1;
```

Fig. 5. Critical Section Example

To check if Process B is eventually allowed to access x when it is waiting for it, we check the property FairArbiter $\rightarrow \mathsf{G}(\text{Bwaiting} \rightarrow \mathsf{F}\,\neg\text{Bwaiting})$ where FairArbiter $= \mathsf{G}\,\mathsf{F}(\texttt{arbiter} = A) \wedge \mathsf{G}\,\mathsf{F}(\texttt{arbiter} = B))$ and Bwaiting is true whenever Process B is in Lines 3 or 7. As the implication leads to an negation of FairArbiter we get a nondeterministic automaton. Our algorithm cannot find a strategy for the product game of the program and this automaton (See Fig. 1).

We solve this problem by manually changing the arbiter to switch processes infinitely often. Freeing `turn1B` in Line 2 of Process A with domain `{false,true}` now leads to the correct answer, `turn1B = true`. Note that this repair also works for the original model. This repair can also be found by checking for violations of the critical section, which can be stated as a simple invariant and therefore does not require a modification of the system.

4.4 Processor

In order to compare the efficiency of repair algorithm to that of model checking, we have introduced a fault in a 16-bit version of a simple unpipelined DLX-style processor. The fault is in the ALU and the property checks that the ALU works correctly.

On a 2.8GHz Linux machine with 2GB of RAM, the model checking run needs 230 seconds to check that the property does not hold on the incorrect version. The repair algorithm finds a repair in 200 seconds, and the repair is verified to be correct by the model checker (an unnecessary precaution) in 210 seconds; all runs use around 1.2GB.

5 Conclusions

We have considered the problem of fixing a program to adhere to its specification, given a suspicion of the fault. We proceed by building the product of a game corresponding to the broken program and the automaton reflecting the specification. If the product game has a winning strategy, we can repair the program. However, a strategy may not exist for the product even if a repair exists because of nondeterminism in the automaton. We could circumvent this problem by determinizing the automaton, but the cost is exponential and for many combinations of program and specification, nondeterminism turns out not to be problematic.

A winning finite state strategy correspond to a repair that introduces new state. We reject the possibility of changing the program logic and instead turn to the problem of finding a memoryless strategy. We have shown that deciding whether a memoryless strategy exists is NP-complete, and we have presented a conservative heuristic that conjoins the strategies for the different states of the automaton. We have described a heuristic that finds an efficient repair for a given memorless strategy.

The algorithm is of a complexity that is comparable to that of model checking, which makes us optimistic as to the practical applicability of the approach. We have implemented a symbolic version of the algorithm and the initial experimental results show that the algorithm finds readable repairs in acceptable time, though improvements in the implementation are still possible.

The algorithm is complete for invariants as they have deterministic automata consisting of one state and in fact we can solve them using the linear algorithm for guarantee games.

A natural extension of this work would be to evaluate the effect of determinizing the automaton before computing a strategy. It would also be interesting to see in how far we can minimize the negative effects of using a finite state strategy, e.g., by using a dependent variable analysis [HD93] to minimize the amount of added state. Finally, it would be interesting to see in how far the approach can be extended to push-down games that would result from an attempt to repair Boolean programs that appear in a SLAM-style abstraction/refinement approach [BR01]. We are looking into further improvements in the efficiency of the implementation.

References

[AL01] R. Alur and S. La Torre. Deterministic generators and games for LTL fragments. In *Symposium on Logic in Computer Science (LICS'01)*, pages 291–302, 2001.

[B+96] R. K. Brayton et al. VIS: A system for verification and synthesis. In T. Henzinger and R. Alur, editors, *Eighth Conference on Computer Aided Verification (CAV'96)*, pages 428–432. Springer-Verlag, Rutgers University, 1996. LNCS 1102.

[BEGL99] F. Buccafurri, T. Eiter, G. Gottlob, and N. Leone. Enhancing model checking in verification by AI techniques. *Artificial Intelligence*, 112:57–104, 1999.

[BNR03] T. Ball, M. Naik, and S. K. Rajamani. From symptom to cause: Localizing errors in counterexample traces. In *30th Symposium on Principles of Programming Languages (POPL 2003)*, pages 97–105, January 2003.

[BR01] T. Ball and S. K. Rajamani. Automatically validating temporal safety properties of interfaces. In M.B. Dwyer, editor, *8th International SPIN Workshop*, pages 103–122, Toronto, May 2001. Springer-Verlag. LNCS 2057.

[CGP99] E. M. Clarke, O. Grumberg, and D. A. Peled. *Model Checking*. MIT Press, Cambridge, MA, 1999.

[CKW05] R. Chen, D. Köb, and F. Wotawa. A comparison of fault explanation and localization. unpublished, 2005.

[FHW80] S. Fortune, J. Hopcroft, and J. Wyllie. The directed subgraph homeomorphism problem. *Theoretical Computer Science*, 10:111–121, 1980.

[GPVW95] R. Gerth, D. Peled, M. Y. Vardi, and P. Wolper. Simple on-the-fly automatic verification of linear temporal logic. In *Protocol Specification, Testing, and Verification*, pages 3–18. Chapman & Hall, 1995.

[Gro04] A. Groce. Error explanation with distance metrics. In *International Conference on Tools and Algorithms for Construction and Analysis of Systems (TACAS'04)*, pages 108–122, Barcelona, Spain, March-April 2004. LNCS 2988.

[GV03] A. Groce and W. Visser. What went wrong: Explaining counterexamples. In *Model Checking of Software: 10th International SPIN Workshop*, pages 121–135. Springer-Verlag, May 2003. LNCS 2648.

[Har05] A. Harding. *Symbolic Strategy Synthesis For Games With LTL Winning Conditions.* PhD thesis, University of Birmingham, 2005. Unpublished.

[HD93] A. J. Hu and D. Dill. Reducing BDD size by exploiting functional dependencies. In *Proceedings of the Design Automation Conference*, pages 266–271, Dallas, TX, June 1993.

[HS96] G. D. Hachtel and F. Somenzi. *Logic Synthesis and Verification Algorithms.* Kluwer Academic Publishers, Boston, MA, 1996.

[JRS02] H. Jin, K. Ravi, and F. Somenzi. Fate and free will in error traces. In *International Conference on Tools and Algorithms for Construction and Analysis of Systems (TACAS'02)*, pages 445–459, Grenoble, France, April 2002. LNCS 2280.

[KV98] O. Kupferman and M. Y. Vardi. Freedom, weakness, and determinism: From linear-time to branching-time. In *Proc. 13th IEEE Symposium on Logic in Computer Science*, June 1998.

[Mai00] M. Maidl. The common fragment of CTL and LTL. In *Proc. 41th Annual Symposium on Foundations of Computer Science*, pages 643–652, 2000.

[MSW00] C. Mateis, M. Stumptner, and F. Wotawa. A value-based diagnosis model for Java programs. In *Proceedings of the Eleventh International Workshop on Principles of Diagnosis*, 2000.

[PR89] A. Pnueli and R. Rosner. On the synthesis of a reactive module. In *Proc. Symposium on Principles of Programming Languages (POPL)*, pages 179–190, 1989.

[RBS00] K. Ravi, R. Bloem, and F. Somenzi. A comparative study of symbolic algorithms for the computation of fair cycles. In W. A. Hunt, Jr. and S. D. Johnson, editors, *Formal Methods in Computer Aided Design*, pages 143–160. Springer-Verlag, November 2000. LNCS 1954.

[RW89] P. J. G. Ramadge and W. M. Wonham. The control of discrete event systems. *Proceedings of the IEEE*, 77:81–98, 1989.

[SB00] F. Somenzi and R. Bloem. Efficient Büchi automata from LTL formulae. In E. A. Emerson and A. P. Sistla, editors, *Twelfth Conference on Computer Aided Verification (CAV'00)*, pages 248–263. Springer-Verlag, Berlin, July 2000. LNCS 1855.

[ST03] R. Sebastiani and S. Tonetta. "more deterministic" vs. "smaller" büchi automata for efficient LTL model checking. In *Correct Hardware Design and Verification Methods (CHARME'03)*, pages 126–140, Berlin, October 2003. Springer-Verlag. LNCS 2860.

[SW96] M. Stumptner and F. Wotawa. A model-based approach to software debugging. In *Proceedings on the Seventh International Workshop on Principles of Diagnosis*, 1996.

[Tho95] W. Thomas. On the synthesis of strategies in infinite games. In *Proc. 12th Annual Symposium on Theoretical Aspects of Computer Science*, pages 1–13. Springer-Verlag, 1995. LNCS 900.

Improved Probabilistic Models for 802.11 Protocol Verification

Amitabha Roy and K. Gopinath

Department of Computer Science and Automation, Indian Institute of Science, Bangalore
{aroy, gopi}@csa.iisc.ernet.in

Abstract. The IEEE 802.11 protocol is a popular standard for wireless local area networks. Its medium access control layer (MAC) is a carrier sense multiple access with collision avoidance (CSMA/CA) design and includes an exponential backoff mechanism that makes it a possible target for probabilistic model checking. In this work, we identify ways to increase the scope of application of probabilistic model checking to the 802.11 MAC. Current techniques model only specialized cases of minimum size. To work around this problem, we identify properties of the protocol that can be used to simplify the models and make verification feasible. Using these observations, we present generalized probabilistic timed automata models that are independent of the number of stations. We optimize these through a novel abstraction technique while preserving probabilistic reachability measures. We substantiate our claims of a significant reduction due to our optimization with results from using the probabilistic model checker PRISM.

1 Introduction

The IEEE 802.11 protocol [1] is a popular standard for wireless networks. Its medium access control layer (MAC) is a carrier sense multiple access with collision avoidance (CSMA/CA) design and includes an exponential backoff mechanism that makes it an ideal target for probabilistic model checking. This protocol has been modeled using a range of techniques such as finite state machines and probabilistic timed automata [2].

The 802.11 protocol suffers from a potential livelock problem, demonstrated formally in [3], which is mitigated only by the presence of a finite retry limit for each data packet. The livelock arises because it is possible, although improbable, for two stations to behave symmetrically and continuously collide until they drop their respective packets on exceeding the retry limit. In such a scenario, it is useful to bound the probability of such pathologically symmetric behavior. This motivates the application of probabilistic model checking to the problem of computing probabilities of desired and undesired behavior in the protocol. Two primary properties of interest are: the probability of the number of retries reaching a certain count and the probability of meeting a *soft* deadline.

A recent solution to the problem of obtaining these probabilities has been proposed in [2]. It models a limited (but critical) aspect of the protocol using Probabilistic Timed Automata (PTA) [4] and exploits available tools, namely, the Probabilistic Symbolic Model Checker (PRISM) [5] for computing the probability values and the real time model checker Uppaal [6] as a proof assistant. Results on the probability of the backoff counter on a station reaching a particular value and the probability of a packet being

K. Etessami and S.K. Rajamani (Eds.): CAV 2005, LNCS 3576, pp. 239–252, 2005.

transmitted within a certain deadline are presented. This work, however, models only a specialized case of two stations (sender destination pairs). When we extended the models to 3 stations (and 3 corresponding destinations), which is a practical sized network topology, we found it computationally infeasible to model check properties of interest. Also, the model has an inaccurate assumption that the packet length can vary on every retransmission.

The aim of this work is twofold. First, we present a more accurate and generalized model for the protocol that is parameterized by the number of stations. Second, we set up a logical framework to exploit protocol specific redundancies. Under this framework, we perform a number of provably correct optimizations that reduce the generalized multi station model. The optimizations involve abstracting away the deterministic waits and considering only a subset of the allowed packet sizes that nevertheless captures all the relevant behavior. In addition, we duplicate the model reduction technique of [2] for the multi station problem.

Our reduced models are immediately verifiable in PRISM and require no further tools. It is also possible to use tools like RAPTURE [7] on the reduced PTA models (see [8] for our experiences with using RAPTURE). Our results show a reduction in state space over the existing solution for two stations. We are also able to successfully model check a topology of three station that was infeasible with the current models.

The organization of the paper is as follows. We begin with the modeling formalism used in this paper. We present the generalized models for the multi station 802.11 problem and discuss the behavior of the protocol. Next, we present a notion of equivalence in probabilistic systems that abstracts away deterministic paths in the system but preserves probabilistic reachability. We give sufficient requirements for equivalence both at the level of untimed probabilistic systems and probabilistic timed automata. Based on this framework, we present our set of reductions to the generalized model for the multi station problem. We also show that we can verify soft deadlines inspite of these optimizations. We conclude with results that detail state space reduction as well as case studies for a three station topology.

2 Modeling Formalism

We need a modeling formalism that can represent the 802.11 protocol at sufficient depth and is amenable to transformations for more efficient verification. We have been guided by the existing work in [2] in our choice of Probabilistic Timed Automata to model the 802.11 protocol.

We introduce Probabilistic Timed Automata (PTA) [4], Probabilistic Systems (PS) [2, 9] and fully probabilistic systems (FPS). All these have been surveyed in [10] with special reference to their relationship in the context of probabilistic model checking.

Let χ be a set of non-negative real valued variables called clocks. Call Z the set of zones over χ, which is the set of all possible atomic constraints of the form $x \sim c$ and $(x - y) \sim c$ and their closure under conjunction. Here $x, y \in \chi$, $\sim \in \{<, \leq, >, \geq\}$ and $c \in \mathbb{N}$, where $\mathbb{N}$ is the set of natural numbers. A clock valuation v is the assignment of values in $\mathbb{R}_{\geq 0}$(where $\mathbb{R}_{\geq 0}$ is the set of non-negative reals) to all clocks in χ. The concept of a clock valuation v satisfying a zone Y, indicated as $v \lhd Y$, is naturally derived by assigning values to each clock in the zone and checking whether all constraints are satisfied.

Definition 1. *A probabilistic timed automaton is a tuple* $(L, \bar{l}, \chi, \Sigma, I, P)$ *where* L *is a finite set of states,* $\bar{l}$ *is the initial state,* χ *is the set of clocks and* Σ *is a finite set of labels used to label transitions. The function* I *is a map* $I : L \rightarrow Z$ *called the invariant condition. The probabilistic edge relation* P *is defined as* $P \subseteq L \times Z \times \Sigma \times Dist(2^{\chi} \times L)$*, where* $Dist(2^{\chi} \times L)$ *is the set of all probability distributions, each elementary outcome of which corresponds to resetting some clocks to zero and moving to a state in* L*. We call a distinguished (not necessarily non-null) subset* Σ^u *of the set of events as* urgent events.

A critical feature of PTAs that makes them powerful modeling tools is that each transition presents *probabilistic choice* in the PTA while different outgoing probabilistic transitions from a state present *non-deterministic* choice in the PTA. Hence, a PTA can model non-determinism, which is inherent in the composition of asynchronous parallel systems.

Composition of PTAs is a cross product of states with the condition that the composed PTAs must synchronize on shared actions. For a detailed description see [2]. A feature of PTAs that is useful for higher-level modeling is urgent channels. Urgent channels are a special set of edge labels (symbols) such that time cannot be allowed to pass in a state when synchronization on an urgent channel is possible. We next define a probabilistic system (PS) (which is the same as the simple probabilistic automaton of [9]).

Definition 2. *A probabilistic system (PS), is a tuple* $(S, \bar{s}, \Sigma, Steps)$ *where* S *is the set of states,* $\bar{s}$ *is the start state,* Σ *is a finite set of labels and Steps is a function* $Steps : S \rightarrow 2^{\Sigma \times Dist(S)}$ *where* $Dist(S)$ *is the set of all distributions over* S*.*

Definition 3. *Given a PTA* $\mathcal{T} = (L, \bar{l}, \chi, \Sigma, I, P)$*, the* semantics *of* $\mathcal{T}$ *is the PS* $[[\mathcal{T}]] = (S, \bar{s}, Act, Steps)$*, where* $S \subseteq L \times \mathbb{R}^{|\chi|}_{\geq 0}$ *is the set of states with the restrictions* $(s, v) \in S$ *iff* $(s \in L$ *and* $v \lhd I(s))$ *and* $\bar{s} = (\bar{l}, 0)$*.* $Act = \mathbb{R}_{>0} \cup \Sigma$*. This reflects either actions corresponding to time steps* $(\mathbb{R}_{>0})$ *or actions from the PTA* (Σ)*. Steps is the least set of probabilistic transitions containing, for each* $(l, v) \in S$*, a set of action distribution pairs* (σ, μ) *where* $\sigma \in Act$ *and* μ *is a probability distribution over* S*. Steps for a state* $s = (l, v)$ *is defined as follows.*
I. for each $t \in \mathbb{R}_{>0}$*,* $(t, \mu) \in Steps(s)$ *iff*

1. $\mu(l, v + t) = 1$ *and* $v + t' \lhd I(l)$ *for all* $0 \leq t' \leq t$*.*
2. *For every probabilistic edge of the form* $(l, g, \sigma, -) \in P$*, if* $v + t' \lhd g$ *for any* $0 \leq t' \leq t$*, then* σ *is non-urgent.*

II. for each $(l, g, \sigma, p) \in P$*, let* $(\sigma, \mu) \in Steps(s)$ *iff* $v \lhd g$ *and for each* $(l', v') \in S$*:* $\mu(l', v') = \Sigma_{X \subseteq \chi \& v' = v[X:=0]}\, p(X, l')$*, the sum being over all clock resets that result in the valuation* v'*.*

A critical result [11], analogous to the region construction result for timed automata, states that it is sufficient to assume only integer increments when all zones are closed (there are no strict inequalities). Hence, the definition given above is modified to $S \subseteq L \times \mathbb{N}^{|\mathcal{X}|}$ and $Act = \mathbb{N} \cup \Sigma$. Under integer semantics, the size of the state space is proportional to the largest constant used. For the rest of this paper, we will assume integer semantics. Note that, in the presence of non-determinism, the probability measure of a path in a PS is undefined. Hence, define an adversary or scheduler that resolves non-determinism as follows:

Definition 4. *An adversary of the PS* $\mathcal{P} = (S, \bar{s}, Act, Steps)$ *is a function* $f : S \to \bigcup_{s \in S} Steps(s)$ *where* $f(s) \in Steps(s)$.

We only consider *simple* adversaries that do not change their decision about an outgoing distribution every time a state is revisited, their sufficiency has been shown in [12]. A simple adversary induces a Fully Probabilistic System (FPS) as defined below.

Definition 5. *A simple adversary A of a PS* $\mathcal{P} = (S, \bar{s}, Act, Steps)$ *induces an FPS or Discrete Time Markov Chain* $\mathcal{P}^A = (S, \bar{s}, P)$. *Here,* $P(s) = A(s)$, *the unique outgoing probability distribution for each* $s \in S$, *where we drop the edge label on the transition.*

Given a PS $\mathcal{M}$ and a set of "target states" F, consider an adversary A and the corresponding FPS $\mathcal{M}^A$. A probability space ($Prob^A$) may be defined on $\mathcal{M}^A$ via a cylinder construction [13]. A path ω in $\mathcal{M}^A$ is simply a (possibly infinite) sequence of states $\bar{s}s_1s_2...$ such that there is a transition of non-zero probability between any two consecutive states in the path. For model checking, we are interested in
$ProbReach^A(F) \stackrel{def}{=} Prob^A\{\omega \in Path^A_\infty \mid \exists i \in \mathbb{N} \text{ where } \omega(i) \in F\}$. F is the desired set of target states, $\omega(i)$ is the ith state in the path ω and $Path^A_\infty$ represents all infinite paths in $\mathcal{M}^A$. Define $MaxProbReach^M(F)$ and $MinProbReach^M(F)$ as the supremum and infimum respectively of $\{ProbReach^A(F)\}$ where the quantification is over all adversaries. This definition does not take into account sink states with no outgoing transitions. However, these states can easily be handled by adding self loops.

Properties of interest at the PTA level are specified using Probabilistic Computational Tree Logic (PCTL) formulas [14]. We limit ourselves to restricted syntax (but non trivial) PCTL formulas, expressible as $P_{\sim\lambda}\{\Diamond p\}$, where $\sim \in \{<, >, \leq, \geq\}$, λ is the constant probability bound that is being model checked for and p is a proposition defined for every state in the state space. These PCTL formulas translate directly into a probabilistic reachability problem on the semantic PS corresponding to the PTA. The reason for this restriction is that, in the case of the 802.11 protocol, the properties of interest, including the real time ones, are all expressible in this form. In this restricted form of PCTL, we indicate numerical equivalence using the following notation.

Definition 6. *Two PSs* $\mathcal{P}_1$ *and* $\mathcal{P}_2$ *are equivalent under probabilistic reachability of their respective target states* F_1 *and* F_2, *denoted by* $\mathcal{P}_1 \stackrel{PS}{\equiv}_{F_1,F_2} \mathcal{P}_2$ *when* $MaxProbReach^{\mathcal{P}_1}(F_1) = MaxProbReach^{\mathcal{P}_2}(F_2)$
and $MinProbReach^{\mathcal{P}_1}(F_1) = MinProbReach^{\mathcal{P}_2}(F_2)$.

Definition 7. $PTA_1 \stackrel{PTA}{\equiv}_{\phi_1,\phi_2} PTA_2$ *when* $[[PTA_1]] \stackrel{PS}{\equiv}_{F_1,F_2} [[PTA_2]]$. *The criterion for marking target states is that* F_1 *corresponds to the target states in the reachability problem for the PCTL formula* ϕ_1, *while* F_2 *corresponds to the target states for the PCTL formula* ϕ_2.

3 Probabilistic Models of 802.11 Protocol

In this section, we present generalized probabilistic models of the 802.11 basic access MAC protocol assuming no hidden nodes[1]. The model for the *multi-station* 802.11 problem consists of the station model and a shared channel, shown in Figures 2 part (a) and 1 part(b) respectively. We assume familiarity with conventions used in graphical representation of timed automata. The states marked with a 'u' are urgent states while that marked by concentric circles is the start state. The station models are replicated to represent multiple sender-destination pairs. Some critical state variables are: *bc* that holds the current backoff counter value, tx_len that holds the chosen transmission length and *backoff* that represents the current remaining time in backoff. The function $RANDOM(bc)$ is a modeling abstraction that assigns a random number in the current contention window. Similarly, $NON\_DET(TX\_MIN, TX\_MAX)$ assigns a non-deterministic packet length between TX_MIN and TX_MAX, which are the minimum and maximum allowable packet transmission times respectively. The values used for verification are from the Frequency Hopping Spread Spectrum (FHSS) physical layer [1]. The transmission rate for the data payload is 2 Mbps.

The station automaton shown in Figure 2, begins with a data packet whose transmission time it selects non-deterministically in the range from $258\mu s$ to $15750\mu s$. On sensing the channel free for a Distributed InterFrame Space ($DIFS = 128\mu s$), it enters the *Vulnerable* state, where it switches its transceiver to transmit mode and begins transmitting the signal. The *Vulnerable* state also accounts for propagation delay. It moves to the *Transmit* state after a time $VULN = 48\mu s$ with a synchronization on *send*. After completing transmission, the station moves to *Test_channel* via one of the two synchronizations, *finish_correct* on a successful transmission and *finish_garbled* on an unsuccessful transmission. The channel keeps track of the status of transmissions, going into a garbled state whenever more than one transmission occurs simultaneously. The station incorporates the behavior of the destination and diverges depending on whether the transmission was successful, or not. If the transmission was successful, the portion of the station corresponding to the destination waits for a Short InterFrame Space ($SIFS = 28\mu s$) before transmitting an ack, which takes $ACK = 183\mu s$.

On an unsuccessful transmission, the station waits for the acknowledgment timeout of $ACK\_TO = 300\mu s$. It then enters a backoff phase, where it probabilistically selects a random backoff period *backoff*$= RANDOM(bc)$, with uniform probability, a value from the contention window (CW) given by the range $[0, (C + 1).2^{bc} - 1]$, where C is the minimum CW ($15\mu s$ for the FHSS physical layer). The backoff counter (bc) is incremented each time the station enters backoff. The backoff counter is frozen when a station detects a transmission on the medium while in backoff.

It may be noted that the channel model in [2] is aware of exactly which stations are transmitting; for n stations, there are 2^n possibilities leading to the channel having $\Omega(2^n)$ state space. Our design recognizes the fact that it is sufficient for the channel to be aware of the number of transmitters using the tx_count variable. Hence our channel model has atmost a constant number of states plus a linear factor in terms of n leading to $O(n)$ states.

[1] In the absence of hidden nodes [15], the channel is a shared medium visible to all the stations.

Also, we start with an abstracted station model, which incorporates the deterministic destination. The validity of this abstraction for the two station case has been shown in [2]. The extension to the multi station case is given in [8].

4 Reducing State Space by Compression of Deterministic Paths

In the 802.11 protocol, there are numerous cases where the component automata representing the system simply count time or where different resolutions of non-determinism lead to the same state but through different paths. If we are verifying an untimed property then such execution fragments increase state space without any contribution to probabilistic reachability. We discovered on studying these models that it is possible to derive alternative *optimized* probabilistic timed automata that avoid the cost of such unnecessary deterministic behavior by compressing these deterministic paths into equivalent but shorter paths. The problem is the lack of a suitable formalism to support our optimizations. This section provides a framework that can be used to justify the equivalence of our optimized models to the original ones.

We assume that the state space is a subset of an implicit global set of states. This allows operations such as intersection and union between the set of states of two different automata. In particular, for this paper we consistently name states across the automata we consider. Our objective is to formalize "deterministic" behavior of interest. The key relationship used in this formalization is a specialization of dominators as defined in [7]. We refer to this restricted version of dominators as "deterministic dominators" in the rest of this paper.

Definition 8. *For a distribution π over the* finite *elementary event set X, define the support of the distribution as $supp(\pi) = \{x \in X \mid \pi(x) > 0\}$*

Definition 9. *Given a PS consisting of the set of states S, define $\prec_D$ as the smallest relation in $S \times S$ satisfying the following: $\forall s \in S \; s \prec_D s$ and $\forall t \in S \; [\forall(a,\pi) \in Steps(s) : \exists x \;\; (supp(\pi) = \{x\}) \wedge (x \prec_D t) \Rightarrow s \prec_D t]$*

If the relation $s \prec_D t$ holds then we say that t is the deterministic dominator of s.

An example of a deterministic dominator is shown in the PSs of Figure 1 part(a), where $S \prec_D T$.

Definition 10. *Given distributions P_1 over S_1 and P_2 over S_2, define $P_1 \stackrel{dist}{\equiv} P_2$ when $supp(P_1) = supp(P_2) = S$ and $\forall s \in S$ we have $P_1(s) = P_2(s)$.*

Based on the notion of equivalence of distributions, we define the notion of equivalence of *sets* of distributions. Let $Steps_1$ be a set of labeled distributions over S_1 and $Steps_2$ be a set of labeled distributions over S_2.

Definition 11. *$Steps_1 \stackrel{dist}{\equiv} Steps_2$ whenever $\forall(a,\mu_1) \in Steps_1 \; \exists(b,\mu_2) \in Steps_2$ such that $\mu_1 \stackrel{dist}{\equiv} \mu_2$ and $\forall(a,\mu_2) \in Steps_2 \; \exists(b,\mu_1) \in Steps_1$ with $\mu_2 \stackrel{dist}{\equiv} \mu_1$.*

Definition 12. *A path in the PS $\mathcal{P} = (S, \overline{s}, \Sigma, Steps)$ is a sequence of state-action pairs $(s_1,a_1),(s_2,a_2)..(s_{n+1})$ such that $\forall i \in \{1..n\}$ we have $\exists(a_i,\mu) \in Steps(s_i)$ such that $\mu(s_{i+1}) > 0$.*

4.1 Deterministic Path Compression in Probabilistic Systems

Consider the two PSs of Figure 1 part(a), each of which has the start state U. It should be clear that each of $MaxProbReach(X)$ and $MinProbReach(X)$ takes the same value in both the systems since we have only removed (compressed) the deterministic segment $B \rightarrow C$.

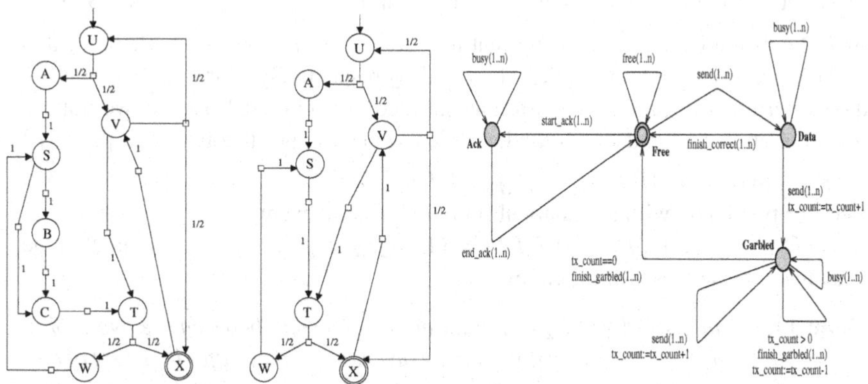

Fig. 1. (a)Two Related Probabilistic Systems (left); (b)PTA model for the Channel - Generalized for the multiple station case(right)

We formalize this notion of deterministic path compression at the level of PSs in theorem 1.

Consider two *finite* Probabilistic Systems $PS_1 = (S_1, \overline{s}, Act, Steps_1)$ and $PS_2 = (S_2, \overline{s}, Act, Steps_2)$ with an identical set of actions. All transitions in $Steps_1$ and $Steps_2$ are simple transitions of the form (s, a, μ) where s is the originating state, $a \in Act$ and μ is a probability distribution over the state space. Note that the S_1 and S_2 are necessarily not disjoint because of the common start state $\overline{s}$.

Definition 13. *If, for some $s \in S_1 \cap S_2$, $Steps_1(s) \overset{dist}{\equiv} Steps_2(s)$ does not hold then s is a point of disagreement between the two PSs.*

Theorem 1 (Equivalence in PSs). *Given two PSs $PS_1(S_1, \overline{s}, Act, Steps_1)$ and $PS_2(S_2, \overline{s}, Act, Steps_2)$ satisfying the following conditions:*

1. *For any state $s \in S_1 \cap S_2$, if s is a point of disagreement then $\exists t \in S_1 \cap S_2$ such that, t is not a point of disagreement and in each of the systems, $s \prec_D t$.*
2. *Let $F_1 \subseteq S_1$ and $F_2 \subseteq S_2$ be sets of target states we are model checking for. We impose the condition $S_1 \cap S_2 \cap F_1 = S_1 \cap S_2 \cap F_2$. For every $s \in S_1 \cap S_2$, which is a point of disagreement we have the following: For the postulated deterministic dominator t and for every state u on any path in PS_1 between s and t, $u \in F_1 \Rightarrow (s \in F_1) \vee (t \in F_1)$. Similarly, for every state u on any path in PS_2 between s and t, $u \in F_2 \Rightarrow (s \in F_2) \vee (t \in F_2)$.*

Under these conditions, $PS_1 \overset{PS}{\equiv}_{F_1,F_2} PS_2$.

The proof follows from first principles by setting up a bijective mapping between paths in the two PSs. The complete proof is available in [8].

4.2 A Comparison Framework for PTAs

Given PTA_1 and PTA_2 and their respective restricted PCTL requirements ϕ_1 and ϕ_2, we need a set of conditions under which we may claim $PTA_1 \overset{PTA}{\equiv}_{\phi_1,\phi_2} PTA_2$. By Definition 7, this is equivalent to showing that $[[PTA_1]] \overset{PS}{\equiv}_{F_1,F_2} [[PTA_2]]$, where F_1 and F_2 are the corresponding target states of ϕ_1 and ϕ_2 respectively. Our optimizations are based on deterministic path compression as outlined in Section 4.1. Hence, we impose requirements on PTA_1 and PTA_2 under which we can apply theorem 1 to $[[PTA_1]]$ and $[[PTA_2]]$ to deduce $[[PTA_1]] \overset{PS}{\equiv}_{F_1,F_2} [[PTA_2]]$.

Consider two PTAs with an identical set of clocks and events: $PTA_1 = (L_1, \overline{l_1}, \chi, \Sigma, I_1, P_1)$ and $PTA_2 = (L_2, \overline{l_2}, \chi, \Sigma, I_2, P_2)$. We assume that the automata have the same set of urgent events, Σ^u.

Definition 14. *A state $s \in L_1 \cap L_2$ is a point of disagreement between the two probabilistic timed automata if either they differ on the invariant or they differ in the set of outgoing transitions or both. Taking a transition out of a state s as the tuple $(s, z, \sigma, P(2^\chi \times L))$, call two transitions different if they disagree on either the guard z, or the event label on the transition σ, or the distribution $P(2^\chi \times L)$.*

The semantic PSs are $[[PTA_1]]$ and $[[PTA_2]]$ respectively. Let $States([[PTA_1]])$ and $States([[PTA_2]])$ denote states of the semantic PSs for PTA_1 and PTA_2 respectively. The states in the semantic PS are tuples (s, v) where s is a state of the PTA and v is a clock valuation.

Lemma 1. *A state $(s, v) \in States([[PTA_1]]) \cap States([[PTA_2]])$ as a point of disagreement (with regard to condition 1 of theorem 1) between the two PS implies that s is a point of disagreement between PTA_1 and PTA_2.*

The condition that labels should also be identical might seem too restrictive considering that we are only interested in probabilistic reachability. However, the next set of lemmas will show that when composing PTAs labels are important.

Most real world systems and the 802.11 protocol in particular are modeled as a composition of PTAs. In a composed system, the above lemma will only tell us whether a particular common state in the PTA can generate a point of disagreement in the semantic PS. This common state represents the composed state of all the PTAs composing the model. The next few lemmas extend lemma 1 to the scenario of composed probabilistic timed automata.

Definition 15. *Consider two PTAs formed of compositions, as follows.*
$PTA_1 = PTA_1^1 \parallel PTA_2^1 \parallel PTA_3^1 \parallel .. \parallel PTA_n^1$ *and*
$PTA_2 = PTA_1^2 \parallel PTA_2^2 \parallel PTA_3^2 \parallel .. \parallel PTA_n^2$.
Define the difference set as the set $D \subseteq \{1, 2, .., n\}$ such that $\forall i \in D : PTA_i^1 \neq PTA_i^2$ and $\forall i \notin D : PTA_i^1 = PTA_i^2$. By equality we mean exactly the same automaton in both the compositions (component wise equality of the tuples defining them).

Definition 16. *We define the specific difference set for the index $i \in D$ as $D_i \subseteq states(PTA_i^1) \cap states(PTA_i^2)$ where D_i is the set of states that disagree across the automata as outlined in definition 14. For every $i \notin D$ set $D_i = \emptyset$.*

Lemma 2. *Consider the composed PTA models of Definition 15. Let S_{common} be the set of common states between PTA_1 and PTA_2. A composed state in S_{common}, say $(l_1, l_2, .., l_n)$ is a point of disagreement between PTA_1 and PTA_2 implies that at least one automaton is in its specific difference set.*

In the composed PTAs of definition 15, each state in the semantic PS for a PTA is a combination of states and clock valuations of the individual PTA in the composition. The next lemma combines lemmas 1 and 2.

Lemma 3 (PTA level requirements).
A state in $States([[PTA_1]]) \cap States([[PTA_2]]) = (l_1, l_2.., l_n, v)$ as a point of disagreement implies that for at least one $i \in \{1..n\}$, the common state l_i of both PTA_i^1 and PTA_i^2 is an element of their specific disagreement set.

Lemma 3 identifies precisely those states in the *component* PTA that *may* cause a disagreement in the PS for the composed system.

4.3 Proof Technique

We will use the framework in this section to prove the correctness of our reduced models. Although our objective is the 802.11 protocol, the concept of deterministic path compression has been developed in a generalized manner anticipating its application to other protocols.

To prove that a reduced PTA model (PTA_2) corresponding to the original PTA model (PTA_1) is correct, we need to prove that $PTA_1 \overset{PTA}{\equiv}_{\phi_1,\phi_2} PTA_2$. Here ϕ_1 and ϕ_2 are the corresponding PCTL formulas in the two models. For our purposes $\phi_1 = \phi_2$ since we are interested in proving that we will arrive at the same result for the same particular PCTL formula. We proceed with the proof in the following manner.

1. Identify the difference set (Definition 15). Compute the specific difference set of each component automaton in the difference set using Definition 16. This is easily done by a visual inspection of the automata.
2. Identify composed states where one or more automata are in their specific difference set. At this point we use protocol specific proofs to limit such combinations to a manageable size. From Lemma 2 we know the set of composed states obtained in this step is a superset of the actual difference set across the composed PTA.
3. For each composed state, we argue about the possible evolution of the untimed model obtained through Definition 3. We show that
i) There is the same deterministic dominator in each of $[[PTA_1]]$ and $[[PTA_2]]$. This is usually the hardest part of the proof. However, we use the fact that the deterministic dominator state in the PS is expressible as the combination of a composed state and clock valuation in the PTA. Hence the proofs are in terms of the PTA rather than the PS. We generally show that each component automaton reaches the state in the composition and progress can only be made when the entire model is in the composed state.

ii) Final states in $[[PTA_1]]$ and $[[PTA_2]]$, corresponding to the PCTL formulas ϕ_1 and ϕ_2 respectively, are distributed as specified in condition 2 of Theorem 1.
iii) PTA_1 and PTA_2 have the same start state.

From Lemma 3 we know that this is sufficient for Theorem 1 to hold. Hence we conclude that at the level of PTAs $PTA_1 \overset{PTA}{\equiv}_{\phi_1,\phi_2} PTA_2$.

Deterministic Path Compression, at the level of PSs, bears similarity to weak bisimulation [9] that can abstract away internal actions. However, a notable difference in our approach from weak bisimulation is that we are able to change invariants on states in the PTA. This corresponds to removing time steps (Definition 3) in the corresponding semantic PS. These time steps are *not* internal actions because composed PSs must synchronize on time steps to maintain the semantics of PTA composition. A possibility would be to apply weak bisimulation to the final composed model but this would mean fixing the number of stations in the composition. The reduced models would no longer be valid for the general multi station problem.

5 Reducing the 802.11 Station Automaton

For the 802.11 problem, we optimize the station automaton in multiple steps, starting from the original abstract station model of Figure 2 part (a). In each case, the set of final states correspond to the PCTL formula $\phi = P_{<\lambda}[\Diamond(bc = k)]$, which expresses the property that the backoff counter of some station reaches k. For every reduction from PTA_1 to PTA_2, we prove the correctness of our optimizations by showing that $PTA_1 \overset{PTA}{\equiv}_{\phi,\phi} PTA_2$. Due to space constraints, we defer complete proofs to [8] and only motivate the key ideas. Our proofs are driven by behavior exhibited by the 802.11 PTA models. For example, a key aspect of many of our proofs is the fact that 802.11 backoff counters are frozen when a busy channel is detected. We can essentially ignore stations in backoff when the channel is busy. These proofs have been constructed to be independent of the number of stations in the composition.

Our first optimization removes the *SIFS* wait following a successful transmission. The original model is $AbsLAN = AbsStn_1 \parallel AbsStn_2 \parallel .. \parallel AbsStn_n \parallel Chan$ and the reduced model is $IntLAN = IntStn_1 \parallel IntStn_2 \parallel .. \parallel IntStn_n \parallel Chan$. The intermediate station model *IntStn* has the *SIFS* wait removed and is shown in Figure 2 part (b). The difference set (see Definition 15) includes all the stations and does not include the channel, which is unchanged. The specific difference set is only the *Test_Channel* urgent state immediately after asserting *finish_correct*. The key idea of the proof is as follows: All the other stations will detect the busy channel and move into the *Wait_until_free* or *Wait_until_free_II* state. The successfully completing station will move into the *Done* state while the rest of the stations will move either into *Wait_for_DIFS* or *Wait_for_DIFS_II* states, which gives us a deterministic dominator in both the automata (*AbsLAN* and *IntLAN*). In the proof, we exploit the fact that in the 802.11 protocol, the backoff counters are frozen when a transmission is detected on the channel. This is modeled by the station in *Backoff* moving into the *Wait_until_free_II* state.

In the final reduced station model, used in our experiments, the *DIFS* wait has also been removed. Proving the deterministic dominator relationship is a little more com-

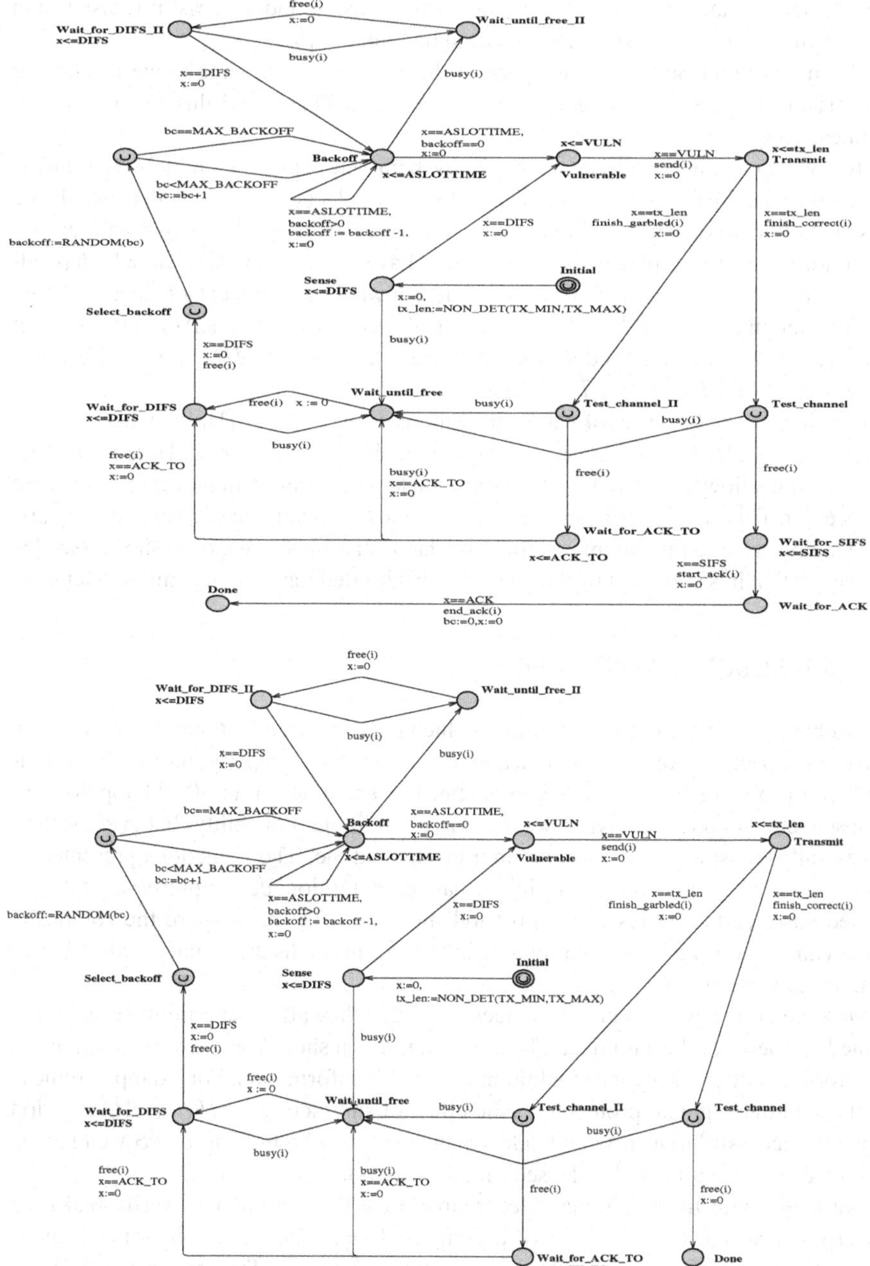

Fig. 2. (a) PTA model for an Abstract Station representing both the sender and destination (top); (b) PTA model for an Intermediate Abstracted and Reduced Station - ACK protocol removed (bottom)

plicated here because we need to consider both collision and successful transmission cases. A discussion of the steps involved can be found in [8].

The major contributor of state space in the protocol is the large range of allowed transmission lengths. The range is from $315\mu s$ to $15717\mu s$ and this proves to be a significant impediment.

To overcome this problem, we begin by parameterizing our models as follows. Rather than having a non-deterministic edge that selects packet lengths, which are subsequently held constant, we *parameterize* the models by packet length and remove the non-deterministic choice. Hence, we now have a *series* of PTA models depending on the choice of parameterizations. The allowable assignment of packet (transmission) lengths is from Par^{full}, the set of all possible parameterizations. Each of $tx\_len_1, .., tx\_len_n$ is assigned a value from the interval $[TX\_MIN, TX\_MAX]$. Formally, $Par^{full} = [TX\_MIN, TX\_MAX]^n$.

Consider the reduced set of parameterizations $Par^{reduced} \subset Par^{full}$ where $tx\_len_1 = TX\_MIN$ and $tx\_len_{i+1} - tx\_len_i \leq VULN, 1 \leq i < n$. Here we restrict the maximum allowable increase in transmission length of one station over its immediate predecessor. This eliminates many parameterizations that would have assigned transmission lengths close to maximum resulting in a large state space. We have shown (see [8] for details) that it is sufficient to consider only this limited range of transmission lengths.

6 Soft Deadline Verification

The probability of meeting soft deadlines, which is the minimum probability of a station delivering a packet within a certain deadline, is a real time property that can be formulated as a probabilistic reachability problem. For example, in an 802.11 topology of three senders and three receivers, we are interested in the probability that *every* station successfully transmits its packet within a given deadline. The reductions presented in this paper, which depend on deterministic path compression, do not preserve total time elapsed since certain states in the probabilistic timed automata where the composite model can spend time have been removed. As a result, paths are replaced with shorter (time wise) versions.

However, one key aspect of our reductions is that they affect deterministic and well-defined segments of the automata. The intuition is that it should be possible to "compensate" for the reductions by using additional available information. For example, removing the acknowledgment protocol has the effect of subtracting a $SIFS + ACK$ period for every successful transmission made. On the other hand removing $DIFS$ wait results in subtracting $DIFS$ from the elapsed time for any transmission made.

We begin with the traditional "decoration" of a PTA in order to verify real time properties. Assume the existence of a composed state $Done$, which is the composition of the state $Done$ across the components the model. Decorating the PTA involves adding a global clock (say y) to the system that counts total time elapsed and a state $Deadline\_exceeded$. Edges are added from each state other than $Done$, with guard $y \geq deadline$ to $Deadline\_exceeded$. Every invariant other than at $Done$ and $Deadline\_exceeded$ is taken in conjunction with $y \leq deadline$. The objective is to model check for the PCTL formula $P_{>\lambda}[\Diamond Done]$, which expresses the soft deadline property. We defer further discussion of the details to [8] due to lack of space.

7 Results

Our verification platform is a 1.2 GHz Pentium III server with 1.5 GB of ECC memory and running Linux 2.4. Our experiments used the Multi-Terminal Binary Decision Diagram (MTBDD) engine of PRISM. All properties were checked with an accuracy of 10^{-6}, which means that the model checker stops when probabilities returned by successive iterations differ by, or less than, this value.

The growth in state space for the multi station problem is shown in Table 2 part (a). The optimized two station models show a significant improvement in size when compared with the models of [2]. Unoptimized models for three and four stations cannot even be built by the model checker within the resources provided. The obtained upper bounds on the probability of the backoff counter reaching a certain value are shown in Table 1. The values for a three station model are higher due to increased contention for the channel. Verification costs for our optimized models are clearly lower.

Table 1. Probability of backoff counter reaching a specified value in 2 station and 3 station cases

Backoff Counter	2original (secs)	2optimized (secs)	Maximum probability	3optimized Iterations	3opt (secs)	Maximum probability
1	0.69	0.09	1.0	285	1428	1.0
2	8.95	1.15	0.18359375	107	124	0.59643554
3	37.37	6.29	0.0170326	259	1250	0.104351032
4	113.25	29.12	7.9424586e-4	506	14183	0.008170952
5	327.04	120.5	1.8566660e-5	525	37659	2.83169319e-4
6	970.38	508.26	2.1729427e-7	947	246874	2.85355921e-5

Table 2. State space sizes for the backoff counter problem and soft deadline problem results

Stations	2Orig	2Opt	3	4
States	5958233	393958	1084111823	1377418222475
Transitions	16563234	958378	3190610466	5162674182210
Choices	11437956	598412	1908688031	2958322202754

(a) State space size

G.729 type	Time (sec)	Min Probability
1	613	0
2	52388	0.0117

(b) Soft deadline results

We include results from an example case study involving soft deadlines. Consider three overlapping 802.11 wireless networks each servicing seven 802.11 stations. Assume voice data being distributed to all stations from a 100 Mbps 802.3 LAN through the wireless network using either of two subtypes of the G.729 [16] voice encoding scheme. A soft deadline for meeting the resultant bandwidth constraints can be formulated; for details see [8]. The probability of meeting this deadline is shown in Table 2 part (b).

8 Conclusion

In this paper, we have introduced generalized probabilistic timed automata models for the 802.11 MAC and optimized them using deterministic path compression, a novel technique to remove protocol redundancies. We have been somewhat successful, using this optimization in tackling the state space problem for the 802.11 wireless LAN protocol. We have also shown that it is still possible to compute the minimum probability of meeting soft deadlines with the optimized models.

Future extenstions to this effort are to model check four or more stations as well as consider extensions to the basic access protocol considered here.

References

1. The Institute of Electrical and Inc. Electronics Engineers. *IEEE Std. 802.11 - Wireless LAN Medium Access Control(MAC) and Physical Layer (PHY) specifications*, 1999.
2. Marta Kwiatkowska, Gethin Norman, and Jeremy Spronston. Probabilistic model checking of the IEEE 802.11 wireless local area network protocol. In *Proc. PAPM/PROBMIV'02*, volume 2399, pages 169–187. Springer, LNCS, 2002.
3. Moustafa Youssef, Arunchandar Vasan, and Raymond Miller. Specification and analysis of the dcf and pcf protocols in the 802.11 standard using systems of communicating machines. In *IEEE ICNP 2002*, November 2002.
4. Marta Kwiatkowska, Gethin Norman, Roberto Segala, and Jeremy Sproston. Automatic verification of real-time systems with discrete probability distributions. *Lecture Notes in Computer Science*, 1601:75–95, 1999.
5. M. Kwiatkowska, G. Norman, and D. Parker. PRISM: Probabilistic symbolic model checker. In T. Field, P. Harrison, J. Bradley, and U. Harder, editors, *Proc. 12th International Conference on Modelling Techniques and Tools for Computer Performance Evaluation (TOOLS'02)*, volume 2324 of *LNCS*, pages 200–204. Springer, 2002.
6. Kim Guldstrand Larsen, Paul Pettersson, and Wang Yi. UPPAAL in a nutshell. In *International Journal on Software Tools for Technology Transfer*, volume 1, pages 134–152, 1997.
7. P.R. D'Argenio, Bertrand Jeannet, Henrik E. Jensen, and Kim G. Larsen. Reduction and refinement strategies for probabilistic analysis. In *Process Algebra and Probabilistic Methods. Performance Modeling and Verification : Second Joint International Workshop PAPM-PROBMIV 2002*, volume 2399. LNCS, 2002.
8. http://agni.csa.iisc.ernet.in/~gopi/aroy/paper.pdf.
9. Roberto Segala and Nancy Lynch. Probabilistic simulations for probabilistic processes. *Nordic Journal of Computing*, 2(2):250–273, 1995.
10. Marta Kwiatkowska. Model checking for probability and time:from theory to practice invited paper. In *Proc. 18th IEEE Symposium on Logic in Computer Science (LICS'03)*, pages 351–360. IEEE Computer Society Press, 2003.
11. Marta Kwiatkowska, Gethin Norman, and Jeremy Sproston. Probabilistic model checking of the 802.11 wireless local area network protocol. Technical Report CSR-02-05, School of Computer Science,University of Birmingham, 2002.
12. Christel Baier and Marta Z. Kwiatkowska. Model checking for a probabilistic branching time logic with fairness. *Distributed Computing*, 11(3):125–155, 1998.
13. John G. Kemeney, J. Laurie Snell, and Anthony W. Knapp. *Denumerable Markov Chains*. Springer Verlag, 1976.
14. Hans Hansson and Bengt Jonsson. A logic for reasoning about time and reliability. *Formal Aspects of Computing*, 6(5):512–535, 1994.
15. I. F. Akyildiz, W. Su, Y. Sankarasubramaniam, and E. Cayirci. Wireless sensor networks: a survey. *Comput. Networks*, 38(4):393–422, 2002.
16. International Telecommunication Union. *Coding of speech at 8 kbit/s using conjugate-structure algebraic-code-excited linear-prediction (CS-ACELP)*, 1996.

Probabilistic Verification for “Black-Box” Systems*

Håkan L.S. Younes

Computer Science Department, Carnegie Mellon University,
Pittsburgh, PA 15213, USA

Abstract. We explore the concept of a “black-box” stochastic system, and propose an algorithm for verifying probabilistic properties of such systems based on very weak assumptions regarding system dynamics. Properties are expressed as formulae in a probabilistic temporal logic. Our presentation is a generalization of and an improvement over recent work by Sen et al. on probabilistic verification for “black-box” systems.

1 Introduction

Stochastic processes are used to model phenomena in nature that involve an element of chance (the throwing of a die) or are too complex to fully capture in a deterministic fashion (the duration of a call in a telephone system). Certain classes of stochastic processes have been studied extensively in the performance evaluation and model checking communities. Numerous temporal logics, such as TCTL [1], PCTL [8], and CSL [2, 3], exist for expressing interesting properties of various types of stochastic processes. Model checking algorithms have been developed for verifying properties of discrete-time Markov chains [8], continuous-time Markov chains [3, 11], semi-Markov processes [10], generalized semi-Markov processes [1], and stochastic discrete event systems in general [15].

Given a stochastic process, we want to know if certain probabilistic properties hold. For instance, we may ask whether the probability of exhausting bandwidth over a communication link is below 0.01. We can also introduce deadlines, for example that a message arrives at its destination within 15 seconds with probability at least 0.8. Properties of this type can be verified using either numerical methods or statistical sampling techniques, as discussed by Younes et al. [14]. Numerical methods provide highly accurate results, but rely on strong assumptions regarding the dynamics of the systems they are used to analyze. Statistical techniques require only that the dynamics of a system can be simulated. They can thus be used for a larger class of stochastic processes, but results are only probabilistic and attaining high accuracy can to be costly.

For some systems, it may not even be feasible to assume that we can simulate their behavior. Sen et al. [12] consider the verification problem for such “black-box” systems. Here, “black-box” means that the system cannot be controlled to

* Supported in part by the US Army Research Office (ARO), under contract no. DAAD190110485, and the Royal Swedish Academy of Engineering Sciences (IVA).

K. Etessami and S.K. Rajamani (Eds.): CAV 2005, LNCS 3576, pp. 253–265, 2005.

generate execution traces, or trajectories, on demand starting from arbitrary states. This is a reasonable assumption, for instance, for a system that has already been deployed and for which we are given only a set of trajectories generated during actual execution of the system. We are then asked to verify a probabilistic property of the system based on the information provided to us as a fixed set of trajectories. Statistical solution techniques are certainly required to solve this problem. The statistical method described by Younes and Simmons [15] (see also [13–Chap. 5]) cannot be used to verify "black-box" systems, however, because it depends on the ability to generate trajectories on demand.

Sen et al. [12] present an alternative solution method for verification of "black-box" systems based on statistical hypothesis testing with fixed sample sizes. In this paper, we improve upon their algorithm by making sure to always accept the most likely hypothesis, and we correct their procedure for verifying nested probabilistic properties. Differences between the two approaches are discussed in detail in Sect. 5.

We focus our attention on systems with piecewise constant trajectories. The class of stochastic discrete event systems, defined in Sect. 2, satisfies this constraint. Sect. 3 introduces the *unified temporal stochastic logic* (UTSL), which can be used to express probabilistic and temporal properties of stochastic discrete event systems. UTSL represents a unification of Hansson and Jonsson's [8] PCTL, which has a semantics defined for discrete-time Markov chains, and Baier et al.'s [3] version of CSL (excluding the steady-state operator), which has a semantics defined for continuous-time Markov chains.

Sect. 4 presents an algorithm for the verification of "black-box" systems. Our algorithm, like that of Sen et al. [12], provides no *a priori* guarantees regarding accuracy. Instead, the algorithm computes a p-value for the result, which is a measure of confidence. The algorithm is essentially finding the most likely answer to a model checking problem given a fixed set of trajectories. This is the best we can do, provided that we cannot generate trajectories for the system as we see fit and are restricted to using a predetermined set of trajectories.

The algorithm presented in this paper is complementary to the statistical model checking algorithm presented by Younes and Simmons [15], and is useful under different assumptions. If we cannot generate trajectories for a system on demand, then the algorithm presented here still allows us to reach conclusions regarding the behavior of the system. If, however, we can simulate the dynamics of the system, then we are better off with the approach of Younes and Simmons as it gives us full control over the probability of obtaining an incorrect result.

2 Stochastic Discrete Event Systems

A *stochastic process* is any process that evolves over time, and whose evolution one can follow and predict in terms of probability [4]. At any point in time, a stochastic process is said to occupy some state. If we attempt to observe the state of a stochastic process at a specific time, the outcome of such an observation is governed by some probability law. Mathematically, a stochastic process is defined as a family of random variables.

Definition 1 (Stochastic Process). *Let S and T be two sets. A* stochastic process *is a family of random variables $\mathcal{X} = \{X_t \mid t \in T\}$, with each random variable X_t having range S.*

The index set T in Definition 1 represents time and is typically the set of non-negative integers, $\mathbb{Z}^*$, for discrete-time stochastic processes and the set of non-negative real numbers, $[0, \infty)$, for continuous-time stochastic processes. The set S represents the states that the stochastic process can occupy, and this can be an infinite, or even uncountable, set.

The definition of a stochastic process as a family of random variables is quite general and includes systems with both continuous and discrete dynamics. We will focus our attention on a limited, but important, class of stochastic processes: *stochastic discrete event systems.* This class includes any stochastic process that can be thought of as occupying a single state for a duration of time before an *event* causes an instantaneous state transition to occur. The canonical example of such a process is a queuing system, with the state being the number of items currently in the queue. The state changes at the occurrence of an event representing the arrival or departure of an item.

2.1 Trajectories

A random variable $X_t \in \mathcal{X}$ represents the chance experiment of observing the stochastic process $\mathcal{X}$ at time t. If we record our observations at consecutive time points for all $t \in T$, then we have a *trajectory*, or *sample path*, for $\mathcal{X}$. Our work in probabilistic verification is centered around the verification of temporal logic formulae over trajectories for stochastic discrete event systems. The terminology and notation introduced here is used extensively in later sections.

Definition 2 (Trajectory). *A* trajectory *for a stochastic process $\mathcal{X}$ is any sequence of observations $\{x_t \in S \mid t \in T\}$ of the random variables $X_t \in \mathcal{X}$.*

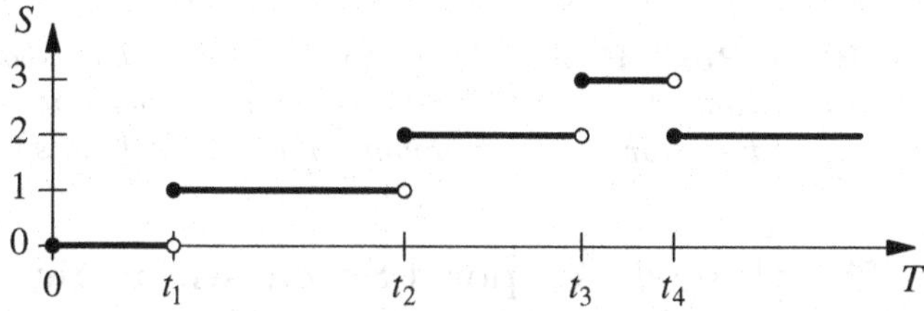

Fig. 1. A trajectory for a simple queuing system with arrival events occurring at t_1, t_2 and t_3 and a departure event occurring at t_4.

The trajectory of a stochastic discrete event system is *piecewise constant* and can therefore be represented as a sequence $\sigma = \{\langle s_0, t_0\rangle, \langle s_1, t_1\rangle, \ldots\}$, with $s_i \in S$ and $t_i \in T \setminus \{0\}$. Zero is excluded to ensure that only a single state can be occupied at any point in time. Fig. 1 plots part of a trajectory for a simple queuing system. Let

$$T_i = \begin{cases} 0 & \text{if } i = 0 \\ \sum_{j=0}^{i-1} t_j & \text{if } i > 0 \end{cases} , \tag{1}$$

i.e. T_i is the time at which state s_i is entered and t_i is the duration of time for which the process remains in s_i before an event triggers a transition to state s_{i+1}. A trajectory σ is then a sequence of observations of $\mathcal{X}$ with $x_t = s_i$ for $T_i \leq t < T_i + t_i$. According to this definition, trajectories of stochastic discrete event systems are *right-continuous.* A finite trajectory is a sequence $\sigma = \{\langle s_0, t_0\rangle, \ldots, \langle s_n, \infty\rangle\}$ where s_n is an *absorbing* state, meaning that no events can occur in s_n and that $x_t = s_n$ for all $t \geq T_n$.

2.2 Measurable Stochastic Discrete Event Systems

Of utmost importance to probabilistic verification is the definition of a *probability measure* over sets of trajectories for a system. The set of trajectories must be *measurable.* Formally, a *measurable space* is a set Ω with a σ-algebra $\mathcal{F}_\Omega$ of subsets of Ω [7]. A *probability space* is a measurable space $\langle \Omega, \mathcal{F}_\Omega\rangle$ and a probability measure μ.

For stochastic discrete event systems, the elements of the σ-algebra are sets of trajectories with common *prefix.* A prefix of $\sigma = \{\langle s_0, t_0\rangle, \langle s_1, t_1\rangle, \ldots\}$ is a sequence $\sigma_{\leq\tau} = \{\langle s'_0, t'_0\rangle, \ldots, \langle s'_k, t'_k\rangle\}$, with $s'_i = s_i$ for all $i \leq k$, $\sum_{i=0}^{k} t'_i = \tau$, $t'_i = t_i$ for all $i < k$, and $t'_k < t_k$. Let $Path(\sigma_{\leq\tau})$ denote the set of trajectories with common prefix $\sigma_{\leq\tau}$. This set must be measurable, and we assume that a probability measure μ over sets of trajectories with common prefix exists. This requirement is not a problem in practice. In general, a stochastic discrete event system is measurable if the sets S and T are measurable.

The precise definition of μ depends on the specific probability structure of the stochastic process being studied. A stochastic process is a Markov chain if $\mu(Path(\{\langle s_0, t_0\rangle, \ldots, \langle s_k, t_k\rangle\})) = \mu(Path(\{\langle s_k, 0\rangle\}))$ for all trajectory prefixes $\{\langle s_0, t_0\rangle, \ldots, \langle s_k, t_k\rangle\}$. We define a "black-box" probabilistic system in terms of what we know (or rather, do not know) regarding the probability measure μ.

Definition 3 ("Black-Box" Probabilistic System). *A "black-box" probabilistic system is a stochastic discrete event system for which the probability measure μ over sets of trajectories with common prefix is not fully specified.*

3 UTSL: The Unified Temporal Stochastic Logic

A stochastic discrete event system is a triple $\langle S, T, \mu\rangle$. We assume a factored representation of S, with a set of state variables SV and a value assignment function $V(s, x)$ providing the value of $x \in SV$ in state s. The domain of x is the set $D_x = \bigcup_{s\in S} V(s, x)$ of possible values that x can take on. We define the syntax of UTSL for a factored stochastic discrete event system $\mathcal{M} = \langle S, T, \mu, SV, V\rangle$ as

$$\Phi ::= x \sim v \;\big|\; \neg\Phi \;\big|\; \Phi \wedge \Phi \;\big|\; \mathcal{P}_{\bowtie\theta}[\mathcal{X}^I\, \Phi] \;\big|\; \mathcal{P}_{\bowtie\theta}[\Phi\, \mathcal{U}^I\, \Phi] ,$$

where $x \in SV$, $v \in D_x$, $\sim \in \{\leq, =, \geq\}$, $\theta \in [0,1]$, $\bowtie \in \{\leq, \geq\}$, and $I \subset T$. Additional UTSL formulae can be derived in the usual way. For example, $\bot \equiv (x = v) \wedge \neg(x = v)$ for some $x \in SV$ and $v \in D_x$, $\top \equiv \neg\bot$, $\Phi \vee \Psi \equiv \neg(\neg\Phi \wedge \neg\Psi)$, $\Phi \rightarrow \Psi \equiv \neg\Phi \vee \Psi$, $\mathcal{P}_{\bowtie\theta}[\Phi\, \mathcal{U}\, \Psi] \equiv \mathcal{P}_{\bowtie\theta}[\Phi\, \mathcal{U}^T\, \Psi]$, and $\mathcal{P}_{<\theta}[\varphi] \equiv \neg\mathcal{P}_{\geq\theta}[\varphi]$.

The standard logic operators have their usual meaning. $\mathcal{P}_{\bowtie\theta}[\varphi]$ asserts that the probability measure over the set of trajectories satisfying the path formula φ is related to θ according to $\bowtie$. Path formulae are constructed using the temporal path operators X^I ("next") and $\mathcal{U}^I$ ("until"). The path formula $X^I\, \Phi$ asserts that the next state transition occurs $t \in I$ time units into the future and that Φ holds in the next state, while $\Phi\, \mathcal{U}^I\, \Psi$ asserts that Ψ becomes true $t \in I$ time units into the future while Φ holds continuously prior to t.

The validity of a UTSL formula, relative to a factored stochastic discrete event system $\mathcal{M}$, is defined in terms of a satisfaction relation $\models_{\mathcal{M}}$:

$$\begin{array}{rll}
\{\langle s_0, t_0\rangle, \ldots, \langle s_k, t_k\rangle\} & \models_{\mathcal{M}} x \sim v & \text{iff } V(s_k, x) \sim v \\
\sigma_{\leq\tau} & \models_{\mathcal{M}} \neg\Phi & \text{iff } \sigma_{\leq\tau} \not\models_{\mathcal{M}} \Phi \\
\sigma_{\leq\tau} & \models_{\mathcal{M}} \Phi \wedge \Psi & \text{iff } (\sigma_{\leq\tau} \models_{\mathcal{M}} \Phi) \wedge (\sigma_{\leq\tau} \models_{\mathcal{M}} \Psi) \\
\sigma_{\leq\tau} & \models_{\mathcal{M}} \mathcal{P}_{\bowtie\theta}[\varphi] & \text{iff } \mu(\{\sigma \in \mathit{Path}(\sigma_{\leq\tau}) \mid \sigma, \tau \models_{\mathcal{M}} \varphi\}) \bowtie \theta
\end{array}$$

$$\begin{array}{ll}
\sigma, \tau \models_{\mathcal{M}} X^I\, \Phi & \text{iff } \exists k \in \mathbb{N}.\big((T_{k-1} \leq \tau) \wedge (\tau < T_k) \wedge (T_k - \tau \in I) \wedge (\sigma_{\leq T_k} \models_{\mathcal{M}} \Phi)\big) \\
\sigma, \tau \models_{\mathcal{M}} \Phi\, \mathcal{U}^I\, \Psi & \text{iff } \exists t \in I.\big((\sigma_{\leq\tau+t} \models_{\mathcal{M}} \Psi) \wedge \forall t' \in T.\big((t' < t) \rightarrow (\sigma_{\leq\tau+t'} \models_{\mathcal{M}} \Phi)\big)\big)
\end{array}$$

The semantics of $\Phi\, \mathcal{U}^I\, \Psi$ requires that Φ holds continuously, i.e. at all time points, along a trajectory until Ψ is satisfied. This is consistent with the semantics of time-bounded until for TCTL [1]. Depending on the probability measure μ, Φ may hold immediately at the entry of a state s and also immediately after a transition from s to s', but still not hold continuously while the system remains in s. Conversely, Ψ may hold at some point in time while the system remains in s, and not hold immediately upon entry to s nor immediately after a transition from s to s'. It is therefore not sufficient, in general, to verify Φ and Ψ at discrete points along a trajectory. It is sufficient to do so, however, for Markov chains. Our semantics for UTSL interpreted over general stochastic discrete event systems therefore coincides with the semantics for PCTL interpreted over discrete-time Markov chains [8] and CSL interpreted over continuous-time Markov chains [3], provided we choose the time domain T appropriately.

A UTSL model checking problem is a triple $\langle\mathcal{M}, s, \Phi\rangle$, with the problem being to verify whether Φ holds for $\mathcal{M}$ if execution starts in state s, i.e. $\{\langle s, 0\rangle\} \models_{\mathcal{M}} \Phi$. We use $s \models \Phi$ as a short form for the latter, leaving out $\mathcal{M}$ when it is clear from the context which system is involved in the model checking problem.

4 Statistical Verification Algorithm

A stochastic discrete event system $\mathcal{M}$ is a "black-box" system if we lack an exact definition of the probability measure μ over sets of trajectories of $\mathcal{M}$ (Definition 3) and we cannot sample trajectories according to μ. Thus, to solve a verification problem $s \models \Phi$ for $\mathcal{M}$, we must rely on an external source to provide a sample set of n trajectories for $\mathcal{M}$ that is representative of the probability measure μ. We further assume that we are provided only with *truncated* trajectories, because infinite trajectories would require infinite memory to store.

We use statistical hypothesis testing to verify properties of a "black-box" system given a sample of n truncated trajectories. Since we rely on statistical techniques, we will typically not know with certainty if the result we produce is correct. The method we present for verification of "black-box" systems computes a p-value for a verification result, which is a value in the interval $[0, 1]$ with values closer to 0 representing higher confidence in the result [9–pp. 255–256].

4.1 Verification Without Nested Probabilistic Operators

Given a state s, verification of a UTSL formula $x \sim v$ is trivial. We can simply read the value assigned to x in s and compare it to v. We consider the remaining three cases in more detail, starting with the probabilistic operator $\mathcal{P}_{\bowtie\theta}[\cdot]$. The objective is to produce a Boolean result annotated with a p-value.

Probabilistic Operator. Consider the problem of verifying the UTSL formula $\mathcal{P}_{\bowtie\theta}[\varphi]$ in state s of a stochastic discrete event system $\mathcal{M}$. Let X_i be a random variable representing the verification of the path formula φ over a trajectory for $\mathcal{M}$ drawn according to the probability measure $\mu(\mathit{Path}(\{\langle s, 0\rangle\}))$. If we choose $X_i = 1$ to represent the fact that φ holds over a random trajectory, and $X_i = 0$ to represent the opposite fact, then X_i is a *Bernoulli variate* with parameter $p = \mu(\{\sigma \in \mathit{Path}(\{\langle s, 0\rangle\}) \mid \sigma, 0 \models \varphi\})$, i.e. $\Pr[X_i = 1] = p$ and $\Pr[X_i = 0] = 1 - p$. To verify $\mathcal{P}_{\bowtie\theta}[\varphi]$, we can make observations of X_i and use statistical hypothesis testing to determine if $p \bowtie \theta$ is likely to hold. An observation of X_i, denoted x_i, is the verification of φ over a specific trajectory σ_i. If σ_i satisfies the path formula φ, then $x_i = 1$, otherwise $x_i = 0$.

In our case, we are given n truncated trajectories for a "black-box" system that we can use to generate observations of X_i. Each observation is obtained by verifying the path formula φ over one of the truncated trajectories. This is straightforward given a truncated trajectory $\{\langle s_0, t_0\rangle, \ldots, \langle s_{k-1}, t_{k-1}\rangle, s_k\}$, provided that φ does not contain any probabilistic operators. For $\varphi = \mathcal{X}^I\ \Phi$, we just check if $t_0 \in I$ and $s_1 \models \Phi$. For $\varphi = \Phi\ \mathcal{U}^I\ \Psi$, we traverse the trajectory until we find a state s_i such that one of the following conditions holds, with T_i defined as in (1) to be the time at which state s_i is entered:

1. $(s_i \models \neg\Phi) \wedge ((T_i \notin I) \vee (s_i \models \neg\Psi))$
2. $(T_i \in I) \wedge (s_i \models \Psi)$
3. $((T_i, T_{i+1}) \cap I \neq \emptyset) \wedge (s_i \models \Phi) \wedge (s_i \models \Psi)$

In the first case, $\Phi\ \mathcal{U}^I\ \Psi$ does not hold over the trajectory, while in the last two cases the time-bounded until formula does hold. Note that we may not always be able to determine the value of φ over all trajectories because the trajectories that are provided to us are assumed to be truncated.

We consider the case $\mathcal{P}_{\geq\theta}[\varphi]$ in detail, noting that $\mathcal{P}_{\leq\theta}[\varphi]$ can be handled in the same way simply by reversing the value of each observation. We want to test the hypothesis $H_0 : p \geq \theta$ against the alternative hypothesis $H_1 : p < \theta$ by using the n observations $x_1, \ldots, x_n$ of $X_1, \ldots, X_n$. To do so, we specify a constant c. If $\sum_{i=1}^{n} x_i$ is greater than c, then hypothesis H_0 is accepted, i.e. $\mathcal{P}_{\geq\theta}[\varphi]$ is determined to hold. Otherwise, if the given sum is at most c, then hypothesis H_1 is accepted, meaning that $\mathcal{P}_{\geq\theta}[\varphi]$ is determined not to hold. The constant c should be chosen so that it becomes roughly equally likely to accept H_0 as H_1 if p equals θ. The pair $\langle n, c\rangle$ is referred to as a *single sampling plan* [6, 5].

The probability distribution of a sum of n Bernoulli variates with parameter p is a binomial distribution with cumulative distribution function $F(c; n, p) = \sum_{i=0}^{c} \binom{n}{i} p^i (1-p)^{n-i}$. Using a single sampling plan $\langle n, c\rangle$, we accept hypothesis H_1 with probability $F(c; n, p)$ and hypothesis H_0 with probability $1 - F(c; n, p)$. Ideally, we should choose c such that $F(c; n, \theta) = 0.5$, but it is not always possible to attain equality because the binomial distribution is a discrete distribution. The best we can do is to choose c such that $|F(c; n, \theta) - 0.5|$ is minimized.

We now have a way to decide whether to accept or reject the hypothesis that $\mathcal{P}_{\geq\theta}[\varphi]$ holds, but we also want to report a p-value reflecting the confidence in our decision. The p-value is defined as the probability of the sum of observations being at least as extreme as the one obtained provided that the hypothesis that was not accepted holds. The p-value for accepting H_0 when $\sum_{i=1}^{n} x_i = d$ is $\Pr[\sum_{i=1}^{n} X_i \geq d \mid p < \theta]$, which is less than $F(n-d; n, 1-\theta) = 1 - F(d-1; n, \theta)$. The p-value for accepting H_1 is $\Pr[\sum_{i=1}^{n} X_i \leq d \mid p \geq \theta]$, which is at most $F(d; n, \theta)$. The following theorem justifies our choice of the constant c [13–Theorem 7.1]:

Theorem 1 (Minimization of p-value). *By choosing c to minimize the value of $|F(c; n, \theta) - 0.5|$ when testing $H_0 : p \geq \theta$ against $H_1 : p < \theta$ using a single sampling plan $\langle n, c\rangle$, the hypothesis with the lowest p-value is always accepted.*

In practice, it is unnecessary to compute c. It is easier simply to compute the p-value of each hypothesis and accept the hypothesis with the lowest p-value.

Example 1. Consider the problem of verifying $\Phi = \mathcal{P}_{\geq 0.9}\left[\top\ \mathcal{U}^{[0,100]}\ x{=}1\right]$ in a state satisfying $x{=}0$ for a "black-box" system that in reality is the continuous-time Markov chain shown in Fig. 2. The probability measure of trajectories starting in state $x{=}0$ and satisfying $\top\ \mathcal{U}^{[0,100]}\ x{=}1$ is $1 - e^{-1} \approx 0.63$, so the UTSL formula does not hold, but we would of course not know this unless we had access to the model. Assume that we are given a set of 100 truncated trajectories, of which 63 satisfy and 37 do not satisfy the path formula $\top\ \mathcal{U}^{[0,100]}\ x{=}1$. Thus, $n = 100$ and $d = 63$. The p-value for H_0 is $1 - F(62; 100, 0.9) \approx 1 - 10^{-13}$, while the p-value for H_1 is $F(63, 100, 0.9) \approx 5.48 \cdot 10^{-13}$. The hypothesis with the lowest p-value is H_1, so we conclude that Φ does not hold.

In the analysis so far we have assumed that the value of φ can be determined over all n truncated trajectories. Now, assume that we are unable to verify the path formula φ over some of the n truncated trajectories. This would happen

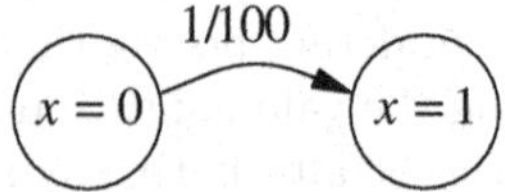

Fig. 2. A simple two-state continuous-time Markov chain

if we verify $\Phi\ \mathcal{U}^I\ \Psi$ over a trajectory that has been truncated before either $\neg\Phi \vee \Psi$ is satisfied or time exceeds all values in I. We cannot simply ignore such trajectories: it is assumed that the *entire* set of n trajectories is representative of the measure μ, but the subset of truncated trajectories for which we can determine the value of φ is not guaranteed to be a representative sample.

Example 2. Consider the same problem as in Example 1. Assume that we are given a set of 100 trajectories for the system that all have been truncated before time 50. Some of the trajectories, on average 39 in every 100, will satisfy $\top\ \mathcal{U}^{[0,100]}\ x{=}1$, while the remaining truncated trajectories will not contain sufficient information to determine the validity of $\top\ \mathcal{U}^{[0,100]}\ x{=}1$ over these trajectories. An analysis based solely on the trajectories over which the path formula can be decisively verified would be severely biased. If the number of positive observations is exactly 39, with 61 undetermined observations, we would wrongly conclude that Φ holds with p-value $1 - F(38; 39, 0.9) \approx 0.0164$, which implies a fairly high confidence in the result.

Let n' be the number of observations whose value we can determine and let d' be the sum of these observations. We then know that the sum of all observations, d, is at least d' and at most $d' + n - n'$. If $d' > c$, then hypothesis H_0 can safely be accepted. Instead of a single p-value, we associate an interval of possible p-values with the result: $[F(n' - d'; n, 1 - \theta), F(n - d'; n, 1 - \theta)]$. Conversely, if $d' + n - n' \leq c$, then hypothesis H_1 can be accepted with p-value in the interval $[F(d'; n, \theta), F(d' + n - n'; n, \theta)]$. In all other cases it is not clear which hypothesis should be accepted. We could then say that we do not have enough information to make an informed choice. Alternatively, we could accept one of the hypotheses with its associated p-value interval. We prefer to always make some choice, and we recommend choosing H_0 if $F(n - d'; n, 1 - \theta) \leq F(d' + n - n'; n, \theta)$ and H_1 otherwise. This strategy minimizes the maximum possible p-value. Alternatively, we could minimize the minimum possible p-value by instead choosing H_0 if $F(n' - d'; n, 1 - \theta) \leq F(d; n, \theta)$ and H_1 otherwise.

Example 3. Consider the same situation as in Example 2, with 39 positive and 61 undetermined observations. The p-value for accepting $\Phi = \mathcal{P}_{\geq 0.9}[\top\ \mathcal{U}^{[0,100]}\ x{=}1]$ as true lies in the interval $[F(0; 100, 0.1), F(61, 100, 0.1)] \approx [2.65 \cdot 10^{-5}, 1 - 3.77 \cdot 10^{-15}]$. For the opposite decision, we get $[F(39; 100, 0.9), F(100; 100, 0.9)] \approx [1.59 \cdot 10^{-35}, 1]$. Both intervals are almost equally uninformative, so no matter what decision we make, we will have a low confidence in the result. This is in sharp contrast to the faulty analysis suggested in Example 2, which lead to an acceptance of Φ as true with a low p-value.

Composite State Formulae. To verify $\neg\Phi$, we first verify Φ. If we conclude that Φ has a certain truth value with p-value pv, then we conclude that $\neg\Phi$ has the opposite truth value with the same p-value. To motivate this, consider the case $\neg\mathcal{P}_{\geq\theta}[\varphi]$. To verify $\mathcal{P}_{\geq\theta}[\varphi]$, we test the hypothesis $H_0 : p \geq \theta$ against $H_1 : p < \theta$ as stated above. Note, however, that $\neg\mathcal{P}_{\geq\theta}[\varphi] \equiv \mathcal{P}_{<\theta}[\varphi]$, which could be posed as the problem of testing the hypothesis $H_0' : p < \theta$ against $H_1' : p \geq \theta$. Since $H_0' = H_1$ and $H_1' = H_0$, we can simply negate the result of verifying $\mathcal{P}_{\geq\theta}[\varphi]$ while maintaining the same p-value (cf. [12]).

For a conjunction $\Phi \wedge \Psi$, we have to consider four cases. First, if we verify Φ to hold with p-value pv_Φ and Ψ to hold with p-value pv_Ψ, then we conclude that $\Phi \wedge \Psi$ holds with p-value $\max(pv_\Phi, pv_\Psi)$. Thus, we are no more confident in the result for $\Phi \wedge \Psi$ than we are in the results for the individual conjuncts. Second, if we verify Φ not to hold with p-value pv_Φ, while verifying that Ψ holds, then we base the decision for the conjunction on the result for Φ alone and conclude that $\Phi \wedge \Psi$ does not hold with p-value pv_Φ. The third case is analogous to the second with Φ and Ψ interchanged. Finally, if we verify Φ not to hold with p-value pv_Φ and Ψ not to hold with p-value pv_Ψ, then we conclude that $\Phi \wedge \Psi$ does not hold with p-value $\min(pv_\Phi, pv_\Psi)$. In this case, we have two sources (not necessarily independent) telling us that the conjunction is false. We have no reason to be less confident in the result for the conjunction than in the result for each of the conjuncts, hence the minimum.

For a mathematical derivation of the given expressions, we consider the formula $\mathcal{P}_{\geq\theta_1}[\varphi_1] \wedge \mathcal{P}_{\geq\theta_2}[\varphi_2]$. Let d_i denote the number of trajectories that satisfy φ_i. Provided we accept the conjunction as true, which means we accept each conjunct as true, the p-value for the result is

$$\Pr[\sum_{i=1}^{n} X_i^{(1)} \geq d_1 \wedge \sum_{i=1}^{n} X_i^{(2)} \geq d_2 \mid p_1 < \theta_1 \vee p_2 < \theta_2] \ . \tag{2}$$

To compute this p-value, consider the three ways in which $p_1 < \theta_1 \vee p_2 < \theta_2$ can be satisfied (cf. [12]). We know from elementary probability theory that $\Pr[A \wedge B] \leq \min(\Pr[A], \Pr[B])$ for arbitrary events A and B. From this fact, and assuming that pv_i is the p-value associated with the verification result for $\mathcal{P}_{\geq\theta_i}[\varphi_i]$, we derive the following:

1. $\Pr[\sum_{i=1}^{n} X_i^{(1)} \geq d_1 \wedge \sum_{i=1}^{n} X_i^{(2)} \geq d_2 \mid p_1 < \theta_1 \wedge p_2 < \theta_2] \leq \min(pv_1, pv_2)$
2. $\Pr[\sum_{i=1}^{n} X_i^{(1)} \geq d_1 \wedge \sum_{i=1}^{n} X_i^{(2)} \geq d_2 \mid p_1 < \theta_1 \wedge p_2 \geq \theta_2] \leq \min(pv_1, 1) = pv_1$
3. $\Pr[\sum_{i=1}^{n} X_i^{(1)} \geq d_1 \wedge \sum_{i=1}^{n} X_i^{(2)} \geq d_2 \mid p_1 \geq \theta_1 \wedge p_2 < \theta_2] \leq \min(1, pv_2) = pv_2$

We take the maximum over these three cases to obtain a bound for (2), which gives us $\max(pv_1, pv_2)$. For the same formula, but now assuming we have verified both conjuncts to be false, we compute the p-value as

$$\Pr[\sum_{i=1}^{n} X_i^{(1)} \leq d_1 \wedge \sum_{i=1}^{n} X_i^{(2)} \leq d_2 \mid p_1 \geq \theta_1 \wedge p_2 \geq \theta_2] \leq \min(pv_1, pv_2) \ . \tag{3}$$

If one conjunct has been verified to be false with p-value pv and the other conjunct has been verified to be true with p-value pv', then the conjunction is determined to be false with p-value pv. This is because the result for the entire conjunction depends only on the conjunct that has been verified to be false.

4.2 Verification with Nested Probabilistic Operators

If we allow nested probabilistic operators, verification of UTSL formulae for "black-box" stochastic discrete event systems becomes much harder. Consider the formula $\mathcal{P}_{\geq \theta}[\top \; \mathcal{U}^{[0,100]} \; \mathcal{P}_{\geq \theta'}[\varphi]]$. In order to verify this formula, we must test if $\mathcal{P}_{\geq \theta'}[\varphi]$ holds at some time $t \in [0, 100]$ along the set of trajectories that we are given. Unless the time domain T is such that there is a finite number of time points in a finite interval, then we potentially have to verify $\mathcal{P}_{\geq \theta'}[\varphi]$ at an infinite or even uncountable number of points along a trajectory, which clearly is infeasible. Even if $T = \mathbb{Z}^*$, so that we only have to verify nested probabilistic formulae at a finite number of points, we still have to take the entire prefix of the trajectory into account at each time point. We are given a fixed set of trajectories, and we can use only the subset of trajectories with a matching prefix to verify a nested probabilistic formula. It is thus likely that we will have few trajectories available to use for verifying nested probabilistic formulae. In the worst case, there will be only a single matching prefix, in which case the uncertainty in the result will be overwhelming.

Only if we assume that the "black-box" system is a Markov chain, which is a rather strong assumption, can we hope to have a significant number of trajectories available for the verification of nested probabilistic formulae. This is because, under the Markov assumption, we only have to take the last state along a trajectory prefix into consideration. Consequently, *any* suffix of a truncated trajectory starting at a specific state s can be regarded as representative of the probability measure $\mu(\{\langle s, 0\rangle\})$ for a Markov chain.

Another complicating factor for verifying $\mathcal{P}_{\geq \theta}[\varphi]$, where φ contains nested probabilistic operators, is that we cannot verify φ over trajectories without some uncertainty in the result. This means that we no longer obtain observations of the random variables X_i, as defined above, but instead we observe some other random variables Y_i, related to X_i through bounds on the observation error.

To compute a p-value for nested verification, we assume that $\Pr[Y_i = 0 \mid X_i = 1] \leq \alpha$ and $\Pr[Y_i = 1 \mid X_i = 0] \leq \beta$. We can make this assumption if we introduce indifference regions in the verification of nested probabilistic formulae and use the procedure described by Younes [13–Chap. 5] to verify path formulae over truncated trajectories. We have the following bounds [13–Lemma 5.7]: $p(1-\alpha) \leq \Pr[Y_i = 1] \leq 1 - (1-p)(1-\beta)$. The p-value for accepting $\mathcal{P}_{\geq \theta}[\varphi]$ as true when the sum of the observations is d is $\Pr[\sum_{i=1}^{n} Y_i \geq d \mid p < \theta]$, which is less than $F(n-d; n, (1-\theta)(1-\beta))$. The p-value for the opposite decision is $\Pr[\sum_{i=1}^{n} Y_i \leq d \mid p \geq \theta]$, which is at most $F(d; n, \theta(1-\alpha))$. Since $F(d; n, p)$ increases as p decreases, we see that the p-value increases as the error bounds α and β increase, which makes perfect sense. As was suggested earlier, we can minimize the p-value of the verification result by computing the p-values of both hypotheses and accept the one with the lowest p-value.

We can let the user specify a parameter δ_0 that controls the relative width of the indifference regions. A nested probabilistic formula $\mathcal{P}_{\geq\theta}[\varphi]$ is verified with an indifference region of half-width $\delta = \delta_0\theta$ if $\theta \leq 0.5$ and $\delta = \delta_0(1-\theta)$ otherwise. The verification is carried out using acceptance sampling as before, but with hypotheses $H_0 : p \geq \theta + \delta$ and $H_1 : p \leq \theta - \delta$. Instead of reporting a p-value, as is done for top-level probabilistic operators, we report bounds for the type I error probability of the sampling plan in use if H_1 is accepted and the type II error probability if H_0 is accepted. In our case, assuming a sampling plan $\langle n, c\rangle$ is used, the type I error bound is $1 - F(c; n, \theta + \delta)$ and the type II error bound is $F(c; n, \theta - \delta)$. As error bounds for the computation of the p-value for a top-level probabilistic operator, we simply take the maximum error bounds for the verification of the path formula over all trajectories.

5 Comparison with Related Work

The idea of using statistical hypothesis testing for verification of "black-box" systems was first proposed by Sen et al. [12]. This section highlights the differences between their approach and the approach presented in this paper.

First, consider the verification of a probabilistic formula $\mathcal{P}_{\geq\theta}[\varphi]$. Our approach is essentially the same as theirs: given a constant c, accept if $\sum_{i=1}^{n} X_i > c$ and reject otherwise. Their choice of c is different, however, and is based on the normal approximation for the binomial distribution. Their acceptance condition is $\sum_{i=1}^{n} X_i \geq n\theta$, which corresponds to choosing c to be $\lceil n\theta \rceil - 1$. Their algorithm, as a consequence, will under some circumstances accept a hypothesis with a larger p-value than the alternative hypothesis. By choosing c as we do, without relying on the normal approximation, we guarantee that the hypothesis with the smallest p-value is always accepted (Theorem 1). Consider $\mathcal{P}_{\geq 0.01}[\varphi]$, for example, with $n = 501$ and $d = 5$. Our procedure would accept the formula as true with p-value 0.562, while the algorithm of Sen et al. would reject it as false with p-value 0.614. It is important to note that their choice of c does not impact the soundness of their algorithm, but it may lead to counterintuitive results.

The second improvement over the method presented by Sen et al. is in the calculation of the p-value for the verification of a conjunction $\Phi \wedge \Psi$ when both conjuncts have been verified to be false. They state that the p-value is bounded by $pv_\Phi + pv_\Psi$, which is correct but unnecessarily conservative. There is no reason to believe that the confidence in the result for $\Phi \wedge \Psi$ would be *lower* (i.e. the p-value *higher*) if we are convinced that both conjuncts are false. We have shown that the p-value in this case is bounded by $\min(pv_\Phi, pv_\Psi)$.

Sen et al., in their handling of nested probabilistic operators, confuse the p-value with the probability of accepting a false hypothesis (generally referred to as the type I or type II error of a sampling plan). The p-value is *not* a bound on the probability of a certain test procedure accepting a false hypothesis. In fact, the test that both they and we use does not provide any useful bound on the probability of accepting a false hypothesis. Their analysis relies heavily on the ability to bound the probability of accepting a false hypothesis, and we have presented a way to provide such bounds by introducing indifference regions (rather than computing p-values) for nested probabilistic operators.

In addition, Sen et al. are vague regarding the assumptions needed for their approach to produce reliable answers. The fact that they treat any portion of a trajectory starting in s, regardless of the portion preceding s, as a sample from the same distribution, hides a rather strong assumption regarding the dynamics of their "black-box" systems. As we have pointed out, this is not a valid assumption unless we know that the system is a Markov chain. They also assume that truncated trajectories are sufficiently long so that a path formula can be verified fully over each truncated trajectory. We have removed this assumption and we have presented a procedure for handling situations when the value of a path formula cannot be determined over all truncated trajectories.

Finally, the empirical analysis offered by Sen et al. easily gives the reader the impression that a low p-value can be guaranteed for a verification result simply by increasing the sample size, even though the authors correctly state that a certain p-value *never* can be guaranteed. If we are unlucky, we may make observations that give us a large p-value even in cases when this is unlikely, and a large p-value may even be the most likely outcome in some cases. The empirical results of Sen et al. cannot be replicated reliably because there is no fixed procedure by which one can determine the sample size required to achieve a certain p-value. Their results give the false impression that their procedure is sequential, i.e. that the sample size automatically adjusts to the difficulty of attaining a certain p-value, when in reality they selected the reported sample sizes *manually* based on prior empirical testing (K. Sen, personal communication, May 20, 2004). It is therefore misleading to say that an algorithm for "black-box" verification is "faster" than a statistical model checking algorithm that is designed to realize certain *a priori* performance characteristics (such as the algorithm described by Younes and Simmons [15]).

6 Discussion

Sen et al. [12] were first to consider the problem of probabilistic verification for "black-box" systems. We have generalized their idea to a wider class of probabilistic systems that can be characterized as stochastic discrete event systems. Our most important contribution is to have given a clear definition of what constitutes a "black-box" system, and to have made explicit any assumptions making feasible the application of statistical hypothesis testing as a solution technique for verification of such systems.

The algorithm presented in this paper should not be thought of as an alternative to the statistical model checking algorithm proposed by Younes and Simmons [15] and empirically evaluated by Younes et al. [14]. The two algorithms are complementary rather than competing, and are useful under disparate sets of assumptions. If we cannot generate trajectories for a system on demand, then the algorithm presented here allows us to still reach conclusions regarding the behavior of the system. If, however, we know the dynamics of a system well enough to enable simulation, then we are better off with the alternative approach as it gives full control over the probability of obtaining an incorrect result.

References

1. Alur, R., Courcoubetis, C., and Dill, D. L. Model-checking for probabilistic real-time systems. In *Proc. 18th International Colloquium on Automata, Languages and Programming*, volume 510 of *LNCS*, pages 115–126. Springer, 1991.
2. Aziz, A., Sanwal, K., Singhal, V., and Brayton, R. K. Model-checking continuous-time Markov chains. *ACM Transactions on Computational Logic*, 1(1):162–170, 2000.
3. Baier, C., Haverkort, B. R., Hermanns, H., and Katoen, J.-P. Model-checking algorithms for continuous-time Markov chains. *IEEE Transactions on Software Engineering*, 29(6):524–541, 2003.
4. Doob, J. L. *Stochastic Processes.* John Wiley & Sons, 1953.
5. Duncan, A. J. *Quality Control and Industrial Statistics.* Richard D. Irwin, fourth edition, 1974.
6. Grubbs, F. E. On designing single sampling inspection plans. *Annals of Mathematical Statistics*, 20(2):242–256, 1949.
7. Halmos, P. R. *Measure Theory.* Van Nostrand Reinhold Company, 1950.
8. Hansson, H. and Jonsson, B. A logic for reasoning about time and reliability. *Formal Aspects of Computing*, 6(5):512–535, 1994.
9. Hogg, R. V. and Craig, A. T. *Introduction to Mathematical Statistics.* Macmillan Publishing Co., fourth edition, 1978.
10. Infante López, G. G., Hermanns, H., and Katoen, J.-P. Beyond memoryless distributions: Model checking semi-Markov chains. In *Proc. 1st Joint International PAPM-PROBMIV Workshop*, volume 2165 of *LNCS*, pages 57–70. Springer, 2001.
11. Kwiatkowska, M., Norman, G., and Parker, D. Probabilistic symbolic model checking with PRISM: A hybrid approach. *International Journal on Software Tools for Technology Transfer*, 6(2):128–142, 2004.
12. Sen, K., Viswanathan, M., and Agha, G. Statistical model checking of black-box probabilistic systems. In *Proc. 16th International Conference on Computer Aided Verification*, volume 3114 of *LNCS*, pages 202–215. Springer, 2004.
13. Younes, H. L. S. *Verification and Planning for Stochastic Processes with Asynchronous Events.* PhD thesis, Computer Science Department, Carnegie Mellon University, 2005. CMU-CS-05-105.
14. Younes, H. L. S., Kwiatkowska, M., Norman, G., and Parker, D. Numerical vs. statistical probabilistic model checking. *International Journal on Software Tools for Technology Transfer*, 2005. Forthcoming.
15. Younes, H. L. S. and Simmons, R. G. Probabilistic verification of discrete event systems using acceptance sampling. In *Proc. 14th International Conference on Computer Aided Verification*, volume 2404 of *LNCS*, pages 223–235. Springer, 2002.

On Statistical Model Checking of Stochastic Systems

Koushik Sen, Mahesh Viswanathan, and Gul Agha

Department of Computer Science,
University of Illinois at Urbana-Champaign
{ksen, vmahesh, agha}@uiuc.edu

Abstract. Statistical methods to model check stochastic systems have been, thus far, developed only for a sublogic of continuous stochastic logic (CSL) that does not have steady state operator and unbounded until formulas. In this paper, we present a statistical model checking algorithm that also verifies CSL formulas with unbounded untils. The algorithm is based on Monte Carlo simulation of the model and hypothesis testing of the samples, as opposed to sequential hypothesis testing. We have implemented the algorithm in a tool called VESTA, and found it to be effective in verifying several examples.

1 Introduction

Stochastic models and temporal logics such as continuous stochastic logic (CSL) [1, 3] and probabilistic computation tree logic (PCTL) [9] are widely used to model practical systems and analyze their performance and reliability. There are two primary approaches to analyzing the stochastic behavior of such systems: *numerical* and *statistical*. In the numerical approach, the formal model of the system is *model checked* for correctness with respect to the specification using symbolic and numerical methods. Model checkers for different classes of stochastic processes and specification logics have been developed [10, 13, 12, 4, 5, 14, 2]. Although the numerical approach is highly accurate, it suffers from memory problem due to state-space explosion and being computationally intensive. An alternate method, proposed in [18], is based on Monte Carlo simulation of the model and performing sequential hypothesis testing on the sample generated. In [15], this method was extended to statistically verify black-box, deployed systems that can only be passively observed. Being statistical, these methods are less precise: they only provide probabilistic guarantees of correctness.

Both statistical approaches (presented in [18, 15]), considered a sublogic of continuous stochastic logic (CSL) that excludes steady state operator and *unbounded until operator*. In this paper, we extend the statistical verification method to verify CSL (or PCTL) formulas that may have unbounded until connectives. Specifically, we consider a sublogic of CSL (and PCTL) that contains all the logical connectives, except for the steady-state operator and present a model checking algorithm for it. As in [18], we assume we have a model that can

K. Etessami and S.K. Rajamani (Eds.): CAV 2005, LNCS 3576, pp. 266–280, 2005.

be simulated on a need basis. The samples generated by Monte Carlo simulation are subjected to hypothesis testing. However, unlike [18], we do simple hypothesis testing as opposed to sequential hypothesis testing. Simple hypothesis testing is easily amenable to parallelism, since the sampling and statistical tests can be done in parallel. We exploit parallelism in our implementation of the algorithm.

We make no inherent assumptions about the model that is being verified, other than it can be simulated using discrete event simulation, and that the model checking problem is well defined with respect to CSL (or PCTL). Thus, our algorithm can be successfully applied to Discrete Time Markov Chains, Continuous Time Markov Chains, and Semi Markov Chains. However, it is unclear whether our method can be applied to Generalized Semi Markov Processes (GSMP). This is because there is no well understood definition of a probability space on execution paths of a GSMP such that the model checking problem is well-defined, i.e., path formulas in CSL define measurable sets.

The rest of the paper is organized as follows. In Section 2, we give our assumptions about the system being analyzed, and present the syntax and semantics of CSL (and PCTL). The model checking algorithm is presented in Section 3. The algorithm is inductive, based on the structure of the formula being verified, and we present the details of the algorithm for all the CSL connectives in our sublogic, though our analysis of the previously considered operators (such as conjunction, negation, next, bounded until, and the probabilistic operator) is similar to that presented in [18], the decision procedures we use differ. Section 4 contains details of our implementation in the VESTA tool and the results of our experimental analysis of the tool. Finally, we conclude in Section 5.

2 Model and Logic

We consider stochastic models that meet the following requirements:

1. Sample execution paths can be generated through discrete-event simulation. Execution paths will be a sequences of the form $\pi = s_0 \xrightarrow{t_0} s_1 \xrightarrow{t_1} s_2 \xrightarrow{t_2} \cdots$ where each s_i is a state of the model and $t_i \in \mathbb{R}_{>0}$ is the time spent in the state s_i before moving to the state s_{i+1}.
2. A probability space can be defined on the execution paths of the model in such a way that the paths satisfying any path formula in our concerned logic (CSL or PCTL), is measurable.
3. The number of states of the system is finite.

It has been shown that commonly used models such as continuous-time Markov chains (CTMC) [17], semi-Markov chains (SMC) [7,14], which are a generalization of CTMC, meet the above requirements. While we believe our algorithm will work for any model that satisfies the above conditions, in order to establish the mathematical concepts and notation clearly, we focus on SMCs.

Let AP be a set of finite atomic propositions. A labelled semi-Markov chain (SMC) is a tuple $\mathcal{M} = (S, s_I, \mathbf{P}, \mathbf{Q}, L)$ where S is a finite set of states, s_I is the initial state, $\mathbf{P}\colon S \times S \to [0,1]$ is a *transition probability matrix* such that $\sum_{s' \in S} \mathbf{P}(s,s') = 1$ for each s in S, $\mathbf{Q}\colon S \times S \to (\mathbb{R}_{\geq 0} \to [0,1])$ is a matrix of continuous cumulative probability distribution functions such that $\mathbf{P}(s,s') = 0$ implies for all t, $\mathbf{Q}(s,s',t) = 1$, and $L\colon S \to 2^{AP}$ is a labelling function that maps every state to a set of atomic propositions.

If for any two states s and s', $\mathbf{P}(s,s') > 0$ then there is a transition from s to s', and the probability of the transition is given by $\mathbf{P}(s,s')$. Thus we can see $(S, s_I, \mathbf{P}, L)$ as the discrete-time Markov chain embedded in the SMC $\mathcal{M}$. Once a next state s' from the current state s is sampled according to the matrix $\mathbf{P}$, the sojourn time in the state s is determined according to the cumulative probability distribution function $\mathbf{Q}(s,s',t)$. The probability to move from state s to s' within t units of time given that s' is sampled as the next state is given by $\mathbf{Q}(s,s',t)$. Note that if all the probability distribution functions in the matrix $\mathbf{Q}$ are exponential then the SMC becomes a CTMC.

A sequence $\pi = s_0 \xrightarrow{t_0} s_1 \xrightarrow{t_1} s_2 \xrightarrow{t_2} \cdots$ is called a path of $\mathcal{M}$, if $s_0 = s_I$, $s_i \in S$, $t_i \in \mathbb{R}_{\geq 0}$, and $\mathbf{P}(s_i, s_{i+1}) > 0$ for all $i \geq 0$. We denote the ith state in an execution π by $\pi[i] = s_i$, and the time spent in the ith state by $\delta(\pi, i) = t_i$. The time at which the execution enters state $\pi[i+1]$ is given by $\tau(\pi, i+1) = \sum_{j=0}^{j=i} \delta(\pi, j)$. The state of the execution at time t (if the sum of sojourn times in all states in the path exceeds t), denoted by $\pi(t)$, is the state s_i such that i is the smallest number for which $t \leq \tau(\pi, i+1)$. We let $Path(s)$ be the set of paths starting at state s.

Let $s_0, s_1, \ldots, s_k \in S$ with $\mathbf{P}(s_i, s_{i+1}) > 0$ for all $0 \leq i < k$. Let $I_0, I_1, I_2, \ldots I_{k-1}$ be non-empty intervals in $\mathbb{R}_{\geq 0}$. Then $C(s_0, I_0, s_1, \ldots I_{k-1}, s_k)$ denotes a *cylinder set* consisting of all paths $\pi \in Path(s_0)$ such that $\pi[i] = s_i$ (for $0 \leq i \leq k$), and $\delta(\pi, i) \in I_i$ (for $i < k$). Let $\mathcal{B}$ be the smallest σ-algebra on $Path(s_0)$ which contains all the cylinders $C(s_0, I_0, s_1, \ldots I_{k-1}, s_k)$. The measure μ on cylinder sets can be inductively defined as $\mu(C(s_0)) = 1$ and for $k > 0$ as

$$\begin{aligned}&\mu(C(s_0, I_0, s_1, \ldots I_{k-1}, s_k)) \\ &\quad = \mu(C(s_0, I_0, s_1, \ldots s_{k-1})) \cdot \mathbf{P}(s_{k-1}, s_k) \cdot (\mathbf{Q}(s_{k-1}, s_k, u) - \mathbf{Q}(s_{k-1}, s_k, \ell))\end{aligned}$$

where $\ell = \inf I_k$ and $u = \sup I_k$. The probability measure on $\mathcal{B}$ is then defined as the unique measure that agrees with μ (as defined above) on the cylinder sets.

2.1 CSL and PCTL Syntax and Semantics

Continuous stochastic logic (CSL) is introduced in [1] as a logic to express probabilistic properties of continuous time Markov chains (CTMCs). We adopt a sublogic of CSL that excludes the steady-state probabilistic operator. Let ϕ represents a *state* formula and ψ represents a *path* formula. Then:

$$\phi ::= \mathit{true} \mid a \in AP \mid \neg\phi \mid \phi \wedge \phi \mid \mathcal{P}_{\bowtie p}(\psi) \qquad \psi ::= \phi\, \mathcal{U}\, \phi \mid \phi\, \mathcal{U}^{\leq t} \phi \mid \mathbf{X}\phi \mid \mathbf{X}^{\leq t}\phi$$

where AP is the set of atomic propositions, $\bowtie \in \{<, \leq, >, \geq\}$, $p \in [0,1]$, and $t \in \mathbb{R}_{\geq 0}$. The notion that a state s (or a path π) *satisfies* a formula ϕ is denoted by $s \models \phi$ (or $\pi \models \phi$), and is defined inductively as follows:

$s \models true$		$s \models a$	iff $a \in AP(s)$
$s \models \neg\phi$	iff $s \not\models \phi$	$s \models \phi_1 \wedge \phi_2$	iff $s \models \phi_1$ and $s \models \phi_2$
$s \models \mathcal{P}_{\bowtie p}(\psi)$	iff $Prob\{\pi \in Path(s) \mid \pi \models \psi\} \bowtie p$		
$\pi \models \mathbf{X}\phi$	iff $\tau(\pi, 1) < \infty$ and $\pi[1] \models \phi$		
$\pi \models \mathbf{X}^{\leq t}\phi$	iff $\tau(\pi, 1) \leq t$ and $\pi[1] \models \phi$		
$\pi \models \phi_1\, \mathcal{U}\, \phi_2$	iff $\exists x \in \mathbb{R}_{\geq 0}\, (\pi(x) \models \phi_2$ and $\forall y \in [0, x).\, \pi(y) \models \phi_1)$		
$\pi \models \phi_1\, \mathcal{U}^{\leq t} \phi_2$	iff $\exists x \in [0, t].\, (\pi(x) \models \phi_2$ and $\forall y \in [0, x).\, \pi(y) \models \phi_1)$		

It can shown that for any path formula ψ and any state s, the set $\{\pi \in Path(s) \mid \pi \models \psi\}$ is measurable [14]. A formula $\mathcal{P}_{\bowtie p}(\psi)$ is satisfied by a state s if $Prob[$path starting at s satisfies $\psi] \bowtie p$. The path formula $\mathbf{X}\phi$ holds over a path if ϕ holds at the second state on the path. The formula $\phi_1\, \mathcal{U}^{\leq t} \phi_2$ is true over a path π if ϕ_2 holds in some state along π at a time $x \in [0, t]$, and ϕ holds at all prior states.

Note that if we change the time domain in the above logic from $\mathbb{R}_{\geq 0}$ to natural numbers $\mathbb{N}$, we get the logic PCTL (stands for probabilistic computation tree logic) [9]. The model-checking algorithm that we describe next is correct for both time domains. Therefore, we can use the model-checking algorithm for verifying properties expressed in both CSL and PCTL. In case of model-checking a PCTL formula, we will assume that the model provided is discrete-time with unit time associated with every transition.

3 Statistical Model Checking

Our model checking algorithm, $\mathcal{A}$, proceeds recursively based on the structure of the formula. Before describing the details of the algorithm, we present the theorem that formally states the correctness of the algorithm. The statement of the theorem is instructive in understanding the subsequent analysis. The algorithm $\mathcal{A}$ takes as input a stochastic model $\mathcal{M}$, a formula ϕ in CSL, error bounds α^* and β^*, and three other parameters δ_1, δ_2, and p_s. The result of model checking on these parameters, denoted by $\mathcal{A}^{\delta_1,\delta_2,p_s}(\mathcal{M}, \phi, \alpha^*, \beta^*)$, can be either *true* or *false*. The algorithm provides the following correctness guarantees.

Theorem 1. *If the model $\mathcal{M}$ satisfies the following conditions*

C1: *For every subformula of the form $\mathcal{P}_{\geq p}\psi$ in the formula ϕ and for every state s in $\mathcal{M}$, the probability that a path from s satisfies ψ must not lie in the range $[\frac{p-\delta_1-\alpha^*}{1-\alpha^*}, \frac{p+\delta_1}{1-\beta^*}]$;*

C2: *For any subformula of the form $\phi_1\, \mathcal{U}\, \phi_2$ and for every state s in $\mathcal{M}$, the probability that a path from s satisfies $\phi_1\, \mathcal{U}\, \phi_2$ must not lie in the range $(0, \frac{\delta_2}{(1-p_s)^N}]$, where N is the number of states in the model $\mathcal{M}$.*

Then the algorithm provides the following guarantees

$$\text{R1}: \quad \begin{array}{l} Prob[\mathcal{A}^{\delta_1,\delta_2,p_s}(\mathcal{M}, \phi, \alpha^*, \beta^*) = true \mid \mathcal{M} \not\models \phi] \leq \alpha^* \\ Prob[\mathcal{A}^{\delta_1,\delta_2,p_s}(\mathcal{M}, \phi, \alpha^*, \beta^*) = false \mid \mathcal{M} \models \phi] \leq \beta^* \end{array}$$

Condition C1 requires that the model be such that for any subformula $\mathcal{P}_{\geq p}\psi$, the probability of ψ being satisfied at a state be bounded away from p. Condition C2 requires that either an until formula does not hold in a state or it holds with some probability that is bounded away from 0. Under such circumstances, we guarantee that the probability of error of $\mathcal{A}$ is within the required bounds.

A few points about the algorithm are in order. First, the requirement that the model satisfy condition C1, is something that previous stochastic model checking algorithms also have. Second, the error bounds α^* and β^* are parameters to the algorithm. Hence, we can improve the confidence in the algorithm's answer to be as close to 1 as we like. Third, the bounds required in conditions C1 and C2 depend on the parameters δ_1, δ_2, and p_s given to the algorithm. Thus, they can be tuned based on the model and formula being analyzed, to ensure that C1 and C2 are satisfied. Typically, for our experiments, we picked $\delta_1 = \delta_2 = 0.01$ and $p_s = 0.1$. Note that one may easily pick p_s to be c/N where N is the number of states and c is some positive constant. This will ensure that the upper bound of the range in condition C2 is $\frac{\delta_2}{(1-c/N)^N} \leq \delta_2 2e^c$ (proved in [16]), which can be made as close to 0 as desired by a suitable choice of c. Note that making p_s smaller comes with a price: if we make p_s very small, the expected length of the samples increases. This can increase the computation cost, something we also observed in our experiments. However, techniques such as caching and discounting optimization (discussed in Section 4) helped us to considerably reduce the computation cost for small p_s.

We make the following notational simplifications in the rest of the paper. The parameters δ_1, δ_2, and p_s are global to the algorithm $\mathcal{A}$; therefore, we will omit the superscript δ_1, δ_2, p_s from $\mathcal{A}^{\delta_1,\delta_2,p_s}(\mathcal{M}, \phi, \alpha^*, \beta^*)$ and write it simply as $\mathcal{A}(\mathcal{M}, \phi, \alpha^*, \beta^*)$. The value of the error bounds α and β will change for the invocation of $\mathcal{A}$ on various subformulas; therefore, we will carry them with $\mathcal{A}$. The result of model-checking a state formula ϕ at a state s will be denoted by $\mathcal{A}(s, \phi, \alpha, \beta)$; similarly, the result of model-checking a path formula ψ over a path π will be denoted by $\mathcal{A}(\pi, \psi, \alpha, \beta)$. Note that $\mathcal{A}(\mathcal{M}, \phi, \alpha^*, \beta^*)$ is same as $\mathcal{A}(s_I, \phi, \alpha^*, \beta^*)$.

3.1 Probabilistic Operator: Computing $\mathcal{A}(s, \mathcal{P}_{\bowtie p}(\psi), \alpha, \beta)$

We use statistical hypothesis testing [11] to verify a probabilistic property $\phi = \mathcal{P}_{\bowtie p}(\psi)$ at a given state s. Without loss of generality, we show our procedure for $\phi = \mathcal{P}_{\geq p}(\psi)$. Note that $\mathcal{P}_{<p}(\psi)$ is the same as $\neg\mathcal{P}_{\geq p}(\psi)$ and $<$ (or $>$) is essentially the same as $\leq$ (or $\geq$). Let p' be the probability that ψ holds over a random path starting at s. We say that $s \models \mathcal{P}_{\geq p}(\psi)$ if and only if $p' \geq p$ and $s \not\models \mathcal{P}_{\geq p}(\psi)$ if and only if $p' < p$.

We want to decide whether $s \models \mathcal{P}_{\geq p}(\psi)$ or $s \not\models \mathcal{P}_{\geq p}(\psi)$. By condition C1, we know that p' cannot lie in the range $[\frac{p-\delta_1-\alpha}{1-\alpha}, \frac{p+\delta_1}{1-\beta}]$, which implies that p' cannot lie in the range $[p - \delta_1, p + \delta_1]$. Accordingly, we set up the following experiment. Let $H_0\colon p' < p-\delta_1$ be the *null hypothesis* and $H_1\colon p' > p+\delta_1$ be the *alternative hypothesis*. Let n be the number of execution paths sampled from the state s. We will show how to estimate n from the different given parameters. Let

$X_1, X_2, \ldots, X_n$ be a random sample having Bernoulli distribution with unknown mean $p' \in [0,1]$ i.e., for each $i \in [1,n]$, $Prob[X_i = 1] = p'$. Then the sum $Y = X_1 + X_2 + \ldots + X_n$ has binomial distribution with parameters n and p'. We say that x_i, an observation of the random variable X_i, is 1 if the ith sample path from s satisfies ψ and 0 otherwise. In the experiment, we reject $H_0\colon p' < p - \delta_1$ and say $\mathcal{A}(s, \phi, \alpha, \beta) = true$ if $\frac{\sum x_i}{n} \geq p$; otherwise, we reject $H_1\colon p' \geq p$ and say $\mathcal{A}(s, \phi, \alpha, \beta) = false$ if $\frac{\sum x_i}{n} < p$. Given the above experiment, to meet the requirement R1 of $\mathcal{A}$, we must have

$$\begin{aligned} Prob[\text{accept } H_1 \mid H_0 \text{ holds}] &= Prob[Y/n \geq p \mid p' < p - \delta_1] \leq \alpha \\ Prob[\text{accept } H_0 \mid H_1 \text{ holds}] &= Prob[Y/n < p \mid p' > p + \delta_1] \leq \beta \end{aligned}$$

Accordingly, we can choose the unknown parameter n for this experiment such that $Prob[Y/n \geq p \mid p' < p - \delta_1] \leq Prob[Y/n \geq p \mid p' = p - \delta_1] \leq \alpha$ and $Prob[Y/n < p \mid p' \geq p + \delta_1] \leq Prob[Y/n < p \mid p' = p + \delta_1] \leq \beta$. In other words, we want to choose the smallest n such that both $Prob[Y/n \geq p] \leq \alpha$ when Y is binomially distributed with parameters n and $p - \delta_1$, and $Prob[Y/n < p] \leq \beta$ when Y is binomially distributed with parameters n and $p + \delta_1$, holds. Such an n can be chosen by standard statistical methods.

3.2 Nested Probabilistic Operators: Computing $\mathcal{A}(s, \mathcal{P}_{\bowtie p}(\psi), \alpha, \beta)$

The above procedure for hypothesis testing works if the truth value of ψ over a sample path determined by the algorithm is the same as the actual truth value. However, in the presence of nested probabilistic operators in ψ, $\mathcal{A}$ cannot determine the satisfaction of ψ over a sample path exactly. Therefore, we modify the hypothesis test so that we can use the inexact truth values of ψ over the sample paths.

Let the random variable X be 1 if a sample path π from s actually satisfies ψ in the model and 0 otherwise. Let the random variable Z be 1 for a sample path π if $\mathcal{A}(\pi, \psi, \alpha, \beta) = true$ and 0 if $\mathcal{A}(\pi, \psi, \alpha, \beta) = false$. In our algorithm, we cannot get samples from the random variable X; instead, our samples come from the random variable Z. Let X and Z have Bernoulli distributions with parameters p' and p'' respectively. Let $Z_1, Z_2, \ldots, Z_n$ be a random sample from the Bernoulli distribution with unknown mean $p'' \in [0,1]$. We say that z_i, an observation of the random variable Z_i, is 1 if $\mathcal{A}(\pi_i, \psi, \alpha, \beta) = true$ for i^{th} sample path π_i from s and 0 otherwise.

We want to test the null hypothesis $H_0\colon p' < p - \delta_1$ against the alternative hypothesis $H_1\colon p' > p + \delta_1$. Using the samples from Z we can estimate p''. However, we need an estimation for p' in order to decide whether $\phi = \mathcal{P}_{\geq p}(\psi)$ holds in state s or not. To get an estimate for p' we note that the random variables X and Z are related as follows: $Prob[Z = 1 \mid X = 0] \leq \alpha'$ and $Prob[Z = 0 \mid X = 1] \leq \beta'$, where α' and β' are the error bounds within which $\mathcal{A}$ verifies the formula ψ over a sample path from s. We can set $\alpha' = \alpha$ and $\beta' = \beta$. By elementary probability theory, we have

$$Prob[Z = 1] = Prob[Z = 1 \mid X = 0]Prob[X = 0] + Prob[Z = 1 \mid X = 1]Prob[X = 1]$$

Therefore, we can approximate $p'' = Prob[Z = 1]$ as follows:

$$Prob[Z = 1] \leq \alpha(1 - p') + 1 \cdot p' = p' + (1 - p')\alpha$$
$$Prob[Z = 1] \geq Prob[Z = 1 \mid X = 1]Prob[X = 1] \geq (1 - \beta)p' = p' - \beta p'$$

This gives the following range in which p'' lies: $p' - \beta p' \leq p'' \leq p' + (1 - p')\alpha$.

By condition C1, we know that p' cannot lie in the range $[\frac{p-\delta_1-\alpha}{1-\alpha}, \frac{p+\delta_1}{1-\beta}]$. Accordingly, we set up the following experiment. Let H_0: $p' < \frac{p-\delta_1-\alpha}{1-\alpha}$ be the *null hypothesis* and $H_1: p' > \frac{p+\delta_1}{1-\beta}$ be the *alternative hypothesis*. Let us say that we accept H_1 if our observation is $\frac{\sum z_i}{n} \geq p$ and we accept H_0 if $\frac{\sum z_i}{n} < p$. By the requirement of algorithm $\mathcal{A}$, we want $Prob[\text{accept } H_1 \mid H_0 \text{ holds}] \leq \alpha$ and $Prob[\text{accept } H_0 \mid H_1 \text{ holds}] \leq \beta$. Hence, we want $Prob[\frac{\sum Z_i}{n} \geq p \mid p' < \frac{p-\delta_1-\alpha}{1-\alpha}] \leq Prob[\frac{\sum Z_i}{n} \geq p \mid \frac{p''-\alpha}{1-\alpha} \leq \frac{p-\delta_1-\alpha}{1-\alpha}] = Prob[\frac{\sum Z_i}{n} \geq p \mid p'' < p - \delta_1] \leq Prob[\frac{\sum Z_i}{n} \geq p \mid p'' = p - \delta_1] \leq \alpha$. Similarly, we want $Prob[\frac{\sum Z_i}{n} < p \mid p'' = p + \delta_1] \leq \beta$. Note that $\sum Z_i$ is distributed binomially with parameters n and p''. We choose the smallest n such that the above requirements for $\mathcal{A}$ are satisfied.

3.3 Negation and Conjunction: $\mathcal{A}(s, \neg\phi, \alpha, \beta)$ and $\mathcal{A}(s, \phi_1 \wedge \phi_2, \alpha, \beta)$

For the verification of a formula $\neg\phi$ at a state s, we recursively verify ϕ at state s. If we know the decision of $\mathcal{A}$ for ϕ at s, we can say that $\mathcal{A}(s, \neg\phi, \alpha, \beta) = \neg\mathcal{A}(s, \phi, \beta, \alpha)$.

For conjunction, we first compute $\mathcal{A}(s, \phi_1, \alpha_1, \beta_1)$ and $\mathcal{A}(s, \phi_2, \alpha_2, \beta_2)$. If one of $\mathcal{A}(s, \phi_1, \alpha_1, \beta_1)$ or $\mathcal{A}(s, \phi_2, \alpha_2, \beta_2)$ is *false*, we say $\mathcal{A}(s, \phi_1 \wedge \phi_2, \alpha, \beta) = \mathit{false}$. Now:

$$\begin{aligned}
&Prob[\mathcal{A}(s, \phi_1 \wedge \phi_2, \alpha, \beta) = \mathit{false} \mid s \models \phi_1 \wedge \phi_2]^1 \\
&= Prob[\mathcal{A}(s, \phi_1, \alpha_1, \beta_1) = \mathit{false} \vee \mathcal{A}(s, \phi_2, \alpha_2, \beta_2) = \mathit{false} \mid s \models \phi_1 \wedge \phi_2] \\
&\leq Prob[\mathcal{A}(s, \phi_1, \alpha_1, \beta_1) = \mathit{false} \mid s \models \phi_1 \wedge \phi_2] + Prob[\mathcal{A}(s, \phi_2, \alpha_2, \beta_2) = \mathit{false} \mid s \models \phi_1 \wedge \phi_2] \\
&= Prob[\mathcal{A}(s, \phi_1, \alpha_1, \beta_1) = \mathit{false} \mid s \models \phi_1] + Prob[\mathcal{A}(s, \phi_2, \alpha_2, \beta_2) = \mathit{false} \mid s \models \phi_2] \\
&\leq \beta_1 + \beta_2 = \beta \text{ [by the requirement R1 of } \mathcal{A}]
\end{aligned}$$

The equality of the expressions in the third and fourth line of the above derivation follows from the fact that if $s \models \phi_1 \wedge \phi_2$ then the state s actually satisfies $\phi_1 \wedge \phi_2$; hence, $s \models \phi_1$ and $s \models \phi_2$. We set $\beta_1 = \beta_2 = \beta/2$.

If both $\mathcal{A}(s, \phi_1, \alpha_1, \beta_1)$ and $\mathcal{A}(s, \phi_2, \alpha_2, \beta_2)$ are *true*, we say $\mathcal{A}(s, \phi_1 \wedge \phi_2, \alpha, \beta) = \mathit{true}$. Then, we have

$$\begin{aligned}
&Prob[\mathcal{A}(s, \phi_1 \wedge \phi_2, \alpha, \beta) = \mathit{true} \mid s \not\models \phi_1 \wedge \phi_2] \\
&\leq \max(Prob[\mathcal{A}(s, \phi_1 \wedge \phi_2, \alpha, \beta) = \mathit{true} \mid s \not\models \phi_1], Prob[\mathcal{A}(s, \phi_1 \wedge \phi_2, \alpha, \beta) = \mathit{true} \mid s \not\models \phi_2]) \\
&\leq \max(Prob[\mathcal{A}(s, \phi_1, \alpha_1, \beta_1) = \mathit{true} \mid s \not\models \phi_1], Prob[\mathcal{A}(s, \phi_2, \alpha_2, \beta_2) = \mathit{true} \mid s \not\models \phi_2] \\
&\leq \max(\alpha_1, \alpha_2)
\end{aligned}$$

We set $\alpha_1 = \alpha_2 = \alpha$.

[1] Note that this is not a conditional probability, because $s \models \phi_1 \wedge \phi_2$ is not an event.

3.4 Unbounded Until: Computing $\mathcal{A}(\pi, \phi_1 \,\mathcal{U}\, \phi_2, \alpha, \beta)$

Consider the problem of checking if a path π satisfies an until formula $\phi_1 \,\mathcal{U}\, \phi_2$. We know that if π satisfies $\phi_1 \mathcal{U} \phi_2$ then there will be a finite prefix of π which will witness this satisfaction; namely, a finite prefix terminated by a state satisfying ϕ_2 and preceded only by states satisfying ϕ_1. On the other hand, if π does not satisfy $\phi_1 \mathcal{U} \phi_2$ then π may have no finite prefix witnessing this fact; in particular it is possible that π only visits states satisfying $\phi_1 \wedge \neg\phi_2$. Thus, to check the non-satisfaction of an until formula, it seems that we have to sample infinite paths.

Our first important observation in overcoming this challenge is to note that set of paths with non-zero measure that do not satisfy $\phi_1 \mathcal{U} \phi_2$ have finite prefixes that are terminated by states s from which there is *no* path satisfying $\phi_1 \,\mathcal{U}\, \phi_2$, i.e., $s \models \mathcal{P}_{=0}(\phi_1 \mathcal{U} \phi_2)$. We therefore set about trying to first address the problem of statistically verifying if a state s satisfies $\mathcal{P}_{=0}(\phi_1 \,\mathcal{U}\, \phi_2)$. It turns out that this special combination of a probabilistic operator and an unbounded until is indeed easier to statistically verify. Observe that by sampling finite paths from a state s, we can witness the fact that s does not satisfy $\mathcal{P}_{=0}(\phi_1 \mathcal{U} \phi_2)$. Suppose we have a model that satisfies the following promise: either states satisfy $\mathcal{P}_{=0}(\phi_1 \mathcal{U} \phi_2)$ or states satisfy $\mathcal{P}_{>\delta}(\phi_1 \mathcal{U} \phi_2)$, for some positive real δ. Now, in this promise setting, if we sample an adequate number of finite paths and none of those witness the satisfaction then we can statistically conclude that the state satisfies $\mathcal{P}_{=0}(\phi_1 \mathcal{U} \phi_2)$ because we are guaranteed that either a significant fraction of paths will satisfy the until formula or none will.

There is one more challenge: we want to sample finite paths from a state s to check if $\phi_1 \,\mathcal{U}\, \phi_2$ is satisfied. However, we do not know *a priori* a bound on the lengths of paths that may satisfy the until formula. We provide a mechanism to sample finite paths of any length by sampling paths with a stopping probability.

We are now ready to present the details of our algorithm for the unbounded until operator. We first show how the special formula $\mathcal{P}_{=0}(\phi_1 \,\mathcal{U}\, \phi_2)$ can be statistically checked at a state. We then show how to use the algorithm for the special case to verify unbounded until formulas.

Computing $\mathcal{A}(s, \mathcal{P}_{=0}(\phi_1 \,\mathcal{U}\, \phi_2), \alpha, \beta)$. To compute $\mathcal{A}(s, \mathcal{P}_{=0}(\phi_1 \mathcal{U} \phi_2), \alpha, \beta)$, we first compute $\mathcal{A}(s, \neg\phi_1 \wedge \neg\phi_2, \alpha, \beta)$. If the result is *true*, we say $\mathcal{A}(s, \mathcal{P}_{=0}(\phi_1 \,\mathcal{U}\, \phi_2), \alpha, \beta) =$ *true*. Otherwise, if the result is *false*, we have to check if the probability of a path from s satisfying $\phi_1 \,\mathcal{U}\, \phi_2$ is non-zero. For this we set up an experiment as follows.

Let p be the probability that a random path from s satisfies $\phi_1 \,\mathcal{U}\, \phi_2$. Let the *null hypothesis* be $H_0 \colon p > \delta_2$ and the *alternative hypothesis* be $H_1 \colon p = 0$ where δ_2 is the small real, close to 0, provided as parameter to the algorithm. The above test is one-sided: we can check the satisfaction of the formula $\phi_1 \mathcal{U} \phi_2$ along a path by looking at a finite prefix of a path; however, if along a path $\phi_1 \wedge \neg\phi_2$ holds only, we do not know when to stop and declare that the path does not satisfy $\phi_1 \mathcal{U} \phi_2$. Therefore, checking the violation of the formula along a path may not terminate if the formula is not satisfied by the path. To mitigate this problem, we modify the model by associating a stopping probability p_s with every state s in the model. While sampling a path from a state, we stop and return the path so far simulated with probability p_s. This allows one to generate paths of finite length from any state in the model.

Formally, we modify the model $\mathcal{M}$ as follows: we add a terminal state $s_\perp$ to the set S of all states of $\mathcal{M}$. Let $S' = S \cup \{s_\perp\}$. For every state $s \in S$, we define $\mathbf{P}(s, s_\perp) = p_s$, $\mathbf{P}(s_\perp, s_\perp) = 1$, and for every pair of states $s, s' \in S$, we modify $\mathbf{P}(s, s')$ to $\mathbf{P}(s, s')(1 - p_s)$. For every state $s \in S$, we pick some arbitrary probability distribution function for $\mathbf{Q}(s, s_\perp, t)$ and $\mathbf{Q}(s_\perp, s_\perp, t)$. We further assume that $L(s_\perp)$ is the set of atomic propositions such that $s_\perp \not\models \phi_2$. This in turn implies that any path (there is only one path) from $s_\perp$ do not satisfy $\phi_1 \,\mathcal{U}\, \phi_2$. Let us denote this modified model by $\mathcal{M}'$. Given this modified model, the following result holds:

Theorem 2. *If a path from any state $s \in S$ in the model $\mathcal{M}$ satisfies $\phi_1 \,\mathcal{U}\, \phi_2$ with some probability, p, then a path sampled from the same state in the modified model $\mathcal{M}'$ will satisfy the same formula with probability at least $p(1-p_s)^N$, where $N = |S|$.*

Proof is given in [16].

By condition C2 of algorithm $\mathcal{A}$, p does not lie in the range $(0, \frac{\delta_2}{(1-p_s)^N}]$. In other words, the modified probability $p(1 - p_s)^N$ $(= p'$, say) of a path from s satisfying the formula $\phi_1 \,\mathcal{U}\, \phi_2$ does not lie in the range $(0, \delta_2]$. To take into account the modified model with stopping probability, we modify the experiment to test whether a path from s satisfies $\phi_1 \,\mathcal{U}\, \phi_2$ as follows. We change the *null hypothesis* to $H_0\colon p' > \delta_2$ and the *alternative hypothesis* to $H_1\colon p' = 0$.

Let n be the number of finite execution paths sampled from the state s in the modified model. Let $X_1, X_2, \ldots, X_n$ be a random sample having Bernoulli distribution with mean $p' \in [0, 1]$ i.e., for each $j \in [1, n]$, $Prob[X_j = 1] = p'$. Then the sum $Y = X_1 + X_2 + \ldots + X_n$ has binomial distribution with parameters n and p'. We say that x_j, an observation of the random variable X_j, is 1 if the jth sample path from s satisfies $\phi_1 \,\mathcal{U}\, \phi_2$ and 0 otherwise. In the experiment, we reject $H_0\colon p' > \delta_2$ if $\frac{\sum x_j}{n} = 0$; otherwise, if $\frac{\sum x_j}{n} > 0$, we reject $H_1\colon p' = 0$. Given the above experiment, to make sure that the error in decisions is bounded by α and β, we must have

$$Prob[\text{accept } H_1 \mid H_0 \text{ holds}] = Prob[Y/n = 0 \mid p' > \delta_2] \leq \alpha$$
$$Prob[\text{accept } H_0 \mid H_1 \text{ holds}] = Prob[Y/n \geq 1 \mid p' = p] = 0 \leq \beta$$

Hence, we can choose the unknown parameter n for this experiment such that $Prob[Y/n = 0 \mid p' > \delta_2] \leq Prob[Y/n = 0 \mid p' = \delta_2] \leq \alpha$ i.e., n is the smallest natural number such that $(1 - \delta_2)^n \leq \alpha$.

Note that in the above analysis we assumed that $\phi_1 \,\mathcal{U}\, \phi_2$ has no nested probabilistic operators; therefore, it can be verified over a path without error. However, in the presence of nested probabilistic operators, we need to modify the experiment in a way similar to that given in section 3.2.

Computing $\mathcal{A}(\pi, \phi_1 \,\mathcal{U}\, \phi_2, \alpha, \beta)$. Once we know how to compute $\mathcal{A}(s, \mathcal{P}_{=0}(\phi_1 \mathcal{U} \phi_2), \alpha, \beta)$, we can give a procedure to compute $\mathcal{A}(\pi, \phi_1 \mathcal{U} \phi_2, \alpha, \beta)$

as follows. Let S be the set of states of the model. We partition S into the sets S^{true}, S^{false}, and $S^?$ and characterize the relevant probabilities as follows:

$S^{true} = \{s \in S \mid s \models \phi_2\}$
$S^{false} = \{s \in S \mid$ it is not the case that $\exists k$ and $\exists s_1 s_2 \ldots s_k$ such that $s = s_1$ and there is a non-zero probability of transition from s_i to s_{i+1} for $1 \leq i < k$ and $s_i \models \phi_1$ for all $1 \leq i < k$, and $s_k \in S^{true}\}$
$S^? = S - S^{true} - S^{false}$

Theorem 3.

$$\begin{aligned}
&Prob[\pi \in Path(s) \mid \pi \models \phi_1 \,\mathcal{U}\, \phi_2] \\
&= Prob[\pi \in Path(s) \mid \exists k \text{ and } s_1 s_2 \ldots s_k \text{ such that } s_1 s_2 \ldots s_k \text{ is a prefix of } \pi \text{ and} \\
&\qquad s_1 = s \text{ and } s_i \in S^? \text{ for all } 1 \leq i < k \text{ and } s_k \in S^{true}] \\
&Prob[\pi \in Path(s) \mid \pi \not\models \phi_1 \,\mathcal{U}\, \phi_2] \\
&= Prob[\pi \in Path(s) \mid \exists k \text{ and } s_1 s_2 \ldots s_k \text{ such that } s_1 s_2 \ldots s_k \text{ is a prefix of } \pi \text{ and} \\
&\qquad s_1 = s \text{ and } s_i \in S^? \text{ for all } 1 \leq i < k \text{ and } s_k \in S^{false}]
\end{aligned}$$

Proof of a similar theorem is given in [8].

Therefore, to check if a sample path $\pi = s_1 s_2 s_3 \ldots$ (ignoring the time-stamps on transitions) from state s satisfies (or violates) $\phi_1 \,\mathcal{U}\, \phi_2$, we need to find a k such that $s_k \in S^{true}$ (or $s_k \in S^{false}$) and for all $1 \leq i < k$, $s_i \in S^?$. This is done iteratively as follows:

```
i ← 1
while(true){
   if s_i ∈ S^true then return true;
   else if s_i ∈ S^false then return false;
   else i ← i + 1; }
```

The above procedure will terminate with probability 1 because, by Theorem 3, the probability of reaching a state in S^{true} or S^{false} after traversing a finite number of states in $S^?$ along a random path is 1.

To check whether a state s_i belongs to S^{true}, we compute $\mathcal{A}(s, \phi_2, \alpha_i, \beta_i)$; if the result is *true*, we say $s_i \in S^{true}$. The check for $s_i \in S^{false}$ is essentially computing $\mathcal{A}(s_i, \mathcal{P}_{=0}(\phi_1 \,\mathcal{U}\, \phi_2), \alpha_i, \beta_i)$. If the result is *true* then $s_i \in S^{false}$; else, we sample the next state s_{i+1} and repeat the loop as in the above pseudo-code.

The choice of α_i and β_i in the above decisions depends on the error bounds α and β with which we wanted to verify $\phi_1 \,\mathcal{U}\, \phi_2$ over the path π. By arguments similar to conjunction, it can be shown that we can choose each α_i and β_i such that $\alpha = \sum_{i \in [1,k]} \alpha_i$ and $\beta = \sum_{i \in [1,k]} \beta_i$ where k is the length of the prefix of π that has been used to compute $\mathcal{A}(\pi, \phi_1 \,\mathcal{U}\, \phi_2, \alpha, \beta)$. Since, we do not know the length k before-hand we choose to set $\alpha_i = \alpha/2^i$ and $\beta_i = \beta/2^i$ for $1 \leq i < k$, and $\alpha_k = \alpha/2^{k-1}$ and $\beta_k = \beta/2^{k-1}$.

An interesting and simple technique for the verification of the unbounded until proposed by H. Younes (personal communications) based on theorem 2 is as follows. Let p denote the probability measure of the set of paths that start in s and satisfy $\phi_1 \,\mathcal{U}\, \phi_2$. Let p' be the corresponding probability measure for the modified model with stopping probability p_s in each state. Then by theorem 2, we have $p \geq p' \geq p(1-p_s)^N$, where N is the number of states in the model. These bounds on p can be used to verify the formula $\mathcal{P}_{\geq\theta}(\phi_1 \,\mathcal{U}\, \phi_2)$ in the same way as we deal with nested probabilistic operators.

However, there are trade-offs between these two approaches. The simple approach described in the last paragraph has the advantage of being conceptually clearer. The disadvantage of the simpler approach, on the other hand, is that we have to provide the exact value of N as input to the algorithm, which may not be available for a complex model. Our original algorithm does not expect the user to provide N; rather, it expects that the user will provide a suitable value of p_s so that condition C2 in theorem 1 holds. Moreover, the bounds on p' given in theorem 2 holds for the worst case. If we consider the worst case lower bound for p', which is dependent exponentially on N, then the value of p_s that needs to be picked to ensure that $\theta - \delta < (\theta + \delta)(1 - p_s)^N$ might be very small and sub-optimal resulting in large verification time. Note that our method for the verification of $\mathcal{P}_{=0}(\phi_1 \mathcal{U} \phi_2)$ can be used as a technique for verifying properties of the form $\mathcal{P}_{\geq 1}(\psi)$ and $\mathcal{P}_{\leq 0}(\psi)$ which were not handled by any previous statistical approaches.

3.5 Bounded Until: Computing $\mathcal{A}(\pi, \phi_1 \,\mathcal{U}^{\leq t} \phi_2, \alpha, \beta)$

The satisfaction or violation of a bounded until formula $\phi_1 \mathcal{U}^{\leq t} \phi_2$ over a path π can be checked by looking at a finite prefix of the path. Specifically, in the worst case, we need to consider all the states $\pi[i]$ such that $\tau(\pi, i) \leq t$. The decision procedure can be given as follows:

$i \leftarrow 0$
<u>while</u>(<u>true</u>){
  <u>if</u> $\tau(\pi, i) > t$ <u>then</u> <u>return</u> *false*;
  <u>else</u> <u>if</u> $\pi[i] \models \phi_2$ <u>then</u> <u>return</u> *true*;
  <u>else</u> <u>if</u> $\pi[i] \not\models \phi_1$ <u>then</u> <u>return</u> *false*;
  <u>else</u> $i \leftarrow i + 1$; }

where the checks $\pi[i] \models \phi_2$ and $\pi[i] \not\models \phi_1$ are replaced by $\mathcal{A}(\pi[i], \phi_2, \alpha_i, \beta_i)$ and $\mathcal{A}(\pi[i], \neg\phi_1, \alpha_i, \beta_i)$, respectively. The choice of α_i and β_i are done as in the case of unbounded until.

3.6 Bounded and Unbounded Next: Computing $\mathcal{A}(\pi, \mathbf{X}^{\leq t}\phi, \alpha, \beta)$ and $\mathcal{A}(\pi, \mathbf{X}\phi, \alpha, \beta)$

For unbounded next, $\mathcal{A}(\pi, \mathbf{X}\phi, \alpha, \beta)$ is same as the result of $\mathcal{A}(\pi[1], \phi, \alpha, \beta)$. For bounded next, $\mathcal{A}(\pi, \mathbf{X}^{\leq t}\phi, \alpha, \beta)$ returns *true* if $\mathcal{A}(\pi[1], \phi, \alpha, \beta) = \mathit{true}$ and $\tau(\pi, 1) \leq t$. Otherwise, $\mathcal{A}(\pi, \mathbf{X}^{\leq t}\phi, \alpha, \beta)$ returns *false*.

3.7 Computational Complexity

The expected length of the samples generated by the algorithm depends on the various probability distributions associated with the stochastic model in addition to the parameters $\alpha, \beta, p_s, \delta_1$, and δ_2. Therefore, an upper bound on the expected length of samples cannot be estimated without knowing the probability distributions associated with the stochastic model. This implies that the computational complexity analysis of our algorithm cannot be done in a model independent way. However, in the next section and in [16], we provide experimental results which illustrate the performance of the algorithm.

4 Implementation and Experimental Evaluation

We have implemented the above algorithm in Java as part of the tool called VeStA (available from `http://osl.cs.uiuc.edu/~ksen/vesta/`). A stochastic model can be specified by implementing a Java interface, called `State`. The model-checking module of VeStA implements the algorithm $\mathcal{A}$. It can be executed in two modes: single-threaded mode and multithreaded mode. The single threaded mode is suitable for a single processor machine; the multithreaded mode exploits the parallelism of the algorithm when executed on a multi-processor machine. While verifying a formula of the form $\mathcal{P}_{\bowtie p}(\psi)$, the verification of ψ over each sample path is independent of each other. This allows us to run the verification of ψ over each sample path in a separate thread, possibly running on a separate processor.

We successfully used the tool to verify several DTMC (discrete-time Markov chains) and CTMC (continuous-time Markov chains) models. We report the performance of our tool in the verification of unbounded until formulas over a DTMC model. The performance of our tool in verifying two CTMC model is provided in the [16]. The experiments were done on a single-processor 2GHz Pentium M laptop with 1GB SDRAM running Windows XP.

IPv4 ZeroConf Protocol: We picked the DTMC model of the IPv4 ZeroConf Protocol described in [6]. We next describe the model briefly without explaining its actual relation to the protocol. The DTMC model has $N+3$ states: $\{s_0, s_1, \ldots, s_n, ok, err\}$. From the initial state s_0, the system can go to two states: state s_1 with probability q and state ok with probability $1-q$. From each of the states s_i ($i \in [1, N-1]$) the system can go to two possible states: state s_{i+1} with probability r and state s_0 with probability $1-r$. From the state s_N the system can go to the state err with probability r or return to state s_0 with probability $1-r$. Let the atomic proposition a be true if the system is in the state err and false in any other state. The property that we considered is $\mathcal{P}_{\bowtie p}(true\,\mathcal{U}\,a)$.

The result of our experiment is plotted in Figure 1. In the plot x–axis represents N in the above model and y–axis represents the running time of the algorithm. The solid line represents the performance of the tool when it is used without any optimization. We noticed that computing $\mathcal{A}(s, \mathcal{P}_{=0}(\phi_1\,\mathcal{U}\,\phi_2), \alpha, \beta)$ at every state along a path while verifying an unbounded until formula has a large performance overhead. Therefore, we used the following optimization that reduces the number of times we compute $\mathcal{A}(s, \mathcal{P}_{=0}(\phi_1\,\mathcal{U}\,\phi_2), \alpha, \beta)$.

Discount Optimization: Instead of computing $\mathcal{A}(s, \mathcal{P}_{=0}(\phi_1\,\mathcal{U}\,\phi_2), \alpha, \beta)$ at every state along a path, we can opt to perform the computation with certain probability say $p_d = 0.1$, called *discount probability*. Note that once a path reaches a state $s \in S^{false}$, any other state following s in the path also belongs to S^{false}. Therefore, this way of *discounting the check* of $s \in S^{false}$, or computing $\mathcal{A}(s, \mathcal{P}_{=0}(\phi_1 \mathcal{U} \phi_2), \alpha, \beta)$, does not influence the correctness of the algorithm. However, the average length of sample paths required to verify unbounded until increases. The modified algorithm for checking unbounded until becomes

$i \leftarrow 1$
while(**true**){
  if $s_i \in S^{true}$ **then return** *true*;
  else if $rand(0.0, 1.0) \leq p_d$ **then if** $s_i \in S^{false}$ **then return** *false*;
  else $i \leftarrow i + 1$; }

The two dashed lines in the plot show the performance of the algorithm when the discount probability is $p_d = 0.1$ and $p_d = 0.5$.

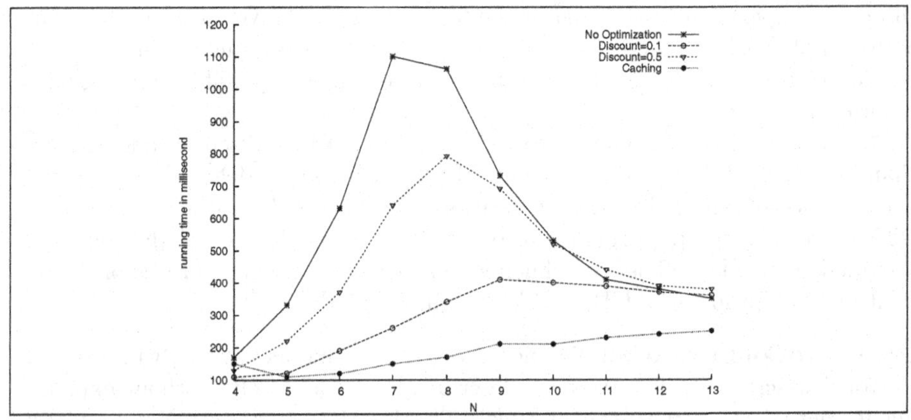

Fig. 1. Performance Measure for Verifying Unbounded Until Formula

Caching Optimization: If the algorithm has already computed and cached $\mathcal{A}(s, \phi, \alpha, \beta)$, any future computation of $\mathcal{A}(s, \phi, \alpha', \beta')$ can use the cached value provided that $\alpha \leq \alpha'$ and $\beta \leq \beta'$. However, note that we must maintain a constant size cache to avoid state-space explosion problem. The plot shows the performance of the tool with caching turned on (with no discount optimization).

The experiments show that the tool is able to handle a relatively large state space; it does not suffer from memory problem due to state-explosion because states are sampled as required and discarded when not needed. Specifically, it can be shown that the number of states stored in the memory at any time is linearly proportional to the maximum depth of nesting of probabilistic operators in a CSL formula. Thus the implementation can scale up with computing resources without suffering from traditional memory limitation due to state-explosion problem.

5 Conclusion

The statistical model-checking algorithm we have developed for stochastic models has at least four advantages over previous work. First, our algorithm can model check CSL formulas which have *unbounded untils*. Second, boundary case formulas of the form $\mathcal{P}_{\geq 1}(\psi)$ and $\mathcal{P}_{\leq 0}(\psi)$ can be verified using the technique presented for the verification of $\mathcal{P}_{=0}(\phi_1 \mathcal{U} \phi_2)$. Third, our algorithm is inherently parallel. Finally, the algorithm does not suffer from memory problem due to state-space explosion, since we do not need to store the intermediate states of an execution. However, our algorithm also has at least two limitations. First, the algorithm cannot guarantee the accuracy that numerical techniques achieve. Second, if we try to increase the accuracy by making the error bounds very small, the running time increases considerably. Thus our technique should be seen as an alternative to numerical techniques to be used only when it is infeasible to use numerical techniques, for example, in large-scale systems.

Acknowledgements

The second author was supported in part by DARPA/AFOSR MURI Award F49620-02-1-0325 and NSF 04-29639. The other two authors were supported in part by ONR Grant N00014-02-1-0715.

References

1. A. Aziz, K. Sanwal, V. Singhal, and R. K. Brayton. Verifying continuous-time Markov chains. In *Proc. of Computer Aided Verification (CAV'96)*, volume 1102 of *LNCS*, pages 269–276, 1996.
2. R. Alur, C. Courcoubetis, and D. Dill. Model-checking for probabilistic real-time systems (extended abstract). In *Proceedings of the 18th International Colloquium on Automata, Languages and Programming (ICALP'91)*, volume 510 of *LNCS*, pages 115–126. Springer, 1991.
3. A. Aziz, K. Sanwal, V. Singhal, and R. Brayton. Model-checking continuous-time Markov chains. *ACM Transactions on Computational Logic*, 1(1):162–170, 2000.
4. C. Baier, E. M. Clarke, V. Hartonas-Garmhausen, M. Z. Kwiatkowska, and M. Ryan. Symbolic model checking for probabilistic processes. In *Proc. of the 24th International Colloquium on Automata, Languages and Programming (ICALP'97)*, volume 1256 of *LNCS*, pages 430–440, 1997.
5. C. Baier, J. P. Katoen, and H. Hermanns. Approximate symbolic model checking of continuous-time Markov chains. In *International Conference on Concurrency Theory*, volume 1664 of *LNCS*, pages 146–161, 1999.
6. H. C. Bohnenkamp, P. van der Stok, H. Hermanns, and F. W. Vaandrager. Cost-optimization of the ipv4 zeroconf protocol. In *International Conference on Dependable Systems and Networks (DSN'03)*, pages 531–540. IEEE, 2003.
7. E. Cinlar. *Introduction to Stochastic Processes.* Prentice-Hall Inc., 1975.
8. C. Courcoubetis and M. Yannakakis. The complexity of probabilistic verification. *Journal of ACM*, 42(4):857–907, 1995.

9. H. Hansson and B. Jonsson. A logic for reasoning about time and reliability. *Formal Aspects of Computing*, 6(5):512–535, 1994.
10. H. Hermanns, J. P. Katoen, J. Meyer-Kayser, and M. Siegle. A Markov chain model checker. In *Tools and Algorithms for Construction and Analysis of Systems (TACAS'00)*, pages 347–362, 2000.
11. R. V. Hogg and A. T. Craig. *Introduction to Mathematical Statistics.* Macmillan, New York, NY, USA, fourth edition, 1978.
12. M. Z. Kwiatkowska, G. Norman, and D. Parker. Prism: Probabilistic symbolic model checker, 2002.
13. M. Z. Kwiatkowska, G. Norman, R. Segala, and J. Sproston. Verifying quantitative properties of continuous probabilistic timed automata. In *Conference on Concurrency Theory (CONCUR'00)*, volume 1877 of *LNCS*, pages 123–137, 2000.
14. G. G. I. López, H. Hermanns, and J.-P. Katoen. Beyond memoryless distributions: Model checking semi-markov chains. In *Proceedings of the Joint International Workshop on Process Algebra and Probabilistic Methods, Performance Modeling and Verification*, volume 2165 of *LNCS*, pages 57–70. Springer-Verlag, 2001.
15. K. Sen, M. Viswanathan, and G. Agha. Statistical model checking of black-box probabilistic systems. In *16th conference on Computer Aided Verification (CAV'04)*, volume 3114 of *LNCS*, pages 202–215. Springer, July 2004.
16. K. Sen, M. Viswanathan, and G. Agha. On statistical model checking of probabilistic systems. Technical Report UIUCDCS-R-2004-2503, University of Illinois at Urbana Champaign, 2005.
17. W. J. Stewart. *Introduction to the Numerical Solution of Markov Chains.* Princeton, 1994.
18. H. L. S. Younes and R. G. Simmons. Probabilistic verification of discrete event systems using acceptance sampling. In *Proc. of Computer Aided Verification (CAV'02)*, volume 2404 of *LNCS*, pages 223–235, 2002.

The AVISPA Tool for the Automated Validation of Internet Security Protocols and Applications*

A. Armando[1], D. Basin[2], Y. Boichut[3], Y. Chevalier[4], L. Compagna[1], J. Cuellar[5], P. Hankes Drielsma[2], P.C. Heám[3], O. Kouchnarenko[3], J. Mantovani[1], S. Mödersheim[2], D. von Oheimb[5], M. Rusinowitch[4], J. Santiago[4], M. Turuani[4], L. Viganò[2], and L. Vigneron[4]

[1] AI-Lab, DIST, Università di Genova, Italy
[2] Information Security Group, ETH Zurich, Switzerland
[3] LIFC, Université de Franche-Comté, Besancon, France
[4] LORIA-INRIA-Lorraine, Nancy, France
[5] Siemens AG, CT IC 3, Munich, Germany

Abstract. AVISPA is a push-button tool for the automated validation of Internet security-sensitive protocols and applications. It provides a modular and expressive formal language for specifying protocols and their security properties, and integrates different back-ends that implement a variety of state-of-the-art automatic analysis techniques. To the best of our knowledge, no other tool exhibits the same level of scope and robustness while enjoying the same performance and scalability.

1 Introduction

With the spread of the Internet and network-based services, the number and scale of new security protocols under development is out-pacing the human ability to rigorously analyze and validate them. To speed up the development of the next generation of security protocols, and to improve their security, it is of utmost importance to have tools that support the rigorous analysis of security protocols by either finding flaws or establishing their correctness. Optimally, these tools should be completely automated, robust, expressive, and easily usable, so that they can be integrated into the protocol development and standardization processes to improve the speed and quality of these processes.

A number of (semi-)automated protocol analysis tools have been proposed, e.g. [1, 4, 6, 7, 13, 14], which can analyze small and medium-scale protocols such as those in the Clark/Jacob library [10]. However, scaling up to large scale Internet security protocols is a considerable challenge, both scientific and technological. We have developed a push-button tool for the *A*utomated *V*alidation of *I*nternet

* This work was supported by the FET Open Project IST-2001-39252 and the BBW Project 02.0431, "AVISPA: Automated Validation of Internet Security Protocols and Applications" (`www.avispa-project.org`).

K. Etessami and S.K. Rajamani (Eds.): CAV 2005, LNCS 3576, pp. 281–285, 2005.

*S*ecurity-sensitive *P*rotocols and *A*pplications, the *AVISPA Tool*[1], which rises to this challenge in a systematic way by (i) providing a modular and expressive formal language for specifying security protocols and properties, and (ii) integrating different back-ends that implement a variety of automatic analysis techniques ranging from *protocol falsification* (by finding an attack on the input protocol) to *abstraction-based verification* methods for both finite and infinite numbers of sessions. To the best of our knowledge, no other tool exhibits the same scope and robustness while enjoying the same performance and scalability.

2 The AVISPA Tool

As displayed in Fig.1, the AVISPA Tool is equipped with a web-based graphical user interface (`www.avispa-project.org/software`) that supports the editing of protocol specifications and allows the user to select and configure the different back-ends of the tool. If an attack on a protocol is found, the tool displays it as a message-sequence chart. For instance, Fig.1 shows part of the specification of Siemens' H.530 protocol (top-right window) and the attack that AVISPA has found (bottom window), reported on in [3]. The interface features specialized menus for both novice and expert users. An XEmacs mode for editing protocol specifications is available as well.

The AVISPA Tool consists of independently developed modules, interconnected as shown at the bottom left of Fig.1. A protocol designer interacts with the tool by specifying a *security problem* (a protocol paired with a security property that it is expected to achieve) in the *High-Level Protocol Specification Language HLPSL* [8]. The HLPSL is an expressive, modular, role-based, formal language that allows for the specification of control flow patterns, data-structures, alternative intruder models, complex security properties, as well as different cryptographic primitives and their algebraic properties. These features make HLPSL well suited for specifying modern, industrial-scale protocols.

The HLPSL enjoys both a declarative semantics based on a fragment of the Temporal Logic of Actions [12] and an operational semantics based on a translation into the rewrite-based formalism *Intermediate Format IF*. HLPSL specifications are translated into equivalent IF specifications by the *HLPSL2IF translator*. An IF specification describes an infinite-state transition system amenable to formal analysis. IF specifications can be generated both in an untyped variant and in a typed one, which abstracts away type-flaw attacks (if any) from the protocol; this is particularly useful as in many cases type-flaws can be prevented in the actual implementation of a protocol [11]. IF specifications are input to the back-ends of the AVISPA Tool, which implement different analysis techniques. The current version of the tool integrates the following four back-ends.

[1] The AVISPA Tool is a successor to the AVISS Tool [1], which automated the analysis of security protocols like those in the Clark/Jacob library. The AVISPA Tool significantly extends its predecessor's scope, effectiveness, and performance.

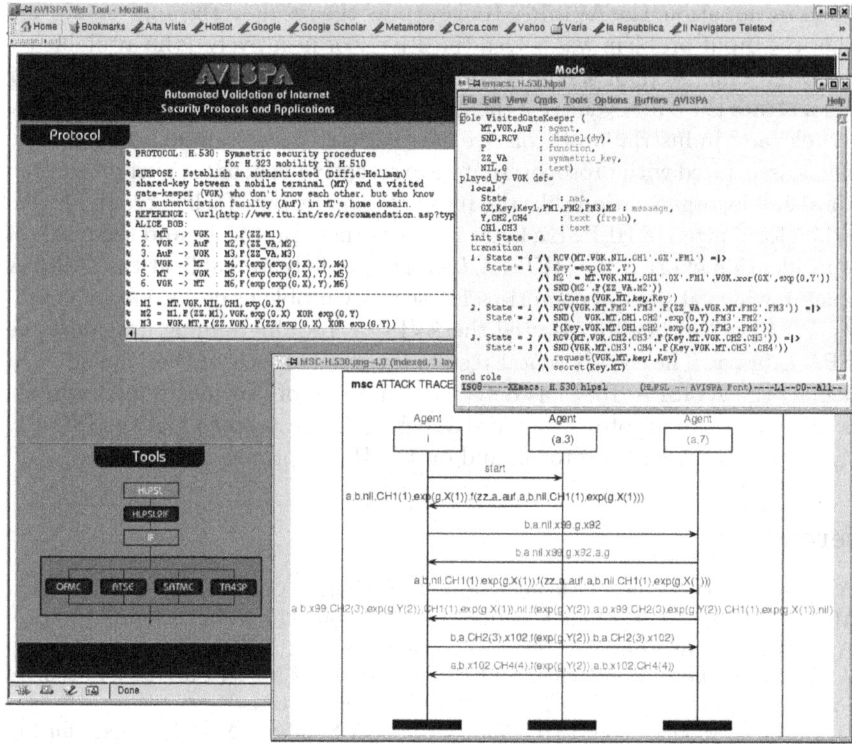

Fig. 1. A screen-shot of the AVISPA Tool

The **On-the-fly Model-Checker (OFMC)** [3] performs protocol falsification and bounded verification by exploring the transition system described by an IF specification in a demand-driven way. OFMC implements a number of correct and complete symbolic techniques. It supports the specification of algebraic properties of cryptographic operators, and typed and untyped protocol models.

The **Constraint-Logic-based Attack Searcher (CL-AtSe)** applies constraint solving as in [9], with some powerful simplification heuristics and redundancy elimination techniques. CL-AtSe is built in a modular way and is open to extensions for handling algebraic properties of cryptographic operators. It supports type-flaw detection and handles associativity of message concatenation.

The **SAT-based Model-Checker (SATMC)** [2] builds a propositional formula encoding a bounded unrolling of the transition relation specified by the IF, the initial state and the set of states representing a violation of the security properties. The propositional formula is then fed to a state-of-the-art SAT solver and any model found is translated back into an attack.

The **TA4SP (Tree Automata based on Automatic Approximations for the Analysis of Security Protocols)** back-end [5] approximates the intruder knowledge by using regular tree languages and rewriting. For secrecy properties, TA4SP can show whether a protocol is flawed (by under-approximation) or whether it is safe for any number of sessions (by over-approximation).

Upon termination, the AVISPA Tool outputs the result of the analysis stating whether the input problem was solved (positively or negatively), the available resources were exhausted, or the problem was not tackled for some reason. In order to demonstrate the effectiveness of the AVISPA Tool on a large collection of practically relevant, industrial protocols, we have selected a substantial set of security problems associated with protocols that have recently been, or are currently being standardized by organizations like the Internet Engineering Task Force IETF. We have then formalized in HLPSL a large subset of these protocols, and the result of this specification effort is the *AVISPA Library* (publicly available at the AVISPA web-page), which at present comprises 112 security problems derived from 33 protocols. We have thoroughly assessed the AVISPA Tool by running it against the AVISPA Library. The experimental results are summarized in the appendix. In particular, the AVISPA Tool has detected a number of previously unknown attacks on some of the protocols analyzed, e.g. on some protocols of the ISO-PK family, on the IKEv2-DS protocol, and on the H.530 protocol.

References

1. A. Armando, D. Basin, M. Bouallagui, Y. Chevalier, L. Compagna, S. Mödersheim, M. Rusinowitch, M. Turuani, L. Viganò, L. Vigneron. The AVISS Security Protocol Analysis Tool. In *Proc. CAV'02*, LNCS 2404. Springer, 2002.
2. A. Armando and L. Compagna. SATMC: a SAT-based Model Checker for Security Protocols. In *Proc. JELIA'04*, LNAI 3229. Springer, 2004.
3. D. Basin, S. Mödersheim, L. Viganò. OFMC: A Symbolic Model-Checker for Security Protocols. *International Journal of Information Security*, 2004.
4. B. Blanchet. An efficient cryptographic protocol verifier based on prolog rules. In *Proc. CSFW'01*. IEEE Computer Society Press, 2001.
5. Y. Boichut, P.-C. Heam, O. Kouchnarenko, F. Oehl. Improvements on the Genet and Klay Technique to Automatically Verify Security Protocols. In *Proc. AVIS'04*, ENTCS, to appear.
6. L. Bozga, Y. Lakhnech, M. Perin. Hermes: An Automatic Tool for the Verification of Secrecy in Security Protocols. In *Proc. CAV'03*, LNCS 2725. Springer, 2003.
7. The CAPSL Integrated Protocol Environment: `www.csl.sri.com/~millen/`.
8. Y. Chevalier, L. Compagna, J. Cuellar, P. Hankes Drielsma, J. Mantovani, S. Mödersheim, L. Vigneron. A High Level Protocol Specification Language for Industrial Security-Sensitive Protocols. In *Proc. SAPS'04*. Austrian Computer Society, 2004.
9. Y. Chevalier and L. Vigneron. Automated Unbounded Verification of Security Protocols. In *Proc. CAV'02*, LNCS 2404. Springer, 2002.
10. J. Clark and J. Jacob. A Survey of Authentication Protocol Literature: Version 1.0, 17. Nov. 1997. URL: `www.cs.york.ac.uk/~jac/papers/drareview.ps.gz`.
11. J. Heather, G. Lowe, S. Schneider. How to prevent type flaw attacks on security protocols. In *Proc. CSFW'00*. IEEE Computer Society Press, 2000.
12. L. Lamport. The temporal logic of actions. *ACM Transactions on Programming Languages and Systems*, 16(3):872–923, 1994.
13. L. C. Paulson. The Inductive Approach to Verifying Cryptographic Protocols. *Journal of Computer Security*, 6(1):85–128, 1998.
14. D. Song. Athena: A new efficient automatic checker for security protocol analysis. In *Proc. CSFW'99*. IEEE Computer Society Press, 1999.

Appendix: Experimental Results

The following table displays the results of running the AVISPA Tool against the 112 security problems from 33 protocols in the AVISPA Library. For each of the protocols, the table gives the number of security problems (#P), and for each back-end, the number of problems successfully analyzed with the given resources[2] (P), the number of problems for which attacks are detected (A), and the time (T) spent by the back-end to find the attacks or to report that no attack exists in the given (bounded) scenario, where "-" indicates that the back-end does not support the analysis of that problem. For SATMC, we list both the time spent to generate the SAT formula (TE) and that spent to solve the formula (TS). Note that the times of unsuccessful attempts (due to time out or memory out) are not taken into account. By running the TA4SP back-end

Problems		OFMC			CL-atse			SATMC			
Protocol	#P	P	A	T	P	A	T	P	A	TE	TS
UMTS_AKA	3	3	0	0,02	3	0	0,01	3	0	0,11	0,00
AAAMobileIP	7	7	0	0,75	7	0	0,20	7	0	1,32	0,01
ISO-PK1	1	1	1	0,02	1	1	0,00	1	1	0,05	0,00
ISO-PK2	1	1	0	0,05	1	0	0,00	1	0	1,62	0,00
ISO-PK3	2	2	2	0,04	2	2	0,01	2	2	0,27	0,00
ISO-PK4	2	2	0	0,54	2	0	0,03	2	0	1.153	1,16
LPD-MSR	2	2	2	0,02	2	2	0,02	2	2	0,17	0,02
LPD-IMSR	2	2	0	0,08	2	0	0,01	2	0	0,43	0,01
CHAPv2	3	3	0	0,32	3	0	0,01	3	0	0,55	0,00
EKE	3	3	2	0,19	3	2	0,04	3	2	0,22	0,00
TLS	3	3	0	2,20	3	0	0,32	3	0	-	0,00
DHCP-delayed	2	2	0	0,07	2	0	0,00	2	0	0,19	0,00
Kerb-Cross-Realm	8	8	0	11,86	8	0	4,14	8	0	113,60	1,69
Kerb-Ticket-Cache	6	6	0	2,43	6	0	0,38	6	0	495,66	7,75
Kerb-V	8	8	0	3,08	8	0	0,42	8	0	139,56	2,95
Kerb-Forwardable	6	6	0	30,34	6	0	10,89	0	0	-	-
Kerb-PKINIT	7	7	0	4,41	7	0	0,64	7	0	640,33	11,65
Kerb-preauth	7	7	0	1,86	7	0	0,62	7	0	373,72	2,57
CRAM-MD5	2	2	0	0,71	2	0	0,74	2	0	0,40	0,00
PKB	1	1	1	0,25	1	1	0,01	1	1	0,34	0,02
PKB-fix	2	2	0	4,06	2	0	44,25	2	0	0,86	0,02
SRP_siemens	3	3	0	2,86	0	0	-	0	0	-	-
EKE2	3	3	0	0,16	0	0	-	0	0	-	-
SPEKE	3	3	0	3,11	0	0	-	0	0	-	-
IKEv2-CHILD	3	3	0	1,19	0	0	-	0	0	-	-
IKEv2-DS	3	3	1	5,22	0	0	-	0	0	-	-
IKEv2-DSx	3	3	0	42,56	0	0	-	0	0	-	-
IKEv2-MAC	3	3	0	8,03	0	0	-	0	0	-	-
IKEv2-MACx	3	3	0	40,54	0	0	-	0	0	-	-
h.530	3	1	1	0,64	0	0	-	0	0	-	-
h.530-fix	3	3	0	4.278	0	0	-	0	0	-	-
lipkey-spkm-known	2	2	0	0,23	0	0	-	0	0	-	-
lipkey-spkm-unknown	2	2	0	7,33	0	0	-	0	0	-	-

on a subset of the AVISPA Library, the AVISPA Tool is able to establish in a few minutes that a number of protocols in the library (namely, EKE, EKE2, IKEv2-CHILD, IKEv2-MAC, TLS, UMTS_AKA, CHAPv2) guarantee secrecy.

[2] Results are obtained by each single back-end with a resource limit of 1 hour CPU time and 1GB memory, on a Pentium IV 2.4GHz under Linux.

The ORCHIDS Intrusion Detection Tool*

Julien Olivain and Jean Goubault-Larrecq

LSV/CNRS UMR 8643 & INRIA Futurs projet SECSI & ENS Cachan,
61 avenue du président-Wilson, F-94235 Cachan Cedex,
Phone: +33-1 47 40 75 50, Fax: +33-1 47 40 24 64
olivain@lsv.ens-cachan.fr

Abstract. ORCHIDS is an intrusion detection tool based on techniques for fast, on-line model-checking. Temporal formulae are taken from a temporal logic tailored to the description of intrusion signatures. They are checked against merged network and system event flows, which together form a linear Kripke structure.

Introduction: Misuse Detection as Model-Checking. ORCHIDS is a new intrusion detection tool, capable of analyzing and correlating events over time, in real time. Its purpose is to detect, report, and take countermeasures against intruders. The core of the engine is originally based on the language and algorithm in the second part of the paper by Muriel Roger and Jean Goubault-Larrecq [6]. Since then, the algorithm evolved: new features (committed choices, synchronization variables), as well as extra abstract interpretation-based optimizations, and the correction of a slight bug in op.cit., appear in the unpublished report [1]. Additional features (cuts, the "without" operator) were described in the unpublished deliverable [2]. Finally, contrarily to the prototype mentioned in [6], ORCHIDS scales up to real-world, complex intrusion detection.

The starting point of the ORCHIDS endeavor is that intrusion detection, and specifically *misuse detection*, whereby bad behavior (so-called *attacks*) is specified in some language and alerts are notified when bad behavior is detected, is essentially a *model-checking* task. The Kripke model to be analyzed is an *event flow* (collected from various logs, and other system or network sources), and complex attack *signatures* are described in an application-specific temporal logic.

Let us give an example of a modern attack [5]. Far from being a gedankenexperiment, this really works in practice and has already been used to penetrate some systems. We also insist that, as systems get more and more secure, we are faced with more and more complex attacks, and [5] is just one representative. The schema on the right displays what a modular kernel (e.g., Linux) does when a user program (here with pid 100) calls an unimplemented functionality.

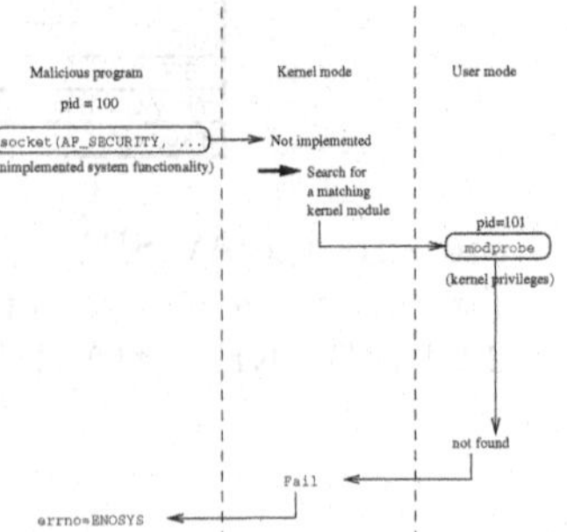

* Partially supported by the RNTL Project DICO, the ACI jeunes chercheurs "Sécurité informatique, protocoles crypto. et détection d'intrusions" and the ACI cryptologie "Psi-Robuste".

K. Etessami and S.K. Rajamani (Eds.): CAV 2005, LNCS 3576, pp. 286–290, 2005.

The kernel will search for a kernel module that implements this functionality, calling the `modprobe` utility to search and install the desired module. If `modprobe` does not find any matching module, an error code is reported to the user program.

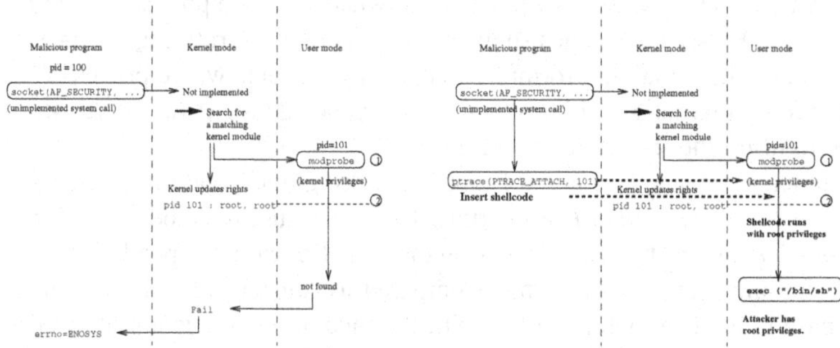

While this is how this is meant to work, some versions of Linux suffer from a race condition (above, left): while `modprobe` has all kernel privileges, the kernel updates the owner tables to make `modprobe` root-owned while `modprobe` has already started running. So there is a small amount of time where the malicious program has complete control over the kernel process `modprobe`: between timepoints ① and ②. The malicious program takes this opportunity to attach the `modprobe` process through the standard Unix debugging API function `ptrace`, inserting a *shellcode* (malicious code) inside `modprobe`'s code. When `modprobe` resumes execution, it will execute any code of the intruder's choosing, with full root privileges (above, right).

Challenges in On-line, Real-Time Model-Checking. Intrusion detection requires specific logics to describe attack signatures, and specific model-checking algorithms.

Compared to standard misuse detection tools, a temporal logic allows one to describe behavior involving several events over time: standard misuse detection tools (e.g., anti-virus software or simple network intrusion detection systems) match a library of patterns against single events, and emit an alert once single so-called *dangerous* events occur. More and more attacks nowadays involving complex, correlated sequences of events, which are usually individually benign. In the `ptrace` attack, *no* individual event (calling an unimplemented system call, or `ptrace`, etc.) is dangerous per se.

The signature language of ORCHIDS extends [6–Section 4]. Among other things, it allows one to write temporal formulas of the typical form $F_1 \wedge \Diamond(F_2 \wedge \Diamond(F_3 \ldots) \vee F'_2 \wedge \Diamond(F'_3 \ldots))$, where $\Diamond$ is the strict "there exists in the future" operator. In general, more complex formulae can be written, using operators resembling Wolper's ETL [7]—except going through a transition denotes either no time-passing at all (ϵ-transitions), or $\Diamond$ (not $\bigcirc$ as in ETL). Such formulae are described internally as automata; we just give a signature for the `ptrace` exploit as an illustration. (Some other attacks such as the `do_brk` exploit [3] require committed choices, or other features of ORCHIDS not described in [6]. To save space, we don't recount them here.) A formula matching the `ptrace` exploit is the following automaton, described in slightly idealized form:

$$\begin{array}{ccccccc} \texttt{Attach}(X,Y,Z) & \xrightarrow{\Diamond} & \texttt{Exec}(Y) & \xrightarrow{\Diamond} & \texttt{Syscall}(X,Y) & \xrightarrow{\Diamond} & \texttt{Getregs}(X,Y) \\ & & & & \Diamond\downarrow & \swarrow\Diamond & \\ & & & & \texttt{Poketext}(X,Y) & \xrightarrow{\Diamond} & \texttt{Detach}(X,Y) \end{array} \quad (1)$$

where X, Y, Z are existentially quantified first-order variables meant to match the attacker's pid, the target's pid (i.e., `modprobe`'s pid), and the attacker's effective uid respectively; where `Attach`(X, Y, Z) abbreviates a formula (not shown) matching any single event displaying a call to `ptrace` by process X owned by Z, on process Y, with the `ATTACH` command, `Exec`(Y) matches single events where `/sbin/modprobe` is `execed` with pid Y, and the remaining formulas match single events where process X issues a call to `ptrace` on target Y, with respective commands `SYSCALL`, `GETREGS`, `POKETEXT` (used to insert the shellcode), and `DETACH`.

Compared to other more standard uses of model-checking, the logic of ORCHIDS is constrained to only specify *eventuality* properties. This is because the model-checker needs to to work *on-line*, that is, by always working on some finite (and expanding over time) prefix of an infinite sequence of events. Compared to standard model-checking algorithms, e.g., based on Büchi automata for LTL, the model-checker is not allowed to make multiple passes over the sequence of events (e.g., we cannot rebuild a product automaton each time a new event is added); in general, intrusion detection tasks are submitted to very stringent efficiency requirements, both in time and in space.

Second, the logic of ORCHIDS includes some first-order features. As witnessed by the use of variables X, Y, Z in (1), this logic can be seen as an existential fragment of a first-order temporal logic.

Finally, such a model-checker cannot just report the *existence* of matches, but must enumerate all matches among a given representative subset, with the corresponding values of the existential variables, build an alert for each match and possibly trigger countermeasures. This is the *raison d'être* behind the `Getregs`(X, Y) formula in (1); if we only wanted a yes/no answer, this would just be redundant, and could be erased from the automaton; here, this is used to be able to report whether the attacker issued at least one call to `ptrace(PTRACE_GETREGS)` or not during the attack.

The model-checking task for the logic of ORCHIDS is NP-hard (it includes that of [6–Section 4]), but can be done using an efficient, on-line and real-time algorithm [2, 1]. Moreover, this algorithm is *optimal* in the following sense: for every attack signature (formula F), if at least one attack (sequence of possibly non-contiguous events) is started at event e_0 that matches F, then exactly one attack is reported amongst these, the one with the so-called *shortest run*. The latter is usually the most meaningful attack among all those that match. The notion of shortest run was refined in ORCHIDS, and now appears as a particular case of *cuts* [2]; this gives more control as to which unique attack we wish to isolate amongst those that match.

Related Work. There are many other formalisms attempting to detect complex intrusion detection scenarios, using means as diverse as Petri nets, parsing schemata, continuous data streams, etc. Perhaps one of the most relevant is run-time monitoring (or cousins: F. Schneider's security automata and variants, and security code weaving), where the event flow is synchronized at run-time with a *monitor* automaton describing paths to bad states. The ORCHIDS approach is certainly close to the latter (although arrows in e.g., (1) are more complex than simple automaton transitions); shortest runs and cuts, which introduce priorities between paths in the monitor, and the fact that only one optimal path among equivalent paths is reported, is a useful refinement.

Implementation. The ORCHIDS engine is implemented in C. At the core of ORCHIDS lies a fast virtual machine for a massively-forking virtual parallel machine, and a byte-code compiler from formulae (such as (1)) to this virtual machine. ORCHIDS uses a hierarchy of input modules to subscribe to, and to parse incoming events, classified by input source and/or event format. A main event dispatcher reads from polled and real-time I/O, reads sequences of events in `syslog` format, `snare`, `sunbsm`, `apache` and other various formats, coming from log files or directly through dedicated network connections, and feeds the relevant events to the core engine. ORCHIDS is able to do both system-level and network-based intrusion detection, simultaneously.

Here are a few figures of ORCHIDS on an instance of the `ptrace` attack:

Time :	Real time :	1267s
	CPU Time :	370.810s
	CPU usage :	29.27%
Resources :	Memory (peak) :	2.348 MB
	Signalisation network load :	1.5 GB
Analyzer :	Loading and rule compilation :	< 5 ms
	Processed events :	4 058 732

To stress the detection engine, the attack was hidden in the middle of a huge amount of normal `ptrace` debugging events, generated by tracing the compilation of the whole *GCC C Compiler* (with the command line `tar xzvf gcc-3.3.2.tar.gz ; cd gcc-3.3.2 ; ./configure ; cd gcc ; strace -F -f make`).

Conclusion. The `ptrace` attack above is one of the typical attacks that ORCHIDS can detect. Experiments are going on at LSV to test ORCHIDS on actual network traffic and system event flows.

From the point of view of security, a good news is that, contrarily to most misuse intrusion detection systems, ORCHIDS is able to detect intrusions that were not previously known (contrarily to popular belief on misuse IDSs). E.g., the signature we use for the `do_brk` attack [3], which tests whether some process managed to gain root privilege without calling any of the adequate system calls, detected the recent (Jan. 2005) Linux `uselib` attack.

For more information, see the Web page [4].

References

1. J. Goubault-Larrecq. Un algorithme pour l'analyse de logs. Research Report LSV-02-18, Lab. Specification and Verification, ENS de Cachan, Cachan, France, Nov. 2002. 33 pages.
2. J. Goubault-Larrecq, J.-P. Pouzol, S. Demri, L. Mé, and P. Carle. Langages de détection d'attaques par signatures. Sous-projet 3, livrable 1 du projet RNTL DICO. Version 1, June 2002. 30 pages.
3. A. Morton and P. Starzetz. Linux kernel `do_brk` function boundary condition vulnerability. `http://www.securityfocus.com/bid/9138`, Dec. 2003. References CAN-2003-0961 (CVE), BugTraq Id 9138.
4. J. Olivain. ORCHIDS—real-time event analysis and temporal correlation for intrusion detection in information systems. `http://www.lsv.ens-cachan.fr/orchids/`, 2004.

5. W. Purczyński. Linux kernel privileged process hijacking vulnerability. `http://www.securityfocus.com/bid/7112`, Mar. 2003. BugTraq Id 7112.
6. M. Roger and J. Goubault-Larrecq. Log auditing through model checking. In *Proc. 14th IEEE Computer Security Foundations Workshop (CSFW'01), Cape Breton, Nova Scotia, Canada, June 2001*, pages 220–236. IEEE Comp. Soc. Press, 2001.
7. P. Wolper. Temporal logic can be more expressive. *Information and Control*, 56(1/2):72–99, 1983.

TVOC: A Translation Validator for Optimizing Compilers

Clark Barrett[1], Yi Fang[1], Benjamin Goldberg[1], Ying Hu[1], Amir Pnueli[1], and Lenore Zuck[2]

[1] New York University
{barrett, yifang, goldberg, yinghu, amir}@cs.nyu.edu
[2] University of Illinois, Chicago
lenore@cs.uic.edu

Abstract. We describe a tool called TVOC, that uses the *translation validation* approach to check the validity of compiler optimizations: for a given source program, TVOC proves the equivalence of the source code and the target code produced by running the compiler. There are two phases to the verification process: the first phase verifies loop transformations using the proof rule PERMUTE; the second phase verifies structure-preserving optimizations using the proof rule VALIDATE. Verification conditions are validated using the automatic theorem prover CVC Lite.

1 Introduction

Verifying the correctness of modern optimizing compilers is challenging because of their size, complexity, and evolution over time. *Translation Validation* [8] is a novel approach that offers an alternative to the verification of translators in general and of compilers in particular. Rather than verifying the compiler itself, one constructs a *validating tool* that, after every run of the compiler, formally confirms that the target code produced is a correct translation of the source program. A number of tools and techniques have been developed for compiler validation based on translation validation[7, 8, 10]. In this paper, we introduce TVOC, a tool for translation validation for compilers.

2 System Architecture

Fig. 1 shows the overall design of TVOC. TVOC accepts as input a source program S and target program T, both in the WHIRL intermediate representation, a format used by Intel's Open Research Compiler (ORC) [9] among others. Just as compilers perform optimizations in multiple passes, it is reasonable to break the validation into multiple phases, each using a different proof rule and focusing on a different set of optimizations. Currently, TVOC uses two phases to validate optimizations performed by the compiler. Below, we explain these two phases in more detail. Fig. 2 shows a program called TEST that we will use as a running example. The transformation in question is loop fusion plus the addition of an extra branch condition before the loop.

K. Etessami and S.K. Rajamani (Eds.): CAV 2005, LNCS 3576, pp. 291–295, 2005.

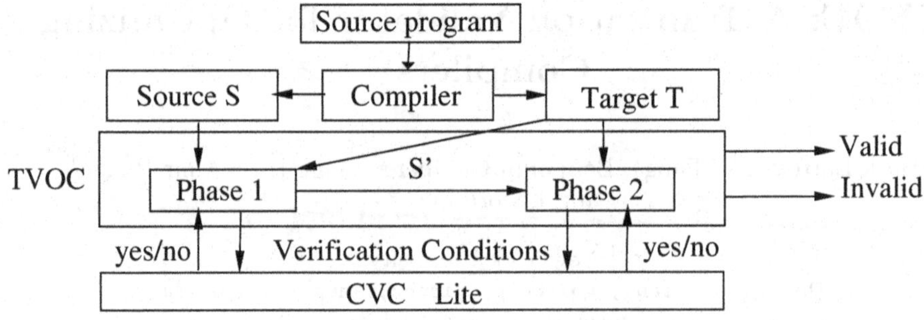

Fig. 1. The architecture of TVOC

```
do i = 0 to N
    A[i] = 0;

do i = 0 to N
    B[i] = 1;
```

```
do i = 0 to N {
    A[i] = 0;
    B[i] = 1;
}
```

```
if N ≥ 0 {
    do i = 0 to N {
        A[i] = 0;
        B[i] = 1;
    }
}
```

Fig. 2. S, S' and T for Program TEST

3 Phase 1: Reordering Transformations

In phase 1, TVOC focuses on reordering transformations. These are transformations which simply permute the order in which statements are executed, without adding or removing any statements. Examples of reordering transformations include loop interchange, loop fusion and distribution, and tiling [2]. Reordering transformations are validated using the proof rule PERMUTE, which, given a bijective function defining the permutation, produces a set of verification conditions which ensure the correctness of the transformation. Essentially, the verification conditions specify that every pair of statements whose order is exchanged by the permutation have the same result regardless of the order in which they are executed.

TVOC automatically determines the loop transformations by comparing the number and structure of loops in the source and target. This approach is described in [5, 6] and works quite well in practice. Note that if TVOC guesses wrong, this can only lead to false negatives, never to false positives. The validation performed is always sound. For program TEST, if i_1 is a loop index variable for the first loop and i_2 is a loop index variable for the second loop, the permutation function reorders two statements exactly when $i_2 < i_1$. The verification condition can thus be expressed as follows, where $\sim$ denotes program equivalence: $(i_2 < i_1) \longrightarrow A[i_1] = 0;\ B[i_2] = 1 \ \sim\ B[i_2] = 1;\ A[i_1] = 0$. The validity of this verification condition can be checked automatically by CVC Lite [3].

Phase 1 also detects transformations such as skewing, peeling and alignment. Even though these do not actually reorder the statements, they do change the structure of the loops and so it is necessary to handle these transformations before moving on to phase 2, which assumes that S' and T have the same loop structure.

4 Phase 2: Structure-Preserving Transformations

Phase 2 handles so-called structure-preserving transformations by applying rule VALIDATE. This rule is quite versatile and can handle a wide variety of standard optimizations and transformations [1], including the insertion or deletion of statements. The main requirement is that the loop structure be the same in the source and target programs.

Two important mappings are required to apply rule VALIDATE, a *control* mapping and a *data* mapping. The control mapping is formed by finding a correspondance between a subset of locations in the target T and a subset of locations in the source S'. These locations are called *cut-points.* The sets of cut-points must include the initial and final locations in S' and T and at least one location from every loop. The other required mapping is the data mapping. Some of the source variables are identified as *observable.* These are the variables whose values must be preserved in order for a transformation to be correct. The data mapping gives a value for each observable source variable in terms of expressions over target variables. TVOC generates the control and data mappings automatically.

Fig. 3 shows program TEST annotated with cut-points. Assuming A and B are the observable variables, the data mapping simply maps A to a and B to b.

```
CP0 :  do I = 0 to N {
CP1 :      A[I] = 0;
           B[I] = 1;
       }
CP2 :
```

```
cp0 :  if n ≥ 0 {
           do i = 0 to n {
cp1 :          a[i] = 0;
               b[i] = 1;
           }
       }
cp2 :
```

Fig. 3. Cut-points for program TEST

Validation of the source against the target is done by checking that the data mapping is preserved along every target path between a pair of cut-points. The overall correctness follows by induction [4, 10]. Initially, TVOC tries to show that all variables correspond at all program locations. When it finds that the data mapping is not preserved for a given variable at some cut-point, that variable is removed from the data mapping at that location. As long as all of the observable variables are still in the data mapping at the final cut-point, the validation succeeds.

For the example, in Fig. 3, there are four possible target paths: $0 \to 1$, $0 \to 2$, $1 \to 1$ and $1 \to 2$. Therefore, four verification conditions must be checked by CVC Lite. Each verification condition checks that if the data mapping holds, and the corresponding source and target transitions are taken, then the data mapping still holds. Transitions are modeled using logical equations with *primed* variables denoting the values of variables after the transition. The verification condition for the transition from 1 to 1 is shown below:

$$
\begin{gathered}
A = a \;\wedge\; B = b \,\wedge \\
a' = write(a, i, 0) \wedge b' = write(b, i, 1) \wedge i' = i + 1 \wedge i + 1 \leq n \wedge n' = n \wedge \\
A' = write(A, I, 0) \wedge B' = write(B, I, 1) \wedge I' = I + 1 \wedge I + 1 \leq N \wedge N' = N \\
\longrightarrow \\
A' = a' \;\wedge\; B' = b'.
\end{gathered}
$$

In the general case, the data mapping may not be inductive, so additional invariants may be needed to establish that it holds. TVOC calculates a simple invariant for each cut-point based on data flow analysis. These invariants are often sufficient to establish the induction. Another complication is that because of branching, there may be multiple paths between two cut-points. In this case, TVOC uses the disjunction of the path transition relations. This allows TVOC for example to correctly identify a transformation in which multiple source paths are merged into a single target path.

5 Conclusions and Future Work

At this point, TVOC still has some limitations: there are some optimizations and language features that cannot yet be validated. For instance, we are still in the process of adding support for procedures and pointers.

Although TVOC has primarily been used as a research prototype and experimental platform for theoretical work, we are hoping it will be of use and interest to a broader community. In addition, we hope to receive feedback and suggestions for further improvement. We are thus making it freely available together with basic examples and documentation at http://www.cs.nyu.edu/acsys/tv/.

References

1. A. Aho, R. Sethi, and J. Ullman. *Compilers Principles, Techniques, and Tools.* Addison Wesley, 1988.
2. R. Allen and K. Kennedy. *Optimizing Compilers for Modern Architectures.* Morgan Kaufmann, 2002.
3. C. Barrett and S. Berezin. CVC Lite: A new implementation of the cooperating validity checker. In *CAV*, July 2004.
4. R. Floyd. Assigning meanings to programs. In *Symposia in Applied Mathematics*, volume 19:19–32, 1967.
5. B. Goldberg, L. Zuck, and C. Barrett. Into the loops: Practical issues in translation validation for optimizing compilers. In *COCV*, Apr. 2004.
6. Y. Hu, C. Barrett, B. Goldberg, and A. Pnueli. Validating more loop optimizations. In *COCV*, Apr. 2005.
7. G. Necula. Translation validation of an optimizing compiler. In *PLDI*, 2000.

8. A. Pnueli, M. Siegel, and E. Singerman. Translation validation. In *TACAS'98*, pages 151–166, 1998.
9. S. C. R.D.-C. Ju and C. Wu. Open research compiler (orc) for the itanium processor family. In *Micro 34*, 2001.
10. L. Zuck, A. Pnueli, B. Goldberg, C. Barrett, Y. Fang, and Y. Hu. Translation and run-time validation of loop transformations. *FMSD*, 2005.

Cogent: Accurate Theorem Proving for Program Verification

Byron Cook[1], Daniel Kroening[2], and Natasha Sharygina[3]

[1] Microsoft Research
[2] ETH Zurich
[3] Carnegie Mellon University

Abstract. Many symbolic software verification engines such as SLAM and ESC/JAVA rely on automatic theorem provers. The existing theorem provers, such as SIMPLIFY, lack precise support for important programming language constructs such as pointers, structures and unions. This paper describes a theorem prover, COGENT, that accurately supports all ANSI-C expressions. The prover's implementation is based on a machine-level interpretation of expressions into propositional logic, and supports finite machine-level variables, bit operations, structures, unions, references, pointers and pointer arithmetic. When used by SLAM during the model checking of over 300 benchmarks, COGENT's improved accuracy reduced the number of SLAM timeouts by half, increased the number of true errors found, and decreased the number of false errors.

1 Introduction

Program verification engines, such as symbolic model checkers and advanced static checking tools, often employ automatic theorem provers for symbolic reasoning. For example, the static checkers ESC/JAVA [1] and BOOGIE [2] use the SIMPLIFY [3] theorem prover to verify user-supplied invariants. The SLAM [4] software model-checker uses ZAPATO [5] for symbolic simulation of C programs. The BLAST [6] and MAGIC [7] tools use SIMPLIFY.

Most automatic theorem provers used in program verification are based on either Nelson-Oppen or Shostak's combination methods. These methods combine various decision procedures to provide a rich logic for mathematical reasoning. However, when applied to software verification, the fit between the program verifier and the theorem prover is not ideal. The problem is that the theorem provers are typically geared towards efficiency in the mathematical theories, such as linear arithmetic over the integers. In reality, program verifiers rarely need reasoning for unbounded integers, and the restriction to linear arithmetic is too limiting. Moreover, because linear arithmetic over the integers is not a convex theory (a restriction imposed by Nelson-Oppen and Shostak), the real numbers are often used instead. Software programs, however, use the reals even less than they do the integers.

The program verifiers must provide support for language features that are not easily mapped into the logics supported by the existing theorem provers. These features include pointers, pointer arithmetic, structures, unions, and the potential relationship between these features. When using provers such as SIMPLIFY,

K. Etessami and S.K. Rajamani (Eds.): CAV 2005, LNCS 3576, pp. 296–300, 2005.

the program verification tools typically approximate the semantics of these features with axioms over the symbols used during the encoding. However, using such axioms has a drawback—axioms can interact badly with the performance heuristics that are often used by provers during axiom-instantiation. Additionally, because bit vectors and arrays are not convex theories, many provers do not support them. In those that can, the link between the non-convex decision procedures can be unsatisfactory. As an example, checking equality between a bit-vector and an integer variable is typically not supported.

Another problem that occurs when using prover such as SIMPLIFY or ZAPATO is that, when a query is not valid, the provers do not supply concrete counterexamples. Some provers provide partial information on counterexamples. However, in program verification this information rarely leads to concrete valuations to the variables in a program, which is what a programmer most wants when a program verification tool reports a potential bug in the source code. For this reason, model checkers such as SLAM, BLAST, and MAGIC do not provide valuations to the program variables when an error trace is presented to the user.

This paper addresses the following question: *When verifying programs, can we abandon the Nelson-Oppen/Shostak combination framework in favor of a prover that performs a basic and precise translation of program expressions into propositional logic?*

We present a tool, called COGENT, that implements an eager and accurate translation of ANSI-C expressions (including features such as bitvectors, structures, unions, pointers and pointer arithmetic) into propositional logic. COGENT then uses a propositional logic SAT-solver to prove or disprove the query. Because COGENT's method is based on this eager translation to propositional logic, the models found by SAT-solvers can be directly converted to counterexamples to the original C input query. We evaluated COGENT's performance in SLAM, COMFORT [8], and BOOGIE. The experimental evidence indicates that COGENT's approach can be successfully used in lieu of conventional theorem provers.

2 Encoding into Propositional Logic

COGENT operates by eagerly translating expressions into propositional logic, and then using a propositional logic SAT-solver. COGENT is inspired by the success of CBMC and UCLID. UCLID encodes separation logic and uninterpreted functions eagerly into propositional logic. It does not, however, support bitvector logic. CBMC is a bounded model checker for C programming language and eagerly compiles bitvector arithmetic into propositional logic. COGENT is also used as a decision procedure for the SATABS [9] model checker. COGENT is a theorem prover intended for use in an abstraction framework such as SLAM or MAGIC, and thus, does not implement any abstraction by itself.

In hardware verification, the encoding of arithmetic operators such as shifting, addition, and even multiplication into propositional logic using arithmetic circuit descriptions is a standard technique. We use a similar approach in COGENT, with several modifications:

- In addition to the features supported by the existing tools, COGENT's translation allows the program verification tools to accurately reason about arithmetic overflow, bit operations, structures, unions, pointers and pointer arithmetic.
- COGENT uses non-determinism to accurately model the ambiguity in the ANSI-C standard, i.e., for the representation of signed types. This differs from the support for bitvectors from theorem provers such as CVC-LITE [10].
- We use non-determinism to improve the encodings of some functions, such as multiplication and division, in a way that is optimized for SAT-solvers.

The technical details of COGENT's encoding for ANSI-C expressions including the use of non-determinism for accuracy and efficiency, can be found in [11].

3 Experimental Evaluation

Experiments with symbolic software model checking. We have integrated COGENT with SLAM and compared the results to SLAM using its current theorem prover, ZAPATO. We ran SLAM/COGENT on 308 model checking benchmarks. The results are summarized in Fig. 1.

SLAM/COGENT outperforms SLAM/ZAPATO. Notably, the number of cases where SLAM exceeded the 1200s time threshold was reduced by half. As a result, two additional device driver bugs were found. The cases where SLAM failed to refine the abstraction [12] were effectively unchanged. During SLAM's execution, the provers actually returned different results in some cases. This is expected, as the provers support different logics. For this reason, there are queries that ZAPATO can prove valid and COGENT reports as invalid (e.g., when overflow is ignored by ZAPATO), and vice-versa (e.g., when validity is dependent on pointer arithmetic or non-linear uses of multiplication). Overall, we found that COGENT is more than 2x slower than ZAPATO. On 2000 theorem proving queries ZAPATO executed for 208s, whereas COGENT ran for 522s. Therefore, the performance improvement in Fig. 1 is indicative that, while COGENT is slower, COGENT's increased accuracy allows SLAM to do less work overall.

During the formalization of the kernel API usage properties that SLAM is used to verify [4], a large set of properties were removed or not actively pursued due to inaccuracies in SLAM's theorem prover. For this reason the results in Fig. 1 are not fully representative of the improvement in accuracy that SLAM/COGENT can give. In order to further demonstrate this improved accuracy, we developed

Model checking result	SLAM/ZAPATO	SLAM/COGENT
Property passes	243	264
Time threshold exceeded	39	17
Property violations found	17	19
Cases of abstraction-refinement failure	9	8

Fig. 1. Comparison of SLAM/ZAPATO to SLAM/COGENT on 308 device driver correctness model checking benchmarks. The time threshold was set to 1200 seconds

and checked several new safety properties that could not be accurately checked with SLAM/ZAPATO. For more information on this property and a previously unknown bug that was found see [11].

Experiments with extended static checking. We have also integrated COGENT with BOOGIE [2], which is an implementation of Detlef *et al.*'s notion of *extended static checking* [1] for the C# programming language. BOOGIE computes *verification conditions* that are checked by an automatic theorem prover.

We have applied COGENT to these verification conditions generated by BOOGIE and compared the performance to SIMPLIFY. The results were effectively the same. For more information on this application and, in particular, how we handle the nested quantifiers that appear in the BOOGIE queries, see [11]. We make [11], our tool, and bitvector benchmark files available on the web[1] in order to allow other researchers to reproduce our results.

4 Conclusion

Automatic theorem provers are often used by program verification engines. However, the logics implemented by these theorem provers are not a good fit for the program verification domain. In this paper, we have presented a new prover that accurately supports the type of reasoning that program verification engines require. COGENT's strategy is to directly encode input queries into propositional logic. This encoding accurately supports bit operations, structures, unions, pointers and pointer arithmetic, and pays particular attention to the sometimes subtle semantics described in the ANSI-C standard. Our evaluation of COGENT demonstrates that it improves the accuracy of BOOGIE, and both the performance and accuracy of SLAM. Additionally, COGENT provides concrete counterexamples in the case of failed proofs. To the best of our knowledge, COGENT is the only theorem prover that accurately supports pointer arithmetic, unions, structures and bitvectors and produces concrete counterexamples for a logic suitable for program verification.

References

1. Flanagan, C., Leino, K.R.M., Lillibridge, M., Nelson, G., Saxe, J.B., Stata, R.: Extended static checking for Java. In: PLDI. (2002)
2. Barnett, M., DeLine, R., Fahndrich, M., Leino, K.R.M., Schulte, W.: Verification of object-oriented programs with invariants. JOT **3** (2004) 27–56
3. Detlefs, D., Nelson, G., Saxe, J.B.: Simplify: A theorem prover for program checking. Technical Report HPL-2003-148, HP Labs (2003)
4. Ball, T., Cook, B., Levin, V., Rajamani, S.K.: SLAM and Static Driver Verifier: Technology transfer of formal methods inside Microsoft. In: IFM. (2004)
5. Ball, T., Cook, B., Lahiri, S.K., Zhang, L.: Zapato: Automatic theorem proving for predicate abstraction refinement. In: CAV. (2004)

[1] `http://www.inf.ethz.ch/personal/kroening/cogent/`

6. Henzinger, T.A., Jhala, R., Majumdar, R., Qadeer, S.: Thread modular abstraction refinement. In: CAV, Springer Verlag (2003) 262–274
7. Chaki, S., Clarke, E., Groce, A., Strichman, O.: Predicate abstraction with minimum predicates. In: CHARME. (2003)
8. Ivers, J., Sharygina, N.: Overview of ComFoRT, a model checking reasoning framework. Technical Report CMU/SEI-2004-TN-018, CMU (2004)
9. Clarke, E., Kroening, D., Sharygina, N., Yorav, K.: SATABS: SAT-based predicate abstraction for ANSI-C. In: TACAS. (2005) to appear.
10. Stump, A., Barrett, C., Dill, D.: CVC: a cooperating validity checker. In: CAV 02: International Conference on Computer-Aided Verification. (2002) 87–105
11. Cook, B., Kroening, D., Sharygina, N.: Accurate theorem proving for program verification. Technical Report 473, ETH Zurich (2005)
12. Ball, T., Cook, B., Das, S., Rajamani, S.K.: Refining approximations in software predicate abstraction. In: TACAS. (2004)

F-SOFT: Software Verification Platform

F. Ivančić, Z. Yang*, M.K. Ganai, A. Gupta, I. Shlyakhter, and P. Ashar**

NEC Laboratories America, 4 Independence Way,
Suite 200, Princeton, NJ 08540
fsoft@nec-labs.com

1 Introduction

In this paper, we describe our verification tool F-SOFT which is developed for the analysis of C programs. Its novelty lies in the combination of several recent advances in formal verification research including SAT-based verification, static analyses and predicate abstraction. As shown in the tool overview in Figure 1, we translate a program into a Boolean model to be analyzed by our verification engine DIVER [4], which includes BDD-based and SAT-based model checking techniques. We include various static analyses, such as computing the control flow graph of the program, program slicing with respect to the property, and performing range analysis as described in Section 2.2. We model the software using a Boolean representation, and use customized heuristics for the SAT-based analysis as described in Section 2.1. We can also perform a localized predicate abstraction with register sharing as described in Section 2.3, if the user so chooses. The actual analysis of the resulting Boolean model is performed using DIVER. If a counter-example is discovered, we use a testbench generator that automatically generates an executable program for the user to examine the bug in his/her favorite debugger. The F-SOFT tool has been applied on numerous case studies and publicly available benchmarks for sequential C programs. We are currently working on extending it to handle concurrent programs.

2 Tool Features

In this section, we describe the software modeling approach in F-SOFT and the main tool features. We perform an automatic translation of the given program to a Boolean model representation by considering the control flow graph (CFG) of the program, which is derived after some front-end simplifications performed by the CIL tool [9]. The transitions between basic blocks of the CFG are captured by control logic, and bit-level assignments to program variables are captured by data logic in the resulting Boolean model. We support primitive data types, pointers, static arrays and records, and dynamically allocated objects (up to a user-specified bound). We also allow modeling of bounded recursion by

* The author is at Western Michigan University.

** The author is now with Real Intent.

K. Etessami and S.K. Rajamani (Eds.): CAV 2005, LNCS 3576, pp. 301–306, 2005.

including a bounded function call stack in the Boolean model. Assuming the program consists of n basic blocks, we represent each block by a label consisting of $\lceil \log n \rceil$ bits, called the program counter (pc) variables. A bounded model checking (BMC) analysis is performed by unrolling the block-wise execution of the program. Similar block-based approaches have been explored in a non-BMC setting for software model checking [3, 11]. However, by incorporating basic-block unrolling into a SAT-based BMC framework, we are able to take advantage of the latest SAT-solvers, while also improving performance by customizing the SAT-solver heuristics for software models. More details of our software modeling approach can be found in [6].

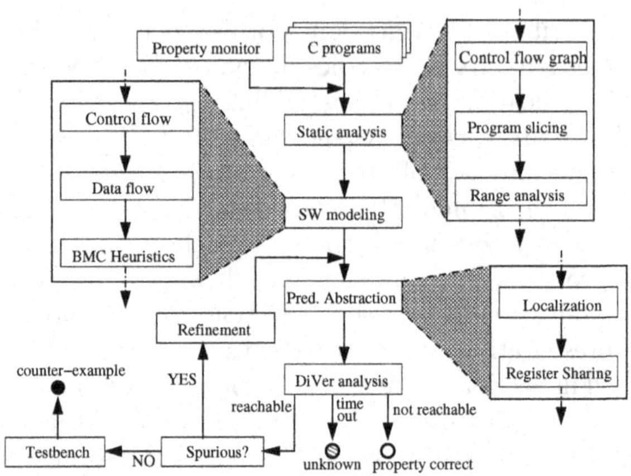

Fig. 1. F-Soft tool overview

2.1 Customized Heuristics for SAT-Based BMC

The Boolean models automatically generated by our software modeling approach contain many common features. We have proposed several heuristics in order to improve the efficiency of SAT-based BMC on such models [6]. In particular, a useful heuristic is a one-hot encoding of the pc variables, called selection bits. A selection bit is set if and only if the corresponding basic block is active. This provides a mechanism for word-level, rather than bit-level, pc decisions by the SAT solver. Furthermore, by increasing the decision score of the selection bits (or the pc variable bits), in comparison to other variables, the SAT-solver can be guided toward making decisions on the control location first. We also add constraints obtained from the CFG, to eliminate impossible predecessor-successor basic block combinations. These constraints capture additional high-level information, which helps to prune the search space of the SAT-solver.

Experimental results for use of these heuristics on a network protocol case study (checking the equivalence of a buggy Linux implementation of the Point-to-Point protocol against its RFC specification) are shown in Figure 2. For these experiments, the bug was found by SAT-based BMC at a depth of 119, and the figure shows the cumulative time in seconds up to each depth. All experiments were performed on a 2.8GHz dual-processor Linux machine with 4GB of memory. The graph labeled *standard* represents the default decision heuristics implemented in the DIVER tool, while the other three graphs show the effect of specialized heuristics – higher scoring of pc variables (*score*), one-hot encoding of pc variables (*one-hot*), and addition of constraints for CFG transitions (*trans*). The advantage of the the one-hot encoding heuristic can be seen clearly.

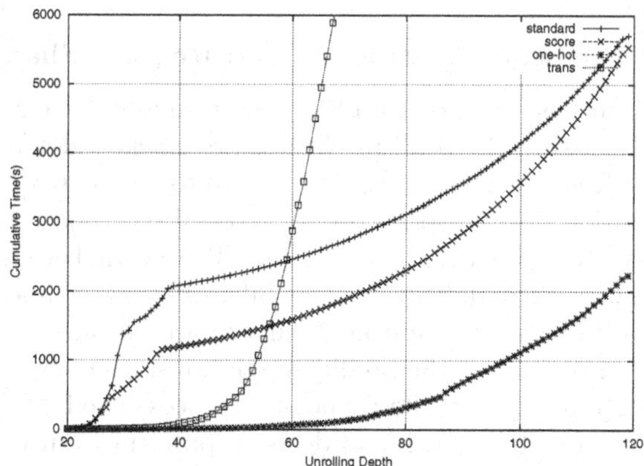

Fig. 2. Cumulative time comparison of SAT-based BMC heuristics for PPP

2.2 Range Analysis

F-SOFT includes several automatic approaches for determining lower and upper bounds for program variables using range analysis techniques [12]. The range information can help in reducing the number of bits needed to represent program variables in the translated Boolean model, thereby improving the efficiency of verification. For example, rather than requiring a 32 bit representation for every `int` variable, we can use the range information to reduce the number of bits for these variables. As discussed in the next section, F-SOFT also provides an efficient SAT-based approach for performing predicate abstraction. In this context too, SAT-based enumeration for predicate abstraction [8] can be improved by using tighter ranges for concrete variables, derived by using our automatic range analysis techniques.

Our main method is based on the framework suggested in [10], which formulates each range analysis problem as a system of inequality constraints between symbolic bound polynomials. It then reduces the constraint system to a linear program (LP), such that the solution provides symbolic lower and upper bounds for the values of all integer variables. This may require over-approximating some program constructs to derive conservative bounds. Our second approach to computing ranges exploits the fact that in a bounded model checking run of depth k, the range information needs to be sound only for traces up to length k. This *bounded range analysis* technique is able to find tighter bounds on many program variables that cannot be bounded using the LP solver-based technique.

These range analysis techniques in F-SOFT have been applied to many examples, including a network protocol (PPP), an aircraft traffic alert system (TCAS), a mutual exclusion algorithm (Bakery), and an array manipulation example. For these control-intensive examples, we found that the LP-based range analysis technique reduced the number of state bits in the translated Boolean model by 60% on average. The bounded range analysis technique produced an additional 53% reduction on average. These resulted in considerable time savings in verification using both BDD-based and SAT-based methods.

2.3 Localized Predicate Abstraction and Register Sharing

Predicate abstraction has emerged as a popular technique for extracting finite-state models from software [1]. If all predicates are tracked globally in the program, the analysis often becomes intractable due to too many predicate relationships. Our contribution [7] is inspired by the lazy abstraction and localization techniques implemented in BLAST [5]. While BLAST makes use of interpolation, we use weakest pre-conditions along infeasible traces and the proof of unsatisfiability of a SAT solver to automatically find predicates relevant at each program location. Since most of the predicate relationships relevant at each program location are obtained from the refinement process itself, this significantly reduces the number of calls to back-end decision procedures in the abstraction computation.

The performance of BDD-based model checkers depends crucially on the number of state variables. Due to predicate localization most predicates are useful only in certain parts of the program. The state variables corresponding to these predicates can be *shared* to represent different predicates in other parts of the abstraction. However, maximal register sharing may result in too many abstraction refinement iterations; e.g., if the value of a certain predicate needs to be tracked at multiple program locations. We make use of a simple heuristic for deciding when to assign a *dedicated* state variable for a predicate in order to track it globally. While it is difficult to compare the performance of these techniques in F-SOFT with BLAST under controlled conditions, our experiments [7] indicated that the maximum number of active predicates at any program location are comparable for the two tools, even though BLAST uses a more complex refinement technique based on computation of Craig interpolants.

We have also applied our predicate abstraction techniques in F-SOFT to a large case study (about 32KLoC) consisting of a serial 16550-based RS-232 device driver from WINDDK 3790 for Windows-NT. We checked the correct lock usage property, i.e. lock acquires and releases should be alternating. Of the 93 related API functions, F-SOFT successfully proved the correctness of 72 functions in about 2 hours (no bugs found so far!).

3 Comparison to Other Tools

The most closely related tool to ours is CBMC [2], which also translates a C program into a Boolean representation to be analyzed by a back-end SAT-based

BMC. However, there are many differences. One major difference is that we generate a Boolean model of the software that can be analyzed by both bounded and unbounded model checking methods, using SAT solvers and BDDs. Another major difference in the software modeling is our block-based approach using a pc variable, rather than a statement-based approach in CBMC. (In our controlled experiments, the block-based approach provides a typical 25% performance improvement over a statement-based approach.) Additionally, the translation to a Boolean model in CBMC requires unwinding of loops up to some bound, a full inlining of functions, and cannot handle recursive functions. In contrast, our pc-based translation method does not require unwinding of loops, avoids multiple inlining, and can also handle bounded recursion. This allows our method to scale better than CBMC on larger programs, especially those with loops. The practical advantages over CBMC were demonstrated in a recent paper [6], where we also used specialized heuristics in the SAT solver to exploit the structure in software models.

We also differentiate our approach by use of light-weight pre-processing analyses such as program slicing and range analysis. Program slicing has been successfully used in other software model checkers [3, 11] as well. Although range analysis techniques have been used for other applications [10], to the best of our knowledge we are the first to use them for software model checking. In practice, it significantly reduces the number of bits needed to represent program variables in the translated Boolean model, compared to using a full bitwidth encoding, as in CBMC. Finally, F-SOFT also allows abstraction of the software program using predicate abstraction and localization techniques. These are inspired by other model checkers [1, 5].

Acknowledgements. We thank Srihari Cadambi, Aleksandr Zaks and Himanshu Jain for their help in development of the F-SOFT platform.

References

1. T. Ball, R. Majumdar, T.D. Millstein, and S.K. Rajamani. Automatic predicate abstraction of C programs. In *PLDI*, pages 203–213, 2001.
2. E.M. Clarke, D. Kroening, and F. Lerda. A tool for checking ANSI-C programs. In *TACAS*, 2004.
3. J. C. Corbett et al. Bandera: Extracting finite-state models from java source code. In *Int. Conf. on Software Engineering*, pages 439–448, 2000.
4. M.K. Ganai, A. Gupta, and P. Ashar. DIVER: SAT-based model checking platform for verifying large scale systems. In *TACAS*, volume 3340 of *LNCS*. Springer, 2005.
5. T.A. Henzinger, R. Jhala, R. Majumdar, and K. McMillan. Abstractions from proofs. In *POPL*, pages 232–244. ACM Press, 2004.
6. F. Ivančić, Z. Yang, M. Ganai, A. Gupta, and P. Ashar. Efficient SAT-based bounded model checking for software verification. In *Symposium on Leveraging Formal Methods in Applications*, 2004.
7. H. Jain, F. Ivančić, A. Gupta, and M.K. Ganai. Localization and register sharing for predicate abstraction. In *TACAS*, volume 3340 of *LNCS*. Springer, 2005.

8. S.K. Lahiri, R.E. Bryant, and B. Cook. A symbolic approach to predicate abstraction. In *Computer Aided Verification*, volume 2725 of *LNCS*. Springer, 2003.
9. G.C. Necula et al. CIL: Intermediate language and tools for analysis and transformation of C programs. In *International Conference on Compiler Construction*, volume 2304 of *LNCS*, pages 213–228. Springer-Verlag, 2002.
10. R. Rugina and M.C. Rinard. Symbolic bounds analysis of pointers, array indices, and accessed memory regions. In *PLDI*, pages 182–195, 2000.
11. W. Visser, K. Havelund, G. Brat, S. Park, and F. Lerda. Model checking programs. *Automated Software Engineering Journal*, 10(2), 2003.
12. A. Zaks, I. Shlyakhter, F. Ivančić, H. Cadambi, Z. Yang, M. Ganai, A. Gupta, and P. Ashar. Range analysis for software verification. 2005. In submission.

Yet Another Decision Procedure for Equality Logic

Orly Meir[1] and Ofer Strichman[2]

[1] Computer science department, Technion , Israel
orlym@cs.technion.ac.il
[2] Information Systems Engineering, Technion, Israel
ofers@ie.technion.ac.il

Abstract. We introduce a new decision procedure for Equality Logic. The procedure improves on Bryant and Velev's SPARSE method [4] from CAV'00, in which each equality predicate is encoded with a Boolean variable, and then a set of transitivity constraints are added to compensate for the loss of transitivity of equality. We suggest the Reduced Transitivity Constraints (RTC) algorithm, that unlike the SPARSE method, considers the *polarity* of each equality predicate, i.e. whether it is an equality or disequality when the given equality formula φ^E is in Negation Normal Form (NNF). Given this information, we build the Equality Graph corresponding to φ^E with two types of edges, one for each polarity. We then define the notion of *Contradictory Cycles* to be cycles in that graph that the variables corresponding to their edges cannot be simultaneously satisfied due to transitivity of equality. We prove that it is sufficient to add transitivity constraints that only constrain Contradictory Cycles, which results in only a small subset of the constraints added by the SPARSE method. The formulas we generate are smaller and define a larger solution set, hence are expected to be easier to solve, as indeed our experiments show. Our new decision procedure is now implemented in the UCLID verification system.

1 Introduction

Equality Logic with Uninterpreted Functions is a major decidable theory used in verification of infinite-state systems. Well-formed expressions in this logic are Boolean combinations of Equality predicates, where the equalities are defined between *term-variables* (variables with some infinite domain) and Uninterpreted Functions. The Uninterpreted Functions can be reduced to equalities via either Ackermann's [1] or Bryant et al.'s reduction [2] (from now on we will say Bryant's reduction), hence the underling theory that is left to solve is that of Equality Logic.

There are many examples of using Equality Logic and Uninterpreted Functions in the literature. Proving equivalence of circuits after *custom-design* or *retiming* (a process in which the layout of the circuit is changed in order to improve computation speed) is a prominent example [3, 6]. *Translation Validation* [15], a process in which the input and output of a compiler are proven to be semantically equivalent is another example of using this logic. Almost all theorem

K. Etessami and S.K. Rajamani (Eds.): CAV 2005, LNCS 3576, pp. 307–320, 2005.

provers that we are aware of support this logic, either explicitly or as part of their support of more expressive logics.

Related work. The importance of this logic led to several suggestions for decision procedures in the last few years [17, 9, 13, 2, 4, 16], almost all of which are surveyed in detail in the full version of this article [11]. Due to space limitations here we will only mention the most relevant prior work by Bryant and Velev [4], called the SPARSE method. In the SPARSE method, each equality predicate is replaced with a new Boolean variable, which results in a purely propositional formula that we denote by $\mathcal{B}$ ($\mathcal{B}$ for $\mathcal{B}$oolean). Transitivity constraints over these Boolean variables are then conjoined with $\mathcal{B}$, to recover the transitivity of equality that is lost in the Boolean encoding. So, for example, given the equality formula: $v_1 = v_2 \wedge v_2 = v_3 \wedge \neg(v_1 = v_3)$ the SPARSE method reduces it to the Boolean formula $\mathcal{B} = e_{1,2} \wedge e_{2,3} \wedge \neg e_{1,3}$ and conjoins $\mathcal{B}$ with the transitivity constraints $e_{1,2} \wedge e_{2,3} \rightarrow e_{1,3}, e_{1,2} \wedge e_{1,3} \rightarrow e_{2,3}$ and $e_{1,3} \wedge e_{2,3} \rightarrow e_{1,2}$. The conjoined formula is satisfiable if and only if the original formula is satisfiable.

In order to decide which constraints are needed, following the SPARSE method one needs to build a graph in which each equality predicate is an edge and each variable is a vertex. With a simple analysis of this graph the necessary constraints are derived. This is where our method is different from the SPARSE method: unlike the graph considered by the SPARSE method, the graph we build has two kinds of edges: one for equalities and one for disequalities, assuming the Equality formula is given to us in Negation Normal Form (NNF) . Given this extra information, about the *polarity* of each equality predicate, we are able to find a small subset of the constraints that are generated by the SPARSE method, that are still sufficient to preserve correctness. This results in a much simpler formula that is easier for SAT to solve, at least in theory.

We base our procedure on a theorem that we state and prove in Section 4. The theorem refers to what we call *Simple Contradictory Cycles*, which are simple cycles that have exactly one disequality edge. In such cycles, the theorem claims, we need to prevent an assignment that assigns FALSE to the disequality edge and TRUE to the rest. And, most importantly, these are the *only kind* of constraints necessary. The proof of this theorem relies on a certain property of NNF formulas called *monotonicity with respect to satisfiability* that we present in Section 3. In Section 5 we show an algorithm that computes in polynomial time a set of constraints that satisfy the requirements of our theorem. In Section 6 we present experimental results. Our new procedure is now embedded in the UCLID [5] verification tool and is hence available for usage. In Section 7 we conclude the paper and present directions for future research.

2 Reducing Equality Logic to Propositional Logic

We consider the problem of deciding whether an Equality Logic formula φ^{E} is satisfiable. The following framework is used by both [4] and the current work to reduce this decision problem to the problem of deciding a propositional formula:

1. Let E denote the set of equality predicates appearing in φ^{E}. Derive a Boolean formula $\mathcal{B}$ by replacing each equality predicate $(v_i = v_j) \in E$ with a new Boolean variable $e_{i,j}$. Encode disequality predicates with negations, e.g., encode $i \neq j$ with $\neg e_{i,j}$.
2. Recover the lost transitivity of equality by conjoining $\mathcal{B}$ with explicit *transitivity constraints* jointly denoted by $\mathcal{T}$ ($\mathcal{T}$ for $\mathcal{T}$ransitivity). $\mathcal{T}$ is a formula over $\mathcal{B}$'s variables and, possibly, auxiliary variables.

The Boolean formula $\mathcal{B} \wedge \mathcal{T}$ should be satisfiable if and only if φ^{E} is satisfiable. Further, we should be able to construct a satisfying assignment to φ^{E} from an assignment to the $e_{i,j}$ variables. A straightforward method to build $\mathcal{T}$ in a way that will satisfy these requirements is to add a constraint for every cyclic comparison between variables, which disallow TRUE assignment to exactly $k-1$ predicates in a k-long simple cycle.

In [4] three different methods to build $\mathcal{T}$ are suggested, all of which are better than this straightforward approach, and are described in some detail also in [11]. We need to define *Non-Polar Equality Graph* in order to explain the SPARSE method, which is both theoretically and empirically the best of the three:

Definition 1 (Non-polar Equality Graph). *Given an Equality Logic formula φ^{E}, the* Non-Polar Equality Graph *corresponding to φ^{E} is an undirected graph (V, E) where each node $v \in V$ corresponds to a variable in φ^{E}, and each edge $e \in E$ corresponds to an equality or disequality predicate in φ^{E}.*

The graph is called *non-polar* to distinguish it from the graph that we will use later, in which there is a distinction between edges that represent equalities and those that represent disequalities. We will simply say Equality Graph from now on in both cases, where the meaning is clear from the context.

The SPARSE method is based on a theorem, proven in [4], stating that it is sufficient to add transitivity constraints only to *chord-free* cycles (a chord is an edge between two non-adjacent nodes). A *chordal* graph, also known as *triangulated graph,* is a graph in which every cycle of size four or more has a chord. In such a graph only triangles are chord-free cycles. Every graph can be made chordal by adding auxiliary edges in linear time. The SPARSE method begins by making the graph chordal, while referring to each added edge as a new auxiliary $e_{i,j}$ variable. It then adds three transitivity constraints for each triangle. We will denote the transitivity constraints generated by the SPARSE method with $\mathcal{T}^S$.

Example 1. Figure 1 presents an Equality Graph before and after making it chordal. The added edge $e_{0,6}$ corresponds to a new auxiliary variable $e_{0,6}$ that appears in $\mathcal{T}^S$ but not in $\mathcal{B}$. After making the graph chordal, it contains 4 triangles and hence there are 12 constraints in $\mathcal{T}^S$. For example, for the triangle (v_1, v_2, v_3) the constraints are: $e_{1,2} \wedge e_{2,3} \rightarrow e_{1,3}$, $e_{1,3} \wedge e_{2,3} \rightarrow e_{1,2}$ and $e_{1,2} \wedge e_{1,3} \rightarrow e_{2,3}$.

□

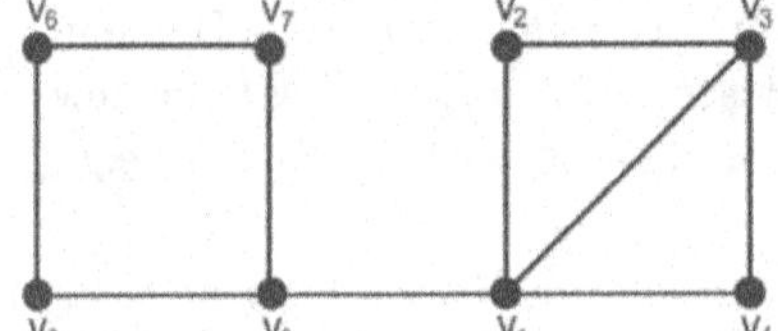

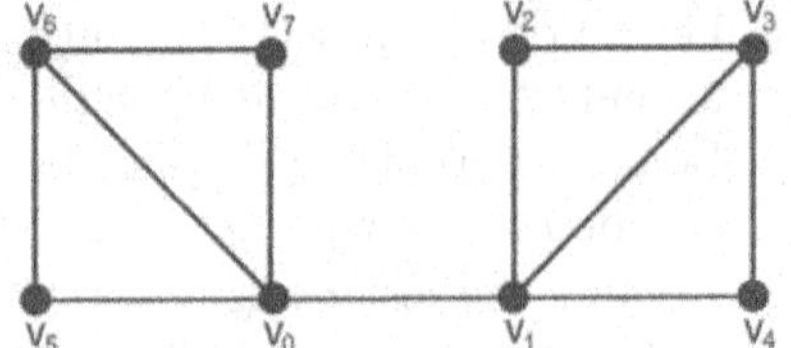

Fig. 1. A non-chordal Equality Graph (left) and its chordal version

We will show an algorithm for constructing a Boolean formula $\mathcal{T}^R$ (the superscript R is for Reduced) which is, similarly to $\mathcal{T}^S$, a conjunction of transitivity constraints, but contains only a subset of the constraints in $\mathcal{T}^S$. $\mathcal{T}^R$ is not logically equivalent to $\mathcal{T}^S$; it has a larger solution set. Yet it maintains the property that $\mathcal{B} \wedge \mathcal{T}^R$ is satisfiable if and only if φ^{E} is satisfiable, as we will later prove. This means that $\mathcal{T}^R$ not only has a subset of the constraints of $\mathcal{T}^S$, but it also defines a less constrained search space (has more solutions than $\mathcal{T}^S$). Together these two properties are likely to make the SAT instance easier to solve. Since the complexity of both our algorithm and the SPARSE method are similar, we can claim dominance over the SPARSE method, although practically, due to the unpredictability of SAT, such claims are never 100% true.

3 Basic Definitions

We will assume that our Equality formula φ^{E} is given in Negation Normal Form (NNF), which means that negations are only applied to atoms, or equality predicates in our case. Every formula can be transformed to this form in linear time in the size of the formula. Given an NNF formula, we denote by $E_=$ the set of (unnegated) equality predicates, and by $E_{\neq}$ the set of disequalities (negated) equality predicates. Our decision procedure, as the SPARSE method, relies on graph-theoretic concepts. We will also use Equality Graphs, but redefine them so they refer to polarity information. Specifically, each of the sets $E_=$, $E_{\neq}$ corresponds in this graph to a different set of edges. We overload these notations so they refer both to the set of predicates and to the edges that represent them in the Equality Graph.

Definition 2 (Equality Graph). *Given an Equality Logic formula φ^{E}, the* Equality Graph *corresponding to φ^{E}, denoted by $G^{\mathrm{E}}(\varphi^{\mathrm{E}})$, is an undirected graph $(V, E_=, E_{\neq})$ where each node $v \in V$ corresponds to a variable in φ^{E}, and each edge in $E_=$ and $E_{\neq}$ corresponds to an equality or disequality from the respective equality predicates sets $E_=$ and $E_{\neq}$. By convention $E_=$ edges are dashed and $E_{\neq}$ edges are solid.*

As before, every edge in the Equality Graph corresponds to a variable $e_{i,j} \in \mathcal{B}$. It follows that when we refer to an assignment of an edge, we actually refer to an assignment to its corresponding variable. Also, we will simply write G^{E} to denote an Equality Graph if we do not refer to a specific formula.

Example 2. In Figure 2 we show an Equality Graph $G^{\mathrm{E}}(\varphi^{\mathrm{E}})$ corresponding to the non-polar version shown in Figure 1, assuming some Equality Formula φ^{E} for which $E_= : \{(v_5 = v_6), (v_6 = v_7), (v_7 = v_0), (v_1 = v_2), (v_2 = v_3), (v_3 = v_4)\}$ and $E_{\neq} : \{(v_0 \neq v_5), (v_0 \neq v_1), (v_1 \neq v_4), (v_1 \neq v_3)\}$. □

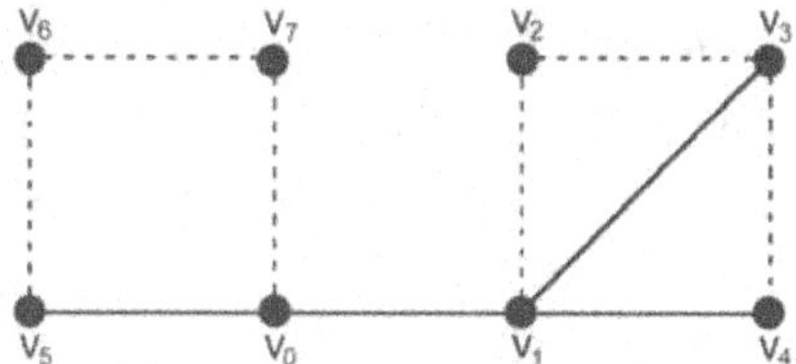

Fig. 2. The Equality Graph $G^{\mathrm{E}}(\varphi^{\mathrm{E}})$ corresponding to the non-polar version of the same graph shown in Figure 1

We now define two types of paths in Equality Graphs.

Definition 3 (Equality Path). *An* Equality Path *in an Equality Graph G^E is a path made of $E_=$ (dashed) edges. We denote by $x =^* y$ the fact that x has an Equality Path to y in G^E, where $x, y \in V$.*

Definition 4 (Disequality Path). *A* Disequality Path *in an Equality Graph G^E is a path made of $E_=$ (dashed) edges and a single $E_{\neq}$ (solid) edge. We denote by $x \neq^* y$ the fact that x has a Disequality Path to y in G^E, where $x, y \in V$.*

Similarly, we will use a *Simple Equality Path* and a *Simple Disequality Path* when the path is required to be loop-free. In Figure 2 it holds, for example, that $v_0 =^* v_6$ due to the simple path v_0, v_7, v_6; $v_0 \neq^* v_6$ due to the simple path v_0, v_5, v_6; and $v_7 \neq^* v_6$ due to the simple path v_7, v_0, v_5, v_6.

Intuitively, Equality Path between two variables implies that it might be required to assign both variables an equal value in order to satisfy the formula. A Disequality Path between two variables implies the opposite: it might be required to assign different values to these variables in order to satisfy the formula. For this reason the case in which both $x =^* y$ and $x \neq^* y$ hold in $G^{\mathrm{E}}(\varphi^{\mathrm{E}})$, requires special attention. We say that the graph, in this case, contains a *Contradictory Cycle.*

Definition 5 (Contradictory Cycle). *A Contradictory Cycle in an Equality Graph is a cycle with exactly one disequality (solid) edge.*

Several characteristics of Contradictory Cycles are: 1) For every pair of nodes x, y in a Contradictory Cycle, it holds that $x =^* y$ and $x \neq^* y$. 2) For every Contradictory Cycle C, either C is *simple* or a subset of its edges forms a Simple Contradictory Cycle. We will therefore refer only to simple Contradictory Cycles from now on. 3) It is impossible to satisfy simultaneously all the predicates that correspond to edges of a Contradictory Cycle. Further, this is the only type of subgraph with this property.

The reason that we need polarity information is that it allows us to use the following property of NNF formulas.

Theorem 1 (Monotonicity of NNF). *Let ϕ be an NNF formula and α be an assignment such that $\alpha \models \phi$. Let the* positive set *S of α be the positive literals in ϕ assigned* TRUE *and the negative literals in ϕ assigned* FALSE*. Every assignment α' with a positive set S' such that $S \subseteq S'$ satisfies ϕ as well.*

The same theorem was used, for example, in [14]. As an aside, when this theorem is applied to CNF formulas, which are a special case of NNF, it is exactly the same as the *pure literal rule.*

4 Main Theorem

The key idea that is formulated by Theorem 2 below and later exploited by our algorithm can first be demonstrated by a simple example.

Example 3. For the Equality Graph below (left), the SPARSE method generates $\mathcal{T}^S$ with three transitivity constrains (recall that it generates three constraints for each triangle in the graph, regardless of the edges' polarity). We claim, however, that the single transitivity constraint $\mathcal{T}^R = (e_{0,2} \wedge e_{1,2} \rightarrow e_{0,1})$ is sufficient.

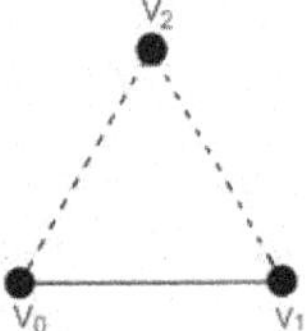

	α^R	α^S
$e_{0,1}$	TRUE	TRUE
$e_{1,2}$	TRUE	TRUE
$e_{0,2}$	FALSE	TRUE

To justify this claim, it is sufficient to show that for every assignment α^R that satisfies $\mathcal{B} \wedge \mathcal{T}^R$, there exists an assignment α^S that satisfies $\mathcal{B} \wedge \mathcal{T}^S$. Since this, in turn, implies that φ^{E} is satisfiable as well, we get that φ^{E} is satisfiable if and only if $\mathcal{B} \wedge \mathcal{T}^R$ is satisfiable. Note that the 'only if' direction is implied by the fact that we use a subset of the constraints defined by $\mathcal{T}^S$.

We are able to construct such an assignment α^S because of the monotonicity of NNF (recall that the polarity of the edges in the Equality Graph are according to their polarity in the NNF representation of φ^{E}). There are only two satisfying assignments to $\mathcal{T}^R$ that do not satisfy $\mathcal{T}^S$. One of these assignments is shown in the α^R column in the table to the right of the drawing. The second column shows a corresponding assignment α^S, which clearly satisfies $\mathcal{T}^S$. But we still need to prove that every formula $\mathcal{B}$ that corresponds to the above graph, is still satisfied by α^S if it was satisfied by α^R. For example, for $\mathcal{B} = (\neg e_{0,1} \vee e_{1,2} \vee e_{0,2})$, both $\alpha^R \models \mathcal{B} \wedge \mathcal{T}^R$ and $\alpha^S \models \mathcal{B} \wedge \mathcal{T}^S$ hold. Intuitively, this is guaranteed to be true because α^S is derived from α^R by flipping an assignment of a positive (un-negated) predicate ($e_{0,2}$) from FALSE to TRUE. We can equivalently flip an assignment to a negated predicate ($e_{0,1}$ in this case) from TRUE to FALSE.

A formalization of this argument requires a reference to the monotonicity of NNF (Theorem 1): Let S and S' denote the positive sets of α^R and α^S respectively. Then in this case $S = \{e_{1,2}\}$ and $S' = \{e_{1,2}, e_{0,2}\}$. Thus $S \subset S'$ and hence, according to Theorem 1, $\alpha^R \models \mathcal{B} \rightarrow \alpha^S \models \mathcal{B}$. □

We need several definitions in order to generalize this example into a theorem.

Definition 6 (A constrained Contradictory Cycle). *Let $C = (e_s, e_1, \ldots, e_n)$ be a Contradictory Cycle where e_s is the solid edge. Let ψ be a formula over the Boolean variables in $\mathcal{B}$ that encodes the edges of C. C is said to be* constrained *in ψ if the assignment $(e_s, e_1, \ldots, e_n) \leftarrow (F, T, \ldots, T)$ contradicts ψ.*

Recall that we denote by $\mathcal{T}^S$ the formula that imposes transitivity constraints in the SPARSE method, as defined in [4] and described in Section 2. Further, recall that the SPARSE method works with chordal graphs, and therefore all constraints are over triangles. Our method also makes the graph chordal, and the constraints that we generate are also over triangles, although we will not use this fact in Theorem 2, in order to make it more general.

Definition 7 (A Reduced Transitivity Constraints function $\mathcal{T}^R$). *A Reduced Transitivity Constraints (RTC) function $\mathcal{T}^R$ is a conjunction of transitivity constraints that maintains these two requirements:*

R1 For every assignment α^S, $\alpha^S \models \mathcal{T}^S \rightarrow \alpha^S \models \mathcal{T}^R$ (the solution set of $\mathcal{T}^R$ includes all the solutions to $\mathcal{T}^S$).
R2 $\mathcal{T}^R$ constrains all the simple Contradictory Cycles in the Equality Graph G^E.

R1 implies that $\mathcal{T}^R$ is less constrained than $\mathcal{T}^S$. Consider, for example, a chordal Equality graph in which all edges are solid (disequalities): in such a graph there are no Contradictory Cycles and hence no constraints are required. In this case $\mathcal{T}^R$ = TRUE, while $\mathcal{T}^S$ includes three transitivity constraints for each triangle.

Theorem 2 (Main). *An Equality formula φ^E is satisfiable if and only if $\mathcal{B} \wedge \mathcal{T}^R$ is satisfiable.*

Due to R1, the proof of the 'only if' direction ($\Rightarrow$) is trivial. To prove the other direction we show in [11] an algorithm for reconstructing an assignment α^S that satisfies $\mathcal{T}^S$ from a given assignment α^R that only satisfies $\mathcal{T}^R$.

5 The Reduced Transitivity Constraints Algorithm

We now introduce an algorithm that generates a formula $\mathcal{T}^R$, which satisfies the two requirements R1 and R2 that were introduced in the previous section.

The RTC algorithm processes *Biconnected Components* (BCC) [7] in the given Equality Graph.

Definition 8 (Maximal Biconnected Component). *A* Biconnected Component *of an undirected graph is a maximal set of edges such that any two edges in the set lie on a common simple cycle.*

We can focus on BCCs because we only need to constrain cycles, and in particular Contradictory Cycles. Each BCC that we consider contains a solid edge e_s and all the Contradictory Cycles that it is part of. In line 5 of RTC we make the BCC chordal. Since making the graph chordal involves adding edges, prior to this step, in line 4, we add solid edges from G^{E} that can serve as chords. After the graph is chordal we call GENERATE-CONSTRAINTS, which generates and adds to some local cache all the necessary constraints for constraining all the Contradictory Cycles in this BCC with respect to e_s. When GENERATE-CONSTRAINTS returns, all the constraints that are in the local cache are added to some global cache. The conjunction of the constraints in the global cache is what RTC returns as $\mathcal{T}^R$.

RTC (Equality Graph $G^{\mathrm{E}}(V, E_=, E_{\neq})$)
1: global-cache = $\emptyset$
2: **for all** $e_s \in E_{\neq}$ **do**
3: Find $B(e_s)$ = maximal BCC in G^{E} made of e_s and $E_=$ edges;
4: Add to $B(e_s)$ all edges from $E_{\neq}$ that connect vertices in $B(e_s)$;
5: Make the graph $B(e_s)$ chordal; ▷ (The chords can be either solid or dashed)
6: GENERATE-CONSTRAINTS ($B(e_s)$, e_s);
7: global-cache = global-cache ∪ local-cache;
8: $\mathcal{T}^R$ = conjunction of all constraints in the global cache;
9: return $\mathcal{T}^R$;

GENERATE-CONSTRAINTS (Equality Graph $G^{\mathrm{E}}(V, E_=, E_{\neq})$, edge $e \in G^{\mathrm{E}}$)
for all triangles $(e_1, e_2, e) \in G^{\mathrm{E}}$ such that

- $e_1 \wedge e_2 \rightarrow e$ is not in the local cache
- $source(e) \neq e_1 \wedge source(e) \neq e_2$

do
$source(e_1) = source(e_2) = e$;
Add $e_1 \wedge e_2 \rightarrow e$ to the local cache;
GENERATE-CONSTRAINTS (G^{E}, e_1); ▷ expand e_1
GENERATE-CONSTRAINTS (G^{E}, e_2); ▷ expand e_2

GENERATE-CONSTRAINTS iterates over all triangles that include the solid edge $e_s \in E_{\neq}$ with which it is called first. It then attempts to implicitly *expand* each such triangle to larger cycles that include e_s. This expansion is done in the recursive calls of GENERATE-CONSTRAINTS. Given the edge e, which is part of a cycle, it tries to make the cycle larger by replacing e with two edges that 'lean' on this edge, i.e. two edges e_1, e_2 that together with e form a triangle. This is why we refer to this operation as expansion. There has to be an indication in which 'direction' we can expand the cycle, because otherwise when considering e.g. e_1, we would replace it with e and e_2 and enter an infinite loop. For this reason we maintain the *source* of each edge. The *source* of an edge is the edge that it replaces. In the example above when replacing e with e_1, e_2, $source(e_1) = source(e_2) = e$. So in the next recursive call, where e_1 is the considered edge, due to the second condition in line 1 we *do not* expand it through the triangle (e, e_1, e_2).

Each time we replace the given edge e by two other edges e_1, e_2, we also add a transitivity constraint $e_1 \wedge e_2 \rightarrow e$ to the local cache. Informally, one may see this constraint as enforcing the transitivity of the expanded cycle, by using the transitivity enforcement of the smaller cycle. In other words, this constraint guarantees that if the expanded cycle violates transitivity, then so does the smaller one. Repeating this argument all the way down to triangles, gives us an inductive proof that transitivity is enforced for all cycles. A formal proof of correctness of RTC appears in [11].

Example 4. Figure 3 (left) shows the result of the iterative application of line 3 in RTC for each solid edge in the graph shown in Figure 2. By definition, after this step each BCC contains exactly one solid edge. Figure 3 (right) demonstrates the application of lines 4 and 5 in RTC: in line 4 we add $e_{1,3}$, and in line 5 we add $e_{0,6}$, the only additional chords necessary in order to make all BCCs chordal. The progress of GENERATE-CONSTRAINTS for this example is shown in Table 1.

Table 1. The progress of GENERATE-CONSTRAINTS when given the graph of Figure 3 (not including steps where the function returns because the triangle contains the source of the expanded edge). In line 5 the constraint is already in the local cache, and hence not added again

Iteration	Component	edge to expand	source of edge	Triangle	added constraint
1	a	$e_{0,5}$	-	$(e_{0,5}, e_{5,6}, e_{0,6})$	$e_{0,6} \wedge e_{5,6} \rightarrow e_{0,5}$
2	a	$e_{0,6}$	$e_{0,5}$	$(e_{0,6}, e_{6,7}, e_{0,7})$	$e_{6,7} \wedge e_{0,7} \rightarrow e_{0,6}$
3	b	$e_{1,4}$	-	$(e_{1,4}, e_{3,4}, e_{1,3})$	$e_{1,3} \wedge e_{3,4} \rightarrow e_{1,4}$
4	b	$e_{1,3}$	$e_{1,4}$	$(e_{1,3}, e_{2,3}, e_{1,2})$	$e_{1,2} \wedge e_{2,3} \rightarrow e_{1,3}$
5	c	$e_{1,3}$	-	$(e_{1,3}, e_{2,3}, e_{1,2})$	$e_{1,2} \wedge e_{2,3} \rightarrow e_{1,3}$

□

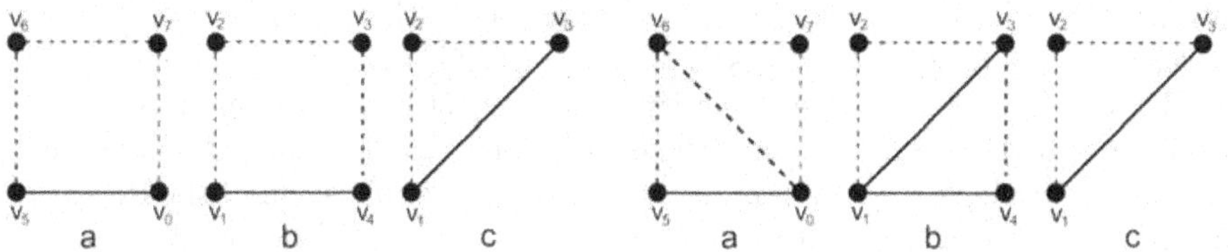

Fig. 3. The BCCs found in line 3 (left) and after lines 4 and 5 in RTC (right)

5.1 Complexity of RTC and Improvements

Lines 3-5 in RTC can all be done in time linear in the size of the graph (including the process of finding BCCs [7]). The number of iterations of the main loop in RTC is bounded by the number of solid edges in the graph. GENERATE-CONSTRAINTS, in each iteration of its main loop, either adds a new constraint or moves to the next iteration without further recursive calls. Since the number of possible constraints is bounded by three times the number of triangles in the graph, the number of recursive calls in GENERATE-CONSTRAINTS is bounded accordingly.

Improvements: To reduce complexity, we only use a global cache, which reduces the number of added constraints and the overall complexity, since we never generate the same constraint twice and stop the recursion calls earlier if we encounter a constraint that was generated in a previous BCC. The correctness proof for this improvement is rather complicated and appears in the full version of this paper [11].

We are also currently examining an algorithm that is more strict than RTC in adding constraints: RTC constrains *all* contradictory cycles, not only the simple ones, which we know is sufficient according to Theorem 2. This algorithm checks whether the cycle that is currently expanded is simple or not. This leads to certain complications that require to continue exploring the graph even when encountering a constraint that is already in the cache. This, in turn, can lead to a worst-case exponential time algorithm, that indeed removes many redundant constraints but is rarely better than RTC according to our experiments, when considering the total solving time. Whether there exists an equivalent algorithm that works in polynomial time is an open question.

6 Experimental Results

UCLID **benchmarks.** Our decision procedure is now integrated in the UCLID [5] verification system. UCLID is a tool for analyzing the correctness of models of hardware and software systems. It can be used to model and verify infinite-state systems with variables of integer, Boolean, function, and array types. The applications of UCLID explored to date include microprocessor design verification, analyzing software for security exploits, verification of a compiler through Translation Validation and verifying distributed algorithms.

UCLID reports to RTC the edges of the Equality Graph corresponding to the verified formula including their polarity, and RTC returns a list of transitivity constraints. The Boolean encoding (the generation of $\mathcal{B}$), the elimination of Uninterpreted Functions, various simplifications and the application of the Positive Equality algorithm [2], are all applied by UCLID as before. The comparison to the SPARSE method of [4], which is also implemented in this tool and fed exactly the same formula, is therefore fair.

We used all the relevant UCLID benchmarks that we are aware of (all of which happen to be unsatisfiable). We compared RTC and the SPARSE method using the two different reduction methods of Uninterpreted Functions: Ackermann's reduction [1] and Bryant's reduction [2]. This might cause a bias in our results not in our favor: the reduction of Uninterpreted Functions to Equality Logic results in Equality Graphs with specific characteristics. In [11], we explain the difference between the two reductions and why this influences our results. Here we will only say that when Bryant's reduction is used, all edges corresponding to comparisons between arguments of functions are 'double', meaning that they are both solid and dashed. In such a case RTC has no advantage at all, since every cycle is a contradictory cycle. This does not mean that when using this reduction method RTC is useless: recall that we claim for theoretical dominance over the SPARSE method. It only means that the advantage of RTC is going to be visible if there is a large enough portion of the Equality Graph that is not related to the reduction of Uninterpreted Functions, rather to the formula itself.

Table 2. RTC vs. the SPARSE method using Bryant's reduction with positive equalities (top) and Ackermann's reduction (bottom). Each benchmark set corresponds to a number of benchmark files in the same family. The column 'uclid' refers to the total running time of the decision procedure without the SAT solving time

Benchmark	#	SPARSE method				RTC			
set	files	Constraints	uclid	zChaff	total	Constraints	uclid	zChaff	total
TV	9	16719	148.48	1.08	149.56	16083	151.1	0.96	152.0
Cache.inv	4	3669	47.28	40.78	88.06	3667	54.26	38.62	92.8
Dlx1c	3	7143	18.34	2.9	21.24	7143	20.04	2.73	22.7
Elf	3	4074	27.18	2.08	29.26	4074	28.81	1.83	30.6
OOO	6	7059	26.85	46.42	73.27	7059	29.78	45.08	74.8
Pipeline	1	6	0.06	37.29	37.35	6	0.08	36.91	36.99
Total	26	38670	268.19	130.55	398.7	38032	284.07	126.13	410.2
TV	9	103158	1467.76	5.43	1473.2	9946	1385.61	0.69	1386.3
Cache.inv	4	5970	48.06	42.39	90.45	5398	54.65	44.14	98.7
Dlx1c	3	46473	368.12	11.45	379.57	11445	350.48	8.88	359.36
Elf	5	43374	473.32	28.99	502.31	24033	467.95	28.18	496.1
OOO	6	20205	78.27	29.08	107.35	16068	79.5	24.35	103.8
Pipeline	1	96	0.17	46.57	46.74	24	0.18	46.64	46.8
q2	1	3531	30.32	46.33	76.65	855	32.19	35.57	67.7
Total	29	222807	2466.02	210.24	2676.2	67769	2370.56	188.45	2559.0

The SAT-solver we used for both RTC and the SPARSE method was ZCHAFF (2004 edition) [12]. For each benchmark we show the number of generated transitivity constraints, the time it took ZCHAFF to solve the SAT formula, the run time of UCLID, which includes RTC but not ZCHAFF time and the total run time. Table 2 (top) compares the two algorithms, when UCLID uses Bryant's reduction with Positive Equality. Indeed, as expected, in this setting the advantage of RTC is hardly visible: the number of constraints is a little smaller comparing to what is generated by the SPARSE method (while the time that takes RTC and the SPARSE method to generate the transitivity constraints is almost identical, with a small advantage to the SPARSE method), and correspondingly the runtime of ZCHAFF is smaller, although not significantly. We once again emphasize that we consider this as an artifact of the specific benchmarks we found; almost all equalities in them are associated with the reduction of the Uninterpreted Functions. As future research we plan to integrate in our implementation the method of Rodeh et al. [16] which, while using Bryant's reduction, not only produces drastically smaller Equality Graphs, but also does not necessarily require a double edge for each comparison of function instances. This is expected to mostly neutralize this side effect of Bryant's reduction. Table 2 (bottom) compares the two algorithms when Ackermann's reduction is used. Here the advantage of RTC is seen clearly, both in the number of constraints and the overall solving times. In particular, note the reduction from a total of 222,807 constraints to 67,769 constraints.

Random formulas. In another set of experiments we generated hundreds of random formulas and respective Equality Graphs, while keeping the ratio of vertices to edges similar to what we found in the real benchmarks (about 1 vertex to 4 edges). Each benchmark set was built as follows. Given n vertices, we randomly generated 16 different graphs with $4n$ random edges, and the polarity of each edge was chosen randomly according to a predefined ratio p. We then generated a random CNF formula $\mathcal{B}$ with $16n$ clauses (each clause with up to 4 literals) in which each literal corresponds to one of the edges. Finally, we generated two formulas, $\mathcal{T}^S$ and $\mathcal{T}^R$ corresponding to the transitivity constraints generated by the SPARSE and RTC methods respectively, and sent the concatenation of $\mathcal{B}$ with each of these formulas to three different SAT solvers, HaifaSat [8], Siege_v4 [10] and zChaff 2004.

In the results depicted in Table 3 we chose $n = 200$ (in the UCLID benchmarks n was typically a little lower than that). Each set of experiments (corresponding to one cell in the table) corresponds to the average results over the 16 graphs, and a different ratio p, starting from 1 solid to 10 dashed, and ending with 10 solids to 1 dashed. We set the timeout to 600 seconds and added this number in case the solver timed-out. We occasionally let SIEGE run without a time limit (with both RTC and SPARSE), just in order to get some information about instances that none of solvers could solve in the given limit. All instances were satisfiable (in the low ratio of solid to dashed, namely 1:2 and 1:5 we could not solve any of the instances with any of the solvers even after several hours). The conclusions from the table are that (1) in all tested ratios RTC generates less constraints than SPARSE. As expected, this is more apparent when the ratio is further than 1:1; there are very few contradictory cycles in this kind of graphs. (2) with all three SAT solvers it took longer to solve $\mathcal{B} \wedge \mathcal{T}^S$ than to solve $\mathcal{B} \wedge \mathcal{T}^R$.

While it is quite intuitive why the instances should be easier to solve when the formula is satisfiable — the solutions space RTC defines is much larger, it is less clear when the formula is unsatisfiable. In fact, SAT solvers are frequently faster when the input formula contains extra information that further prunes the search space. Nevertheless, the experiments above on UCLID benchmarks (which, recall, are all unsatisfiable) and additional results on random formulas (see [11]) show that RTC is still better in unsatisfiable instances. We speculate that the reason for this is the following. Let T represent all transitivity constraints that

Table 3. RTC vs. the SPARSE method in random satisfiable formulas listed by the ratio of solid to dashed edges

ratio	constraints		zChaff		HaifaSat		siege_v4	
solid:dashed	Sparse	RTC	Sparse	RTC	Sparse	RTC	Sparse	RTC
1:10	373068.8	181707.8	581.1	285.6	549.2	257.4	1321.6	506.4
1:5	373068.8	255366.6	600.0	600.0	600.0	600.0	600.0	600.0
1:2	373068.8	308346.5	600.0	600.0	600.0	600.0	600.0	600.0
1:1	373068.8	257852.6	5.2	0.4	5.9	3.0	1.2	0.1
2:1	373068.8	123623.4	0.1	0.01	0.6	0.22	0.01	0.01
5:1	373068.8	493.9	0.1	0.01	0.6	0.01	0.01	0.01
10:1	373068.8	10.3	0.1	0.01	0.6	0.01	0.01	0.01
average	373068.8	161057.3	255.2	212.3	251.0	208.7	360.4	243.8

are in $\mathcal{T}^S$ but not in $\mathcal{T}^R$. Assuming $\mathcal{B}$ is satisfiable, it can be proven that $\mathcal{B} \wedge T$ is satisfiable as well [11]. This means that any proof of unsatisfiability must rely on clauses from $\mathcal{T}^R$. Apparently in practice it is rare that the SAT solver finds shortcuts through the T clauses.

7 Conclusions and Directions for Future Research

We presented a new decision procedure for Equality Logic, which builds upon and improves previous work by Bryant and Velev in [4, 3]. The new procedure generates a set of transitivity constraints that is, at least in theory, easier to solve. The experiments we conducted show that in most cases it is better in practice as well, and in any case does not make it worse, at least not in more than a few seconds. RTC does not make full use of Theorem 2, as it constrains all Contradictory Cycles rather than only the simple ones. We have another version of the algorithm, not presented in the article due to lack of space, that handles this problem, but with an exponential price. As stated before, the question whether there exists a polynomial algorithm that does the same or it is inherently a hard problem, is left open.

Acknowledgement. We are exceptionally grateful to Sanjit Seshia for the many hours he invested in hooking our procedure to UCLID, and for numerous insightful conversations we had on this and related topics.

References

1. W. Ackermann. *Solvable cases of the Decision Problem.* Studies in Logic and the Foundations of Mathematics. North-Holland, Amsterdam, 1954.
2. R. Bryant, S. German, and M. Velev. Exploiting positive equality in a logic of equality with uninterpreted functions. In *Proc. 11th Intl. Conference on Computer Aided Verification (CAV'99)*, 1999.

3. R. Bryant, S. German, and M. Velev. Processor verification using efficient reductions of the logic of uninterpreted functions to propositional logic. *ACM Transactions on Computational Logic*, 2(1):1–41, 2001.
4. R. Bryant and M. Velev. Boolean satisfiability with transitivity constraints. In *Proc. 12th Intl. Conference on Computer Aided Verification (CAV'00)*, volume 1855 of *LNCS*, 2000.
5. R. E. Bryant, S. K. Lahiri, and S. A. Seshia. Modeling and verifying systems using a logic of counter arithmetic with lambda expressions and uninterpreted functions. In *Proc. 14th Intl. Conference on Computer Aided Verification (CAV'02)*, 2002.
6. J. R. Burch and D. L. Dill. Automatic verification of pipelined microprocessor control. In *Proc. 6th Intl. Conference on Computer Aided Verification (CAV'94)*, volume 818 of *LNCS*, pages 68–80. Springer-Verlag, 1994.
7. T. Cormen, C. Leiserson, and R. Rivest. *Introduction to Algorithms*, chapter 26, page 563. MIT press, 2000.
8. R. Gershman and O. Strichman. Cost-effective hyper-resolution for preprocessing cnf formulas. In T. Walsh and F. Bacchus, editors, *Theory and Applications of Satisfiability Testing (SAT'05)*, 2005.
9. A. Goel, K. Sajid, H. Zhou, A. Aziz, and V. Singhal. BDD based procedures for a theory of equality with uninterpreted functions. In A. Hu and M. Vardi, editors, *CAV98*, volume 1427 of *LNCS*. Springer-Verlag, 1998.
10. L.Ryan. Efficient algorithms for clause-learning SAT solvers. Master's thesis, Simon Fraser University, 2004.
11. O. Meir and O. Strichman. Yet another decision procedure for equality logic (full version), 2005. ie.technion.ac.il/~ofers/cav05_full.ps.
12. M. Moskewicz, C. Madigan, Y. Zhao, L. Zhang, and S. Malik. Chaff: Engineering an efficient SAT solver. In *Proc. Design Automation Conference (DAC'01)*, 2001.
13. A. Pnueli, Y. Rodeh, O. Shtrichman, and M. Siegel. Deciding equality formulas by small-domains instantiations. In *Proc. 11th Intl. Conference on Computer Aided Verification (CAV'99)*, LNCS. Springer-Verlag, 1999.
14. A. Pnueli, Y. Rodeh, O. Strichman, and M. Siegel. The small model property: How small can it be? *Information and computation*, 178(1):279–293, Oct. 2002.
15. A. Pnueli, M. Siegel, and O. Shtrichman. Translation validation for synchronous languages. In K. Larsen, S. Skyum, and G. Winskel, editors, *ICALP'98*, volume 1443 of *LNCS*, pages 235–246. Springer-Verlag, 1998.
16. Y. Rodeh and O. Shtrichman. Finite instantiations in equivalence logic with uninterpreted functions. In *Computer Aided Verification (CAV)*, 2001.
17. R. Shostak. An algorithm for reasoning about equality. *Communications of the ACM*, 21(7):583 - 585, July 1978.

DPLL(T) with Exhaustive Theory Propagation and Its Application to Difference Logic

Robert Nieuwenhuis and Albert Oliveras*

Abstract. At CAV'04 we presented the DPLL(T) approach for satisfiability modulo theories T. It is based on a general DPLL(X) engine whose X can be instantiated with different theory solvers $Solver_T$ for conjunctions of literals.

Here we go one important step further: we require $Solver_T$ to be able to detect *all* input literals that are T-consequences of the partial model that is being explored by DPLL(X). Although at first sight this may seem too expensive, we show that for *difference logic* the benefits compensate by far the costs.

Here we describe and discuss this new version of DPLL(T), the DPLL(X) engine, and our $Solver_T$ for difference logic. The resulting very simple DPLL(T) system importantly outperforms the existing techniques for this logic. Moreover, it has very good scaling properties: especially on the larger problems it gives improvements of orders of magnitude w.r.t. the existing state-of-the-art tools.

1 Introduction

During the last years the performance of decision procedures for the satisfiability of propositional formulas has improved spectacularly. Most state-of-the-art SAT solvers [MMZ$^+$01, GN02] today are based on different variations of the Davis-Putnam-Logemann-Loveland (DPLL) procedure [DP60, DLL62].

But, in many verification applications, satisfiability problems arise for logics that are more expressive than just propositional logic. In particular, decision procedures are required for (specific classes of) ground first-order formulas with respect to theories T such as equality with uninterpreted functions (EUF), the theory of the integer/real numbers, or of arrays or lists.

Normally, for *conjunctions* of theory literals there exist well-studied decision procedures. For example, such a *theory solver* for the case where T is equality (i.e., for EUF logic) can use *congruence closure*. It runs in $O(n \log n)$ time [DST80], also in the presence of successor and predecessor functions [NO03]. Another example is *difference logic* (sometimes also called *separation logic*) over the integers or reals, where atoms take the form $a - b \leq k$, being a and b variables and k a constant. In difference logic the satisfiability of conjunctions of such literals can be decided in $O(n^3)$ time by the Bellman-Ford algorithm.

* Technical Univ. of Catalonia, Barcelona, `www.lsi.upc.es/~roberto|~oliveras`.
Partially supported by Spanish Min. of Educ. and Science through the LogicTools project (TIN2004-03382, both authors), and FPU grant AP2002-3533 (Oliveras).

K. Etessami and S.K. Rajamani (Eds.): CAV 2005, LNCS 3576, pp. 321–334, 2005.

However, it is unclear in general which is the best way to handle arbitrary Boolean or CNF formulas over theory (and propositional) literals. Typically, the problem is attacked by trying to combine the strengths of the DPLL approach for dealing with the boolean structure, with the strengths of the specialized procedures for handling conjunctions of theory literals.

One well-known possibility is the so-called *lazy approach* [ACG00, dMR02] [BDS02, FJOS03, BBA+05]. In this approach, each theory atom is simply abstracted by a distinct propositional variable, and a SAT solver is used to find a propositional model. This model is then checked against the theory by using the solver for conjunctions of literals. Theory-inconsistent models are discarded from later consideration by adding an appropriate *theory lemma* to the original formula and restarting the process. This is repeated until a model compatible with the theory is found or all possible propositional models have been explored. The main advantage of such lazy approaches is their flexibility: they can easily combine new decision procedures for different logics with new SAT solvers. Nowadays, most lazy approaches have tighter integrations in which partial propositional models are checked incrementally against the theory while they are built by the SAT solver. This increases efficiency at the expense of flexibility.

However, these lazy approaches suffer from the drawbacks of *insufficient constraint propagation* and *blind search* [dMR04]: essentially, the theory information is used only to *validate* the search a posteriori, not to *guide* it a priori.

In practice, for some theories these lazy approaches are outperformed by the so-called *eager* techniques, where the input formula is translated, in a single satisfiability-preserving step, into a propositional CNF, which is checked by a SAT solver for satisfiability. However, such eager approaches require sophisticated ad-hoc translations for each logic. For example, for EUF there exist the *per-constraint* encoding [BV02], the *small domain* encoding [PRSS99, BLS02], and several hybrid approaches [SLB03]. Similarly, for difference logic, sophisticated range-allocation approaches have been defined in order to improve the translations [TSSP04]. But, in spite of this, on many practical problems the translation process or the SAT solver run out of time or memory (see [dMR04]).

1.1 The DPLL(T) Approach of [GHN+04]

As a way to overcome the drawbacks of the lazy and eager approaches, at CAV'04 we proposed DPLL(T) [GHN+04]. It consists of a general DPLL(X) engine, whose parameter X can be instantiated with a solver (for conjunctions of literals) $Solver_T$ for a given theory T, thus producing a DPLL(T) decision procedure.

One essential aspect of DPLL(T) is that $Solver_T$ not only validates the choices made by the SAT engine (as in the lazy approaches). It also eagerly detects literals of the input CNF that are T-consequences of the current partial model, and sends them to the DPLL(X) engine for propagation. Due to this, for the EUF logic the DPLL(T) approach not only outperforms the lazy approaches, but also all eager ones, as soon as equality starts playing a significant role in the

EUF formula [GHN+04][1]. On the other hand, DPLL(T) is similar in flexibility to the lazy approaches: other logics can be dealt with by simply plugging in their theory solvers into the DPLL(X) engine, provided that these solvers conform to a minimal and simple interface.

In the DPLL(T) version of [GHN+04], $Solver_T$ is allowed to fail sometimes to detect that a certain input literal l is a T-consequence of literals $l_1, \ldots, l_n$ in the current partial model. Then, only when the DPLL(X) engine actually makes $\neg l$ true, as a decision literal, or as a unit propagated literal, and communicates this to $Solver_T$, it is detected that the partial model is no longer T-consistent. Then $Solver_T$ warns the DPLL(X) engine, who has several different ways of treating such situations. One possibility is to backjump to the level where l actually became T-entailed, and propagate it there. This mechanism alone gives one a complete DPLL(T) decision procedure. But in order to make it more efficient, it is usually better to *learn* the corresponding theory lemma $l_1 \wedge \ldots \wedge l_n \rightarrow l$. In other similar branches of the DPLL search the literal l can then be propagated earlier. Altogether, such concrete situations of non-exhaustiveness of $Solver_T$ are essentially handled as in the lazy approaches.

The reason why in [GHN+04] the approach was defined considering a possibly non-exhaustive $Solver_T$ was due to our experiments with EUF. More precisely, for *negative* equality consequences we found it expensive to detect them exhaustively, whereas all positive literals were propagated.

1.2 DPLL(T) with Exhaustive Theory Propagation

At least for difference logic, it is indeed possible to go one important step further in this idea: in this paper we describe a DPLL(T) approach where $Solver_T$ is required to detect and communicate to DPLL(X) *all* literals of the input formula that are T-consequences of the partial model that is being explored. This assumption makes the DPLL(X) engine much simpler and efficient than before, because it can propagate these literals in exactly the same way as for standard unit propagation in DPLL, and no theory lemma learning is required at all.

The DPLL(X) engine then becomes essentially a propositional SAT solver. The only difference is a small interface with $Solver_T$. DPLL(X) communicates to $Solver_T$ each time the truth value of a literal is set, and $Solver_T$ answers with the list of literals that are new T-consequences. DPLL(X) also communicates to $Solver_T$, each time a backjump takes place, how many literals of the partial interpretation have been unassigned. As in most modern DPLL systems, backjumping is guided by an *implication graph* [MSS99], but of course here some arrows in the graph correspond to theory consequences. Therefore, for building the graph, DPLL(X) also needs $Solver_T$ to provide an *Explain*(l) operation, returning, for each T-consequence l it has communicated to DPLL(X), a (preferably small) subset of the true literals that implied l. This latter requirement to our $Solver_T$ coincides with what solvers in the lazy approach must do for returning the theory lemmas.

[1] And our implementations are now again much faster than reported at CAV'04.

Due to the fact that DPLL(X) is here nothing more than a standard DPLL-based SAT solver, the approach has become again more flexible, because it is now easy to convert any new DPLL-based SAT solver into a DPLL(X) engine. Moreover, there is at least one important theory for which the exhaustiveness requirement does not make $Solver_T$ too slow: here we give extensive experimental evidence showing that for difference logic our approach outperforms all existing systems, and moreover has better scaling properties. Especially on the larger problems it gives improvements of orders of magnitude.

This paper is structured as follows. In Section 2 we give a precise formulation of DPLL(T) with exhaustive theory propagation. In Section 3 we show how our relatively simple solver for difference logic is designed in order to efficiently fulfill the requirements. Section 4 gives all experimental results, and we conclude in Section 5.

2 DPLL(T): Basic Definitions and Notations

A procedure for Satisfiability Modulo Theories (SMT) is a procedure for deciding the satisfiability of ground (in this case, CNF) formulas in the context of a background theory T. By *ground* we mean containing no variables—although possibly containing constants not in T (which can also be seen as Skolemized existential variables).

A *theory* T is a satisfiable set of closed first-order formulas. We deal with (partial Herbrand) interpretations M as sets of ground literals such that $\{A, \neg A\} \subseteq M$ for no ground atom A. A ground literal l is *true* in M if $l \in M$, is *false* in M if $\neg l \in M$, and is *undefined* otherwise. A ground clause C is true in M if $C \cap M \neq \emptyset$. It is false in M, denoted $M \models \neg C$, if all its literals are false in M. Similarly, we define in the standard way when M satisfies (is a model of) a theory T. If F and G are ground formulas, *G is a T-consequence of F* written $F \models_T G$, if $T \cup F \models G$. The decision problem that concerns us here is whether a ground formula F is *satisfiable in* a theory T, that is, whether there is a model M of $T \cup F$. Then we say that M is a T-model of F.

2.1 Abstract Transition Rules

Here we define DPLL(T) with exhaustive theory propagation by means of the *abstract DPLL* framework, introduced in [NOT05] (check this reference for details). Here a DPLL procedure is modelled by a transition relation over states. A state is either *fail* or a pair $M \parallel F$, where F is a finite set of clauses and M is a sequence of literals that is seen as a partial interpretation. Some literals l in M will be *annotated* as being *decision literals*; these are the ones added to M by the Decide rule given below, and are sometimes written l^{d}. The transition relation is defined by means of rules.

Definition 1. *The* DPLL system with exhaustive theory propagation *consists of the following transition rules:*

UnitPropagate :

$$M \parallel F, C \vee l \quad \Longrightarrow \quad M\, l \parallel F, C \vee l \quad \textbf{if} \begin{cases} M \models \neg C \\ l \text{ is undefined in } M \end{cases}$$

Decide :

$$M \parallel F \quad \Longrightarrow \quad M\, l^{\mathsf{d}} \parallel F \quad \textbf{if} \begin{cases} l \text{ or } \neg l \text{ occurs in a clause of } F \\ l \text{ is undefined in } M \end{cases}$$

Fail :

$$M \parallel F, C \quad \Longrightarrow \quad \mathit{fail} \quad \textbf{if} \begin{cases} M \models \neg C \\ M \text{ contains no decision literals} \end{cases}$$

Backjump :

$$M\, l^{\mathsf{d}}\, N \parallel F, C \quad \Longrightarrow \quad M\, l' \parallel F, C \quad \textbf{if} \begin{cases} M\, l^{\mathsf{d}}\, N \models \neg C, \text{ and there is} \\ \text{some clause } C' \vee l' \text{ s.t.:} \\ \quad F \models_T C' \vee l' \text{ and } M \models \neg C' \\ \quad l' \text{ is undefined in } M \\ \quad l' \text{ or } \neg l' \text{ occurs in } F \end{cases}$$

T-Propagate :

$$M \parallel F \quad \Longrightarrow \quad M\, l \parallel F \quad \textbf{if} \begin{cases} M \models_T l \\ l \text{ or } \neg l \text{ occurs in a clause of } F \\ l \text{ is undefined in } M \end{cases}$$

Learn :

$$M \parallel F \quad \Longrightarrow \quad M \parallel F, C \quad \textbf{if} \begin{cases} \text{all atoms of } C \text{ occur in } F \\ F \models_T C \end{cases}$$

Forget :

$$M \parallel F, C \quad \Longrightarrow \quad M \parallel F \quad \textbf{if} \; \{ F \models_T C$$

Restart :

$$M \parallel F \quad \Longrightarrow \quad \emptyset \parallel F$$

These rules express how the search state of a DPLL procedure evolves. Without T-Propagate, and replacing everywhere $\models_T$ by $\models$, they model a standard propositional DPLL procedure. Note that this is equivalent to considering T to be the empty theory: then T-Propagate never applies. The propagation and decision rules extend the current partial interpretation M with new literals, and if in some state $M \parallel F$ there is a *conflict*, i.e., a clause of F that is false in M, always either Fail applies (if there are no decision literals in M) or Backjump applies (if there is at least one decision literal in M). In the latter case, the *backjump clause*

$C' \vee l'$ can be found efficiently by constructing a *conflict graph.* Good backjump clauses allow one to return to low *decision levels*, i.e., they maximize the number of literals in N. Usually such backjump clauses are learned by the Learn rule, in order to prevent future similar conflicts. The use of Forget is to free memory by removing learned clauses that have become less active (e.g., cause less conflicts or propagations).

These first five rules terminate (independently of any strategies or priorities) and termination of the full system is easily enforced by limiting the applicability of the other three rules (e.g., if all Learn steps are immediately after Backjump steps, and Restart is done with increasing periodicity). If we say that a state is *final* if none of the first five rules applies, the following theorem is proved in a similar way to what is done in [NOT05].

Theorem 2. *Let $\Longrightarrow$ denote the transition relation of the DPLL system with exhaustive theory propagation where T-Propagate is applied eagerly, i.e., no other rule is applied if T-Propagate is applicable, and let $\Longrightarrow^*$ be its transitive closure.*

1. *$\emptyset \parallel F \Longrightarrow^*$ fail if, and only if, F is unsatisfiable in T.*
2. *If $\emptyset \parallel F \Longrightarrow^* M \parallel F'$, where $M \parallel F'$ is final, then M is a T-model of F.*

2.2 Our Particular Strategy

Of course, actual DPLL implementations may use the above rules in more restrictive ways, using particular application strategies. For example, many systems will eagerly apply UnitPropagate and minimize the application of Decide, but this is not necessary: any strategy will be adequate for Theorem 2 to hold.

We now briefly explain the particular strategy used by our DPLL(T) implementation, and the roles of the DPLL(X) engine and of $Solver_T$ in it.

For the initial setup of DPLL(T), one can consider that it is $Solver_T$ that reads the input CNF, then stores the list of all literals occurring in it, and hands it over to DPLL(X) as a purely propositional CNF. After that, DPLL(T) implements the rules as follows:

- Each time DPLL(X) communicates to $Solver_T$ that the truth value of a literal has been set, due to UnitPropagate or Decide, $Solver_T$ answers with the list of all input literals that are new T-consequences. Then, for each one of these consequences, T-Propagate is immediately applied.
- If T-Propagate is not applicable, then UnitPropagate is eagerly applied by DPLL(X) (this is implemented using the two-watched-literals scheme).
- DPLL(X) applies Fail or Backjump if, and only if, a conflict clause C is detected, i.e., a clause C that is false in M. As said, if there is some decision literal in M, then it is always Backjump that is applied. The application of Backjump is guided by an *implication graph.* Each literal of the conflict clause C is false in M because its negation l is in M, which can be due to one of three possible rules:
  - UnitPropagate: l is true because, in some clause $D \vee l$, every literal in D is the negation of some l' in M.

- T-Propagate: l has become true because it is a T-consequence of other literals l' in M.
- Decide: l has been set true by Decide.

In the cases of UnitPropagate and T-Propagate, recursively the l' are again true due to the same three possible reasons. By working backwards in this way from the literals of C, one can trace back the reasons of the conflict. A conflict graph is nothing but a representation of these reasons. By analyzing a subset of it, one can find adequate backjump clauses [MSS99]. But for building the graph, for the case of the T-Propagate implications, $Solver_T$ must be able to return the set of l' that T-entailed l. This is done by the $Explain(l)$ operation provided by $Solver_T$.
After each backjump has taken place in DPLL(X), it tells $Solver_T$ how many literals of the partial interpretation have been unassigned.

- Immediately after each Backjump application, the Learn rule is applied for learning the backjump clause.
- In our current implementation, DPLL(X) applies Restart when certain system parameters reach some limits, such as the number of conflicts or lemmas, the number of new units derived, etc.
- Forget is applied by DPLL(X) after each restart (and only then), removing at least half of the lemmas according to their activity (number of times involved in a conflict since last restart). The 500 newest lemmas are not removed.
- DPLL(X) applies Decide only if none of the other first five rules is applicable. The heuristic for chosing the decision literal is as in Berkmin [GN02]: we take an unassigned literal that occurs in an as recent as possible lemma, and in case of a draw, or if there is no such literal in the last 100 lemmas, the literal with the highest VSIDS measure is taken [MMZ+01] (where each literal has a counter increased by each participation in a conflict, and from time to time all counters are divided by a constant).

3 Design of $Solver_T$ for Difference Logic

In this section we address the problem of designing $Solver_T$ for a DPLL(T) system deciding the satisfiability of a CNF formula F in difference logic (sometimes also called separation logic). In this logic, the domain can be the integers, rationals or reals (as we will see, the problem is essentially equivalent in all three cases), and atoms are of the form $a \leq b+k$, where a and b are variables over this domain and k is a constant.

Note that, over the integers, atoms of the form $a < b+k$ can be equivalently written as $a \leq b+(k-1)$. A similar transformation exists for rationals and reals, by decreasing k by a small enough amount that depends only on the remaining literals ocurring in the input formula [Sch87]. Hence, negations can also be removed, since $\neg(a \leq b+k)$ is equivalent to $b < a-k$, as well as equalities $a = b+k$, which are equivalent to $a \leq b+k \ \wedge \ a \geq b+k$. Therefore, we will consider that all literals are of the form $a \leq b+k$.

Given a conjunction of such literals, one can build a directed weighted graph whose nodes are the variables, and with an edge $a \xrightarrow{k} b$ for each literal $a \leq b+k$. It is easy to see that, independently of the concrete arithmetic domain (i.e., integers, rationals or reals), such a conjunction is unsatisfiable if, and only if, there is a cycle in the graph with negative accumulated weight. Therefore, once the problem has all its literals of the form $a \leq b + k$, the concrete domain does not matter any more.

Despite its simplicity, difference logic has been used to express important practical problems, such as verification of timed systems, scheduling problems or the existence of paths in digital circuits with bounded delays.

3.1 Initial Setup

As said, for the initial setup of DPLL(T), it is $Solver_T$ that reads the input CNF, then stores the list of all literals occurring in it, and hands it over to DPLL(X) as a purely propositional CNF.

For efficiency reasons, it is important that in this CNF the relation between literals and their negations is made explicit. For example, if $a \leq b + 2$ and $b \leq a - 3$ occur in the input, then, since (in the integers) one is the negation of the other, they should be abstracted by a propositional variable and its negation. This can be detected by using a canonical form during this setup process. For instance, one can impose that always the smallest variable, say a, has to be at the left-hand side of the $\leq$ relation, and thus we would have $a \leq b + 2$ and $\neg(a \leq b + 2)$, and abstract them by p and $\neg p$ for some propositional variable p.

$Solver_T$ will keep a data structure recording all such canonized input literals like $a \leq b + 2$ and its abstraction variable p. Moreover, for reasons we will see below, it keeps for each variable the list of all input literals it occurs in, together with the length of this list.

3.2 DPLL(X) Sets the Truth Value of a Literal

When the truth value of a literal is set, $Solver_T$ converts the literal into the form $a \leq b + k$ and adds the corresponding edge to the aforementioned directed weighted graph. Since there is a one-to-one correspondence between edges and such literals, and between the graph and the conjunction of the literals, we will sometimes speak about literals that are (T-)consequences of the graph. Here we will write $a_0 \xrightarrow{k\,*} a_n$ if there is a path in the graph of the form

$$a_0 \xrightarrow{k_1} a_1 \xrightarrow{k_2} \dots \xrightarrow{k_{n-1}} a_{n-1} \xrightarrow{k_n} a_n$$

with $n \geq 0$ and where $k = 0 + k_1 + \dots k_n$ is called the length of this path.

Note that one can assume that DPLL(X) does not communicate to $Solver_T$ any redundant edges, since such consequences would already have been communicated by $Solver_T$ to DPLL(X). Similarly, DPLL(X) will not communicate to $Solver_T$ any edges that are inconsistent with the graph. Therefore, there will be no cycles of negative length.

Here, $Solver_T$ must return to DPLL(X) all input literals that are new consequences of the graph once the new edge has been added. Essentially, for detecting the new consequences of a new edge $a \xrightarrow{k} b$, $Solver_T$ needs to check all paths

$$a_i \xrightarrow{k_i\ *} a \xrightarrow{k} b \xrightarrow{k'_j\ *} b_j$$

and see whether there is any input literal that follows from $a_i \leq b_j+(k_i+k+k'_j)$, i.e., an input literal of the form $a_i \leq b_j + k'$, with $k' \geq k_i + k + k'_j$.

For checking all such paths from a_i to b_j that pass through the new edge from a to b, we need to be able to find all nodes a_i from which a is reachable, as well as the nodes b_j that are reachable from b. Therefore, we keep the graph in double adjacency list representation: for each node n, we keep the list of outgoing edges as well as the one of incoming edges. Then a standard single-source-shortest-path algorithm starting from a can be used for computing all a_i with their corresponding minimal k_i (and similarly for the b_j).

What worked best in our experience to finally detect all entailed literals is the following. We use a simple depth-first search, where each time a node is reached for the first time it is marked, together with the accumulated distance k, and, each time it is reached again with some k', the search stops if $k' \geq k$ (this terminates because there are no cycles of negative length).

While doing this, the visited nodes are pushed onto two stacks, one for the a_i's and another one for the b_j's, and it is also counted, for each one of those two stacks, how many input literals these a_i's (and b_j's) occur in (remember that there are precomputed lists for this, together with their lengths).

Then, if, w.l.o.g., the a_i's are the ones that occur in less input literals, we check, for each element in the list of input literals containing each a_i, whether the other constant is some of the found b_j, and whether the literal is entailed or not (this can be checked in constant time since previously all b_j have been marked).

3.3 Implementation of Explain

As said, for building the implication graph, DPLL(X) needs $Solver_T$ to provide an *Explain*(l) operation, returning, for each T-consequence l it has communicated to DPLL(X), a preferably small subset of the literals that implied l.

For implementing this, we proceed as follows. Whenever the m-th edge is added to the directed weighted graph, the edge is annotated with its associated insertion number m. In a similar fashion, when a literal l is returned as a consequence of the m-th edge, this m is recorded together with l. Now assume l is of the form $a \leq b + k$, and the explanation for l is required. Then we search a path in the graph from a to b of length at most k, using a depth-first search as before. Moreover, in this search we will not traverse any edges with insertion number greater than m. This not only improves efficiency, but it is it is also needed for not returning "too new" explanations, which may create cycles in the implication graph, see [GHN$^+$04].

4 Experimental Evaluation

Experiments have been done with all benchmarks we know of for difference logic, both real-world and hand-made ones[2]. The table below contains runtimes for five suites of benchmark families: the SAL Suite [dMR04], the MathSAT Suite (see `mathsat.itc.it`), and the DLSAT one [CAMN04] come from verification by bounded model checking of timed automated and linear hybrid systems and from the job shop scheduling problem (the `abz` family of DLSAT). The remaining two suites are hand-made. The Diamond Suite is from the problem generator of [SSB02], where problem `diamondsN` has N edges per diamond, generating between 10 and 18 diamonds (i.e., 9 problems per family), forcing unsatisfiability over the integers. The DTP Suite is from [ACGM04].

We compare with three other systems: ICS 2.0 (`ics.csl.sri.com`), MathSAT [BBA+05][3] and TSAT++ (see [ACGM04] and `ai.dist.unige.it/Tsat`, we thank Claudio Castellini for his help with this system). For the handmade problems, TSAT++ has been used in the setting recommended by the authors for these problems; for the other problems, we used the best setting we could find (as recommended to us by the authors). DPLL(T) has been used on all problems in the same standard setting, as described in this paper.

We have included ICS and not others such as CVC [BDS02], CVC-Lite [BB04], UCLID [LS04], because, according to [dMR04], ICS either dominates them or gives similar results. It has to be noted that UCLID could perhaps improve its performance by using the most recent range allocation techniques of [TSSP04], and that ICS applies a more general solver for linear arithmetic, rather than a specialized solver for difference logic as MathSAT, TSAT++ and DPLL(T) do.

On all benchmark families, DPLL(T) is always significantly better than all other systems. It is even orders of magnitude faster, especially on the larger problems, as soon as the theory becomes relevant, i.e., when in, say, at least 10 percent of the conflicts the theory properties play any role. This is the case for all problem families except lpsat and the FISCHER problems of the MathSAT Suite.

Results are in seconds and are aggregated per family of benchmarks, with times greater than 100s rounded to whole numbers. All experiments were run on a 2GHz 512MB Pentium-IV under Linux. Each benchmark was run for one hour, i.e., 3600 seconds. An annotation of the form (n t) or (n m) in a column indicates respectively that the system timed out or ran out of memory on n benchmarks. Each timeout or memory out is counted as 3600s.

---

[2] Individual results for each benchmark can be found at `www.lsi.upc.es/~oliveras`, together with all the benchmarks and an executable of our system.

[3] V3.1.0, Nov 22, 2004, see `mathsat.itc.it`, which features a new specialized solver for difference logic. We have no exhaustive results yet of the even more recent V3.1.1 of Jan 12, 2005 on all the larger problems. It appears to be slightly faster than V3.1.0 on some problems, but with results relative to DPLL(T) similar to V3.1.0. We will keep up-to-date results on `www.lsi.upc.es/~oliveras`.

Benchmark family	# Problems in family	ICS	MathSAT	TSAT++	DPLL(T)
SAL Suite:					
lpsat	20	636	185	490	135
bakery-mutex	20	39.44	17.91	9.93	0.5
fischer3-mutex	20	(7t) 27720	363	(2t) 14252	259
fischer6-mutex	20	(10t) 39700	(7t) 27105	(11t) 40705	4665
fischer9-mutex	20	(12t) 43269	(9t) 33380	(13t) 48631	(2t) 14408
MathSAT Suite:					
FISCHER9	10	187	187	172	86.68
FISCHER10	11	1162	962	3334	380
FISCHER11	12	(1t) 5643	4037	(2t) 9981	3091
FISCHER12	13	(3t) 11100	(2t) 8357	(4t) 14637	(1t) 6479
FISCHER13	14	(4t) 14932	(3t) 12301	(5t) 18320	(2t) 10073
FISCHER14	15	(5t) 18710	(4t) 15717	(6t) 218891	(3t) 14253
PO4	11	14.57	33.98	28.01	2.68
PO5	13	(10m) 36004	269	220	23.8
DLSAT Suite:					
abz	12	(2t) 11901	218	49.02	5.29
ba-max	19	770	211	233	14.55
Diamond Suite:					
diamonds4	9	(2m) 11869	9018	501	312
diamonds6	9	(2m) 9054	2926	742	193
diamonds10	9	(2m) 11574	(1t) 4249	1567	207
diamonds20	9	(4m, 1t) 19286	5050	(1t) 6073	219
DTP Suite:					
DTP-175	20	(8t) 45060	37.63	35.69	0.77
DTP-210	20	(20t) 72000	50.74	112	5.27
DTP-240	20	(20t) 72000	36.53	191	6.86

4.1 Scaling Properties

To illustrate the scaling properties of our approach, below we include two graphical representations of the behaviour of MathSAT and DPLL(T) on the fischer6-mutex family, which is a typical real-world suite for which large benchmarks exist where the theory plays a relevant role (the other such suites give similar graphics).

The diagram on the left below compares both systems on the problems of size between 10 and 20 on a normal time scale of up to 100,000 seconds. MathSAT did not finish any of the problems 18, 19 and 20 in 210,000 seconds, whereas DPLL(T) (almost invisible) takes 603, 1108 and 1778 seconds on them, respectively. The diagram on the right expresses the same results on a logarithmic scale, in order to get a better impression of the asymptotic behaviour of DPLL(T).

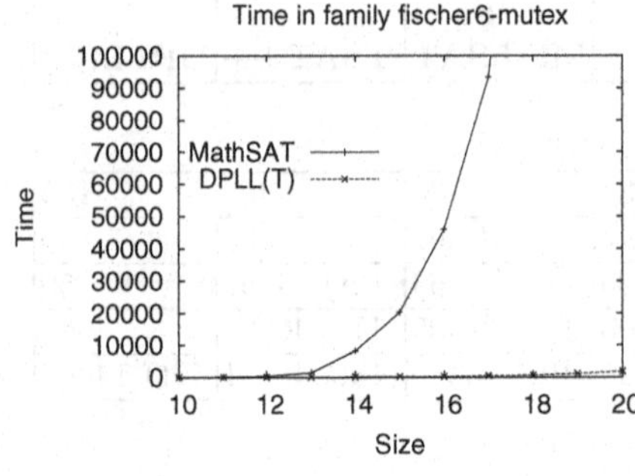

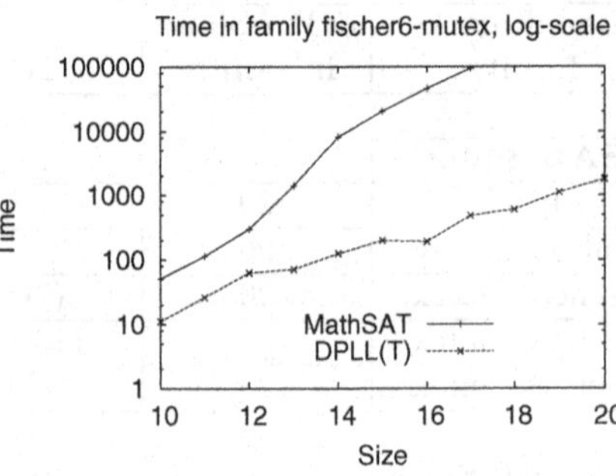

5 Conclusions and Further Work

We have shown that it is possible to deal with Satisfiability Modulo Theories (SMT) in a clean and modular way, even if the information for the theory under consideration is used exhaustively for propagating implied literals. Although at first sight one might get the impression that this may be too expensive, we have shown that, at least for difference logic, this is not the case.

Future work concerns other theories for which exhaustive theory propagation may be useful, and others where a hybrid approach has to be applied, i.e., where some classes of unit T-consequences are assumed to be detected and other are handled more lazily.

References

[ACG00] A. Armando, C. Castellini, and E. Giunchiglia. SAT-based procedures for temporal reasoning. In *Procs 5th European Conf. on Planning (Durham, UK)*, LNCS 1809 pages 97–108. Springer, 2000.

[ACGM04] A. Armando, C. Castellini, E. Giunchiglia, and M. Maratea. A SAT-based Decision Procedure for the Boolean Combination of Difference Constraints. In *7th Int. Conf. Theory and Appl. of Sat Testing(SAT 2004)*. LNCS, 2004.

[BB04] C. Barrett and S. Berezin. CVC lite: A new implementation of the cooperating validity checker. In *16th Int. Conf. Computer Aided Verification, CAV'04* LNCS 3114, pages 515–518. Springer, 2004.

[BBA+05] M. Bozzano, R. Bruttomesso, A. Cimatti, T. Junttila, P .v. Rossum, S. Schulz, and R. Sebastiani. An incremental and layered procedure for the satisfiability of linear arithmetic logic. In *TACAS'05*, 2005.

[BDS02] C. Barrett, D. Dill, and A. Stump. Checking satisfiability of first-order formulas by incremental translation into sat. In *Procs. 14th Intl. Conf. on Computer Aided Verification (CAV)*, LNCS 2404, 2002.

[BLS02] R. Bryant, S. Lahiri, and S. Seshia. Modeling and verifying systems using a logic of counter arithmetic with lambda expressions and uninterpreted functions. In *Procs. 14th Intl. Conference on Computer Aided Verification (CAV)*, LNCS 2404, 2002.

[BV02] R. Bryant and M. Velev. Boolean satisfiability with transitivity constraints. *ACM Trans. Computational Logic*, 3(4):604–627, 2002.

[CAMN04] S. Cotton, E. Asarin, O. Maler, and P. Niebert. Some progress in satisfiability checking for difference logic. In *FORMATS 2004 and FTRTFT 2004*, LNCS 3253, pages 263–276, 2004.

[DLL62] M. Davis, G. Logemann, and D .Loveland. A machine program for theorem-proving. *Comm. of the ACM*, 5(7):394–397, 1962.

[dMR02] L. de Moura and H. Rueß. Lemmas on demand for satisfiability solvers. In *Procs. 5th Int. Symp. on the Theory and Applications of Satisfiability Testing, SAT'02*, pages 244–251, 2002.

[dMR04] L. de Moura and H. Ruess. An experimental evaluation of ground decision procedures. In *16th Int. Conf. on Computer Aided Verification, CAV'04*, LNCS 3114, pages 162–174. Springer, 2004.

[DP60] M. Davis and H. Putnam. A computing procedure for quantification theory. *Journal of the ACM*, 7:201–215, 1960.

[DST80] P. Downey, R. Sethi, and R. Tarjan. Variations on the common subexpressions problem. *Journal of the ACM*, 27(4):758–771, 1980.

[FJOS03] C. Flanagan, R. Joshi, X. Ou, and J. Saxe. Theorem proving using lazy proof explanation. In *Procs. 15th Int. Conf. on Computer Aided Verification (CAV)*, LNCS 2725, 2003.

[GHN+04] H. Ganzinger, G. Hagen, R. Nieuwenhuis, A. Oliveras, and C. Tinelli. DPLL(T): Fast decision procedures. In *16th Int. Conf. on Computer Aided Verification, CAV'04*, LNCS 3114, pp 175–188, 2004.

[GN02] E. Goldberg and Y. Novikov. BerkMin: A fast and robust SAT-solver. In *Design, Automation, and Test in Europe (DATE '02)*, pages 142–149, 2002.

[LS04] S. Lahiri and S. Seshia. The UCLID Decision Procedure. In *Computer Aided Verification, 16th International Conference, (CAV'04)*, Lecture Notes in Computer Science, pages 475–478. Springer, 2004.

[MMZ+01] M. Moskewicz, C. Madigan, Y. Zhao, L. Zhang, and S. Malik. Chaff: Engineering an Efficient SAT Solver. In *Proc. 38th Design Automation Conference (DAC'01)*, 2001.

[MSS99] J. Marques-Silva and K. Sakallah. GRASP: A search algorithm for propositional satisfiability. *IEEE Trans. Comput.*, 48(5):506–521, 1999.

[NO03] Robert Nieuwenhuis and Albert Oliveras. Congruence closure with integer offsets. In M Vardi and A Voronkov, eds, *10h Int. Conf. Logic for Programming, Artif. Intell. and Reasoning (LPAR)*, LNAI 2850, pp 78–90, 2003.

[NOT05] R. Nieuwenhuis, A. Oliveras, and C. Tinelli. Abstract DPLL and Abstract DPLL Modulo Theories. In *11h Int. Conf. Logic for Programming, Artif. Intell. and Reasoning (LPAR)*, LNAI 3452, 2005.

[PRSS99] A. Pnueli, Y. Rodeh, O. Shtrichman, and M. Siegel. Deciding equality formulas by small domains instantiations. In *Procs. 11th Int. Conf. on Computer Aided Verification (CAV)*, LNCS 1633, pages 455–469, 1999.

[Sch87] A. Schrijver. *Theory of Linear and Integer Programming.* John Wiley and Sons, New York, 1987.

[SLB03] S. Seshia, S. Lahiri, and R. Bryant. A hybrid SAT-based decision procedure for separation logic with uninterpreted functions. In *Procs. 40th Design Automation Conference (DAC)*, pages 425–430, 2003.

[SSB02] O. Strichman, S. Seshia, and R. Bryant. Deciding separation formulas with SAT. In *Procs. 14th Intl. Conference on Computer Aided Verification (CAV)*, LNCS 2404, pages 209–222, 2002.

[TSSP04] M. Talupur, N. Sinha, O. Strichman, and A. Pnueli. Range allocation for separation logic. In *16th Int. Conf. on Computer Aided Verification, CAV'04*, LNCS 3114, pp 148–161, 2004.

Efficient Satisfiability Modulo Theories via Delayed Theory Combination*

Marco Bozzano[1], Roberto Bruttomesso[1], Alessandro Cimatti[1], Tommi Junttila[2], Silvio Ranise[3], Peter van Rossum[4], and Roberto Sebastiani[5]

[1] ITC-IRST, Povo, Trento, Italy
{bozzano, bruttomesso, cimatti}@itc.it
[2] Helsinki University of Technology, Finland
Tommi.Junttila@tkk.fi
[3] LORIA and INRIA-Lorraine, Villers les Nancy, France
Silvio.Ranise@loria.fr
[4] Radboud University Nijmegen, The Netherlands
petervr@sci.kun.nl
[5] DIT, Università di Trento, Italy
roberto.sebastiani@unitn.it

Abstract. The problem of deciding the satisfiability of a quantifier-free formula with respect to a background theory, also known as Satisfiability Modulo Theories (*SMT*), is gaining increasing relevance in verification: representation capabilities beyond propositional logic allow for a natural modeling of real-world problems (e.g., pipeline and RTL circuits verification, proof obligations in software systems).

In this paper, we focus on the case where the background theory is the combination $T_1 \cup T_2$ of two simpler theories. Many *SMT* procedures combine a boolean model enumeration with a decision procedure for $T_1 \cup T_2$, where conjunctions of literals can be decided by an integration schema such as Nelson-Oppen, via a structured exchange of interface formulae (e.g., equalities in the case of convex theories, disjunctions of equalities otherwise).

We propose a new approach for $SMT(T_1 \cup T_2)$, called Delayed Theory Combination, which does not require a decision procedure for $T_1 \cup T_2$, but only individual decision procedures for T_1 and T_2, which are directly integrated into the boolean model enumerator. This approach is much simpler and natural, allows each of the solvers to be implemented and optimized without taking into account the others, and it nicely encompasses the case of non-convex theories. We show the effectiveness of the approach by a thorough experimental comparison.

1 Introduction

Many practical verification problems can be expressed as satisfiability problems in decidable fragments of first-order logic. In fact, representation capabilities beyond propo-

* This work has been partly supported by ISAAC, an European sponsored project, contract no. AST3-CT-2003-501848, by ORCHID, a project sponsored by Provincia Autonoma di Trento, and by a grant from Intel Corporation. The work of T. Junttila has also been supported by the Academy of Finland, projects 53695 and 211025.

K. Etessami and S.K. Rajamani (Eds.): CAV 2005, LNCS 3576, pp. 335–349, 2005.

sitional logic enable a natural modeling of real-world problems (e.g., pipeline and RTL circuits verification, proof obligations in software systems).

The field has been devoted a lot of interest and has recently acquired the name *Satisfiability Modulo Theories* (*SMT*). *SMT* can be seen as an extended form of propositional satisfiability, where propositions are constraints in a specific theory. A prominent approach which underlies several systems (e.g., MATHSAT [16,6], DLSAT [7], DPLL(T) [13], TSAT++ [28,2], ICS [14,11], CVCLITE [8,4], haRVey [9]), is based on extensions of propositional SAT technology: a SAT engine is modified to enumerate boolean assignments, and integrated with a decision procedure for the theory.

The above schema, which we denote as Bool+T, is also followed when the background theory T turns out to be the combination $T_1 \cup T_2$ of two simpler theories — for instance, Equality and Uninterpreted Functions ($\mathcal{E}$) and Linear Arithmetic ($\mathcal{LA}$). The decision procedure to decide a combination of literals in T is typically based on an integration schema such as Nelson-Oppen (NO) [18] (we denote the resulting schema as Bool+no(T_1, T_2)), starting from decision procedures for each T_i, and combining them by means of a structured exchange of interface formulae.

In this paper, we propose a new approach for the $SMT(T_1 \cup T_2)$ problem, called *Delayed Theory Combination*. The main idea is to avoid the integration schema between T_1 and T_2, and tighten the connection between each T_i and the boolean level. While the truth assignment is being constructed, it is checked for consistency with respect to each theory in isolation. This can be seen as constructing two (possibly inconsistent) partial models for the original formula; the "merging" of the two partial models is enforced, on demand, since the solver is requested to find a complete assignment to the *interface equalities*.

We argue that this approach, denoted as Bool+$T_1 + T_2$, has several advantages over Bool+no(T_1, T_2). First, the whole framework is much simpler to analyze and implement; each of the solvers can be implemented and optimized without taking into account the others; for instance, when the problem falls within one T_i, the solver behaves exactly as Bool+T_i. Second, the approach does not rely on the solvers being deduction-complete. This enables us to explore the trade-off between which deduction is beneficial for efficiency and which is in fact hampering the search – or too difficult to implement. Third, the framework nicely encompasses the case of non-convex theories: in the no(T_1, T_2) case, a backtrack search is used to take care of the disjunctions that need to be managed. We experimentally show that our approach is competitive and often superior to the other state of the art approaches based on Nelson-Oppen integration.

This paper is structured as follows. We first present some background and overview the Bool+T procedure in Sect. 2. Then we discuss the $T_1 \cup T_2$ case by means of the Nelson-Oppen combination schema in Sect. 3. We present our approach Bool+T_1+T_2 in Sect. 4. Then we describe the implementation of Bool+T_1+T_2 for the case of $\mathcal{LA} \cup \mathcal{E}$ in Sect. 5 and some related work in Sect. 6. We discuss the experimental evaluation in Sect. 7. Finally, we draw some conclusions and discuss some future work in Sect. 8.

2 Satisfiability Modulo Theories

Satisfiability Modulo a Theory is the problem of checking the satisfiability of a quantifier-free (or ground) first-order formula with respect to a given first-order theory

T. Theories of interest are, e.g., the theory of difference logic $\mathcal{DL}$, where constraints have the form $x - y \leq c$; the theory $\mathcal{E}$ of equality and uninterpreted functions, whose signature contains a finite number of uninterpreted function and constant symbols, and such that the equality symbol $=$ is interpreted as the equality relation; the quantifier-free fragment of Linear Arithmetic over the rationals (or, equivalently, over the reals), hereafter denoted with $\mathcal{LA}(Rat)$; the quantifier-free fragment of Linear Arithmetic over the integers, hereafter denoted with $\mathcal{LA}(Int)$.

Figure 1 presents Bool+T, a (much simplified) decision procedure for $SMT(T)$. The function *Atoms* takes a ground formula ϕ and returns the set of atoms which occurs in ϕ. We use the notation ϕ^p to denote the *propositional abstraction* of ϕ, which is formed by the function *fol2prop* that maps propositional variables to themselves, ground atoms into fresh propositional variables, and is homomorphic w.r.t. boolean operators and set inclusion. The function *prop2fol* is the inverse of *fol2prop*. We use β^p to denote a propositional assignment, i.e. a conjunction (a set) of propositional literals. The idea underlying the algorithm is that the truth assignments for the propositional abstraction of ϕ are enumerated and checked for satisfiability in T. The procedure either concludes satisfiability if one such model is found, or returns with failure otherwise. The function *pick_total_assign* returns a total assignment to the propositional variables in ϕ^p, that is, it assigns a truth value to all variables in $\mathcal{A}^p$. The function T-*satisfiable*(β) detects if the set of conjuncts β is T-satisfiable: if so, it returns (sat, $\emptyset$); otherwise, it returns (unsat, π), where $\pi \subseteq \beta$ is a T-unsatisfiable set, called a *theory conflict set*. We call the negation of a conflict set, a *conflict clause*.

The algorithm is a coarse abstraction of the ones underlying TSAT++, MathSAT, DLSAT, DPLL(T), CVCLite, haRVey, and ICS. The test for satisfiability and the extraction of the corresponding truth assignment are kept separate in this description only for the sake of simplicity. In practice, enumeration is carried out on *partial assignments*, by means of efficient boolean reasoning techniques, typically by means of a DPLL-algorithm (but see also [9] for an approach based on BDDs). Additional improvements are *early pruning*, i.e., partial assignments which are not T-*satisfiable* are pruned (since no refinement can be T-*satisfiable*); theory conflicts discovered by the theory solver can be passed as conflict clauses to the boolean solver, and trigger non-chronological backjumping; such conflict clauses can also be *learned*, and induce the

```
function Bool+T (φ: quantifier-free formula)
    A^p ⟵ fol2prop(Atoms(φ))
    φ^p ⟵ fol2prop(φ)
    while Bool-satisfiable(φ^p) do
        β^p ⟵ pick_total_assign(A^p, φ^p)
        (ρ, π) ⟵ T-satisfiable(prop2fol(β^p))
        if ρ = sat then return sat
        φ^p ⟵ φ^p ∧ ¬fol2prop(π)
    end while
    return unsat
end function
```

Fig. 1. A simplified view of enumeration-based T-satisfiability procedure: Bool+T

discovery of more compact learned clauses; finally, *theory deduction* can be used to reduce the search space by explicitly returning truth values for unassigned literals, as well as constructing/learning implications. The interested reader is pointed to [6] for details and further references.

3 $SMT(T_1 \cup T_2)$ via Nelson-Oppen Integration

In many practical applications of $SMT(T)$, the background theory is a combination of two theories T_1 and T_2. For instance, $\mathcal{DL}$ and $\mathcal{E}$; $\mathcal{LA}(Rat)$ and $\mathcal{E}$; $\mathcal{LA}(Int)$ and $\mathcal{E}$; $\mathcal{LA}(Int)$, $\mathcal{E}$ and the theory of arrays. Many recent approaches to $SMT(T_1 \cup T_2)$ (e.g. CVCLITE, ICS) rely on the adaptation of the Bool+T schema, by instantiating T-*satisfiable* with some decision procedure for the satisfiability of $T_1 \cup T_2$, typically based on the Nelson-Oppen integration schema (see Figure 2, left). In the following, we briefly recall the most relevant issues pertaining to the combination of decision procedures. (For a more complete discussion we refer the reader to [20].) [1]

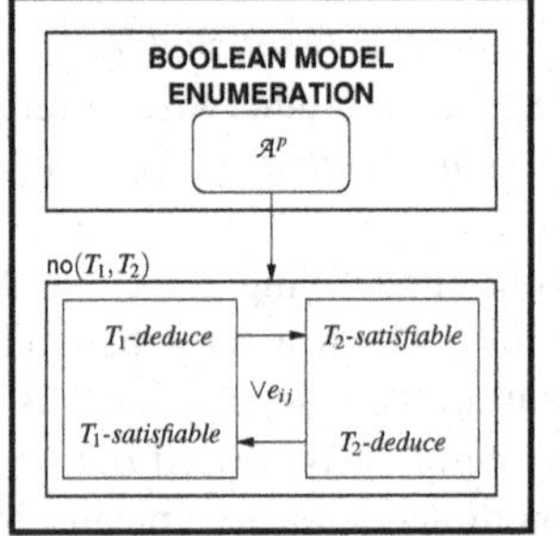

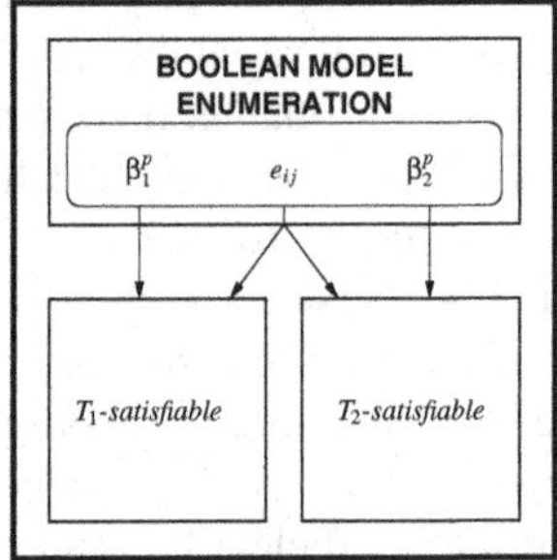

Fig. 2. The different schemas for $SMT(T_1 \cup T_2)$

Let Σ_1 and Σ_2 be two disjoint signatures, and let T_i be a Σ_i-theory for $i = 1,2$. A $\Sigma_1 \cup \Sigma_2$-term t is an *i-term* if it is a variable or it has the form $f(t_1, ..., t_n)$, where f is in Σ_i and $n \geq 0$ (notice that a variable is both a 1-term and a 2-term). A non-variable subterm s of an i-term is *alien* if s is a j-term, and all superterms of s are i-terms, where $i, j \in \{1,2\}$ and $i \neq j$. An i-term is *i-pure* if it does not contain alien subterms. A literal is i-pure if it contains only i-pure terms. A formula is said to be *pure* iff every literal occurring in the formula is i-pure for some $i \in \{1,2\}$. The process of *purification* maps any formula ϕ into an equisatisfiable pure formula ϕ' by introducing new variables and definitions to rename non-pure/alien terms. Especially, if ϕ is a conjunction of literals, then ϕ' can be written as $\phi_1 \wedge \phi_2$ s.t. each ϕ_i is a conjunction of i-pure literals. In the following, we call

[1] Notice that the Nelson-Oppen schema of Figure 2, left, is a simplified one. In actual implementations (e.g., CVCLITE, ICS) more than two theories can be handled at a time, and the interface equalities are exchanged between theory solvers by exploiting sophisticated techniques (see e.g. [10] for details).

interface variables of a pure formula ϕ' the set of all variables $c_1, \ldots, c_n \in Var(\phi')$ that occur in both 1-pure and 2-pure literals in ϕ', and we define e_{ij} as the *interface equality* $c_i = c_j$.

A Σ-theory T is called *stably-infinite* iff for any T-satisfiable Σ-formula ϕ, there exists a model of T whose domain is infinite and which satisfies ϕ. A *Nelson-Oppen* theory is a stably-infinite theory which admits a satisfiability algorithm. E.g., $\mathcal{E}$, $\mathcal{DL}$, $\mathcal{LA}(Rat)$, and $\mathcal{LA}(Int)$ are all Nelson-Oppen theories. A conjunction Γ of Σ-literals is *convex* in a Σ-theory T iff for any disjunction $\bigvee_{i=1}^{n} x_i = y_i$ (where x_i, y_i are variables) we have that $T \cup \Gamma \models \bigvee_{i=1}^{n} x_i = y_i$ iff $T \cup \Gamma \models x_i = y_i$ for some $i \in \{1, ..., n\}$. A Σ-theory T is *convex* iff all the conjunctions of Σ-literals are convex. Note that, while $\mathcal{E}$ and $\mathcal{LA}(Rat)$ are convex theories, $\mathcal{LA}(Int)$ is not: e.g., given the variables x, x_1, x_2, the set $\{x_1 = 1, x_2 = 2, x_1 \leq x, x \leq x_2\}$ entails $x = x_1 \vee x = x_2$ but neither $x = x_1$ nor $x = x_2$.

Given two signature-disjoint Nelson-Oppen theories T_1 and T_2, the Nelson-Oppen combination schema [18], in the following referred to as $\mathsf{no}(T_1, T_2)$, allows one to solve the satisfiability problem for $T_1 \cup T_2$ (i.e. the problem of checking the $T_1 \cup T_2$-satisfiability of conjunctions of $\Sigma_1 \cup \Sigma_2$-literals) by using the satisfiability procedures for T_1 and T_2. The procedure is basically a structured interchange of information inferred from either theory and propagated to the other, until convergence is reached. The schema requires the exchange of information, the kind of which depends on the *convexity* of the involved theories. In the case of convex theories, the two solvers communicate to each other interface equalities. In the case of non-convex theories, the $\mathsf{no}(T_1, T_2)$ schema becomes more complicated, because the two solvers need to exchange *arbitrary disjunctions of interface equalities*, which have to be managed within the decision procedure by means of case splitting and of *backtrack* search.

We notice that the ability to carry out deductions is often crucial for efficiency: each solver must be able to derive the (disjunctions of) interface equalities e_{ij} entailed by its current facts ϕ. When this capability is not available, it can be replaced by "guessing" followed by a satisfiability check with respect to T_i.

Example 1. Let T_1 be $\mathcal{E}$ and T_2 be $\mathcal{LA}(Int)$, and consider the following *SMT* problem for the purified formula, $V = \{x, w_1, w_2\}$ being the set of interface variables:

$$\phi = \neg(f(x) = f(w_1)) \wedge (A \leftrightarrow \neg(f(x) = f(w_2))) \wedge 1 \leq x \wedge x \leq 2 \wedge w_1 = 1 \wedge w_2 = 2.$$

Suppose we first assign the boolean variable A to true (branch 1), so that ϕ simplifies into a conjunction of literals $\phi_1 \wedge \phi_2$, s.t., $\phi_1 = \neg(f(x) = f(w_1)) \wedge \neg(f(x) = f(w_2))$ and $\phi_2 = 1 \leq x \wedge x \leq 2 \wedge w_1 = 1 \wedge w_2 = 2$. Then the $\mathsf{no}(T_1, T_2)$ schema runs as follows:

1. The literals of ϕ_1 are processed, T_1-satisfiability is reported, and no equality is derived.
2. The literals of ϕ_2 are processed, T_2-satisfiability is reported, and the disjunction $x = w_1 \vee x = w_2$ is returned.
3. The disjunction induces a case-splitting; first, $x = w_1$ is passed to the solver for T_1:
   (a) $\phi_1 \wedge x = w_1$ is T_1-unsatisfiable, since $\neg(f(x) = f(w_1)) \wedge x = w_1$ is;
   then, $x = w_2$ is passed to the satisfiability procedure for T_1:
   (b) $\phi_1 \wedge x = w_2$ is T_1-unsatisfiable, since $\neg(f(x) = f(w_2)) \wedge x = w_2$ is.
   The T_1-solver may be able to return the conflict clauses C_1: $\neg(x = w_1) \vee f(x) = f(w_1)$ and C_2: $\neg(x = w_2) \vee f(x) = f(w_2)$ to the boolean solver, which learns them to drive future search.
4. $\mathsf{no}(T_1, T_2)$ returns the $T_1 \cup T_2$-unsatisfiability of $\phi_1 \wedge \phi_2$, and the procedure backtracks.

Then we assign A to false (branch 2), so that ϕ_1 becomes $\neg(f(x) = f(w_1)) \wedge (f(x) = f(w_2))$. Hence the $\mathsf{no}(T_1, T_2)$ combination schema reruns steps 1, 2, and 3(a) as in branch 1. (Notice that, if the conflict clause C_1 has been generated, then $\neg(x = w_1)$ is added to branch 2 by the boolean solver, so that step 2 generates only $x = w_2$, and hence step 3(a) is skipped.) Then, $x = w_2$ is passed to the satisfiability procedure for T_1, which states that $\phi_1 \wedge x = w_2$ is T_1-satisfiable, and that no new interface equalities are deducible. Hence $\phi_1 \wedge \phi_2$ in branch 2 is $T_1 \cup T_2$-satisfiable, so that the original formula ϕ is $T_1 \cup T_2$-satisfiable.

4 $SMT(T_1 \cup T_2)$ via Delayed Theory Combination

We propose a new approach to $SMT(T_1 \cup T_2)$, which does not require the direct combination of decision procedures for T_1 and T_2. The Boolean solver Bool is coupled with a satisfiability procedure T_i*-satisfiable* for each T_i (see Fig. 2, right), and each of the theory solvers works in isolation, without direct exchange of information. Their mutual consistency is ensured by conjoining the purified formula with a suitable formula, containing only the interface equalities e_{ij}, even if these do not occur in the original problem; such a formula encodes all possible equivalence relations over the interface variables in the purified formula. The enumeration of assignments includes not only the atoms in the formula, but also the interface atoms of the form e_{ij}. Both theory solvers receive, from the boolean level, the same truth assignment for e_{ij}: under such conditions, the two "partial" models found by each decision procedure can be merged into a model for the input formula. We call the approach *Delayed Theory Combination* (DTC): the synchronization between the theory reasoners is delayed until the e_{ij}'s are associated a value. We denote this schema as Bool$+T_1+T_2$.

function Bool$+T_1+T_2$ (ϕ_i: *quantifier-free formula*)
1 $\phi \longleftarrow purify(\phi_i)$
2 $\mathcal{A}^p \longleftarrow fol2prop(Atoms(\phi) \cup E(interface\_vars(\phi)))$
3 $\phi^p \longleftarrow fol2prop(\phi)$
4 **while** Bool-*satisfiable* (ϕ^p) **do**
5 $\quad \beta_1^p \wedge \beta_2^p \wedge \beta_e^p = \beta^p \longleftarrow pick\_total\_assign(\mathcal{A}^p, \phi^p)$
6 $\quad (\rho_1, \pi_1) \longleftarrow T_1\text{-}satisfiable\ (prop2fol(\beta_1^p \wedge \beta_e^p))$
7 $\quad (\rho_2, \pi_2) \longleftarrow T_2\text{-}satisfiable\ (prop2fol(\beta_2^p \wedge \beta_e^p))$
8 $\quad$ **if** $(\rho_1 = \mathsf{sat} \wedge \rho_2 = \mathsf{sat})$ **then return** sat **else**
9 $\qquad$ **if** $\rho_1 = \mathsf{unsat}$ **then** $\phi^p \longleftarrow \phi^p \wedge \neg fol2prop(\pi_1)$
10 $\qquad$ **if** $\rho_2 = \mathsf{unsat}$ **then** $\phi^p \longleftarrow \phi^p \wedge \neg fol2prop(\pi_2)$
11 **end while**
12 **return** unsat
end function

Fig. 3. A simplified view of the Delayed Theory Combination procedure for $SMT(T_1 \cup T_2)$

A simplified view of the algorithm is presented in Fig. 3. Initially (lines 1–3), the formula is purified, the interface variables c_i are identified by *interface_vars*, the interface equalities e_{ij} are created by E and added to the set of propositional symbols $\mathcal{A}^p$, and the propositional abstraction ϕ^p of ϕ is created. Then, the main loop is entered (lines 4–11): while ϕ^p is propositionally satisfiable (line 4), we select a satisfying truth assignment β^p (line 5). We remark that truth values are associated not only to atoms in ϕ, but also to the e_{ij} atoms, even though they do not occur in ϕ. β^p is then (implicitly) separated into $\beta_1^p \wedge \beta_e^p \wedge \beta_2^p$, where *prop2fol*$(\beta_i^p)$ is a set of i-pure literals and *prop2fol*(β_e^p) is a set of e_{ij}-literals. The relevant part of β^p are checked for consistency against each theory (lines 6–7); T_i*-satisfiable* (β) returns a pair (ρ_i, π_i), where ρ_i is unsat iff β is unsatisfiable in T_i, and sat otherwise. If both calls to T_i*-satisfiable* return sat, then the formula is satisfiable. Otherwise, when ρ_i is unsat, then π_i is a theory conflict set, i.e. $\pi_i \subseteq \beta$ and π_i is T_i-unsatisfiable. Then, ϕ^p is strengthened to exclude truth assignments which may fail in the same way (line 9–10), and the loop is resumed. Unsatisfiability is returned (line 12) when the loop is exited without having found a model.

To see why Bool+T_1+T_2 is a decision procedure for $SMT(T_1 \cup T_2)$, let us first consider the case where ϕ is a conjunction of literals. In this case, we claim that the correctness and completeness of Bool+T_1+T_2 reduces to that of a nondeterministic version of Nelson-Oppen combination schema (see e.g. [27]). The traditional, deterministic Nelson-Oppen schema relies on the exchange of entailed interface equalities, i.e. discovering that e_{ij} is entailed by the set of literals ϕ modulo the theory T_i. In the non-deterministic case, the same deduction is simulated by "guessing" that e_{ij} holds, and then checking whether $\phi \wedge \neg e_{ij}$ is T_i-unsatisfiable. Similar reasoning applies in the dual case where we "guess" that e_{ij} is false. In Bool+T_1+T_2, the selection of the truth assignment on line 5 corresponds to guessing a truth value for each of the e_{ij}, while the calls to T_i*-satisfiable* of lines 6 and 7 check the consistency of this guess with respect to each T_i. According to [27], $T_1 \cup T_2$-satisfiability can be concluded when both checks return sat. Otherwise, another guess should be attempted: this is carried out by strengthening the formula with the conflict clause (lines 9–10), and selecting a different total assignment to the e_{ij}. This result can be generalized to the case when ϕ is an arbitrary formula. We consider that ϕ is satisfiable iff there exists a satisfying assignment to its literals, which is also $T_1 \cup T_2$-satisfiable. It is not difficult to see that the set of assignments enumerated by the algorithm is the same set obtained by enumerating the assignments of Atoms(ϕ), and then extending it with a complete assignment over the e_{ij}.

For lack of space, the algorithm is described in Fig. 3 at a high level of abstraction. In practice, enumeration is carried out by means of a DPLL-based SAT engine, and all the optimizations discussed for Bool+T can be retained. For a thorough discussion of these issues, we refer the reader to an extended version of this paper [5]. Here, we only emphasize the role of theory deduction, where a call to T_i*-satisfiable*, when satisfiable, can return in π_i a set of theory deductions (i.e. theory-justified implications, which may in turn force truth values on unassigned literals, thus further constraining the boolean search space).

Example 2. Consider the formula and the situation of Example 1. As before, we first assign A to true (branch 1), so that $\neg(f(x) = f(w_2))$. We suppose that the SAT solver branches, in order, on $w_1 = w_2$, $x = w_1$, $x = w_2$, assigning them the true value first.

1. Choosing $w_1 = w_2$ causes a T_2-inconsistency be revealed by early-pruning calls to the theory solvers, so that the conflict clause C_3: $\neg(w_1 = 1) \vee \neg(w_2 = 2) \vee \neg(w_1 = w_2)$ is learned, and the SAT solvers backtracks to $\neg(w_1 = w_2)$, which does not cause inconsistency.

2. Similarly, choosing $x = w_1$ causes a T_1-inconsistency, the conflict clause C_1 of example 1 is learned, and the SAT solvers backtracks to $\neg(x = w_1)$, which does not cause inconsistency.
3. Similarly, choosing $x = w_2$ causes a T_1-inconsistency, the conflict clause C_2 of example 1 is learned, and the SAT solvers backtracks to $\neg(x = w_2)$.
4. $\neg(x = w_1)$ and $\neg(x = w_2)$ cause a T_2-inconsistency, so that branch 1 is closed.

Then we assign A to false (branch 2), so that $f(x) = f(w_2)$. Hence $\neg(x = w_1)$ and $\neg(w_1 = w_2)$ are immediately assigned by unit-propagation on C_1 and C_3. Thus, after splitting on $x = w_2$ we have a satisfying assignment.

Notice that (i) when a *partial* assignment on e_{ij}'s is found unsatisfiable under some T_i (e.g., $w_1 = w_2$ in branch 1, step 1), then all its *total* extensions are T_i-unsatisfiable, so that there is no need for further boolean search on the other e_{ij}'s. Therefore techniques like early pruning, learning and theory deduction allow for restricting the search on *partial* assignments; (ii) the extra boolean component of search caused by the non-convexity of $\mathcal{LA}(Int)$ has been merged into the top-level boolean search, so that it can be handled efficiently by the top-level DPLL procedure.

The following observations indicate what are the advantages of DTC.

Simplicity. The overall schema is extremely simple. Nothing is needed beyond decision procedures for each T_i, and no complicated integration schema between the T_i is required. Furthermore, when the input problem is fully contained within one T_i, the setup reduces nicely to Bool+T_i. All features from the DPLL framework such as early pruning, theory driven backjumping and learning, deduction, and split control can be used.

Bool vs. theory. The interaction between the boolean level and each theory is tightened, thus taking into account the fact that the Boolean structure of the quantifier-free formula can severely dominate the complexity of $T_1 \cup T_2$-satisfiability. In contrast, Nelson-Oppen privileges the link between T_1 and T_2, while in fact $SMT(T_1 \cup T_2)$ problems may feature complex interactions between the boolean level and each of the T_i.

Multiple Theories. The DTC approach can be easily extended to handle the combination of $n > 2$ component theories. We only need to dispatch each satisfiability procedure the conjunction of pure literals extended with a total assignment on the interface equalities e_{ij} and return the satisfiability of the formula if all report satisfiability. In case some of the procedures report unsatisfiability, the conflict sets are added to the formula and a new propositional assignment is considered. We see no practical difficulty to implement the DTC schema for $n > 2$ theories, although we have not yet investigated this experimentally.

Deduction. The NO schema relies on theory solvers being deduction-complete, that is, being able to always infer all the (disjunctions of) e_{ij}'s which are entailed in the theory by the input set of theory literals. However, deduction completeness can be sometimes hard to achieve (e.g. it may greatly complicate the satisfiability algorithms), and computationally expensive to carry out. In the DTC approach, the theory solvers do not have to be deduction-complete. This enables us to explore the trade-off between which deduction is beneficial to efficiency and which is in fact hampering the search – or too difficult to implement.

Non-convexity. The DTC schema captures in a very natural way the case of non-convex theories. The Nelson-Oppen schema implements case-splitting on the disjunction of equalities entailed by each T_i and this case splitting is separate from the management of the boolean splitting. Therefore, the combination schema becomes very complex: one has to deal with the fact that disjunctions of e_{ij} need to be exchanged. Besides complicating the deduction mechanism of each theory, a stack-based search with backtracking has to be performed. In DTC the search on the "top-level" boolean component of the problem and the search on the "non-convex" component are dealt with in an "amalgamated" framework, and positively interact with each other, so that to maximize the benefit of the optimizations of state-of-the art SAT procedures.

Theory Conflict. The construction of conflict sets may be a non-trivial task within a single theory. The problem is even harder in the case of $T_1 \cup T_2$, since the construction of a conflict set must take into account the conflict obtained in one theory, as well as the interface equalities that have been exchanged. In our framework, this complication is avoided altogether: a conflict for the combined theories is naturally induced by the interaction between the conflict in one theory and the mechanisms for conflict management in the boolean search.

As possible drawbacks, we notice that DTC requires the *whole* formula to be purified, and the upfront introduction of $O(n^2)$ interface constraints e_{ij}. However, many of these may not occur in the purified formula; and even though the truth assignment of the interface equalities has to be guessed by the boolean level, which potentially increases the boolean search space, early pruning, learning and deduction can help to limit the increase in the search. On the whole, we expect that the DTC schema will make it easier the task of extending *SMT* tools to handle combination of theories while ensuring a high-degree of efficiency. In fact, the DTC approach does not need dedicated mechanisms to exchange selected formulae nor to handle non-convex theories, thereby greatly simplifying the implementation task. On the one hand, we believe that systems based on our approach can be made competitive with more traditional systems on theories where deduction of entailed facts can be efficiently done, by adapting techniques developed for SAT solvers. On the other hand, the DTC approach offers a flexible framework to explore the different trade-offs of deduction for theories where deriving entailed facts is computationally expensive.

5 Delayed Theory Combination in Practice: MATHSAT $(\mathcal{E} \cup \mathcal{LA})$

We implemented the Delayed Theory Combination schema presented in the previous section in MATHSAT [6]. MATHSAT is an SMT solver for each of the theories $\mathcal{DL}$, $\mathcal{LA}(Rat)$, $\mathcal{LA}(Int)$, and $\mathcal{E}$. Furthermore, it is also an SMT solver for $(\mathcal{E} \cup \mathcal{LA}(Rat))$ and for $(\mathcal{E} \cup \mathcal{LA}(Int))$, where uninterpreted symbols are eliminated by means of Ackermann's expansion [1]. MATHSAT is based on an enhanced version of the Bool+T schema (see [6] for further details).

We instantiated the Delayed Theory Combination schema to deal with $\mathcal{E} \cup \mathcal{LA}(Rat)$ and with $\mathcal{E} \cup \mathcal{LA}(Int)$. During preprocessing, the formula is purified, the interface variables c_i are identified, and the interface equalities e_{ij} are added to the solver. The most important points to be emphasized are related to the management of the interface atoms:

- in order to delay the activation of e_{ij} atoms, we instructed the SAT solver not to branch on them until no other choice is left; (by suitably initializing the activity vector controlling the VSIDS splitting strategy [17]);
- once the search finds a truth assignment that satisfies ϕ^p and is also T_1- and T_2-satisfiable, we are not done: to guarantee correctness, we need an assignment also for those e_{ij}'s that still do not have a value. This is provided by the SAT solver used in MATHSAT, which constructs total assignments over the propositional variables that are declared;
- before any new split, the current (partial) assignment is checked for T_1- and T_2-satisfiability, and the procedure backtracks if it is found unsatisfiable. In this way, the SAT solver enumerates total assignments on e_{ij}'s only if strictly necessary;
- depending on the search, it is possible that e_{ij} are given values not only by branching, but also by boolean constraint propagation on learned clauses, or even by theory deduction. In fact, the e_{ij} interface equalities are also fed into the congruence closure solver, which also implements forward deduction [6] and therefore is able to assign forced truth values (e.g., to conclude the truth of $c_1 = c_2$ from the truth of $x = c_1$, $y = c_2$, and $x = y$). This reduces branching at boolean level, and limits the delay of combination between the theories;
- when e_{ij} is involved in a conflict, it is treated like the other atoms by the conflict-driven splitting heuristic: its branching weight is increased and it becomes more likely to be split upon. Furthermore, the conflict clause is learned, and it is thus possible to prevent incompatible configurations between interface atoms and the other propositions;
- the initial value attempted for each unassigned e_{ij} is false. If c_i and c_j were in the same equivalence class because of equality reasoning, then e_{ij} had already been forced to true by equality reasoning. Thus c_i and c_j belong to different equivalence classes in the congruence closure solver and setting e_{ij} to false will not result in expensive merging of equivalence classes nor otherwise change the state of the solver. However, conflicts can result in the arithmetic solver.

6 Related Work

To our knowledge, the integration schema we describe in this paper has not been previously proposed elsewhere. Most closely related are the following systems, which are able to deal with combination of theories, using variants of Bool+no(T_1, T_2). CVCLITE [8, 4] is a library for checking validity of quantifier-free first-order formulas over several interpreted theories, including $\mathcal{LA}(Rat)$, $\mathcal{LA}(Int)$, $\mathcal{E}$, and arrays, replacing the older tools SVC and CVC. VERIFUN [12] is a similar tool, supporting domain-specific procedures for $\mathcal{E}$, $\mathcal{LA}$, and the theory of arrays. ZAPATO [3] is a counterexample-driven abstraction refinement tool, able to decide the combination of $\mathcal{E}$ and a specific fragment of $\mathcal{LA}(Int)$. ICS [14, 11] is able to deal with uninterpreted function symbols and a large variety of theories, including arithmetic, tuples, arrays, and bit-vectors. ICS [21,24] somewhat departs from the Bool+no(T_1, T_2) schema, by mixing Shostak approach (by merging canonizers for individual theories into a global canonizer), with Nelson-Oppen integration schema (to deal with non-Shostak's theories).

Other approaches implementing Bool+T for a single theory are [28,7,13]. The work in [13] proposes a formal characterization of the Bool+T approach, and an efficient instantiation to a decision procedure for $\mathcal{E}$ (based on an incremental and backtrackable congruence closure algorithm [19], which is also implemented in MATHSAT). Despite its generality for the case of a single theory, the approach is bound to the Bool+T schema, and requires an integration between theory solvers to deal with $SMT(T_1 \cup T_2)$.

A different approach to SMT is the "eager" reduction of a decision problem for T to propositional SAT. This approach has been successfully pioneered by UCLID [29, 23], a tool incorporating a decision procedure for $\mathcal{E}$, arithmetic of counters, separation predicates, and arrays. This approach leverages on the accuracy of the encodings and on the effectiveness of propositional SAT solvers, and performs remarkably well for certain theories. However, it sometimes suffers from a blow-up in the encoding to propositional logic, see for instance a comparison in [13] on $\mathcal{E}$ problems. The bottleneck is even more evident in the case of more expressive theories such as $\mathcal{LA}$ [26,25], and in fact UCLID gives up the idea of a fully eager encoding [15]. The most relevant subcase for this approach is $\mathcal{DL} \cup \mathcal{E}$, which is addressed in [22]. Unfortunately, it was impossible to make a comparison due to the unavailability of the benchmarks (only the benchmarks after Ackermann's expansion were made available to us).

7 Experimental Evaluation

We ran the implementation of MATHSAT with Delayed Theory Combination (hereafter called MATHSAT-DTC) against the alternative implementation based on Ackermann's expansion (hereafter called MATHSAT-ACK), and the competitor tools ICS (v.2.0) and CVCLITE (v.1.1.0). (We also tried to use the unstable version of CVCLITE, which is somewhat more efficient, but it was unable to run the tests due to internal errors). Unfortunately, there is a general lack of test suites on $\mathcal{E} \cup \mathcal{LA}$ available. For instance, the tests in [22] were available only after Ackermann's expansion, so that the $\mathcal{E}$ component has been removed. We also analyzed the tests in the regression suite for CVCLITE [8], but they turned out to be extremely easy. We defined the following benchmarks suites.

Modular Arithmetic. Simulation of arithmetic operations (succ, pred, sum) modulo N. Some basic variables range between 0 and N; the problem is to decide the satisfiability of (the negation of) known mathematical facts. Most problems are unsat. The test suite comes in two versions: one purely $\mathcal{E}$, where the behaviour of arithmetic operations is "tabled" (e.g., $s(0) = 1, \ldots, s(N) = 0$); one in $\mathcal{E} \cup \mathcal{LA}$, where each arithmetic operation has also a characterization via $\mathcal{LA}$ and conditional expressions (e.g., $p(x,y) = \textit{if } (x+y<N) \textit{ then } x+y \textit{ else } x+y-N$) take into account overflows.

Random Problems. We developed a random generator for SMT($\mathcal{E} \cup \mathcal{LA}(Rat)$) problems. The propositional structure is a 3-CNF; the atoms can be either fully proposi-

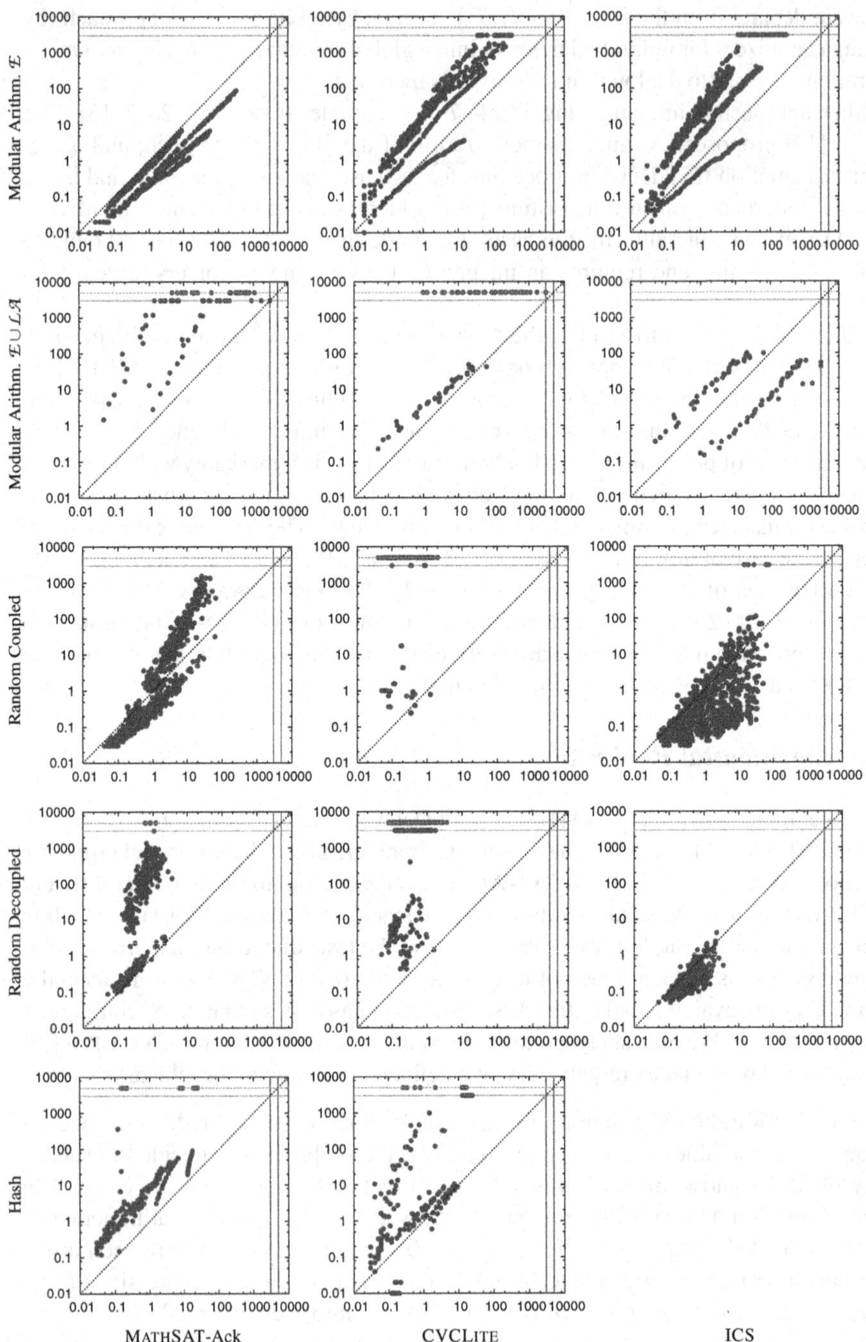

Fig. 4. Execution time ratio: the X and Y axes report MATHSAT-DTC and each competitor's times, respectively (logarithmic scale). A dot above the diagonal means a better performance of MATHSAT-DTC and viceversa. The two uppermost horizontal lines and the two rightmost vertical lines represent, respectively, out-of-memory (higher) or timed-out (lower)

tional, equalities between two terms, or a comparison between a term and a numerical constant. A basic term is an individual variable between $x_1,\ldots,x_n$; a compound terms x_i, with $i > n$, is either the application of an uninterpreted function symbol (e.g. $f(x_{j_1},\ldots,x_{j_n})$), or a ternary linear polynomial with random coefficients to previously defined terms. The generator depends on the *coupling*: high coupling increases the probability that a subterm of the term being generated is a compound term rather than a variable. We denote a class of problem as RND(vartype, n, clauses, coupling); for each configuration of the parameters we defined 20 random samples.

Hash. The suite contains some problems over hash tables modeled as integer-valued bijective functions over finite sets of integers.

We ran the four tools on over 3800 test formulae. The experiments were run on a 2-processor INTEL Xeon 3 GhZ machine with 4 Gb of memory, running Linux RedHat 7.1. The time limit was set to 1800 seconds (only one processor was allowed to run for each run) and the memory limit to 500 MB. An executable version of MATHSAT and the source files of all the experiments performed in the paper are available at [16].

The results are reported in Fig. 4. The columns show the comparison between MATHSAT-DTC and MATHSAT-ACK, CVCLITE, ICS; the rows correspond to the different test suites. MATHSAT-DTC dominates CVCLITE on all the problems, and MATHSAT-ACK on all the problems except the ones on Modular Arithmetic on $\mathcal{E}$. [2] The comparison with ICS is limited to problems in $\mathcal{E} \cup \mathcal{LA}(Rat)$, i.e. the first four rows (the Hash suite is in $\mathcal{E} \cup \mathcal{LA}(Int)$ and ICS, being incomplete over the integers, returns incorrect results). In the first row, MATHSAT-DTC generally outperforms ICS. On the second row, MATHSAT-DTC behaves better than ICS on part of the problems, and worse on others. In the third and fourth rows, MATHSAT-DTC is slower than ICS on simpler problems, but more effective on harder ones (for instance, it never times out); this is more evident in the third row, due to the fact that the problems in the fourth row are simpler (most of them were run within one second).

8 Conclusions and Future Work

In this paper we have proposed a new approach for tackling the problem of Satisfiability Modulo Theories (SMT) for the combination of theories. Our approach is based on delaying the combination, and privileging the interaction between the boolean component and each of the theories. This approach is much simpler to analyze and implement; each of the solvers can be implemented and optimized without taking into account the others; furthermore, our approach does not rely on the solvers being deduction-complete, and it nicely encompasses the case of non-convex theories. We have implemented the approach in the MATHSAT [6] solver for the combination of the theories of Equality and Uninterpreted Functions ($\mathcal{E}$) and Linear Arithmetic, over the rationals ($\mathcal{LA}(Rat)$) and the integers ($\mathcal{LA}(Int)$), and we have shown its effectiveness experimentally.

[2] The tests for CVCLITE on the "random coupled" benchmark (3rd row, 2nd column in Fig. 4) are not complete, because on nearly all samples CVCLITE produced either a time-out or a out-of-memory, so that we could not complete on time the whole run on the 2400 formulas of the benchmark.

As future work, we plan to further improve MATHSAT by investigating new ad hoc optimizations for $\mathcal{LA}(Rat) \cup \mathcal{E}$ and $\mathcal{LA}(Int) \cup \mathcal{E}$. In particular, the most evident limitation of the approach presented in this paper is the upfront introduction of interface equalities. We believe that this potential bottleneck could be avoided by means of a lazy approach, which will be the objective of future research. We also want to provide a more extensive experimental evaluation on additional sets of benchmarks. Finally, we plan to apply our framework for the verification of RTL circuit designs, where the combination of $\mathcal{LA}(Int)$ and $\mathcal{E}$ is essential for representing complex designs.

References

1. W. Ackermann. *Solvable Cases of the Decision Problem.* North Holland Pub. Co., 1954.
2. A. Armando, C. Castellini, E. Giunchiglia, and M. Maratea. A SAT-based Decision Procedure for the Boolean Combination of Difference Constraints. In *Proc. SAT'04*, 2004.
3. T. Ball, B. Cook, S.K. Lahiri, and L. Zhang. Zapato: Automatic Theorem Proving for Predicate Abstraction Refinement. In *CAV 2004*, volume 3114 of *LNCS*. Springer, 2004.
4. C. Barrett and S. Berezin. CVC Lite: A New Implementation of the Cooperating Validity Checker. In *CAV 2004*, volume 3114 of *LNCS*. Springer, 2004.
5. M. Bozzano, R. Bruttomesso, A. Cimatti, T. Junttila, S. Ranise, P.van Rossum, and R. Sebastiani. Efficient Theory Combination via Boolean Search. Technical Report T05-04-02, ITC-IRST, 2005.
6. M. Bozzano, R. Bruttomesso, A. Cimatti, T. Junttila, P. van Rossum, S. Schulz, and R. Sebastiani. An incremental and Layered Procedure for the Satisfiability of Linear Arithmetic Logic. In *TACAS 2005*, volume 3440 of *LNCS*. Springer, 2005.
7. S. Cotton, E. Asarin, O. Maler, and P. Niebert. Some Progress in Satisfiability Checking for Difference Logic. In *FORMATS/FTRTFT 2004*, volume 3253 of *LNCS*. Springer, 2004.
8. CVC, CVCLITE and SVC. `http://verify.stanford.edu/{CVC,CVCL,SVC}`.
9. D. Deharbe and S. Ranise. Light-Weight Theorem Proving for Debugging and Verifying Units of Code. In *Proc. SEFM'03*. IEEE Computer Society Press, 2003.
10. D. Detlefs, G. Nelson, and J.B. Saxe. Simplify: A Theorem Prover for Program Checking. Technical Report HPL-2003-148, HP Laboratories, 2003.
11. J.-C. Filliâtre, S. Owre, H. Rueß, and N. Shankar. ICS: Integrated Canonizer and Solver. In *CAV 2001*, volume 2102 of *LNCS*. Springer, 2001.
12. C. Flanagan, R. Joshi, X. Ou, and J.B. Saxe. Theorem Proving using Lazy Proof Explication. In *CAV 2003*, volume 2725 of *LNCS*. Springer, 2003.
13. H. Ganzinger, G. Hagen, R. Nieuwenhuis, A. Oliveras, and C. Tinelli. DPLL(T): Fast decision procedures. In *CAV 2004*, volume 3114 of *LNCS*. Springer, 2004.
14. ICS. `http://www.icansolve.com`.
15. D. Kroening, J. Ouaknine, S. A. Seshia, , and O. Strichman. Abstraction-Based Satisfiability Solving of Presburger Arithmetic. In *CAV 2004*, volume 3114 of *LNCS*. Springer, 2004.
16. MATHSAT. `http://mathsat.itc.it`.
17. M. W. Moskewicz, C. F. Madigan, Y. Zhao, L. Zhang, and S. Malik. Chaff: Engineering an efficient SAT solver. In *Proc. DAC'01*, pages 530–535. ACM, 2001.
18. G. Nelson and D.C. Oppen. Simplification by Cooperating Decision Procedures. *ACM Trans. on Programming Languages and Systems*, 1(2):245–257, 1979.
19. R. Nieuwenhuis and A. Oliveras. Congruence Closure with Integer Offsets. In *LPAR 2003*, number 2850 in LNAI. Springer, 2003.
20. S. Ranise, C. Ringeissen, and D.-K. Tran. Nelson-Oppen, Shostak, and the Extended Canonizer: A Family Picture with a Newborn. In *ICTAC 2004*, volume 3407 of *LNCS*, 2005.

21. H. Rueß and N. Shankar. Deconstructing Shostak. In *Proc. LICS'01*, pages 19–28. IEEE Computer Society, 2001.
22. S.A. Seshia and R.E. Bryant. Deciding Quantifier-Free Presburger Formulas Using Parameterized Solution Bounds. In *Proc. LICS'04*. IEEE, 2004.
23. S.A. Seshia, S.K. Lahiri, and R.E. Bryant. A Hybrid SAT-Based Decision Procedure for Separation Logic with Uninterpreted Functions. In *DAC 2003*. ACM, 2003.
24. N. Shankar and H. Rueß. Combining Shostak Theories. In *RTA 2002*, volume 2378 of *LNCS*. Springer, 2002.
25. O. Strichman. On Solving Presburger and Linear Arithmetic with SAT. In *FMCAD 2002*, volume 2517 of *LNCS*. Springer, 2002.
26. O. Strichman, S. Seshia, and R. Bryant. Deciding separation formulas with SAT. In *CAV 2002*, volume 2404 of *LNCS*. Springer, 2002.
27. C. Tinelli and M. Harandi. A New Correctness Proof of the Nelson-Oppen Combination Procedure. In *Proc. FroCos'96*. Kluwer Academic Publishers, 1996.
28. TSAT++. `http://www.ai.dist.unige.it/Tsat`.
29. UCLID. `http://www-2.cs.cmu.edu/~uclid`.

Symbolic Systems, Explicit Properties: On Hybrid Approaches for LTL Symbolic Model Checking

Roberto Sebastiani[1,*], Stefano Tonetta[1,*], and Moshe Y. Vardi[2,**]

[1] DIT, Università di Trento
{rseba,stonetta}@dit.unitn.it
[2] Dept. of Computer Science, Rice University
vardi@cs.rice.edu

Abstract. In this work we study *hybrid* approaches to LTL symbolic model checking; that is, approaches that use explicit representations of the property automaton, whose state space is often quite manageable, and symbolic representations of the system, whose state space is typically exceedingly large. We compare the effects of using, respectively, (i) a purely symbolic representation of the property automaton, (ii) a symbolic representation, using logarithmic encoding, of explicitly compiled property automaton, and (iii) a partitioning of the symbolic state space according to an explicitly compiled property automaton. We apply this comparison to three model-checking algorithms: the doubly-nested fixpoint algorithm of Emerson and Lei, the reduction of emptiness to reachability of Biere et al., and the singly-nested fixpoint algorithm of Bloem et al. for weak automata. The emerging picture from our study is quite clear, hybrid approaches outperform pure symbolic model checking, while partitioning generally performs better than logarithmic encoding. The conclusion is that the hybrid approaches benefits from state-of-the-art techniques in semantic compilation of LTL properties. Partitioning gains further from the fact that the image computation is applied to smaller sets of states.

1 Introduction

Linear-temporal logic (LTL) [26] is a widely used logic to describe infinite behaviors of discrete systems. Verifying whether an LTL property is satisfied by a finite transition system is a core problem in Model Checking (MC). Standard automata-theoretic MC techniques consider the formula φ that is the negation of the desired behavior and construct a generalized Büchi automaton (GBA) B_φ with the same language. Then, they compute the product of this automaton B_φ with the system S and check for emptiness. To check emptiness, one has to compute the set of *fair states*, i.e. those states of the

* Supported in part by ORCHID, a project sponsored by Provincia Autonoma di Trento, and by a grant from Intel Corporation.

** Supported in part by NSF grants CCR-9988322, CCR-0124077, CCR-0311326, IIS-9908435, IIS-9978135, EIA-0086264, and ANI-0216467, by BSF grant 9800096, by Texas ATP grant 003604-0058-2003, and by a grant from the Intel Corporation.

K. Etessami and S.K. Rajamani (Eds.): CAV 2005, LNCS 3576, pp. 350–363, 2005.

product automaton that are extensible to a fair path. The main obstacle to model checking is the *state-space explosion*; that is, the product is often too large to be handled.

Explicit-state model checking uses highly optimized LTL-to-GBA compilation, cf. [11, 13, 14, 17, 18, 19, 21, 29, 30], which we refer to as *semantic compilation*. Such compilation may involve an exponential blow-up in the worst case, though such blow-up is rarely seen in practice. Emptiness checking is performed using nested depth-first search [10]. To deal with the state-explosion problem, various state-space reductions are used, e.g., [25, 31].

Symbolic model checking (SMC) [6] tackles the state-explosion problem by representing the product automaton symbolically, usually by means of (ordered) BDDs. The compilation of the property to symbolically represented GBA is purely *syntactic*, and its blow-up is linear (which induces an exponential blow-up in the size of the state space), cf. [9]. Symbolic model checkers typically compute the fair states by means of some variant of the doubly-nested-fixpoint Emerson-Lei algorithm (EL) [12, 15, 27]. For "weak" property automata, the doubly-nested fixpoint algorithm can be replaced by a singly-nested fixpoint algorithm [3]. An alternative algorithm [1] reduces emptiness checking to reachability checking (which requires a singly-nested fixpoint computation) by doubling the number of symbolic variables.

Extant model checkers use either a pure explicit-state approach, e.g., in SPIN [22], or a pure symbolic approach, e.g., in NuSMV[7]. Between these two approaches, one can find *hybrid* approaches, in which the property automaton, whose state space is often quite manageable, is represented explicitly, while the system, whose state space is typically exceedingly large, is represented symbolically. For example, the singly-nested fixpoint algorithm of [3] is based on an explicit construction of the property automaton. (See [2, 8] for other hybrid approaches.)

In [28], motivated by previous work on *generalized symbolic trajectory evaluation* (GSTE) [34], we proposed a hybrid approach to LTL model checking, referred to as *property-driven partitioning* (PDP). In this approach, the property automaton A_φ is constructed explicitly, but its product with the system is represented in a partitioned fashion. If the state space of the system is $\mathcal{S}$ and that of the property automaton is $\mathcal{B}$, then we maintain a subset $Q \subseteq \mathcal{S} \times \mathcal{B}$ of the product space as a collection $\{Q_b : b \in \mathcal{B}\}$ of sets, where each $Q_b = \{s \in \mathcal{S} : (s,b) \in Q\}$ is represented symbolically. Thus, in PDP, we maintain an array of BDDs instead of a single BDD to represent a subset of the product space. Based on extensive experimentation, we argued in [28] that PDP is superior to SMC, in many cases demonstrating exponentially better scalability.

While the results in [28] are quite compelling, it is not clear why PDP is superior to SMC. On one hand, one could try to implement PDP in a purely symbolic manner by ensuring that the symbolic variables that represent the property-automaton state space precede the variables that represent the system state space in the BDD variable order. This technique, which we refer to as *top ordering*, would, in effect, generate a separate BDD for each block in the partitioned product space, but without generating an explicit array of BDDs, thus avoiding the algorithmic complexity of PDP. It is possible that, under such variable order, SMC would perform comparably (or even better) than PDP[1].

[1] We are grateful to R.E. Bryant and F. Somenzi for making this observation.

On the other hand, it is possible that the reason underlying the good performance of PDP is not the partitioning of the state space, but, rather, the explicit compilation of the property automaton, which yields a reduced state space for the property automaton. So far, however, no detailed comparison of hybrid approaches to the pure symbolic approach has been published. (VIS [4] currently implements a hybrid approach to LTL model checking. The property automaton is compiled explicitly, but then represented symbolically, using the so-called *logarithmic encoding*, so SMC can be used. No comparison of this approach to SMC, however, has been published). Interestingly, another example of property-based partitioning can be found in the context of explicit-state model checking [20].

In this paper we undertake a systematic study of this spectrum of representation approaches: purely symbolic representation (with or without top ordering), symbolic representation of semantically compiled automata (with or without top ordering), and partitioning with respect to semantically compiled automata (PDP). An important observation here is that PDP is orthogonal to the choice of the fixpoint algorithm. Thus, we can study the impact of the representation on different algorithms; we use here EL, the reduction of emptiness to reachability of [1], and the singly-nested fixpoint algorithm of [3] for weak property automata. The focus of our experiments is on measuring *scalability*. We study scalable systems and measure how running time scales as a function of the system size. We are looking for a multiplicative or exponential advantage of one algorithm over another one.

The emerging picture from our study is quite clear, hybrid approaches outperform pure SMC. Top ordering generally helps, but not as much as semantic compilation. PDP generally performs better than symbolic representation of semantically compiled automata (even with top ordering). The conclusion is that the hybrid approaches benefit from state-of-the-art techniques in semantic compilation of LTL properties. Such techniques includes preprocessing simplification by means of rewriting [13, 30], postprocessing state minimization by means of simulations [13, 14, 21, 30], and midprocessing state minimization by means of alternating simulations [17, 18]. In addition, empty-language states of the automata can be discarded. PDP gains further from the fact that the image computation is applied on smaller sets of states. The comparison to SMC with top ordering shows that managing partitioning symbolically is not as efficient as managing it explicitly.

Section 2 contains required background on explicit-state and symbolic model checking. Section 3 describes hybrid approaches to symbolic model checking. Section 4 contains experimental results. Finally, Section 5 contains some concluding remarks.

2 Background

2.1 Explicit-State LTL Model Checking

Let *Prop* be a set of propositions. We take Σ to be equal to 2^{Prop}. A fair transition system (FTS) is a tuple $\langle \mathcal{S}, \mathcal{S}_0, T, \Sigma, \mathcal{L}, \mathcal{F}^{\mathcal{S}} \rangle$, where $\mathcal{S}$ is a set of states, $\mathcal{S}_0 \subseteq \mathcal{S}$ are the initial states, $T \subseteq \mathcal{S} \times \mathcal{S}$ is the transition relation, $\mathcal{L} : \mathcal{S} \rightarrow \Sigma$ is a labeling function, and $\mathcal{F}^{\mathcal{S}} \subseteq 2^{\mathcal{S}}$ is the set of fairness constraints (each set in $\mathcal{F}^{\mathcal{S}}$ should be visited infinitely often). A generalized Büchi automaton (GBA) is a tuple $\langle \mathcal{B}, b_0, \Sigma, \delta, \mathcal{F}^{\mathcal{B}} \rangle$, where $\mathcal{B}$ is a set of states, $b_0 \in \mathcal{B}$ is the initial state, $\delta \in \mathcal{B} \times \Sigma \times \mathcal{B}$ is the transition relation, and $\mathcal{F}^{\mathcal{B}} \subseteq 2^{\mathcal{B}}$ is the set of fairness constraints. The product between an FTS S and a GBA B is the FTS $\langle \mathcal{P}, \mathcal{P}_0, T^{\mathcal{P}}, \Sigma, \mathcal{L}^{\mathcal{P}}, \mathcal{F}^{\mathcal{P}} \rangle$, where $\mathcal{P} = \mathcal{S} \times \mathcal{B}$; $\mathcal{P}_0 = \mathcal{S}_0 \times \{b_0\}$; $(p_1, p_2) \in T^{\mathcal{P}}$ iff $p_1 = (s_1, b_1)$, $p_2 = (s_2, b_2)$, $(s_1, s_2) \in T$, $\mathcal{L}(s_1) = a$, and $(b_1, a, b_2) \in \delta$; $\mathcal{L}^{\mathcal{P}}(p) = a$ iff $p = (s, b)$ and $\mathcal{L}(s) = a$; $\mathcal{F}^{\mathcal{P}} = \{F^S \times \mathcal{B}\}_{F^S \in \mathcal{F}^S} \cup \{\mathcal{S} \times F^{\mathcal{B}}\}_{F^{\mathcal{B}} \in \mathcal{F}^{\mathcal{B}}}$.

LTL model checking is solved by compiling the negation φ of a property into a GBA B^{φ} and checking the emptiness of the product P between the FTS S and B^{φ} [32]. In explicit-state model checking, emptiness checking is performed by state enumeration: a depth-first search can detect if there exists a fair strongly-connected component reachable from the initial states [10].

2.2 Symbolic LTL Model Checking

Suppose that for an FTS $\langle \mathcal{S}, \mathcal{S}_0, T, \Sigma, \mathcal{L}, \mathcal{F} \rangle$ there exists a set of symbolic (Boolean) variables V such that $\mathcal{S} \subseteq 2^V$, i.e. a state s of $\mathcal{S}$ is an assignment to the variables of V. We can think of a subset Q of $\mathcal{S}$ as a predicate on the variables V. Since $a \in \Sigma$ can be associated with the set $\mathcal{L}^{-1}(a) \subseteq \mathcal{S}$, a can be thought of as a predicate on V too. Similarly, the transition relation T is represented by a predicate on the variables $V \cup V'$, where V' contains one variable v' for every $v \in V$ (v' represents the next value of v). In the following, we will identify a set of states or a transition relation with the predicate that represents it.

Given two FTS $S^1 = \langle \mathcal{S}^1, \mathcal{S}^1_0, T^1, \Sigma, \mathcal{L}^1, \mathcal{F}^1 \rangle$ with $\mathcal{S}^1 \subseteq 2^{V^1}$ and $S^2 = \langle \mathcal{S}^2, \mathcal{S}^2_0, T^2, \Sigma, \mathcal{L}^2, \mathcal{F}^2 \rangle$ with $\mathcal{S}^2 \subseteq 2^{V^2}$, the composition of S^1 and S^2 is the FTS $\langle \mathcal{S}^{\mathcal{P}}, \mathcal{S}^{\mathcal{P}}_0, T^{\mathcal{P}}, \Sigma, \mathcal{L}^{\mathcal{P}}, \mathcal{F}^{\mathcal{P}} \rangle$, where $\mathcal{S}^{\mathcal{P}} \subseteq 2^{V^{\mathcal{P}}}$, $V^{\mathcal{P}} = V^1 \cup V^2$, $\mathcal{S}^{\mathcal{P}}(v_1, v_2) = \mathcal{S}^1(v_1) \wedge \mathcal{S}^2(v_2) \wedge (L^1(v_1) \leftrightarrow L^2(v_2))$, $\mathcal{S}^{\mathcal{P}}_0(v_1, v_2) = \mathcal{S}^1_0(v_1) \wedge \mathcal{S}^2_0(v_2)$, $T^{\mathcal{P}}(v_1, v_2, v_1', v_2') = T^1(v_1, v_1') \wedge T^2(v_2, v_2')$, $\mathcal{L}^{\mathcal{P}}(v_1, v_2) = L^1(v_1)$, $\mathcal{F}^{\mathcal{P}} = \mathcal{F}^1 \cup \mathcal{F}^2$.

Again, the negation φ of an LTL property is compiled into an FTS, such that the product with the system contains a fair path iff there is a system's violation of the property. The standard compilation produces an FTS $\langle \mathcal{S}^{\varphi}, \mathcal{S}^{\varphi}_0, T^{\varphi}, \Sigma, \mathcal{L}^{\varphi}, \mathcal{F}^{\varphi} \rangle$, where $\mathcal{S}^{\varphi} = 2^{V^{\varphi}}$, $V^{\varphi} = Atoms(\varphi) \cup Extra(\varphi)$, so that $Atoms(\varphi) \subseteq Prop$ are the atoms of φ, $Extra(\varphi) \cap V = \emptyset$ and $Extra(\varphi)$ contains one variable for every temporal connective occurring in φ [6, 9, 33]. We call this *syntactic compilation*.

To check language containment, a symbolic model checker implements a fixpoint algorithm [6]. Sets of states are manipulated by using basic set operations such as intersection, union, complementation, and the preimage and postimage operations. Since sets are represented by predicates on Boolean variables, intersection, union and complementation are translated into resp. $\wedge$, $\vee$ and $\neg$. The preimage and postimage operations are translated into the following formulas:

$$preimage(Q) = \exists v'((Q[v'/v])(v') \wedge T(v, v'))$$
$$postimage(Q) = (\exists v(Q(v) \wedge T(v, v')))[v/v']$$

The most used representation for predicates on Boolean variables are Binary Decision Diagrams (BDDs) [5]. For a given variable order, BDDs are canonical representations. However, the order may affect considerably the size of the BDDs. By means of BDDs, set operations can be performed efficiently.

3 Hybrid Approaches

Between the two approaches described in Section 2, *hybrid* approaches represent the system symbolically and the property automaton explicitly. Thus, they semantically compile the LTL formula into a GBA. This can be either encoded into an FTS or used to drive PDP. Notice that the choice between the two does not affect the set of states visited. Indeed, the product representation is completely orthogonal to the model-checking algorithm.

Logarithmic Encoding. Given the GBA $B = \langle \mathcal{B}, b_0, \Sigma, \delta, \mathcal{F} \rangle$ corresponding to the formula φ, we can compile B into the FTS $\langle \mathcal{S}^B, \mathcal{S}_0^B, T^B, \Sigma, \mathcal{L}^B, \mathcal{F}^B \rangle$, where $\mathcal{S}^B = 2^{V^B}$, $V^B = Extra(B) \cup Atoms(\varphi)$, $Extra(B) \cap Prop = \emptyset$ and $|Extra(B)| = log(|\mathcal{B}|)$, $\mathcal{S}_0^B$ represents $\{b_0\}$, $T^B(s,a,s',a')$ is true iff $(s,a,s') \in \delta$, $\mathcal{L}^B(s,a) = a$ and finally every $F^B \in \mathcal{F}^B$ represents the correspondent set $F \in \mathcal{F}$. Intuitively, we number the states of the GBA and then use binary notation to refer to the states symbolically. This is referred to as *logarithmic encoding*.

Property-Driven Partitioning. Given an FTS S and a GBA B, we can consider the partitioning of the product state space: $\{\mathcal{P}_b\}_{b \in \mathcal{B}}$, where $\mathcal{P}_b = \{p \in \mathcal{P} : p = (s,b)\}$. Thus, a subset Q of $\mathcal{P}$ can be represented by the following set of states of S: $\{Q_b\}_{b \in \mathcal{B}}$, where $Q_b = \{s : (s,b) \in Q\}$. If $Q^1 = \{Q_b^1\}_{b \in \mathcal{B}}$ and $Q^2 = \{Q_b^2\}_{b \in \mathcal{B}}$, we translate the set operations used in symbolic algorithms into:

$$Q^1 \wedge Q^2 := \{Q_b^1 \wedge Q_b^2\}_{b \in \mathcal{B}} \quad Q^1 \vee Q^2 := \{Q_b^1 \vee Q_b^2\}_{b \in \mathcal{B}} \quad \neg Q := \{\neg Q_b\}_{b \in \mathcal{B}}$$
$$preimage(Q) := \{\bigvee_{(b,a,b') \in \delta} preimage(Q_{b'}) \wedge a\}_{b \in \mathcal{B}}$$
$$postimage(Q) := \{\bigvee_{(b',a,b) \in \delta} postimage(Q_{b'} \wedge a)\}_{b \in \mathcal{B}}$$

All symbolic model-checking algorithms that operate on the product FTS can be partitioned according to the property automaton, operating on a BDD array rather than on a single BDD (see [28]).

Hypothesis. Our hypothesis is that hybrid approaches combine the best features of explicit-state and symbolic model checking techniques. On one hand, they use a symbolic representation for the system and a symbolic algorithm, which may benefit from the compact representation of BDDs. On the other hand, they may benefit from state-of-the-art techniques in LTL-to-Büchi compilation, which aim at optimizing the state space of the property automaton, and prune away redundant and empty-language parts. Optimizations include preprocessing simplification by means of rewriting [13, 30]; post-processing minimization by means of simulations [13, 14, 21, 30], and midprocessing minimization by means of alternating simulation [17, 18].

In addition, PDP has the advantage of using a partitioned version of the product state space. Partitioned methods usually gain from the fact that the image operation is applied to smaller sets of states, cf. [16]. Furthermore, PDP enables traversing the product state space without computing it explicitly. The experiments reported in the next section test our hypothesis.

4 Experimental Results

We tested the different product representations on two scalable systems with their LTL properties, by using three different model-checking algorithms. Every plot we show in this paper is characterized by three elements: the system S, the LTL property φ and the model-checking algorithm used.

4.1 Systems, Properties and Model Checking Algorithms

The two systems and their properties are inspired by case studies of the Bandera Project (`http://bandera.projects.cis.ksu.edu`). The first system is a gas-station model. There are N customers who want to use one pump. They have to prepay an operator who then activates the pump. When the pump has charged, the operator give the change to the customer. We will refer to this system as `gas`. The second system is a model of a stack with the standard pop and push functions. In this case, scalability is given by the maximum size N of the stack. The properties of the two systems are displayed in Tab. 1.

The first model checking algorithm we used is the classic Emerson-Lei (EL) algorithm [12], which computes the set of fair states. There are many variants of this algorithm [15, 27], but all are based on a doubly-nested fixpoint computation: an outer loop updates an approximation of the set of fair states until a fixpoint is reached; at every iteration of the inner loop, a number of inner fixpoints is computed, one for every fairness constraint; every inner fixpoint prunes away those states that cannot reach the corresponding fairness constraint inside the approximation.

Table 1. LTL properties

`gas.prop1`	$G((pump\_started1 \;\&\; ((!pump\_charged1)\ U\ operator\_prepaid\_2))$ $\rightarrow ((!operator\_activate\_1)\ U\ (operator\_activate\_2 \mid G!operator\_activate\_1)))$
`gas.prop2`	$(G(pump\_started1 \rightarrow$ $((!operator\_prepaid\_1)\ U\ (operator\_change\_1 \mid G!operator\_prepaid\_1))))$ $\rightarrow (G((pump\_started1 \;\&\; ((!pump\_charged1)\ U\ operator\_prepaid\_2))$ $\rightarrow ((!operator\_activate\_1)\ U\ (operator\_activate\_2 \mid G!operator\_activate\_1)))$
`gas.prop3`	$((!operator\_prepaid\_2)\ U\ operator\_prepaid\_1)$ $\rightarrow (!pump\_started2\ U\ (pump\_started1 \mid G(!pump\_started2)))$
`gas.prop4`	$G(pump\_started1$ $\rightarrow ((!pump\_started2)\ U\ (pump\_charged1 \mid G(!pump\_started2))))$
`stack.prop1`	$G(callPushd1 \;\&\; ((!returnPopd1)\ U\ callTop\_Down)$ $\rightarrow F(callTop\_Down \;\&\; F(callProcessd1)))$
`stack.prop2`	$G((callPush \;\&\; (!returnPop\ U\ callEmpty))$ $\rightarrow F(callEmpty \;\&\; F(returnEmptyFalse)))$
`stack.prop3`	$G((callPushd1 \;\&\; F(returnEmptyTrue)) \rightarrow (!returnEmptyTrue\ U\ returnPopd1))$
`stack.prop4`	$G((callPushd1 \;\&\; ((!returnPopd1)\ U\ (callPushd2 \;\&$ $((!returnPopd1 \;\&\; !returnPopd2)\ U\ callTop\_Down))))$ $\rightarrow F(callTop\_Down \;\&\; F(callProcessd2 \;\&\; FcallProcessd2)))$
`stack.prop5`	$G((callPushd1 \;\&\; (!returnPopd1\ U\ callPushd2))$ $\rightarrow (!returnPopd1\ U\ (!returnPopd2 \mid G!returnPopd1)))$

The second algorithm is a reduction of liveness checking to safety checking (l2s) [1]. The reduction is performed by doubling the number of symbolic variables. This way, it is possible to choose non-deterministically a state from which we look for a fair loop. We can check the presence of such a loop by a reachability analysis. To assure that the loop is fair, one has to add a further symbolic variable for every fairness constraint.

The third technique (weak-safety) consists of checking if the automaton is simple enough to apply a single fixpoint computation in order to find a fair loop [3]. If the automaton is weak, we can define a set $\mathcal{B}$ of states such that there exists a fair path if and only if there exists a loop inside $\mathcal{B}$ reachable from an initial state. If the automaton is terminal (the property is safety), we can define a set $\mathcal{B}$ of states such that there exists a fair path if and only if $\mathcal{B}$ is reachable from an initial state.

4.2 LTL to Büchi Automata Conversion

In this section, we focus the attention on the compilation of LTL formulas into (generalized) Büchi automata. For syntactic compilation, we used `ltl2smv`, distributed together with NuSMV. As for semantic compilation, we used MODELLA, which uses also some techniques described in [13, 14, 19, 30]. In Tab. 2, we reported the size of the automata used in the tests.

Note that the automata created by MODELLA are degeneralized, i.e. they have only one fairness constraint. Degenerilization involves a blow-up in the number of states that is linear in the number of fairness constraints (without degeneralization, the same linear factor shows up in the complexity of emptiness testing).

Recall that l2s doubles the number of symbolic variables in order to reduce emptiness to reachability. This is equivalent to squaring the size of the state space. Since in PDP we work directly with the state space of the property automaton, we need to square the explicit state space, while doubling the number of symbolic variables that describe the system. We provide details in the full version of the paper. In order to apply the third technique, we checked which automata were weak or terminal: we found that automata corresponding to stack.prop1, stack.prop2 and stack.prop4 were weak, and that the au-

Table 2. Automata details

property	ltl2smv		modella		
	extra variables	fairness constraints	states	extra variables ($\lceil\log(\text{states})\rceil$)	fairness constraints
gas.prop1	4	4	6	3	1
gas.prop2	7	7	32	5	1
gas.prop3	3	3	4	2	1
gas.prop4	3	3	6	3	1
stack.prop1	4	4	4	2	1
stack.prop2	4	4	4	2	1
stack.prop3	3	3	6	3	1
stack.prop4	6	6	9	4	1
stack.prop5	4	4	5	3	1

tomata corresponding to gas.prop1, gas.prop3, gas.prop4, stack.prop3 and stack.prop5 were terminal.

4.3 Hybrid Approaches

Hereafter, `log-encode` stands for the logarithmic encoding of the explicit representation of the automata. Note that an explicit LTL-to-Büchi compiler usually uses fewer symbolic variables than standard syntactic compilation (Tab. 2). Nevertheless, one may think that the syntactic compilation, whose transition constraints are typically simpler, is more suitable for symbolic model checking. As we see below, this is not the case.

We use `top-order` to denote the option of putting the symbolic variables of the property automaton at the top of the variable ordering. Consider a BDD d that represents a set Q of states of the product and a state b of the property automaton. Let b correspond to an assignment to the symbolic variables of the property automaton. If you follow this assignment in the structure of d, you find a sub-BDD, which corresponds to the set Q_b. Thus, by traversing the product state space with the option `top-order`, every BDD will contain an implicit partitioning of the set of states it represents.

Finally, we consider the PDP representation of the product state space. PDP uses the same automaton encoded by `log-encode` to partition the state space. Unlike `top-order`, the partitioning is handled explicitly (see [28]).

4.4 Results

We used NuSMV as platform to perform out tests. We run NuSMV on the Rice Terascale Cluster (RTC)[2], a TeraFLOP Linux cluster based on Intel Itanium 2 Processors. A timeout has been fixed to 72 hours for each run. The execution time (in seconds) has been plotted in log scale against the size of the system. The results are shown in Figs. 1-26.[3] Every plot corresponds to one system, one property, one model checking algorithm. Figs. 1-9 show the results of EL algorithm. Figs. 10-18 show the results of l2s[4] . Figs. 19-26 show the results of BRS (in these plots, syntactic compilation uses EL).

Analyzing the plots, we see that syntactic compilation performs always worse than semantic compilation. In the case of the `stack` system, the gap is considerable. The `top-order` option typically helps logarithmic encoding, while in the case of syntactic compilation it is less reliable: in some cases (see Figs. 14,17,18), it degrades the performance a lot. PDP usually performs better than `log-encode`, even if combined with `top-order`.

In conclusion, the results confirm our hypothesis: hybrid approaches perform better than standard techniques, independently of the model checking algorithm adopted. Moreover, they usually benefit from partitioning. Finally, by handling the partitioning explicitly, we get a further gain. This last point shows that accessing an adjacency list of successors may perform better than existentially quantifying the variables of a BDD.

---

[2] `http://www.citi.rice.edu/rtc/`

[3] All examples, data and tools used in these tests, as well as larger plots and the full version of the paper, are available at `http://www.science.unitn.it/~stonetta/CAV05`.

[4] We are grateful to Armin Biere and Viktor Schuppan for providing us with their tools in order to test the combination of "liveness to safety" with automata-theoretic approaches.

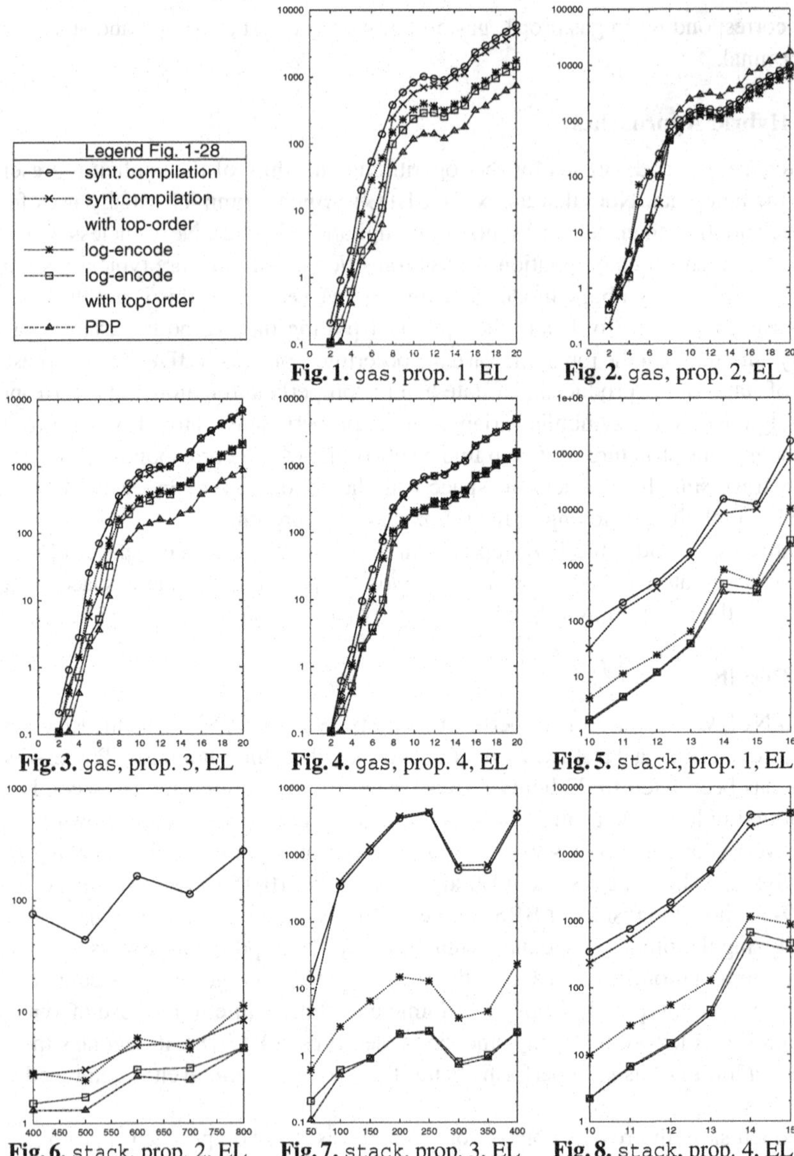

Fig. 1. gas, prop. 1, EL

Fig. 2. gas, prop. 2, EL

Fig. 3. gas, prop. 3, EL

Fig. 4. gas, prop. 4, EL

Fig. 5. stack, prop. 1, EL

Fig. 6. stack, prop. 2, EL

Fig. 7. stack, prop. 3, EL

Fig. 8. stack, prop. 4, EL

4.5 Scaling Up the Number of Partitions

In the previous section, we have seen that PDP has the best performance among the techniques we tested. However, a doubt may arise about the feasibility of the partitioning

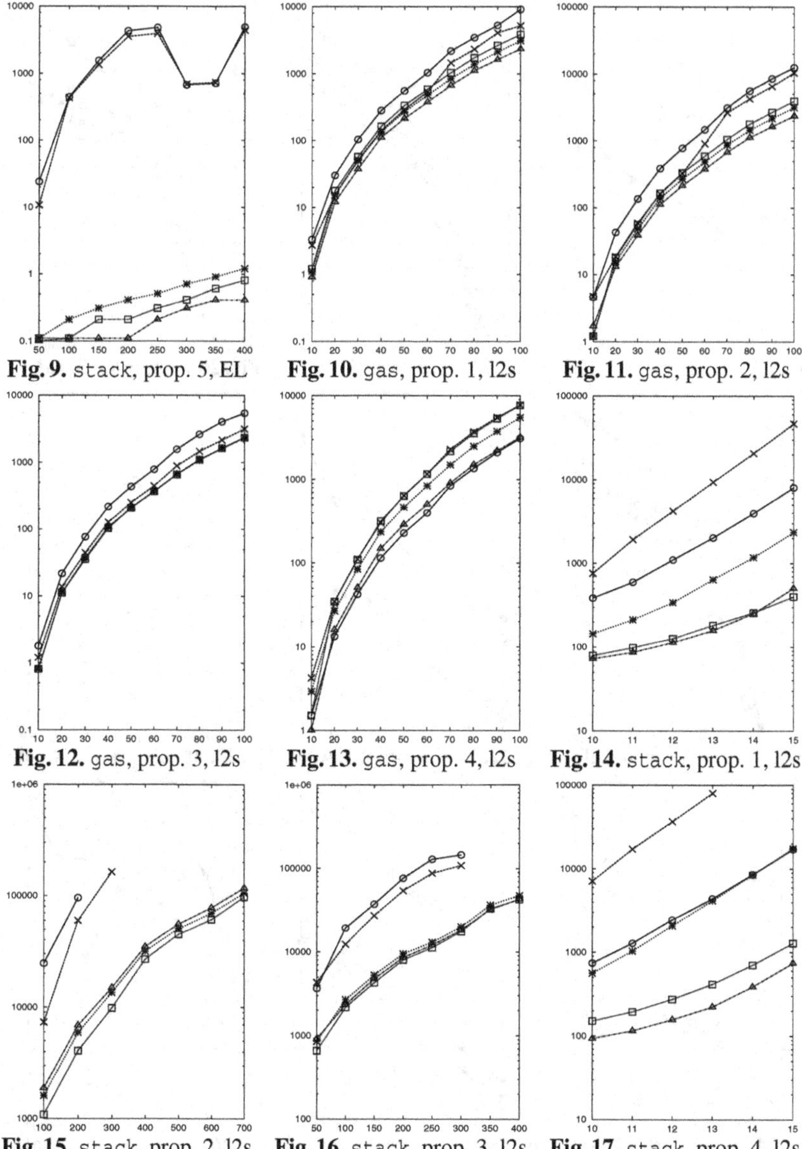

Fig. 9. stack, prop. 5, EL **Fig. 10.** gas, prop. 1, l2s **Fig. 11.** gas, prop. 2, l2s

Fig. 12. gas, prop. 3, l2s **Fig. 13.** gas, prop. 4, l2s **Fig. 14.** stack, prop. 1, l2s

Fig. 15. stack, prop. 2, l2s **Fig. 16.** stack, prop. 3, l2s **Fig. 17.** stack, prop. 4, l2s

when the number of partitions grows. For this reason, we looked for some LTL properties whose corresponding automaton has a large number of states. We took as example a property used in the PAX Project (`http://www.informatik.uni-kiel.de/~kba/pax`): $((GF\,p0 \rightarrow GF\,p1)\&(GF\,p2 \rightarrow GF\,p0)\&(GF\,p3 \rightarrow GF\,p2)\&(GF\,p4 \rightarrow GF\,p2)\&(GF\,p5 \rightarrow GF\,p3)\&(GF\,p6 \rightarrow GF(p5|p4))\&(GF\,p7 \rightarrow GF\,p6)\&(GF\,p1 \rightarrow GF\,p7)) \rightarrow GF\,p8$. Trying to compile this property into a GBA, we faced an interesting problem: no com-

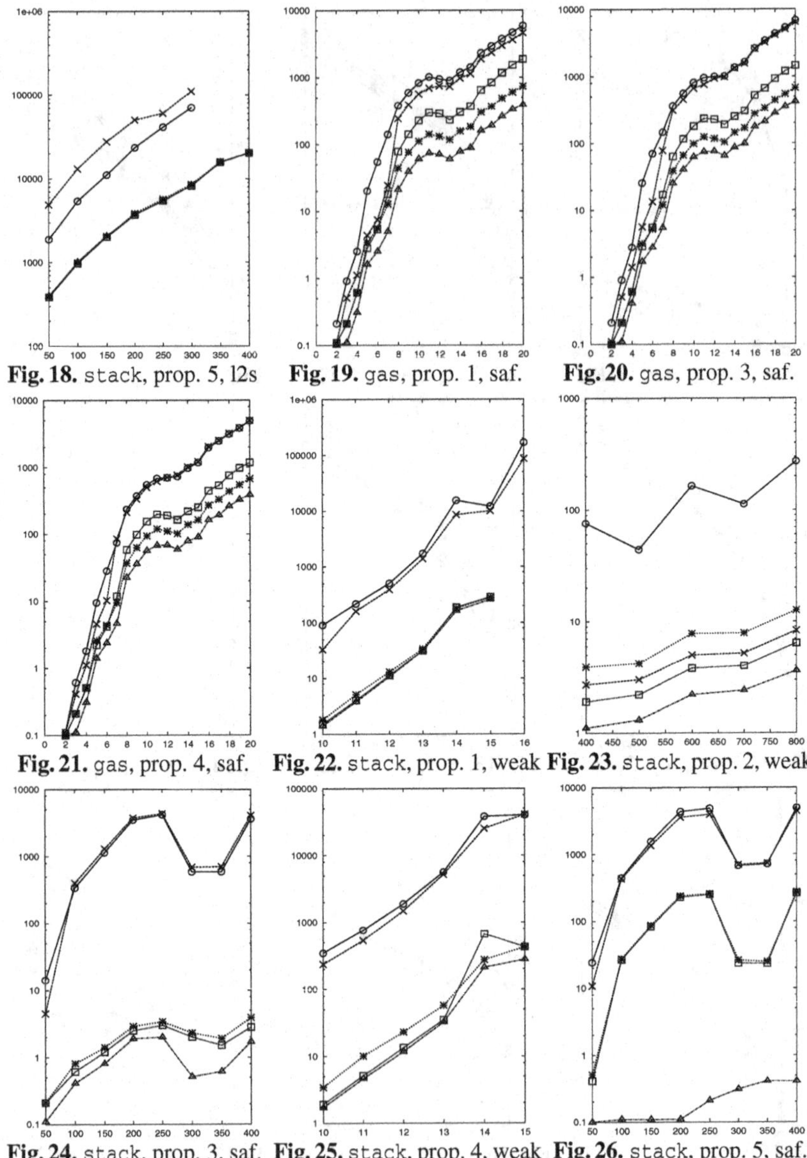

Fig. 18. `stack`, prop. 5, l2s **Fig. 19.** `gas`, prop. 1, saf. **Fig. 20.** `gas`, prop. 3, saf.

Fig. 21. `gas`, prop. 4, saf. **Fig. 22.** `stack`, prop. 1, weak **Fig. 23.** `stack`, prop. 2, weak

Fig. 24. `stack`, prop. 3, saf. **Fig. 25.** `stack`, prop. 4, weak **Fig. 26.** `stack`, prop. 5, saf.

piler we tried managed to translate this property in reasonable time[5]. For this reason, we built a new compiler specialized for this kind of properties (Boolean combination of *GF* formulas). The resulting automaton has 1281 states. We checked this property on the leader election algorithm LCR, cf. [23]. We instantiated the propositions in order

[5] Actually, the only translator that succeeded was `ltl2tgba` (`http://spot.lip6.fr`). However, we had to disable simulation-based reduction so that the resulting automaton had more than 70000 states and even parsing such an automaton took more than model checking time.

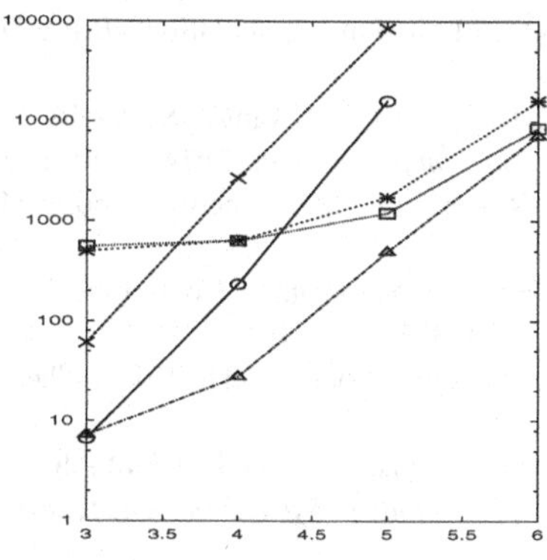

Fig. 27. LCR, large prop. (true), EL

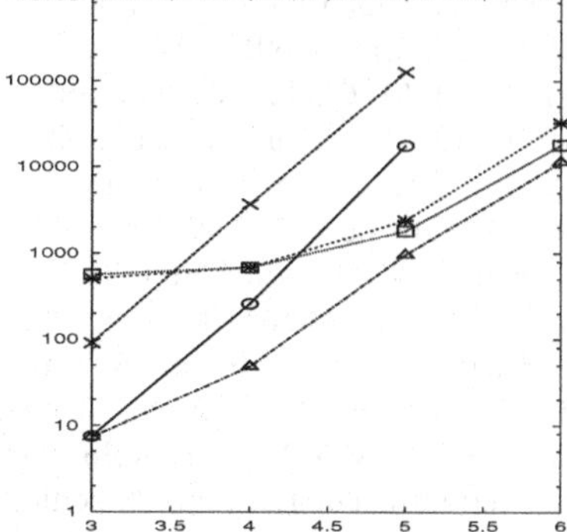

Fig. 28. LCR, large prop. (false), EL

to make the property true in one case, false in another. The results are plotted in Figs. 27-28. Note that the pattern is the same as in the previous results. More importantly, partitioning does not seem to be affected by the number of partitions. Notice that the logarithmic encoding pays an initial overhead for encoding symbolically the automaton. However, as the size of the system grows, this technique outperforms syntactic compilation.

5 Conclusions

The main finding of this work is that hybrid approaches to LTL symbolic model checking outperform pure symbolic model checking. Thus, a uniform treatment of the system under verification and the property to be verified is not desirable. We believe that this finding calls for further research into the algorithmics of LTL symbolic model checking. The main focus of research in this area has been either on the implementation of BDD operations, cf. [24], or on symbolic algorithms for FTS emptiness, cf. [27], ignoring the distinction between system and property. While ignoring this distinction allows for simpler algorithms, it comes with a significant performance penalty.

References

1. A. Biere, C. Artho, and V. Schuppan. Liveness Checking as Safety Checking. *Electr. Notes Theor. Comput. Sci.*, 66(2), 2002.
2. A. Biere, E. M. Clarke, and Y. Zhu. Multiple State and Single State Tableaux for Combining Local and Global Model Checking. In *Correct System Design*, pp 163–179, 1999.
3. R. Bloem, K. Ravi, and F. Somenzi. Efficient Decision Procedures for Model Checking of Linear Time Logic Properties. In *CAV*, pp 222–235, 1999.
4. R. K. Brayton, G. D. Hachtel, A. Sangiovanni-Vincentelli, F. Somenzi, A. Aziz, S. T. Cheng, S. Edwards, S. Khatri, Y. Kukimoto, A. Pardo, S. Qadeer, R. K. Ranjan, S. Sarwary, T. R. Shiple, G. Swamy, and T. Villa. VIS: a System for Verification and Synthesis. In *CAV*, pp 428–432, 1996.

5. R. E. Bryant. Graph-Based Algorithms for Boolean Function Manipulation. *IEEE Trans. Computers*, 35(8):677–691, 1986.
6. J.R. Burch, E.M. Clarke, K.L. McMillan, D.L. Dill, and L.J. Hwang. Symbolic Model Checking: 10^{20} States and Beyond. *Information and Computation*, 98(2):142–170, 1992.
7. A. Cimatti, E.M. Clarke, F. Giunchiglia, and M. Roveri. NuSMV: a new Symbolic Model Verifier. In *CAV*, pp 495 – 499, 1999.
8. A. Cimatti, M. Roveri, and P. Bertoli. Searching Powerset Automata by Combining Explicit-State and Symbolic Model Checking. In *TACAS*, pp 313–327, 2001.
9. E. M. Clarke, O. Grumberg, and K. Hamaguchi. Another Look at LTL Model Checking. *Formal Methods in System Design*, 10(1):47–71, 1997.
10. C. Courcoubetis, M.Y. Vardi, P. Wolper, and M. Yannakakis. Memory-Efficient Algorithms for the Verification of Temporal Properties. *Formal Methods in System Design*, 1(2/3):275–288, 1992.
11. N. Daniele, F. Guinchiglia, and M.Y. Vardi. Improved automata generation for linear temporal logic. In *CAV*, pp 249–260, 1999.
12. E.A. Emerson and C.L. Lei. Efficient Model Checking in Fragments of the Propositional μ-Calculus. In *LICS*, pp 267–278, 1986.
13. K. Etessami and G. J. Holzmann. Optimizing Büchi Automata. In *CONCUR*, pp 153–167, 2000.
14. K. Etessami, T. Wilke, and R. A. Schuller. Fair Simulation Relations, Parity Games, and State Space Reduction for Büchi Automata. In *ICALP*, pp 694–707, 2001.
15. K. Fisler, R. Fraer, G. Kamhi, M.Y. Vardi, and Z. Yang. Is there a best symbolic cycle-detection algorithm? In *TACAS*, pp 420–434, 2001.
16. R. Fraer, G. Kamhi, B. Ziv, M. Y. Vardi, and L. Fix. Prioritized Traversal: Efficient Reachability Analysis for Verification and Falsification. In *CAV*, pp 389–402, 2000.
17. C. Fritz and T. Wilke. State Space Reductions for Alternating Büchi Automata. In *FSTTCS*, pp 157–168, 2002.
18. P. Gastin and D. Oddoux. Fast LTL to Büchi Automata Translation. In *CAV*, pp 53–65, 2001.
19. D. Giannakopoulou and F. Lerda. From States to Transitions: Improving Translation of LTL Formulae to Büchi Automata. In *FORTE*, pp 308–326, 2002.
20. P. Godefroid and G. J. Holzmann. On the Verification of Temporal Properties. In *PSTV*, pp 109–124, 1993.
21. S. Gurumurthy, R. Bloem, and F. Somenzi. Fair Simulation Minimization. In *CAV*, pp 610–624, 2002.
22. G.J. Holzmann. *The SPIN model checker: Primer and reference manual.* Addison Wesley, 2003.
23. N. A. Lynch. *Distributed Algorithms.* Morgan Kaufmann Publishers Inc., 1996.
24. H. Ochi, K. Yasuoka, and S. Yajima. Breadth-first manipulation of very large binary-decision diagrams. In *ICCAD*, pp 48–55, 1993.
25. Doron Peled. Combining Partial Order Reductions with On-the-fly Model-Checking. In *CAV*, pp 377–390, 1994.
26. A. Pnueli. The temporal logic of programs. In *FOCS*, pp 46–57, 1977.
27. K. Ravi, R. Bloem, and F. Somenzi. A Comparative Study of Symbolic Algorithms for the Computation of Fair Cycles. In *FMCAD*, pp 143–160, 2000.
28. R. Sebastiani, E. Singerman, S. Tonetta, and M. Y. Vardi. GSTE is Partitioned Model Checking. In *CAV*, pp 229–241, 2004.
29. R. Sebastiani and S. Tonetta. "More Deterministic" vs. "Smaller" Büchi Automata for Efficient LTL Model Checking. In *CHARME*, pp 126–140, 2003.
30. F. Somenzi and R. Bloem. Efficient Büchi Automata from LTL Formulae. In *CAV*, pp 247–263, 2000.

31. A. Valmari. Error Detection by Reduced Reachability Graph Generation. In *ATPN*, 1988.
32. M.Y. Vardi and P. Wolper. An Automata-Theoretic Approach to Automatic Program Verification. In *LICS*, pp 332–344, 1986.
33. M.Y. Vardi and P. Wolper. Reasoning about Infinite Computations. *Information and Computation*, 115(1):1–37, 1994.
34. J. Yang and C.-J.H. Seger. Generalized Symbolic Trajectory Evaluation - Abstraction in Action. In *FMCAD*, pp 70–87, 2002.

Efficient Monitoring of ω-Languages

Marcelo d'Amorim* and Grigore Roşu

Department of Computer Science,
University of Illinois at Urbana-Champaign, USA
{damorim, grosu}@cs.uiuc.edu

Abstract. We present a technique for generating efficient monitors for ω-regular-languages. We show how Büchi automata can be reduced in size and transformed into special, statistically optimal nondeterministic finite state machines, called *binary transition tree finite state machines* (*BTT-FSMs*), which recognize precisely the minimal bad prefixes of the original ω-regular-language. The presented technique is implemented as part of a larger monitoring framework and is available for download.

1 Introduction

There is increasing recent interest in the area of *runtime verification* [17, 31], an area which aims at bridging testing and formal verification. In runtime verification, monitors are generated from system requirements. These monitors observe online executions of programs and check them against requirements. The checks can be either *precise*, with the purpose of detecting existing errors in the observed execution trace, or *predictive*, with the purpose of detecting errors that have not occurred in the observed execution but were "close to happen" and could possibly occur in other executions of the (typically concurrent) system. Runtime verification can be used either during testing, to catch errors, or during operation, to detect and recover from errors. Since monitoring unavoidably adds runtime overhead to a monitored program, an important technical challenge in runtime verification is that of synthesizing *efficient* monitors from specifications.

Requirements of systems can be expressed in a variety of formalisms, not all of them necessarily easily monitorable. As perhaps best shown by the immense success of programming languages like Perl and Python, regular patterns can be easily devised and understood by ordinary software developers. ω-regular-languages [5, 33] add infinite repetitions to regular languages, thus allowing one to specify properties of reactive systems [23]. The usual acceptance condition in finite state machines (FSM) needs to be modified in order to recognize infinite words, thus leading to Büchi automata [8]. Logics like linear temporal logics (LTL) [23] often provide a more intuitive and compact means to specify system requirements than ω-regular patterns. It is therefore not surprising that a large amount of work has been dedicated to generating (small) Büchi automata from, and verifying programs against, LTL formulae [15, 33, 11, 13].

* This author is supported by CAPES grant# 15021917.

K. Etessami and S.K. Rajamani (Eds.): CAV 2005, LNCS 3576, pp. 364–378, 2005.

Based on the belief that ω-languages represent a powerful and convenient formalism to express requirements of systems, we address the problem of generating efficient monitors from ω-languages expressed as Büchi automata. More precisely, we generate monitors that recognize the *minimal bad prefixes* [22] of such languages. A bad prefix is a *finite* sequence of events which cannot be the prefix of any accepting trace. A bad prefix is minimal if it does not contain any other bad prefix. Therefore, our goal is to develop efficient techniques that read events of the monitored program incrementally and precisely detect when a *bad prefix* has occurred. Dual to the notion of bad prefix is that of a good prefix, meaning that the trace will be accepted for any infinite extension of the prefix.

We present a technique that transforms a Büchi automaton into a special (nondeterministic) finite state machine, called a *binary transition tree finite state machine* (*BTT-FSM*), that can be used as a monitor: by maintaining a set of possible states which is updated as events are available. A sequence of events is a bad prefix iff the set of states in the monitor becomes empty. One interesting aspect of the generated monitors is that they may contain a special state, called *neverViolate*, which, once reached, indicates that the property is *not monitorable* from that moment on. That can mean either that the specification has been fulfilled (e.g., a specification $\diamond(x > 0)$ becomes fulfilled when x is first seen larger than 0), or that from that moment on there will always be some possible continuation of the execution trace. For example, the monitor generated for $\square(a \rightarrow \diamond b)$ will have exactly one state, *neverViolate*, reflecting the intuition that liveness properties cannot be monitored.

As usual, a program state is abstracted as a set of relevant atomic predicates that hold in that state. However, in the context of monitoring, the evaluation of these atomic predicates can be the most expensive part of the entire monitoring process. One predicate, for example, can say whether the vector $v[1...1000]$ is sorted. Assuming that each atomic predicate has a given evaluation cost and a given probability to hold, which can be estimated apriori either by static or by dynamic analysis, the BTT-FSM generated from a Büchi automaton executes a "conditional program", called a *binary transition tree* (*BTT*), evaluating atomic predicates *by need* in each state in order to statistically optimize the decision to which states to transit. One such BTT is shown in Fig. 2.

The work presented in this paper is part of a larger project focusing on *monitoring-oriented programming* (*MOP*) [6, 7] which is a tool-supported software development framework in which monitoring plays a foundational role. MOP aims at reducing the gap between specification and implementation by integrating the two through monitoring: specifications are checked against implementations at runtime, and recovery code is provided to be executed when specifications are violated. MOP is specification-formalism-independent: one can add one's favorite or domain-specific requirements formalism via a generic notion of *logic plug-in*, which encapsulates a formal logical syntax plus a corresponding monitor synthesis algorithm. The work presented in this paper is implemented and provided as part of the LTL logic plugin in our MOP framework. It is also available for online evaluation and download on the MOP website [1].

Some Background and Related Work. Automata theoretic model-checking is a major application of Büchi automata. Many model-checkers, including most notably SPIN [19], use this technique. A significant effort has been put into the construction of small Büchi automata from LTL formulae. Gerth *et al.* [15] show a tableaux procedure to generate on-the-fly Büchi automata of size $2^{O(|\varphi|)}$ from LTL formulae φ. Kesten *et al.* [20] describe a backtracking algorithm, also based on tableaux, to generate Büchi automata from formulae involving both past and future modalities (PTL), but no complexity results are shown. It is known that LTL model-checking is PSPACE-complete [30] and PTL is as expressive and as hard as LTL [24], though exponentially more succinct [24]. Recently, Gastin and Oddoux [13] showed a procedure to generate standard Büchi automata of size $2^{O(|\varphi|)}$ from PTL via alternating automata. Several works [11, 15] describe simplifications to reduce the size of Büchi automata. Algebraic simplifications can also be applied *apriori* on the LTL formula. For instance, $a\ \mathcal{U}\ b \wedge c\ \mathcal{U}\ b \equiv (a \wedge c)\ \mathcal{U}\ b$ is a valid LTL congruence that will reduce the size of the generated Büchi automaton. All these techniques producing small automata are very useful in our monitoring context because the smaller the original Büchi automaton for the ω-language, the smaller the BTT-FSM. Simplifications of the automaton *with respect to monitoring* are the central subject of this paper.

Kupferman *et al.* [22] classify safety according to the notion of *informativeness*. Informative prefixes are those that "tell the whole story": they witness the violation (or validation) of a specification. Unfortunately, not all bad prefixes are informative; e.g., the language denoted by $\square(a \vee \circ(\square c)) \wedge \square(b \vee \circ(\square \neg c))$ does not include any word whose prefix is $\{a, b\}, \{a\}, \{\neg c\}$. This is a (minimal) bad but not informative prefix, since it does not witness the violation taking place in the next state. One can use the construction described in [22] to build an automaton of size $O(2^{2^{|\varphi|}})$ which recognizes all bad prefixes but, unfortunately, this automaton may be too large to be stored. Our fundamental construction is similar in spirit to theirs but we do not need to apply a subset construction on the input Büchi since we already maintain the set of possible states that the running program can be in. Geilen [14] shows how Büchi automata can be turned into monitors. The construction in [14] builds a tableaux similar to [15] in order to produce an FSM of size $O(2^{|\varphi|})$ for recognizing informative prefixes. Here we detect *all* the minimal bad prefixes, rather than just the informative ones. Unlike in model-checking where a user hopes to see a counter-example that witnesses the violation, in monitoring critical applications one wants to detect a violation *as soon as it occurs*.

RCTL [4] is an interesting language for safety properties combining regular expressions and CTL. One can easily generate efficient monitors for RCTL. However, [4] focused on on-the-fly model-checking of RCTL properties, while here we focus on online monitoring of properties expressed as ω-languages.

Temporal logics have different interpretations on finite and infinite traces as shown in [27]. For instance, the formula $\square(\diamond a \wedge \diamond \neg a)$ is satisfiable in infinite trace LTL but unsatisfiable in its finite trace version [27]. Ruf *et al.* [28] present a finite-trace fragment of MTL [32] with just the "metric" operators always

($\Box_{[t_1,t_2]}\varphi$) and eventually ($\Diamond_{[t_1,t_2]}\varphi$), meaning that the property φ holds at all times or, respectively, at some time between t_1 and t_2, but without a metric until operator $\_\,\mathcal{U}_{[t_1,t_2]}\,\_$. A similar metric temporal logic, TXP, is presented in [10]. Our goal in this paper is *not* to present a novel logic, especially one with a finite trace semantics, neither to generate monitors from logical formulae. Instead, we consider already existing Büchi automata and show how to transform them into efficient non-deterministic monitors. One can use off-the-shelf techniques to generate Büchi automata from formulae in different logics, or reuse them from complementary model-checking efforts.

The technique illustrated here is implemented as a plug-in in the MOP *runtime verification* (*RV*) framework [6, 7]. Other RV tools include JAVA-MAC [21], JPAX [16], JMPAX [29], and EAGLE [3]. JAVA-MAC uses a special interval temporal logic as the specification language, while JPAX and JMPAX support variants of LTL. These systems instrument the JAVA bytecode to emit events to an external monitor observer. JPAX was used to analyze NASA's K9 Mars Rover code [2]. JMPAX extends JPAX with predictive capabilities. EAGLE is a finite-trace temporal logic and tool for runtime verification, defining a logic similar to the μ-calculus with data-parameterization.

2 Preliminaries: Büchi Automata

Büchi automata and their ω-languages have been studied extensively during the past decades. They are well suited to program verification because one can check satisfaction of properties represented as Büchi automata statically against transition systems [33, 8]. LTL is an important but proper subset of ω-languages.

Definition 1. *A (nondeterministic) standard* ***Büchi automaton*** *is a tuple* $\langle \Sigma, S, \delta, S_0, \mathcal{F} \rangle$*, where* Σ *is an* ***alphabet****,* S *is a set of* ***states****,* $\delta\colon S \times \Sigma \to 2^S$ *is a* ***transition function****,* $S_0 \subseteq S$ *is the set of* ***initial states****, and* $\mathcal{F} \subseteq S$ *is a set of* ***accepting*** *states.*

In practice, Σ typically refers to events or actions in a system to be analyzed.

Definition 2. *A Büchi automaton* $\mathcal{A} = \langle \Sigma, S, \delta, S_0, \mathcal{F} \rangle$ *is said to* ***accept*** *an infinite word* $\tau \in \Sigma^\omega$ *iff there is some* ***accepting run*** *in the automaton, that is, a map* $\rho\colon \mathcal{N}at \to S$ *such that* $\rho_0 \in S_0$*,* $\rho_{i+1} \in \delta(\rho_i, \tau_i)$ *for all* $i \geq 0$*, and* $inf(\rho) \cap \mathcal{F} \neq \emptyset$*, where* $inf(\rho)$ *contains the states occurring infinitely often in* ρ*. The* ***language of*** $\mathcal{A}$*,* $\mathcal{L}(\mathcal{A})$*, consists of all words it accepts.*

Therefore, ρ can be regarded as an infinite path in the automaton that starts with an initial state and contains at least one accepting state appearing infinitely often in the trace. Fig. 1 shows a nondeterministic Büchi automaton for the ω-regular expression $(a+b)^*b^\omega$ that contains all the infinite words over a and b with finitely many as.

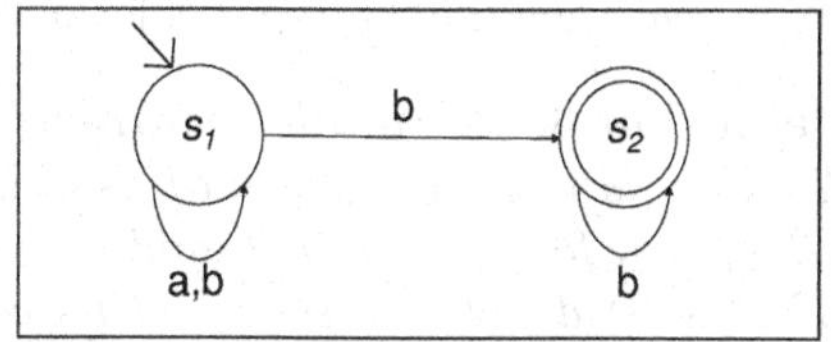

Fig. 1. Büchi automaton recognizing the ω-regular expression $(a+b)^*b^\omega$

Definition 3. *Let $\mathcal{L}(\mathcal{A})$ be the language of a Büchi automaton $\mathcal{A}=\langle \Sigma, S, \delta, S_0, \mathcal{F}\rangle$. A finite word $x \in \Sigma^*$ is a* **bad prefix of** $\mathcal{A}$ *iff for any $y \in \Sigma^\omega$ the concatenation $xy \notin \mathcal{L}(\mathcal{A})$. A bad prefix is* **minimal** *if no other bad prefix is a prefix of it.*

Therefore, no bad prefix of the language of a Büchi automaton can be extended to an accepted word. Similarly to [8], from now on we may tacitly assume that Σ is defined in terms of propositions over atoms. For instance, the self-transitions of s_1 in Fig. 1 can be represented as one self-transition, $a \vee b$.

3 Multi-transitions and Binary Transition Trees

Büchi automata cannot be used unchanged as monitors. For the rest of the paper we explore structures suitable for monitoring as well as techniques to transform Büchi automata into such structures. Deterministic multi-transitions (*MT*) and binary-transition trees (*BTTs*) were introduced in [18, 27]. In this section we extend their original definitions with nondeterminism.

Definition 4. *Let S and A be sets of* **states** *and* **atomic predicates**, *respectively, and let P_A denote the set of* **propositions** *over atoms in A, using the usual boolean operators. If $\{s_1, s_2, ..., s_n\} \subseteq S$ and $\{p_1, p_2, ..., p_n\} \subseteq P_A$, we call the n-tuple $[p_1\colon s_1, p_2\colon s_2, ..., p_n\colon s_n]$ a* **(nondeterministic) multi-transition (MT)** *over P_A and S. Let $MT(P_A, S)$ denote the set of MTs over P_A and S.*

Intuitively, if a monitor is in a state associated to an MT $[p_1\colon s_1, p_2\colon s_2, ..., p_n\colon s_n]$ then $p_1, p_2, ..., p_n$ can be regarded as guards allowing the monitor to nondeterministically transit to one of the states $s_1, s_2, ..., s_n$.

Definition 5. *Maps $\theta\colon A \to \{true, false\}$ are called* **A-events**, *or simply events. Given an A-event θ, we define its* **multi-transition extension** *as the map $\theta_{MT} : MT(P_A, S) \to 2^S$, where $\theta_{MT}([p_1 : s_1, p_2 : s_2, ..., p_n : s_n]) = \{s_i \mid \theta \models p_i\}$.*

The role of A-events is to transmit the monitor information regarding the running program. In any program state, the map θ assigns atomic propositions to *true* iff they hold in that state, otherwise to *false*. Therefore, A-events can be regarded as abstractions of the program states. Moreover, technically speaking, A-events are in a bijective map to P_A. For an MT μ, the set of states $\theta_{MT}(\mu)$ is often called the set of *possible continuations* of μ under θ.

Example 1. If $\mu = [a \vee \neg b\colon s_1, \neg a \wedge b\colon s_2, c\colon s_3]$, and $\theta(a)$=*true*, $\theta(b)$=*false*, and $\theta(c)$=*true*, then the set of possible continuations of μ under θ, $\theta_{MT}(\mu)$, is $\{s_1, s_3\}$.

Definition 6. *A* **(nondeterministic) binary transition tree (BTT)** *over A and S is inductively defined as either a set in 2^S or a structure of the form $a\ ?\ \beta_1 : \beta_2$, for some atom a and for some binary transition trees β_1 and β_2. Let $BTT(A, S)$ denote the set of BTTs over the set of states S and atoms A.*

Definition 7. *Given an event θ, we define its* **binary transition tree extension** *as the map $\theta_{BTT}\colon BTT(A, S) \to 2^S$, where:*

$\theta_{BTT}(Q) = Q$ *for any set of states* $Q \subseteq S$,
$\theta_{BTT}(a\ ?\ \beta_1\ :\ \beta_2) = \theta_{BTT}(\beta_1)$ *if* $\theta(a) = true$, *and*
$\theta_{BTT}(a\ ?\ \beta_1\ :\ \beta_2) = \theta_{BTT}(\beta_2)$ *if* $\theta(a) = false$.

Definition 8. *A BTT* β ***implements*** *an MT* μ, *written* $\beta \models \mu$, *iff for any event* θ, *it is the case that* $\theta_{BTT}(\beta) = \theta_{MT}(\mu)$.

Example 2. The BTT $b?\ (a?\ (c?\ s_1\ s_3 : s_1) : (c?\ s_2\ s_3 : s_2)) : (c?\ s_1\ s_3 : s_3)$ implements the multi-transition shown in Example 1.

Fig. 2 represents this BTT graphically. The right branch of the node labeled with **b** corresponds to the BTT expression $(c\ ?\ s_1 s_3 : s_3)$, and similarly for the left branch and every other node. Atomic predicates can be any host programming language boolean expressions. For example, one may be interested if a variable x is positive or if a vector $v[1...100]$ is sorted. Some atomic predicates typically are more expensive to evaluate than others. Since our purpose is to generate *efficient monitors*, we need to take the evaluation costs of atomic predicates into consideration. Moreover, some predicates can hold with higher probability than others; for example, some predicates may be simple "sanity checks", such as checking whether the output of a sorting procedure is indeed sorted. We next assume that atomic predicates are given evaluation costs and probabilities to hold. These may be estimated *apriori*, either statically or dynamically.

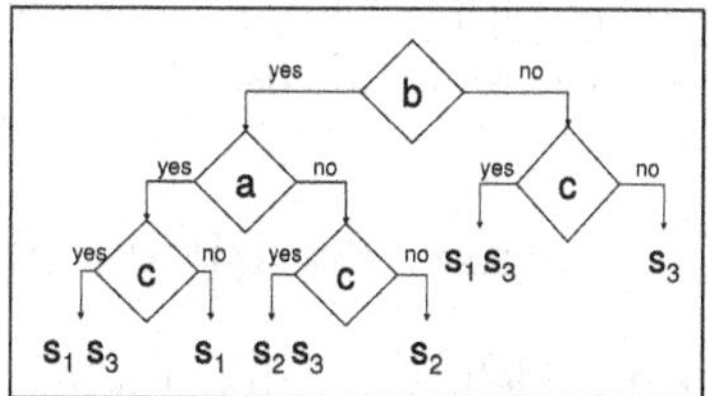

Fig. 2. BTT corresponding to the MT in Example 1

Definition 9. *If* $\varsigma : A \to \mathcal{R}^+$ *and* $\pi : A \to [0,1]$ *are cost and probability functions for events in* A, *respectively, then let* $\gamma_{\varsigma,\pi} : BTT(A,S) \to \mathcal{R}^+$ *defined as:*
$\gamma_{\varsigma,\pi}(Q) \ =\ 0$ *for any* $Q \subseteq S$, *and*
$\gamma_{\varsigma,\pi}(a\ ?\ \beta_1\ :\ \beta_2) \ =\ \varsigma(a) + \pi(a) * \gamma_{\varsigma,\pi}(\beta_1) + (1 - \pi(a)) * \gamma_{\varsigma,\pi}(\beta_2)$,
be the **expected (evaluation) cost** function on $BTTs$ in $BTT(A,S)$.

Example 3. Given $\varsigma = \{(a,10),(b,5),(c,20)\}$ and $\pi = \{(a,0.2),(b,0.5),(c,0.5)\}$, the expected evaluation cost of the BTT defined in Example 2 is 30.

With the terminology and motivations above, the following problem develops as an interesting and important problem in monitor synthesis:

Problem: Optimal $BTT(A,S)$.
Input: A multi-transition $\mu = [p_1 : s_1, p_2 : s_2, ..., p_n : s_n]$ with associated cost $\varsigma : A \to \mathcal{R}^+$ and probability $\pi : A \to [0,1]$.
Output: A minimal cost BTT β with $\beta \models \mu$.

Binary decision trees (BDTs) and diagrams (BDDs) have been studied as models and data-structures for several problems in artificial intelligence [25] and program verification [8]. [9] discusses BDTs and how they relate to $BTTs$. Moret [25] shows that a simpler version of this problem, using BDTs, is NP-hard.

In spite of this result, in general the number of atoms in formulae is relatively small, so it is not impractical to exhaustively search for the optimal *BTT*. We next informally describe a backtracking algorithm that we are currently using in our implementation to compute the minimal cost *BTT* by exhaustive search. Start with the sequence of all atoms in A. Pick one atom, say a, and make two recursive calls to this procedure, each assuming one boolean assignment to a. In each call, pass the remaining sequence of atoms to test, and simplify the set of propositions in the multi-transition according to the value of a. The product of the *BTTs* is taken when the recursive calls return in order to compute all *BTTs* starting with a. This procedure repeats until no atom is left in the sequence. We select the minimal cost *BTT* amongst all computed.

4 Binary Transition Tree Finite State Machines

We next define an automata-like structure, formalizing the desired concept of an *effective runtime monitor*. The transitions of each state are all-together encoded by a *BTT*, in practice the statistically optimal one, in order for the monitor to efficiently transit as events take place in the monitored program. Violations occur when one cannot further transit to any state for any event. A special state, called *neverViolate*, will denote a configuration in which one can no longer detect a violation, so one can stop the monitoring session if this state is reached.

Definition 10. *A* ***binary transition tree finite state machine (BTT-FSM)*** *is a tuple* $\langle A, S, btt, S_0\rangle$, *where* A *is a set of atoms,* S *is a set of states potentially including a special state called "neverViolate", btt is a map associating a BTT in BTT(A,S) to each state in* S *where btt(neverViolate)={neverViolate} when neverViolate* $\in S$, *and* $S_0 \subseteq S$ *is a subset of initial states.*

Definition 11. *Let* $\langle A, S, btt, S_0\rangle$ *be a BTT-FSM. For an event* θ *and* $Q, Q' \subseteq S$, *we write* $Q \xrightarrow{\theta} Q'$ *and call it a* ***transition between sets of states****, whenever* $Q' = \bigcup_{s\in Q} \theta_{BTT}(btt(s))$. *A* ***trace of events*** $\theta_1\theta_2...\theta_j$ *generates a* ***sequence of transitions*** $Q_0 \xrightarrow{\theta_1} Q_1 \xrightarrow{\theta_2} ... \xrightarrow{\theta_j} Q_j$ *in the BTT-FSM, where* $Q_0 = S_0$ *and* $Q_i \xrightarrow{\theta_{i+1}} Q_{i+1}$, *for all* $0 \le i < j$. *The trace is* ***rejecting*** *iff* $Q_j = \{\}$.

Note that no finite extension of a trace $\theta_1\theta_2...\theta_j$ will be ***rejected*** if *neverViolate* $\in Q_j$. The state *neverViolate* denotes a configuration in which violations can no longer be detected for any finite trace extension. This means that the set Q_k will not be empty, for any $k > j$, when *neverViolate* $\in Q_j$. Therefore, the monitoring session can stop at event j if *neverViolate* $\in Q_j$, because we are only interested in violations of requirements.

5 Generating a *BTT-FSM* from a Büchi Automaton

Not any property can be monitored. For example, in order to check a liveness property one needs to ensure that certain propositions hold infinitely often, which cannot be verified at runtime. This section describes how to transform a Büchi automaton into an efficient *BTT-FSM* that rejects precisely the minimal bad prefixes of the denoted ω-language.

Definition 12. *A* ***monitor FSM (MFSM)*** *is a tuple* $\langle\Sigma, S, \delta, S_0\rangle$*, where* $\Sigma = P_A$ *is an alphabet,* S *is a set of states potentially including a special state "neverViolate",* $\delta\colon S\times\Sigma \to 2^S$ *is a transition function with* $\delta(neverViolate, true) = \{neverViolate\}$ *when* $neverViolate \in S$*, and* $S_0 \subseteq S$ *are initial states.*

Note that we take Σ to be P_A, the set of propositions over atoms in A. Like *BTT-FSMs*, *MFSMs* may also have a special *neverViolate* state.

Definition 13. *Let* $Q_0 \xrightarrow{\theta_1} Q_1 \xrightarrow{\theta_2} \ldots \xrightarrow{\theta_j} Q_j$ *be a sequence of transitions in the MFSM* $\langle\Sigma, S, \delta, S_0\rangle$*, generated from* $t{=}\theta_1\theta_2...\theta_j$*, where* $Q_0{=}S_0$ *and* $Q_{i+1}{=}\bigcup_{s\in Q_i}\{\delta(s,\sigma) \mid \theta_{i+1} \models \sigma\}$*, for all* $0{\le}i{<}j$*. We say that the MFSM* ***rejects*** t *iff* $Q_j = \{\}$*.*

No finite extension of t will be ***rejected*** if $neverViolate \in Q_j$.

From Büchi to *MFSM*. We next describe two simplification procedures on a Büchi automaton that are sound w.r.t. monitoring, followed by the construction of an *MFSM*. The first procedure identifies segments of the automaton which cannot lead to acceptance and can therefore be safely removed. As we will show shortly, this step is necessary in order to guarantee the soundness of the monitoring procedure. The second simplification identifies states with the property that if they are reached then the corresponding requirement cannot be violated by any *finite* extension of the trace, so monitoring is ineffective from there on. Note that reaching such a state does not necessarily mean that a good prefix has been recognized, but only that the property is *not monitorable* from there on.

Definition 14. *Let* $\langle\Sigma, S, \delta, S_0, \mathcal{F}\rangle$ *be a Büchi automaton,* C *a connected component of its associated graph, and nodes(C) the states associated to* C*. We say that* C *is* ***isolated*** *iff for any* $s \in$ *nodes(C) and* $\sigma \in \Sigma$*, it is the case that* $\delta(s,\sigma) \subseteq$ *nodes(C). We say that* C *is* ***total*** *iff for any* $s \in$ *nodes(C) and event* θ*, there are transitions* σ *such that* $\theta \models \sigma$ *and* $\delta(s,\sigma) \cap$ *nodes(C)* $\neq \emptyset$*.*

Therefore, there is no way to escape from an isolated connected component, and regardless of the upcoming event, it is always possible to transit from any node of a total connected component to another node in that component.

Removing Bad States. The next procedure removes states of the Büchi automaton which cannot be part of any accepting run (see Definition 2). Note that any state appearing in such an accepting run must eventually *reach* an accepting state. This procedure is fundamentally inspired by strongly-connected-component-analysis [20, 33], used to check emptiness of the language denoted by a Büchi automaton. Given a Büchi automaton $\mathcal{A} = \langle\Sigma, S, \delta, S_0, \mathcal{F}\rangle$, let $U \subseteq S$ be the largest set of states such that the language of $\langle\Sigma, S, \delta, U, \mathcal{F}\rangle$ is empty. The states in U are unnecessary in $\mathcal{A}$, because they cannot change its language. Fortunately, U can be calculated effectively as the set of states that *cannot reach* any cycle in the graph associated to $\mathcal{A}$ which contains at least one accepting state in $\mathcal{F}$. Fig. 3 shows an algorithm to do this.

```
INPUT : A Büchi automaton 𝒜
OUTPUT : A smaller Büchi automaton 𝒜' such that ℒ(𝒜') = ℒ(𝒜).
REMOVE_BAD_STATES :
    for each maximal connected component C of 𝒜
      if (C is isolated and nodes(C) ∩ ℱ=∅) then mark all states in C "bad"
    DFS_MARK_BAD ; REMOVE_BAD
```

Fig. 3. Removing bad states

The loop identifies maximal isolated connected components which do not contain any accepting states. The nodes in these components are marked as "bad". The procedure DFS_MARK_BAD performs a depth-first-search in the graph and marks nodes as "bad" when all outgoing edges lead to a "bad" node. Finally, the procedure REMOVE_BAD removes all the bad states. The runtime complexity of this algorithm is dominated by the computation of maximal connected components. In our implementation, we used Tarjan's $O(V + E)$ double DFS [8]. The proof of correctness is simple and it appears in [9]. The Büchi automaton $\mathcal{A}'$ produced by the algorithm in Fig. 3 has the property that there is some proper path from any of its states to some accepting state. One can readily generate an *MFSM* from a Büchi automaton $\mathcal{A}$ by first applying the procedure REMOVE_BAD_STATES in Fig. 3, and then ignoring the acceptance conditions.

Theorem 1. *The MFSM generated from a Büchi automaton $\mathcal{A}$ as above rejects precisely the minimal bad prefixes of $\mathcal{L}(\mathcal{A})$.*

Proof. Let $\mathcal{A}=\langle\Sigma, S, \delta, S_0, \mathcal{F}\rangle$ be the original Büchi automaton, let $\mathcal{A}'=\langle\Sigma, S', \delta', S'_0, \mathcal{F}\rangle$ be the Büchi automaton obtained from $\mathcal{A}$ by applying the algorithm in Fig. 3, and let $\langle\Sigma, S', \delta', S'_0\rangle$ be the corresponding *MFSM* of $\mathcal{A}'$. For any finite trace $t = \theta_1...\theta_j$, let us consider its corresponding sequence of transitions in the *MFSM* $Q_0\overset{\theta_1}{\rightarrow}...\overset{\theta_j}{\rightarrow}Q_j$, where Q_0 is S'_0. Note that the trace t can also be regarded as a sequence of letters in the alphabet Σ of $\mathcal{A}$, because we assumed Σ is P_A and because there is a bijection between propositions in P_A and A-events. All we need to show is that t is a bad prefix of $\mathcal{A}'$ if and only if $Q_j=\emptyset$. Recall that $\mathcal{A}'$ has the property that there is some non-empty path from any of its states to some accepting state. Thus, one can build an infinite path in $\mathcal{A}'$ starting with any of its nodes, with the property that some accepting state occurs infinitely often. In other words, Q_j is not empty iff the finite trace t is the prefix of some infinite trace in $\mathcal{L}(\mathcal{A}')$. This is equivalent to saying that Q_j is empty iff the trace t is a bad prefix in $\mathcal{A}'$. Since Q_j empty implies $Q_{j'}$ empty for any $j>j'$, it follows that the *MFSM* rejects precisely the minimal bad prefixes of $\mathcal{A}$. □

Theorem 1 says that the *MFSM* obtained from a Büchi automaton as above can be used as a monitor for the corresponding ω-language. Indeed, one only needs to maintain a current set of states Q, initially S'_0 , and transform it accordingly as new events θ are generated by the observed program: if $Q\overset{\theta}{\rightarrow}Q'$ then set Q to Q'; if Q ever becomes empty then report violation. Theorem 1 tells us that a violation will be reported as soon as a bad prefix is encountered.

Collapsing Never-Violate States. Reducing runtime overhead is crucial in runtime verification. There are many situations when the monitoring process can be safely stopped, because the observed finite trace cannot be finitely extended to any bad prefix. The following procedure identifies states in a Büchi automaton which cannot lead to the violation of any *finite* computation. For instance, the Büchi automaton in Fig. 4 can only reject infinite words in which the state s_2 occurs finitely many times; moreover, at least one transition is possible at any moment. Therefore, the associated *MFSM* will never report a violation, even though there are infinite words that are not accepted. We call such an automaton *non-monitorable.* This example makes it clear that if a state like s_1 is ever reached by the monitor, it does *not* mean that we found a good prefix, but that we could *stop looking* for bad prefixes.

Let $\mathcal{A}=\langle\Sigma, S, \delta, S_0, \mathcal{F}\rangle$ be a Büchi automaton *simplified with* `REMOVE_BAD_STATES`. The procedure in Fig. 5 finds states which, if reached by a monitor, then the monitor can no longer detect violations regardless of what events will be observed in the future.

The procedure first identifies the total connected components. According to the definition of totality, once a monitor reaches a state of a total connected component, the monitor will have the possibility to always transit within that connected component, thus never getting a chance to report violation. All states of a total component can therefore be marked as "never violate". Other states can also be marked as such if, for any events, it is possible to transit from them to states already marked "never violate"; that is the reason for the disjunction in the second conditional. The procedure finds such nodes in a depth-first-search. Finally, `COLLAPSE-NEVER_VIOLATE` collapses all components marked "never violate", if any, to a distinguished node, *neverViolate*, having just a *true* transition to itself. If any collapsed node was in the initial set of states, then the entire automaton is collapsed to *neverViolate.* The procedure `GENERATE_MFSM` produces an *MFSM* by ignoring accepting conditions.

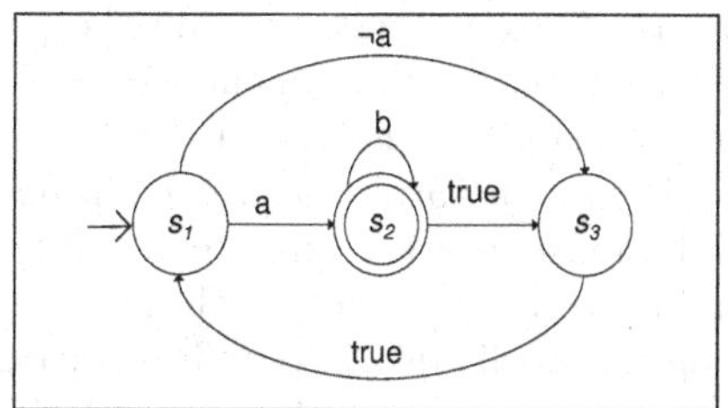

Fig. 4. Non-monitorable automaton

Taking as input this *MFSM*, say $\langle\Sigma, S', \delta', S'_0\rangle$, cost function ς, and probability function π, `GENERATE_BTT-FSM` constructs a *BTT-FSM* $\langle A, S', btt, S'_0\rangle$, where A corresponds to the set of atoms from which the alphabet Σ is built, and the map *btt*, here represented by a set of pairs, is defined as follows:

$$btt = \{(neverViolate, \{neverViolate\}) \mid neverViolate \in S'\} \cup$$
$$\{(s, \beta_s) \mid s \in S'\text{-}\{neverViolate\} \wedge \beta_s \models \mu_s\}, \text{ where}$$

β_s optimally implements μ_s w.r.t. ς and π, with $\mu_s = \oplus(\bigcup\{[\sigma : s'] \mid s' \in \delta'(s, \sigma)\})$

```
INPUT  : A Büchi automaton 𝒜, cost function ς, and probability function π.
OUTPUT : An effective BTT-FSM monitor rejecting the bad prefixes of ℒ(𝒜).
COLLAPSE_NEVER_VIOLATE :
    for each maximal connected component C of 𝒜
      if ( C is total ) then mark all states in C as "never violate"
    for each s in depth-first-search visit
      if ( ⋁{σ | δ(s,σ) contains some state marked "never violate"} )
      then mark s as "never violate"
    COLLAPSE-NEVER_VIOLATE ; GENERATE_MFSM ; GENERATE_BTT-FSM
```

Fig. 5. Collapsing non-monitorable states

The symbol $\oplus$ denotes concatenation on a set of multi-transitions. Optimal *BTTs* β_s are generated like in Section 3. Proof of correctness appears in [9].

6 Monitor Generation and MOP

We have shown that one can generate from a Büchi automaton a *BTT-FSM* recognizing precisely its bad prefixes. However, it is still necessary to integrate the *BTT-FSM* monitor within the program to be observed. Runtime overhead is introduced by instrumentation and is also dependent on the selection of cost and probabilities assigned to atoms by the user.

Monitoring-oriented programming (MOP) [7] aims at merging specification and implementation through generation of runtime monitors from specifications and integration of those within implementation. In MOP, the task of generating monitors is divided into defining a logic engine and a language shell. The logic engine is concerned with the translation of specifications given as logical formulae into monitoring (pseudo-)code. The shell is responsible for the integration of the monitor within the application.

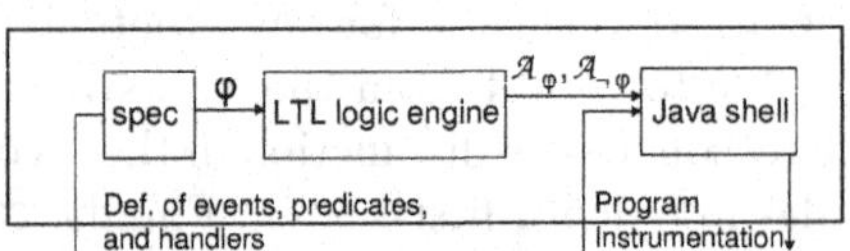

Fig. 6. Generation of monitors in MOP

Fig. 6 captures the essence of the synthesis process of LTL monitors in MOP using the technique described in this paper. The user defines specifications either as annotations in the code or in a separate file. The specification contains definitions of events and state predicates, as well as LTL formulae expressing trace requirements. These formulae treat events and predicates as atomic propositions. Handlers are defined to track violation or validation of requirements. For instance, assume the events a and b denote the login and the logoff of the same user, respectively. Then the formula $\Box(a \rightarrow \circ(\neg a\ \mathcal{U}\ b))$ states that the user cannot be logged in more than once. A violation handler could be declared to track the user who logged in twice. The logic engine is responsible for the translation of the formulae φ and $\neg\varphi$ into two *BTT-FSM* monitors. One detects violation and the other validation of φ. Note that if the user is just interested in validation (no violation handler), then only the automaton for negation is generated. Finally, the language shell reads the definition of events and instruments the code so that the monitor will receive the expected notifications.

We used LTL2BA [26] to generate standard Büchi automata from LTL formulae. The described procedures are implemented in JAVA. This software and a WWW demo are available from the MOP website [1].

6.1 Evaluation

Table 1 shows *BTT-FSM* monitors for some LTL formulae. The *BTT* definition corresponding to a state follows the arrow ($\rightsquigarrow$). Initial states appear in brackets. For producing this table, we used the same cost and probabilities for all events and selected the smallest *BTT*. The first formula cannot be validated by monitoring and presents the permanent possibility to be violated; that is why its *BTT-FSM* does not have a *neverViolate* state. The second formula can never be violated since event a followed by event b can always occur in the future, so its *BTT-FSM* consists of just one state *neverViolate*. The last formula shows that our procedure does not aim at distinguishing validating from non-violating prefixes.

Table 1. *BTT-FSMs* generated from temporal formulae

Temporal Formula	*BTT-FSM*
$\Box(a \rightarrow b\,\mathcal{U}\,c)$	$[s_0] \rightsquigarrow c\ ?\ (b\ ?\ s_0s_1 : s_0) : (a\ ?\ (b\ ?\ s_1 : \emptyset) : (b\ ?\ s_0s_1 : s_0))$ $s_1 \rightsquigarrow b\ ?\ (c\ ?\ s_0s_1 : s_1) : (c\ ?\ s_0 : \emptyset)$
$\Box(a \rightarrow \Diamond b)$	$[neverViolate] \rightsquigarrow \{neverViolate\}$
$a\,\mathcal{U}\,b\,\mathcal{U}\,c$	$[s_0] \rightsquigarrow c\ ?\ neverViolate : (a\ ?\ (b\ ?\ s_0s_1 : s_0) : (b\ ?\ s_1 : \emptyset))$ $s_1 \rightsquigarrow c\ ?\ neverViolate : (b\ ?\ s_1 : \emptyset)$ $neverViolate \rightsquigarrow \{neverViolate\}$

Table 2 shows that our technique can not only identify non-monitorable formulae, but also reduce the cost of monitoring by collapsing large parts of the Büchi automaton. We use the symbols ♡, ♣, and ♠ to denote, respectively, the effectiveness of `REMOVE_BAD_STATES`, the first, and the second loop of `COLLAPSE_NEVER_VIOLATE`. The first group contains non-monitorable formulae. The next contains formulae where monitor size could not be reduced by our procedures. The third group shows formulae where our simplifications could significantly reduce the monitor size. The last group shows examples of "accidentally" safe and "pathologically" safe formulae from [22]. A formula φ is accidentally safe iff not all bad prefixes are "informative" [22] (i.e., can serve as a witness for violation) but all computations that violate φ have an informative bad prefix. A formula φ is pathologically safe if there is a computation that violates φ and has no informative bad prefix. Since we detect *all* minimal bad prefixes, informativeness does not play any role in our approach. Both formulae are monitorable. For the last formula, in particular, a minimal bad prefix will be detected as soon as the monitor observes a $\neg a$, having previously observed a $\neg b$. One can generate and visualize the *BTT-FSMs*of all these formulae, and many others, online at [1].

Table 2. Number of states and transitions before and after monitoring simplifications

Temporal Formula	# states	# transitions	symplif.
$\diamond a$	2 , 1	3 , 1	♣
$a\ \mathcal{U}\ \circ(\diamond b)$	3 , 1	5, 1	♣♠
$\Box(a \wedge b \rightarrow \diamond c)$	2 , 1	4 , 1	♣
$a\,\mathcal{U}\ (b\,\mathcal{U}\ (c\,\mathcal{U}\ (\diamond d)))$	2 , 1	3 , 1	♣
$a\,\mathcal{U}\ (b\,\mathcal{U}\ (c\,\mathcal{U}\ \Box(d \rightarrow \diamond e)))$	5 , 1	15 , 1	♣♠
$\neg\ a\,\mathcal{U}\ (b\,\mathcal{U}\ (c\,\mathcal{U}\ \Box(d \rightarrow \diamond e)))$	12 , 1	51 , 1	♣
$\neg\ \diamond a$	1 , 1	1 , 1	
$\Box(a \rightarrow b\,\mathcal{U}\ c)$	2 , 2	4 , 4	
$a\,\mathcal{U}\ (b\,\mathcal{U}\ (c\,\mathcal{U}\ d))$	4 , 4	10 , 10	
$a \wedge \circ(\diamond b) \wedge \diamond(\Box e)$	5 , 4	11 , 6	♣
$a \wedge \circ(\diamond b) \wedge \circ(\diamond c) \wedge \diamond(\Box e)$	9 , 6	29 , 12	♣
$a \wedge \circ(\diamond b) \wedge \circ(\diamond c) \wedge \circ(\diamond d) \wedge \diamond(\Box e)$	17 , 10	83 , 30	♣
$a \wedge \circ(\neg(\Box(b \rightarrow c\,\mathcal{U}\ d))) \wedge \diamond(\Box e)$	7 , 5	20 , 10	♣
$\Box(a \vee \circ(\Box c)) \wedge \Box(b \vee \circ(\Box\neg c))$	3 , 3	5 , 5	
$(\Box(a \vee \diamond(\Box c)) \wedge \Box(b \vee \diamond(\Box\neg c))) \vee \Box a \vee \Box b$	12 , 6	43 , 22	♡♣

7 Conclusions

Not all properties a Büchi automaton can express are monitorable. This paper describes transformations that can be applied to extract the monitorable components of Büchi automata, reducing their size and the cost of runtime verification. The resulting automata are called *monitor finite state machines* (*MFSMs*). The presented algorithms have polynomial running time in the size of the original Büchi automata and have already been implemented. Another contribution of this paper is the definition and use of *binary transition trees* (*BTTs*) and corresponding finite state machines (*BTT-FSMs*), as well as a translation from *MFSMs* to *BTT-FSMs*. These special-purpose state machines encode optimal evaluation paths of boolean propositions in transitions.

We used LTL2BA [26] to generate Büchi automata from LTL, and JAVA to implement the presented algorithms. Our algorithms, as well as a graphical HTML interface, are available at [1]. This work is motivated by, and is part of, a larger project aiming at promoting monitoring as a foundational principle in software development, called *monitoring-oriented programming* (MOP). In MOP, the user specifies formulae, atoms, cost and probabilities associated to atoms, as well as violation and validation handlers. Then all these are used to automatically generate monitors and integrate them within the application.

This work is concerned with monitoring *violations* of requirements. In the particular case of LTL, *validations* of formulae can also be checked using the same technique by monitoring the negation of the input formula. Further work includes implementing the algorithm defined in [13] for generating Büchi automata of size $2^{O(|\varphi|)}$ from PTL, combining multiple formulae in a single automaton as showed by Ezick [12] so as to reduce redundancy of proposition evaluations, and applying further (standard) NFA simplifications to *MFSM*.

References

1. MOP website, LTL plugin. http://fsl.cs.uiuc.edu/mop/repository.jsp?ltype=LTL.
2. C. Artho, D. Drusinsky, A. Goldberg, K. Havelund, M. Lowry, C. Păsăreanu, G. Roşu, W. Visser, and R. Washington. Automated Testing using Symbolic Execution and Temporal Monitoring. *Theoretical Computer Sci.*, to appear, 2005.
3. H. Barringer, A. Goldberg, K. Havelund, and K. Sen. Rule-Based Runtime Verification. In *Proceedings of VMCAI'04*, volume 2937 of *LNCS*, pages 44–57, 2004.
4. I. Beer, S. Ben-David, and A. Landver. On-the-Fly Model Checking of RCTL Formulas. In *Proceedings of CAV '98*, pages 184–194, London, UK, 1998. Springer.
5. J. R. Büchi. *On a Decision Method in Restricted Second Order Arithmetic.* Logic, Methodology and Philosophy of Sciences. Stanford University Press, 1962.
6. F. Chen, M. d'Amorim, and G. Roşu. A Formal Monitoring-Based Framework for Software Development and Analysis. In *Proceedings of ICFEM'04*, volume 3308 of *LNCS*, pages 357–372, 2004.
7. F. Chen and G. Roşu. Towards Monitoring-Oriented Programming: A Paradigm Combining Specification and Implementation. In *Proceedings of RV'03*, volume 89 of *ENTCS*, pages 106–125, 2003.
8. E. M. Clarke, O. Grumberg, and D. A. Peled. *Model Checking.* The MIT Press, Cambridge, Massachusetts, 1999.
9. M. d'Amorim and G. Roşu. Efficient monitoring of ω-languages. Technical Report UIUCDCS-R-2005-2530, University of Illinois Urbana-Champaign, March 2005.
10. S. Dudani, J. Geada, G. Jakacki, and D. Vainer. Dynamic Assertions Using TXP. *ENTCS*, 55(2), 2001.
11. K. Etessami and G. Holzmann. Optimizing Büchi Automata. In *Proc. of Int. Conf. on Concurrency Theory*, volume 1877 of *LNCS*, pages 153–167. Springer, 2000.
12. J. Ezick. An Optimizing Compiler for Batches of Temporal Logic Formulas. In *Proceedings of ISSTA'04*, pages 183–194. ACM Press, 2004.
13. P. Gastin and D. Oddoux. LTL with Past and Two-Way Very-Weak Alternating Automata. In *Proceedings of MFCS'03*, number 2747 in LNCS, pages 439–448. Springer, 2003.
14. M. Geilen. On the Construction of Monitors for Temporal Logic Properties. In *Proceedings of RV'01*, volume 55 of *ENTCS*. Elsevier Science, 2001.
15. R. Gerth, D. Peled, M. Y. Vardi, and P. Wolper. Simple on-the-fly Automatic Verification of Linear Temporal Logic. In *Proceedings of the 15th IFIP WG6.1 International Symposium on Protocol Specification, Testing and Verification XV*, pages 3–18. Chapman & Hall, Ltd., 1996.
16. K. Havelund and G. Roşu. Monitoring Java Programs with Java PathExplorer. In *Proceedings of RV'01*, volume 55 of *ENTCS*. Elsevier Science, 2001.
17. K. Havelund and G. Roşu. *Workshops on Runtime Verification (RV'01, RV'02, RV'04)*, volume 55, 70(4), to appear of *ENTCS*. Elsevier, 2001, 2002, 2004.
18. K. Havelund and G. Roşu. Synthesizing Monitors for Safety Properties. In *Proceedings of TACAS'02*, volume 2280 of *LNCS*, pages 342–356. Springer, 2002.
19. G. Holzmann. The Model Checker SPIN. *IEEE Transactions on Software Engineering*, 23(5):279–295, 1997.
20. Y. Kesten, Z. Manna, H. McGuire, and A. Pnueli. A Decision Algorithm for Full Propositional Temporal Logic. In *Proceedings of CAV'93*, volume 697 of *LNCS*, pages 97–109. Springer, 1993.
21. M. Kim, S. Kannan, I. Lee, and O. Sokolsky. Java-MaC: a Run-time Assurance Tool for Java. In *Proceedings of RV'01*, volume 55 of *ENTCS*. Elsevier Sci., 2001.

22. O. Kupferman and M. Y. Vardi. Model Checking of Safety Properties. In *Proceedings of CAV '99*, volume 1633 of *LNCS*, pages 172–183. Springer, 1999.
23. Z. Manna and A. Pnueli. *Temporal Verification of Reactive Systems: Safety.* Springer, New York, 1995.
24. N. Markey. Temporal Logic with Past is Exponentially more Succinct. *EATCS Bulletin*, 79:122–128, 2003.
25. B. Moret. Decision Trees and Diagrams. *ACM Comp. Surv.*, 14(4):593–623, 1982.
26. D. Oddoux and P. Gastin. LTL2BA. http://www.liafa.jussieu.fr/~oddoux/ltl2ba/.
27. G. Roşu and K. Havelund. Rewriting-Based Techniques for Runtime Verification. *Journal of Automated Software Engineering*, 12(2):151–197, 2005.
28. J. Ruf, D. Hoffmann, T. Kropf, and W. Rosenstiel. Simulation-Guided Property Checking Based on Multi-Valued AR-Automata. In *Proceedings of DATE'01*, pages 742–749, London, UK, 2001. IEEE Computer Society.
29. K. Sen, G. Roşu, and G. Agha. Online Efficient Predictive Safety Analysis of Multithreaded Programs. In *Proceedings of TACAS'04*, volume 2988 of *LNCS*, pages 123–138. Springer, 2002.
30. A. P. Sistla and E. M. Clarke. The Complexity of Propositional Linear Temporal Logics. *Journal of the ACM*, 32(3):733–749, 1985.
31. O. Sokolsky and M. Viswanathan. *Workshop on Runtime Verification (RV'03)*, volume 89 of *ENTCS*. Elsevier, 2003.
32. P. Thati and G. Roşu. Monitoring Algorithms for Metric Temporal Logic. In *Proceedings of RV'04*, volume (to appear) of *ENTCS*. Elsevier Science, 2004.
33. P. Wolper. Constructing Automata from Temporal Logic Formulas: a Tutorial. volume 2090 of *LNCS*, pages 261–277. Springer, 2002.

Verification of Tree Updates for Optimization

Michael Benedikt[1], Angela Bonifati[2], Sergio Flesca[3], and Avinash Vyas[1]

[1] Bell Laboratories
[2] Icar CNR, Italy
[3] D.E.I.S., University of Calabria

Abstract. With the rise of XML as a standard format for representing tree-shaped data, new programming tools have emerged for specifying transformations to tree-like structures. A recent example along this line are the update languages of [16, 15, 8] which add tree update primitives on top of the declarative query languages XPath and XQuery. These tree update languages use a "snapshot semantics", in which all querying is performed first, after which a generated sequence of concrete updates is performed in a fixed order determined by query evaluation. In order to gain efficiency, one would prefer to perform updates as soon as they are generated, before further querying. This motivates a specific verification problem: given a tree update program, determine whether generated updates can be performed before all querying is completed. We formalize this notion, which we call "Binding Independence". We give an algorithm to verify that a tree update program is Binding Independent, and show how this analysis can be used to produce optimized evaluation orderings that significantly reduce processing time.

1 Introduction

The rise of XML as a common data format for storing structured documents and data has spurred the development of new languages for manipulating tree-structured data, such as XSLT and XQuery. In this work, we deal with a new class of languages for specifying *updates* – programs that describe changes to an input tree. Specification and processing of updates to tree-structured data is a critical data management task. In the XML context, updates have long been implementable in node-at-a-time fashion within navigational interfaces such as DOM, but languages for specifying bulk updates are now emerging. Several language proposals based on extensions of the declarative languages XPath and XQuery have been put forward in the literature [16, 15, 8, 7], and the World Wide Web consortium is well underway in extending XQuery, the XML standard query language, with the capability of expressing updates over XML data. Since XML documents are basically trees, and since the update primitives of these languages cannot violate the tree structure, we refer to these as *tree update languages*. A sample declarative tree update program, in the syntax of [15] is shown below:

```
U1 :    for $i in //open_auction
        insert $i/initial/text into $i/current
        delete $i/bidder
```

//openauction is an XPath expression returning the set of openauction nodes in the tree, hence the opening for loop binds the variable $i to every openauction node in

K. Etessami and S.K. Rajamani (Eds.): CAV 2005, LNCS 3576, pp. 379–393, 2005.

turn. In the body of the loop, the XPath expression $i/initial/text returns the subtree underneath a text node lying below a initial child of a node bound to variable $i at this iteration of the loop. The expression $i/bidder returns all the bidder nodes below the node bound to $i. Informally, example U1 states that below each current child of an openauction node a copy of the subtree rooted at a certain text node is inserted, and that each bidder node lying below a openauction element should be deleted. The effect of this program over an instance, is shown in Figure 1(a) and (b).

Previous tree update language proposals differ in many details, but they agree on a critical semantic issue regarding how program evaluation is to be ordered. The current proposals generally center upon the *snapshot semantics* [15], which specifies the use of two logical phases of processing: in the first all evaluation of query expressions is done, yielding an ordered set of point updates. In the second phase the sequence of updates is applied in the specified order. In the example above, a sequence consisting of a list of insertions and deletions will be generated, based on the ordering of the results of //openauction and the other queries; this sequence will be applied in that order to the tree.

The snapshot semantics has a number of attractive features; it is easier to reason about, consistent with the semantics of declarative relational update languages such as SQL, and it averts the possibility of ill-formed reads arising at runtime. The main drawback is that the naive implementation of it is very inefficient. In a straightforward implementation the intermediate results must all be materialized before any writes are performed. To increase performance, one would prefer a more pipelined chaining of reads to subsequent writes – an *interleaved semantics*. Our approach to this problem is to maintain the use of the snapshot semantics, but to verify that an interleaved implementation does not violate the semantics of a given program. We concentrate on determining *statically* whether updates generated from a program can be applied as soon as they are generated. We denote this property *Binding Independence*, and our main contribution is an algorithm for verifying it.

In example U1, our analysis detects that evaluation order of U1 can be rearranged to perform updates as soon as they are generated: that is, U1 is Binding Independent. Intuitively, this is because the insert and delete operations in one iteration do not affect the evaluation of expressions in subsequent iterations. More generally, we formalize a notion of *non-interference* of an update with an expression. We show that non-interference implies Binding Independence, and then present algorithms that decide non-interference properties. In this paper, we concentrate on a subset of the language of [15], but our techniques are applicable to other tree update language proposals that use snapshot semantics.

Optimization based on specification-time verification is particularly attractive for bulk updates in XML, given that they are often defined well in advance of their execution and are used to specify computing-intensive modifications to data that may take minutes or even hours on current update processors. Thus the contributions of the paper are: (*i*) a formalization of Binding Independence, a property of programs that is critical to update optimization, (*ii*) the notion of non-interference of programs, and an algorithm for reducing Binding Independence to a series of non-interference properties, (*iii*) an algorithm for deciding non-interference and (*iv*) experiments investigating the feasibility of the verification.

Related Work. Tree update languages are similar to tree transducers, whose verification is studied in [1, 2]. These works are similar to ours in that they concern capturing the iteration of one transducer with the single action of another transducer. However, the expressiveness of the respective formalisms is incomparable: update languages work on ordered trees with no bound on rank, while [1, 2] deal with fixed-ranked trees; the iteration here is a bounded looping construct, while in [1, 2] it is a transitive closure. The works differ also in the notion of "capturing" (equality up to isomorphism vs. language containment) and the application (optimization vs. model checking). There has been considerable work on static analysis of other tree query and transformation languages. In the XML setting a good summary, focusing on the type-checking problem, can be found in [14]. [10] presents a system for doing static analysis of XSLT. Because XQuery and XSLT cannot perform destructive updates, their analysis is much different than ours. Still, [10, 5] include techniques for performing conservative satisfiability tests on trees that could be used in conjunction with our analysis.

The main technique in our analysis is transforming dynamic assertions into static ones. This idea is certainly an ancient one in program analysis (e.g. [3]). Distinctive features in our setting include the fact that a tree pattern query language, XPath, is part of the programming formalism we analyze; also that the update operations stay within the domain of trees, making both the reduction and the final static test simpler.

Organization. Section 2 gives the data model and presents the update language studied in this paper, a variant of the language of [15]. Section 3 defines the verification problem we are interested in and overviews our solution. Section 4 describes our implementation and experimental results on the static analyses.

2 Trees, Queries, and Tree Update Languages

In this section, we review the basics of the data model and the fragment of the XPath query language considered in this work.

Data Model. We deal here with node-labeled trees. Because we think of these as abstractions of XML documents, we refer to labels as *tags*, and generally use D (for document) to range over trees. Each node has additionally a unique identity, referred to as its *node identifier* or nodeId. Moreover, trees are ordered according to the *document order* for nodes, which is the order returned by an in-order depth-first traversal of the tree. An example of one of our trees is given in Figure 1(a).

XPath. A key component of update languages is the use of patterns or queries to identify nodes. Although our analysis could work for many tree pattern languages, for simplicity we use a subset of the XPath language. XPath consists of *expressions*, each of which defines a map from a node in a tree to an ordered set of output nodes from the same tree, and *filters*, which define predicates on nodes in the tree. The ordering of the output of our XPath expressions will always be via the depth-first traversal ordering of the input tree, so we will not show it explicitly. In this paper, a top-level XPath expres-

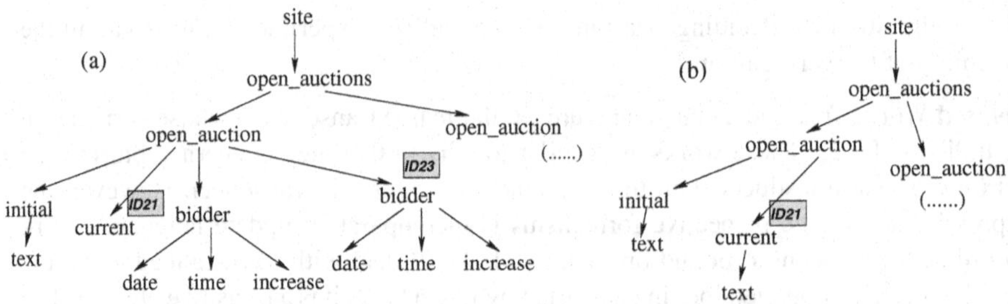

Fig. 1. An example XML tree, before (a) and after (b) the update U1

sion is either a basic expression or a union $E_1 \cup \ldots \cup E_n$ of basic expressions. Basic expressions are built up from rules $E = E/E$, $E = /A$, $E = //A$, $E = /*$, $E = //*$, and $E = [F]$. Here A is any label and F is any filter (defined below). An expression /A returns all the children labeled A of the input node, while //A returns all the A descendants of an input node. The expression /* returns all children of a node, while //* returns all descendants. / is the composition operator on binary relations and [F] is the identity restricted to nodes satisfying filter F. A filter is either a basic expression E, [label=A] for A a tag, or a conjunction of filters. The filter E holds exactly when E returns nonempty at a node, while the label comparison has the obvious meaning. Following convention, we often omit the composition operator for brevity: e.g. writing /A/B rather than ((/A)/(/B)) for the XPath query that returns all B children of A children of an input node. We use XP to denote the XPath language above. As seen in the opening example, our update programs deal with XPath expressions with variables in them. We use XP($\boldsymbol{x}$) to denote the language built up as above but with the additional rule $E = x_i$, where x_i is a variable in $\boldsymbol{x}$. We let XP_V denote an XPath expression with variables. Such expressions are evaluated relative to an assignment of a nodeId in a tree to each variable, with the expression x_i returning exactly the node associated with the nodeId bound to x_i under the assignment, or $\emptyset$ if there is no such node. An expression with variables in $\boldsymbol{x}$ will be denoted $E(\boldsymbol{x})$. For a tree D, we let $E(\boldsymbol{a})(D)$ be the evaluation of E at the root of D in a context where x_i is assigned a_i.

Schemas and DTDs. Our algorithms can take into account constraints on the input tree. Our most general notion of constraint will be a non-deterministic bottom-up tree automaton on unranked trees. This corresponds roughly to the expressiveness of the schemas supported by the industry standard XML Schema; hence we refer to an automaton as a *schema*. Our implementation requires the schema to be given as a Document Type Definition (DTD) from XML. A DTD enumerates a finite set of labels that can be used, and for each label a regular expression over the label alphabet which constrains the children of a node with label. A DTD thus describes a very restricted kind of regular language of unranked trees, where the state depends only on the label. The examples in this paper are based on the XMark DTD [13], used for benchmarking XML tools.

Templates. Finally, in order to present our core update language, we will need functions that construct trees from XP_V expressions. A *template* is a tree whose nodes are labeled with literal tags or $\mathrm{XP_V}$ expressions, with the latter appearing only at leaves. A template τ is evaluated relative to a tree D and an assignment b of variables to nodeIds in D. The result of evaluation is $\tau(D,b) = \Theta$, where Θ is the forest formed by replacing each node in τ that is an XP expression E with the sequence of trees resulting from the evaluation of E relative to D, b.

Tree Update Language. We present the syntax of the tree update language TUpdate we use throughout the paper. This language is an abstraction of that presented in [15]. The top-level update constructs we deal with are as follows:

UpdateStatement ::= SimpleUpdate | ComplexUpdate
ComplexUpdate ::= for var in **XPathExpr ComplexUpdate| UpdateBlock**
UpdateBlock ::= **SimpleUpdate**$^+$
SimpleUpdate ::= ("insert" **cExpr** ("after" | "before") **tExpr**) | ("insert" **cExpr** "into" **tExpr**) |
("delete" **tExpr**) | ("replace" **tExpr** "with" **cExpr**)

Here **XPathExpr** and **tExpr** are $\mathrm{XP_V}$ expressions, while **cExpr** is a template. Intuitively, **tExpr** computes the target location where the update is taking place, while **cExpr** constructs a new tree which is to be inserted or replaced at the target of the update.

We now review the semantics of tree update programs in the style of [16, 15]. The semantics of all existing update proposals [16, 15, 8, 12] consists first of a description of how individual updates apply, and secondly how query evaluation is used to generate an ordered sequence of individual updates. Following this, our semantics will be via a transition system, with two kinds of transitions, one for application of individual updates and the other for reducing complex updates to simpler ones based on queries. We will give both these transitions, and then discuss the order in which transitions fire.

Concrete Update API. Let D be a tree, f be a forest (ordered sequence of trees), and n a node identifier. A *concrete update* u, is one of the following operations: *(i)* $u = \mathrm{InsAft}(n, f)$ or $u = \mathrm{InsBef}(n, f)$: when applied to a tree D the operation returns a new tree, such that, if $n \in D$, the trees in f are inserted immediately after (before) the node with id n in the parent node of n, in the same order as in the forest f. If $n \notin D$, the operation just returns D (we omit the similar requirement on the updates below); *(ii)* $u = \mathrm{InsInto}(n, f)$: when applied to D, the operation returns a new tree such that, if $n \in D$, the trees in f are inserted after the last child of node n; *(iii)* $u = \mathrm{Del}(n)$: the operation returns a new tree obtained from D by removing the sub-tree rooted at n; *(iv)* $u = \mathrm{Replace}(n, f)$: the operation returns a new tree such that, if $n \in D$, the trees in f replace the sub-tree rooted in the node n (in the ordering given by f). In all cases above, fresh nodeIds are generated for inserted nodes.

Single-step processing of programs. We now present the next main component of update evaluation, the operator that reduces a single partially-evaluated update to a sequence of simpler ones.

An *expression binding* for an update u is a mapping associating a set of tuples to occurrences of XPath expressions in u. A tuple will be either a nodeId in the original tree or a tree constructed from the original one (e.g., a copy of the subtree below a node).

A *bound update* is a pair (b, u) where u is an **UpdateStatement** and b is an expression binding for u. The *update reduction operator* $[\cdot]$ takes a bound update and produces a sequence of bound updates and concrete updates. We refer to such a sequence as an *update sequence*. We define $[p]$ for a bound update $p = (b, u)$ as follows. If $p =$ (for var in E u', b), we form $[p]$ by evaluating E to get nodes $n_1 \ldots n_k$, and return the sequence whose i^{th} element is (b_i, u') , where b_i extends b by assigning var to n_i. If u is an update block $u_1 \ldots u_l$, then $[p]$ returns $(b, u_1) \ldots (b, u_l)$. If u is a simple update with no bindings for the expressions in u, $[p]$ is formed by first evaluating the template in u (in case of replace or insert) to get a forest, and evaluating the target expressions in u to get one or more target node identifiers. We then proceed as follows: for an insert or replace if the target expression evaluated to more than one target node, $[p]$ is the empty sequence, otherwise $[p]$ is (b', u_0), where b' extends b by binding the remaining variables according to the evaluation just performed. For a delete, let nodeIds $n_1 \ldots n_j$ be the result of evaluation of the target expression. $[p]$ is $(b_1, u) \ldots (b_j, u)$, where b_i extends b by assigning the target expression of the delete to n_i. Finally, if $p = (b, u)$ is a bound update in which u is simple and every expression is already bound, then $[p]$ is simply the concrete update formed by replacing the expressions in u with the corresponding nodeId or forest given by the bindings.

Processing Order for Complex Updates. We are now ready to define the semantics of programs, using two kinds of transitions acting on a *program state*, which consists of a tree and an update sequence.

An *evaluation step* on a program state $(D, \mathrm{us} = p_1 \ldots p_n)$ is a transition to (D, us') where the new update sequence us$'$ is formed by picking a bound update $p = (b, u)$ from the update sequence and replacing p by $[p]$ in the sequence. If ps is the program state before such an evaluation step and ps$'$ is the result of the step, we write ps $\leadsto^e_p$ ps$'$. For example, the processing of the update U = for $x in /A/B insert $x/C into /B at program state $\mathrm{ps}_0 = (D, \mathrm{p}_0 = (\emptyset, U))$ would begin with the step: $\mathrm{ps}_0 \leadsto^e_{p_0} \mathrm{ps}_1$ where ps_1 is: D, $\{p_1$=(⟨ $x:i$_1$ ⟩, insert $x/C into /B); p_2 = (⟨ $x:i$_2$ ⟩, insert $x/C into /B) $\}$ and where the nodeIds $\{i_1, i_2\}$ are the result of evaluating $/A/B$. An *application step* simply consumes a concrete update u from the update sequence and replaces the tree D by the result of applying u to D. We write ps $\leadsto^a_u$ ps$'$

An *evaluation sequence* is any sequence of steps $\leadsto^e$ and $\leadsto^a$ as above, leading from the initial tree and update statement to some tree with empty update sequence. The final tree is the *output of the sequence*. In general, different evaluation sequences may produce distinct outputs. As mentioned in the introduction, all existing proposals use a snapshot semantics which restricts to evaluation sequences such that *(i)* (*snapshot rule*) all available evaluation transitions $\leadsto^e$ must be applied before any application step $\leadsto^a$ is performed, and *(ii)* (*ordering rule*) the application steps $\leadsto_a$ must then be applied in exactly the order given in the update sequence - that is, we always perform $\leadsto^a_p$ starting at the initial concrete update in the update sequence. It is easy to see that this results in a unique output for each update. We say $(D, U) \leadsto^{snap} D'$ if $(D, \{(\emptyset, U)\}$ rewrites to $(D', \emptyset)$ via a sequence of $\leadsto^e$ and $\leadsto^a$ transitions, subject to the conditions above.

3 Optimized Evaluation and Verification

Naturally, an implementation of the snapshot semantics will differ from the conceptual version above: e.g. multiple evaluation or concrete update steps can be folded into one, and cursors over intermediate tables containing query results will be used, rather than explicit construction of the update sequence. However, even a sophisticated implementation may be inefficient if it respects the snapshot rule *(i)* above. The snapshot rule forces the evaluation of all embedded expressions to occur: this can be very expensive in terms of space. Furthermore, it may be more efficient to apply delete operations as soon as they are generated, since these can dramatically reduce the processing time in further evaluations.

The *eager evaluation* of an update u is the evaluation formed by dropping the snapshot rule and replacing it with the requirement *(i')* that whenever the update sequence has as initial element a concrete update p, we perform the application step $\rightsquigarrow_p^a$. It is easy to see that *(i')* also guarantees that there is at most one outcome of every evaluation. We denote the corresponding rewriting relation by $\rightsquigarrow^{eager}$.

We say that a program U is *Binding Independent* (BI) if any evaluation sequence for u satisfying requirement the ordering rule *(ii)* produces the same output modulo an isomorphism preserving any nodeIds from the input tree. Note that if two trees are isomorphic in this sense, then no user query can distinguish between them. Clearly, if an update is BI we can use $\rightsquigarrow^{eager}$ instead of $\rightsquigarrow^{snap}$. Similarly, we say that a program U is BI with respect to a schema (automaton or DTD) if the above holds for all trees D satisfying the schema. The example U1 is BI with respect to the XMark DTD (a fact which our analysis verifies). A simple example of an update that is not BI is:

```
U2 :    for $i in //openauction,for $ j in //openauction,
        insert $i into $j
```

Indeed, the eager evaluation of U2 can increase the size of the tree exponentially, since at each \$i element we duplicate every openauction element in the tree. A simple argument shows that snapshot evaluation can increase the size of the tree only polynomially. Unfortunately, one cannot hope to decide whether an arbitrary TUpdate program is BI. That is, we have:

Theorem 1. *The problem of deciding whether a TUpdate program is Binding Independent with respect to an automaton is undecidable.*

The proof is by a reduction to solvability of diophantine equations, and is omitted for space reasons. We thus turn to the main goal of the paper: a static analysis procedure that gives sufficient conditions for BI. These conditions will also guarantee that the number of evaluation steps needed to process the update under eager evaluation is no greater than its time under snapshot evaluation.

Binding Independence Verification Algorithm. We give a conservative reduction of BI testing to the decidable problem of satisfiability testing for *XPath equations*. Given $\boldsymbol{x}$ a sequence of variables, a *system of XPath equations in* $\boldsymbol{x}$ is a conjunction of statements either of the form $x_i : E_i$, where E_i is in XP($x_1 \ldots x_{i-1}$), or of one of the forms $lab(x) = A$, $lab(x) \neq A$, $x_i \neq x_j$ for $i \neq j$. Given a tree D and sequence of nodeIds

$a_1 \ldots a_n$, we say $\boldsymbol{a}$ satisfies the equations if a_i is in the result of E_i evaluated in a context where $\boldsymbol{x}$ interpreted by $\boldsymbol{a}$, and if the label and inequality conjuncts are satisfied. A system of equations $H(\boldsymbol{x})$ is unsatisfiable iff for all trees D there is no $\boldsymbol{a}$ satisfying H in D. We define the notion of unsatisfiability with respect to a schema analogously. Our goal is an algorithm that, given a TUpdate program U will produce a set of systems of XPath equations $S_1 \ldots S_n$ such that: each S_i is unsatisfiable implies U is BI.

Non-interference. Intuitively, an update is BI if performing concrete updates that are generated from a program does not impact the evaluation of other XPath expressions. For example U1, we can see that in order to verify BI it suffices to check that: i) for each a_0 in //openauction, the update ($i:a$_0$, insert $i/initial/text into $i/current) does not change the value of the expression $i/initial/text, $i/current, or $i/bidder, where in the last expression $i can be bound to any a_1 in //openauction, and in the first two to any $a_1 \neq a_0$ ii) for each a$_0$ in //openauction, ($i:a$_0$, delete $i/bidder) does not effect $i/initial/text, or $i/current for any $i, and does not effect $i/bidder when $i is bound to $a_1 \neq a_0$. The above suffices to show BI, since it implies that performing any evaluation step after an update gives the same result as performing the evaluation before the update.

We say a TUpdate program U is *non-interfering* if: for every D, for each two distinct tuples $\boldsymbol{a}$ and $\boldsymbol{a}'$ that can be generated from binding the for loops in U on D, for each simple update u in U and every XPath expression E in U, $E(\boldsymbol{a}')(D)$ returns the same set as $E(\boldsymbol{a}')(u(\boldsymbol{a})(D))$, and if the above holds for $\boldsymbol{a} = \boldsymbol{a}'$ if E is not in u. Note that both eager and snapshot semantics agree on what $u(\boldsymbol{a})(D)$ means for a simple update u. The discussion previously is summarized in the observation: *if U is non-interfering, then U is BI*. Furthermore, if U is non-interfering, the eager evaluation terminates in at most the number of steps needed to evaluate U under snapshot evaluation. The condition is not necessary. Thus far we have found that BI updates arising in practice (i.e. in the uses of our update engine within projects at Lucent Technologies) are non-interfering. Moreover, non-interference can be tested effectively; however, to gain additional efficiency, we provide only a conservative test in our implementation.

Non-interference breaks down into a number of assertions about the invariance of expressions under updates, each of which needs to be verified separately. A *delete non-interference assertion* is of the form $(C(\boldsymbol{x}), u(\boldsymbol{x}), M(\boldsymbol{x}, \boldsymbol{y}))$ where $C(\boldsymbol{x})$ is a system of XPath equations, M is a system of equations in XP$(\boldsymbol{x}, \boldsymbol{y})$, and u is a SimpleUpdate. The system M is the *monitored system* of the assertion while C is the *context system*. An *insert non-interference assertion* has the same form.

A delete non-interference assertion is valid iff for all trees D $\boldsymbol{a}$ satisfying $C(\boldsymbol{x})$ in D, for every $\boldsymbol{b}$ in D, we have $D \models M(\boldsymbol{a}, \boldsymbol{b}) \rightarrow u(\boldsymbol{a})(D) \models M(\boldsymbol{a}, \boldsymbol{b})$. That is, u does not delete anything from the monitored system. An insert non-interference assertion is valid iff for all trees D, $\boldsymbol{a}$ satisfying $C(\boldsymbol{x})$ in D, and for every $\boldsymbol{b}$ in $u(\boldsymbol{a})D$, $u(\boldsymbol{a})(D) \models M(\boldsymbol{a}, \boldsymbol{b}) \rightarrow D \models M(\boldsymbol{a}, \boldsymbol{b})$. That is, u does not add anything to the monitored system. Note that if u is a delete, then we need only consider delete non-interference assertions, since the XPath queries we deal with are monotone; similarly, if u is an insert, we consider only insert non-interference assertions. Hence we drop the word "insert" or "delete" before non-interference assertions for these simple updates, implicitly assuming the non-vacuous case. We write non-interference assertions in tabular form. For example, the non-interference assertion below, generated from U1, states that a delete in U1 for an index $i does not effect the expression $i/current for any other value of $i:

C= $\$i_1$://openauction	u= delete $\$i_1$/bidder	M= $\$i_1 \neq \$i_2$; $\$i_2$://openauction; $z:$\$i_2$/current

Non-interference of U amounts to verifying a set of non-interference assertions, one for each triple consisting of a simple update in U, an XPath expression in U, and an index that witnesses that the context variables are distinct. To increase precision, we can exclude considering non-interference assertions where u is a delete and E is the target expression of u: this broadening of the definition of non-interference is sound, since if $u(\boldsymbol{a})$ deletes from $E(\boldsymbol{a}')$ this does not effect the final evaluation but merely accelerates it.

From Non-interference to Satisfiability. Validity of non-interference assertions still requires reasoning about updates over multiple trees, while we wish to reason about XPath satisfiability over a single tree. Our main result is a reduction of non-interference assertions to satisfiability tests. This reduction makes use of a fundamental property of the snapshot semantics: under this semantics elements in the output tree are in one-to-one correspondence with tuples of elements in the input tree.

Consider the non-interference assertion generated from U1 in the table above. To check this it suffices to confirm that the deleted items do not overlap with the monitored expression $\$i_2$/current. So the non-interference assertion is equivalent to the joint unsatisfiability of the equations: $\$i_1$://openauction; $\$i_2$://openauction; $\$i_1 \neq \$i_2$; $z: $\$i_1$/bidder//*; $z:$\$i_2$/current. This system is unsatisfiable because $z cannot be both a descendant of $\$i_1$ and a child of $\$i_2 \neq \$i_1$, and this is easily detected by our satisfiability test. In general, for delete operations, a non-interference assertion requires checking whether the system Γ is unsatisfiable, where Γ contains the context and monitored equations, and equations $o:$te//*$. Here te is the target expression of the delete, and $o is the variable appearing in an XPath equation in the monitored system (for a delete, this will consist of inequalities plus one XPath equation).

The analysis for inserts requires a much more complex transformation. We give the intuition for this by example, leaving details for the full paper. Consider the non-interference assertion generated from U1, which states that the insert into $i/current does not effect $i/initial/text:

C=$i://openauction	u = insert $i/initial/text into $i/current	M = $\$i'$://openauction; $\$i' \neq \$i$; $z:$\$i'$/initial/te

We want to derive a collection of systems of equations such that they are all unsatisfiable iff this assertion holds. We start by normalizing the assertion so that all equations are *basic*: a basic equation is either a label test, an inequality, or of the form $x:$y/* or $x:$y//*. That is, all the XPath expressions consist of just a single step. We do this by introducing additional variables for intermediate steps in all path expressions.

C	lab($i)=openauction; $k:$i/*; lab($k)=initial; $l:$k/*; lab($l)=text; $m:$i/*; lab($m)=current;
u	insert $l into $m
M	$\$i' \neq \$i$; lab($\$i'$)=openauction; $\$k'$:$\$i'$/*; lab($\$k'$)=initial; $\$l'$:$\$k'$/*; lab($\$l'$)=text;

So this assertion says that for any values of i, k, l, m satisfying the equations at the top, the operation in the center does not insert any new witness for the equations on the bottom. Note that there is a further approximation being done here, since instead of checking whether the output of an XPath expression changes, we check whether there is a change to a vector of variables that projects onto that output. This approximation allows us to reduce non-interference to a satisfiability test, while an exact non-interference test would require a (EXPTIME complete [9]) containment test in the presence of a schema.

To reason about these assertions, we consider the possible ways in which a new witness set for the monitored equations can occur. Continuing with our example, let D be some tree, i, k, l, m be witnesses for the context equations in D, and $D'(i, k, l, m)$ be the tree resulting from the insert above. Every node in D' is either a node from the initial tree D (an "old" witness) or was inserted by the operation insert $1 into $m. In general, nodes n arising from an insert or replace can be classified by which node of the insert or replace template they arose from. They are either matched by a literal node tn of a template, or they are matched by a node p that lies inside a copy of the subtree t_a of D rooted at node a, where a was matched by some variable v associated with template node tn of the insert operation. In either of the last two cases, we say that n is *generated by template node* tn. In the second case we say the node p is the *pre-witness of* n: that is, p is the element of the old tree that was copied to get n. We write $p = \mathsf{pre}(n)$. In the case n is an old witness, we say $\mathsf{pre}(n) = n$, and in the case n is associated with a literal template node, we set $\mathsf{pre}(n)$ to be the insertion point where the constructed witness was appended. We can classify our witness tuple by means of a *witness map*: this is a function F assigning to each variable in the monitored equations either an element of the insert or replace template, or the keyword old.

In the example above, one of the witness maps is: $F(\mathrm{i}') = F(\mathrm{k}') = \mathsf{old}, F(\mathrm{l}') = tn$ where tn is the only template node of the insert. We reduce the number of maps considered by enforcing some simple consistency conditions needed for a map to have the possibility of generating a witness. For example, not all variables can be mapped to old, if there is equation $lab(x) = A$ in M, and x is mapped by F to a literal node of a template, then the label of that node must be the literal A.

In the case above, these rules imply that the map above is the only witness map that could yield a witness violating the non-interference assertion, because the template node is a text node and hence cannot witness a non-text node. Figure 2 illustrates the situation: a) shows the initial tree before the insert, with the inserted tree and insert point highlighted. b) shows the tree resulting from the insert, and c) shows the pattern needed to witness the interference assertion in the new tree, according to this witness map. Note that the monitored equations assert that k' is the parent of l'. So we have an old node k'

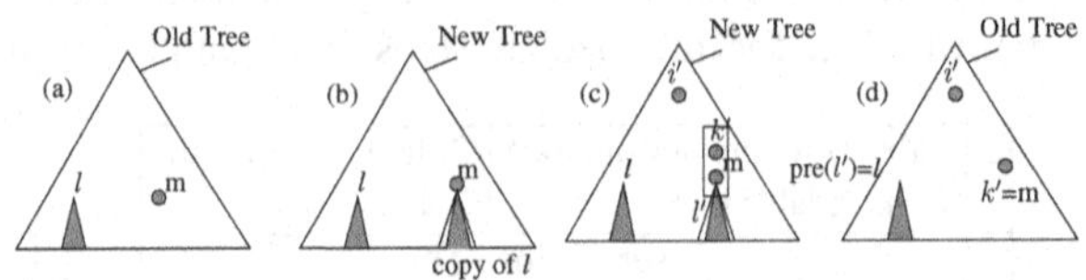

Fig. 2. A pattern and its precondition relative to a witness map

that is the parent of a newly-inserted node l′. From the picture, it is clear that this can happen only if k′ is actually the target of the insert, namely m, while l′ is a copy of the root l of the inserted tree. Hence in the original tree D, the pre-witnesses for i′, k′, l′ are shown in Figure 2d); since k′, i′ are old witnesses, we write i′ instead of pre(i′) in the figure. The pre-witnesses of i′, k′ are a pair satisfying the context equations, but with pre(k′) constrained to be m; the pre-witness of l' will be l. Figure 2d) thus shows what the old tree must look like. The set of equations corresponding to this is shown below. The equations are unsatisfiable, since $m =$ pre(k′) but they have distinct labels.

---

lab($i)=openauction; $k:$i/*; lab($k)=initial; $l:$k/*; lab($l)=text; $m:$i/*; lab($m)=current; $i′ ≠ $i; lab($i′)=openauction; pre($k′):$i′/*; lab(pre($k′))=initial; pre($k′) =$m; pre($l′)=$l;

Given a witness map F and assertion $A = (H(\boldsymbol{x}), u(\boldsymbol{x}), M(\boldsymbol{x}, \boldsymbol{y}))$, we can now state more precisely our goal: to get a set of equations $K(\boldsymbol{x}, \boldsymbol{y}')$ such that for any tree D and $\boldsymbol{a}$ satisfying H in D, for any $\boldsymbol{b}'$ in D, $K(\boldsymbol{a}, \boldsymbol{b}')$ holds iff there is $\boldsymbol{b}$ such that $H(\boldsymbol{a}, \boldsymbol{b})$ holds in $D' = u(\boldsymbol{a})(D)$ and pre(b_i) $= \mathrm{b}'_i$. As the example shows, we get this set of equations by unioning the context equations with a rewriting of the monitored equations. Details are given in the full paper.

Theorem 2. *For every non-interference assertion A we can generate a collection of systems of equations* $S_1 \ldots S_n$ *such that A is valid iff each of the* S_i *are unsatisfiable.*

Accounting for a schema. The analysis above checks that an update program U is Binding Independent when run on *any* tree D. Of course, since many programs are not BI on an arbitrary input, it is essential to do a more precise analysis that verifies BI only for input trees satisfying a given automata or DTD S. It is tempting to think that relativizing to a schema requires one only to do the satisfiability test relative to the schema. That is, one might think that a program U is BI w.r.t. schema S if for every tree D satisfying S, for any concrete update u generated from U and any path expression E with parameters from D, E has the same value on D as it does on $u(D)$. However, this is not the case. Consider the update U: for $x in //A insert $x into $x//C insert $x into $x//B delete A/[/B and /C]. Suppose that we wish to consider whether or not U is BI with respect to a given schema S. It is clear that we need to know that instances of the insert do not produce a new witness to A/[/B and /C]. Thus, we need to prove that under eager evaluation there is no evaluation sequence adding a new witness pattern consisting of A,B, and C nodes. But the final witness to this pattern will result from an update to some intermediate tree D', which may not satisfy S. Hence to reduce BI analysis to non-interference of concrete updates *over trees D satisfying the schema*, we must deal with the impact of *sequences* of concrete updates on D.

For integer k, a TUpdate U is *k non-interfering with respect to a schema S* if for every D satisfying S *i)* no delete or replace operation generated from U deletes a witness to an XPath expression in U for a distinct binding, and *ii)* for every sequence $u_1(\boldsymbol{a}^1) \ldots u_k(\boldsymbol{a}^k)$, where u_i are simple inserts or replaces in U and $\boldsymbol{a}^i$ are tuples satisfying the for loop bindings in D, for every expression E, and every $\boldsymbol{b}$ satisfying the bindings and distinct from all $\boldsymbol{a}^i$, $E(\boldsymbol{b})(D) = E(\boldsymbol{b})(D')$, where D' is the result of applying each $u_i^+(\boldsymbol{a}_i)$ to D. Here u^+ for $u =$ replace E with τ is defined to be insert τ into E, and $u^+ = u$ for other simple updates. Informally, k non-interfering means that no single update deletes a witness to an XPath expression in U, and no sequence of k

updates inserts a witness. It is easy to see that programs with this property for *every* k are Binding Independent w.r.t. S. The following result gives a bound on k: its proof is given in the full paper.

Theorem 3. *A program U is BI with respect to S if it is k-non-interfering, with respect to S, where k is the maximum of the number of axis steps in any expression E.*

From the theorem, we can see that Binding Independence of U w.r.t. schema S can be reduced to polynomially many non-interference assertions, where this notation is extended to allow a collection of updates. If we consider the update U1 with regard to schema-based BI verification, we need to check assertions such as:

C	\$i$_1$://openauction;	\$i$_2$://openauction;	\$i$_3$://openauction;
$\mathcal{U}$	insert \$i$_1$/initial/text into \$i$_1$/current	insert \$i$_2$/initial/text into \$i$_2$/current	insert \$i$_3$/initial/text
M	\$i$'$://openauction;	\$i$' \neq$ \$i$_1$,i$_2$,i$_3$;	\$z:\$i$'$/initial/text;

These new non-interference assertions are reduced to satisfiability through the use of witness maps and rewriting as previously – we now map nodes in the monitored equations to template nodes in any of the updates.

(Un)Satisfiability Test. The previous results allow us to reduce BI analysis to a collection of unsatisfiability tests of systems of XPath equations on a single tree. Unsatisfiability can be seen decidable via appeal to classical decidability results on trees [17]. Although we could have made use of a third party satisfiability test for logics on trees (e.g. the MONA system [4], although this deals only with satisfiability over ranked trees), we found it more convenient to craft our own test. Our satisfiability problem is in CO-NP; in contrast MONA implements a satisfiability test for a much more powerful logic, whose worst-case complexity is non-elementary. For the quantifier-free XPath equations considered here, the satisfiability problem is known to be NP-complete [6]. From this, we can show that non-interference is CO-NP hard.

Since an exact test is CO-NP, we first perform a conservative unsatisfiability test which simply extracts the descendant relations that are permitted by the schema (for a DTD, this is done by taking the transitive closure of the dependency graph) and then checks each axis equation for consistency with these relations: this test is linear in the size of the equations, and if all equations generated by the reduction are unsatisfiable, we have verified Binding Independence. Our exact test uses a fairly standard automata-theoretic method. The basic idea is to "complete" a system of equations S to get a system S' in which: i) the dependency relation between variables forms a tree, ii) distinct variables are related by inequations, and variables that are siblings within the tree are related by a total sibling ordering iii) if x is a variable then there is at most one variable y that is related to x by an equation y: x//*. The significance of complete systems is that they can be translated in linear time into a tree automaton. There are many completions of a given system, and we can enumerate them by making choices for the relations among variables. Although the number of completions is necessarily exponential in the worst case, in the presence of a schema we can trim the number significantly by making only those choices consistent with the schema dependency graph. In the absence of a schema, any propositionally consistent complete equation system is satisfiable; thus we can test satisfiability by checking for existence of a complete consistent extension. In the presence of a schema, we translate complete systems into automata, and then take a product. Consider the standard encoding of an ordered unranked tree T by a binary tree T': in this encoding a node $n' \in T'$ represents a node $n \in T$, with the left child c' of n' corresponding to the first child of n, and the right child of n' corresponding to the following sibling of n in T (this sibling ordering is given as part of the complete system). Relative to this coding, we translate a complete system into a system of equations over binary trees. Our translation maps an XPath equation ρ to a "binary XPath equation" ρ' , where these equations mention the axes $\downarrow_{\mathsf{left}}, \downarrow_{\mathsf{right}}, \downarrow^*_{\mathsf{right}} \dots$ For example, an equation of the form \$x:\$y/* maps to an equation \$x:\$y/$\downarrow_{\mathsf{left}}/\downarrow^*_{\mathsf{right}}$. The resulting binary equations are again complete, and can thus be translated easily into a bottom-up non-deterministic tree automaton over finite trees.

We have thus arrived at a collection of automata A_i representing complete binary systems extending our original system S. We can likewise transform the schema S into an automaton A_S accepting exactly the binary encodings of trees conforming to S. A standard product construction then yields an automaton A'_i accepting exactly those trees conforming to D for which S returns a result, and a simple fixed point algorithm is used to see if the language returned by an A'_i is nonempty [11].

4 Experimental Results

The overall flow of the verification and its use is shown in Figure 3. At verification time, a program is parsed and then goes through the stages of: i) generating non-interference assertions, ii) for each assertion generating the witness maps, iii) for each assertion and witness map, performing rewriting to get a system of equations which needs to be found unsatisfiable. Each system produced is tested for satisfiability with respect to the DTD, if one is present. If a system is found satisfiable, analysis terminates; in this case, nothing is known about the program. If all systems are unsatisfiable, the analysis outputs that the program is verified to be BI. At runtime, the program is processed by our modification of the Galax-based XML update engine. A flag is passed with the program telling whether the program is BI; if so, the eager evaluation is used. The verification algorithms are in Java, while the runtime, like the rest of Galax, is in OCAML.

We ran our analysis algorithms on a testbed of sample updates, corresponding in size and complexity to those used in our application of the XML update language of [15] at Lucent Technologies. In Table 1 we show the verification times as the number of steps in the update increases. The times are based on a Pentium 4 with a 1GB RAM and 2.80GHz CPU running XP: in each case, the verification runs in seconds. The times are an average over 1-4 updates, 90% BI and 10% non-BI. We were interested also in tracking the two potential sources of combinatorial blow-up in our algorithms: the first

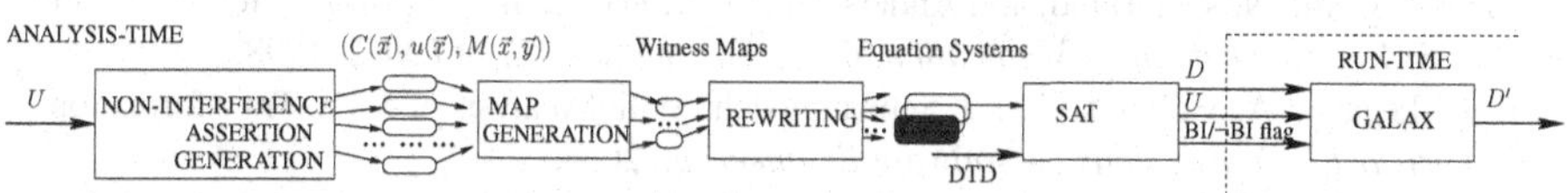

Fig. 3. Architecture of Static Analysis-time and Run-time in Galax

Table 1. Results of Analysis on a query with variable number of steps

Query Steps	Verification Time(ms)	Nr. of Equation Systems
9	4422	7
10	2390	15
11	5125	15
12	6953	17
13	8250	17
14	10984	17
15	8719	17
16	15701	17
17	25046	17
18	29781	17
19	31281	17

is the number of witness maps to be considered, which determines the number of equation systems that need to be generated. The second is the complexity of the satisfiability test. The first is controlled by the consistency rules for witness map assignment, and our preliminary results (also shown in the figure) show that our rules keep the number of equations systems, and hence calls to satisfiability, low, generally in single digits. The complexity of the satisfiability test is controlled principally by filtering using an approximate test and secondly by using the DTD dependency graph to limit the number of completions. The latter is particularly useful given that DTDs tend to give strong restrictions on the tags that can appear in a parent/child relationship. Currently, our approximate test is quite crude, and eliminates only a small percentage of the equation systems. However, the XMark DTD reduces the number of completions significantly – in our sample updates, to at most several hundred. This results in low time for the aggregate test, since for complete systems the satisfiability test is linear.

Acknowledgements. We thank Jérôme Siméon for many helpful discussions on update semantics, and Andrea Pugliese for his support in implementation of the static analysis routines. We are also very grateful to Glenn Bruns and Patrice Godefroid for invaluable comments on the draft.

References

1. A. Bouajjani and T. Touili. Extrapolating Tree Transformations. In *Proceedings of CAV*, 2002.
2. D. Dams, Y. Lakhnech, and M. Steffen. Iterating Transducers for Safety of Data-Abstractions. In *Proceedings of CAV*, 2001.
3. E. W. Dijkstra. *A Discipline of Programming*. Prentice-Hall, 1976.
4. Jacob Elgaard, Nils Klarlund, and Anders Moller. Mona 1.x: new techniques for WS1S and WS2S. In *Computer Aided Verification, CAV '98*, volume 1427 of *LNCS*, 1998.
5. C. Kirkegaard, A. Moller, and M. I. Schwartzbach. Static Analysis of XML Transformations in Java. *IEEE Transactions on Software Engineering*, 2004.
6. L. V. S. Lakshmanan, G. Ramesh, H. Wang, and Z. Zhao. On Testing Satisfiability of Tree Pattern Queries. In *Proc. of VLDB*, 2004.

7. A. Laux and L. Martin. XUpdate - XML Update Language., 2000. http://www.xmldb.org/xupdate/xupdate-wd.html.
8. P. Lehti. Design and Implementation of a Data Manipulation Processor. Diplomarbeit, Technische Universitat Darmstadt, 2002. http://www.lehti.de/beruf/diplomarbeit.pdf.
9. F. Neven and T. Schwentick. XPath Containment in the Presence of Disjunction, DTDs, and Variables. In *Proc. of ICDT*, pages 315–329, 2003.
10. Mads Olesen. Static validation of XSLT, 2004. http://www.daimi.au.dk/madman/xsltvalidation.
11. Grzegorz Rozenberg and Arto Salomaa. *Handbook of formal languages, volume 3: beyond words*. Springer Verlag, 1997.
12. M. Rys. Bringing the Internet to Your Database: Using SQLServer 2000 and XML to Build Loosely-Coupled Systems. In *Proc. of ICDE*, pages 465–472, 2001.
13. A. Schmidt, F. Waas, M. Kersten, M. Carey, I. Manolescu, and R. Busse. XMark: A benchmark for XML data management. In *Proc. of VLDB*, 2002.
14. Michael Schwartzbach and Anders Moller. The design space of type checkers for XML transformation languages. In *Proc. of ICDT*, 2005.
15. G. Sur, J. Hammer, and J. Siméon. An XQuery-Based Language for Processing Updates in XML. In *PLAN-X*, 2004. See http://www.cise.ufl.edu/research/mobility.
16. I. Tatarinov, Z. Ives, A.Y. Halevy, and D.S. Weld. Updating XML. In *Proc. of ACM SIGMOD*, 2001.
17. J.W. Thatcher and J.B. Wright. Generalized finite automata with an application to a decision problem of second-order logic. *Math. Systems Theory*, 2:57–82, 1968.

Expand, Enlarge and Check... Made Efficient*

Gilles Geeraerts, Jean-François Raskin, and Laurent Van Begin**

Université Libre de Bruxelles – Département d'Informatique – CPI 212
Boulevard du Triomphe, B–1050 Bruxelles, Belgium
{gigeerae, jraskin, lvbegin}@ulb.ac.be

Abstract. The coverability problem is decidable for the class of well-structured transition systems. Until recently, the only known algorithm to solve this problem was based on symbolic backward reachability. In a recent paper, we have introduced the theory underlying a new algorithmic solution, called 'Expand, Enlarge and Check', which can be implemented in a forward manner. In this paper, we provide additional concepts and algorithms to turn this theory into efficient forward algorithms for monotonic extensions of Petri nets and Lossy Channels Systems. We have implemented a prototype and applied it on a large set of examples. This prototype outperforms a previous fine tuned prototype based on backward symbolic exploration and shows the practical interest of our new algorithmic solution.

1 Introduction

Model-checking is nowadays widely accepted as a powerful technique for the automatic verification of reactive systems that have natural finite state abstractions. However, many reactive systems are only naturally modelled as infinite-state systems. Consequently, a large (and successful) research effort has recently focused on the application of model-checking techniques to infinite-state models such as FIFO channel systems [2], (extensions of) Petri nets and automata with counters [14], broadcast protocols [7], etc.

One of the positive results is the decidability of the *coverability problem* for *well-structured transition systems* (WSTS for short). WSTS enjoy an infinite set of states that is well-quasi ordered by $\leq$ and their transition relation is monotonic w.r.t $\leq$. Examples of such systems are Petri nets and their monotonic extensions [4, 14], broadcast protocols [6], lossy channel systems [2]. The *coverability problem* asks whether a given WSTS S can reach a state of a given $\leq$-upward closed set of states U.

A general algorithm (i.e. a procedure that always terminates) is known to solve the coverability problem for WSTS [1, 9]. It symbolically manipulates upward-closed sets of states, obtained by unrolling the transition relation in a

* This work has been partially supported by the FRFC grant 2.4530.02. of the National Belgian Fund for Scientific Research (FNRS).

** Supported by a "First Europe" grant EPH3310300R0012 of the Walloon Region.

K. Etessami and S.K. Rajamani (Eds.): CAV 2005, LNCS 3576, pp. 394–407, 2005.

backward fashion. Unfortunately, backward search is seldom efficient in practice [12], and the only complete forward approach known so far is the Karp-Miller algorithm that can only be applied to a small subclass of WSTS: Petri nets. All the previous attempts to generalize this procedure have led to incomplete forward approaches that are either not guaranteed to terminate (e.g.: [6], as shown in [7]) or that can be inconclusive due to over-approximation [3].

Nevertheless, we have recently proposed a new schema of algorithms, called 'Expand, Enlarge and Check' (EEC for short), to solve the coverability problem for a large class of WSTS (those that enjoy reasonable effectiveness requirements, see [11] for the details). EEC works basically as follows. It constructs a sequence of pairs of approximations of the set of reachable states: an under-approximation (built during the 'Expand phase') and an over-approximation (built during the 'Enlarge' phase). Some basic results from the theory of well-quasi ordering and recursively enumerable sets allow us to show that positive instances of the coverability problem are answered by the sequence of under-approximations while negative instances are answered by the over-approximations after a finite number of iterations. The theory and the proofs are very elegant and furthermore the schema is really promising from the practical point of view because it can be implemented in a forward manner.

In this paper, we show that, indeed, EEC can be turned into an efficient algorithm to solve the coverability problem in a forward manner. In particular, we show how to implement the EEC efficiently for the two most practically important classes of WSTS in the literature: monotonic extensions of Petri Nets (EPN for short) and for Lossy Channel Systems (LCS for short). Those two classes are useful for the analysis of parametric systems and communication protocols. To obtain efficient algorithms from the EEC schema, we have to get over two obstacles: first, during the 'Expand' phase, we have to analyze finite graphs that can be very large. Second, during the 'Enlarge' phase, we have to approximate sets of successors efficiently. To solve the first problem, we show that we can always turn a WSTS into a *lossy* WSTS that respects the same coverability properties and for which the graph during the 'Expand' phase is monotonic. The coverability problem can often be solved efficiently in monotonic graphs because (roughly) only $\leq$-maximal states of the graph must be explored. We provide an efficient algorithm for that exploration. This algorithm is also applicable during the 'Enlarge' phase in the case of EPN. We show in the sequel that it dramatically improves the practical efficiency of the method. The second problem is difficult for LCS only. We provide here a way to construct efficiently the most precise approximations of the set of the successors of a downward-closed set of LCS configurations.

On the basis of those two conceptual tools, we have implemented a prototype to analyze coverability properties of EPN and LCS. We have applied the prototype to a large set of examples taken in the literature and compared its performances with our fine-tuned implementation of the backward search in the case of EPN. For LCS, the only available tools are implementing either a potentially non-terminating analysis or an over-approximation algorithm that is not guaranteed to conclude due to over-approximation. The performance of our prototype are very encouraging and often much better than those of the backward search prototype.

The rest of the paper is organized as follows. In Section 2, we recall some basic notions about well-quasi orderings, WSTS and the coverability problem. In Section 3, we summarize the results of our previous paper about the EEC schema. In Section 4, we show how to efficiently explore monotonic graphs to establish coverability properties and show that the graphs that we have to analyze during the 'Expand' phase are monotonic when the lossy abstraction is applied. In Section 5, we show how EPN and LCS can be analyzed efficiently with the EEC schema, and provide practical evidence that it can compete advantageously with other techniques. Finally, we draw some conclusions in section 6.

Due to the lack of space, the proofs have been omitted in the present version of the paper. A full version of the paper and complete experimental results (including the data) can be found at: `http://www.ulb.ac.be/di/ssd/ggeeraer/eec/`

2 Preliminaries

In this section, we recall some fundamental results about *well-quasi orderings* and *well-structured transition systems* (the systems we analyze here). We show how to *finitely* represent upward- and downward-closed sets of states (which will allow us to devise *symbolic* algorithms), and discuss And-Or graphs and monotonic graphs (useful to represent abstractions of systems).

Well Quasi-Orderings and Adequate Domains of Limits. A *well quasi ordering* $\leq$ on C (wqo for short) is a *reflexive* and *transitive* relation s. t. for any infinite sequence $c_0 c_1 \ldots c_n \ldots$ of elements in C, there exist i and j, with $i < j$ and $c_i \leq c_j$. We note $c_i < c_j$ if $c_i \leq c_j$ but $c_j \not\leq c_i$.

Let $\langle C, \leq \rangle$ be a well-quasi ordered set. A *$\leq$-upward closed set* $U \subseteq C$ is such that for any $c \in U$, for any $c' \in C$ such that $c \leq c'$, $c' \in U$. A *$\leq$-downward-closed set* $D \subseteq C$ is such that for any $c \in D$, for any $c' \in C$ such that $c' \leq c$, $c' \in D$. The set of *$\leq$-minimal* elements $\mathsf{Min}(U)$ of a set $U \subseteq C$ is a minimal set such that $\mathsf{Min}(U) \subseteq U$ and $\forall s' \in U : \exists s \in \mathsf{Min}(U) : s \leq s'$. The next proposition is a consequence of wqo:

Proposition 1. *Let $\langle C, \leq \rangle$ be a wqo set and $U \subseteq C$ be an $\leq$-upward closed set, then:* $\mathsf{Min}(U)$ *is finite and* $U = \{c \mid \exists c' \in \mathsf{Min}(U) : c' \leq c\}$.

Thus, any $\leq$-upward closed set can be *effectively represented* by its finite set of minimal elements. To obtain a finite representation of $\leq$-downward-closed sets, we must use well-chosen limit elements $\ell \notin C$ that represent $\leq$-downward closures of infinite increasing chains of elements.

Definition 1 ([11]). *Let $\langle C, \leq \rangle$ be a well-quasi ordered set and L be a set s.t. $L \cap C = \emptyset$. The tuple $\langle L, \sqsubseteq, \gamma \rangle$ is called an* adequate domain of limits *for $\langle C, \leq \rangle$ if the following conditions are satisfied: (L_1: representation mapping) $\gamma : L \cup C \rightarrow$*

2^C *associates to each element in* $L \cup C$ *a* $\leq$*-downward-closed set* $D \subseteq C$*, and for any* $c \in C$*,* $\gamma(c) = \{c' \in C \mid c' \leq c\}$*.* γ *is extended to sets* $S \subseteq L \cup C$ *as follows:* $\gamma(S) = \cup_{c \in S}\gamma(c)$*; (*$\mathsf{L}_2$*: top element) There exists a special element* $\top \in L$ *such that* $\gamma(\top) = C$*; (*L_3*: precision order) The set* $L \cup C$ *is partially ordered by* $\sqsubseteq$*, where:* $d_1 \sqsubseteq d_2$ *iff* $\gamma(d_1) \subseteq \gamma(d_2)$*; (*$\mathsf{L}_4$*: completeness) for any* $\leq$*-downward-closed set* $D \subseteq C$*, there exists a finite set* $D' \subseteq L \cup C$*:* $\gamma(D') = D$*.*

Well-Structured Transition Systems and Coverability Problem. A *transition system* is a tuple $S = \langle C, c_0, \rightarrow\rangle$ where C is a (possibly infinite) set of states, $c_0 \in C$ is the initial state, $\rightarrow \subseteq C \times C$ is a transition relation. We note $c \rightarrow c'$ for $\langle c, c'\rangle \in \rightarrow$. For any state c, $\mathsf{Post}(c)$ denotes the set of one-step successors of c, i.e. $\mathsf{Post}(c) = \{c' | c \rightarrow c'\}$, this function is extended to sets: for any $C' \subseteq C$, $\mathsf{Post}(C') = \bigcup_{c \in C'} \mathsf{Post}(c)$. Without loss of generality, we assume that $\mathsf{Post}(c) \neq \emptyset$ for any $c \in C$. A *path* of S is a sequence of states $c_1, c_2, \ldots, c_k$ such that $c_1 \rightarrow c_2 \rightarrow \cdots \rightarrow c_k$. A state c' is reachable from a state c, noted $c \rightarrow^* c'$, if there exists a path $c_1, c_2, \ldots, c_k$ in S with $c_1 = c$ and $c_k = c'$. Given a transition system $S = \langle C, c_0, \rightarrow\rangle$, $\mathsf{Reach}(S)$ denotes the set $\{c \in C \mid c_0 \rightarrow^* c\}$.

Definition 2. *A transition system* $S = \langle C, c_0, \rightarrow\rangle$ *is a* well-structured transition system *(*WSTS*) [1, 9] for the quasi order* $\leq \subseteq C \times C$ *(noted:* $S = \langle C, c_0, \rightarrow, \leq\rangle$*) if: (*$\mathsf{W}_1$*: well-ordering)* $\leq$ *is a well-quasi ordering and (*W_2*: monotonicity) for any* $c_1, c_2, c_3 \in C$*:* $c_1 \leq c_2$ *and* $c_1 \rightarrow c_3$ *implies* $\exists c_4 \in C : c_3 \leq c_4$ *and* $c_2 \rightarrow c_4$*. It is* lossy *if its transition relation satisfies the following additional property: (*W_3*)* $\forall c_1, c_2, c_3 \in C$ *such that* $c_1 \rightarrow c_2$ *and* $c_3 \leq c_2$*, we have* $c_1 \rightarrow c_3$*.*

Problem 1. The *coverability problem for well-structured transition systems* is defined as follows: 'Given a well-structured transition system S and the $\leq$-upward closed set $U \subseteq C$, determine whether $\mathsf{Reach}(S) \cap U \neq \emptyset$'

To solve the coverability problem, we use the notion of covering set:

Definition 3. *For any* WSTS $S = \langle C, c_0, \rightarrow, \leq\rangle$*, the* covering set *of* S *(*$\mathsf{Cover}(S)$*), is the* $\leq$*-downward closure of* $\mathsf{Reach}(S)$*:* $\mathsf{Cover}(S) = \{c | \exists c' \in \mathsf{Reach}(S) : c \leq c'\}$*.*

Proposition 2 ([14]). *For any* WSTS $S = \langle C, c_0, \rightarrow, \leq\rangle$*,* $\mathsf{Cover}(S)$ *is such that for any* $\leq$*-upward closed set* $U \subseteq C$*:* $\mathsf{Reach}(S) \cap U = \emptyset$ *iff* $\mathsf{Cover}(S) \cap U = \emptyset$*.*

Finite Representation. For any WSTS $S = \langle C, c_0, \rightarrow, \leq\rangle$ with an adequate domain of limits $\langle L, \sqsubseteq, \gamma\rangle$ for $\langle C, \leq\rangle$, by property L_4 of Definition 1, there exists a finite subset $\mathsf{CS}(S) \subseteq L \cup C$ s.t. $\gamma(\mathsf{CS}(S)) = \mathsf{Cover}(S)$. In the sequel, $\mathsf{CS}(S)$ is called a *coverability set* of the covering set $\mathsf{Cover}(S)$ and finitely represents that set.

Lossiness Abstraction. Any WSTS can be turned into a lossy WSTS that respects the same coverability property. Definition 4 and Proposition 3 formalize this:

Definition 4. *The lossy version of a* WSTS $S = \langle C, c_0, \rightarrow, \leq \rangle$ *is the lossy* WSTS $\mathsf{lossy}(S) = \langle C, c_0, \rightarrow_\ell, \leq \rangle$ *where* $\rightarrow_\ell = \{(c, c') \mid \exists c'' \in C : c \rightarrow c'' \wedge c' \leq c''\}$.

Proposition 3. *For any* WSTS $S = \langle C, c_0, \rightarrow, \leq \rangle$: $\mathsf{Cover}(S) = \mathsf{Cover}(\mathsf{lossy}(S))$*; and for any* $\leq$*-upward closed set* $U \subseteq C$: $\mathsf{Reach}(S) \cap U = \emptyset$ *iff* $\mathsf{Cover}(\mathsf{lossy}(S)) \cap U = \emptyset$.

Abstractions. The EEC algorithm considers two kinds of abstractions. To represent them, we introduce two types of graphs. First, a $\overline{\preccurlyeq}$*-monotonic graph* is a finite graph $\langle V, \Rightarrow, v_i \rangle$ where V is a set of nodes, $\Rightarrow \subseteq V \times V$ is the transition relation and $v_i \in V$ is the initial node. That graph is associated with an order $\overline{\preccurlyeq} \subseteq V \times V$ such that for any $v_1, v_2, v_3 \in V$ with $v_1 \Rightarrow v_2$ and $v_1 \overline{\preccurlyeq} v_3$, there exists $v_4 \in V$ with $v_2 \overline{\preccurlyeq} v_4$ and $v_3 \Rightarrow v_4$. Notice that $\overline{\preccurlyeq}$-monotonic graphs are finite WSTS. Second, an *And-Or graph* is a tuple $G = \langle V_A, V_O, v_i, \Rightarrow \rangle$ where $V = V_A \cup V_O$ is the (finite) set of nodes (V_A is the set of "And" nodes and V_O is the set of "Or" nodes), $V_A \cap V_O = \emptyset$, $v_i \in V_O$ is the initial node, and $\Rightarrow \subseteq (V_A \times V_O) \cup (V_O \times V_A)$ is the transition relation s.t. $\forall v \in V_A \cup V_O$, there exists $v' \in V_A \cup V_O$ with $(v, v') \in \Rightarrow$.

Definition 5. *A* compatible unfolding *of an And-Or graph* $G = \langle V_A, V_O, v_i, \Rightarrow \rangle$ *is an infinite labelled tree* $T_G = \langle N, root, B, \Lambda \rangle$ *where: (i)* N *is the set of nodes of* T_G*, (ii)* $root \in N$ *is the root of* T_G*, (iii)* $B \subseteq N \times N$ *is the transition relation of* T_G*, (iv)* $\Lambda : N \rightarrow V_A \cup V_0$ *is the labelling function of the nodes of* T_G *by nodes of* G *that respects the three following compatibility conditions (*Λ *is extended to sets of nodes in the usual way):* (C_1)$\Lambda(root) = v_i$*;* (C_2) *for all* $n \in N$ *such that* $\Lambda(n) \in V_A$*, we have that (a) for all nodes* $v' \in V_O$ *such that* $\Lambda(n) \Rightarrow v'$*, there exists one and only one* $n' \in N$ *such that* $B(n, n')$ *and* $\Lambda(n') = v'$*, and conversely (b) for all nodes* $n' \in N$ *such that* $B(n, n')$*, we have* $\Lambda(n) \Rightarrow \Lambda(n')$*.* ($\mathsf{C}_3$) *for all* $n \in N$ *such that* $\Lambda(n) \in V_O$*, we have that: there exists one and only one* $n' \in N$ *such that* $B(n, n')$*, and* $\Lambda(n) \Rightarrow \Lambda(n')$*.*

Problem 2. The *And-Or Graph Avoidability Problem* is defined as: 'Given an And-Or graph $G = \langle V_A, V_O, v_i, \Rightarrow \rangle$ and $E \subseteq V_A \cup V_O$, is there $T = \langle N, root, B, \Lambda \rangle$, a compatible unfolding of G, s.t. $\Lambda(N) \cap E = \emptyset$?' When it is the case, we say that E is *avoidable* in G. It is well-known that this problem is complete for *PTIME.*

3 Expand, Enlarge and Check

This section recalls the fundamentals of the EEC algorithm [11]. The principle of this algorithm consists to build a sequence of pairs of approximations. The first one, is an under-approximation of the set of reachable states, and allows one to decide positive instances of the coverability problem. The latter one over-approximates the reachable states and is suitable to decide negative instances.

More precisely, given a WSTS $S = \langle C, c_0, \rightarrow, \leq \rangle$, and a set of limits L, the algorithm considers in parallel a sequence of subsets of C: $C_0, C_1, \ldots$ and a sequence of limit elements: $L_0, L_1, \ldots$ s.t. (*i*) $\forall i \geq 0 : C_i \subseteq C_{i+1}$, (*ii*) $\forall c \in \mathsf{Reach}(S) : \exists i \geq 0 : c \in C_i$, and (*iii*) $c_0 \in C_0$; and (*iv*) $\forall i \geq 0 : L_i \subseteq L_{i+1}$, (*v*)

$\forall \ell \in L : \exists i \geq 0 : \ell \in L_i$ and (*vi*) $\top \in L_0$. Given a set C_i, one can construct an *exact partial reachability graph* (EPRG for short) $\mathsf{EPRG}(S, C_i)$ which is an under-approximation of the system. Similarly, given a set L_i, one builds an over-approximation of the system under the form of an And-Or Graph:

Definition 6. *Given a* WSTS $S = \langle C, c_0, \rightarrow, \leq \rangle$ *and a set* $C' \subseteq C$, *the* EPRG *of* S *is the transition system* $\mathsf{EPRG}(S, C') = \langle C', c_0, (\rightarrow \cap (C' \times C')) \rangle$.

Definition 7. *Given a* WSTS $S = \langle C, c_0, \rightarrow, \leq \rangle$, *an adequate domain of limits* $\langle L, \sqsubseteq, \gamma \rangle$ *for* $\langle C, \leq \rangle$, *a finite subset* $C' \subseteq C$ *with* $c_0 \in C'$, *and a finite subset* $L' \subseteq L$ *with* $\top \in L'$, *the And-Or graph* $G = \langle V_A, V_O, v_i, \Rightarrow \rangle$, *noted* $\mathsf{Abs}(S, C', L')$, *is s.t.:* (A_1) $V_O = L' \cup C'$; (A_2) $V_A = \{S \in 2^{L' \cup C'} \setminus \{\emptyset\} \mid \nexists d_1 \neq d_2 \in S : d_1 \sqsubseteq d_2\}$; ($\mathsf{A}_3$) $v_i = c_0$; ($\mathsf{A}_{4.1}$) *for any* $n_1 \in V_A, n_2 \in V_O$: $(n_1, n_2) \in \Rightarrow$ *if and only if* $n_2 \in n_1$; ($\mathsf{A}_{4.2}$) *for any* $n_1 \in V_O, n_2 \in V_A$: $(n_1, n_2) \in \Rightarrow$ *if and only if (i)* $\mathsf{Post}(\gamma(n_1)) \subseteq \gamma(n_2)$ *and (ii)* $\neg \exists n \in V_A : \mathsf{Post}(\gamma(n_1)) \subseteq \gamma(n) \subset \gamma(n_2)$.

Remark 1. The over-approximations are And-Or graphs instead of plain graphs. The reason is that, in Definition 1, we do not impose strong properties on the limits. Hence, the set of successors of an element $c \in L' \cup C'$ may not have a (unique) most precise approximation as a subset of $L' \cup C'$. Every over-approximation is able to simulate the successors in the WSTS, but some of them may lead to bad states, while others don't (which will be established by the And-Or graph).

Theorem 1 states the adequacy of these abstractions. Theorem 2 tells us that we will eventually find the right abstractions to decide the coverability problem. The EEC algorithm directly follows: it enumerates the pairs of C_i and L_i, and, for each of them, (1 – 'Expand') builds $\mathsf{EPRG}(S, C_i)$, (2 – 'Enlarge') builds $\mathsf{Abs}(S, C_i, L_i)$ and (3 – 'Check') looks for an error trace in $\mathsf{EPRG}(S, C_i)$ and checks the avoidability of the bad states in $\mathsf{Abs}(S, C_i, L_i)$ (see [11] for details).

Theorem 1. *Given a* WSTS $S = \langle C, c_0, \rightarrow, \leq \rangle$ *with adequate domain of limits* $\langle L, \sqsubseteq, \gamma \rangle$, *and an* $\leq$*-upward-closed set* $U \subseteq C$: $\forall i \geq 0$: **If** $\mathsf{Reach}(\mathsf{EPRG}(S, C_i)) \cap U \neq \emptyset$ **then** $\mathsf{Reach}(S) \cap U \neq \emptyset$. **If** U *is avoidable in* $\mathsf{Abs}(S, C_i, L_i)$, **then** $\mathsf{Reach}(S) \cap U = \emptyset$.

Theorem 2. *Given a* WSTS $S = \langle C, c_0, \rightarrow, \leq \rangle$ *with adequate domain of limits* $\langle L, \sqsubseteq, \gamma \rangle$, *and an* $\leq$*-upward-closed set* $U \subseteq C$: **If** $\mathsf{Reach}(S) \cap U \neq \emptyset$, **then** $\exists i \geq 0 : \mathsf{Reach}(\mathsf{EPRG}(S, C_i)) \cap U \neq \emptyset$. **If** $\mathsf{Reach}(S) \cap U = \emptyset$, **then** $\exists i \geq 0$ *s.t.* U *is avoidable in* $\mathsf{Abs}(S, C_i, L_i)$.

Propositions 4 and 5 give properties of these abstractions. The latter says that, if C' is $\leq$-downward-closed and S is lossy, $\mathsf{EPRG}(S, C')$ is a finite $\leq$-monotonic graph. Section 4 shows how to efficiently explore these graphs.

Proposition 4. *Let* $S = \langle C, c_0, \rightarrow, \leq \rangle$ *be a* WSTS *and* $\langle L, \sqsubseteq, \gamma \rangle$ *be an adequate domain of limits, for* S. *Let* $\mathsf{Abs}(S, C', L') = \langle V_A, V_O, v_i, \Rightarrow \rangle$ *be an And-Or graph for some* $C' \subseteq C$ *and* $L' \subseteq L$. *For any* $v_1, v_2, v_3 \in V_A \cup V_O$ *s.t.* $v_1 \Rightarrow v_2$ *and* $\gamma(v_1) \subseteq \gamma(v_3)$, *there exists* $v_4 \in V_A \cup V_O$ *s.t.* $v_3 \Rightarrow v_4$ *and* $\gamma(v_2) \subseteq \gamma(v_4)$.

Proposition 5. *Given a* lossy WSTS $S = \langle C, c_0, \rightarrow, \leq \rangle$, *and a* $\leq$*-downward-closed set* $C' \subseteq C$: $\mathsf{EPRG}(S, C')$ *is a* $\leq$*-monotonic graph.*

4 Efficient Exploration of $\overline{\preccurlyeq}$-Monotonic Graphs

This section is devoted to the presentation of Algorithm 1 which efficiently decides the coverability problem on $\overline{\preccurlyeq}$-monotonic graphs. It is based on ideas borrowed from the algorithm to compute the minimal coverability set of Petri nets, presented in [8]. However, as recently pointed out in [10], this latter algorithm is flawed and may in certain cases compute an under-approximation of the actual minimal coverability set. Algorithm 1 corrects this bug in the context of finite graphs. At the end of the section, we show how to exploit it in EEC.

Algorithm 1 receives a $\overline{\preccurlyeq}$-monotonic graph $\mathcal{G} = \langle V, \Rightarrow, v_i \rangle$ and constructs a finite tree $\mathcal{T} = \langle N, n_0, B, \Lambda \rangle$, with set of nodes N, root node $n_0 \in N$, set of arcs $B \subseteq N \times N$ (in the following we denote by B^* the transitive closure of B) and labelling function $\Lambda : N \mapsto V$. We denote by $\mathsf{leaves}(\mathcal{T})$ the set of leaves of $\mathcal{T}$; by $\mathsf{subtree}(n)$, the maximal sub-tree of $\mathcal{T}$ rooted in $n \in N$; and by $\mathsf{nodes}(\mathcal{T})$ the set of nodes of $\mathcal{T}$. Given a tree $\mathcal{T}$, and two nodes n and n', the function $\mathsf{Replace\_subtree}(n, n', \mathcal{T}, \mathit{to\_treat})$ replaces, in $\mathcal{T}$, the subtree $\mathsf{subtree}(n)$ by $\mathsf{subtree}(n')$ and removes from *to_treat* the nodes $n'' \in (\mathsf{leaves}(\mathsf{subtree}(n)) \setminus \mathsf{leaves}(\mathsf{subtree}(n'))) \cap \mathit{to\_treat}$. We also attach a predicate $\mathsf{removed}(n)$ to each node n of a tree, which is initially *false* for any node. When $\mathsf{removed}(n)$ is true, the node n is *virtually* removed from the tree. It is however kept in memory, so that it can be later put back in the tree (this makes sense since the bug in [8]

Data : $\mathcal{G} = \langle V, \Rightarrow, v_i \rangle$: $\overline{\preccurlyeq}$-monotonic graph; $U \subseteq V$: $\overline{\preccurlyeq}$-upw.-cl. set of states.
Result : `true` when U is reachable in $\mathcal{G}$; `false` otherwise.
begin
  Let $\mathcal{T} = \langle N, n_0, B, \Lambda \rangle$ be the tree computed as follows:
  to_treat $= \{n_0\}$ such that $\Lambda(n_0) = v_i$, $N = \{n_0\}$, $B = \emptyset$;
  while *to_treat* $\neq \emptyset$ **do**
    while *to_treat* $\neq \emptyset$ **do**
      choose and **remove** n in *to_treat* ;
      foreach *successor* v *of* $\Lambda(n)$ **do**
        Add n' with $\Lambda(n') = v$ as successor of n;
1   **if** $\nexists n'' \in N : B^*(n'', n') \wedge \Lambda(n') \overline{\preccurlyeq} \Lambda(n'')$ **then** add n' to *to_treat*;
        else $\mathsf{removed}(n') =$ **true**;
      Apply reduction rules (see Algorithm 2);
    /* reuse of nodes formerly computed */
2   **while** $\exists n, n' \in N : \neg\mathsf{removed}(n) \wedge \mathsf{removed}(n') \wedge \neg\mathsf{covered}(\Lambda(n'), N) \wedge B(n, n')$ **do** $\mathsf{removed}(n') =$ `false` ;
    /*construction of new nodes */
3   **while** $\exists n \in (N \setminus \mathit{to\_treat}) : \exists v \in V : \Lambda(n) \Rightarrow v \wedge \neg\mathsf{removed}(n) \wedge \neg\mathsf{covered}(v, N)$ **do** add n to *to_treat*;
  if $\exists n \in N : \mathsf{removed}(n) =$ `false`, $\Lambda(n) \in U$ **then return** `true`;
  else return `false`;
end

Algorithm 1: Coverability

while $\exists n, n' \in N : \Lambda(n)\overline{\preccurlyeq}\Lambda(n')$ **do**

1 **if** $\neg B^*(n, n') \wedge \neg\mathsf{removed}(n) \wedge \neg\mathsf{removed}(n')$ **then**
  foreach $n'' \in \mathsf{nodes}(\mathsf{subtree}(n))$ **do** $\mathsf{removed}(n'') = \mathtt{true}$;
  $\mathit{to\_treat} \leftarrow \mathit{to\_treat} \setminus \mathsf{nodes}(\mathsf{subtree}(n))$;

2 **else if** $B^*(n, n') \wedge \neg\mathsf{removed}(n) \wedge \neg\mathsf{removed}(n')$ **then**
  Let $S = \{n'' \in \mathsf{leaves}(\mathsf{subtree}(n')) \mid n'' \notin \mathit{to\_treat}\}$;
  $\mathsf{Replace\_subtree}(n, n', \mathcal{T}, \mathit{to\_treat})$;
  foreach $n'' \in S$ **do**
    if $\nexists n' \in N : B^*(n', n'') \wedge \Lambda(n'')\overline{\preccurlyeq}\Lambda(n')$ **then** add n'' to $\mathit{to\_treat}$;

Algorithm 2: Reduction rules

occurs when nodes are deleted by mistake). The function $\mathsf{covered}(v, N)$ returns $\mathtt{true}$ iff there is a node $n \in N$ with $v\overline{\preccurlyeq}\Lambda(n)$ and $\mathsf{removed}(n) = \mathtt{false}$.

Sketch of the Algorithm. The tree built by Algorithm 1 is the reachability tree of the $\overline{\preccurlyeq}$-monotonic graph $\mathcal{G}$ on which some reduction rules are applied in order to keep maximal elements only, (so that the labels of the tree eventually computed form a coverability set of $\mathcal{G}$). The sketch of the algorithm is as follows. The inner **while** loop constructs the tree by picking up a node n from *to_treat* and adding its successors. When a successor n' is smaller than or equal to one of its ancestors n'' ($\Lambda(n')\overline{\preccurlyeq}\Lambda(n'')$), we stop the development of n' (line 1). Then, reduction rules (Algorithm 2) are applied: *(i)* when the tree contains two nodes n and n' such that $\Lambda(n)\overline{\preccurlyeq}\Lambda(n')$ and n is not an ancestor of n', $\mathsf{subtree}(n)$ does not need to be developed anymore and is *removed* (that is, all the nodes n'' of $\mathsf{subtree}(n)$ are tagged: $\mathsf{removed}(n'') = \mathtt{true}$, and removed from *to_treat*); *(ii)* when the tree contains two nodes n and n' such that $\Lambda(n)\overline{\preccurlyeq}\Lambda(n')$ and n is an ancestor of n', we replace $\mathsf{subtree}(n)$ by $\mathsf{subtree}(n')$. As mentioned above, the inner **while** loop may fail to compute a coverability set of $\mathcal{G}$ and may only compute an under-approximation. To cope with this problem, we test, at the end of the inner **while** loop whether a coverability set has been computed. More precisely (line 2), we look at all the nodes n' such that $\mathsf{removed}(n') = \mathtt{true}$ and that are direct successors of a node n actually in the tree (i.e.: $\mathsf{removed}(n) = \mathtt{false}$). When we find that such an n' is not covered by a node actually in the tree, we set $\mathsf{removed}(n')$ back to $\mathtt{false}$. This step is iterated up to stabilization. Then (line 3), we add into *to_treat* the nodes n with $\mathsf{removed}(n) = \mathtt{false}$ such that (i) the successor nodes of n have not been developed yet and (ii) there exists one successor v of $\Lambda(n)$ that is not covered by nodes actually in the tree. If *to_treat* is not empty at the end of these steps, it means that the inner **while** loop has computed an under-approximation of the coverability set. In that case, it is iterated again. Otherwise, when *to_treat* is empty, it is easy to see that for each node n in the tree such that $\mathsf{removed}(n) = \mathtt{false}$ all the successors of $\Lambda(n)$ are covered by nodes n' of the tree such that $\mathsf{removed}(n') = \mathtt{false}$. Since the root node of the tree covers v_i, we conclude that $\{v \mid \exists$ a node n of the tree: $\Lambda(n) = v, \mathsf{removed}(n) = \mathtt{false}\}$ is a coverability set.

The next theorem states the correctness of Algorithm 1:

Theorem 3. *Algorithm 1, when applied to the $\overline{\preccurlyeq}$-monotonic graph $\mathcal{G}$ and the $\overline{\preccurlyeq}$-upward closed set U, always terminates and returns* `true` *if and only if there exists a node $v \in U$ such that v is reachable from v_i in $\mathcal{G}$.*

Remark 2. When $\Rightarrow$ is computable, Algorithm 1 can compute $\mathcal{T}$ without disposing of the whole graph $\mathcal{G}$ (v_i only is necessary). In that case, Algorithm 1 efficiently explores a (possibly small) portion of a (potentially large) $\overline{\preccurlyeq}$-monotonic graph without building it entirely.

Application to EEC. Thanks to Proposition 5, we can apply Algorithm 1 to any EPRG built at the 'Expand' phase, if the WSTS is lossy (but by Proposition 3, we can always take the lossy version of any WSTS), and the sets C_i are $\preccurlyeq_e$-downward-closed. We show in Section 5 that this is not restrictive in practice.

Algorithm 1 is also useful to improve the 'Enlarge' phase in the case where the And-Or graph is *degenerated.* An And-Or graph is degenerated whenever each Or-node has only one successor. Hence a degenerated And-Or graph $G = \langle V_A, V_O, v_i, \Rightarrow\rangle$ is equivalent to a plain graph $G' = \langle V_O, v_i, \Rightarrow'\rangle$ where we have $v \Rightarrow' v'$ if an only if $\exists v'' \in V_A : v \Rightarrow v'' \Rightarrow v'$. From Proposition 4, G' is a $\sqsubseteq$-monotonic graph, for any WSTS with adequate domain of limits $\langle L, \sqsubseteq, \gamma\rangle$.

5 Expand, Enlarge and Check in Practice

Checking the practical usability of EEC by implementing it is an essential step. Indeed, even if we dispose of a nice theoretical result that shows the completeness of EEC, the theoretical complexity of the problems addressed here remain *non-primitive recursive* [13]. In this section, we specialize EEC to obtain efficient procedures for the coverability problem on two classes of WSTS: the monotonic extensions of Petri nets (EPN) and the lossy channel systems (LCS).

Since And-Or graphs for EPN are always degenerated [11], we can exploit the efficient procedure described in Section 4 in both the 'Expand' and the 'Enlarge' phase. As far as LCS are concerned, the main difficulty relies in the construction of the And-Or graph: the 'Expand' phase requests an efficient procedure to compute the most precise successors of any Or-node.

5.1 Extended Petri Nets

We consider monotonic extensions of the well-known Petri net model (such as Petri nets with transfer arcs, a.s.o., see [4]). Due to the lack of space, we refer the reader to [11] for the syntax. An EPN P defines a WSTS $S = \langle \mathbb{N}^k, \mathbf{m}_0, \rightarrow\rangle$ where k is the number of places of P, $\mathbf{m}_0$ is the initial marking of P and $\rightarrow\subseteq \mathbb{N}^k \times \mathbb{N}^k$ is a transition relation induced by the transitions of the EPN (see [11] for details).

Domain of Limits. To apply the schema of algorithm to extensions of Petri nets, we proposed in [11] to consider the domain of limits $\langle \mathcal{L}, \preccurlyeq_e, \gamma\rangle$ where $\mathcal{L} = (\mathbb{N} \cup \{+\infty\})^k \setminus \mathbb{N}^k$, $\preccurlyeq_e \subseteq (\mathbb{N} \cup \{+\infty\})^k \times (\mathbb{N} \cup \{+\infty\})^k$ is such that $\langle m_1, \ldots, m_k\rangle \preccurlyeq_e$

$\langle m'_1, \ldots, m'_k \rangle$ if and only if $\forall 1 \leq i \leq k : m_i \leq m'_i$ (where $\leq$ is the natural order over $\mathbb{N} \cup \{+\infty\}$. In particular: $c < +\infty$ for all $c \in \mathbb{N}$). γ is defined as: $\gamma(\mathbf{m}) = \{\mathbf{m}' \in \mathbb{N}^k \mid \mathbf{m}' \preccurlyeq_e \mathbf{m}\}$. The sequences of C_i's and L_i's are defined as follows: (D_1) $C_i = \{0, \ldots, i\}^k \cup \{\mathbf{m} | \mathbf{m} \preccurlyeq_e \mathbf{m}_0\}$, i.e. C_i is the set of markings where each place is bounded by i (plus the $\preccurlyeq_e$-downward closure of the initial marking); (D_2) $L_i = \{\mathbf{m} \in \{0, \ldots i, +\infty\}^k \mid \mathbf{m} \notin \mathbb{N}^k\}$.

Efficient Algorithm. To achieve an efficient implementation of EEC, and according to Proposition 3, we consider the lossy version of EPN (that are lossy WSTS) to decide the coverability problem on EPN. As the sets C_i are $\preccurlyeq_e$-downward-closed, we use the algorithm of Section 4 to efficiently compute the 'Expand' phase.

The 'Enlarge' phase is improved by using the method of [11] to compute the successors of any Or-node of the And-Or graph. Moreover, the And-Or graphs are always degenerated in the case of (lossy) EPN [11], hence we also apply Algorithm 1 during that phase. Note that, although the set of successors of a state of a lossy EPN can be large, $\preccurlyeq_e$-monotonic graphs and And-Or graphs allow us to consider the maximal successors only.

Experiments. We have implemented the techniques described so far in a prototype capable of analyzing EPN. We have run the prototype on about 30 examples[1] from the literature. Table 1 reports on selected results. The case studies retained here are mainly abstractions of multi-threaded Java programs (from [14]).

When applied to these examples, the basic symbolic backward algorithm of [1] seldom produces a result within the time limit of 1 hour of CPU time we have fixed (column **Pre**). A heuristic presented in [5] uses place-invariants to guide the search and improves the performance of the prototype (which has been fined tuned during several years of research). Still, it might not terminate on some examples (column **Pre+Inv**). On the other hand, we have implemented EEC with a basic exploration of the abstractions (column $\mathbf{EEC}_1$). The performance increase is already noticeable when compared to the basic backward approach. Moreover, when we apply the efficient exploration presented in Section 4, our prototype perfoms much better, on all the examples (column $\mathbf{EEC}_2$). Our experiments prove the practical superiority of the forward analysis at work in EEC.

Other tools such as FAST and LASH can analyze the same examples by using a forward procedure. Remark that these tools can handle a broader class of systems than EEC. In practice, FAST does not always terminate on our examples[2].

5.2 Lossy Channel Systems

Lossy channel systems (LCS) are systems made up of a finite number of automata which communicate through lossy FIFO channels, by writing to or reading from the channels when a transition is fired. This model is well-studied, see e.g. [3, 2]. In particular, the Simple Regular Expressions (sre), a symbolic representation

[1] See http://www.ulb.ac.be/di/ssd/ggeeraer/eec

[2] See http://www.lsv.ens-cachan.fr/fast/example.php.

Table 1. results obtained on INTEL XEON 3Ghz with 4Gb of memory : **cat.**: category of example (PNT = Petri nets with transfer arcs, PN = (unbounded) Petri net); **P**: number of places; **T**: number of transitions; **EEC**$_1$: basic EEC with complete exploration of the graph; **EEC**$_2$: EEC with efficient exploration of Section 4; **Pre + Inv**: Backward approach with invariants; **Pre**: same without invariants. Times in second

Example					EEC$_1$	EEC$_2$		Pre+Inv	Pre
cat.	name	P	T	Safe	Time	Time	Mem (Kb)	Time	Time
PNT	Java	44	37	×	10.39	8.47	23,852	1.40	1276.56
PNT	delegatebuffer	50	52	√	↑↑	180.78	116,608	↑↑	↑↑
PNT	queuedbusyflag	80	104	√	341	28.87	21,388	↑↑	↑↑
PN	pncsacover	31	36	×	800	7.54	13,704	40.83	↑↑

for downward-closed sets of states of LCS, have been defined. Algorithms to symbolically compute classical operations, such as the union, intersection or the Post, have been devised. In the sequel, we will rely on this background.

Preliminaries. In order to keep the following discussion compact, we will consider, without loss of generality, a LCS $\mathcal{C}$ made up of a single automaton (with set of states Q) and a single FIFO channel (initially empty, with alphabet Σ). A state of $\mathcal{C}$ is a pair $\langle q, w\rangle$, where $q \in Q$ is the state of the automaton, and $w \in \Sigma^*$ is the content of the channel. Let $S_{\mathcal{C}}$ be the set of states of $\mathcal{C}$. A transition of $\mathcal{C}$ is of the form $\langle s_1, Op, s_2\rangle$ where $s_1, s_2 \in Q$ and Op is $!a$ (add a to the channel), or $?a$ (consume a on the channel), or *nop* (no modification of the channel), for any $a \in \Sigma$. The semantics is the classical one, see [3]. The w.q.o. $\preccurlyeq_w \subseteq \Sigma^* \times \Sigma^*$ is defined as follows: $w_1 \preccurlyeq_w w_2$ iff w_1 is a (non-necessarily contiguous) subword of w_2. A *downward-closed regular expression* (dc-re) is a regular expression that is either $(a+\varepsilon)$ for some $a \in \Sigma$, or $(a_1+a_2+\ldots+a_n)^*$ for $\{a_1, a_2, \ldots, a_n\} \subseteq \Sigma$. Given a dc-re d, $\alpha(d)$ (the *alphabet of* d) is the set of all the elements of Σ that occur in d. A *product* (of dc-re) is either ε or an expression of the form $d_1 \cdot d_2 \cdot \ldots \cdot d_n$, where $d_1, d_2, \ldots, d_n$ are dc-re. Given a product p, $[\![p]\!] \subseteq \Sigma^*$ denotes the ($\preccurlyeq_w$-downward-closed) language generated by p, and $|p|$, denotes its size, i.e., the number of dc-re that compose it (for $w \in \Sigma^*$, $|w|$ is defined the usual way). Let $P(\Sigma)$ denote the set of all products built from Σ.

Domain of Limits. Let $\mathcal{L}(\Sigma, Q)$ denote the set of limits $\{\langle q, p\rangle | q \in Q, p \in P(\Sigma)\} \cup \{\top\}$. For any $\langle q, p\rangle \in \mathcal{L}(\Sigma, Q)$, $[\![\langle q, p\rangle]\!]$ denotes the set of states $\langle q, w\rangle \in S_{\mathcal{C}}$ such that $w \in [\![p]\!]$. We define the function $\gamma : \mathcal{L}(\Sigma, Q) \to 2^{S_{\mathcal{C}}}$ such that (i) $\gamma(\top) = Q \times \Sigma^*$ and (ii) $\gamma(\langle q, p\rangle) = [\![\langle q, p\rangle]\!]$, for any $\langle q, p\rangle \in \mathcal{L}(\Sigma, Q) \setminus \{\top\}$.We define $\overline{\sqsubseteq} \subseteq \mathcal{L}(\Sigma, Q) \times \mathcal{L}(\Sigma, Q)$ as follows : $c_1 \overline{\sqsubseteq} c_2$ if and only if $\gamma(c_1) \subseteq \gamma(c_2)$. When $c_1 \overline{\sqsubseteq} c_2$ but $c_2 \overline{\not\sqsubseteq} c_1$, we write $c_1 \overline{\sqsubset} c_2$.

Let us now define the sets of concrete and limit elements we will consider at each step. We define $C_i = \{\langle q, w\rangle \mid \langle q, w\rangle \in S_{\mathcal{C}}, |w| \leq i\}$, i.e. C_i is the set of states where the channel contains at most i characters. Similarly, we define L_i as follows: $L_i = \{\langle q, p\rangle \in \mathcal{L}(\Sigma, Q) \mid |p| \leq i\} \cup \{\top\}$, i.e. L_i contains the limits where a product of length at most i represents the channel (plus $\top$).

Efficient Algorithm. In the case of LCS, the And-Or graph one obtains is, in general, not degenerated. Hence, the techniques presented in Section 4 can be used along the 'Expand' phase only (the C_is are $\preccurlyeq_w$-downward-closed and the WSTS induced by LCS are lossy). In the sequel, we try nonetheless to improve the 'Enlarge' phase by showing how to directly compute (i.e. without enumeration of states) the set of (most precise) successors of any Or-node. Notice that following the semantics of LCS, the Post operation can add at most one character to the channel. Hence, we only need to be able to approximate precisely any $c \in L_{i+1} \cup C_{i+1}$ by elements in $L_i \cup C_i$.

Over-Approximation of a Product. Given a product $p \neq \varepsilon$ and a natural number $i \geq 1$ such that $|p| \leq i+1$, let us show how to directly compute, the most complete and most precise set of products that over-approximate p, and whose size is at most i. For this purpose, we first define an auxiliary function $L(p)$. Let $p = d_1 \cdot d_2 \cdots d_n$ be a product.

$L(p) = \bigcup_{1 \leq i \leq n-1} \{d_1 \cdots d_{i-1} \cdot (c_1 + \ldots + c_m)^* \cdot d_{i+2} \cdots d_n | \{c_1, \ldots, c_m\} = \alpha(d_i) \cup \alpha(d_{i+1})\}$. We can now define $\mathsf{Approx}(p,i)$ for $|p| \leq i+1$ and $i \geq 1$. $\mathsf{Approx}(p,i) = \{p\}$ when $|p| \leq i$, and $\mathsf{Approx}(p,i) = \{q \in L(p) \mid \nexists q' \in L(p) : q' \sqsubseteq q\}$ when $|p| = i+1$.

Proposition 6. *Given a natural number i and a product of* dc-re *p such that $|p| \leq i+1$, for all products of* dc-re *p' such that (i) $[\![p]\!] \subseteq [\![p']\!]$; (ii) $|p'| \leq i$ and (iii) $p' \notin \mathsf{Approx}(p,i)$: $\exists p'' \in \mathsf{Approx}(p,i) : [\![p'']\!] \subseteq [\![p']\!]$.*

Hence, Approx allows us to over-approximate any limit element of L_{i+1} by elements of L_i. In order to handle elements of C_{i+1}, we extend the definition of Approx as follows. Let i be a natural number and $w = a_1 \ldots a_n \in \Sigma^*$ (with $n \leq i+1$) be a word, then $\mathsf{Approx}(w,i) = w$ when $n \leq i$, and $\mathsf{Approx}(w,i) = \mathsf{Approx}(p_w,i)$ with $p_w = (a_1 + \varepsilon) \cdots (a_n + \varepsilon)$ otherwise. Remark that w and p_w both define the same $\preccurlyeq_w$-downward-closed set, and Proposition 6 remains valid.

When the LCS has more than one channel, a state (limit) associates a word (or a product of dc-re) to each channel. It that case, the best approximation can be computed by taking the product of the best approximations for each channel.

Experiments. We have built a prototype to decide the coverability problem for LCS. It implements the improvements of the 'Expand' and 'Enlarge' phases presented above. Another improvement in the construction of the And-Or graph consists in computing only the states that are reachable from the initial state.

Table 2. Results obtained on INTEL XEON 3Ghz with 4Gb of memory : **S** and **E**: number of states and edges of the graph ; **C**: number of channels; **EEC**: execution time (in second) of an implantation of EEC

Case study	S	E	C	EEC	Case study	S	E	C	EEC
ABP	48	192	2	0.18	BRP_3	480	2,460	2	0.35
BRP_1	480	2,460	2	0.19	BRP_4	480	2,460	2	0.41
BRP_2	480	2,460	2	0.19	BRP_5	640	3,370	2	0.19

Table 2 reports on the performance of the prototype when applied to various examples of the literature: the Alternating Bit Protocol (ABP), and the Bounded Retransmission Protocol (BRP), on which we verify five different properties [3]. Table 2 shows very promising results with our simple prototype.

6 Conclusion

In this paper we have pursued a line of research initiated in [11] with the introduction of the 'Expand, Enlarge and Check' algorithm. We have shown in the present work that, for a peculiar subclass of WSTS, one can derive efficient practical algorithms from this theoretical framework. We have presented an efficient method to decide the coverability problem on monotonic graphs. This solution fixes a bug, for the finite case, in the minimal coverability tree algorithm of [8]. It can always be applied to improve the 'Expand' phase. In the case of *extended Petri nets*, it can also be used to improve the 'Enlarge' phase. In the case of *lossy channel systems*, we have also shown how to improve the 'Expand' phase, by building the And-Or graph in an efficient way. We have implemented these techniques in two prototypes, working in a *forward* fashion. Their excellent behaviours clearly demonstrate the practical interest of EEC.

Acknowledgements. We are deeply grateful to Ahmed Bouajjani and Mihaela Sighireanu, who have given us access to their C++ library to manipulate sre.

References

1. P. A. Abdulla, K. Cerans, B. Jonsson, and Y.-K. Tsay. General Decidability Theorems for Infinite-state Systems. In *Proc. of LICS'96*, pages 313–321. IEEE, 1996.
2. Parosh Abdulla, Aurore Annichini, and Ahmed Bouajjani. Symbolic verification of lossy channel systems: Application to the bounded retransmission protocol. In *Proc. of TACAS'99*, number 1579 in LNCS, pages 208–222. Springer-Verlag, 1999.
3. P. A. Abdulla, A. Collomb-Annichini, A. Bouajjani, and B. Jonsson. Using forward reachability analysis for verification of lossy channel systems. *Form. Methods Syst. Des.*, 25(1):39–65, 2004.
4. G. Ciardo. Petri nets with marking-dependent arc multiplicity: properties and analysis. In *Proc. of ICATPN'94*, vol. 815 of *LNCS*, pages 179–198. Springer, 1994.
5. G. Delzanno, J.-F. Raskin, and L. Van Begin. Attacking Symbolic State Explosion. In *Proc. of CAV 2001*, vol. 2102 of *LNCS*, pages 298–310. Springer, 2001.
6. E. A. Emerson and K. S. Namjoshi. On Model Checking for Non-deterministic Infinite-state Systems. In *Proc. of LICS '98*, pages 70–80. IEEE, 1998.
7. J. Esparza, A. Finkel, and R. Mayr. On the Verification of Broadcast Protocols. In *Proc. of LICS'99*, pages 352–359. IEEE, 1999.
8. A. Finkel. The minimal coverability graph for Petri nets. In *Proc. of APN'93*, vol. 674 of *LNCS*, pages 210–243. Springer, 1993.
9. A. Finkel and P. Schnoebelen. Well-structured transition systems everywhere! *Theoretical Computer Science*, 256(1-2):63–92, 2001.

10. A. Finkel G. Geeraerts, J.-F. Raskin, and L. Van Begin. A counter-example to the minimal coverability tree algorithm *Technical report ULB 535.* `http://www.ulb.ac.be/di/ssd/ggeeraer/papers/FGRV05-Coverability.pdf`
11. G. Geeraerts, J.-F. Raskin, and L. Van Begin. Expand, Enlarge and Check: new algorithms for the coverability problem of WSTS. In *Proc. of FSTTCS'04*, vol. 3328 of LNCS, pages 287–298. Springer-Verlag, 2004.
12. T. A. Henzinger, O. Kupferman, and S. Qadeer. From *pre*historic to *post*modern symbolic model checking. *Formal Methods in System Design*, 23(3):303–327, 2003.
13. Ph. Schnoebelen. Verifying Lossy Channel Systems has Nonprimitive Recursive Complexity. *Information Processing Letters*, 83(5), 251–261, 2002
14. L. Van Begin. Efficient Verification of Counting Abstractions for Parametric systems. *PhD thesis*, Université Libre de Bruxelles, Belgium, 2003.

IIV: An Invisible Invariant Verifier*

Ittai Balaban[1], Yi Fang[1], Amir Pnueli[1], and Lenore D. Zuck[2]

[1] New York University, New York
{balaban, yifang, amir}@cs.nyu.edu
[2] University of Illinois at Chicago
lenore@cs.uic.edu

1 Introduction

This paper describes the *Invisible Invariant Verifier* (IIV)—an automatic tool for the generation of inductive invariants, based on the work in [4, 1, 2, 6]. The inputs to IIV are a parameterized system and an invariance property p, and the output of IIV is "success" if it finds an inductive invariant that strengthens p and "fail" otherwise. IIV can be run from *http://eeyore.cs.nyu.edu/servlets/iiv.ss*.

Invisible Invariants. *Uniform verification of parameterized systems* is one of the most challenging problems in verification. Given $S(N) : P[1] \parallel \cdots \parallel P[N]$, a parameterized system, and a property p, uniform verification attempts to verify that $S(N)$ satisfies p for every $N > 1$. When p is an invariance property, the proof rule INV of [3] can be applied. In order to prove that assertion p is an invariant of program P, the rule requires devising an auxiliary assertion φ that is *inductive* (i.e. is implied by the initial condition and is preserved under every computation step) and that strengthens (implies) p. The work in [4, 1] introduced the method of *invisible invariants*, that offers a method for automatic generation of the auxiliary assertion φ for parameterized systems, as well as an efficient algorithm for checking the validity of the premises of INV.

The generation of invisible invariants is based on the following idea: it is often the case that an auxiliary assertion φ for a parameterized system $S(N)$ is a boolean combination of assertions of the form $\forall i_1, \ldots, i_m : [1..N].q(\vec{i})$. We construct an instance of the parameterized system taking a fixed value N_0 for the parameter N. For the finite-state instantiation $S(N_0)$, we compute, using BDDs, the set of reachable states, denoted by *reach*. Initially, we search for a universal assertion for $m = 1$, i.e., of the type $\forall i.q(i)$. Fix some $k \leq N_0$, and let r_k be the projection of *reach* on process $P[k]$, obtained by discarding references to variables that are local to all processes other than $P[k]$. We take $q(i)$ to be the generalization of r_k obtained by replacing each reference to a local variable $P[k].x$ by a reference to $P[i].x$. The obtained $q(i)$ is our initial candidate for the body of the inductive assertion $\varphi : \forall i.q(i)$. The procedure can be easily generalized to generate assertions for higher values of m.

Having obtained a candidate for φ, we still have to check its inductiveness and verify that it implies the invariance property p. As is established in [4, 1], our system enjoys

* This research was supported in part by NSF grant CCR-0205571 and ONR grant N00014-99-1-0131.

K. Etessami and S.K. Rajamani (Eds.): CAV 2005, LNCS 3576, pp. 408–412, 2005.

a small-model property, indicating that for the assertions we generate, it suffices to validate on small instantiations (whose size depend on the system and the candidate assertion) in order to conclude validity on arbitrary instantiations. Thus, the user never needs to see the auxiliary assertion φ. Generated by symbolic BDD-techniques, the representation of the auxiliary assertions is often unreadable and non-intuitive, and it usually does not contribute to a better understanding of the program or its proof. Because the user never sees it, we refer to this method as the "method of *invisible invariants*."

The Systems to which IIV is Applicable. As our computational model, we take a *bounded-data discrete systems* of [4, 1]. For a given N, we allow boolean and finite-range scalars denoted by **bool**, integers in the range $[1..N]$, denoted by **index**, integers in the range $[0..N]$, denoted by **data**, arrays of the type **index** $\mapsto$ **bool**, and arrays of the type **index** $\mapsto$ **data**. *Atomic formulae* may compare two variables of the same type. Thus, if y and y' are same type, then $y \leq y'$ is an atomic formula, and so is $z[y] = x$ for an array z: **index** $\mapsto$ **bool** and x: **bool**. *Formulae*, used in the transition relation and the initial condition, are obtained from the atomic formulae by closing them under negation, disjunction, and existential quantifiers, for appropriately typed quantifiers.

System Architecture. The TLV (Temporal Logic Verifier) system ([5]) is a flexible environment for verification of finite state systems based on BDD-techniques. TLV reads programs written in the SMV input language or in, translates them to OBDDs and then enters an interactive mode where OBDDs can be manipulated. The interactive mode includes a scripting language, TLV-BASIC, which also parses SMV expressions. IIV is built on top of TLV. The main module of IIV is an `invariant generator`, written in TLV-BASIC. Users interface with IIV by providing a description of a parametrized system $S(N)$ (definition of variables, initial condition, transition relation, etc.) and an invariant property, both of which are written as SMV expressions. Users are also expected to give additional information that configures the invariant generator, such as the size of instantiation of the system from which the inductive invariant is generated, maximal number of quantifiers of $\forall$-assertions to be generated, and the set of processes that is not generic. IIV performs invisible verification in two phases: It generates a candidate inductive invariant and, according to its structure, computes the size of the model that has the small model property; In the second phase, IIV performs the necessary validity check on an instantiation of the system computed in the first step.

Protocol	# of BDD nodes	N_0	*reach* time	*reach* size	`gen_inv` time	`gen_inv` size	# of alt.	N_1
enter_pme	256688	11	210.00s	3860	49.00s	3155	4	11
bdd_pme	16160	7	33.69s	2510	0.46s	842	2	8
bakery	53921	5	0.09s	860	0.53s	860*	1	3
token ring	1229	7	0.03s	72	0.02s	72*	1	3
Szymanski	3463	7	0.07s	119	0.01s	100	1	4

Table 1. Some run-time results of IIV

Performance of IIV. Using IIV we have established safety properties of a number of parametrized systems with various types of variables. Other than safety properties such as mutual exclusion, we have deduced properties such as bounded overtaking, as well as certain liveness properties that are reducible to safety properties with auxiliary variables. In our examples the invariants generated by the tool were boolean combinations of up to four universal assertions (the next section elaborates on boolean combinations).

Our experience has shown that the process of computing a candidate invariant from a BDD containing *reach* is rather efficient, compared with the process of computing *reach*. For instance, in a system with a state space of 2^{55}, it took 210 seconds to compute *reach* and 49 seconds to generate a nine-quantifier invariant from it. It is usually the case that a small instantiation (less than 8) suffices for invariant generation (step 1), while validity checking (step 2) requires much larger instantiations. Since checking validity is considerably more efficient than computing *reach*, the validity checking is rarely (if ever) the cause of bad performance. Table 1 describes some of our results. The third column, N_0, is the size of the instantiation used for invariant generation. The fourth and fifth column describes the time it took to compute *reach* and the number of BDD-nodes in it. The next two columns describe how long it took to generate an inductive invariant and its size; a $*$ indicates that the invariant computed is exactly *reach*. The "alt." column describes the number of alternations between universally and existentially quantified parts of the assertion (this is discussed in the next section). Finally, N_1 is the size in the instantiation used for validity checking.

2 Generating Invariants

Generating $\forall$-assertions. We fix a system S and a safety property p. Given a BDD f representing a set of concrete states on a finite-state instantiation $S(N_0)$ and an integer m, module `proj_gen` computes a formula α of the form $\alpha : \forall j_1, \ldots, j_m . q(\vec{j})$ that is an approximation of f. Under appropriate symmetry assumptions about f, α will often be an over-approximation of f. It returns a BDD that is the instantiation of α to $S(N_0)$, i.e., $\bigwedge_{j_1,\ldots,j_m:[1..N_0]} q(\vec{j})$. Intuitively, f is projected onto some selected m processes, and α is computed as the generalization of those m processes to any m processes. We thus choose m pairwise disjoint process indices $r_1, \ldots, r_m$, and compute α so that "whatever is true in f for $r_1, \ldots, r_m$ will be true in a for arbitrary $j_1, \ldots, j_m$".

Analysis Fact(s)	Conjunct(s) Contributed to $\beta_{r,j}$
v: **bool**	$v' = v$
a: **index** $\mapsto$ **bool**	$a'[j] = a[r]$
v_1, v_2: **index** or **data**	$(v_1' < v_2' \iff v_1 < v_2)$, $(v_1' = v_2' \iff v_1 = v_2)$
a, b: **index** $\mapsto$ **data**	$(a[j]' < b'[j] \iff a[r] < b[r])$, $(a'[j] = b'[j] \iff a[r] = b[r])$
v_1: **data** a: **index** $\mapsto$ **data**	$(v_1' < a'[j] \iff v_1 < a[r])$, $(v_1' = a'[j] \iff v_1 = a[r])$
v: **index**	$(v' = r \iff v = j)$,

Table 2. Rules for construction of $\beta_{r,j}$

For simplicity, we assume $m = 1$. Fix a process index r. The projection/generalization $\bigwedge_{j:[1..N_0]} q(j)$ is computed as follows: For each $j \in [1..N_0]$ an assertion $\beta_{r,j}$ is constructed over $V \cup V'$ that describes, in the "primed part", the projection onto r generalized to j. Then, $q(j)$ is computed as the *unprimed version* of $\exists V.f \wedge \beta_{r,j}$. The expression $\beta_{r,j}$ is a conjunction constructed by analyzing, for each program variable, its type in f. Individual conjuncts are contributed by the rules shown in Fig. 2. The construction relies on the fact that equality and inequality are the only operations allowed between **index** and **data** terms. Thus the rules in Fig. 2 only preserve the ordering between these term types. The first two rules preserve values of non-parameterized variables, the next six rules preserve ordering among **index** and **data** variables. The last rule preserves ordering between every **index** variable v and r.

For systems with special processes whose behavior differs from the rest, we must generalize from a generic process r to the processes that are identical to it, and preserve states of special processes. In cases that the program or property are sensitive to the ordering between process indices, the last rule should be extended to preserve also inequalities of the form $v < j$. In this case, $P[1]$ and $P[N]$ should be treated as special processes. In cases of ring architectures and $m \geq 3$, it may be necessary to preserve cyclic, rather than linear, ordering. Thus $(r_1, r_2, r_3) = (1, 2, 3)$ should be mapped on $(j_1, j_2, j_3) = (2, 4, 6)$ as well as on $(j_1, j_2, j_3) = (4, 6, 2)$.

Determining m. Given a set of states f and a constant M, module gen_forall computes an over-approximation of f of the form $\alpha_m : \forall j_1, \ldots, j_m . q(j_1, \ldots, j_m)$, for some m such that either $m < M$ and α_{m+1} is equivalent to α_m, or $m = M$. This is justified by the observation that for higher values of m, α_m approximates f more precisely. If M is too close to N_0, α_M may fail to generalize for $N > N_0$. We choose $M = N_0 - 2$ and $M = (N_0 - 1)/2$ for systems with, and without, **index** variables, respectively. Experience has shown that gen_forall rarely returns assertions with $m > 3$.

Generating Boolean combinations of $\forall$-assertions. Often $\forall$-assertions are not sufficient for inductiveness and strengthening, requiring fine-tuning. This is done by gen_inv, shown in Fig. 1, which computes candidate invariants as boolean combinations of $\forall$-assertions. This module is initially called with the candidate φ: $(\psi_0 \wedge p)$, where ψ_0 is the assertion gen_forall(*reach*). It successively refines φ until either an inductive version is found, or a fix-point is reached, indicating failure.

An iteration of gen_inv alternates between candidate invariants that are over– and under-approximations of *reach*. To see this, recall that for any assertion, gen_forall serves to over-approximate it. Thus, lines (2)–(3) remove non-inductive states from φ, possibly including some reachable states. Lines (5)–(8) then "return" to φ the reachable states that were removed from it.

gen_inv(i, φ)
1 : **if** φ *is inductive* **return** φ
else
2 : ψ_{2i-1} := gen_forall($\varphi \wedge EF \neg\varphi$)
3 : $\varphi := \varphi \wedge \neg\psi_{2i-1}$
4 : **if** φ *is inductive* **return** φ
else
5 : ψ_{2i} := gen_forall($reach \wedge \neg\varphi$)
6 : **if** $\psi_{2i-1} = \psi_{2i}$
7 : *conclude failure*
else
8 : **return** gen_inv($i + 1$, $\varphi \vee \psi_{2i}$)

Fig. 1. Module gen_inv

2.1 Checking Validity

For an assertion α, let A_α and E_α be the number of universal and existential quantified variables in α, respectively. Let φ be a candidate invariant for a system with initial condition Θ and transition relation ρ. According to the small model theorem, we compute $N_1 = max(E_\Theta + A_\varphi, E_\rho + A_\varphi + E_\varphi, A_\varphi + A_p)$ such that establishing the validity of inductive premises on the instantiation of size N_1 implies the validity on instantiations of arbitrary size. Having computed N_1, we instantiate the assertion φ on $S(N_1)$ (which is easily constructed via proj_gen), and use a model-checker to verify its validity.

References

1. T. Arons, A. Pnueli, S. Ruah, J. Xu, and L. Zuck. Parameterized verification with automatically computed inductive assertions. In CAV'01, pages 221–234. LNCS 2102, 2001.
2. Y. Fang, N. Piterman, A. Pnueli, and L. Zuck. Liveness with invisible ranking. In *Proc. of the 5th conference on Verification, Model Checking, and Abstract Interpretation*, volume 2937, pages 223–238, Venice, Italy, January 2004.
3. Z. Manna and A. Pnueli. *Temporal Verification of Reactive Systems: Safety*. New York, 1995.
4. A. Pnueli, S. Ruah, and L. Zuck. Automatic deductive verification with invisible invariants. In TACAS'01, pages 82–97. LNCS 2031, 2001.
5. E. Shahar. *The TLV Manual*, 2000. http://www.cs.nyu.edu/acsys/tlv.
6. L. Zuck and A. Pnueli. Model checking and abstraction to the aid of parameterized systems. *Computer Languages, Systems, and Structures*, 30(3–4):139–169, 2004.

Action Language Verifier, Extended*

Tuba Yavuz-Kahveci[1], Constantinos Bartzis[2], and Tevfik Bultan[3]

[1] University of Florida
[2] Carnegie Mellon University
[3] UC, Santa Barbara

1 Introduction

Action Language Verifier (ALV) is an infinite state model checker which specializes on systems specified with linear arithmetic constraints on integer variables. An Action Language specification consists of integer, boolean and enumerated variables, parameterized integer constants and a set of modules and actions which are composed using synchronous and asynchronous composition operators [3, 7]. ALV uses symbolic model checking techniques to verify or falsify CTL properties of the input specifications. Since Action Language allows specifications with unbounded integer variables, fixpoint computations are not guaranteed to converge. ALV uses conservative approximation techniques, reachability and acceleration heuristics to achieve convergence.

Originally, ALV was developed using a Polyhedral representation for linear arithmetic constraints [4]. In the last couple of years we extended ALV by adding an automata representation for linear arithmetic constraints [2]. ALV also uses BDDs to encode boolean and enumerated variables. These symbolic representations can be used in different combinations. For example, polyhedral and automata representations can be combined with BDDs using a disjunctive representation. ALV also supports efficient representation of bounded arithmetic constraints using BDDs [2]. Other extensions to ALV include several techniques to improve the efficiency of fixpoint computations such as marking heuristic and dependency analysis, and automated counting abstraction for verification of arbitrary number of finite state processes [7].

2 Symbolic Representations

ALV uses the Composite Symbolic Library [8] as its symbolic manipulation engine. Composite Symbolic Library provides an abstract interface which is inherited by every symbolic representation that is integrated to the library. ALV encodes the transition relation and sets of states using a disjunctive, composite representation, which uses the same interface and handles operations on multiple symbolic representations.

Polyhedral vs. Automata Representation: Current version of the Composite Symbolic Library uses two different symbolic representations for integer variables: 1) *Polyhedral representation*: In this approach the valuations of integer variables are represented in a disjunctive form where each disjunct corresponds to a convex polyhedron

* This work is supported by NSF grant CCR-0341365.

K. Etessami and S.K. Rajamani (Eds.): CAV 2005, LNCS 3576, pp. 413–417, 2005.

and each polyhedron corresponds to a conjunction of linear arithmetic constraints. This approach is extended to full Presburger arithmetic by including divisibility constraints (which is represented as an equality constraint with an existentially quantified variable). 2) *Automata representation*: In this approach a Presburger arithmetic formula on v integer variables is represented by a v-track automaton that accepts a string if it corresponds to a v-dimensional integer vector (in binary representation) that satisfies the formula. Both of these symbolic representations are integrated to the Composite Symbolic Library by implementing the intersection, union, complement, backward and forward image operations, and subsumption, emptiness and equivalence tests, which are required by the abstract symbolic interface. We implemented the polyhedral representation by writing a wrapper around the Omega Library [1]. We implemented the automata representation using the automata package of the MONA tool [6] and based on the algorithms discussed in [2].

BDD Representation for Bounded Integers: We also integrated algorithms for constructing efficient BDDs for linear arithmetic formulas to ALV [2]. The size of the BDD for a linear arithmetic formula is linear in the number of variables and the number of bits used to encode each variable, but can be exponential in the number of *and* and *or* operators [2]. This bounded representation can be used in three scenarios: 1) all the integer variables in a specification can be bounded, 2) infinite state representations discussed above may exhaust the available resources during verification, or 3) infinite state fixpoint computations may not converge. Note that, for cases 2 and 3, verification using the bounded representation does not guarantee that the property holds for the unbounded case, i.e., the bounded representation is used for finding counter-examples.

Polymorphic Verification: Due to the object oriented design of the ALV, implementation of the model checking algorithms are polymorphic. This enables the users to choose different encodings without recompiling the tool. For example, one can first try the polyhedral encoding and if the verification takes too long or the memory consumption is too much the same specification can be checked using the automata encoding. The user specifies the encoding to be used as a command line argument to the ALV. When there are no integer variables in the specification or if the bounded BDD representation for integers is used, ALV automatically runs as a BDD based model checker.

3 Fixpoint Computations

ALV is a symbolic model checker for CTL. It uses the least and greatest fixpoint characterizations of CTL operators to compute the truth set of a given temporal property. It uses iterative fixpoint computations starting from the fixpoint for the innermost temporal operator in the formula. At the end, it checks if all the initial states are included in the truth set. ALV supports both the $\{EX, EG, EU\}$ basis and the $\{EX, EU, AU\}$ basis for CTL. ALV uses various heuristics to improve the performance of the fixpoint computations. We discuss some of them below. The reader is referred to [7] for the experimental analysis of these heuristics.

Marking Heuristic: Since composite representation is disjunctive, during the least fixpoint computations the result of the kth iteration includes the disjuncts from the $k-1$st iteration. A naive approach that applies the image computation to the result of the kth iteration to obtain the result of the $k+1$st iteration performs redundant computations, i.e., it recomputes the image for the disjuncts coming from the result of the $k-1$th iteration. We alleviate this problem by marking the disjuncts coming from the $k-1$st iteration when we compute the result of the kth iteration [7]. Hence, at the $k+1$st iteration, we only compute the images of the disjuncts that are not marked, i.e., disjuncts that were added in the kth iteration. Markings are preserved during all the operations that manipulate the disjuncts and they are also useful during subsumption check and simplification. When we compare the result of the current iteration to the previous one, we only check if the unmarked disjuncts are subsumed by the previous iteration. During the simplification of the composite representation (which reduces the number of disjuncts) we try to merge two disjuncts only if one of them is unmarked.

Dependency Analysis: Typically, in software specifications, the transition relation corresponds to a disjunction of a set of atomic actions. Since the image computation distributes over disjunctions, during fixpoint computation one can compute the image of each action separately. It is common to have pairs of actions a_1 and a_2 such that, when we take the backward-image of a_2 with respect to true and then take the backward-image of a_1 with respect to the result, we get **false**. I.e., there are no states s and s' such that s' is reachable from s by execution of a_1 followed by execution of a_2. This implies that, during the kth iteration of a backward (forward) fixpoint computation, when we take the backward-image (forward-image) of a_1 (a_2) with respect to the result of the backward-image (forward-image) of a_2 (a_1) from the $k-1$st iteration, the result will be **false**. We use a dependency analysis to avoid such redundant image computations [7]. First, before we start the fixpoint computation, we identify the dependencies among the actions using the transition relation. Then, during the fixpoint computation, we tag the results of the image computations with the labels of the actions that produce them, and avoid the redundant image computations using the dependency information.

Approximations, Reachability, and Accelerations: For the infinite state systems that can be specified in Action Language, model checking is undecidable. Action Language Verifier uses several heuristics to achieve convergence: 1) Truncated fixpoint computations to compute lower bounds for least fixpoints and upper bounds for greatest fixpoints, 2) Widening heuristics (both for polyhedra and automata representations) to compute upper bounds for least fixpoints (and their duals to compute lower bounds for greatest fixpoints), 3) Approximate reachability analysis using a forward fixpoint computation and widening heuristics, 4) Accelerations based on loop-closures which extract disjuncts from the transition relation that preserve the boolean and enumerated variables but modify the integer variables, and then compute approximations of the transitive closures of the integer part.

4 Counting Abstraction

We integrated the counting abstraction technique [5] to ALV in order to verify properties of parameterized systems with arbitrary number of finite state modules. When a module is marked to be parameterized, ALV generates an abstract transition system in which the local states of the parameterized module are abstracted away (by removing all the local variables) but the number of instances in each local state is counted by introducing an auxiliary integer variable for each local state. An additional parameterized constant is introduced to denote the number of instances of the module. Counting abstraction preserves the CTL properties that do not involve the local states of the abstracted processes. When we verify properties of a system using counting abstraction we know that the result will hold for any number of instances of the parameterized module and if we generate a counter-example it corresponds to a concrete counter-example. Note that counting abstraction technique works only for modules with finite number of local states.

5 An Example

Here, we will briefly describe the verification of the concurrency control component of an airport ground traffic control simulation program (this and other examples and the ALV tool are available at `http://www.cs.ucsb.edu/~bultan/composite/`). The simulation program uses an airport ground network model which consists of two runways (16R, 16L) and 11 taxiways. The Action Language specification has one main module and two submodules representing departing and arriving airplanes. We use integer variables to denote the number of airplanes in each runway and taxiway. A local enumerated variable for each submodule denotes the locations of the airplanes. A set of actions for each submodule specifies how the airplanes move between the runways and taxiways based on the airport topology. The specification has 13 integer variables and 2 and 4 boolean variables for each instantiation of the departing and arriving airplane modules, respectively (these boolean variables are generated by the ALV compiler to encode the enumerated variables).

The property "At any time there is at most one airplane in either runway," is expressed as `AG(num16R<=1 and num16L<=1)`. ALV verified this property on an instance with 8 departing and 8 arriving airplanes (13 integer variables, 48 boolean variables) in 1.20 seconds using 46.5 MBytes of memory (on a 2.8 GHertz Pentium 4 processor with 2 GBytes of main memory). We also verified this property on the parameterized specification for arbitrary number of arriving and departing airplanes using automated counting abstraction (which generates 20 additional integer variables and 2 parameterized integer constants). ALV verified the property above on the parameterized instance in 9.38 seconds using 6.7 MBytes of memory using the option to compute an approximation of the reachable states (using widening) and the marking heuristic.

References

1. The Omega project. Available at `http://www.cs.umd.edu/projects/omega/`
2. C. Bartzis. *Symbolic Representations for Integer Sets in Automated Verification.* PhD thesis, University of California, Santa Barbara, 2004.
3. T. Bultan. Action language: A specification language for model checking reactive systems. In *Proc. ICSE 2000*, pages 335–344, June 2000.
4. T. Bultan and T. Yavuz-Kahveci. Action language verifier. In *Proc. of ASE 2001*, pages 382–386, November 2001.

5. G. Delzanno. Automatic verification of parameterized cache coherence protocols. In *Proc. CAV 2000*, pages 53–68, 2000.
6. J. G. Henriksen, J. Jensen, M. Jorgensen, N. Klarlund, R. Paige, T. Rauhe, and A. Sandholm. Mona: Monadic second-order logic in practice. In *Proc. TACAS 1995*, 1995.
7. T. Yavuz-Kahveci. *Specification and Automated Verification of Concurrent Software Systems*. PhD thesis, University of California, Santa Barbara, 2004.
8. T. Yavuz-Kahveci and T. Bultan. A symbolic manipulator for automated verification of reactive systems with heterogeneous data types. *STTT*, 5(1):15–33, November 2003.

Romeo: A Tool for Analyzing Time Petri Nets

Guillaume Gardey[1], Didier Lime[2], Morgan Magnin[1], and Olivier (H.) Roux[1]

[1] IRCCyN, CNRS UMR 6597, Nantes, France
{Morgan.Magnin, Guillaume.Gardey, Olivier-h.Roux}@irccyn.ec-nantes.fr
[2] Aalborg University - CISS, Denmark
didier@cs.aau.dk

Abstract. In this paper, we present the features of ROMEO, a Time Petri Net (TPN) analyzer. The tool ROMEO allows state space computation of *TPN* and on-the-fly model-checking of reachability properties. It performs translations from *TPNs* to Timed Automata (*TAs*) that preserve the behavioural semantics (timed bisimilarity) of the *TPNs*. Besides, our tool also deals with an extension of Time Petri Nets (*Scheduling-TPNs*) for which the valuations of transitions may be stopped and resumed, thus allowing the modeling preemption.

Keywords: Time Petri nets, model-checking, state-space, DBM, polyhedron, scheduling, stopwatch.

1 Introduction

Time Petri Nets (*TPNs*) are a classical formalism, with Timed Automata (*TAs*), to design reactive systems. *TPNs* extend classical Petri nets with temporal intervals associated with transitions. They benefit from an easy representation of real-time systems features (synchronization, parallelism ...). State reachability and boundedness is proven to be undecidable for arbitrary *TPNs*. However, state reachability is decidable for bounded *TPNs*, which is sufficient for virtually all practical purposes.

In real-time applications, it is often necessary to memorize the progress status of an action when this one is suspended then resumed. In this class of models, some extensions of Time Petri Nets have been proposed to express the preemptive scheduling of tasks. Roux and Déplanche [1] propose an extension for Time Petri Nets (*Scheduling-TPNs*) that consists of mapping into the Petri net model the way the different schedulers of the system activate or suspend the tasks. For a fixed priority scheduling policy, *Scheduling-TPNs* introduce two new attributes associated to each place that respectively represent allocation (processor or resource) and priority (of the modeled task). Bucci *et al.* [2] propose a similar model: Preemptive Time Petri Net (*Preemptive-TPN*) by mapping the scheduling policies onto transitions.

K. Etessami and S.K. Rajamani (Eds.): CAV 2005, LNCS 3576, pp. 418–423, 2005.

2 The Tool Romeo

The purposes of the tool ROMEO [1] (available for Linux, MacOSX and Windows platforms) are the analysis and simulation of reactive systems modelled by *TPNs* or *Scheduling-TPNs*. It consists of: (1) a graphical user interface (GUI) (written in TCL/Tk) to edit and design *TPNs*, and (2) computation modules (GPN and MERCUTIO, written in C++).

2.1 System Design

In a system modelling activity, the ROMEO GUI allows to model reactive systems or preemptive reactive systems using *TPNs* or *Scheduling-TPNs*. Both benefit from an easy graphical representation and from an easy representation of common real-time features (parallelism, synchronization, resources management, watch-dogs...).

As a design helper, ROMEO implements on-line simulation (*TPNs*, *Scheduling-TPNs*) and reachability model-checking (*TPNs*). It allows the early detection of some modeling issues during the conception stage.

2.2 On-line Model-Checking

In addition to on-line simulation that makes scenarii testing possible, ROMEO provides an on-line model-checker for reachability. Properties over markings can be expressed and tested. It is then possible to test the reachability of a marking such that it verifies $M(P_1) = 1 \vee M(P_3) \geq 3$ where $M(P_i)$ is the number of tokens in the place P_i of the net. The tool returns a trace leading to such a marking if reachable.

Such a model-checker allows to verify more complex properties (quantitative properties for instance) expressed by observers (which translate a quantitative property into a reachability test), which is the main method used to study the behavior of a *TPN*.

2.3 Off-line Model-Checking

The modeling of a property using observers requires a good knowledge in *TPNs* and, as far as we know, no automatic observers generation is available to help a system designer.

ROMEO implements different theoretical methods to translate the model analyzed into Automata, Timed Automata (*TAs*) or Stopwatch Automata (*SWAs*). The advantages of such translations is that several efficient model-checking tools are available for these models (MEC, ALDEBARAN, UPPAAL, KRONOS, HYTECH). These translations also extend the class of properties that can be model-checked with observers to temporal logic (LTL, CTL) and quantitative temporal logic (TCTL).

---

[1] Download at: `http://www.irccyn.ec-nantes.fr/irccyn/d/fr/equipes/TempsReel/logs`

To our knowledge, the translations of *TPNs* to *TAs* implemented in ROMEO are currently the only existing methods allowing the verification of quantitative time properties (quantitative liveness and TCTL) on *TPNs*.

Structural Translation. ROMEO implements a structural transformation of a *TPN* into a timed-bisimilar synchronized product of *TAs* [3] that can be model-checked with the tool UPPAAL. The translation is optimized to take at its advantage the management of inactive clocks in UPPAAL. It follows that the algorithms implemented in this tool are used efficiently.

State Space Computation Based Translation. A first translation consists in the computation of the state class graphs (SCG) that provide finite representations for the behavior of bounded nets preserving their LTL properties [4]. For bounded *TPNs* the algorithm is based on DBM (Difference Bounds Matrix) data structure whereas, for *Scheduling-TPNs*, the semi-algorithm is based on polyhedra (using the *New Polka* library).

Two different methods are implemented for *TPNs* to generate a *TA* that preserves its semantics (in the sense of *timed bisimilarity*): the first one is derived from *TA* framework [5], the other one from the classical state class graph approach [6]. In the latter method, we reduce the number of clocks needed during the translation, so that the subsequent verification on the resulting *TA* is more efficient. In both methods, the *TAs* are generated in UPPAAL or KRONOS input format.

Concerning *Scheduling-TPNs*, the method introduced in [7] is implemented. It allows a fast translation into a Stopwatch Automaton (SWA) using an over-approximating semi-algorithm (DBM-based). Despite the overapproximation, it has been proven that the SWA is timed-bisimilar to the original *Scheduling-TPN*. The SWA is produced in the HYTECH input format and is computed with a low number of stopwatches. Since the number of stopwatches is critical for the complexity of the verification, the method increases the efficiency of the timed analysis of the system; moreover, in some cases, it may just make the analysis possible while it would be a dead-end to model the system directly with HYTECH.

2.4 Comparisons

The following tables are an overview of the ROMEO features compared to two others main tools used for the analysis of *TPNs* and *TPNs* extension dealing with preemption. They compare the capabilities of the tools in terms of the properties classes that can be handled.

TINA [8] is a tool for the analysis of *TPNs* mainly using state class graphs techniques. ORIS [9] is a tool that analyzes *Preemptive-TPNs* which are equivalent to *Scheduling-TPNs*.

Our major contribution is to bring to *TPNs* frameworks (*Scheduling-TPNs*) methods to efficiently model-check TCTL properties.

Table 1. ROMEO capabilities on *TPNs*

	Reachability	LTL	CTL	Quantitative Liveness [a]	TCTL
TINA	Marking Graph	SCG[b] + MC[c]	Atomic SCG[b] + MC[c]	–	–
ROMEO	On-the-fly checking or Marking Graph	SCG + MC[c] or ZFG[e] + MC[c]	Translation to Timed Automata + UPPAAL [d] or KRONOS		

[a] Includes response properties like $\forall\Box(\varphi \implies \forall\Diamond\Psi)$ where φ or Ψ can contain clock constraints.
[b] SCG = Computation of the State Class Graph.
[c] MC = requires the use of a Model-Checker on the SCG or the ZFG.
[d] Subset of TCTL.
[e] ZFG = Computation of the Zone-based Forward Graph.

Table 2. ROMEO capabilities on *Scheduling-TPNs*

	State-space computation		Timed analysis	
	Overapproximation	Exact abstraction	RTTL	TCTL
ORIS	DBM	–	DBM-SCG[a] + MC[b]	–
ROMEO	DBM	SCG[c]	Efficient translation to timed bisimilar Stopwatch automata + HYTECH	

[a] Computation of a DBM over-approximation of the State Class Graph.
[b] Oris supports exact timeliness analysis of traces (with respect to a linear-time variant of Real-Time Temporal Logic (RTTL).
[c] As for *TPNs*, the SCG preserves LTL properties.

3 Case Study

3.1 Description

In this section, we work on a partial model for the control of an oscillation compensator (hydraulic shock absorber) and a differential blocking on a tractor with a sowing trailer. The partial system consists of processors running a real-time operating system, linked together with a CAN bus.

We used the translation of a *Scheduling-TPN* into a *SWA* whose state space is computed with HYTECH.

We compared the efficiency of our method with a generic direct modelling with HYTECH on this case study. We also tested several simpler and more complex related systems obtained by removing or adding tasks and/or processors. Table 3 gives the obtained results.

Columns 2 and 3 give the number of processors and tasks of the system. Columns 4, 5 and 6 describe the direct modelling in HYTECH results: the number of SWA used to model the system, the number of stopwatches and the time taken by HYTECH to compute the state space. For this generic modelling, we basically used the product of one SWA per task and one SWA for each scheduler. Columns 7 to 10 give the results for our method: the number of locations/transitions, stopwatches of the SWA we generated, and the time taken for its generation. Finally, the last column gives the time used by HYTECH to compute the state space of the SWA generated by our method. Times are given in seconds and NA means that the HYTECH computation could not yield a result on the machine used.

Table 3. Experimental results

	Description		Direct SWA Modelling			Our method[a]				
Ex.	Proc.	Tasks	SWA's	Sw.	t_{HYTECH}	Loc.	Trans.	Sw.	t_{ROMEO}	t_{HYTECH}
1	2	4	8	7	77.8	20	29	3	≤0.1	0.2
2	3	6	11	9	590.3	40	58	4	≤0.1	0.5
3	3	7	12	10	NA	52	84	4	≤0.1	0.7
4	3+CAN	7	13	11	NA	297	575	7	0.3	5.3
5	4+CAN	9	15	13	NA	761	1 677	8	0.9	29.8
6	5+CAN	11	17	15	NA	1 141	2 626	9	6	60.1
7	6+CAN	14	.	.	NA	4 587	12 777	10	59.7	438.8
8	7+CAN	18	.	.	NA	8 817	25 874	12	1 146.7	NA

[a] *Scheduling-TPN* $\stackrel{\text{ROMEO}}{\longrightarrow}$ SWA $\stackrel{\text{HYTECH}}{\longrightarrow}$ state-space

These computations have been performed on a POWERPC G4 1.25GHz with 500MB of RAM.

We observe that the computation on a direct modelling as a product of SWA is quickly untractable (example 3). However, with our method, we are able to deal with systems of much greater size.

References

1. Roux, O.H., Déplanche, A.M.: A t-time Petri net extension for real time-task scheduling modeling. European Journal of Automation (JESA) **36** (2002) 973–987
2. Bucci, G., Fedeli, A., Sassoli, L., Vicario, E.: Time state space analysis of real-time preemptive systems. IEEE transactions on software engineering **30** (2004) 97–111
3. Cassez, F., Roux, O.H.: Structural translation from time Petri nets to timed automata. In: Fourth International Workshop on Automated Verification of Critical Systems (AVoCS'04). ENTCS, London (UK), Elsevier (2004)
4. Berthomieu, B., Diaz, M.: Modeling and verification of time dependent systems using time Petri nets. IEEE trans. on software engineering **17** (1991) 259–273
5. Gardey, G., Roux, O., Roux, O.: State space computation and analysis of time Petri nets. Theory and Practice of Logic Programming (TPLP). Special Issue on Specification Analysis and Verification of Reactive Systems (2005) to appear.

6. Lime, D., Roux, O.H.: State class timed automaton of a time Petri net. In: 10th International Workshop on Petri Nets and Performance Models, (PNPM'03). (2003)
7. Lime, D., Roux, O.H.: A translation based method for the timed analysis of scheduling extended time Petri nets. In: The 25th IEEE RTSS'04, Lisbon, Portugal (2004)
8. Berthomieu, B., Ribet, P.O., Vernadat, F.: The tool tina – construction of abstract state spaces for petri nets and time petri nets. International Journal of Production Research **42** (2004) Tool available at http://www.laas.fr/tina/.
9. Bucci, G., Sassoli, L., Vicario, E.: Oris: A tool for state-space analysis of real-time preemptive systems. Quantitative Evaluation of Systems, First International Conference on (QEST'04) (2004) 70–79

TRANSYT: A Tool for the Verification of Asynchronous Concurrent Systems*

Enric Pastor, Marco A. Peña, and Marc Solé

Department of Computer Architecture,
Technical University of Catalonia,
08860 Castelldefels (Barcelona), Spain

1 Introduction

TRANSYT is a BDD-based tool specifically designed for the verification of timed and untimed asynchronous concurrent systems. TRANSYT system architecture is designed to be modular, open and flexible, such that additional capabilities can be easily integrated. A state of the art BDD package [1] is integrated into the system, and a middleware extension [2] provides support complex BDD manipulation strategies.

TSIF (Transition System Interchange Format) is the main input language of TRANSYT. TSIF is a low-level language for describing asynchronous event-based systems, although synchronous systems can be also covered. Many formalisms can be mapped onto it: digital circuits, Petri nets, etc. TRANSYT integrates specialized algorithms for untimed reachability analysis based on disjunctive Transition Relation (TR) partitioning, and relative-time verification for timed systems. Invariant verification for both timed and untimed systems is fully supported, while CTL model checking is currently supported for untimed systems. TRANSYT provides orders of magnitude improvement over general untimed verification tools like NuSMV [3] and VIS [4], and expands the horizon of timed verification to middle-size real examples.

2 System Functionalities

We provide here a high-level overview of the the most relevant features of TRANSYT. Details of the architecture and algorithms will be provided in Section 3.

User Interaction. TRANSYT works with an interactive shell, processing systems according to command-line options. The user can activate all phases of the verification process (file parsing, system construction, reachability analysis, model checking, simulation, counter-example generation, etc.) with full control of all available options. On top of the interactive shell, a limited but under expansion GUI front-end offers access to all interactive commands, as well as an improved visualization of the systems and the properties under analysis.

* Ministry of Science and Technology TIN 2004-07739-C02-01 and grant AP2001-2819.

K. Etessami and S.K. Rajamani (Eds.): CAV 2005, LNCS 3576, pp. 424–428, 2005.

System Description. TRANSYT can process hierarchical systems formalized (using the TSIF format) as a set of variables to encode the state and *events* to describe the "actions" that the system can execute. Systems can be simultaneously coordinated by variable interchange or event synchronization. Other formalisms can be encoded and easily mapped onto TSIF. Currently we offer a front-end for BLIF [4] and Petri nets [5], and we are working toward a new SMV front-end.

Reachability Analysis. Implements specialized reachability schemes based on disjunctive TRs and uses a mixed BFS/DFS traversal that schedules the application of the TR parts in order to maximize the state generation ratio and minimize BDD peaks. These algorithms have demonstrated orders of magnitude improvement over existing BFS / conjunctive TR traversal schemes (e.g. [3]) when applied to asynchronous concurrent systems. State-of-the art conjunctive TR traversal schemes are also available to efficiently manipulate mixed synchronous/asynchronous systems.

Model Checking. TRANSYT implements fair CTL model checking as defined in [6], and also offers specialized on-the-fly invariant verification. The tool can be configured to detect a minimum number of failures in a single traversal. Failing states are stored to allow selective counter-example generation for all of them.

Semi-formal Verification. In addition to classical reachability analysis, TRANSYT offers an automated two-phase simulation-verification hybrid scheme. Simulation follows a branching scheme that generates traces as divergent as possible (interleaved traces will be rejected). Traces are stored for further analysis. The second phase will select a number of simulation traces as seed of a guided-traversal algorithm. Guided-traversal exploits the behavioral information in the traces to efficiently identify additional states. On-the-fly invariant verification can be carried out during both phases.

Relative-time Verification. TRANSYT offers invariant verification of timed systems based on the *relative-timing* paradigm. TSIF events can be annotated with min-max delays. If it exists, the tool provides a timed counter-example. Otherwise, TRANSYT provides a set of graphic structures that inform the user about how the execution of events is ordered due to timing. Note that not all existing orderings are provided, but just those that are relevant to prove the invariants under verification.

3 Tool Architecture and Algorithms

This section describes the main functional modules in TRANSYT (see Figure 1), the peculiarities of the algorithms implemented in them and their interrelations.

The System Instantiation and Boolean Model Construction provides support for creating the internal representation of the TSIF format. The system is mapped onto a Boolean model after an encoding process, in which TRs, properties, etc. are constructed. Once TRs are built, their causal interrelations can be analyzed

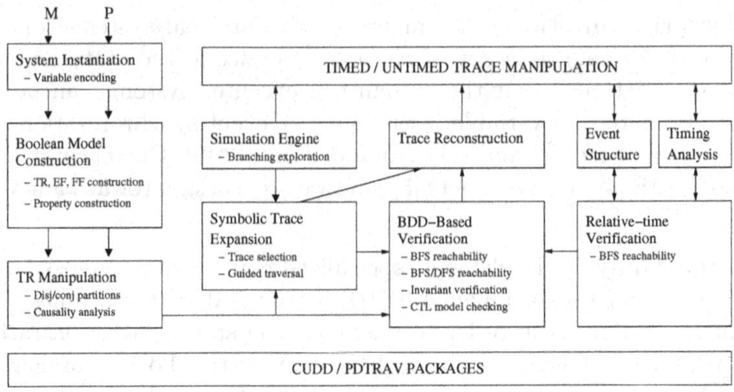

Fig. 1. TRANSYT modular architecture

in order to determine if the application of a TR part may trigger the execution of other TRs. The granularity of the TR partition is decided here depending on TR size, number of parts and detected causality. Different partition schemes can be used according to these parameters.

The BDD-based verification module is the core of TRANSYT. It implements highly efficient traversal schemes based on mixed BFS/DFS algorithms that schedule the application of the disjunctive TR parts. New states generated by one part are immediately reused as source for following parts. If causality is taken into account, this simple scheme provides orders-of-magnitude improvement over BFS traversal. Based on BFS/DFS traversal, on-the-fly invariant verification and fair CTL model checking can be performed on the selected design. Once failures are detected, counter-example traces can be generated and stored —associated to each failing property— for both further manipulation or visualization.

An alternative invariant verification approach, combining simulation and guided-traversal, is provided. Simulation can be executed following a branching strategy that resembles partial-order verification. At each visited state the causality between enabled events is analyzed. In case of detecting concurrent events, only one of the execution traces is followed. In case of conflict (i.e. a choice in the execution path) both execution traces are explored. Exploration continues until no additional states are available or until a certain number of failures have been identified. Causality information can be extracted from traces. Given a trace, its associated causality can be extracted and directly applied to a guided-traversal process. Guided-traversal executes a BFS/DFS reachability analysis applying events in the best order as indicated by causality.

TRANSYT extends symbolic invariant verification to timed systems. The use of *relative timing* [7] eliminates the need to compute the exact timed state space. Instead, the timed behavior of events is captured by means of partial orders that represent relative temporal relations. Timed systems provide delays for all the events in the system; however, many of the constraints imposed by such delays are not actually required. TRANSYT only considers timing information in an *on-demand* basis, as long as it is required to prove a given property.

Moreover, the timing analysis is performed over the subset of events involved in such proof by any external timing analysis algorithm. As a result, the untimed state space of the system is refined incrementally. The tool not only proves or disproves the correctness of the system with respect to a set of invariants, but also provides a set of sufficient relative-time relations that guarantee such correctness or demonstrate a counterexample.

4 Results and Future Directions

TRANSYT is a well-structured platform for the verification of asynchronous concurrent systems. The TSIF front-end provides a flexible entry point for most specification languages relevant to the area. Additional functionalities and algorithms for each phase of the verification flow can be easily integrated. The performance of the tool is satisfactory due to the BDD package and its specific algorithms. Additional information about TRANSYT is available at

`http://research.ac.upc.es/VLSI/transyt/transyt.html`.

TRANSYT has been successfully used to analyze a number systems, both in the timed and untimed domain. Extensive comparisons have been carried out with the state generation engines in NuSMV [3] and VIS [4]. In both cases, orders of magnitude improvements have been obtained [8]. Complex timed systems have been also analyzed using TRANSYT. In particular, several interface FIFO implementations (IPCMOS by S. Schuster and STARI by M.R. Greenstreet) connecting different clock domains have been successfully verified.

Currently, several new functionalities are under development. A mixed conjunctive/disjunctive TR construction and scheduling scheme is being implemented for complex Globally Asynchronous Locally Synchronous (GALS) systems. The CTL verification algorithm is being upgraded to exploit the same causality information used during the reachability process. A restricted version of timed-CTL is being developed to be integrated with the relative-time verification engine. On the user's side, better feedback visualization is being implemented through more powerful visual libraries.

References

1. Somenzi, F.: CUDD: CU decision diagram package release (1998)
2. Cabodi, G., Quer, S.: PdTRAV package politecnico di torino reachability analysis for verification (release 1.2) (1999)
3. Cimatti, A., Clarke, E.M., Giunchiglia, F., Roveri, M.: NuSMV: A new symbolic model checker. International Journal on Software Tools for Technology Transfer **2** (2000) 410–425
4. The VIS Group: VIS: A system for verification and synthesis. In: Proc. International Conference on Computer Aided Verification. Volume 1102 of LNCS., Springer-Verlag (1996) 428–432

5. Cortadella, J., Kishinevsky, M., Kondratyev, A., Lavagno, L., Yakovlev, A.: Petrify: a tool for manipulating concurrent specifications and synthesis of asynchronous controllers. IEICE Transactions on Information and Systems **E80-D** (1997) 315–325
6. Clarke, E.M., Grumberg, O., McMillan, K.L., Zhao, X.: Efficient generation of counterexamples and witnesses in symbolic model checking. In: Proceedings of the 32nd ACM/IEEE conference on Design automation conference. (1995) 427–432
7. Stevens, K., Ginosar, R., Rotem, S.: Relative timing. In: Proc. International Symposium on Advanced Research in Asynchronous Circuits and Systems. (1999) 208–218
8. Solé, M., Pastor, E.: Evaluating symbolic traversal algorithms applied to asynchronous concurrent systems. In: International Conference on Application of Concurrency to System Design (ACSD'04). (2004) 207–216

Ymer: A Statistical Model Checker*

Håkan L.S. Younes

Computer Science Department, Carnegie Mellon University,
Pittsburgh, PA 15213, USA

Abstract. We present Ymer, a tool for verifying probabilistic transient properties of stochastic discrete event systems. Ymer implements both statistical and numerical model checking techniques. We focus on two features of Ymer: distributed acceptance sampling and statistical model checking of nested probabilistic statements.

1 Introduction

Ymer is a tool for verifying probabilistic transient properties of stochastic discrete event systems. Properties are expressed using the logics PCTL [2] and CSL [1]. For example, the CSL property $\neg\mathcal{P}_{\geq 0.01}[\top\ \mathcal{U}^{[0,15.07]}\ faulty{=}n]$ asserts that the probability of n servers becoming faulty within 15.07 seconds is less than 0.01. In general, $\Phi\ \mathcal{U}^{[\tau_1,\tau_2]}\ \Psi$ is a path formula and is evaluated over execution paths for a stochastic system. The formula $\mathcal{P}_{\geq\theta}[\varphi]$, where φ is a path formula, holds if and only if the probability measure of the set of paths that satisfy φ is at least θ. To solve CSL model checking problems, one can attempt to compute the probability measure of a set of paths using numerical techniques, but this is infeasible for systems with complex dynamics (e.g. generalized semi-Markov processes) or large state spaces. Existing CSL model checkers—ETMCC [3] and PRISM [5]—are limited to finite-state Markov chains.

To handle the generality of stochastic discrete event systems, Ymer implements the statistical model checking techniques, based on discrete event simulation and acceptance sampling, for CSL model checking developed by Younes and Simmons [12] (see also [10–Chap. 5]). To verify a formula $\mathcal{P}_{\geq\theta}[\varphi]$, Ymer uses discrete event simulation to generate sample execution paths and verifies the path formula φ over each execution path. The verification result over a sample execution path is the outcome of a chance experiment (Bernoulli trial), which is used as an observation for an acceptance sampling procedure. Ymer implements both sampling with a fixed number of observations and sequential acceptance sampling. Ymer includes support for distributed acceptance sampling, i.e. the use of multiple machines to generate observations, which can result in significant speedup as each observation can be generated independently.

Ymer currently supports time-homogeneous generalized semi-Markov processes specified using an extension of the PRISM input language. PRISM and

* Supported by the Army Research Office (ARO) under contract no. DAAD190110485 and a grant from the Royal Swedish Academy of Engineering Sciences (IVA).

K. Etessami and S.K. Rajamani (Eds.): CAV 2005, LNCS 3576, pp. 429–433, 2005.

ETMCC work only with Markov processes, but support a richer set of properties than Ymer, including steady-state properties and unbounded until operators in path formulae. Ymer can use numerical techniques for continuous-time Markov chains (CTMCs) as it includes the hybrid engine from the PRISM tool for CTMC model checking. Numerical and statistical techniques can be used in combination to solve nested CSL queries for CTMCs as described by Younes et al. [11].

2 Distributed Acceptance Sampling

Statistical solution methods that use samples of independent observations are trivially parallelizable. One can use multiple computers to generate the observations, as noted already by Metropolis and Ulam [7–p. 340], and expect a speedup linear in the added computing power. To ensure that observations are independent, some care needs to be taken when generating pseudorandom numbers on each machine. Ymer uses the scheme proposed by Matsumoto and Nishimura [6], which encodes a process identifier into the pseudorandom number generator. This effectively creates a different generator for each unique identifier.

Ymer adopts a master/slave architecture (Fig. 1) for the distributed verification task. One or more slave processes register their ability to generate observations with a single master process. The master process collects observations from the slave processes and performs an acceptance sampling procedure. Each slave process is assigned a unique identifier by the master process to ensure that the slave processes use different pseudorandom number generators. The right side of Fig. 1 illustrates a typical communication session.

When using distributed sampling with a sequential test, such as Wald's [9] sequential probability ratio test, it is important not to introduce a bias against observations that take a longer time to generate. For probabilistic model checking, each observation involves the generation of a path prefix through discrete event simulation and the verification of a path formula over the generated path prefix. If we simply use observations as they become available, then the guarantees of the acceptance sampling test may no longer hold. For example, negative

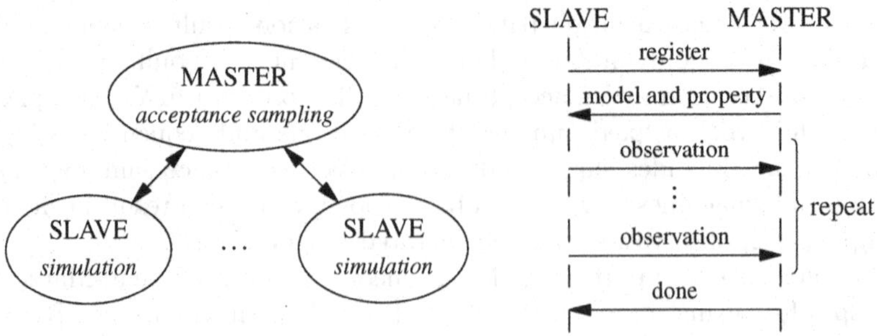

Fig. 1. Master/slave architecture and communication protocol for distributed acceptance sampling

observations for the path formula $\top\ \mathcal{U}^{[0,1000]}\ \Psi$ require simulation for 1000 time units, while positive observations may be fast to generate if Ψ is satisfied early (cf. [10–Example 5.4]).

Such bias is avoided by committing, *a priori*, to the order in which observations are taken into account. Observations that are received out-of-order are buffered until it is time to process them. Ymer maintains a dynamic schedule of the order in which observations are processed. At the beginning, we schedule to receive one observation from each slave process in a specific order. We then reschedule the processing of the next observation for a slave process at the arrival of an observation. This gives us a schedule that automatically adjusts to variations in performance of slave processes without the need for explicit communication of performance characteristics.

To show the effect of distributed sampling, we use the model of an n-station symmetric polling system described by Ibe and Trivedi [4]. In this model, each station has a single-message buffer and the stations are attended by a single server in cyclic order. The server begins by polling station 1. If there is a message in the buffer of station 1, the server starts serving that station. Once station i has been served, or if there is no message at station i when it is polled, the server starts polling station $i+1$ (or 1 if $i=n$). We verify the CSL property $m_1{=}1 \rightarrow \mathcal{P}_{\geq 0.5}[\top\ \mathcal{U}^{[0,20]}\ poll_1]$, which states that if station 1 is full, then it is polled within 20 time units with probability at least 0.5. We do so in the state where station 1 has just been polled and the buffers of all stations are full.

Fig. 2 shows the reduction in verification time for the symmetric polling system when using two machines to generate observations. The first machine is equipped with a 733 MHz Pentium III processor. If we also generate observations, in parallel, on a machine with a 500 MHz Pentium III processor, we get the relative performance indicated by the solid curve. The verification time with two machines is roughly 70 % of the verification time with a single machine. Fig. 3 shows the fraction of observations used from each machine, with m_1 being

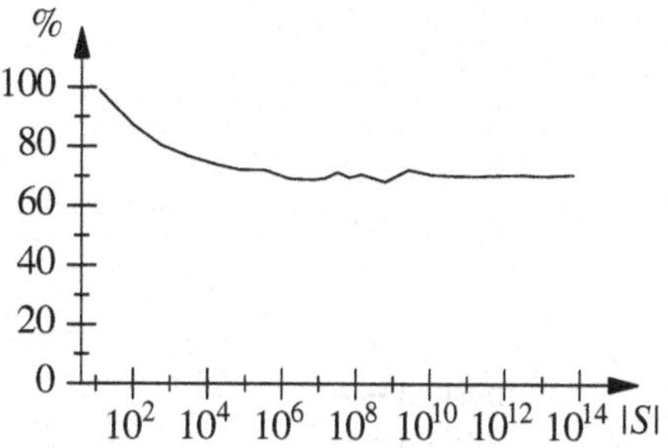

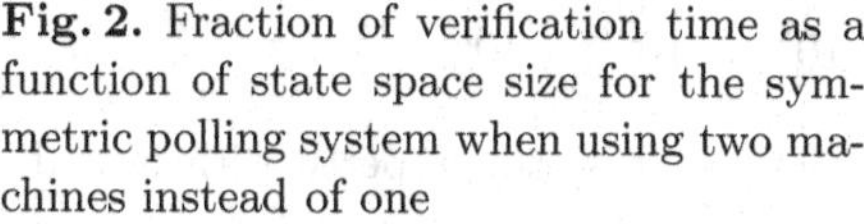
Fig. 2. Fraction of verification time as a function of state space size for the symmetric polling system when using two machines instead of one

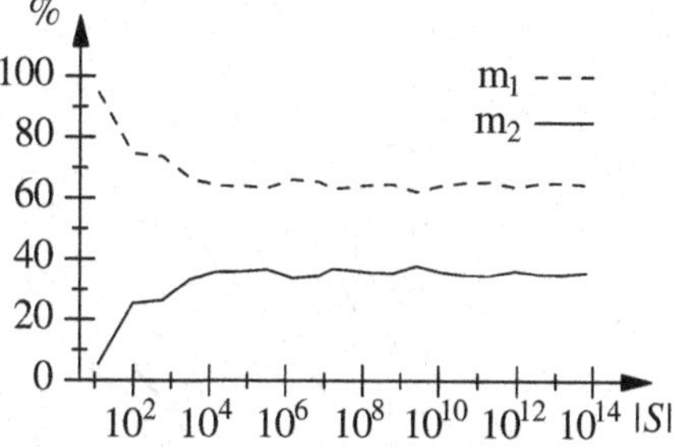

Fig. 3. Distribution of workload as a function of state space size for the symmetric polling system when using two machines to generate observations

the faster of the two machines. We can see that these fractions are in line with the relative performance of the machines.

3 Nested Probabilistic Operators

To illustrate the use of nested probabilistic operators, we consider the robot grid world described by Younes et al. [11]. A robot is moving in an $n \times n$ grid from the bottom left corner to the top right corner. The objective is for the robot to reach the top right corner within 100 time units with probability at least 0.9, while maintaining at least a 0.5 probability of periodically (every 9 time units) communicating with a base station. Let c be a Boolean state variable that is true when the robot is communicating, and let x and y be two integer-valued state variables holding the current location of the robot. The CSL property $\mathcal{P}_{\geq 0.9}[\mathcal{P}_{\geq 0.5}[\top\, \mathcal{U}^{[0,9]}\, c]\, \mathcal{U}^{[0,100]}\, x{=}n \wedge y{=}n]$ expresses the desired objective.

The path formula for the outer probabilistic statement contains a probabilistic operator and cannot be verified without error with statistical techniques. Younes et al. [11] present a mixed solution method using statistical sampling for top-level probabilistic operators and numerical methods for nested probabilistic operators. Younes [10–Sect. 5.2] provides a purely statistical approach, which is made practical through the use of heuristics for selecting observation errors and *memoization* [8] to avoid repeated effort. Ymer implements both techniques.

Fig. 4 plots the verification time for the robot grid world property as a function of state space size. The results were generated on a machine with a 3 GHz Pentium 4 processor. The purely statistical approach is slower for smaller state spaces, but handles larger state spaces than the other two solution methods without exhausting memory resources (800 MB in this case). The dotted line shows where the property goes from being true to being false as the state space grows larger. The use of sequential acceptance sampling gives the peak in the curve for the mixed solution method, but the peak is not present in the curve for the purely statistical method thanks to memoization. The data shows that

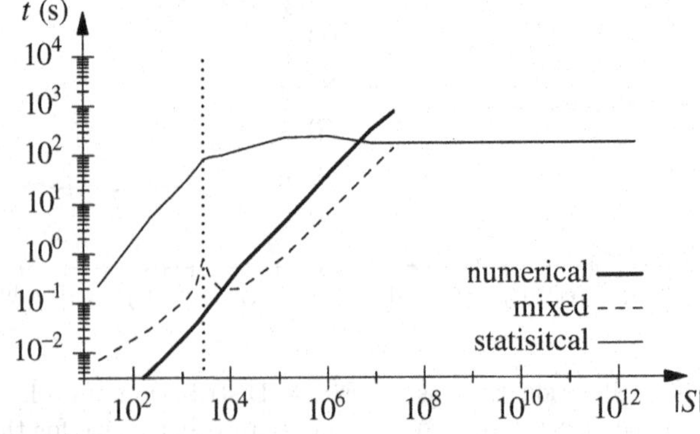

Fig. 4. Comparison of solution methods for robot grid world property with nested probabilistic operators

no method strictly dominates any other method in terms of verification time, although one should keep in mind that the correctness guarantees are different for all three methods. Numerical methods can guarantee high numerical accuracy, while statistical methods provide only probabilistic correctness guarantees.

4 Implementation Details and Availability

Ymer is implemented in C (the random number generator) and C++, and uses the CUDD package for symbolic data structures (BDDs and MTBDDs) used by the hybrid CTMC model checking engine. The part of the code implementing numerical analysis of CTMCs has been adopted from the PRISM tool. Ymer is free software distributed under the GNU General Public License (GPL), and is available for download at http://www.cs.cmu.edu/~lorens/ymer.html.

References

1. Baier, C., Haverkort, B. R., Hermanns, H., and Katoen, J.-P. Model-checking algorithms for continuous-time Markov chains. *IEEE Transactions on Software Engineering*, 29(6):524–541, 2003.
2. Hansson, H. and Jonsson, B. A logic for reasoning about time and reliability. *Formal Aspects of Computing*, 6(5):512–535, 1994.
3. Hermanns, H., Katoen, J.-P., Meyer-Kayser, J., and Siegle, M. A Markov chain model checker. In *Proc. 6th International Conference on Tools and Algorithms for the Construction and Analysis of Systems*, volume 1785 of *LNCS*, pages 347–362. Springer, 2000.
4. Ibe, O. C. and Trivedi, K. S. Stochastic Petri net models of polling systems. *IEEE Journal on Selected Areas in Communications*, 8(9):1649–1657, 1990.
5. Kwiatkowska, M., Norman, G., and Parker, D. Probabilistic symbolic model checking with PRISM: A hybrid approach. *International Journal on Software Tools for Technology Transfer*, 6(2):128–142, 2004.
6. Matsumoto, M. and Nishimura, T. Dynamic creation of pseudorandom number generators. In *Monte-Carlo and Quasi-Monte Carlo Methods 1998*, pages 56–69. Springer, 2000.
7. Metropolis, N. and Ulam, S. M. The Monte Carlo method. *Journal of the American Statistical Association*, 44(247):335–341, 1949.
8. Michie, D. "Memo" functions and machine learning. *Nature*, 218(5136):19–22, 1968.
9. Wald, A. Sequential tests of statistical hypotheses. *Annals of Mathematical Statistics*, 16(2):117–186, 1945.
10. Younes, H. L. S. *Verification and Planning for Stochastic Processes with Asynchronous Events.* PhD thesis, Computer Science Department, Carnegie Mellon University, 2005. CMU-CS-05-105.
11. Younes, H. L. S., Kwiatkowska, M., Norman, G., and Parker, D. Numerical vs. statistical probabilistic model checking. *International Journal on Software Tools for Technology Transfer*, 2005. Forthcoming.
12. Younes, H. L. S. and Simmons, R. G. Probabilistic verification of discrete event systems using acceptance sampling. In *Proc. 14th International Conference on Computer Aided Verification*, volume 2404 of *LNCS*, pages 223–235. Springer, 2002.

Extended Weighted Pushdown Systems

Akash Lal, Thomas Reps, and Gogul Balakrishnan

University of Wisconsin, Madison, Wisconsin 53706
{akash, reps, bgogul}@cs.wisc.edu

Abstract. Recent work on weighted-pushdown systems shows how to generalize interprocedural-dataflow analysis to answer "stack-qualified queries", which answer the question "what dataflow values hold at a program node for a particular set of calling contexts?" The generalization, however, does not account for precise handling of local variables. Extended-weighted-pushdown systems address this issue, and provide answers to stack-qualified queries in the presence of local variables as well.

1 Introduction

An important static-analysis technique is dataflow analysis, which concerns itself with calculating, for each program point, information about the set of states that can occur at that point. For a given abstract domain, the ideal value to compute is the meet-over-all-paths (MOP) value. Kam and Ullman [10] gave a coincidence theorem that provides a sufficient condition for when this value can be calculated for single-procedure programs. Later, Sharir and Pnueli [23] generalized the theorem for multiple-procedure programs, but did not consider local variables. Knoop and Steffen [12] then further extended the theorem to include local variables by modeling the run-time stack of a program. Alternative techniques for handling local variables have been proposed in [17, 19], but these lose certain relationships between local and global variables.

The MOP value over-approximates the set of all possible states that occur at a program point (for all possible calling contexts). Recent work on weighted-pushdown systems (WPDSs) [18] shows how to generalize interprocedural-dataflow analysis to answer "stack-qualified queries" that calculate an over-approximation to the states that can occur at a program point for a given regular set of calling contexts. However, as with Sharir and Pnueli's coincidence theorem, it is not clear if WPDSs can handle local variables accurately. In this paper, we extend the WPDS model to the Extended-WPDS (EWPDS) model, which can accurately encode interprocedural-dataflow analysis on programs with local variables and answer stack-qualified queries on them. The EWPDS model can be seen as generalizing WPDSs in much the same way that Knoop and Steffen generalized Sharir and Pnueli's coincidence theorem.[1]

[1] Recently, with S. Schwoon, we have shown that the computational power of WPDSs is the same as that of EWPDSs. We do not present this result in this paper due to space constraints, but it involves simulating the program run-time stack as a dataflow value.

K. Etessami and S.K. Rajamani (Eds.): CAV 2005, LNCS 3576, pp. 434–448, 2005.

The contributions of this paper can be summarized as follows:

- We give a way of handling local variables in an extension of the WPDS model. The advantage of using (E)WPDSs is that they give a way of calculating dataflow values that hold at a program node for a particular calling context (or set of calling contexts). They can also provide a set of "witness" program execution paths that justify a reported dataflow value.
- We show that the EWPDS model is powerful enough to capture Knoop and Steffen's coincidence theorem. In particular, this means that we can calculate the MOP value (referred to as the interprocedural-meet-over-all-valid-paths, or IMOVP value, for multiple-procedure programs with local variables) for any distributive dataflow-analysis problem for which the domain of transfer functions has no infinite descending chains. For monotonic problems that are not distributive, we can safely approximate the IMOVP value. In addition to this, EWPDSs support stack-qualified IMOVP queries.
- We have extended the WPDS++ library [11] to support EWPDSs and used it to calculate affine relationships that hold between registers in x86 code [2].

A further result was too lengthy to be included in this paper, but illustrates the value of our approach: we have shown that the IMOVP result of [13] for single-level pointer analysis is an instance of our framework.[2] This immediately gives us something new: a way of answering stack-qualified aliasing problems.

The rest of the paper is organized as follows: §2 provides background on WPDSs and explains the EWPDS model; §3 presents algorithms to solve reachability queries in EWPDSs. In §4, we show how to compute the IMOVP value using an EWPDS; §5 presents experimental results; and §6 describes related work.

2 The EXTENDED-WPDS Model

2.1 Pushdown Systems

Definition 1. *A* **pushdown system** *is a triple* $\mathcal{P} = (P, \Gamma, \Delta)$ *where* P *is the set of states or control locations,* Γ *is the set of stack symbols and* $\Delta \subseteq P \times \Gamma \times P \times \Gamma^*$ *is the set of pushdown rules. A* **configuration** *of* $\mathcal{P}$ *is a pair* $\langle p, u\rangle$ *where* $p \in P$ *and* $u \in \Gamma^*$*. A rule* $r \in \Delta$ *is written as* $\langle p, \gamma\rangle \hookrightarrow_{\mathcal{P}} \langle p', u\rangle$ *where* $p, p' \in P$*,* $\gamma \in \Gamma$ *and* $u \in \Gamma^*$*. These rules define a transition relation* $\Rightarrow_{\mathcal{P}}$ *on configurations of* $\mathcal{P}$ *as follows: If* $r = \langle p, \gamma\rangle \hookrightarrow_{\mathcal{P}} \langle p', u\rangle$ *then* $\langle p, \gamma u'\rangle \Rightarrow_{\mathcal{P}} \langle p', uu'\rangle$ *for all* $u' \in \Gamma^*$*. The subscript* $\mathcal{P}$ *on the transition relation is omitted when it is clear from the context. The reflexive transitive closure of* $\Rightarrow$ *is denoted by* $\Rightarrow^*$*. For a set of configurations* C*, we define* $pre^*(C) = \{c' \mid \exists c \in C : c' \Rightarrow^* c\}$ *and* $post^*(C) = \{c' \mid \exists c \in C : c \Rightarrow^* c'\}$*, which are just backward and forward reachability under the transition relation* $\Rightarrow$*.*

We restrict the pushdown rules to have at most two stack symbols on the right-hand side. This means that for every rule $r \in \Delta$ of the form $\langle p, \gamma\rangle \hookrightarrow_{\mathcal{P}} \langle p', u\rangle$, we have

[2] Multi-level pointer analysis problems (the kind that occur in C, C++, and Java programs) can be safely approximated as single-level pointer-analysis problems [14].

$|u| \leq 2$. This restriction does not decrease the power of pushdown systems because by increasing the number of stack symbols by a constant factor, an arbitrary pushdown system can be converted into one that satisfies this restriction [20]. Moreover, pushdown systems with at most two stack symbols on the right-hand side of each rule are sufficient for modeling control flow in programs. We use $\Delta_i \subseteq \Delta$ to denote the set of all rules with i stack symbols on the right-hand side.

It is instructive to see how a program's control flow can be modeled because even though the EWPDS model can work with any pushdown system, it is geared towards performing dataflow analysis in programs. The construction we present here is also followed in [18]. Let $(\mathcal{N}, \mathcal{E})$ be an interprocedural control flow graph where each *call* node is split into two nodes: one is the source of an interprocedural edge to the callee's entry node and the second is the target of an edge from the callee's exit node. $\mathcal{N}$ is the set of nodes in this graph and $\mathcal{E}$ is the set of control-flow edges. Fig. 1(a) shows an example of an interprocedural control-flow graph; Fig. 1(b) shows the pushdown system that models it. The PDS has a single state p, one stack symbol for each node in $\mathcal{N}$, and one rule for each edge in $\mathcal{E}$. We use Δ_1 rules to model intraprocedural edges, Δ_2 rules (also called *push* rules) for *call* edges, and Δ_0 rules (also called *pop* rules) for *return* edges. It is easy to see that a valid path in the program corresponds to a path in the pushdown system's transition system and vice versa.

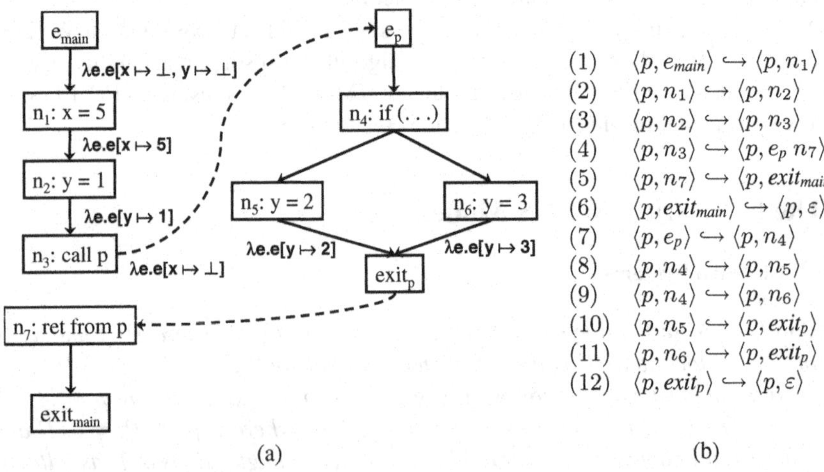

Fig. 1. (a) An interprocedural control flow graph. The e and *exit* nodes represent entry and exit points of procedures, respectively. x is a local variable of $main$ and y is a global variable. Dashed edges represent interprocedural control flow. Edge labels correspond to dataflow facts and are explained in §2.3. (b) A pushdown system that models the control flow of the graph shown in (a)

The number of configurations of a pushdown system is unbounded, so we use a finite automaton to describe a set of configurations.

Definition 2. *Let $\mathcal{P} = (P, \Gamma, \Delta)$ be a pushdown system. A $\mathcal{P}$-**automaton** is a finite automaton $(Q, \Gamma, \rightarrow, P, F)$, where $Q \supseteq P$ is a finite set of states, $\rightarrow \subseteq Q \times \Gamma \times Q$ is the transition relation, P is the set of initial states, and F is the set of final states of* *the automaton. We say that a configuration* $\langle p, u \rangle$ *is accepted by a* $\mathcal{P}$*-automaton if the automaton can accept* u *when it is started in state* p *(written as* $p \xrightarrow{u}{}^{*} q$*, where* $q \in F$*). A set of configurations is called* **regular** *if some* $\mathcal{P}$*-automaton accepts it.*

An important result is that for a regular set of configurations C, both $post^*(C)$ and $pre^*(C)$ are also regular sets of configurations [20, 3, 8].

2.2 Weighted Pushdown Systems

A weighted pushdown system is obtained by supplementing a pushdown system with a weight domain that is a bounded idempotent semiring [18, 4].

Definition 3. *A* **bounded idempotent semiring** *is a quintuple* $(D, \oplus, \otimes, 0, 1)$*, where* D *is a set whose elements are called* **weights***,* 0 *and* 1 *are elements of* D*, and* $\oplus$ *(the combine operation) and* $\otimes$ *(the extend operation) are binary operators on* D *such that*

1. $(D, \oplus)$ *is a commutative monoid with* 0 *as its neutral element, and where* $\oplus$ *is idempotent (i.e., for all* $a \in D$*,* $a \oplus a = a$*).*
2. $(D, \otimes)$ *is a monoid with the neutral element* 1*.*
3. $\otimes$ *distributes over* $\oplus$*, i.e., for all* $a, b, c \in D$ *we have*
   $a \otimes (b \oplus c) = (a \otimes b) \oplus (a \otimes c)$ *and* $(a \oplus b) \otimes c = (a \otimes c) \oplus (b \otimes c)$.
4. 0 *is an annihilator with respect to* $\otimes$*, i.e., for all* $a \in D$*,* $a \otimes 0 = 0 = 0 \otimes a$*.*
5. *In the partial order* $\sqsubseteq$ *defined by:* $\forall a, b \in D$*,* $a \sqsubseteq b$ *iff* $a \oplus b = a$*, there are no infinite descending chains.*

Definition 4. *A* **weighted pushdown system** *is a triple* $\mathcal{W} = (\mathcal{P}, \mathcal{S}, f)$ *where* $\mathcal{P} = (P, \Gamma, \Delta)$ *is a pushdown system,* $\mathcal{S} = (D, \oplus, \otimes, 0, 1)$ *is a bounded idempotent semiring and* $f : \Delta \to D$ *is a map that assigns a weight to each pushdown rule.*

Let $\sigma \in \Delta^*$ be a sequence of rules. Using f, we can associate a value to σ, i.e., if $\sigma = [r_1, \ldots, r_k]$, then we define $v(\sigma) \stackrel{\text{def}}{=} f(r_1) \otimes \ldots \otimes f(r_k)$. Moreover, for any two configurations c and c' of $\mathcal{P}$, we let $path(c, c')$ denote the set of all rule sequences $[r_1, \ldots, r_k]$ that transform c into c'. Weighted pushdown systems are geared towards solving the following two reachability problems.

Definition 5. *Let* $\mathcal{W} = (\mathcal{P}, \mathcal{S}, f)$ *be a weighted pushdown system, where* $\mathcal{P} = (P, \Gamma, \Delta)$*, and let* $C \subseteq P \times \Gamma^*$ *be a regular set of configurations. The* **generalized pushdown predecessor** (GPP) **problem** *is to find for each* $c \in P \times \Gamma^*$*:*

$$\delta(c) \stackrel{\text{def}}{=} \bigoplus\{\, v(\sigma) \mid \sigma \in path(c, c'), c' \in C \,\}.$$

The **generalized pushdown successor** (GPS) **problem** *is to find for each* $c \in P \times \Gamma^*$*:*

$$\delta(c) \stackrel{\text{def}}{=} \bigoplus\{\, v(\sigma) \mid \sigma \in path(c', c), c' \in C \,\}.$$

2.3 Extended Weighted Pushdown Systems

The reachability problems defined in the previous section compute the value of a rule sequence by taking an extend of the weights of each of the rules in the sequence. However, when weighted pushdown systems are used for dataflow analysis of programs [18] then the rule sequences, in general, represent interprocedural paths in a program.

To summarize the weight of such paths, we would have to maintain information about local variables of all unfinished procedures that appear on the path.

We lift weighted pushdown systems to handle local variables in much the same way that Knoop and Steffen [12] lifted conventional dataflow analysis to handle local variables. We allow for local variables to be stored at call sites and then use special merging functions to appropriately combine them with the value returned by a procedure. For a semiring $\mathcal{S}$ on domain D, define a *merging function* as follows:

Definition 6. *A function $g : D \times D \to D$ is a* **merging function** *with respect to a bounded idempotent semiring $\mathcal{S} = (D, \oplus, \otimes, 0, 1)$ if it satisfies the following properties.*

1. **Strictness.** *For all $a \in D$, $g(0, a) = g(a, 0) = 0$.*
2. **Distributivity.** *The function distributes over $\oplus$. For all $a, b, c \in D$,*
$$g(a \oplus b, c) = g(a, c) \oplus g(b, c) \text{ and } g(a, b \oplus c) = g(a, b) \oplus g(a, c)$$
3. **Path Extension.**[3] *For all $a, b, c \in D$, $g(a \otimes b, c) = a \otimes g(b, c)$.*

Definition 7. *An* **extended weighted pushdown system** *is a quadruple $\mathcal{W}_e = (\mathcal{P}, \mathcal{S}, f, g)$ where $(\mathcal{P}, \mathcal{S}, f)$ is a weighted pushdown system and $g : \Delta_2 \to \mathcal{G}$ assigns a merging function to each rule in Δ_2, where $\mathcal{G}$ is the set of all merging functions on the semiring $\mathcal{S}$. We will write g_r as a shorthand for $g(r)$.*

Note that a push rule has both a weight and a merging function associated with it. The merging functions are used to combine the effects of a called procedure with those made by the calling procedure just before the call. As an example, Figure 1 shows an interprocedural control flow graph and the pushdown system that can be used to represent it. We can perform constant propagation (with uninterpreted expressions) on the graph by assigning a weight to each pushdown rule. Let V be the set of all variables in a program and $(\mathbb{Z}_\perp, \sqsubseteq, \sqcap)$ with $\mathbb{Z}_\perp = \mathbb{Z} \cup \{\perp\}$ be the standard constant-propagation semilattice: $\perp \sqsubseteq c$ for all $c \in \mathbb{Z}$ and $\sqcap$ is the greatest-lower-bound operation in this partial order. $\perp$ stands for "not-a-constant". The weight semiring is $\mathcal{S} = (D, \oplus, \otimes, 0, 1)$ where $D = (\mathit{Env} \to \mathit{Env})$ is the set of all environment transformers with an environment being a mapping for all variables: $\mathit{Env} = (V \to \mathbb{Z}_\perp) \cup \{\top\}$. We use $\top$ to denote an infeasible environment. Furthermore, we restrict the set D to contain only $\top$-strict transformers, i.e., for all $d \in D$, $d(\top) = \top$. We can extend the meet operation to environments by taking meet componentwise.

$$\mathit{env}_1 \sqcap \mathit{env}_2 = \begin{cases} \mathit{env}_1 & \text{if } \mathit{env}_2 = \top \\ \mathit{env}_2 & \text{if } \mathit{env}_1 = \top \\ \lambda v.(\mathit{env}_1(v) \sqcap \mathit{env}_2(v)) & \text{otherwise} \end{cases}$$

The semiring operations and constants are defined as follows:

$$0 = \lambda e.\top \qquad w_1 \oplus w_2 = \lambda e.(w_1(e) \sqcap w_2(e))$$
$$1 = \lambda e.e \qquad w_1 \otimes w_2 = w_2 \circ w_1$$

The weights for the PDS that models the program in Fig. 1 are shown as edge labels. A weight of the form $\lambda e.e[x \mapsto 5]$ returns an environment that agrees with the argument, except that x is bound to 5. The environment $\top$ cannot be updated, and thus $(\lambda e.e[x \mapsto 5])\top = \top$.

[3] This property can be too restrictive in some cases; App. A discusses how this property may be dispensed with.

The merging function for call site n_3 will receive two environment transformers: one that summarizes the effect of the caller from its entry point to the call site (e_{main} to n_3) and one that summarizes the effect of the called procedure (e_p to $exit_p$). It then has produce the transformer that summarizes the effect of the caller from its entry point to the return site (e_{main} to n_7). We define it as follows:

$$\begin{aligned} g(w_1, w_2) \;=\; & \textbf{if } (w_1 = 0 \text{ or } w_2 = 0) \textbf{ then } 0 \\ & \textbf{else } \lambda e.e[x \mapsto w_1(e)(x), y \mapsto (w_1 \otimes w_2)(e)(y)] \end{aligned}$$

It copies over the value of the local variable x from the call site, and gets the value of y from the called procedure. Because the merging function has access to the environment transformer just before the call, we do not have to pass the value of local variable x into procedure p. Hence the call stops tracking the value of x using the weight $\lambda e.e[x \mapsto \bot]$.

To formalize this, we redefine the generalized pushdown predecessor and successor problem by changing the definition of the value of a rule sequence. If $\sigma \in \Delta^*$ with $\sigma = [r_1, r_2, \cdots, r_k]$ then let $(r\ \sigma)$ denote the sequence $[r, r_1, \cdots, r_k]$. Also, let $[\,]$ denote the empty sequence. Consider the context-free grammar shown in Fig. 2.

$$\begin{array}{lll} R_0 \to r\ \ (r \in \Delta_0) & \sigma_s \to [\,] \mid R_1 \mid \sigma_s\ \sigma_s & \sigma_i \to R_2 \mid \sigma_b \mid \sigma_i\ \sigma_i \\ R_1 \to r\ \ (r \in \Delta_1) & \sigma_b \to \sigma_s \mid \sigma_b\ \sigma_b & \sigma_d \to R_0 \mid \sigma_b \mid \sigma_d\ \sigma_d \\ R_2 \to r\ \ (r \in \Delta_2) & \quad\;\; \mid R_2\ \sigma_b\ R_0 & \sigma_a \to \sigma_d\ \sigma_i \end{array}$$

Fig. 2. Grammar used for parsing rule sequences. The start symbol of the grammar is σ_a

σ_s is simply R_1^*. σ_b represents a *balanced* sequence of rules that have matched calls (R_2) and returns (R_0) with any number of rules from Δ_1 inbetween. σ_i is just $(R_2 \mid \sigma_b)^+$ in regular-language terminology, and represents sequences that increase stack height. σ_d is $(R_0 \mid \sigma_b)^+$ and represents sequences that decrease stack height. σ_a can derive any rule sequence. We use this grammar to define the value of a rule sequence.

Definition 8. *Given an* EWPDS $\mathcal{W}_e = (\mathcal{P}, \mathcal{S}, f, g)$, *we define the* **value** *of a sequence of rules* $\sigma \in \Delta^*$ *by first parsing the sequence according to the above grammar and then giving a meaning to each production rule.*

$$\begin{array}{ll} 1.\ v(r) \quad\;\; = f(r) & 5.\ v(R_2\ \sigma_b\ R_0) = g_{R_2}(1, v(\sigma_b) \otimes v(R_0)) \\ 2.\ v([\,]) \quad\; = 1 & 6.\ v(\sigma_d\ \sigma_d) \quad\;\; = v(\sigma_d) \otimes v(\sigma_d) \\ 3.\ v(\sigma_s\ \sigma_s) = v(\sigma_s) \otimes v(\sigma_s) & 7.\ v(\sigma_i\ \sigma_i) \quad\;\;\; = v(\sigma_i) \otimes v(\sigma_i) \\ 4.\ v(\sigma_b\ \sigma_b) = v(\sigma_b) \otimes v(\sigma_b) & 8.\ v(\sigma_d\ \sigma_i) \quad\;\; = v(\sigma_d) \otimes v(\sigma_i) \end{array}$$

Here we have used g_{R_2} *as a shorthand for* g_r *where* r *is the terminal derived by* R_2.

The main thing to note in the above definition is the application of merging functions on balanced sequences. Because the grammar presented in Fig. 2 is ambiguous, there might be many parsings of the same rule sequence, but all of them would produce the same value because the extend operation is associative and there is a unique way to balance R_2s with R_0s.

The generalized pushdown problems GPP and GPS for EWPDS are the same as those for WPDS except for the changed definition of the value of a rule sequence. If we let each merging function be $g_r(w_1, w_2) = w_1 \otimes f(r) \otimes w_2$, then the EWPDS reduces to a WPDS. This justifies calling our model an *extended* weighted pushdown system.

3 Solving Reachability Problems in EWPDSs

In this section, we present algorithms to solve the generalized reachability problems for EWPDSs. Throughout this section, let $\mathcal{W}_e = (\mathcal{P}, \mathcal{S}, f, g)$ be an EWPDS where $\mathcal{P} = (P, \Gamma, \Delta)$ is a pushdown system and $\mathcal{S} = (D, \oplus, \otimes, 0, 1)$ is the weight domain. Let C be a fixed regular set of configurations that is recognized by a $\mathcal{P}$-automaton $\mathcal{A} = (Q, \Gamma, \rightarrow_0, P, F)$ such that $\mathcal{A}$ has no transition leading to an initial state. Note that any automaton can be converted to an equivalent one that has no transition into an initial state by duplicating the initial states. We also assume that $\mathcal{A}$ has no ε-transitions.

As in the case of weighted pushdown systems, we construct an annotated automaton from which $\delta(c)$ can be read off efficiently. This automaton is the same as the automaton constructed for simple pushdown reachability [20], except for the annotations. We will not show the calculation of witness annotations because they are obtained in exactly the same way as for weighted pushdown systems [18]. This is because witnesses record the paths that justify a weight and not how the values of those paths were calculated.

3.1 Solving GPP

To solve GPP, we take as input the $\mathcal{P}$-automaton $\mathcal{A}$ that describes the set of configurations on which we want to query the EWPDS. As output, we create an automaton $\mathcal{A}_{pre^*}$ with weights as annotations on transitions, and then read off the values of $\delta(c)$ from the automaton. The algorithm is based on the saturation rule shown below. Starting with the automaton $\mathcal{A}$, we keep applying this rule until it can no longer be applied. Termination is guaranteed because there are a finite number of transitions and the height of the weight domain is bounded as well. For each transition in the automaton being created, we store the weight on it using function l. The saturation rule is the same as that for predecessor reachability in ordinary pushdown systems, except for the weights, and is different from the one for weighted pushdown systems only in the last case, where a merging function is applied.

- If $r = \langle p, \gamma \rangle \hookrightarrow \langle p', \varepsilon \rangle$, then update the annotation on $t = (p, \gamma, p')$ to $l(t) := l(t) \oplus f(r)$. We assume $l(t) = 0$ if the transition t did not exist before.
- If $r = \langle p, \gamma \rangle \hookrightarrow \langle p', \gamma' \rangle$ and there is a transition $t = (p', \gamma', q)$, then update the annotation on $t' = (p, \gamma, q)$ to $l(t') := l(t') \oplus (f(r) \otimes l(t))$.
- If $r = \langle p, \gamma \rangle \hookrightarrow \langle p', \gamma' \gamma'' \rangle$ and there are transitions $t = (p', \gamma', q_1)$ and $t' = (q_1, \gamma'', q_2)$, then update the annotation on $t'' = (p, \gamma, q_2)$ to
$$l(t'') := l(t'') \oplus \begin{cases} f(r) \otimes l(t) \otimes l(t') & \text{if } q_1 \notin P \\ g_r(1, l(t)) \otimes l(t') & \text{otherwise} \end{cases}$$

For convenience, we will write a transition $t = (p, \gamma, q)$ in $\mathcal{A}_{pre^*}$ with $l(t) = w$ as $p \xrightarrow[w]{\gamma} q$. Define the value of a path $q_1 \xrightarrow[w_1]{\gamma_1} q_2 \cdots \xrightarrow[w_n]{\gamma_n} q_{n+1}$ to be $w_1 \otimes w_2 \cdots \otimes w_n$. The following theorem shows how $\delta(c)$ is calculated.

Theorem 1. *For a configuration $c = \langle p, \gamma_1 \gamma_2 \cdots \gamma_n \rangle$, $\delta(c)$ is the combine of the values of all accepting paths $p \xrightarrow{\gamma_1} q_1 \xrightarrow{\gamma_2} \cdots \xrightarrow{\gamma_n} q_n$, $q_n \in F$ in $\mathcal{A}_{pre^*}$.*

We can calculate $\delta(c)$ efficiently using an algorithm similar to the simulation algorithm for NFAs (cf. [1–Algorithm 3.4]).

3.2 Solving GPS

For this section, we shall assume that we can have at most one rule of the form $\langle p, \gamma \rangle \hookrightarrow \langle p', \gamma'\gamma'' \rangle$ for each combination of p',γ', and γ''. This involves no loss of generality because we can replace a rule $r = \langle p, \gamma \rangle \hookrightarrow \langle p', \gamma'\gamma'' \rangle$ with two rules: (a) $r' = \langle p, \gamma \rangle \hookrightarrow \langle p_r, \gamma'\gamma'' \rangle$ with weight $f(r)$ and merging function g_r, and (b) $r'' = \langle p_r, \gamma' \rangle \hookrightarrow \langle p', \gamma' \rangle$ with weight 1, where p_r is a new state. This replacement does not change the reachability problem's answers. Let $lookup(p', \gamma', \gamma'')$ be a function that returns the unique push rule associated with a triple (p', γ', γ'') if there is one.

Before presenting the algorithm, let us consider an operational definition of the value of a rule sequence. The importance of this alternative definition is that it shows the correspondence with the call semantics of a program. For each interprocedural path in a program, we define a stack of weights that contains a weight for each unfinished call in the path. Elements of the stack are from the set $D \times D \times \Delta_2$ (recall that Δ_2 was defined as the set of all push rules in Δ), where (w_1, w_2, r) signifies that (i) a call was made using rule r, (ii) the weight at the time of the call was w_1, and (iii) w_2 was the weight on the call rule.

Let $STACK = D.(D \times D \times \Delta_2)^*$ be the set of all nonempty stacks where the topmost element is from D and the rest are from $(D \times D \times \Delta_2)$. We will write an element $(w_1, w_2, r) \in D \times D \times \Delta_2$ as $(w_1, w_2)_r$. For each rule $r \in \Delta$ of the form $\langle p, \gamma \rangle \hookrightarrow \langle p', u \rangle$, $u \in \Gamma^*$, we will associate a function $[\![r]\!] : STACK \to STACK$. Let $S \in (D \times D \times \Delta_2)^*$.

- If r has one symbol on the right-hand side ($|u| = 1$), then accumulate its weight on the top of the stack: $[\![r]\!]\ (w_1\ S) = ((w_1 \otimes f(r))\ S)$
- If r has two symbols on the right-hand side ($|u| = 2$), then save the weight of the push rule as well as the push rule itself on the stack and start a fresh entry on the top of the stack: $[\![r]\!]\ (w_1\ S) = (1\ (w_1, f(r))_r\ S)$
- If r has no symbols on the right-hand side ($|u| = 0$), then apply the appropriate merging function if there is something pushed on the stack. Otherwise, r represents an unbalanced pop rule and simply accumulate its weight on the stack. Note that we drop the weight of the push rule when we apply the merging function in accordance with case 5 of Defn. 8.

$$[\![r]\!]\ (w_1\ (w_2, w_3)_{r_1}\ S) = ((g_{r_1}(w_2, w_1 \otimes f(r))\ S) \qquad (1)$$
$$[\![r]\!]\ (w_1) = (w_1 \otimes f(r))$$

For a sequence of rules $\sigma = [r_1, r_2, \cdots, r_n]$, define $[\![\sigma]\!] = [\![[r_2, \cdots, r_n]]\!] \circ [\![r_1]\!]$. Let *flatten* $: STACK \to D$ be an operation that computes a weight from a stack as follows:

$$flatten(w_1\ S) = flatten'(S) \otimes w_1 \qquad \begin{array}{ll} flatten'(()) & = 1 \\ flatten'((w_1, w_2)_r\ S) & = flatten'(S) \otimes (w_1 \otimes w_2) \end{array}$$

Example 1. Consider the rule sequence σ that takes the program in Fig. 1 from e_{main} to $exit_p$ via node n_5. If we apply $[\![\sigma]\!]$ to a stack containing just 1, we get a stack of height 2 as follows: $[\![\sigma]\!](1) = ((\lambda e.e[y \mapsto 2])\ (\lambda e.e[x \mapsto 5, y \mapsto 1], \lambda e.e[x \mapsto \perp])_r)$, where r is the push rule that calls procedure p (Rule 4 in Fig. 1(b)). The top of the stack is the weight computed inside p (Rules 7, 8, 10), and the bottom of the stack contains a pair of weights: the first component is the weight computed in *main* just before the call

(Rules 1, 2, 3); the second component is just the weight on the call rule r. If we apply the *flatten* operation on this stack, we get the weight $\lambda e.e[x \mapsto \bot, y \mapsto 2]$ which is exactly the value $v(\sigma)$. When we apply the pop rule r' (Rule 12) to this stack, we get:

$$\begin{aligned}[\![\sigma\, r']\!](1) &= [\![r']\!] \circ [\![\sigma]\!](1) \\ &= (g_r(\lambda e.e[x \mapsto 5, y \mapsto 1], \lambda e.e[y \mapsto 2])) \\ &= (\lambda e.e[x \mapsto 5, y \mapsto 2])\end{aligned}$$

Again, applying *flatten* on this stack gives us $v(\sigma\, r')$. The following lemma formalizes the equivalence between $[\![\sigma]\!]$ and $v(\sigma)$.

Lemma 1. *For any valid sequence of rules σ ($\sigma \in path(c, c')$ for some configurations c and c'), $[\![\sigma]\!]\,(1) = S$ such that $flatten(S) = v(\sigma)$.*

Corollary 1. *For a configuration c, let $\delta_S(c) \subseteq STACK$ be defined as follows:*

$$\delta_S(c) = \{[\![\sigma]\!](1) \mid \sigma \in paths(c', c),\ c' \in C\}.$$

Let C be the set of configurations described by the $\mathcal{P}$-automaton $\mathcal{A}$. Then

$$\delta(c) = \oplus\{flatten(S) \mid S \in \delta_S(c)\}.$$

The above corollary shows that $\delta_S(c)$ has enough information to compute $\delta(c)$ directly. To solve the pushdown successor problem, we take the input $\mathcal{P}$-automaton $\mathcal{A}$ that describes a set of configurations and create an annotated $\mathcal{P}$-automaton $\mathcal{A}_{post^*}$ (one that has weights as annotations on transitions) from which we can read off the value of $\delta(c)$ for any configuration c. The algorithm is again based on a saturation rule. For each transition in the automaton being created, we have a function l that stores the weight on the transition. Based on the above operational definition of the value of a path, we would create $\mathcal{A}_{post^*}$ on pairs of weights, that is, over the semiring $(D \times D, \oplus, \otimes, (0,0), (1,1))$ where $\oplus$ and $\otimes$ are defined component wise. Also, we introduce a new state for each push rule. So the states of $\mathcal{A}_{post^*}$ are $Q \cup \{q_{p',\gamma'} \mid \langle p, \gamma\rangle \hookrightarrow \langle p', \gamma'\gamma''\rangle \in \Delta\}$. Let Q' be the set of new states added. The saturation rule is shown in Fig. 3. To see what the saturation rule is doing, consider a path in $\mathcal{A}_{post^*}$: $\tau = q_1 \xrightarrow{\gamma_1} q_2 \xrightarrow{\gamma_2} \cdots \xrightarrow{\gamma_n} q_{n+1}$. As an invariant of our algorithm, we would have $q_1 \in (P \cup Q')$; $q_2, \cdots, q_k \in Q'$; and $q_{k+1}, \cdots, q_{n+1} \in (Q - P)$ for some $0 \leq k \leq n+1$. This is because of the fact that we never create transitions from a state in P to a state in P, or from a state in Q' to a state in P, or from a state in $Q - P$ to a state in $P \cup Q'$. Now define a new transition label $l'(t)$ as follows: $l'(p, \gamma, q) = lookup(p', \gamma', \gamma)$ if $p \equiv q_{p',\gamma'}$.
Then the path τ describes the *STACK* $vpath(\tau) = (l_1(t_1)\ \ l(t_2)_{l'(t_2)} \cdots\ l(t_k)_{l'(t_k)})$ where $t_i = (q_i, \gamma_i, q_{i+1})$ and $l_1(t)$ is the first component projected out of the weight-pair $l(t)$. This means that each path in $\mathcal{A}_{post^*}$ represents a *STACK* and all the saturation algorithm does is to make the automaton rich enough to encode all *STACK*s in $\delta_S(c)$ for all configurations c. The first and third cases of the saturation rule can be seen as applying $[\![r]\!]$ for rules with one and two stack symbols on the right-hand side, respectively. Applying the fourth case immediately after the second case can be seen as applying $[\![r]\!]$ for pop rules.

Theorem 2. *For a configuration $c = \langle p, u\rangle$, we have,*

$$\delta(c) = \oplus\{flatten(vpath(\sigma_t)) \mid \sigma_t \in paths(p, u, q_f), q_f \in F\}$$

where $paths(p, u, q_f)$ denotes the set of all paths of transitions in $\mathcal{A}_{post^*}$ that go from p to q_f on input u, i.e., $p \xrightarrow{u}{}^{*} q_f$.

- If $r = \langle p, \gamma \rangle \hookrightarrow \langle p', \gamma' \rangle$ and there is a transition $t = (p, \gamma, q)$ with annotation $l(t)$, then update the annotation on transition $t' = (p', \gamma', q)$ to $l(t') := l(t') \oplus (l(t) \otimes (f(r), 1))$. We assume $l(t') = (0, 0)$ if the transition did not exist before.
- If $r = \langle p, \gamma \rangle \hookrightarrow \langle p', \varepsilon \rangle$ and there is a transition $t = (p, \gamma, q)$ with annotation $l(t)$, then update the annotation on transition $t' = (p', \varepsilon, q)$ to $l(t') := l(t') \oplus (l(t) \otimes (f(r), 1))$.
- If $r = \langle p, \gamma \rangle \hookrightarrow \langle p', \gamma' \gamma'' \rangle$ and there is a transition $t = (p, \gamma, q)$ with annotation $l(t)$ then let $t' = (p', \gamma', q_{p',\gamma'})$, $t'' = (q_{p',\gamma'}, \gamma'', q)$ and update annotations on them.

$$\begin{aligned} l(t') &:= l(t') \oplus (1, 1) \\ l(t'') &:= l(t'') \oplus (l(t) \otimes (1, f(r))) \end{aligned}$$

- If there are transitions $t = (p, \varepsilon, q)$ and $t' = (q, \gamma', q')$ with annotations $l(t) = (w_1, w_2)$ and $l(t') = (w_3, w_4)$ then update the annotation on the transition $t'' = (p, \gamma', q')$ to $l(t'') := l(t'') \oplus w$ where w is defined as follows:

$$w = \begin{cases} (g_{lookup(p',\gamma',\gamma'')}(w_3, w_1), 1) & \text{if } q \equiv q_{p',\gamma'} \\ l(t') \otimes l(t) & \text{otherwise} \end{cases}$$

Fig. 3. Saturation rule for constructing $\mathcal{A}_{post^*}$ from $\mathcal{A}$

An easy way of computing the combine in the above theorem is to replace annotation $l(t)$ on each transition t with $l_1(t) \otimes l_2(t)$, the extend of the two weight components of $l(t)$, and then use standard NFA simulation algorithms (cf. [1–Algorithm 3.4]) as we would use for $\mathcal{A}_{pre^*}$.

4 Interprocedural Meet over All Paths

In this section, we show how extended weighted pushdown systems can be used to compute the interprocedural-meet-over-all-paths (IMOVP) solution for a given dataflow analysis problem. We will first define the IMOVP strategy as described in [12] and then show how to solve it using an EWPDS.

We are given a meet semilattice $(\mathcal{C}, \sqcap)$ describing dataflow facts and the interprocedural-control-flow graph of a program $(\mathcal{N}, \mathcal{E})$ where $\mathcal{N}_C, \mathcal{N}_R \subseteq \mathcal{N}$ are the call and return nodes, respectively. We are also given a semantic transformer for each node in the program: $[\![\ ]\!] : \mathcal{N} \to (\mathcal{C} \to \mathcal{C})$, which represents (i.e., over-approximates) the effect of executing a statement in the program. Let $STK = \mathcal{C}^+$ be the set of all nonempty stacks with elements from $\mathcal{C}$. STK is used as an abstract representation of the run-time stack of a program. Define the following operations on stacks.

$newstack : \mathcal{C} \to STK$	creates a new stack with a single element
$push : STK \times \mathcal{C} \to STK$	pushes a new element on top of the stack
$pop : STK \to STK$	removes the top most element of the stack
$top : STK \to \mathcal{C}$	returns the top most element of the stack

We can now describe the interprocedural semantic transformer for each program node: $[\![\ ]\!]^* : \mathcal{N} \to (STK \to STK)$. For $stk \in STK$,

$$[\![n]\!]^*(stk) = \begin{cases} push(pop(stk), [\![n]\!](top(stk))) & \text{if } n \in \mathcal{N} - (\mathcal{N}_C \cup \mathcal{N}_R) \\ push(stk, [\![n]\!](top(stk))) & \text{if } n \in \mathcal{N}_C \\ push(pop(pop(stk)), \mathcal{R}_n(top(pop(stk)), [\![n]\!](top(stk)))) & \text{if } n \in \mathcal{N}_r \end{cases}$$

where $\mathcal{R}_n : \mathcal{C} \times \mathcal{C} \to \mathcal{C}$ is a merging function like we have in EWPDSs. It is applied on dataflow value computed by the called procedure ($[\![n]\!](top(stk))$) and the value computed by the caller at the time of the call ($top(pop(stk))$). This definition assumes that a dataflow fact in $\mathcal{C}$ contains all information that is required by a procedure so that each transformer has to look at only the top of the stack passed to it – except for return nodes, where we look at the top two elements of the stack. Now, define a path transformer as follows. If $p = [n_1\ n_2 \cdots n_k]$ is a valid interprocedural path in the program then $[\![p]\!]^* = [\![[n_2 \cdots n_k]]\!]^* \circ [\![n_1]\!]^*$. This leads to the following definition.

Definition 9. *[12] If $s \in \mathcal{N}$ is the starting node of a program, then for $c_0 \in \mathcal{C}$ and $n \in \mathcal{N}$, the interprocedural-meet-over-all-paths value is defined as follows:*

$$\text{IMOVP}_{c_0}(n) = \sqcap\{[\![p]\!]^*(newstack(c_0)) \mid p \in \mathbf{IP}(s, n)\}$$

where $\mathbf{IP}(s, n)$ represents the set of all valid interprocedural paths from s to n and meet of stacks is just the meet of their topmost values: $stk_1 \sqcap stk_2 = top(stk_1) \sqcap top(stk_2)$.

We now construct an EWPDS $\mathcal{W}_e = (\mathcal{P}, \mathcal{S}, f, g)$ to compute this value when $\mathcal{C}$ has no infinite descending chains, all semantic transformers $[\![n]\!]$ are distributive, and all merging relations $\mathcal{R}_n$ are distributive in each of their arguments. Define a semiring $\mathcal{S} = (D, \oplus, \otimes, 0, 1)$ as $D = [\mathcal{C} \to \mathcal{C}] \cup \{0\}$, which consists of the set of all distributive functions on $\mathcal{C}$ and a special function 0. For $a, b \in D$,

$$a \oplus b = \begin{cases} a & \text{if } b = 0 \\ b & \text{if } a = 0 \\ (a \sqcap b) & \text{otherwise} \end{cases} \qquad a \otimes b = \begin{cases} 0 & \text{if } a = 0 \text{ or } b = 0 \\ (b \circ a) & \text{otherwise} \end{cases} \qquad 1 = \lambda c.c$$

The pushdown system $\mathcal{P}$ is $(\{q\}, \mathcal{N}, \Delta)$ where Δ is constructed by including a rule for each edge in $\mathcal{E}$. First, let $\mathcal{E}_{intra} \subseteq \mathcal{E}$ be the intraprocedural edges and $\mathcal{E}_{inter} \subseteq \mathcal{E}$ be the interprocedural (call and return) edges. Then include the following rules in Δ.

1. For $(n, m) \in \mathcal{E}_{intra}$, include the rule $r = \langle q, n \rangle \hookrightarrow \langle q, m \rangle$ with $f(r) = [\![n]\!]$.
2. For $n \in \mathcal{N}_C$, $(n, m) \in \mathcal{E}_{inter}$ with $n_R \in \mathcal{N}_R$ being the return site for the call at n, include the rule $r = \langle q, n \rangle \hookrightarrow \langle q, m\ n_R \rangle$ with $f(r) = [\![n]\!]$ and
$$g_r(a, b) = \lambda c.\mathcal{R}_n(a(c), (a \otimes [\![n]\!] \otimes b \otimes [\![n_R]\!])(c)).$$
3. For $n \in \mathcal{N}$, if it is an exit node of a procedure, include the rule $r = \langle q, n \rangle \hookrightarrow \langle q, \varepsilon \rangle$ with $f(r) = [\![n]\!]$.

A small technical detail here is that the merging functions defined above need not satisfy the path-extension property given in Defn. 6. In App. A, we give an alternative definition of how to assign a weight to a rule sequence such that the path-extension property is no longer a limitation. This leads us to the following theorem.

Theorem 3. *Let $\mathcal{A}$ be a $\mathcal{P}$-automaton that accepts just the configuration $\langle q, s \rangle$, where s is the starting point of the program and let $\mathcal{A}_{post^*}$ be the automaton obtained by using the saturation rule shown in Fig. 3 on $\mathcal{A}$. Then if $c_0 \in \mathcal{C}$, $n \in \mathcal{N}$, $\delta(c)$ is read off $\mathcal{A}_{post^*}$ in accordance with Thm. 2, we have,*

$$\text{IMOVP}_{c_0}(n) = [\oplus\{\delta(\langle q, n\ u \rangle \mid u \in \Gamma^*\}](c_0).$$

If $L \subseteq \Gamma^*$ is a regular language of stack configurations then $\text{IMOVP}_{c_0}(n, L)$*, which is the* IMOVP *value restricted to only those paths that end in configurations described by L, can be calculated as follows:*

$$\text{IMOVP}_{c_0}(n, L) = [\oplus\{\delta(\langle q, n\ u \rangle \mid u \in L\}](c_0).$$

In case the semantic transformers $[\![.]\!]$ and $\mathcal{R}_n$ are not distributive but only monotonic, then the two combines in Thm. 3 safely approximate $\mathrm{IMOVP}_{c_0}(n)$ and $\mathrm{IMOVP}_{c_0}(n, L)$, respectively. We do not present the proof in this paper, but the essential idea carries over from solving monotonic dataflow problems in WPDSs [18].

5 Experimental Results

In [2], Balakrishnan and Reps present an algorithm to analyze memory accesses in x86 code. Its goal is to determine an over-approximation of the set of values/memory-addresses that each register and memory location holds at each program point. The core dataflow-analysis algorithm used, called value-set analysis (VSA), is not relational, i.e., it does not keep track of the relationships that hold among registers and memory locations. However, when interpreting conditional branches, specifically those that implement loops, it is important to know such relationships. Hence, a separate affine-relation analysis (ARA) is performed to recover affine relations that hold among the registers at conditional branch points; those affine relations are then used to interpret conditional branches during VSA. ARA recovers affine relations involving registers only, because recovering affine relations involving memory locations would require points-to information, which is not available until the end of VSA. ARA is implemented using the affine-relation domain from [16] as a weight domain. It is based on machine arithmetic, i.e., arithmetic module 2^{32}, and is able to take care of overflow.

Before each call instruction, a subset of the registers is saved on the stack, either by the caller or the callee, and restored at the return. Such registers are called the *caller-save* and *callee-save* registers. Because ARA only keeps track of information involving registers, when ARA is implemented using a WPDS, all affine relations involving caller-save and callee-save registers are lost at a call. We used an EWPDS to preserve them across calls by treating caller-save and callee-save registers as local variables at a call; i.e., the values of caller-save and callee-save registers after the call are set to the

Table 1. Comparison of ARA results implemented using EWPDS versus WPDS

					Memory (MB)		Time (s)		Branches with useful information		
Prog	Insts	Procs	Branches	Calls	WPDS	EWPDS	WPDS	EWPDS	WPDS	EWPDS	Improvement
mplayer2	58452	608	4608	2481	27	6	8	9	137	192	57 (42%)
print	96096	955	8028	4013	61	19	20	23	601	889	313 (52%)
attrib	96375	956	8076	4000	40	8	12	13	306	380	93 (30%)
tracert	101149	1008	8501	4271	70	22	24	27	659	1021	387 (59%)
finger	101814	1032	8505	4324	70	23	24	30	627	999	397 (63%)
lpr	131721	1347	10641	5636	102	36	36	46	1076	1692	655 (61%)
rsh	132355	1369	10658	5743	104	36	37	45	1073	1661	616 (57%)
javac	135978	1397	10899	5854	118	43	44	58	1376	2001	666 (48%)
ftp	150264	1588	12099	6833	121	42	43	61	1364	2008	675 (49%)
winhlp32	179488	1911	15296	7845	156	58	62	98	2105	2990	918 (44%)
regsvr32	297648	3416	23035	13265	279	117	145	193	3418	5226	1879 (55%)
notepad	421044	4922	32608	20018	328	124	147	390	3882	5793	1988 (51%)
cmd	482919	5595	37989	24008	369	144	175	444	4656	6856	2337 (50%)

values before the call and the values of other registers are set to the values at the exit node of the callee.

The results are shown in Tab. 1. The column labeled 'Branches with useful information' refers to the number of branch points at which ARA recovered at least one affine relation. The last column shows the number of branch points at which ARA implemented via an EWPDS recovered more affine relations when compared to ARA implemented via a WPDS. Tab. 1 shows that the information recovered by EWPDS is better in 30% to 63% of the branch points that had useful information. The EWPDS version is somewhat slower, but uses less space; this is probably due to the fact that the dataflow transformer from [16] for 'spoiling' the affine relations that involve a given register uses twice the space of a transformer that preserves such relations.

6 Related Work

Some libraries/tools based on model-checking pushdown systems for dataflow analysis are MOPED [7, 21], WPDS [18], and WPDS++ [11]. Weighted pushdown systems have been used for finding uninitialized variables, live variables, linear constant propagation, and the detection of affine relationships. In each of these cases, local variables are handled by introducing special paths in the transition system of the PDS that models the program. These paths skip call sites to avoid passing local variables to the callee. This leads to imprecision by breaking existing relationships between local and global variables. Besides dataflow analysis, WPDSs have also been used for generalized authorization problems [22].

MOPED has been used for performing relational dataflow analysis, but only for finite abstract domains. Its basic approach is to embed the abstract transformer of each program statement into the rules of the pushdown system that models the program. This contrasts with WPDSs, where the abstract transformer is a separate weight associated with a pushdown rule. MOPED associates global variables with states of the PDS and local variables with its stack symbols. Then the stack of the PDS simulates the run-time stack of the program and maintains a different copy of the local variables for each procedure invocation. A simple pushdown reachability query can be used to compute the required dataflow facts. The disadvantage of that approach is that it cannot handle infinite-size abstract domains because then associating an abstract transformer with a pushdown rule would create an infinite number of pushdown rules. An EWPDS is capable of performing an analysis on infinite-size abstract domains as well. The domain used for copy-constant propagation in §2.3 is one such example.

Besides dataflow analysis, model-checking of pushdown systems has also been used for verifying security properties in programs [6, 9, 5]. Like WPDSs, we can use EWPDS for this purpose, but with added precision that comes due to the presence of merging functions.

A result we have not presented in this paper is that EWPDSs can be used for single-level pointer analysis, which enables us to answer stack-qualified aliasing queries. Stack-qualified aliasing has been studied before by Whaley and Lam [24]. However, for recursive programs, they collapse the strongly connected components in the call graph. We do not make any such approximation, and can also answer aliasing queries with respect to a language of stack configurations instead of just a single stack configuration.

The idea behind the transition from a WPDS to an EWPDS is that we attach extra meaning to each run of the pushdown system. We look at a run as a *tree* of matching calls and returns that push and pop values on the run-time stack of the program. This treatment of a program run has also been explored by Müller-Olm and Seidl [15] in an interprocedural dataflow-analysis algorithm to identify the set of all affine relationships. They explicitly match calls and returns to avoid passing relations involving local variables to different procedures. This allowed us to to directly translate their work into an EWPDS, which we have used for the experiments in §5.

References

1. A.V. Aho, R. Sethi, and J.D. Ullman. *Compilers: Principles, Techniques and Tools*. Addison-Wesley, 1985.
2. G. Balakrishnan and T. Reps. Analyzing memory accesses in x86 executables. In *Int. Conf. on Comp. Construct.*, 2004.
3. A. Bouajjani, J. Esparza, and O. Maler. Reachability analysis of pushdown automata: Application to model checking. In *CONCUR*, pages 135–150. Springer-Verlag, 1997.
4. A. Bouajjani, J. Esparza, and T. Touili. A generic approach to the static analysis of concurrent programs with procedures. In *Symp. on Princ. of Prog. Lang.*, pages 62–73, 2003.
5. H. Chen and D. Wagner. MOPS: An infrastructure for examining security properties of software. In *Conf. on Comp. and Commun. Sec.*, November 2002.
6. J. Esparza, A. Kučera, and S. Schwoon. Model-checking LTL with regular valuations for pushdown systems. In *TACAS*, pages 306–339, 2001.
7. J. Esparza and S. Schwoon. A BDD-based model checker for recursive programs. In *Proc. CAV'01*, LNCS 2102, pages 324–336. Springer-Verlag, 2001.
8. A. Finkel, B. Willems, and P. Wolper. A direct symbolic approach to model checking pushdown systems. *Electronic Notes in Theoretical Computer Science*, 9, 1997.
9. T. Jensen, D. Le Métayer, and T. Thorn. Verification of control flow based security properties. In *IEEE Symposium on Security and Privacy*, pages 89–103, 1999.
10. J.B. Kam and J.D. Ullman. Monotone data flow analysis frameworks. *Acta Inf.*, 7(3):305–318, 1977.
11. N. Kidd, T. Reps, D. Melski, and A. Lal. WPDS++: A C++ library for weighted pushdown systems, 2004.
12. J. Knoop and B. Steffen. The interprocedural coincidence theorem. In *Int. Conf. on Comp. Construct.*, pages 125–140, 1992.
13. W. Landi and B. Ryder. Pointer-induced aliasing: A problem classification. In *Symp. on Princ. of Prog. Lang.*, pages 93–103, 1991.
14. W. Landi and B. Ryder. A safe approximate algorithm for interprocedural pointer aliasing. In *Conf. on Prog. Lang. Design and Impl.*, pages 235–248, 1992.
15. M. Müller-Olm and H. Seidl. Precise interprocedural analysis through linear algebra. In *Symp. on Princ. of Prog. Lang.*, 2004.
16. M. Müller-Olm and H. Seidl. Analysis of modular arithmetic. In *European Symp. on Programming*, 2005.
17. T. Reps, S. Horwitz, and M. Sagiv. Precise interprocedural dataflow analysis via graph reachability. In *Symp. on Princ. of Prog. Lang.*, pages 49–61, 1995.

18. T. Reps, S. Schwoon, and S. Jha. Weighted pushdown systems and their application to interprocedural dataflow analysis. In *Static Analysis Symp.*, pages 189–213, 2003.
19. M. Sagiv, T. Reps, and S. Horwitz. Precise interprocedural dataflow analysis with applications to constant propagation. *Theor. Comp. Sci.*, 167:131–170, 1996.
20. S. Schwoon. *Model-Checking Pushdown Systems.* PhD thesis, Technical Univ. of Munich, Munich, Germany, July 2002.
21. S. Schwoon. Moped, 2002. http://www.fmi.uni-stuttgart.de/szs/tools/moped/.
22. S. Schwoon, S. Jha, T. Reps, and S. Stubblebine. On generalized authorization problems. In *Comp. Sec. Found. Workshop*, Wash., DC, 2003. IEEE Comp. Soc.
23. M. Sharir and A. Pnueli. Two approaches to interprocedural data flow analysis. In *Program Flow Analysis: Theory and Applications*. Prentice-Hall, Englewood Cliffs, NJ, 1981.
24. J. Whaley and M. Lam. Cloning-based context-sensitive pointer alias analysis using binary decision diagrams. In *Conf. on Prog. Lang. Design and Impl.*, pages 131–144, 2004.

A Relaxing Merging Function Requirements

This appendix discusses what happens when merging functions do not satisfy the third property in Defn. 6. The *pre** algorithm of §3.1 (used for creating $\mathcal{A}_{pre^*}$) would still compute the correct values for $\delta(c)$ because it parses rule sequences using the grammar from Defn. 8, but the *post** algorithm of §3.2 (used for creating $\mathcal{A}_{post^*}$) would not work because it utilizes a different grammar and relies on the path-extension property to compute the correct value. Instead of trying to modify the *post** algorithm, we will introduce an alternative definition of the value of a rule sequence that is suited for the cases when merging functions do not satisfy the path-extension property. The definition involves changing the productions and valuations of balanced sequences as follows:

$$\begin{array}{lll} \sigma_{b'} \rightarrow [\,] & v(\sigma_{b'}\ \sigma_{b'}) & = v(\sigma_{b'}) \otimes v(\sigma_{b'}) \\ \quad\mid\ \sigma_b\ R_2\ \sigma_b\ R_0 & v(\sigma_b\ R_2\ \sigma_b\ R_0) & = g_{R_2}(v(\sigma_b), v(\sigma_b) \otimes v(R_0)) \\ \sigma_b \rightarrow \sigma_{b'}\ \sigma_s & v(\sigma_{b'}\ \sigma_s) & = v(\sigma_{b'}) \otimes v(\sigma_s) \end{array} \quad (2)$$

The value of a rule sequence as defined above is the same as the value defined by Defn. 8 when merging functions satisfy the path-extension property. In the absence of the property, we need to make sure that merging functions are applied to the weight computed in the caller just before the call and the weight computed by the callee. We enforce this using Eqn. (2). The *STACK* values that are calculated for rule sequences in §3.2 also does the same in Eqn. (1)[Pg. 441]. This means that Lem. 1 still holds and the *post** algorithm correctly solves this more general version of GPS. However, the *pre** algorithm is closely based on Defn. 8 and does not solve the generalized version of GPP based on the above alternative definition.

Incremental Algorithms for Inter-procedural Analysis of Safety Properties

Christopher L. Conway[1], Kedar S. Namjoshi[2], Dennis Dams[2], and Stephen A. Edwards[1]

[1] Department of Computer Science, Columbia University
{conway, sedwards}@cs.columbia.edu
[2] Bell Labs, Lucent Technologies
{kedar, dennis}@research.bell-labs.com

Abstract. Automaton-based static program analysis has proved to be an effective tool for bug finding. Current tools generally re-analyze a program from scratch in response to a change in the code, which can result in much duplicated effort. We present an inter-procedural algorithm that analyzes *incrementally* in response to program changes and present experiments for a null-pointer dereference analysis. It shows a substantial speed-up over re-analysis from scratch, with a manageable amount of disk space used to store information between analysis runs.

1 Introduction

Tools based on model checking with automaton specifications have been very effective at finding important bugs such as buffer overflows, memory safety violations, and violations of locking and security policies. Static analysis tools such as MC/Coverity [1] and Uno [2], and model checking tools such as SLAM [3] are based on inter-procedural algorithms for propagating dataflow information [4, 5, 6, 7]. These algorithms perform a reachability analysis that always starts from scratch. For small program changes—which often have only a localized effect on the analysis—this can be inefficient.

Our main contribution is to present the first, to our knowledge, incremental algorithms for safety analysis of recursive state machines. We demonstrate how these algorithms can be used to obtain simple—yet general and precise—incremental automaton-based program analyses. We give two such algorithms: one that operates in the forward direction from the initial states and another that operates "inside-out" from the locations of the program changes. These have different tradeoffs, as is true of forward and backward algorithms for model checking safety properties. The key to both algorithms is a data structure called a *derivation graph*, which records the analysis process. In response to a program change, the algorithms re-check derivations recorded in this graph, pruning those that have been invalidated due to the change and adding new ones. This repair process results in a new derivation graph, which is stored on disk and used for the following increment.

K. Etessami and S.K. Rajamani (Eds.): CAV 2005, LNCS 3576, pp. 449–461, 2005.

A prototype implementation of these algorithms has been made for the Orion static analyzer for `C` and `C++` programs [8]. Our measurements show significant speedup for both algorithms when compared with a non-incremental version. This comes at the expense of a manageable increase in disk usage for storing information between analysis runs. We expect our algorithms to be applicable to many current program analysis tools.

The algorithms we present are incremental forms of a standard model checking algorithm. As such, their verification result is identical to that of the original algorithm. The implementation is part of a static analysis tool that checks an abstraction of `C` or `C++` code. Thus, there is some imprecision in its results: the analysis may report false errors and miss real ones. However, the incremental algorithms produce reports with the same precision as the non-incremental algorithm.

Incremental model checking may have benefits beyond speeding up analysis. One direction is to trade the speed gain from incremental analysis for higher precision in order to reduce the number of false errors reported. Another direction is to integrate a fine-grained incremental model checker into a program development environment, so that program errors are caught immediately, as has been suggested for testing [9]. A third direction is to use an incremental model checker to enable correct-by-construction development, as suggested by Dijkstra [10]. In this scenario, instead of applying model checking after a program is written, an incremental model checker can maintain and update a proof of correctness during program development. Our work is only a first step towards realizing the full potential of these possibilities.

Experimental data and full proofs of theorems are available in an expanded version of this paper [11].

1.1 An Example

The input to the basic algorithm is a program, described by a collection of control-flow graphs (CFGs), and a checking automaton. The nodes of a CFG represent control locations, while edges are labeled either with simple assignment statements, (side-effect free) assertions, or function calls. In the model checking view, the (possibly non-deterministic) checking automaton "runs" over matched call-return paths in this collection of CFGs, flagging a potential program error whenever the current run enters an error state.

The basic model checking algorithm works by building, on-the-fly, a "synchronous product" graph of the collective CFGs with the automaton. At a function call edge, this product is constructed by consulting a summary cache of entry-exit automaton state pairs for the function. Using this cache has two consequences: it prevents infinite looping when following recursive calls and it exploits the hierarchical function call structure, so that function code is not unnecessarily re-examined.

The key to the incremental version of the algorithm is to observe that the process of forming the synchronous product can be recorded as a derivation

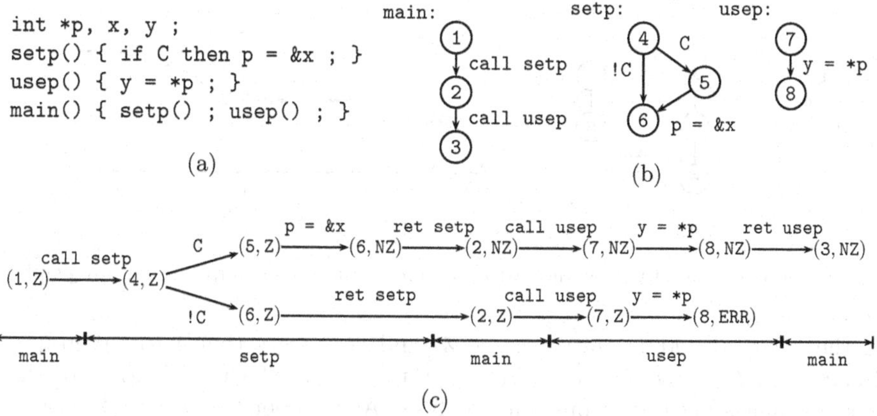

Fig. 1. (a) An example program, (b) its function CFGs, and (c) the derivation graph

graph. After a small change to the CFGs, it is likely that most of the process of forming the synchronous product is a repetition of the earlier effort. By storing the previous graph, this repetitive calculation can be avoided by checking those portions that may have been affected by the change, updating derivations only when necessary.

To illustrate these ideas, consider the program in Fig. 1(a). The correctness property we are interested in is whether the global pointer `p` is initialized to a non-null value before being dereferenced. A simple automaton (not shown) to check for violations of this property has three states: `Z`, indicating `p` may be null; `NZ`, indicating `p` is not null; and the error state `ERR` indicating `p` is dereferenced when it may be null.

Figures 1(b) and 1(c) show, respectively, the CFGs for this program and the resulting derivation graph (in this case a tree). Each derivation graph node is the combination of a CFG node and an automaton state. If condition `C` holds on entry to **`setp`** (the upper branch from the state (4, `Z`) in **`setp`**), the function returns to **`main`** with the automaton state `NZ`, and execution proceeds normally to termination. If `C` does not hold (the lower branch), **`setp`** returns to **`main`** with the automaton state `Z`. On the statement "`y = *p`", the automaton moves to the state `ERR` and an error is reported in **`usep`**.

The incremental algorithm operates on the derivation graph data structure. Besides this graph, its input consists of additions, deletions, and modifications to CFG edges. The basic idea is simple: inspect each derivation step to determine whether it is affected by a change; if so, remove the derivation and re-check the graph from the affected point until a previously explored state is encountered.

For our example, consider the revision obtained by replacing the body of **`setp()`** by "`x++; p = &x;`". The new CFGs are shown in Fig. 2(a). Figure 2(b) shows the incremental effect on the derivation graph. The removal of the `if` statement has the effect of removing the conditional branch edges (dashed) from the graph, making the previous error state unreachable. The addition of `x++`

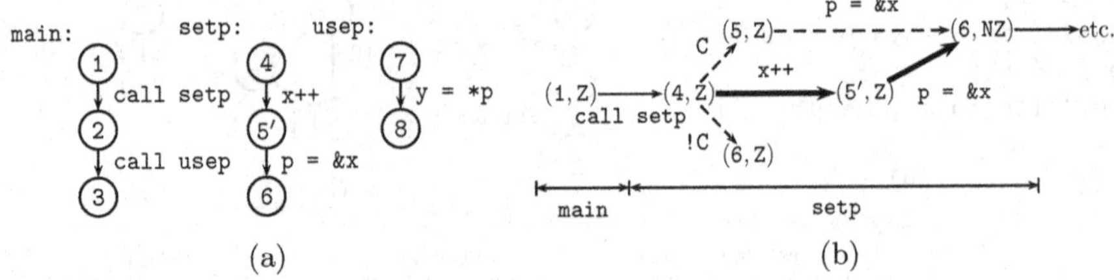

Fig. 2. (a) The revised CFGs and (b) a portion of the incremental derivation graph

has the effect of adding the state (`5′`, `Z`) and two edges (bold) to the graph. After processing these edges, we get to state (`6`, `NZ`), which is identical to the corresponding state in the previous analysis. At this point, we should be able to terminate the analysis. This is a simplified picture: our algorithms actually operate somewhat differently. In particular, the backward algorithm will also inspect the derivation graph in `main`, but not that for `usep`.

2 The Full Analysis Algorithm

A program is given as a set $\mathcal{F}$ of functions, with a distinguished initial function, *main*. Each function is represented by a CFG, which is a tuple (N, Σ, E). Here, N is a finite set of *control locations* containing the distinguished locations $\downarrow$ (entry) and $\uparrow$ (exit); Σ is a set of *(simple) program statements* (assignments and assertions); and E is the set of *edges*. Let Σ' be Σ together with call statements $\{call(f) \mid f \in \mathcal{F}\}$. E is a subset of $(N \backslash \{\uparrow\}) \times \Sigma' \times N$. We require that there are no calls to functions outside $\mathcal{F}$. For simplicity of exposition, we do not represent function call arguments and return values, or variables and their scoping rules. The implementation takes each of these features into consideration.

Next we define the executions of a program. A *position* is a pair (f, n), where f is a function and n is a node in (the CFG for) f. A *(global) program state* is a sequence $(f_1, n_1) \cdots (f_k, n_k)$ of positions, representing a point during execution where control resides at position (f_k, n_k) and $(f_1, n_1) \cdots (f_{k-1}, n_{k-1})$ is the stack of return locations that is in effect at this point. We define a labeled transition system on program states, as follows.

1. $(f_1, n_1) \cdots (f_k, n_k) \xrightarrow{a} (f_1, n_1) \cdots (f_k, n'_k)$ iff (n_k, a, n'_k) is an edge in f_k and a is not a call
2. $(f_1, n_1) \cdots (f_k, n_k) \rightarrow (f_1, n_1) \cdots (f_k, n'_k)(f', \downarrow)$ iff $(n_k, call(f'), n'_k)$ is an edge in f_k
3. $(f_1, n_1) \cdots (f_{k-1}, n_{k-1})(f_k, \uparrow) \rightarrow (f_1, n_1) \cdots (f_{k-1}, n_{k-1})$

An *execution* is a finite path in this transition system that begins with the program state $(main, \downarrow)$, consisting of just the initial position. Such an execution generates a *trace* consisting of the sequence of labels (which are program statements) along it. Note that this is the definition of a recursive state machine [6, 7], restricted to the case of finite executions.

```
ADD-TO-WORKSET(c)
if c is not marked then
    workset ← workset ∪ {c}
    mark c
```

```
FOLLOW-EDGE(c, e)
// c=(f,n,r,q), e=(n,a,n')
if a = call(f') then
    // use summaries; do book-keeping
    ADD-TO-WORKSET((f', ↓, q, q))
    Add c to call-sites(f')
    for q' : ⟨q, q'⟩ ∈ summary(f') do
        ADD-TO-WORKSET((f, n', r, q'))
else
    // follow automaton transition
    for q' : (q, a, q') ∈ Δ do
        ADD-TO-WORKSET((f, n', r, q'))
```

```
STEP(c = (f, n, r, q))
if q ∈ F then
    REPORT-ERROR(c)
if n =↑ then
    // add a summary pair
    Add ⟨r, q⟩ to summary(f)
    workset ← workset ∪ call-sites(f)
else
    // follow a CFG edge
    for e ∈ edges(n) do
        FOLLOW-EDGE(c, e)
```

```
ANALYZE
workset ← {(main, ↓, q, q) | q ∈ Q̂}
while workset ≠ ∅ do
    Remove some c ∈ workset
    STEP(c)
```

Fig. 3. Pseudo-code for the Full Algorithm

Analysis properties are represented by (non-deterministic, error detecting) automata with Σ as input alphabet. An analysis automaton is given by a tuple $(Q, \hat{Q}, \Delta, F)$, where Q is a set of *(automaton) states*, $\hat{Q} \subseteq Q$ is a set of *initial states*, $\Delta \subseteq Q \times \Sigma \times Q$, is a *transition relation*, and $F \subseteq Q$ is a set of *rejecting states*. A *run* of the automaton on a trace is defined in the standard way. A *rejecting run* is a run that includes a rejecting state. Note that in this simplified presentation, the set Σ of program statements does not include function calls and returns, and hence the automata cannot refer to them. In the implementation, transitions that represent function calls and returns (rules 2 and 3 above) carry special labels, and the error detecting automaton can react to them by changing its state, e.g. to perform checks of the arguments passed to a function, or the value returned by it.

We emphasize that an automaton operates on the *syntax* of the program; the relationship with the semantics is up to the automaton writer. For instance, one might define an under-approximate automaton, so that any error reported by the automaton check is a real program error, but it might not catch all real errors. It is more common to define an over-approximate automaton, so that errors reported are not necessarily real ones, but the checked property holds if the automaton does not find any errors.

The pseudo-code for the from-scratch analysis algorithm (Full) is shown in Fig. 3. It keeps *global configurations* in a work-set; each configuration is a tuple (f, n, r, q), where (f, n) is a position and r, q are automaton states. The presence of such a configuration in the work-set indicates that it is possible for a run of the automaton to reach position (f, n) in automaton state q as a result of entering f with automaton state r (the "root" state). In addition, the algorithm keeps a set of summaries for each function, which are entry-exit automaton state pairs, and a set of known call-sites, which are configurations from which the function is called. ANALYZE repeatedly chooses a configuration from the work-set and calls STEP to generate its successors. In STEP, if the automaton is in an error state, a potential error is reported. (In an implementation, the REPORT-ERROR procedure may also do additional work to check if the error is semantically possible.)

Much of the work is done in the FOLLOW-EDGE procedure. For a non-call statement, the procedure follows the automaton transition relation (Line 10). For a function call, the procedure looks up the summary table to determine successor states (Line 6). If there is no available summary, registering the current configuration in *call-sites*(f') and creating a new entry configuration for f' ensures that a summary entry will be created later, at which point this configuration is re-examined (Line 6 in STEP). We assume that visited configurations are kept in a suitable data structure (e.g., a hash-table).

Theorem 1. *The Full algorithm reports an error at a configuration* (f, n, r, q)*, for some* r, q*, if and only if there is a program execution ending at a position* (f, n)*, labeled with trace* t*, such that the automaton has a rejecting run on* t*.*

3 A First Incremental Algorithm: IncrFwd

Input: A textual program change can be reflected in the CFGs as the addition, deletion, or modification of control-flow edges. It can also result in the redefinition of the number and types of variables. Our incremental algorithms expect as input CFG changes, and repair the derivation graph accordingly. Changes to types and variables correspond to automaton modifications. The algorithm can be easily modified for the situation where the property—and not the program—changes, since we are maintaining their joint (i.e., product) derivation graph.
Data Structure: The incremental algorithm records a derivation relation on configurations. This is done in the procedure FOLLOW-EDGE: whenever a new configuration of the form (f, n', r, q') is added after processing a configuration (f, n, r, q) and an edge a, a derivation edge $(f, n, r, q) \vdash_a (f, n', r, q')$ is recorded. This results in a labeled and directed derivation graph. Notice that the derivation graph can be viewed also as a tableau proof that justifies either the presence or absence of reachable error states.

Given as input a set of changes to the CFGs and a derivation graph, the incremental algorithm first processes all the modifications, then the deletions, and finally the additions. This order avoids excess work where new configurations are added only to be retracted later due to CFG deletions.
Modifications: For an edge $e = (n, a, n')$ modified to $e' = (n, b, n')$ in function f, if each derivation of the form $(f, n, r, q) \vdash_a (f, n', r, q')$ holds also for the new statement b—which is checked by code similar to that in FOLLOW-EDGE— there is no need to adjust the derivation graph. Otherwise, the modification is handled as the deletion of edge e and the addition of e'.
Additions: For a new edge $e = (n, a, n')$ in the CFG of f, FOLLOW-EDGE is applied to all configurations of the form $c = (f, n, r, q)$, for some r, q, that are

```
ADD-TO-WORKSET(c)
  if c is not marked then
    workset ← workset ∪ {c}
    mark c

CHECK-EDGE(e = c ⊢_a c')
  // c = (f,n,r,q), c' = (f,n',r,q')
  if (n, a, n') is a deleted edge then
    skip
  elseif a = call(f') then
    // use stored summaries
    ADD-TO-WORKSET((f', ↓, q, q))
    Add c to call-sites(f')
    if ⟨q, q'⟩ is marked in f' then
      ADD-TO-WORKSET(c'); mark e
  else
    ADD-TO-WORKSET(c'); mark e

CHECK-STEP(c = (f, n, r, q))
  if n = ↑ then
    Mark the summary ⟨r, q⟩ in f
    workset ← workset ∪ call-sites(f)
  else
    for each deriv. edge e from c do
      CHECK-EDGE(e)

CHECK-DERIVATIONS(Fns)
  for f ∈ Fns do
    Unmark f's configs, edges,
      summaries, and call sites that
      originate in Fns
  workset ← EXT-INITS(Fns)
  while workset ≠ ∅ do
    Choose and remove c ∈ workset
    CHECK-STEP(c)
  Remove unmarked elements
```

Fig. 4. The IncrFwd algorithm for Deletions

present in the current graph. Consequently, any newly generated configurations are processed as in the full algorithm.

Deletions: Deletion is the non-trivial case. Informally, the idea is to check all of the recorded derivation steps, disconnecting those that are based on deleted edges. The forward-traversing deletion algorithm (IncrFwd) is shown in Fig. 4. The entry point is the procedure CHECK-DERIVATIONS, which is called with the full set of functions, $\mathcal{F}$. The auxiliary function EXT-INITS(F) returns the set of entry configurations for functions in F that arise from a call outside F. The initial configurations for *main* are considered to have external call sites. This gives a checking version of the full analysis algorithm. Checking an existing derivation graph can be expected to be faster than regenerating it from scratch with the full algorithm. The savings can be quite significant if the automaton transitions Δ are computed on-the-fly—notice that the algorithm does not re-compute Δ. The similarity between the Full and IncrFwd algorithms can be formalized in the following theorem.

Theorem 2. *The derivation graph resulting from the IncrFwd algorithm is the same as the graph generated by the Full analysis algorithm on the modified CFGs.*

4 A Second Incremental Algorithm: IncrBack

The IncrFwd algorithm checks derivations in a forward traversal. This might result in unnecessary work: if only function g is modified, functions that are not on any call path that includes g are not affected, and do not need to be

```
RETRACE(c = (f, n, r, q))
if c is not marked then
    return false
elseif f = main then
    return true
else
    return (∃c' = (f', n', r', r):
        c' ∈ call-sites(f) ∧ RETRACE(c'))
```

```
INCR-BACK()
// bottom-up repair
for each SCC C (in reverse
        topological order) do
    if AFFECTED(C) then
        CHECK-DERIVATIONS(C)
// remove unreachable errors
for each error configuration c do
    if (not RETRACE(c)) then
        unmark c
```

Fig. 5. The IncrBack algorithm for Deletions

checked. Moreover, if the change to g does not affect its summary information, even its callers do not need to be checked. Such situations can be detected with an "inside-out" algorithm, based on the maximal strongly connected component (SCC) decomposition of the function call graph. (A non-trivial, maximal SCC in the call graph represents a set of mutually recursive functions.)

The effect of a CFG edge deletion from a function f propagates both upward and downward in the call graph. Since some summary pairs for f may no longer be valid, derivations in f's callers might be invalidated. In the other direction, for a function called by f, some of its entry configurations might now be unreachable.

The SCC-based algorithm (IncrBack) is shown in Fig. 5. It works bottom-up on the SCC decomposition, checking first the lowest (in topological order) SCC that is affected. The function AFFECTED(C) checks whether a function in C is modified, or whether summaries for any external function called from C have been invalidated. For each SCC C, one can inductively assume that summaries for functions below C are valid. Hence, it is only necessary to examine functions in C. This is done by the same CHECK-DERIVATIONS procedure as in Fig. 4, only now applied to a single SCC instead of the full program. Note that CHECK-DERIVATIONS initially invalidates summaries in C that cannot be justified by calls outside C.

This process can result in over-approximate reachability information. Consider a scenario where f calls g. Now suppose that f is modified. The algorithm repairs derivations in f, but does not touch g. However, derivations in f representing calls to g might have been deleted, making corresponding entry configurations for g unreachable. To avoid reporting spurious errors resulting from this over-approximation, the (nondeterministic) RETRACE procedure re-determines reachability for all error configurations.

Theorem 3. *The derivation graph after the IncrBack algorithm is an over-approximation of the graph generated by the full analysis algorithm on the modified CFGs, but has the same set of error configurations.*

5 Complexity and Optimality

The non-incremental algorithm takes time and space linear in the product of the size of the automaton and the size of the collective control-flow graphs. Algorithms with better bounds have been developed [6, 7], but these are based on knowing in advance the number of exit configurations of a function; this is impossible for an on-the-fly state exploration algorithm.

From their similarity to the non-incremental algorithm, it follows that the incremental algorithms cannot do more work than the non-incremental one, so they have the same worst-case bound. However, worst-case bounds are not particularly appropriate, since incremental algorithms try to optimize for the common case. Ramalingam and Reps [12, 13] propose to analyze performance in terms of a quantity $||\delta||$, which represents the difference in reachability after a change. They show that any "local" incremental algorithm like ours has worst-case inputs where the work cannot be bounded by a function of $||\delta||$ alone. At present, the precise complexity of incremental reachability remains an open question [14].

6 Implementation and Experiments

We have implemented the Full, IncrFwd, and IncrBack algorithms in the Orion static analyzer. In the implementation, we take a function as the unit of change. This is done for a number of reasons. It is quite difficult, without additional machinery (such as an incremental parser), to identify changes of finer granularity. It also fits well into the normal program development process. Furthermore, functions scale well as a unit of modification—as the size of a program increases, the relative size of individual functions decreases. In the case of large programs, attempting to identify changes at the CFG or parse tree level may not lead to significant gains.

We present data on five open source applications: sendmail, the model checker spin, spin:tl (spin's temporal logic utility), guievict (an X-Windows process migration tool) and rocks (a reliable sockets utility). We perform an interprocedural program analysis from a single entry function, checking whether global pointers are set before being dereferenced. For sendmail and spin, this analysis is run for a small subset of the program's global pointers in order to reduce the time necessary for the experiments. We simulate the incremental development of code as follows. For each function f in the program, we run the incremental analysis on the program with f removed (i.e., replaced with an empty stub). Then we insert f and run the incremental analysis. The time taken for this incremental analysis is compared with a full analysis of the program with f. We thus have one analysis run for each function in the program; each run represents an incremental analysis for the modification of a single function (in this case, replacing an empty stub with the actual body of the function).

This experiment exercises both the addition and deletion algorithms: the modification of a function is equivalent to deleting and reinserting a call edge at each of its call sites; if the function summary changes, derivations based on the

Table 1. Experimental results

	Lines of code	Reachable functions	No. ptrs analyzed	Full analysis time (s)	Average speedup IncrFwd	Average speedup IncrBack	Incr. data (KB)
sendmail	47,651	336	3	33.75	1.6	**8.6**	73.72
spin	16,540	348	6	24.91	1.3	**10.1**	91.61
spin:tl	2,569	93	2	1.09	1.3	**8.0**	7.01
guievict	4,545	115	1	0.60	1.4	**5.9**	3.54
rocks	4,619	134	1	0.66	1.3	**4.3**	4.36

old summary are deleted and new derivations are generated based on the newly available, now-accurate summary.

The experimental results are shown in Table 1. The overall average speedup for IncrBack is 8.2; the average for IncrFwd is 1.4. IncrFwd improves on Full essentially by "caching" state data between analysis runs. This caching behavior is able to provide modest performance increases, but the average-case performance of the algorithm is unbounded in $||\delta||$. IncrBack is able to improve on the performance of IncrFwd by skipping large portions of the derivation graph, when possible, and using the call graph structure of the program to minimize its workload. This intuition is confirmed by the experimental results.

To better illustrate the performance characteristics of IncrBack, Fig. 6 plots the speedups for each analysis run in terms of percentiles. For each percentage x, we plot the minimum speedup for the best-performing $x\%$ of analysis runs. For example, 50% of analysis runs overall showed a speedup of at least 7.5 (i.e., 7.5 is the median speedup). The legend shows the number of analysis runs (i.e., the number of (statically) reachable functions) for each benchmark. The data on the horizontal axis is plotted in uniform intervals of length $100/N$ for each benchmark. The plateaus evident in the plots for spin, spin:tl, and rocks represent clustering of data values (possibly due to rounding) rather than a sparsity of data points.

There was quite a bit of variation between benchmarks: over 50% of runs on spin showed a speedup of at least 12.4, while the maximum speedup for rocks was only 5.5. It is likely that larger programs will exhibit higher speedups in general. We observed no strong correlation between the the speedup for a function and its size, its depth in the call graph, or its number of callers and callees (see [11]).

The tests we describe here are conservative in the sense that we only analyze functions that are reachable from a single distinguished entry function. Preliminary tests on all of the entry functions in guievict show an average speedup of 11.3 (instead of 5.9)—since many functions are unconnected in the call graph to the modified function, the full algorithm does much unnecessary work.

These tests concentrate on changes that are quite small with respect to the total size of the program. We hypothesize that changes on the order of a single function are a reasonable model of how the analysis would be applied in a development scenario. However, we have also run tests in which 10-50% of the functions in the program are modified in each increment. In these tests, IncrBack

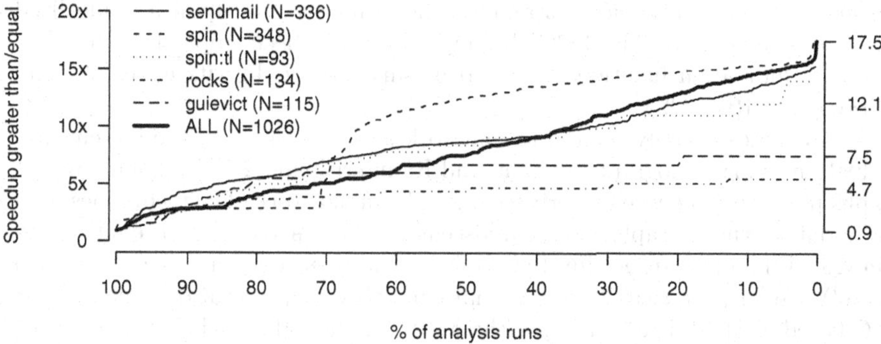

Fig. 6. Distribution of speedups for IncrBack, with quantiles for all at right

showed a more modest average speedup of 2.5, with larger speedups for smaller incremental changes.

Table 1 also shows the size of the incremental data stored after the re-run of the incremental analysis, on the complete program. This data may be written to disk, taking time proportional to the size. In an interactive setting, this time can be considered irrelevant: the user can begin inspecting errors while the tool performs I/O.

7 Related Work and Conclusions

The approach of automaton-based model checking of push-down systems [15, 6, 7] has contributed algorithms for program analysis that are conceptually simple and powerful. We have developed incremental versions of these algorithms and shown that this approach leads to incremental dataflow algorithms that are simple yet precise and general. The algorithms lend themselves to simple implementations showing excellent experimental results: a factor of 8.2 on average for IncrBack, at the cost of a manageable overhead in storage. To the best of our knowledge, the algorithms we propose are the first for inter-procedural, automaton-based static analysis.

There is a strong similarity between the behavior of our checking procedure and tracing methods for garbage collection [16] (cf. [17]). A key difference is the pushdown nature of the derivation graphs, which has no analogy in garbage collection.

Incremental data flow analysis has been studied extensively. Existing data flow algorithms are not directly applicable to model checking, because they either compute less precise answers than their from-scratch counterparts; are applicable only to restricted classes of graphs, such as reducible flow-graphs; or concern specific analyses, such as points-to analysis [18, 19, 20] (cf. the excellent survey by Ramalingam and Reps [21]). Sittampalam et al. [22] suggest an approach to incremental analysis tied to program transformation (cf. [23]). Since analyses are specified on the abstract syntax tree, the technique only applies to idealized Pascal-like languages. The SCC decomposition has been applied to the flow graphs of individual functions to speed up analysis by Horwitz et al. [24] and Marlowe and Ryder [25].

Perhaps most closely related to our work is the research on the incremental evaluation of logic programs by Saha and Ramakrishnan [26, 27]. Their support graphs play the same role as derivation graphs in our work. The techniques used for updating these graphs are reminiscent of Doyle's truth maintenance system [28]. While inter-procedural analysis is readily encoded as a logic program (cf. [6]), we suspect that it may be hard to recover optimizations such as the SCC-based method. Previous algorithms for incremental model checking [29, 30] do not handle either program hierarchy or recursion, working instead with a flat state space. Some tools (e.g., Uno [2], MOPS [31]) pre-compute per-file information; however, the interprocedural analysis is still conducted from scratch.

The Orion tool in which the algorithms are implemented is aimed at producing error reports with a low false-positives ratio. In this context, it seems especially attractive to devote the time gained by incrementalization towards a further improvement of this ratio, especially for inter-procedural analysis.

Acknowledgements. Thanks to Nils Klarlund for many helpful comments on a draft of the paper. We also thank D. Saha and C.R. Ramakrishnan for kindly sending us a draft of their paper [27], Sape Mullender for a useful discussion, and Rupak Majumdar for his comments. This work was supported in part by NSF grant CCR-0341658. Stephen Edwards and his group are supported by an NSF CAREER award, a grant from Intel corporation, an award from the SRC, and from New York State's NYSTAR program.

References

1. Hallem, S., Chelf, B., Xie, Y., Engler, D.: A system and language for building system-specific, static analyses. In: PLDI, Berlin, Germany (2002) 69–82
2. Holzmann, G.: Static source code checking for user-defined properties. In: Integrated Design and Process Technology (IDPT), Pasadena, CA (2002)
3. Ball, T., Rajamani, S.K.: The SLAM toolkit. In: CAV, Paris, France (2001) 260–264
4. Reps, T., Horwitz, S., Sagiv, S.: Precise interprocedural dataflow analysis via graph reachability. In: POPL, San Francisco, CA (1995) 49–61
5. Esparza, J., Schwoon, S.: A BDD-based model checker for recursive programs. In: CAV, Paris, France (2001) 324–336
6. Alur, R., Etessami, K., Yannakakis, M.: Analysis of recursive state machines. In: CAV, Paris, France (2001) 207–220
7. Benedikt, M., Godefroid, P., Reps, T.: Model checking of unrestricted hierarchical state machines. In: ICALP, Crete, Greece (2001) 652–666
8. Dams, D., Namjoshi, K.S.: Orion: High-precision static error analysis for C and C++ programs. Technical report, Bell Labs (2003)

9. Saff, D., Ernst, M.D.: An experimental evaluation of continuous testing during development. In: ISSTA, Boston, MA (2004) 76–85
10. Dijkstra, E.: Guarded commands, nondeterminacy, and formal derivation of programs. Communications of the ACM **18** (1975)
11. Conway, C.L., Namjoshi, K.S., Dams, D., Edwards, S.A.: Incremental algorithms for inter-procedural analysis of safety properties. Technical Report CUCS-018-05, Columbia University, New York, NY (2005)
12. Reps, T.: Optimal-time incremental semantic analysis for syntax-directed editors. In: POPL, Albuquerque, NM (1982) 169–176
13. Ramalingam, G., Reps, T.: On the computational complexity of dynamic graph problems. Theoretical Computer Science **158** (1996) 233–277
14. Hesse, W.: The dynamic complexity of transitive closure is in DynTC^0. Theoretical Computer Science **3** (2003) 473–485
15. Schmidt, D., Steffen, B.: Program analysis *as* model checking of abstract interpretations. In: SAS, Pisa, Italy (1998) 351–380
16. McCarthy, J.: Recursive functions of symbolic expressions and their computation by machine. Communications of the ACM **3** (1960) 184–195
17. Wilson, P.: Uniprocessor garbage collection techniques. In: International Workshop on Memory Management (IWMM), Saint-Malo, France (1992) 1–42
18. Yur, J.S., Ryder, B., Landi, W., Stocks, P.: Incremental analysis of side effects for C software systems. In: ICSE, Los Angeles, CA (1997) 422–432
19. Yur, J.S., Ryder, B., Landi, W.: An incremental flow- and context-sensitive pointer aliasing analysis. In: ICSE, Boston, MA (1999) 442–451
20. Vivien, F., Rinard, M.: Incrementalized pointer and escape analysis. In: PLDI, Snowbird, Utah (2001) 69–82
21. Ramalingam, G., Reps, T.: A categorized bibliography on incremental computation. In: POPL, Charleston, SC (1993) 502–510
22. Sittampalam, G., de Moor, O., Larsen, K.: Incremental execution of transformation specifications. In: POPL, Venice, Italy (2004) 26–38
23. Liu, Y.A., Stoller, S.D., Teitelbaum, T.: Static caching for incremental computation. ACM Trans. on Programming Languages and Systems **20** (1998) 546–585
24. Horwitz, S., Demers, A., Teitelbaum, T.: An efficient general iterative algorithm for dataflow analysis. Acta Informatica **24** (1987) 6790–694
25. Ryder, B., Marlowe, T.: An efficient hybrid algorithm for incremental data flow analysis. In: POPL, San Francisco, CA (1990) 184–196
26. Saha, D., Ramakrishnan, C.: Incremental evaluation of tabled logic programs. In: ICLP, Mumbai, India (2003) 392–406
27. Saha, D., Ramakrishnan, C.: Incremental and demand driven points to analysis using logic programming. Provided by authors (2004)
28. Doyle, J.: A truth maintenance system. Artificial Intelligence **12** (1979) 231–272
29. Sokolsky, O., Smolka, S.: Incremental model checking in the modal mu-calculus. In: CAV, Stanford, CA (1994) 351–363
30. Henzinger, T., Jhala, R., Majumdar, R., Sanvido, M.: Extreme model checking. In: Verification: Theory and Practice, Sicily, Italy (2003) 332–358
31. Chen, H., Wagner, D.: MOPS: an infrastructure for examining security properties of software. In: CCS, Washington, DC (2002) 235–244

A Policy Iteration Algorithm for Computing Fixed Points in Static Analysis of Programs

A. Costan[†], S. Gaubert[*], E. Goubault[+], M. Martel[+], and S. Putot[+]

[†] Polytehnica Bucarest
[*] INRIA Rocquencourt
[+] CEA Saclay

Abstract. We present a new method for solving the fixed point equations that appear in the static analysis of programs by abstract interpretation. We introduce and analyze a policy iteration algorithm for monotone self-maps of complete lattices. We apply this algorithm to the particular case of lattices arising in the interval abstraction of values of variables. We demonstrate the improvements in terms of speed and precision over existing techniques based on Kleene iteration, including traditional widening/narrowing acceleration mecanisms.

1 Introduction and Related Work

One of the important goals of static analysis by abstract interpretation (see Cousot & Cousot [9]) is the determination of invariants of programs. They are generally described by over approximation (abstraction) of the sets of values that program variables can take, at each control point of the program. And they are obtained by solving a system of (abstract) semantic equations, derived from the program to analyze and from the domain of interpretation, or abstraction, i.e. by solving a given fixed point equation in an order-theoretic structure.

Among the classical abstractions, there are the *non-relational* ones, such as the domain of *intervals* [9] (invariants are of the form $v_i \in [c1, c2]$), of *constant propagation* ($v_i = c$), of *congruences* [16] ($v_i \in a\mathbb{Z} + b$). Among the *relational* ones we can mention *polyedra* [28] ($\alpha_1 v_1 + \cdots + \alpha_n v_n \leq c$), *linear equalities* [23] ($\alpha_1 v_1 + \cdots + \alpha_n v_n = c$), *linear equalities modulo* [17] ($\alpha_1 v_1 + \cdots + \alpha_n v_n \equiv a$) or more recently the *octagon* domain [26] ($v_i - v_j \leq c$).

All these domains are (order-theoretic) lattices, for which we could think of designing specific fixed point equation solvers instead of using the classical, and yet not very efficient value iteration algorithms, based on Kleene's iteration. A classical way to improve these computations is to use widening/narrowing operators [10]. They improve the rapidity of finding an over-approximated invariant at the expense of accuracy sometimes; i.e. they reach a post-fixed point or a fixed point, but not always the least fixed point of the semantic equations (we review some elements of this method in Section 2, and give examples in the case of the interval lattice).

K. Etessami and S.K. Rajamani (Eds.): CAV 2005, LNCS 3576, pp. 462–475, 2005.

In this paper, we introduce a new algorithm, based on policy iteration and not value iteration, that correctly and efficiently solves this problem (Section 3). It shows good performances in general with respect to various typical programs, see Section 4.4. We should add that this work started from the difficulty to find good widening and narrowing operators for domains used for characterizing the precision of floating-point computations, used by some of the authors in [15].

Policy iteration was introduced by Howard [21] to solve stochastic control problems with finite state and action space. In this context, a *policy* is a feedback strategy (which assigns to every state an action). The classical policy iteration generalizes Newton's algorithm to the equation $x = f(x)$, where f is monotone, non-differentiable, and convex. The convergence proof is based on the discrete version of the maximum principle for harmonic functions. This method is experimentally efficient, although its complexity is still not well understood theoretically. We refer the reader to the book of Puterman [29] for background.

It is natural to ask whether policy iteration can be extended to the case of zero-sum games: at each iteration, one fixes the strategy of one player, and solves a non-linear (optimal control problem) instead of a linear problem. This idea goes back to Hoffman and Karp [20]. The central difficulty in the case of games is to obtain the convergence, because the classical (linear) maximum principle cannot be applied any more. For this reason, the algorithm of [20] requires positivity conditions on transition probabilities, which do not allow to handle the case of deterministic games. In applications to static analysis, however, even the simplest fixed point problems lead to deterministic game problems. A policy iteration algorithm for deterministic games with ergodic reward has been given by Cochet-Terrasson, Gaubert, and Gunawardena [6, 14]: the convergence proof relies on max-plus spectral theory, which provides nonlinear analogues of results of potential theory.

In the present paper (elaborating on [8]), we present a new policy iteration algorithm, which applies to monotone self-maps of a complete lattice, defined by the infimum of a certain family satisfying a selection principle. Thus, policy iteration is not limited to finding fixed point that are numerical vectors or functions, fixed points can be elements of an abstract lattice. This new generality allows us to handle lattices which are useful in static analysis. For the fixed point problem, the convergence analysis is somehow simpler than in the ergodic case of [6, 14]: we show that the convergence is guaranteed if we compute at each step the least fixed point corresponding to the current policy. The main idea of the proof is that the map which assigns to a monotone map its least fixed point is in some weak sense a morphism with respect to the inf-law, see Theorem 1. This shows that policy iteration can be used to compute the minimal fixed points, at least for a subclass of maps (Theorem 3 and Remark 3).

Other fixed point acceleration techniques have been proposed in the literature. There are mainly three types of fixed point acceleration techniques, as used in static analysis. The first one relies on specific information about the structure of the program under analysis. For instance, one can define refined iteration strategies for loop nests [2], or for interprocedural analysis [1]. These methods are completely orthogonal to the method we are introducing here, which does not use such structural properties. However, they might be combined with policy iteration, for efficient interprocedural analysis for instance. This is beyond the scope of this paper.

Another type of algorithm is based on the particular structure of the abstract domain. For instance, in model-checking, for reachability analysis, particular iteration strategies have been designed, so that to keep the size of the state space representation small (using BDDs, or in static analyzers by abstract interpretation, using binary decision graphs, see [25]), by a combination of breadth-first and depth-first strategies, as in [31]. For boolean equations, some authors have designed specific representations which allow for relatively fast least fixed point algorithms. For instance, [24] uses Bekic-Leszczyloiwski theorem. In strictness analysis, representation of boolean functions by "frontiers" has been widely used, see for instance [22] and [4]. Our method here is general, as hinted in Section 3. It can be applied to a variety of abstract domains, provided that we can find a "selection principle". This is exemplified here on the domain of intervals, but we are confident this can be equally applied to octagons and polyedra.

Last but not least, there are some general purpose algorithms, such as general widening/narrowing techniques, [10], with which we compare our policy iteration technique. There are also incremental or "differential" computations (in order not to compute again the functional on each partial computations) [12], [13]. In fact, this is much like the static partitioning technique some of the authors use in [30]. Related algorithms can be found in [11], [27] and [3].

2 Kleene's Iteration Sequence, Widenings and Narrowings

In order to compare the policy iteration algorithm with existing methods, we briefly recall in this section the classical method based on Kleene's fixed point iteration, with widening and narrowing refinements (see [10]).

Let $(\mathcal{L}, \leq)$ be a complete lattice. We write $\perp$ for its lowest element, $\top$ for its greatest element, $\cup$ and $\cap$ for the meet and join operations, respectively. We say that a self-map f of a complete lattice $(\mathcal{L}, \leq)$ is *monotone* if $x \leq y \Rightarrow f(x) \leq f(y)$. The least fixed point of a monotone f can be obtained by computing the sequence: $x^0 = \perp$, $x^{n+1} = f(x^n)$ $(n \geq 0)$, which is such that $x^0 \leq x^1 \leq \ldots$ If the sequence becomes stationary, i.e., if $x^m = x^{m+1}$ for some m, the limit x^m is the least fixed point of f. Of course, this procedure may be inefficient, and it needs not even terminate in the case of lattices of infinite height, such as the simple interval lattice (that we use for abstractions in Section 4). For this computation to become tractable, *widening* and *narrowing* operators have been introduced, we refer the reader to [10] for a good survey. As we will only show examples on the interval lattice, we will not recall the general theory. Widening operators are binary operators ∇ on $\mathcal{L}$ which ensure that any finite Kleene iteration $x^0 = \perp$, $x^1 = f(x^0)$, $\ldots$, $x^{k+1} = f(x^k)$, followed by an iteration of the form $x^{n+1} = x^n \nabla f(x^n)$, for $n > k$, yields an ultimately stationary sequence,

```
void main() {
  int x=0;            // 1
  while (x<100) {     // 2
    x=x+1;            // 3
  }                   // 4
}
```

$$\begin{aligned} x_1 &= [0,0] \\ x_2 &=]-\infty,99] \cap (x_1 \cup x_3) \\ x_3 &= x_2 + [1,1] \\ x_4 &= [100,+\infty[\cap (x_1 \cup x_3) \end{aligned}$$

Fig. 1. A simple integer loop and its semantic equations

whose limit x^m is a *post fixed point* of f, i.e. a point x such that $x \geq f(x)$. The index k is a parameter of the least fixed point solver. Increasing k increases the precision of the solver, at the expense of time. In the sequel, we choose $k = 10$. Narrowing operators are binary operators Δ on $\mathcal{L}$ which ensure that any sequence $x^{n+1} = x^n \Delta f(x^n)$, for $n > m$, initialized with the above post fixed point x^m, is eventually stationary. Its limit is required to be a fixed point of f but not necessarily the least one.

Consider first the program at the left of Figure 1. The corresponding semantic equations in the lattice of intervals are given at the right of the figure. The intervals $x_1, \dots, x_4$ correspond to the control points $1, \dots, 4$ indicated as comments in the C code. We look for a fixed point of the function f given by the right hand side of these semantic equations. The standard Kleene iteration sequence is eventually constant after 100 iterations, reaching the least fixed point. This fixed point can be obtained in a faster way by using the classical (see [10] again) widening and narrowing operators:

$$[a,b]\nabla[c,d] = [e,f] \text{ with } e = \begin{cases} a & \text{if } a \leq c \\ -\infty & \text{otherwise} \end{cases} \quad \text{and } f = \begin{cases} b & \text{if } d \leq b \\ \infty & \text{otherwise,} \end{cases}$$

$$[a,b]\Delta[c,d] = [e,f] \text{ with } e = \begin{cases} c \text{ if } a = -\infty \\ a \text{ otherwise} \end{cases} \quad \text{and } f = \begin{cases} d \text{ if } b = \infty \\ b \text{ otherwise.} \end{cases}$$

The iteration sequence using widenings and narrowings takes 12 iterations because we chose $k = 10$, and it reaches the least fixed point of f :

$$\begin{aligned} x_2^1 &= [0,0] \\ x_3^1 &= [1,1] \\ x_4^1 &= \bot \\ &\dots \\ x_2^9 &= [0,8] \\ x_3^9 &= [1,9] \\ x_4^9 &= \bot \end{aligned} \qquad \begin{aligned} &\text{(widening)} \\ x_2^{10} &= [0,\infty[\\ x_3^{10} &= [1,\infty[\\ x_4^{10} &= [100,\infty[\end{aligned} \qquad \begin{aligned} &\text{(narrowing)} \\ x_2^{11} &= [0,99[\\ x_3^{11} &= [1,100] \\ x_4^{11} &= [100,100] \end{aligned}$$

3 Policy Iteration Algorithm in Complete Lattices

3.1 Lower Selection

To compute a fixed point of a self-map f of a lattice $\mathcal{L}$, we shall assume that f is effectively given as an infimum of a finite set $\mathcal{G}$ of "simpler" maps. Here, and in the sequel, the infimum refers to the pointwise ordering of maps. We wish to obtain a fixed point of f from the fixed points of the maps of $\mathcal{G}$. To this end, the following general notion will be useful.

Definition 1 (Lower selection). *We say that a set $\mathcal{G}$ of maps from a set X to a lattice $\mathcal{L}$* admits a lower selection *if for all $x \in X$, there exists a map $g \in \mathcal{G}$ such that $g(x) \leq h(x)$, for all $h \in \mathcal{G}$.*

Setting $f = \inf \mathcal{G}$, we see that $\mathcal{G}$ has a lower selection if and only if for all $x \in X$, we have $f(x) = g(x)$ for some $g \in \mathcal{G}$. We next illustrate this definition.

Example 1. Take $\mathcal{L} = \overline{\mathbb{R}}$, and consider the self-map of $\mathcal{L}$, $f(x) = \bigcap_{1 \leq i \leq m} (a_i + x) \cup b_i$, where $a_i, b_i \in \mathbb{R}$. Up to a trivial modification, this is a special case of *min-max function* [18, 6, 19]. The set $\mathcal{G}$ consisting of the m maps $x \mapsto (a_i + x) \cup b_i$ admits a lower selection. We represent on Figure 2 the case where $m = 5$, $b_1 = -5, a_1 = 2.5, b_2 = -3, a_2 = 0.5, b_3 = 1, a_3 = -3, b_4 = 1.5, a_4 = -4, b_5 = 2.5, a_5 = -4.5$. The graph of the map f is represented in bold.

3.2 Universal Policy Iteration Algorithm

In many applications, and specially in static analysis of programs, the smallest fixed point is of interest. We shall denote by f^- the smallest fixed point of a monotone self-map f of a complete lattice $\mathcal{L}$, whose existence is guaranteed by Tarski's fixed point theorem. We first state a simple theoretical result which brings to light one of the ingredients of policy iteration.

Theorem 1. *Let $\mathcal{G}$ denote a family of monotone self-maps of a complete lattice $\mathcal{L}$ with a lower selection, and let $f = \inf \mathcal{G}$. Then $f^- = \inf_{g \in \mathcal{G}} g^-$.*

Theorem 1 is related to a result of [7] concerning monotone self-maps of $\mathbb{R}^n$ that are nonexpansive in the sup-norm (see also the last chapter of [5]).

We now state a very general policy iteration algorithm. The input of the algorithm consists of a finite set $\mathcal{G}$ of monotone self-maps of a lattice $\mathcal{L}$ with a lower selection. When the algorithm terminates, its output is a fixed point of $f = \inf \mathcal{G}$.

Algorithm (PI: Policy iteration in lattices).

1. Initialization. *Set $k = 1$ and select any map $g_1 \in \mathcal{G}$.*
2. Value determination. *Compute a fixed point x^k of g_k.*
3. *Compute $f(x^k)$.*
4. *If $f(x^k) = x^k$, return x^k.*
5. Policy improvement. *Take g_{k+1} such that $f(x^k) = g_{k+1}(x^k)$. Increment k and goto Step 2.*

We next show that the algorithm does terminate when at each step, the smallest fixed-point of g_k, $x^k = g_k^-$ is selected. We call *height* of a subset $\mathcal{X} \subset \mathcal{L}$ the maximal cardinality of a chain of elements of $\mathcal{X}$.

Theorem 2. *Assume that $\mathcal{L}$ is a complete lattice and that all the maps of $\mathcal{G}$ are monotone. If at each step k, the smallest fixed-point $x^k = g_k^-$ of g_k is selected, then the number of iterations of Algorithm PI is bounded by the height of $\{g^- \mid g \in \mathcal{G}\}$, and a fortiori, by the cardinality of $\mathcal{G}$.*

Remark 1. Any $x^k \in \mathcal{L}$ computed by Algorithm PI is a post fixed point: $f(x^k) \leq x^k$. In static analysis of programs, such a x^k yields a valid, although suboptimal, information.

Example 2. We first give a simple illustration of the algorithm, by computing the smallest fixed point of the map f of Example 1. Let us take the first policy $g_5(x) = b_5 \cup (a_5 + x) = 2.5 \cup (-4.5 + x)$, which has two fixed points, $+\infty$ and 2.5. We choose the smallest one, $x^1 = 2.5$. We have $f(x^1) = g_2(x^1)$ where $g_2(x) = b_3 \cup (a_3 + x) = 1 \cup (-3 + x)$. We take for x^2 the smallest fixed point of g_2, $x^2 = 1$. Then, the algorithm stops since $f(x^2) = x^2$. This execution is illustrated in Figure 2. By comparison, the Kleene iteration (right) initialized at the point $-\infty$ takes 11 iterations to reach the fixed point.

A crucial difficulty in the application of the algorithm to static analysis is that even when the smallest fixed points $x^k = g_k^-$ are always chosen, the policy iteration algorithm need *not* return the smallest fixed point of f. For instance, in Example 2, if one takes the initial policy $x \mapsto a_1 \cup (b_1 + x)$ or $x \mapsto a_2 \cup (b_2 + x)$, we get $x^1 = \infty$, and the algorithm stops with a fixed point of f, ∞, which is non minimal. This shows the importance of the initial policy and of the update rule for policies.

Although Algorithm PI may terminate with a nonminimal fixed point, it is often possible to check that the output of the algorithm is actually the smallest fixed point and otherwise improve the results, thanks to the following kind of

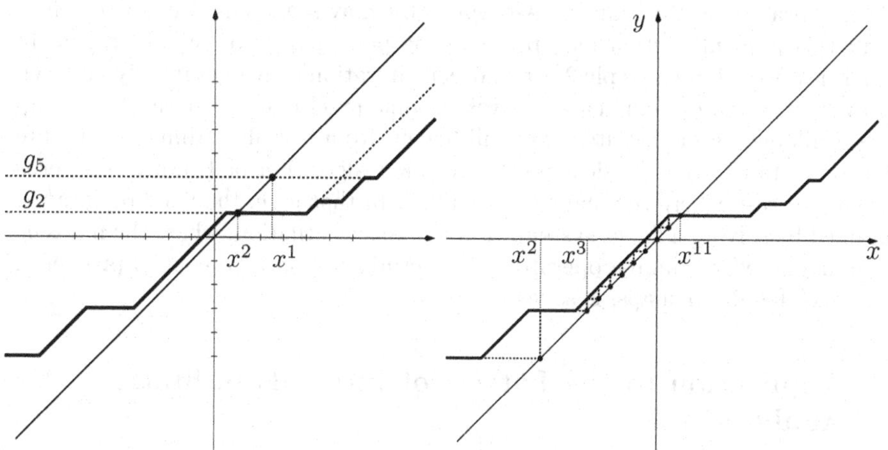

Fig. 2. Policy iteration (left) versus Kleene iteration (right)

results. We consider the special situation where f is a monotone self-map of $\overline{\mathbb{R}}^n$, with a restriction $\mathbb{R}^n \to \mathbb{R}^n$ that is nonexpansive for the sup-norm, meaning that $\|f(x) - f(y)\|_\infty \leq \|x - y\|_\infty$, for all $x, y \in \mathbb{R}^n$. We shall say that such maps f have *Property N*. (For instance, the maps in Example 1 all have Property N.) The following theorem identifies situations where the *uniqueness* of the terminal policy guarantees that the fixed point returned by Algorithm PI is the smallest one.

Theorem 3. *Assume that $\mathcal{G}$ is a finite set of monotone self-maps of $\overline{\mathbb{R}}^n$ that all have Property N, that $\mathcal{G}$ has a lower selection, and let $f = \inf \mathcal{G}$. If Algorithm PI terminates with a finite fixed point $x^k = g_k^-$ such that there is only one $g \in \mathcal{G}$ such that $f(x^k) = g(x^k)$, then, x^k is the smallest finite fixed point of f.*

Remark 2. The nonexpansiveness assumption cannot be dispensed with in Theorem 3. Consider the self-map of $\overline{\mathbb{R}}$, $f(x) = 0 \cap (1 + 2x)$, and take the set $\mathcal{G}$ consisting of the maps $x \mapsto 0$ and $x \mapsto 1 + 2x$. Algorithm PI initialized with the map $g_1 = 0$ stops immediately with the fixed point $x^1 = 0$, and g_1 is the only map g in $\mathcal{G}$ such that $g(0) = f(0)$, but x^1 is a nonminimal finite fixed point of f, since $f(-1) = -1$.

Remark 3. When the policy g such that $f(x^k) = g(x^k)$ is not unique, we can check whether x^k is the smallest finite fixed point of f in the following way. We scan the set of maps $g \in \mathcal{G}$ such that $g(x^k) = f(x^k)$, until we find a fixpoint associated to g smaller than x^k, or all these maps g have been scanned. In the former case, an improved post fixed point of f has been found and this process can be iterated. In the latter case, a small variation of the proof of Theorem 3 shows that x^k is the smallest finite fixed point of f (if all the maps in $\mathcal{G}$ have Property N).

Algorithm PI requires to compute at every step a fixed point x^k of the map g_k, and if possible, the minimal one, g_k^-. An obvious way to do so is to apply Kleene iteration to the map g_k. Although this may seem surprising at the first sight, this implementation may preserve the performance of the algorithm. In fact, it is optimal in Example 2, since Kleene iteration converges in only one step for every map g_k. In many cases, however, some precise information on the map g_k is available, and policy iteration will benefit from fast algorithms to compute x^k. For instance, the classical policy iteration algorithm of Howard, concerns the special case where the maps g_k are affine. In that case, the fixed point x^k is obtained by solving a linear system. A non classical situation, where the maps g_k are dynamic programming operators of deterministic optimal control problems, i.e., max-plus linear maps, is solved in [6, 14].

4 Application to the Lattice of Intervals in Static Analysis

In the sequel, we shall consider the set $\mathcal{I}(\mathbb{R})$ of closed intervals of $\mathbb{R}$. This set, ordered by inclusion, is a complete lattice. It will be convenient to represent an interval $I \in \mathcal{I}(\mathbb{R})$ as $I = [-a,b] := \{x \in \mathbb{R} \mid -a \leq x \leq b\}$ with $a,b \in \mathbb{R} \cup \{\pm\infty\}$. We changed the sign in order to get a monotone map $\psi : I \mapsto (a = -\inf I, b = \sup I)$, from $\mathcal{I}(\mathbb{R}) \to \overline{\mathbb{R}}^2$, converting the inclusion on intervals to the componentwise order on $\overline{\mathbb{R}}^2$. Observe that ψ is a right inverse of $\imath : (a,b) \mapsto [-a,b]$. By extending ψ and $\imath$ to products of spaces, entrywise, we see that any monotone self-map f of $\mathcal{I}(\mathbb{R}^n)$ induces a monotone self-map of $(\overline{\mathbb{R}}^2)^n$, $\psi \circ f \circ \imath$, that we call the *lift* of f. The minimal fixed point of f is the image by $\imath$ of the minimal fixed point of its lift, although our algorithms apply preferably to the map f rather than to its lift.

4.1 The Interval Abstraction

We consider a toy imperative language with the following instructions:

1. loops: `while (condition) instruction;`
2. conditionals: `if (condition) instruction [else instruction];`
3. assignment: `operand = expression;` We assume here that the arithmetic expressions are built on a given set of variables (belonging to the set Var), and use operators +, -, * and /, together with numerical constants (only integers here for more simplicity).

There is a classical [10] Galois connection relating the powerset of values of variables to the product of intervals (one for each variable). This is what gives the correction of the classical [10] abstract semantics $[\![.]\!]$, with respect to the standard collecting semantics of this language. $[\![.]\!]$ is given by a set of equations over the variables $x_1, \ldots, x_n$ of the program that we will show on some examples. Each variable x_i is interpreted as an interval $[-x_i^-; x_i^+]$.

4.2 Selection Property for a Family of Finitely Generated Functions on Intervals

We now define a class of monotone self-maps of $\mathcal{I}(\mathbb{R})$, which is precisely the class of functions arising from the semantic equations of the previous section. This class may be thought of as an extension of the min-max functions introduced in [18]. For an interval $I = [-a,b]$, we set $\uparrow I \stackrel{\text{def}}{=} [-a, \infty[$ and $\downarrow I \stackrel{\text{def}}{=}]-\infty, b]$.

Definition 2. *A finitely generated function of intervals, $(\mathcal{I}(\mathbb{R}))^n \to (\mathcal{I}(\mathbb{R}))^p$, is a map f whose coordinates $f_j : x = (x_1, \ldots, x_n) \mapsto f_j(x)$ are terms of the following grammar G:*

$$CSTE ::= [-a,b] \quad VAR ::= x_i$$

$$\begin{array}{lll} EXPR ::= CSTE & \mid VAR & \mid EXPR + EXPR \mid \\ \quad EXPR * EXPR & \mid EXPR/EXPR & \mid EXPR - EXPR \\ TEST ::= \uparrow EXPR \cap EXPR & \mid \downarrow EXPR \cap EXPR & \mid CSTE \cap EXPR \\ G ::= EXPR & \mid TEST & \mid G \cup G \end{array}$$

where i can take arbitrary values in $\{1, \ldots, n\}$, and a, b can take arbitrary values in $\overline{\mathbb{R}}$.

We write $\mathcal{F}$ for the set of such functions. The variables $x_1, \ldots, x_n$ correspond to the different variables in Var. We set $x_i^- = -\inf x_i$, $x_i^+ = \sup x_i$, so that $x_i = [-x_i^-, x_i^+]$. Non-terminals $CSTE$, VAR, $EXPR$ and $TEST$ do correspond to the semantics of constants, variables, arithmetic expressions, and (simple) tests. For instance, the fixed point equation at the right of Figure 1 is of the form $x = f(x)$ where f is a finitely generated function of intervals.

In order to write maps of $\mathcal{F}$ as infima of simpler maps, when $I = [-a, b]$ and $J = [-c, d]$, we also define $l(I, J) = I$ (l is for "left"), $r(I, J) = J$ (r for "right"), $m(I, J) = [-a, d]$ and $m^{\mathrm{op}}(I, J) = [-c, b]$ (m is for "merge"). These four operators will define the four possible policies on intervals, as shown in Proposition 1 below.

Let $G_\cup$ be the grammar, similar to G except that we cannot produce terms with $\cap$.

$$\begin{array}{rlllll} G_\cup ::= & EXPR & \mid \uparrow EXPR & \mid \downarrow EXPR & \mid G_\cup \cup G_\cup & \mid \\ & l(G_\cup, G_\cup) & \mid r(G_\cup, G_\cup) & \mid m(G_\cup, G_\cup) & \mid m^{\mathrm{op}}(G_\cup, G_\cup) & \end{array}$$

We write $\mathcal{F}_\cup$ for the set of functions defined by this grammar. Terms $l(G, G)$, $r(G, G)$, $m(G, G)$ and $m^{\mathrm{op}}(G, G)$ represent respectively the left, right, m and m^{op} policies.

The intersection of two intervals, and hence, of two terms of the grammar, interpreted in the obvious manner as intervals, is given by the following formula:

$$G_1 \cap G_2 = l(G_1, G_2) \cap r(G_1, G_2) \cap m(G_1, G_2) \cap m^{\mathrm{op}}(G_1, G_2) \tag{1}$$

To a finitely generated function of intervals $f \in \mathcal{F}$, we associate a family $\Pi(f)$ of functions of $\mathcal{F}_\cup$ obtained in the following manner: we replace each occurrence of a term $G_1 \cap G_2$ by $l(G_1, G_2)$, $r(G_1, G_2)$, $m(G_1, G_2)$ or $m^{\mathrm{op}}(G_1, G_2)$. We call such a choice a *policy*. Using Equation (1), we get:

Proposition 1. *If f is a finitely generated function of intervals, the set of policies $\Pi(f)$ admits a lower selection. In particular, $f = \inf \Pi(f)$.*

4.3 Implementation Principles of the Policy Iteration Algorithm

A simple static analyzer has been implemented in C++. It consists of a parser for a simple imperative language (a very simplified C), a generator of abstract semantic equations using the interval abstraction, and the corresponding solver, using the policy iteration algorithm described in Section 3.

A policy is a table that associates to each intersection node in the semantic abstraction, a value modeling which policy is chosen among l, r, m or m^{op}, in Equation (1). There is a number of heuristics that one might choose concerning the initial policy, which should be a guess of the value of $G_1 \cap G_2$ in Equation (1). The choice of the initial policy may be crucial, since some choices of the initial policy may lead eventually to a fixed point which is not minimal. (In such cases, Remark 3 should be used: it yields a heuristics to improve the fixed point, which can be justified rigorously by Theorem 3, when the lift of f has Property N.) The current prototype makes a sensible choice: when a term $G_1 \cap G_2$ is encountered, if a finite constant bound appears in G_1 or G_2, this bound is selected. Moreover, if a $+\infty$ upper bound or $-\infty$ lower bound appears in G_1 or G_2, then, this bound is not selected, unless no other choice is available (in other words, choices that give no information are avoided). When the applications of these rules is not enough to determine the initial policy, we choose the bound arising from the left hand side term. Thus, when $G_1 = [-a, \infty[$, the initial policy for $G_1 \cap G_2$ is $m(G_1, G_2)$, which keeps the lower bound of G_1 and the upper bound of G_2.

The way the equations are constructed, when the terms $G_1 \cap G_2$ correspond to a test on a variable (and thus no constant choice is available for at least one bound), this initial choice means choosing the constraint on the current variable brought on by this test, rather than the equation expressing the dependence of current state of the variable to the other states. These choices often favor as first guess an easily computable system of equations.

We then compute the fixed point of the reduced equations, using if possible specific algorithms. In particular, when the lift of f is a min-max function, shortest path type algorithms may be used, in the spirit of [6, 14]. Linear or convex programming might also be used in some cases. For the time being, we only use a classical Kleene like value iteration algorithm, discussed in Section 4.4.

We then proceed to the improvement of the policy, as explained in Section 3. In short, we change the policy at each node for which a fixed point of the complete system of equations is not reached, and compute the fixed point of the new equations, until we find a fixed point of the complete system of equations. Even when this fixpoint is reached, using Remark 3 can allow to get a smaller fixpoint in some cases, when the current fixpoint is obtained for several policies.

4.4 Examples and Comparison with Kleene's Algorithm

In this section, we discuss a few typical examples, that are experimented using our prototype implementation. We compare the policy iteration algorithm with Kleene's iteration sequence with widenings and narrowings (the very classical one of [10]), called Algorithm K here. For both algorithms, we compare the accuracy of the results and the cost of the solution.

We did not experiment specific algorithms for solving equations in $G_\cup$ (meaning, without intersections), as we consider this to be outside the scope of this paper, so we chose to use an iterative solver (algorithm K$'$) for each policy. Algorithm K$'$ is exactly the same solver as algorithm K, but used on a smaller class of functions, for one policy. Note that the overall speedup of policy iteration algorithms could be improved by using specific solvers instead. So Algorithm PI will run Algorithm K$'$ at every value determination step (Step 2). Of course, using Algorithm K$'$ instead of a specific solver is an heuristics, since the convergence result, Theorem 2, requires that at every value determination step, the smallest fixed point is computed. We decided to widen intervals, both in Algorithms K and K$'$, only after ten standard Kleene iterations. This choice is conventional, and in most examples below, one could argue that an analyzer would have found the right result with only two Kleene iterations. In this case, the speedup obtained by the policy iteration algorithm would be far less; but it should be argued that in most static analyzers, there would be a certain unrolling before trying to widen the result. In the sequel we compare the number of fixpoint iterations and of "elementary operations" performed by algorithms K and PI. We count as elementary operations, the arithmetic operations (+, - etc.), min and max (used for unions and intersections), and tests ($\leq$, $\geq$, $=$, used for checking whether we reach local fixed points during iterations of algorithms K and K′).

A simple typical (integer) loop is shown on Figure 1, together with the equations generated by the analyzer. The original policy is m^{op} in equation 2 in Figure 1 (by equation i, we mean the equation which determines the state of variables at control point i, here x_2), and m in the equation determining x_4, This is actually the right policy on the spot, and we find in one iteration (and 34 elementary operations), the correct result (the least fixed point). This is to be compared with the 12 iterations of Algorithm K (and 200 elementary operations), in Section 2. In the sequel, we put upper indices to indicate at which iteration the abstract value of a variable is shown. Lower indices are reserved as before to the control point number.

The analysis of the program below leads to an actual policy improvement:

```
void main(){                  while (j >= i) { // 3
int i,j;                        i = i+2; // 4
i=1; // 1                       j = -1+j; // 5
j=10; // 2                    } // 6 }
```

Semantic equations at control points 3 and 6 are

$$(i_3, j_3) = (]-\infty, \max(j_2, j_5)] \cap (i_2 \cup i_5),\ \ [\min(i_2, i_5), +\infty[\cap(j_2 \cup j_5))$$
$$(i_6, j_6) = ([\min(j_2, j_5) + 1, +\infty[\cap(i_2 \cup i_5),\ \ ]-\infty, \max(i_2, i_5) - 1] \cap (j_2 \cup j_5))$$

The algorithm starts with policy m^{op} for variable i in equation 3, m for variable j in equation 3, m for variable i equation 6 and m^{op} in equation 6, variable j. The first iteration using Algorithm K′ with this policy, finds the value $(i_6^1, j_6^1) = ([1, 12], [0, 11])$. But the value for variable j given by equation 6, given using the previous result, is $[0, 10]$ instead of $[0, 11]$, meaning that the policy on equation 6 for j should be improved. The minimum (0) for j at equation 6 is reached as the minimum of the right argument of $\cap$. The maximum (10) for j at equation 6 is reached as the maximum of the right argument of $\cap$. Hence the new policy one has to choose for variable j in equation 6 is r. In one iteration of Algorithm K′ for this policy, one finds the least fixed point of the system of semantic equations, which is at line 6, $(i_6^2, j_6^2) = ([1, 12], [0, 10])$. Unfortunately, this fixed point is reached by several policies, and Remark 3 is used, leading to another policy iteration. This in fact does not improve the result since the current fixed point is the smallest one. Algorithm PI uses 2 policy iterations, 5 values iterations and 272 elementary operations. Algorithm K takes ten iterations (and 476 elementary operations) to reach the same result.

Some benchmarks. In the following table, we describe preliminary results that we obtained using Algorithms K and PI on simple C programs, consisting essentially of loop nests. We indicate for each program (available on http://www.di.-ens.fr/~goubault/Politiques) the number of variables, the number of loops, the maximal depth of loop nests, the number of policy iterations slash the total number of potential policies, value iterations and elementary operations for each algorithm (when this applies). The last column indicates the speedup ratio of Algorithm PI with respect to K, measured as the number of elementary operations K needs over the number that PI needs.

Program	vars	loops	depth	pols./tot.	iters.K/PI	ops.K/PI	speedup
`test1`	1	1	1	1/16	12/1	200/34	*5.88*
`test2`	2	1	1	2/256	10/5	476/272	*1.75*
`test3`	3	1	1	1/256	5/2	44/83	*0.51*
`test4`	5	5	1	0/1048576	43/29	2406/1190	*2.02*
`test5`	2	2	2	0/256	164/7	5740/198	*28.99*
`test6`	2	2	2	1/1048576	57/19	2784/918	*3.03*
`test7`	3	3	2	1/4096	62/13	3242/678	*4.78*
`test8`	3	3	3	0/4096	60/45	3916/2542	*1.54*
`test9`	3	3	3	2/4096	185/41	11348/1584	*7.16*
`test10`	4	4	3	3/65536	170/160	11274/10752	*1.05*

The relative performances can be quite difficult to predict (for instance, for `test3`, Algorithm K is about twice as fast as PI, which is the only case in the benchmark), but in general, in nested loops Algorithm PI can outperform Algorithm K by a huge factor. Furthermore, for nested loops, Algorithm PI can even be both faster and more precise than Algorithm K, as in the case of `test7`:

```
int main() {
  int i,j,k;
  i = 0; //1
  k = 9; //2
  j = -100; //3
  while (i <= 100) //4 {
    i = i + 1; //5
    while (j < 20) //6
      j = i+j; //7 //8
    k = 4; //9
    while (k <=3) //10
      k = k+1; //11 //12
  } //13 }
```

Algorithm PI reaches the following fixed point, at control point 13, in 13 value iterations, $i = [101, 101]$, $j = [-100, 120]$ and $k = [4, 9]$ whereas Algorithm K only finds $i = [101, 101]$, $j = [-100, +\infty]$ and $k = [4, 9]$ in 62 iterations. The fact that Algorithm K does not reach the least fixed point can be explained as follows. At control point 4, Algorithm K finds successively:

	then:	up to:	then widening:
$i_4 = [0, 0]$	$i_4 = [0, 1]$	$i_4 = [0, 9]$	$i_4 = [0, +\infty]$
$j_4 = [-100, -100]$	$j_4 = [-100, 20]$	$j_4 = [-100, 28]$	$j_4 = [-100, +\infty]$
$k_4 = [9, 9]$	$k_4 = [4, 9]$	$k_4 = [4, 9]$	$k_4 = [4, 9]$

From now on, there is no way, using further decreasing iterations, to find that j is finite (and less than 20) inside the outer while loop, since this depends on a relation between i and j that cannot be simulated using this iteration strategy.

5 Future Work

We have shown in this paper that policy iteration algorithms can lead to fast and accurate solvers for abstract semantic equations, such as the ones coming from classical problems in static analysis. We still have some heuristics in the choice of initial policies we would like to test (using for example a dynamic initial choice, dependent on the values of variables after the first fixpoint iterations), and the algorithmic consequences of Theorem 3 should be investigated.

One of our aims is to generalize the policy iteration algorithm to more complex lattices of properties, such as the one of octagons (see [26]). We would like also to apply this technique to symbolic lattices (using techniques to transfer numeric lattices, see for instance [32]). Finally, we should insist on the fact that a policy iteration solver should ideally rely on better solvers than value iteration ones, for each of its iterations (i.e. for a choice of a policy). The idea is that, choosing a policy simplifies the set of equations to solve, and the class of such sets of equations can be solved by better specific solvers. In particular, we would like to experiment the policy iteration algorithms again on grammar $G_{\cup}$, so that we would be left with solving, at each step of the algorithm, purely numerical constraints, at least in the case of the interval abstraction. For numerical constraints, we could then use very fast numerical solvers dedicated to large classes of functions, such as linear equations.

References

1. F. Bourdoncle. Abstract interpretation by dynamic partitioning. *Journal of Functional Programming*, 2(4):407–435, 1992.
2. F. Bourdoncle. Efficient chaotic iteration strategies with widenings. Number 735, pages 128–141. Lecture Notes in Computer Science, Springer-Verlag, 1993.
3. B. Le Charlier and P. Van Hentenryck. A universal top-down fixpoint algorithm. Technical Report CS-92-25, Brown University, May 1992.
4. C. Clack and S. L. Peyton Jones. Strictness Analysis — A Practical Approach. In J.-P. Jouannaud, editor, *Functional Programming Languages and Computer Architecture*, LNCS 201, pages 35–49. Springer, Berlin, sept 1985.
5. J. Cochet-Terrasson. *Algorithmes d'itération sur les politiques pour les applications monotones contractantes.* Thèse, École des Mines, Dec. 2001.
6. J. Cochet-Terrasson, S. Gaubert, and J. Gunawardena. A constructive fixed point theorem for min-max functions. *Dynamics and Stability of Systems*, 14(4):407–433, 1999.
7. J. Cochet-Terrasson, S. Gaubert, and J. Gunawardena. Policy iteration algorithms for monotone nonexpansive maps. Draft, 2001.
8. A. Costan. Analyse statique et itération sur les politiques. Technical report, CEA Saclay, report DTSI/SLA/03-575/AC, and Ecole Polytechnique, August 2003.
9. P. Cousot and R. Cousot. Abstract interpretation: A unified lattice model for static analysis of programs by construction of approximations of fixed points. *Principles of Programming Languages 4*, pages 238–252, 1977.
10. P. Cousot and R. Cousot. Comparison of the Galois connection and widening/narrowing approaches to abstract interpretation. JTASPEFL '91, Bordeaux. *BIGRE*, 74:107–110, October 1991.

11. D. Damian. Time stamps for fixed-point approximation. *ENTCS*, 45, 2001.
12. H. Eo and K. Yi. An improved differential fixpoint iteration method for program analysis. November 2002.
13. C. Fecht and H. Seidl. Propagating differences: An efficient new fixpoint algorithm for distributive constraint systems. pages 90–104, 1998.
14. S. Gaubert and J. Gunawardena. The duality theorem for min-max functions. *C. R. Acad. Sci. Paris.*, 326, Série I:43–48, 1998.
15. E. Goubault, M. Martel, and S. Putot. Asserting the precision of floating-point computations: A simple abstract interpreter. *ESOP, LNCS 2305*, 2002.
16. P. Granger. *Analyse de congruences.* PhD thesis, Ecole Polytechnique, 1990.
17. P. Granger. Static analysis of linear congruence equalities among variables of a program. In S. Abramsky and T. S. E. Maibaum, editors, *TAPSOFT '91 (CAAP'91)*, LNCS 493, pages 169–192. Springer-Verlag, 1991.
18. J. Gunawardena. Min-max functions. *Discrete Event Dynamic Systems*, 4:377–406, 1994.
19. J. Gunawardena. From max-plus algebra to nonexpansive maps: a nonlinear theory for discrete event systems. *Theoretical Computer Science*, 293:141–167, 2003.
20. A. J. Hoffman and R. M. Karp. On nonterminating stochastic games. *Management Sci.*, 12:359–370, 1966.
21. R. Howard. *Dynamic Programming and Markov Processes.* Wiley, 1960.
22. L. S. Hunt. *Abstract Interpretation of Functional Languages: From Theory to Practice.* Ph.D. thesis, Department of Computing, Imperial College, London, 1991.
23. M. Karr. Affine relationships between variables of a program. *Acta Informatica*, (6):133–151, 1976.
24. V. Kuncak and K. Rustan M. Leino. On computing the fixpoint of a set of boolean equations. Technical Report MSR-TR-2003-08, Microsoft Research, 2003.
25. L. Mauborgne. Binary decision graphs. In A. Cortesi and G. Filé, editors, *Static Analyis Symposium SAS'99*, LNCS 1694, pp 101-116. Springer-Verlag, 1999.
26. A. Miné. The octagon abstract domain in analysis, slicing and transformation. pages 310–319, October 2001.
27. R. A. O'Keefe. Finite fixed-point problems. In Jean-Louis Lassez, editor, *ICLP '87*, pages 729–743, Melbourne, Australia, May 1987. MIT Press.
28. P. and N. Halbwachs. Discovery of linear restraints among variables of a program.
29. M. L. Puterman. *Markov decision processes: discrete stochastic dynamic programming.* Wiley Series in Probability and Mathematical Statistics: Applied Probability and Statistics. John Wiley & Sons Inc., New York, 1994.
30. S. Putot, E. Goubault, and M. Martel. Static analysis-based validation of floating-point computations. LNCS 2991. Springer-Verlag, 2003.
31. K. Ravi and F. Somenzi. Efficient fixpoint computation for invariant checking. In *International Conference on Computer Design (ICCD '99)*, pages 467–475, Washington - Brussels - Tokyo, October 1999. IEEE.
32. A. Venet. Nonuniform alias analysis of recursive data structures and arrays. In *SAS 2002*, LNCS 2477, pages 36–51. Springer, 2002.

Data Structure Specifications via Local Equality Axioms

Scott McPeak and George C. Necula

University of California, Berkeley
{smcpeak, necula}@cs.berkeley.edu

Abstract. We describe a program verification methodology for specifying global shape properties of data structures by means of axioms involving predicates on scalar fields, pointer equalities, and pointer disequalities, in the neighborhood of a memory cell. We show that such local invariants are both natural and sufficient for describing a large class of data structures. We describe a complete decision procedure for axioms without disequalities, and practical heuristics for the full language. The procedure has the key advantage that it can be extended easily with reasoning for any decidable theory of scalar fields.

1 Introduction

This paper explores a program verification strategy where programs are annotated with invariants, and decision procedures are used to prove them. A key element of such an approach is the specification language, which must precisely capture shape and alias information but also be amenable to automatic reasoning. Type systems and alias analyses are often too imprecise. There are very expressive specification languages (e.g., reachability predicates [15], shape types [4]) with either negative or unknown decidability results. A few systems such as TVLA [19] and PALE [13] have similar expressivity and effectiveness, but use logics with *transitive closure* and thus incur additional restrictions.

We propose to use local equality axioms for data structure specification ("LEADS"), such as "for every list node n, n.`next`.`prev` $= n$", which specifies a doubly-linked list. This simple idea generalizes to describe a wide variety of shapes, as subsequent examples will show. And, as each specification constrains only a bounded fragment of the heap around a distinguished element n (unlike with transitive closure), it is fairly easy to reason about.

There are two main contributions of this work. First, we present a *methodology* for specifying shapes of data structures, using local specifications. The specifications use arbitrary predicates on scalar fields and equality between pointer expressions to constrain the shape of the data structure. We show that such local specifications can express indirectly a number of important global properties.

The second contribution is a *decision procedure* for a class of local shape specifications as described above. The decision procedure is based on the idea that local shape specifications have the property that any counterexamples are

K. Etessami and S.K. Rajamani (Eds.): CAV 2005, LNCS 3576, pp. 476–490, 2005.

also local. This decision procedure is not only simple to implement but fits naturally in a cooperating decision procedure framework that integrates pointer-shape reasoning with reasoning about scalar values, such as linear arithmetic, or uninterpreted functions.

A related contribution is to the field of automated deduction, for dealing with universally quantified assumptions: the matching problem is that of finding sufficient instantiations of universally quantified facts to prove a goal. Performing too few instantiations endangers completeness while performing too many compromises the performance of the algorithm and often even its termination. For the class of universally quantified axioms that we consider here we show a complete and terminating matching rule. This is a valuable result in a field where heuristics are the norm [14, 2].

Our experimental results are encouraging. We show that we can describe the same data structures that are discussed in the PALE publications, with somewhat better performance results; we can also encode some data structures that are not expressible using PALE. We also show that the matching rules are not only complete, but lead to a factor of two improvement in performance over the heuristics used by Simplify [2], a mature automatic theorem prover. Furthermore, unlike matching in Simplify, our algorithm will always terminate.

2 Methodology Example

We follow a standard program verification strategy (e.g., [14]), with programmer-specified invariants for each loop and for the function start (precondition) and end (postcondition). We use a symbolic verification condition generator to extract a verification condition for each path connecting two invariants. The emphasis in this paper is on the specification mechanism for the invariants and the decision procedure for proving the resulting verification conditions.

Suppose we wish to verify the procedure in Figure 1, part of a hypothetical process scheduler written in a Java-like language. It has the job of removing a process from the list of runnable processes, in preparation for putting it into the list of sleeping processes. Each list is doubly-linked.

We capture the data structure invariants using the set of axioms in Figure 1, where the quantifier ranges over list cells. These axioms constitute the data structure invariant, and must hold at the start and end of the function. Axioms A1 and A2 express the local invariant that the `next` and `prev` fields are inverses. Axiom A3 says that all the processes in a list have the same state (`RUN` or `SLP`), and axiom A4 says that all the runnable processes have non-increasing priorities.

To begin verifying `insert`, we need a formal precondition:

$$PRE: \quad \texttt{x} \neq \texttt{null} \ \wedge\ \texttt{x.prev} \neq \texttt{null} \ \wedge\ \texttt{x.state} = \texttt{RUN}$$

The verification condition generator produces verification conditions, which are implications where the left-hand side consists of the function precondition along with the current path predicates, and the right-hand side is the goal to prove.

```
1 // precondition: x is runnable (RUN) and not first in list
2 void remove(Process x) {
3   x.prev.next = x.next;
4   if (x.next)
5     x.next.prev = x.prev;
6   x.state = SLP;
7   x.next = x.prev = null;
8 }
```

$$
\begin{array}{lll}
A1. & \forall p.\ p \neq \texttt{null} \wedge p.\texttt{next} \neq \texttt{null} & \Rightarrow p.\texttt{next.prev} = p \\
A2. & \forall p.\ p \neq \texttt{null} \wedge p.\texttt{prev} \neq \texttt{null} & \Rightarrow p.\texttt{prev.next} = p \\
A3. & \forall p.\ p \neq \texttt{null} \wedge p.\texttt{next} \neq \texttt{null} & \Rightarrow p.\texttt{state} = p.\texttt{next.state} \\
A4. & \forall p.\ p \neq \texttt{null} \wedge p.\texttt{next} \neq \texttt{null} \wedge p.\texttt{state} = \texttt{RUN} & \Rightarrow p.\texttt{prio} \geq p.\texttt{next.prio}
\end{array}
$$

Fig. 1. A scheduler `remove` function and its data structure axioms

We use the standard strategy to show validity of the verification condition by showing that its negation is unsatisfiable. For example, to prove that we do not dereference `null` in `x.next` on line 3, we must show unsatisfiability of $PRE \wedge \texttt{x} = \texttt{null}$. This can be done without any reference to the axioms.

What is harder to show is that the axioms hold when the function returns. Consider first showing that axiom A3 still holds, which is non-trivial since the axiom depends on the mutated fields `next` and `state`. An update $q.\texttt{f} = v$ is modeled by saying that the function modeling field `f` is changed into $\texttt{f}[q \mapsto v]$, with semantics

$$
p.\texttt{f}[q \mapsto v] = \begin{cases} v & \text{if } p = q \\ p.\texttt{f} & \text{otherwise} \end{cases} \qquad \text{(upd)}
$$

The updated values of the `next` and `state` fields relevant to A3 are:

$$
\begin{aligned}
\texttt{next'} &= \texttt{next}[\texttt{x.prev} \mapsto \texttt{x.next}][\texttt{x} \mapsto \texttt{null}] \\
\texttt{state'} &= \texttt{state}[\texttt{x} \mapsto \texttt{SLP}]
\end{aligned}
$$

We have to verify that A3 still holds:

$$
\forall q.\ \ q \neq \texttt{null} \ \wedge\ q.\texttt{next'} \neq \texttt{null} \ \Rightarrow\ q.\texttt{state'} = q.\texttt{next'.state'} \qquad \text{(goal)}
$$

To prove a formula involving updated fields, such as `q.next'`, we first eliminate the field updates by performing the case analysis suggested by the update equation (upd). In each case, what remains to be shown is that a conjunction of literals involving field accesses is unsatisfiable in the presence of some universally quantified local equality axioms.

For our example, there are twelve cases to consider: $q.\texttt{next'}$ has cases $q = \texttt{x}$, $q = \texttt{x.prev} \neq \texttt{x}$, and $q \neq \texttt{x} \wedge q \neq \texttt{x.prev}$; $q.\texttt{state'}$ has cases $q = \texttt{x}$ and $q \neq \texttt{x}$; and $q.\texttt{next'.state'}$ has cases $q.\texttt{next'} = \texttt{x}$ and $q.\texttt{next'} \neq \texttt{x}$. Several cases can be shown unsatisfiable without relying on the axioms.

Four cases require using the axioms; one such case is when $q = \texttt{x.prev} \neq \texttt{x}$ and $q.\texttt{next'} = \texttt{x}$. Consequently $q.\texttt{state'} = q.\texttt{state}$, $q.\texttt{next'} = \texttt{x.next}$ and

Injectivity	$\forall p.\ p \neq \texttt{null} \wedge p.\texttt{a} \neq \texttt{null} \Rightarrow p.\texttt{a.b} = p$
Transitivity	$\forall p.\ p \neq \texttt{null} \wedge p.\texttt{a} \neq \texttt{null} \Rightarrow p.\texttt{a.b} = p.\texttt{b}$
Order	$\forall p.\ p \neq \texttt{null} \wedge p.\texttt{a} \neq \texttt{null} \Rightarrow p.\texttt{a.b} > p.\texttt{b}$
Grid	$\forall p.\ p \neq \texttt{null} \wedge p.\texttt{a} \neq \texttt{null} \wedge p.\texttt{f} \neq \texttt{null} \Rightarrow p.\texttt{a.f} = p.\texttt{f.a}$

Fig. 2. Four important axiom forms

q.next'.state' $=$ x.next.state. We must show q.state $=$ x.next.state. We first instantiate $A2$ at x (written $A2[\texttt{x}/p]$) to derive x.prev.next $=$ x, implying q.next $=$ x. Then we instantiate $A3[q/p]$ to derive q.state $=$ x.state, and finally $A3[\texttt{x}/p]$ to derive x.state $=$ x.next.state.

The essence of the above discussion is that the verification strategy will perform case analysis based on the memory writes and will generate facts that must be proved unsatisfiable using a number of axiom instantiations. The only difficulty is how to decide what instances of axioms to use; a strategy that instantiates too few axioms will not be complete (we might fail to prove unsatisfiability), while a strategy that instantiates too many might not terminate.

2.1 Unrestricted Scalar Predicates

Scalar predicates let us connect the shape of a data structure with the data stored within it. One advantage of our specification strategy is that we we can combine our satisfiability procedure with that of any predicate that works within the framework of a Nelson-Oppen theorem prover [16]. While other approaches often abstract scalars as boolean fields [13, 19], we can reason about them precisely. For example, in order to verify that the function remove shown in Figure 1 preserves the priority ordering axiom A4, we need transitivity of $\geq$, so we use a satisfiability procedure for partial orders. We also use scalar predicates to allow descriptions for different types of objects to coexist (e.g., a list and a tree), by predicating axioms on the object's dynamic type (modeled as a field).

2.2 Useful Axiom Patterns

In the process of specifying data structures, we have identified several very useful axiom patterns; four are shown in Figure 2. For example, axiom A1 of the scheduler example is an instance of the *injectivity* pattern. Such an injectivity axiom implies useful must-not-alias facts such as $x \neq y \wedge x.\texttt{a} \neq \texttt{null} \Rightarrow x.\texttt{a} \neq y.\texttt{a}$. Injectivity can specify tree shapes as well, for example:

$$\forall p.\ p \neq \texttt{null} \wedge p.\texttt{left} \neq \texttt{null} \Rightarrow p.\texttt{left.inv} = p \wedge p.\texttt{left.kind} = L$$
$$\forall p.\ p \neq \texttt{null} \wedge p.\texttt{right} \neq \texttt{null} \Rightarrow p.\texttt{right.inv} = p \wedge p.\texttt{right.kind} = R$$

where kind is a scalar field and $L \neq R$. Such axioms specify that left and right are *mutually injective*, because inv is the inverse of their union. However, note that (to support data structures with sharing) pointers are not *required* to be injective; the user states when and where injectivity holds.

The axioms A3 and A4 from the example are similar in that they relate the value of a certain field across the next field, which is in some sense *transitive*.

A transitivity axiom can be used to say that two memory cells are in separate instances of a data structure; we used axiom A3 to require that the `runnable` and the `sleeping` lists are disjoint. More generally, we can prove the powerful must-not-reach fact $x.\mathtt{b} \neq y.\mathtt{b} \;\Rightarrow\; x.\mathtt{a}^n \neq y.\mathtt{a}^m$, where $x.\mathtt{a}^n$ means the object reached from x after following the `a` field n times. But note that transitivity axioms cannot express must-reach facts.

Axiom A4 is a non-strict *order* axiom. In its strict form it can be used to specify the absence of cycles. In this pattern, any transitive and anti-reflexive binary predicate can be used in place of >.

We defer discussion of the grid pattern to Section 1. A common theme in these patterns is that we use *equalities* and scalar predicates to imply *disequalities*, which are needed to reason precisely about updates. The interplay between equality axioms and the entailed disequalities is central to our approach.

2.3 Ghost Fields

Often, a data structure does not physically have a field that is needed to specify its shape. For example, a singly-linked list does not have the back pointers needed to witness injectivity of the forward pointers. In such cases, we propose to simply add *ghost fields* (also known as auxiliary variables, or specification fields), which are fields that our verification algorithm treats the same as "real" fields, but do not actually exist when the code is compiled and run. Thus, to specify a singly-linked list, we add `prev` as a ghost field and instead specify a doubly-linked list. For our prototype tool, the programmer must add explicit updates to ghost fields. Updates to ghost fields often follow a regular pattern, so are presumably amenable to inference, but in the limit human assistance is required [10].

2.4 Temporary Invariant Breakage

In our tool, the shape descriptions are required to accurately describe the heap at procedure entry and exit, and at all loop invariant points. But some programs *need* their invariants to be broken temporarily at such points. Our solution is to introduce a special ghost global pointer called (say) `broken`, and write axioms of the form

$$\forall p.\;\; p \neq \mathtt{broken} \;\Rightarrow\; Q(p)$$

where $Q(p)$ is the nominal invariant. Then the program can set `broken` to point at whichever object (if any) does not respect the invariant. Once the object's invariant is repaired, `broken` can be set to `null`, meaning all invariants hold.

3 The Specification Language

Figure 3 describes the main syntactic elements of the specification language. This is a two-sorted logic, with pointer values and scalar values. Scalar predicates may have any arity. We use the notation $\mathcal{E}$ for disjunctions of pointer equalities, $\mathcal{D}$ for disjunctions of pointer disequalities, and $\mathcal{C}$ for disjunctions of scalar constraints.

Globals	x	$\in$ Var		Pointer equalities	E	$::=$	$t_1 = t_2$
Variables	p	$\in$ Var		Pointer disequal.	D	$::=$	$t_1 \neq t_2$
Pointer fields	L	$\in$ PField		Scalar fields	S, R	$\in$	SField
Pointer paths	α, β	$::= \epsilon \mid \alpha.L$		Scalar predicates	P	$\in$	Pred
Pointer terms	t, u	$::= \texttt{null} \mid x \mid p.\alpha$		Scalar constraints	C	$::=$	$P(t_1.S, t_2.R)$

Fig. 3. Specification language

Core Language. We have two languages, one a subset of the other. In the core language, a *data structure specification* is a finite set of axioms of the form

$$\forall p.\ \ \mathcal{E} \vee \mathcal{C} \qquad \text{(core)}$$

where p ranges over pointer values. Axioms in the core language cannot have pointer disequalities, but can have scalar field disequalities in $\mathcal{C}$. This language is expressive enough to describe many common structures, including those of Figures 1 and 2. Section 4 describes a satisfiability procedure for this language.

Extended Language. The extended language has axioms of the form

$$\forall p.\ \ \mathcal{E} \vee \mathcal{C} \vee \mathcal{D} \qquad \text{(ext)}$$

This language is more expressive; e.g., it allows us to insist that certain pointers not be `null`, or to describe additional kinds of reachability, or to require that a structure be cyclic, among other things. Unfortunately, the extended language includes specifications with undecidable theories (see below). However, we extend the satisfiability procedure for the core language to handle many extended axioms as well, including all forms that we have encountered in our experiments.

Nullable Subterms. Data structure specification axioms naturally have the following *nullable subterms* (NS) property: for any pointer term $t.L$ or any scalar term $t.S$ that appears in the body of an axiom, the axiom also contains the equality $t = \texttt{null}$ among its disjuncts. This is because fields are not defined at `null`. We require that all axioms have the NS property.

Discussion. The keystone of our technical result is the observation that the NS property ensures the decidability of the axioms in the core language. In contrast, if we allow axioms of the form $\forall p.\ p.\alpha = p.\beta$ (in the core language, but without the NS property), then we could encode any instance of the (undecidable) "word problem" [8] as an axiom set and a satisfiability query.

Intuitively, an axiom with the nullable subterms property can be satisfied by setting to `null` any unconstrained subterms. This avoids having to materialize new terms, which in turn ensures termination. Notice however, that if we allow arbitrary pointer disequalities we can cancel the effect of the NS condition. For example, the axiom

$$\forall p.\ \ p = \texttt{null} \ \vee\ p.\mathsf{a} \neq \texttt{null}$$

forces $t.\mathtt{a}$ to be non-null for any non-null t. Thus the unrestricted use of the disequalities in $\mathcal{D}$ makes satisfiability undecidable. In our experiments we observed that pointer disequalities are needed less frequently than other forms, which motivates separate treatment of the core and extended languages.

4 A Satisfiability Algorithm

The algorithm is essentially a Nelson-Oppen theorem prover, augmented with specific matching rules for instantiating the quantified axioms, and deferred, heuristic treatment of disequalities among uninstantiated terms.

4.1 The Algorithm

The purpose of the algorithm is to determine whether a set of local equality axioms and a set of ground (unquantified) facts is satisfiable. When used on axioms without pointer disequalities (core language) the algorithm always terminates with a definite answer. However, in the presence of axioms with pointer disequalities (extended language) the algorithm may return "maybe satisfiable". Note that pointer disequalities in the ground facts do not endanger completeness.

The basic idea of the algorithm is to exploit the observation that in a data structure described by local axioms, when the facts are satisfiable, they are satisfiable by a "small" model. Essentially, the algorithm attempts to construct such a model by setting any unknown values to null.

The algorithm's central data structure is an equality graph (e-graph) G [16], a congruence-closed representation of the ground facts. We use the notation $t \in G$ to mean term t is *represented* in G, and $G \wedge f$ to mean the e-graph obtained by adding representatives of the terms in formula f to G, and asserting f.

The algorithm must decide which axioms to instantiate and for which terms. We first define when a ground pointer term u matches an equality disjunct $t_1 = t_2$ in an axiom with bound (quantified) variable p, as follows:

- Either $t_1[u/p] \in G$ or $t_2[u/p] \in G$, when neither t_1 nor t_2 is null, or
- t_1 is null and $t_2[u/p] \in G$ (or vice-versa).

We say that a term matches an axiom if it *matches all its pointer equality disjuncts.* An axiom is instantiated with any term that matches the axiom.

These rules implement an "all/most" strategy of instantiation. For example, an axiom

$$\forall p. \ \ldots \ \vee \ p.\alpha.\mathtt{a} = p.\beta.\mathtt{b}$$

must include (because of NS) disjuncts $p.\alpha = \mathtt{null}$ and $p.\beta = \mathtt{null}$. For a ground term u to match this axiom, it must match every equality disjunct (from the definition above), so $u.\alpha$, $u.\beta$, and either $u.\alpha.\mathtt{a}$ or $u.\beta.\mathtt{b}$ must be represented. Consequently, asserting the literal $u.\alpha.\mathtt{a} = u.\beta.\mathtt{b}$ will require representing at most one new term, *but no new equivalence classes.*

If G is an e-graph, and DS is a conjunction (i.e., a set) of disjunctions of pointer disequalities, we define a satisfiability procedure $\mathtt{unsat}(G, DS)$ that returns true if the facts represented in G along with DS and the axioms are

```
1 unsat(G, DS) =
2   if G is contradictory then true
3   elseif DS = (DS' ∧ false) then true
4   elseif a term u ∈ G matches axiom ∀p. ℰ ∨ 𝒞 ∨ 𝒟,
5          not yet instantiated for class of u, then
6     for each t1 = t2 ∈ ℰ,
7       unsat(G ∧ t1[u/p] = t2[u/p], DS);
8     for each P(t1.S, t2.R) ∈ 𝒞,
9       unsat(G ∧ P(t1[u/p].S, t2[u/p].R), DS);
10    unsat(G, DS ∧ 𝒟[u/p])
11  elseif DS = true then
12    raise Satisfiable(G)
13  elseif DS = (DS' ∧ (t1 ≠ t2 ∨ 𝒟))
14         with t1 ∈ G and t2 ∈ G, then
15    unsat(G ∧ t1 ≠ t2, DS');
16    unsat(G, DS' ∧ 𝒟)
17  else   /* search for a cyclic model */
18    for each term t1 ∉ G where t1 ≠ t2 ∈ DS,
19      for each term t3 ∈ G,
20        unsat(G ∧ t1 = t3, DS);
21    raise MaybeSatisfiable   /* give up */
```

Fig. 4. The basic decision algorithm

unsatisfiable, raises the exception `Satisfiable` if it is satisfiable, and raises the exception `MaybeSatisfiable` if the procedure cannot decide satisfiability (in presence of axioms with pointer disequalities). Figure 4 contains the pseudocode for this procedure. This procedure is used by first representing the facts in an e-graph G, and then invoking $\texttt{unsat}(G, \texttt{true})$.

Lines 2 and 3 identify contradictions in the e-graph. The judgment "G is contradictory" may make use of a separate satisfiability procedure for the scalar predicates. We write $DS = (DS' \wedge \texttt{false})$ to deconstruct DS. The heart of the algorithm is in lines 4–10, which instantiate axioms with terms that match, given the matching rules described above, and performs the case analysis dictated by the instantiated axioms. Note that the pointer disequalities are deferred by collecting them in DS (line 10). When line 12 is reached, the axioms are completely instantiated and all cases fully analyzed, but no contradiction has been found. Thus, the original $G \wedge DS$ was satisfiable; the current G is a witness.

Lines 13–16 handle pointer disequalities where both sides are already represented in the e-graph. Finally, lines 17–20 attempt to find a satisfying assignment for the unrepresented terms in DS by setting them equal to other terms that *are* represented. The algorithm searches for cyclic models to accommodate data structures like cyclic lists.

Recalling the proof from Section 2 that A3 holds after `next` and `state` have been modified, we can now explain how the algorithm would prove it. First, the update rules are used to split the proof into cases; among those cases is $q \neq \texttt{x} \wedge q = \texttt{x.prev} \wedge \texttt{x.next} \neq \texttt{x}$, which (along with the precondition) is used to initialize G, and `unsat(`G`, true)` is invoked. Next, the algorithm determines that the term `x` matches axiom $A2$, because `x.prev` $\in G$, and begins asserting its disjuncts. Only the `x.prev.next` $=$ `x` disjunct is not immediately refuted. Asserting this literal causes the new term `x.prev.next` to be represented, by putting it into the same equivalence class as `x`. Since $q =$ `x.prev`, the term q`.next` is now represented, and so q matches $A3$, and $A3[q/p]$ is instantiated. Finally, as `x.next` is represented, $A3[\texttt{x}/p]$ is also instantiated. After these three instantiations, case analysis and reasoning about equality are sufficient.

4.2 Analysis of the Algorithm

Correctness when result is "Unsatisfiable". The algorithm is always right when it claims unsatisfiability, which in our methodology means that the goal is proved. The (omitted) proof is a straightforward induction on the recursion.

Correctness when result is "Satisfiable". When the algorithm raises `Satisfiable(`G'`)`, there is a model Ψ that satisfies the original $G \wedge DS \wedge \mathcal{A}$, where $\mathcal{A}$ is the set of axioms:

$$\Psi(u) = \begin{cases} u^* & \text{if } u \in G' \\ \texttt{null} & \text{otherwise} \end{cases}$$

where by u^* we denote the representative of u in the e-graph G'. Ψ satisfies $\mathcal{A}$ because for every pointer term u (represented or not) and axiom A, either $A[u/p]$ has been instantiated, so G' satisfies $A[u/p]$ (and so does Ψ), or else u does not match A, in which case there is a pointer equality $t_1 = t_2$ in A that does not match. By the definition of matching, there are two cases:

- Neither t_1 nor t_2 are `null`, and $t_1[u/p] \notin G$ and $t_2[u/p] \notin G$. But then $\Psi(t_1[u/p]) = \Psi(t_2[u/p]) = \texttt{null}$, satisfying $A[u/p]$.
- t_1 is `null` and $t_2[u/p] \notin G$. Then $\Psi(t_2[u/p]) = \texttt{null}$, satisfying $A[u/p]$.

That is, the matching rules guarantee that if an axiom has not been instantiated, it can be satisfied by setting unrepresented terms to `null`.

Termination. The essence of the termination argument is that none of the steps of the algorithm increases the number of pointer equivalence classes in the e-graph. Whenever a new pointer term t might be created in the process of extending the e-graph, it is created while adding the fact $t = t'$, where t' is already in the e-graph. This is ensured by the matching rule that requires one side of each equality to be present in the e-graph. Furthermore, if t is of the form $t''.L$, then by the NS property, the disjunct $t'' = \texttt{null}$ is also part of axiom and thus the matching rule requires t'' to be already in the e-graph. Thus t is the only new term and is added to an existing equivalence class. There are only a finite number of equality and scalar constraints over a fixed number of pointer equivalence classes; once all entailed constraints are found, the algorithm halts.

Soundness and completeness on the Core Language. For the core language, the algorithm stays above line 13, because DS is always empty (`true`). As it always terminates, it must always return either Satisfiable or Unsatisfiable.

Complexity. The algorithm has exponential complexity, because of the case analysis that is performed in processing updates and conditional axioms. If we have n nodes in the e-graph representing the facts, a axioms with at most k disjuncts each, then there could be a total of $n \times a$ axiom instantiations. We can think of the algorithm exploring a state space that resembles a tree. Each node in the tree corresponds to an instance of an axiom, and has a branching factor k. Consequently its running time is $O(k^{na} S(n))$, where $S(n)$ is the complexity bound for the underlying satisfiability procedure for scalar constraints.

5 Disequalities

Axioms with disequalities are necessary for specifying some shape properties, such as never-`null` pointers and cyclic structures. These often take the form of *termination conditions*, for example

$$\forall p.\ Q(p) \ \Rightarrow\ p.\mathtt{next} \neq \mathtt{null}$$

This poses a challenge for automated reasoning, as the basic approach is to search for a finite model, so we try to set pointers to `null` wherever possible, but setting p.`next` to `null` is impossible if $Q(p)$ is known to be true.

In the context of the algorithm in Figure 4, this issue arises when we reach line 17: all axioms have been instantiated, and G is consistent, but there remain some disequalities DS among terms not represented in G. We cannot report satisfiability because the consequences of DS have not yet been considered.

One approach, shown in Figure 4, is to explicitly check for a cyclic model: try setting unrepresented terms equal to existing terms. When the axioms describe a cyclic structure, this may be the only way to find a finite model.

Another approach (not shown in the figure for reasons of space) is to simply grow the model, representing the terms in DS by creating new equivalence classes. Of course, doing so jeopardizes termination, since the new equivalence classes may trigger additional axiom instantiations. So, the programmer may specify an expansion horizon k, and the algorithm will then not create an equivalence class more than k "hops" away from the original set of classes. Typically, we use the bound $k = 2$.

If the heuristics fail, the algorithm may report `MaybeSatisfiable`; but the algorithm will never make a false claim (in particular, the expansion bound is not involved in a claim of unsatisfiability).

More generally (and optimistically), it is possible to show for specific axiom sets that the above heuristics are *complete*: that the algorithm will never report `MaybeSatisfiable`. However, it remains future work to develop a systematic way of constructing completeness arguments for axiom sets containing disequalities.

6 Experiments

Our algorithm has been implemented as a modified version of the Simplify [2] theorem prover. To evaluate the expressiveness of our specification language, we compare our prototype verifier to the Pointer Assertion Logic Engine (PALE) [13]. To measure the effectiveness of our decision algorithm, we compare it to the unmodified Simplify. For several example programs, we measure the lines of annotation, which axiom forms are used (from Figure 2, plus disequalities), and the time to verify on a 1.1GHz Athlon Linux PC with 768MB RAM. See Figure 5.

		Annot. lines		Axiom Forms					Verify Time (s)		
example	LOC	PALE	Ours	$\neq$	inj	trans	order	grid	PALE	Simplify	Ours
`bubblesort`	47	10	31		2				1.9	0.9	0.6
`doublylinked`	73	35	69		4	1			2.6	2.9	1.9
`taillist`	73	38	94	3	4	4			2.4	1.8	1.3
`redblacktree`	146	112	224		4		4		19.4	36.5	22.0
`gc_copy`	38		58	1	1			2		50.2	15.6
`btree`	163		185	2	7	4	6			96.7	26.4
`set_as_list`	36		73	1	2	1	4			1.9	1.3
`pc_keyb`	1116		163	2						40.1	38.1
`scull`	534		360	4	5					58.2	46.4

Fig. 5. Programs verified, with comparison to PALE when available

We are able to verify all of the examples distributed with PALE[1], however PALE requires less than half the lines of annotation. There are three reasons: (1) in PALE, the backbone tree is concisely specified by the `data` keyword, whereas our axioms must spell it out with injectivity, (2) PALE specifications use transitive closure, whereas we use the more verbose transitivity axioms, and (3) our language does not assume the program is type-safe (it is C, after all), so we have explicit axioms to declare where typing invariants hold. We plan to add forms of syntactic sugar to address these points.

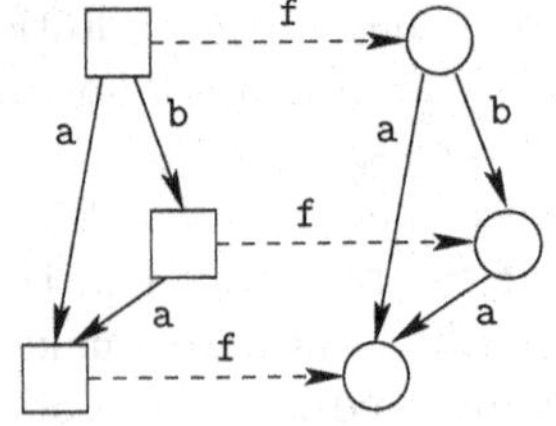

We also selected two data structures that cannot be specified in PALE. `gc_copy` is the copy phase of a copying garbage collector, and has the job of building an isomorphic copy of the from-space, as shown at right. This isomorphism, embodied by the forwarding pointers `f`, is specified by the "grid" or "homomorphism" axiom $\forall p.\ \ldots \Rightarrow p.\mathtt{a}.\mathtt{f} = p.\mathtt{f}.\mathtt{a}$. This axiom (along with injectivity of `f`) describes a data structure where the targets of `f` pointers are isomorphic images of the sources.

[1] In the case of the `taillist` example, the verified property is slightly weaker due to the encoding of reachability via transitivity.

The btree benchmark is a B+-tree implementation, interesting in part because we can verify that the tree is *balanced*, by using scalar constraints

$$\begin{array}{lll}\forall p. & p \neq \texttt{null} \wedge p.\texttt{left} \neq \texttt{null} & \Rightarrow p.\texttt{level} = p.\texttt{left.level} + 1 \\ \forall p. & p \neq \texttt{null} \wedge p.\texttt{right} \neq \texttt{null} & \Rightarrow p.\texttt{level} = p.\texttt{right.level} + 1\end{array}$$

along with disequality constraints that force all leaves to have the same level:

$$\begin{array}{lll}\forall p. & p \neq \texttt{null} \wedge p.\texttt{left} = \texttt{null} & \Rightarrow p.\texttt{level} = 0 \\ \forall p. & p \neq \texttt{null} \wedge p.\texttt{right} = \texttt{null} & \Rightarrow p.\texttt{level} = 0\end{array}$$

However, this specification is also noteworthy because there is no bound k on the size of models as advocated in Section 5: the facts $x.\texttt{level} = 100$ and $x \neq \texttt{null}$ (plus the axioms) are satisfiable only by models with at least 100 elements. Fortunately, such pathological hypotheses do not seem to arise in practice.

The set_as_list example uses a linked list to represent a set. We use a ghost field s, associated with each node in the list, with intended invariant

$$\forall n.\ \ n.\texttt{s} = \{\ x \ \mid\ \exists i \in \mathbb{N}.\ \ n(.\texttt{next})^i.\texttt{data} = x\ \}$$

That is, s contains all data elements at or below the node. But since our language does not allow "$n(.\texttt{next})^i$", we instead write

$$\begin{array}{llll} S1. & \forall n. & n.\texttt{next} \neq \texttt{null} & \Rightarrow n.s = \{n.\texttt{data}\} \cup n.\texttt{next}.s \\ S2. & \forall n. & n.\texttt{next} = \texttt{null} & \Rightarrow n.s = \{n.\texttt{data}\}\end{array}$$

Axiom S1 imposes a lower bound on s, allowing one to conclude (among other things) must-not-reach facts. Axiom S2 imposes an upper bound, and allows conclusion of must-reach facts, but includes a pointer disequality disjunct. To reason about set-theoretic concepts, we use the procedure in [1]. This example highlights the way our technique can integrate with powerful off-the-shelf "scalar" concepts to specify the relationship between shape and data.

Finally, pc_keyb and scull are two Linux device drivers. These real-world examples demonstrate the applicability of the technique, and the benefits of integrated pointer and scalar reasoning; for example, their data structures feature arrays of pointers, which are difficult to model in PALE or TVLA.

An important contribution of this work is the particular matching rules used to instantiate the axioms. Simplify has heuristics for creating matching rules for arbitrary universally-quantified facts. As expected, we find that our matching rules, which instantiate the axioms in strictly fewer circumstances, lead to better performance (compare timing columns "Simplify" and "Ours" in Figure 5). In fact, Simplify's heuristics will often lead to infinite matching loops, especially while trying to find counterexamples for invalid goals. This is not to denounce Simplify's heuristics—they do a good job for a wide variety of axiom sets—just to emphasize that in the case of axioms expressing data structure shape within our methodology, one can have a more efficient and predictable algorithm.

7 Related Work

As explained in Section 1, most existing approaches to specifying shape are either too imprecise or too difficult to reason about automatically. Here, we consider alternative approaches with similar expressiveness and effectiveness.

PALE [13], the Pointer Assertion Logic Engine, uses graph types [7] to specify a data structure as consisting of a spanning tree backbone augmented with auxiliary pointers. One disadvantage is the restriction that the data structure have a tree backbone: disequality constraints that force certain pointers to not be `null` are not possible, since every tree pointer is implicitly nullable, cyclic structures are awkward, and grid structures such as the garbage collector example in Section 1 are impossible. The second disadvantage is that only boolean scalar fields are allowed. Thus, all scalar values must first be abstracted into a set of boolean ghost fields, and updates inserted accordingly.

TVLA [12, 19], the Three Valued Logic Analyzer, uses abstract interpretation over a heap description that includes 1/2 or "don't know" values. It obtains shape precision through the use of *instrumentation predicates*, which are essentially ghost boolean fields with values defined by logical formulas. In general, the programmer specifies how instrumentation predicates evolve across updates, though TVLA can conservatively infer update rules that are often sufficiently precise. The primary advantage of TVLA is it infers loop invariants automatically, by fixpoint iteration. The disadvantage is that the obligation of proving that a shape is preserved across updates is delegated to the instrumentation predicate evolution rules, which are not fully automated. Also, as with PALE, scalar values must be abstracted as boolean instrumentation predicates.

PALE and TVLA include transitive closure operators, and hence can reason directly about reachability, but they pay a price: PALE has non-elementary complexity and requires tree backbones, and TVLA has difficulty evolving instrumentation predicates when they use transitive closure. The difficulties of reasoning about transitive closure have been recently explored by Immerman et. al [6], with significant negative decidability results. Our technique is to approximate reachability using transitivity axioms, giving up some shape precision in exchange for more precision with respect to scalar values.

The shape analysis algorithm of Hackett and Rugina [5] partitions the heap into regions and infers points-to relationships among them. Its shape descriptions are less precise; it can describe singly-linked lists but not doubly-linked lists.

Roles [9] characterize an object by the types it points to, and the types that point at it. Role specifications are similar to our injectivity axioms. The role analysis in [9] provides greater automation but it can express fewer shapes.

Separation logic [18] includes a notion of temporal locality, exploited by a frame rule that allows reasoning about only those heap areas accessed by a procedure. We believe such a notion is essentially orthogonal to, and could be useful with, the spatial locality notions of this paper.

Early work on data structures showed that the property of an object being *uniquely generated* (e.g., every instance of `cons(1,2)` is the same object) has decidable consequences [17], a result related to the decidability of the consequences of the injectivity axioms presented here. However, the early work does not admit more refined notions of shape, as it does not address the use of quantifiers.

Our work uses methods most similar to the Extended Static Checker [3] and Boogie/Spec# [11]. However, while we suspect that specifications similar to elements described here have been written before while verifying programs, we are unaware of any attempts to explore their expressiveness or decidability.

8 Conclusion

We have presented a language for describing data structure shapes along with scalar field relationships. The language is relatively simple because it can only talk about local properties of a neighborhood of nodes, yet is capable of expressing a wide range of global shape constraints sufficient to imply the kind of must-not-alias information needed for strong update reasoning. Furthermore, it is sufficiently tractable to admit a simple decision procedure, extensible with arbitrary decidable scalar predicates. Using this language we have verified a number of small example programs, of both theoretical and practical interest.

References

1. D. Cantone and C. G. Zarba. A new fast decision procedure for an unquantified fragment of set theory. In *First-Order Theorem Proving*, pages 97–105, 1998.
2. D. Detlefs, G. Nelson, and J. B. Saxe. Simplify: A theorem prover for program checking. Technical Report HPL-2003-148, HP Labs, July 2003.
3. D. L. Detlefs, K. R. M. Leino, G. Nelson, and J. B. Saxe. Extended static checking. Technical Report SRC-159, COMPAQ SRC, Palo Alto, USA, Dec. 1998.
4. P. Fradet and D. L. Métayer. Shape types. In *POPL*, pages 27–39, 1997.
5. B. Hackett and R. Rugina. Region-based shape analysis with tracked locations. In *POPL*, pages 310–323, 2005.
6. N. Immerman, A. Rabinovich, T. Reps, M. Sagiv, and G. Yorsh. The boundary between decidability and undecidability for transitive-closure logics. In *CSL*, 2004.
7. N. Klarlund and M. Schwartzbach. Graph types. In *POPL*, pages 196–205, 1993.
8. D. E. Knuth and P. B. Bendix. Simple word problems in universal algebra. In J. Leech, editor, *Computational Problems in Abstract Algebras*, pages 263–297. Pergamon Press, 1970.
9. V. Kuncak, P. Lam, and M. Rinard. Role analysis. In *POPL*, pages 17–32, 2002.
10. V. Kuncak and M. Rinard. Existential heap abstraction entailment is undecidable. In *SAS*, pages 418–438, 2003.
11. K. R. M. Leino and P. Müller. Object invariants in dynamic contexts. In *European Conference on Object-Oriented Programming (ECOOP)*, 2004.
12. T. Lev-Ami and S. Sagiv. TVLA: A system for implementing static analyses. In *Static Analysis Symposium*, pages 280–301, 2000.
13. A. Möller and M. Schwartzbach. The pointer assertion logic engine. In *PLDI*, pages 221–231, 2001.
14. G. Nelson. Techniques for program verification. Technical Report CSL-81-10, Xerox Palo Alto Research Center, 1981.
15. G. Nelson. Verifying reachability invariants of linked structures. In *POPL*, pages 38–47, 1983.

16. G. Nelson and D. C. Oppen. Fast decision procedures based on congruence closure. *JACM*, 27(2):356–364, Apr. 1980.
17. D. C. Oppen. Reasoning about recursively defined data structures. *JACM*, 27(3):403–411, July 1980.
18. J. C. Reynolds. Separation logic: A logic for shared mutable data structures. In *Logic in Computer Science*, pages 55–74, 2002.
19. S. Sagiv, T. W. Reps, and R. Wilhelm. Parametric shape analysis via 3-valued logic. *TOPLAS*, 24(3):217–298, 2002.

Linear Ranking with Reachability*

Aaron R. Bradley, Zohar Manna, and Henny B. Sipma

Computer Science Department, Stanford University,
Stanford, CA 94305-9045
{arbrad, zm, sipma}@theory.stanford.edu

Abstract. We present a complete method for synthesizing *lexicographic linear ranking functions* supported by inductive linear invariants for loops with linear guards and transitions. Proving termination via linear ranking functions often requires invariants; yet invariant generation is expensive. Thus, we describe a technique that discovers just the invariants necessary for proving termination. Finally, we describe an implementation of the method and provide extensive experimental evidence of its effectiveness for proving termination of C loops.

1 Introduction

Guaranteed termination of program loops is necessary in many settings, such as embedded systems and safety critical software. Additionally, proving general temporal properties of infinite state programs requires termination proofs, for which automatic methods are welcome [19, 11, 15]. We propose a termination analysis of linear loops based on the synthesis of lexicographic linear ranking functions supported by linear invariants.

The method exploits the *constraint-based* approach to static analysis. In constraint-based analysis, a property *template* is constrained by high-level conditions that describe the desired property. These high-level conditions induce a constraint system; its solutions are valid instantiations of the template. For example, [3] describes how to generate linear invariants of linear transition systems via the constraint-based approach. In contrast to classical symbolic simulation, constraint-based analyses are not limited to invariants; for example, [4, 5] describes how to apply the constraint-based approach to generate linear ranking functions to prove loop termination.

Our approach to termination analysis has two distinct features over previous work on ranking function synthesis and constraint-based analysis. First, we combine the generation of ranking functions with the generation of invariants to form one constraint solving problem. This combination makes invariant generation *implicit*: the necessary *supporting* invariants for the ranking function are

* This research was supported in part by NSF grants CCR-01-21403, CCR-02-20134, CCR-02-09237, CNS-0411363, and CCF-0430102, by ARO grant DAAD19-01-1-0723, and by NAVY/ONR contract N00014-03-1-0939. The first author was additionally supported by a Sang Samuel Wang Stanford Graduate Fellowship.

K. Etessami and S.K. Rajamani (Eds.): CAV 2005, LNCS 3576, pp. 491–504, 2005.

discovered on demand. In [4,5], the generation of ranking functions was supported by independently generated invariants. Second, we take constraint-based analysis one step further in combining *structural* constraints with *numeric* constraints, which allows us to specify a set of templates for the ranking function components and solve for a *lexicographic* linear ranking function. The numeric constraints arise, as usual, from placing conditions on the template coefficients. The structural constraints arise from requiring a lexicographic ordering among the ranking function components, which constrains the conditions that should be applied. Consequently, our solving strategy alternates between adding or removing ordering constraints and solving the resulting numeric constraint systems. We propose two main components to the solving strategy: first, the numeric constraint solver quickly solves the special form of *parametric linear constraints* that arise; second, the higher-level solver searches for a lexicographic ranking function. The latter is theoretically complete, in that if a lexicographic ordering exists, it will be found; moreover, it is fast in practice.

Automatic synthesis of linear ranking functions has received a fair amount of attention. In [8], Katz and Manna show how to generate constraint systems over loops with linear assertional guards and linear assignments for which solutions are linear ranking functions. Synthesis of linear ranking functions over linear loops with multiple paths and assertional transition relations is accomplished via polyhedral manipulation in [4,5]. In [14], Podelski and Rybalchenko specialize the technique to single-path linear loops without an initial condition, providing an efficient and complete synthesis method based on linear programming. We generalize these previous efforts.

Automatic synthesis of ranking functions is applicable in at least two ways. First, it can serve as the main component of an automated program analysis. We provide empirical evidence of its effectiveness at analyzing loops that arise in C programs. Second, it can support theoretically complete verification frameworks like *verification diagrams* [11] and *transition invariants* [15] (see also [6,9,1] for related ideas). In this context, the user guides the construction of the proof with support from automatic invariant generation and ranking function synthesis. A *verification diagram* is a state-based abstraction of the reachable state-space of a program. A *transition invariant* is a relation-based abstraction of the transition relation of a program. Its form is a disjunctive set of relations. Ramsey's Theorem ensures that if each of the relations is well-founded, then the transition relation is well-founded. Both frameworks identify the semantic behavior of a loop, so that its infinite behavior can be expressed disjunctively. In a verification diagram, a loop might manifest itself in multiple strongly connected components of the diagram, each of which can have a different ranking function. Similarly, in a transition invariant, each disjunct can have a different ranking function. In many cases, these multiple ranking functions are simpler than a single global ranking function, so that it is reasonable to expect that automatic synthesis can usually replace the user in proposing ranking functions.

The rest of the paper is organized as follows. Section 2 introduces basic concepts and mathematical tools. Section 3 presents the constraint generation technique. Section 4 describes the method for synthesizing lexicographic functions in practice, while Section 5 discusses our approach to solving the generated numeric constraint systems. Section 6 presents empirical data from applying our analysis to C programs. Section 7 concludes.

2 Preliminaries

We first define our loop abstraction based on sets of linear transitions. Subsequently, we formalize ranking functions and inductive invariants in the context of loops. Finally, we present Farkas's Lemma.

Definition 1 (Linear Assertion). *An* atom *over a set of variables* $\mathcal{V}$: $\{x_1, \ldots, x_m\}$ *is an affine inequality over* $\mathcal{V}$: $a_1x_1 + a_2x_2 + \cdots + a_mx_m + b \geq 0$. *Letting* $\mathbf{x} = (x_1, x_2, \ldots, x_m, 1)^{\mathrm{T}}$, *we also write* $\mathbf{a}^{\mathrm{T}}\mathbf{x} \geq 0$, *where* $\mathbf{a}_{m+1} = b$. *A linear assertion over* $\mathcal{V}$ *is a conjunction of inequalities over the program variables, written (as a matrix in homogenized form)* $\mathbf{A}\mathbf{x} \geq 0$.

```
int gcd(int y1 > 0, int y2 > 0) :
  while y1 ≠ y2 do
    if y1 > y2 then
      y1 := y1 − y2
    else
      y2 := y2 − y1
  return y1
```

(a)

$$\Theta : \{y_1 \geq 1,\ y_2 \geq 1\}$$
$$\tau_1 : \{y_1 \geq y_2 + 1\} \Rightarrow \{y_1' = y_1 - y_2,\ y_2' = y_2\}$$
$$\tau_2 : \{y_2 \geq y_1 + 1\} \Rightarrow \{y_2' = y_2 - y_1,\ y_1' = y_1\}$$

(b)

Fig. 1. (a) Program GCD for finding the greatest common divisor of two positive integers. **(b)** Path-sensitive abstraction to set of guarded commands

Definition 2 (Guarded Command). *A* guarded command $\tau(\mathcal{V}) : g(\mathcal{V}) \Rightarrow u(\mathcal{V}, \mathcal{V}')$ *over a set of variables* $\mathcal{V}$ *consists of a guard* $g(\mathcal{V})$, *which is a linear assertion over* $\mathcal{V}$, *and an update* $u(\mathcal{V}, \mathcal{V}')$, *which is a linear assertion over primed and unprimed variables in* $\mathcal{V}$. *Letting* $(\mathbf{x}\mathbf{x}') = (x_1, x_2, \ldots, x_m, x_1', x_2', \ldots, x_m', 1)^{\mathrm{T}}$, *we also write* $\tau(\mathbf{x}\mathbf{x}') \geq 0$.

Definition 3 (Loop). *A* loop $L : \langle G,\ \Theta\rangle$ *over* $\mathcal{V}$ *consists of a set of guarded commands* G *over* $\mathcal{V}$ *and an initial condition* Θ, *a linear assertion over* $\mathcal{V}$. *We sometimes write* $\Theta\mathbf{x} \geq 0$, *viewing* Θ *as a homogenized matrix of coefficients.*

Definition 4 (Loop Satisfaction). *A loop* $L : \langle G,\ \Theta\rangle$ *over* $\mathcal{V}$ *satisfies an assertion* φ, *written* $L \models \varphi$, *if* φ *holds in all reachable states of* L.

Example 1. Consider the program GCD in Figure 1**(a)**, which computes the greatest common divisor of two positive integers [10]. Figure 1**(b)** presents the program as a *loop*. Strict inequalities are translated into weak inequalities based on the integer type of the variables.

To show that a loop is terminating, it is sufficient to exhibit a *ranking function*. In this paper we focus on lexicographic linear ranking functions.

Definition 5 (Lexicographic Linear Ranking Function). *A* lexicographic linear ranking function *for a loop* $L : \langle G,\ \Theta\rangle$ *over* $\mathcal{V}$ *is an* n*-tuple of affine expressions* $\langle \mathbf{r_1}^{\mathrm{T}}\mathbf{x},\ \ldots,\ \mathbf{r_n}^{\mathrm{T}}\mathbf{x}\rangle$ *such that for some* $\epsilon > 0$ *and for each* $\tau \in G$*, for some* $i \in \{1, \ldots, n\}$,

(Bounded) $L \models\ \tau(\mathbf{xx'}) \geq 0 \rightarrow \mathbf{r_i}^{\mathrm{T}}\mathbf{x} \geq 0$;
(Ranking) $L \models\ \tau(\mathbf{xx'}) \geq 0 \rightarrow \mathbf{r_i}^{\mathrm{T}}\mathbf{x} - \mathbf{r_i}^{\mathrm{T}}\mathbf{x'} \geq \epsilon$;
(Unaffecting) *for* $j < i$, $L \models\ \tau(\mathbf{xx'}) \geq 0 \rightarrow \mathbf{r_j}^{\mathrm{T}}\mathbf{x} - \mathbf{r_j}^{\mathrm{T}}\mathbf{x'} \geq 0$.

A (non-lexicographic) linear ranking function is simply the case in which $n = 1$.

For some loops, invariants are necessary to prove that a function is actually a ranking function for the loop; we say such invariants are *supporting* invariants. While in theory, supporting invariants may be of any type, we focus on linear invariants in this paper.

Definition 6 (Linear Inductive Invariant). *A (homogenized) linear assertion* $\mathbf{Ix} \geq 0$ *is an inductive invariant of a loop* $L : \langle G,\ \Theta\rangle$ *if it holds at the start of the loop and it is preserved by all guarded commands. Formally, a* linear inductive invariant *satisfies the following conditions:*

(Initiation) $\Theta\mathbf{x} \geq 0 \rightarrow \mathbf{Ix} \geq 0$;
(Consecution) *for every* $\tau \in G$, $\mathbf{Ix} \geq 0 \wedge \tau(\mathbf{xx'}) \geq 0 \rightarrow \mathbf{Ix'} \geq 0$.

As we are working only with linear transitions, linear ranking functions, and linear invariants, Farkas's Lemma [18] will both justify completeness claims and serve as a tool for encoding and solving conditions for synthesizing ranking functions.

Theorem 1 (Farkas's Lemma). *Consider the following system of affine inequalities over real variables* $\mathcal{V} = \{x_1, \ldots, x_m\}$*:*

$$S : \begin{bmatrix} A_{1,1}x_1 + \cdots + A_{1,m}x_m + A_{1,m+1} \geq 0 \\ \vdots \qquad\qquad \vdots \qquad\qquad \vdots \\ A_{n,1}x_1 + \cdots + A_{n,m}x_m + A_{n,m+1} \geq 0 \end{bmatrix}$$

If S *is satisfiable, it entails affine inequality* $c_1x_1 + \cdots + c_mx_m + c_{m+1} \geq 0$ *iff there exist real numbers* $\lambda_1, \ldots, \lambda_n \geq 0$ *such that*

$$c_1 = \sum_{i=1}^{n} \lambda_i A_{i,1} \quad \cdots \quad c_m = \sum_{i=1}^{n} \lambda_i A_{i,m} \quad c_{m+1} \geq \left(\sum_{i=1}^{n} \lambda_i A_{i,m+1}\right).$$

Furthermore, S *is unsatisfiable iff* S *entails* $-1 \geq 0$.

For notational convenience we represent applications of Farkas's Lemma by means of assertions in homogenized form as before, without explicitly mentioning the multipliers λ. Thus, for example, we write

$$\frac{\mathbf{Ax} \geq 0}{\mathbf{Cx} \geq 0} \qquad \text{where} \qquad \mathbf{x} = (x_1, x_2, \ldots, x_m, 1)^{\mathrm{T}}.$$

3 Constraint Generation

Our approach for finding (lexicographic) ranking functions is based on a *template* ranking function, consisting of a (set of) affine expression(s) over $\mathcal{V}$ with unknown coefficients, and a *template* supporting invariant, consisting of an n-conjunct linear assertion with $n(|\mathcal{V}|+1)$ unknown coefficients. Conditions on the templates ensure that any solution to the induced constraint system represents a ranking function and its supporting invariants. Farkas's Lemma provides a means of translating some high-level conditions to numeric constraints. Structural conditions (*i.e.*, ordering constraints among components) are enforced via the specific set of high-level conditions that are applied.

Definition 7 (Template Expression). *A* template expression *over* $\mathcal{V}$ *is an affine expression* $c_1x_1 + \cdots + c_mx_m + c_{m+1}$, *or* $\mathbf{c}^{\mathrm{T}}\mathbf{x}$, *with unknown coefficients* $\mathbf{c}$. *A* template assertion *is a linear assertion* $\bigwedge_i \mathbf{c_i}^{\mathrm{T}}\mathbf{x} \geq 0$, *or* $\mathbf{Cx} \geq 0$.

The application of Farkas's Lemma takes a system of linear assertions and templates and returns a *dual* numeric constraint system over the λ-multipliers and the unknown template coefficients. Given a loop $L : \langle G,\ \Theta\rangle$, the supporting invariant template $\mathbf{Ix} \geq 0$, and lexicographic ranking function template $\{\mathbf{c_1}^{\mathrm{T}}\mathbf{x},\ \ldots, \mathbf{c_n}^{\mathrm{T}}\mathbf{x}\}$, the following Farkas's Lemma *specializations* are applied to encode the appropriate conditions.

(Initiation) The supporting invariant includes the initial condition.

$$\mathbb{I} \stackrel{\text{def}}{=} \frac{\Theta\mathbf{x} \geq \mathbf{0}}{\mathbf{Ix} \geq \mathbf{0}}$$

(Disabled) Transition $\tau_i \in G$ and the invariant may contradict each other, indicating "dead code."

$$\mathbb{D}_i \stackrel{\text{def}}{=} \frac{\begin{array}{ll}\mathbf{Ix} & \geq \mathbf{0}\\ \tau_i(\mathbf{xx'}) & \geq \mathbf{0}\end{array}}{-1 \quad \geq \mathbf{0}}$$

(Consecution) For transition $\tau_i \in G$, if the invariant holds and the transition is taken, then the invariant holds in the next state.

$$\mathbb{C}_i \stackrel{\text{def}}{=} \frac{\begin{array}{ll}\mathbf{Ix} & \geq \mathbf{0}\\ \tau_i(\mathbf{xx'}) & \geq \mathbf{0}\end{array}}{\mathbf{Ix'} \quad \geq \mathbf{0}}$$

(Bounded) For transition $\tau_i \in G$ and ranking function component $\mathbf{c_j}^{\mathrm{T}}\mathbf{x}$, the invariant and transition imply the nonnegativity of the ranking function component.

$$\mathbb{B}_{ij} \stackrel{\text{def}}{=} \frac{\begin{array}{ll}\mathbf{Ix} & \geq \mathbf{0}\\ \tau_i(\mathbf{xx'}) & \geq \mathbf{0}\end{array}}{\mathbf{c_j}^{\mathrm{T}}\mathbf{x} \quad \geq \mathbf{0}}$$

(Ranking) For transition $\tau_i \in G$ and ranking function component $\mathbf{c_j}^{\mathrm{T}}\mathbf{x}$, taking the transition decreases the linear ranking function by at least some positive amount ($\epsilon > 0$).

$$\mathbb{R}_{ij} \stackrel{\text{def}}{=} \frac{\begin{array}{ll}\mathbf{Ix} & \geq \mathbf{0} \\ \tau_i(\mathbf{xx'}) & \geq \mathbf{0}\end{array}}{\mathbf{c_j}^{\mathrm{T}}\mathbf{x} - \mathbf{c_j}^{\mathrm{T}}\mathbf{x'} - \epsilon \geq \mathbf{0}}$$

(Unaffecting) For transition $\tau_i \in G$ and ranking function component $\mathbf{c_j}^{\mathrm{T}}\mathbf{x}$, taking the transition does not increase the linear ranking function.

$$\mathbb{U}_{ij} \stackrel{\text{def}}{=} \frac{\begin{array}{ll}\mathbf{Ix} & \geq \mathbf{0} \\ \tau_i(\mathbf{xx'}) & \geq \mathbf{0}\end{array}}{\mathbf{c_j}^{\mathrm{T}}\mathbf{x} - \mathbf{c_j}^{\mathrm{T}}\mathbf{x'} \geq \mathbf{0}}$$

This specialization is used only if $n > 1$ — *i.e.*, if the ranking function template is lexicographic.

The specializations are applied according to the definitions of inductive invariants and ranking functions discussed in Section 2. In Section 4, we describe an effective algorithm for finding lexicographic ranking functions in practice.

Theorem 2. *Loop $L : \langle G, \Theta \rangle$ has a ℓ-lexicographic linear ranking function supported by an n-conjunct inductive linear invariant iff the constraint system generated by*

$$\mathbb{I} \wedge \bigwedge_{\tau_i \in G} (\mathbb{D}_i \vee (\mathbb{C}_i \wedge \mathbb{B}_{i,\sigma(i)} \wedge \mathbb{R}_{i,\sigma(i)})) \wedge \bigwedge_{\tau_i \in G, j < \sigma(i)} (\mathbb{D}_i \vee \mathbb{U}_{ij})$$

is satisfiable for some σ mapping transition indices to lexical component indices $\{1, \ldots, \ell\}$.

Corollary 1. *Loop $L : \langle G, \Theta \rangle$ has a linear ranking function supported by an n-conjunct inductive linear invariant iff the constraint system generated by*

$$\mathbb{I} \wedge \bigwedge_{\tau_i \in G} (\mathbb{D}_i \vee (\mathbb{C}_i \wedge \mathbb{B}_i \wedge \mathbb{R}_i))$$

is satisfiable.

These claims follow from the completeness of Farkas's Lemma and the definitions of inductive invariants and ranking functions.

The above formulation of the constraint system assumes a single n-conjunct invariant supporting all lexical components. An alternate formulation allows each component to have its own n-conjunct invariant. Specifically, the constraint system may be split into ℓ constraint systems, one for each component j:

$$\mathbb{I} \wedge \bigwedge_{\tau_i \in G} (\mathbb{D}_i \vee \mathbb{C}_i) \wedge \bigwedge_{\tau_i \in G : \sigma(i) = j} (\mathbb{D}_i \vee (\mathbb{B}_{ij} \wedge \mathbb{R}_{ij})) \wedge \bigwedge_{\tau_i \in G : \sigma(i) > j} (\mathbb{D}_i \vee \mathbb{U}_{ij})$$

This separation has two advantages. First, in practice, the multiple smaller systems are easier to solve than the equivalent large system. Second, the inductive invariant template may be instantiated differently for each system, so that a smaller template is sometimes possible. Consequently, each condition contributes constraints over fewer variables to the generated constraint systems.

Example 2. Consider finding a two-lexicographic linear ranking function for GCD, with a two-conjunct supporting invariant. Choosing the mapping σ determines the form of the conditions on the ranking function template $\mathbf{c}^T\mathbf{x}$ and the invariant template $\mathbf{I}\mathbf{x} \geq 0$. For $\sigma(1) = 2$, $\sigma(2) = 1$, we obtain $\mathbb{I} \wedge \mathbb{C}_1 \wedge \mathbb{C}_2 \wedge \mathbb{B}_{1,2} \wedge \mathbb{B}_{2,1} \wedge \mathbb{R}_{1,2} \wedge \mathbb{R}_{2,1} \wedge \mathbb{U}_{1,1}$, where we omit the *disabled* cases, as we often do in practice, so that the dual constraint system is conjunctive. $\mathbb{C}_1$ and $\mathbb{R}_{1,2}$ expand to the following:

$$\mathbb{C}_1 : \begin{array}{l} i_{1,1}y_1 + i_{1,2}y_2 + i_{1,3} \geq 0 \\ i_{2,1}y_1 + i_{2,2}y_2 + i_{2,3} \geq 0 \\ y_1 \geq y_2 + 1 \\ y_1' = y_1 - y_2 \\ y_2' = y_2 \\ \hline i_{1,1}y_1' + i_{1,2}y_2' + i_{1,3} \geq 0 \\ i_{2,1}y_1' + i_{2,2}y_2' + i_{2,3} \geq 0 \end{array} \qquad \mathbb{R}_{1,2} : \begin{array}{l} i_{1,1}y_1 + i_{1,2}y_2 + i_{1,3} \geq 0 \\ i_{2,1}y_1 + i_{2,2}y_2 + i_{2,3} \geq 0 \\ y_1 \geq y_2 + 1 \\ y_1' = y_1 - y_2 \\ y_2' = y_2 \\ \hline c_{2,1}y_1 + c_{2,2}y_2 \geq c_{2,1}y_1' + c_{2,2}y_2' + \epsilon \end{array}$$

Farkas's Lemma dualizes each component of the condition to produce one numerical constraint system over the λ-multipliers and the unknown template coefficients. See Section 5 for details on the form and solution of such constraint systems. Solving the system that arises here reveals the two-component ranking function $\langle y_2 - 2,\ y_1 - 2\rangle$, supported by the invariant $y_1 \geq 1 \ \wedge\ y_2 \geq 1$, which proves termination for GCD.

If we split the constraint system, as described above, into two constraint systems induced by $\mathbb{I} \wedge \mathbb{C}_1 \wedge \mathbb{C}_2 \wedge \mathbb{B}_{1,2} \wedge \mathbb{R}_{1,2} \wedge \mathbb{U}_{1,1}$ and $\mathbb{I} \wedge \mathbb{C}_1 \wedge \mathbb{C}_2 \wedge \mathbb{B}_{2,1} \wedge \mathbb{R}_{2,1}$, then the solution produces the same ranking function $\langle y_2 - 2,\ y_1 - 2\rangle$. However, only a one-conjunct template invariant is needed, as the first component only requires the invariant $y_1 \geq 1$, while the second only requires $y_2 \geq 1$.

4 Lexicographic Linear Ranking Functions

Theorem 2 requires finding a σ mapping transition indices to lexical component indices. While the number of possible σ's is finite — as only at most $|G|$ lexicographic components are required — it is exponentially large in the number of transitions. An implementation could enumerate the possible σ's to find one that induces a satisfiable constraint system, but this option is not practically feasible, nor is it theoretically satisfying. Not only does this approach take too long on loops for which a ranking function exists, but its worst-case input — loops for which no solution exists — occurs frequently in real code. In this section, we describe an effective procedure for deciding whether a loop has a lexicographic linear ranking function.

```
bool has_llrf(L, n) :
  llrf_{L,n}({})

bool rec llrf_{L,n}(o) :
  if sat_{L,n}(o) then
    if complete(o) then return true
    (i, j) := choose_unordered(o)
    return llrf_{L,n}(o ∪ (i < j)) or llrf_{L,n}(o ∪ (i > j))
  else return false
```

Fig. 2. Search strategy for finding a lexicographic linear ranking function, supported by an n-conjunct inductive linear invariant, for loop L

Each transition is assigned its own template component in the lexicographic function so that the discovered function has $|G|$ components, ensuring completeness (although the final function may be compressible). Each transition and its component induces a *bounded* condition and a *ranking* condition. Furthermore, the transitions and proposed invariant template induce *initiation* and *consecution* (and possibly *disabled*) conditions. All of these conditions are independent of the order of the lexicographic components; only the *unaffecting* conditions remain to be determined.

Figure 2 outlines the algorithm. Function *has_llrf* indicates if a loop L : $\langle G, \Theta \rangle$ has a lexicographic linear ranking function supported by an n-conjunct inductive linear invariant. The function $llrf_{L,n}$ takes as input an *order relation* o, which describes the known ordering constraints between components. Initially, this relation is the empty relation. First, $llrf_{L,n}$ checks the feasibility of the current ordering o. The function $sat_{L,n}$ generates the constraint system induced by L, n, and o, returning whether the system is satisfiable. If it is not, then no possible completion of this ordering can induce a satisfiable constraint system, so the search on the current branch terminates. If the constraint system is satisfiable and the order relation is complete, a solution is feasible and the function returns. If the order is not complete, two unordered components are selected and the function is called recursively on the two alternate orderings of these components. The $\cup$ operation returns the transitive closure.

Proposition 1. *Assuming that* $sat_{L,n}$ *is a decision procedure, has_llrf(*L*,* n*) returns* **true** *iff loop* L : $\langle G, \Theta \rangle$ *has a lexicographic linear ranking function supported by an* n*-conjunct inductive linear invariant.*

Example 3. Since each transition is assigned its own template component, we drop the second index of $\mathbb{B}$ and $\mathbb{R}$. Returning to the GCD program of Example 2, the search first generates the constraint systems induced by $\mathbb{I} \wedge \mathbb{C}_1 \wedge \mathbb{C}_2 \wedge \mathbb{B}_1 \wedge \mathbb{R}_1$ and $\mathbb{I} \wedge \mathbb{C}_1 \wedge \mathbb{C}_2 \wedge \mathbb{B}_2 \wedge \mathbb{R}_2$ and checks their feasibility. Finding both systems satisfiable, it adds (arbitrarily) the ordering constraint $1 > 2$ between indices 1 and 2, which results in the constraint systems induced by $\mathbb{I} \wedge \mathbb{C}_1 \wedge \mathbb{C}_2 \wedge \mathbb{B}_1 \wedge \mathbb{R}_1 \wedge \mathbb{U}_{1,2}$ and $\mathbb{I} \wedge \mathbb{C}_1 \wedge \mathbb{C}_2 \wedge \mathbb{B}_2 \wedge \mathbb{R}_2$. Both systems are found satisfiable and, since $\{1 > 2\}$ is a total ordering, the search terminates with ranking function $\langle y_2 - 2, y_1 - 2 \rangle$, supported by the invariants $y_1 \geq 1$ and $y_2 \geq 1$, respectively, where $\sigma(1) = 2$, $\sigma(2) = 1$ (*i.e.*, τ_1 maps to the second component, τ_2 to the first).

5 Solving the Numerical Constraints

Consider the specialization $\mathbb{R}_{ij}$, and expand the transition relation $\tau_i(\mathbf{x}\mathbf{x}')$ to the guard $\mathbf{G_i x} + \mathbf{g_i} \geq \mathbf{0}$ and the update $\mathbf{U_i x} + \mathbf{V_i x'} + \mathbf{u_i} \geq \mathbf{0}$, where $\mathbf{x} = (x_1, \ldots, x_m)^{\mathrm{T}}$. By Farkas's Lemma, $\mathbb{R}_{i,j}$ expands as follows:

$$\mathbb{R}_{ij}: \begin{array}{lr} \mathbf{Ix} & \geq 0 \\ \tau_i(\mathbf{xx'}) & \geq 0 \\ \hline \mathbf{c_j}^{\mathrm{T}}\mathbf{x} - \mathbf{c_j}^{\mathrm{T}}\mathbf{x}' - \epsilon & \geq 0 \end{array} \Rightarrow \begin{array}{r|lr} \lambda_I & \mathbf{Ix} & + \ \mathbf{i} \geq 0 \\ \lambda_G & \mathbf{G_i x} & + \mathbf{g_i} \geq 0 \\ \lambda_U & \mathbf{U_i x} + \ \mathbf{V_i x'} & + \mathbf{u_i} \geq 0 \\ \hline & \mathbf{c_j}^{\mathrm{T}}\mathbf{x} - \mathbf{c_j}^{\mathrm{T}}\mathbf{x}' & - \ \epsilon \geq 0 \end{array}$$

The second table corresponds to the constraints

$$\begin{array}{rl} {\lambda_I}^{\mathrm{T}}\mathbf{I} + {\lambda_G}^{\mathrm{T}}\mathbf{G_i} + {\lambda_U}^{\mathrm{T}}\mathbf{U_i} = \mathbf{c_j} & \\ {\lambda_U}^{\mathrm{T}}\mathbf{V_i} = -\mathbf{c_j} & \qquad \lambda_I, \lambda_G, \lambda_U \geq \mathbf{0} \\ {\lambda_I}^{\mathrm{T}}\mathbf{i} + {\lambda_G}^{\mathrm{T}}\mathbf{g_i} + {\lambda_U}^{\mathrm{T}}\mathbf{u_i} \leq -\epsilon & \qquad \epsilon > 0 \end{array}$$

where $\mathbf{I}$, $\mathbf{i}$, and $\mathbf{c_j}$ are the unknown coefficients. The template invariant coefficients $\mathbf{I}$ and $\mathbf{i}$ appear in nonlinear terms, while the template ranking function coefficients $\mathbf{c_j}$ occur only linearly. This observation holds in general. Thus, the number of template ranking function coefficients has little impact on the complexity of the constraint solving problem. Indeed, if no invariant template is proposed, the constraint solving problem is linear and thus trivial to solve. In this section, we focus on the nonlinear case that arises with a template invariant.

In principle, Tarski's decision procedure for polynomials [21] or CAD [2] can be used to produce solutions of these systems. Sankaranarayanan *et al.*'s work on constraint-based linear invariant generation [3, 16] explores several techniques for solving similar constraint problems that arise in invariant generation; the main practical solution is partly heuristic. We present a principled technique that combines bisection search over the invariant template coefficients with linear constraint solving. It guarantees finding a solution if one exists with integer coefficients of at most some given absolute value.

Our method searches among linear assertions with integer coefficients in a preset range, looking for a linear invariant that makes the constraint system satisfiable. Rather than explicitly enumerating all linear assertions and checking whether they result in a satisfiable constraint system, the method is guided in its enumeration by considering *regions* of coefficients. A *feasibility check* forms a linear overapproximation of the constraint system based on the considered region and checks it for satisfiability. If the overapproximation is found unsatisfiable, it concludes that no assertion in that region is a supporting invariant, thus excluding the entire region from further search. If the region is found feasible, an assertion in the *corner* of the region is chosen and substituted in the constraint system, thus linearizing the constraint system. If the resulting constraint system is satisfiable, the search terminates, as a solution has been found. Otherwise, the region is bisected, and each subregion is handled recursively until a solution is found or the preset depth is reached. An outline of the algorithm is given in Figure 3.

```
bool sat(sys, params) :
  queue := {(1, [-1, 1]^|params|)}
  while |queue| > 0 do
    (depth, r) := choose(queue)
    if feasible(sys, r) then
      if corner(sys, r) then return true
      if depth ≤ D · |params| then
        (r1, r2) := bisect(r)
        queue := queue ∪ {(depth + 1, r1), (depth + 1, r2)}
  return false
```

Fig. 3. Satisfiability check for numerical constraint systems

The feasibility check is computed as follows. Consider a constraint system Φ and a region r consisting of one interval $[\ell_i, u_i]$ for each invariant template coefficient c_i. Each constraint φ in Φ of the form $\cdots \pm c_i\lambda_j + \cdots \geq 0$ is replaced by a constraint φ' in which each c_i is replaced by ℓ_i if $c_i\lambda_j$ occurs negatively and by u_i if $c_i\lambda_j$ occurs positively (recall that $\lambda_j \geq 0$). The resulting linear constraint system Φ' is checked for satisfiability.

Lemma 1. *If Φ is satisfiable for some value of the c_i's in r, then Φ' is satisfiable.*

Consequently, if Φ' is found unsatisfiable, then no solution exists for Φ with coefficients from r; the region r is deemed infeasible.

The linear systems formed during the feasibility check and the check for a solution contain the positive ϵ introduced by the *ranking* specialization. This ϵ may be maximized, resulting in a linear program. The resulting maximum must be positive for the constraint system to be satisfiable. Alternately, ϵ may be set to a constant value, resulting in a linear feasibility check.

The satisfiability check may terminate with a solution, terminate because it hits the maximum depth, or terminate because all regions are found infeasible. If the search terminates only because regions are found infeasible, then no (lexicographic) linear ranking function exists supported by an invariant of the given size. If the maximum depth is ever reached but no solution is found, the result is inconclusive. Assuming a fair *bisect* criterion and that the "lower-left" corner of the region is always chosen when checking a particular solution, we have the following guarantee.

Proposition 2. *sat(sys, params) returns* **true** *iff a supporting invariant exists with integer coefficients in the range $[-2^{D-1}, 2^{D-1})$, for maximum depth $D \geq 1$.*

The forward direction is immediate. For the other direction, first, every linear invariant with rational coefficients may be represented such that all coefficients lie in $[-1, 1]$ and the denominators of coefficients are powers of 2. Second, if *bisect* and *corner* satisfy the stated restrictions, then every combination of such coefficients, with coefficient denominators up to 2^{D-1} and numerators in $[-2^{D-1}, 2^{D-1})$, appears as a corner. Converting these rational coefficients to integers results in integer coefficients in $[-2^{D-1}, 2^{D-1})$. Finally, Lemma 1 ensures that no region containing a solution is pruned.

Invariants from other sources can be used directly by adding them "above the line" of each specialization. For example, polynomial methods exist to generate all invariant linear equalities [7] and many linear inequalities [17]. These invariants strengthen the constraint system without introducing nonlinearities. An invariant template may still be required to enable solving for the harder-to-find supporting invariants. However, one may expect that a smaller template will be sufficient for finding the ranking function, thus reducing the complexity of solving the constraint system.

6 Experimental Results

We implemented our method in O'Caml as a standalone tool. Its input is a set of guarded commands, the initial condition, known invariants, and the size of the supporting invariant template. When successful, it returns a ranking function and its supporting invariants as a witness to termination. By itself, this tool is suitable for analyzing interesting loops like GCD and McCarthy's 91 function. For example, it finds a single ranking function for GCD in about five seconds and a lexicographic ranking function for GCD in about one second. The computation of the lexicographic function is faster because it requires only a one-conjunct template to produce two invariants, while the single ranking function needs two conjuncts. For McCarthy's 91 function, our tool finds the lexicographic ranking function in about a second.

To test our method's general applicability, we implemented a prototype C loop abstracter in CIL [12]. Its input is C source code; its output is a set of abstracted loops, represented as sets of guarded commands. This set of tests measures the performance of our lexicographic ranking function synthesis method without supporting invariants[1]. Thus, all numeric constraint systems are linear.

We implemented three *lexicographic strategies* to guide the synthesis. *One* tries to find a non-lexicographic linear ranking function. *Search* tries to find a non-lexicographic ranking function first, then applies $has\_llrf(L,\ n)$ if that fails. *Set* tries to find a non-lexicographic ranking function first; if that fails, it tries to find a $|G|$-component lexicographic function *with a fixed initial ordering*. The third strategy was implemented for comparison purposes. One important feature of a scalable analysis is that when it fails on a common class of input, it fails quickly. Comparing *Search* with *Set* allows us to assess whether *Search* fails quickly on loops that do not have lexicographic linear ranking functions.

The implementation omits the *disabled* case when generating the constraint systems to avoid introducing disjunctions, which produce multiple numeric constraint systems. In practice, however, the sets of guarded commands extracted by our C loop abstracter contain inconsistent transitions: each guarded command represents a path through the loop, but some of these paths are logically infeasible. Pruning the guarded command set by checking satisfiability of the

[1] Our prototype abstracter does not produce initial conditions for the loops, so no assertions can be proved invariant.

Table 1. Results of tests. Interpret column headings as follows: **Name**: name of program; **LOC**: lines of code *of files successfully parsed and containing loops*, as measured by `wc`; **#L**: number of analyzed loops; **#A**: number of *nontrivial* abstracted loops; **#P**: number of loops proved terminating; **Tm**: time in seconds required to analyze the program; **P/A**: percent of abstracted loops proved terminating; **P/L**: percent of all loops proved terminating. The experimental results are subdivided by the strategies *one*, *set*, and *search*

				One		*Set*		*Search*			
Name	**LOC**	**#L**	**#A**	**#P**	**Tm**	**#P**	**Tm**	**#P**	**P/A**	**P/L**	**Tm**
`small1`	310	8	3	2	2	2	2	2	66	25	2
`vector`	361	13	13	12	2	12	1	12	92	92	2
`serv`	457	9	6	5	1	5	1	5	83	55	2
`dcg`	1K	55	53	53	4	53	4	53	100	96	4
`bcc`	4K	70	18	18	5	18	5	18	100	25	5
`sarg`	7K	110	25	25	77	25	77	25	100	22	77
`spin`	19K	652	124	119	76	119	94	119	95	18	76
`meschach`	28K	911	778	751	64	758	66	758	97	83	64
`f2c`	30K	436	100	98	49	98	48	98	98	22	47
`ffmpeg/libavformat`	33K	451	230	217	55	217	55	217	94	48	55
`gnuplot`	50K	826	312	300	87	301	89	301	96	36	88
`gaim`	57K	594	54	52	93	52	94	52	96	8	94
`ffmpeg/libavcodec`	75K	2223	1885	1863	147	1863	143	1864	98	83	143

guards before starting the main analysis leads to significant time and memory savings. This pruning is essentially the *disabled* case without invariants.

We applied our C loop abstracter and termination tool to a set of thirteen C projects downloaded from NETLIB [13] and SOURCEFORGE [20]. Table 1 displays the results. The timing data are obtained from running the tests on a 3GHz dual-Pentium processor with 2GB of memory. Loops are counted as successfully abstracted if they do not have any trivial guards or updates. The data indicate that our method provides good coverage of successfully abstracted loops (**P/A**) at low cost in time (**Tm**). Moreover, the timing data indicate that the extra power of lexicographic function synthesis comes at almost no cost. Although *Search* invokes the search method on every loop for which *One* fails, its speed is competitive with *One* while proving 9 more loops terminating. Moreover, comparing *Search* with *Set* indicates that the search method fails quickly when it must fail: the feasibility check controls an otherwise expensive search.

7 Conclusion

Our method of ranking function synthesis demonstrates two new ideas. First, the constraint-based analysis style of separating the encoding of requirements from the synthesis itself [4] is extended by incorporating structural and numeric constraints. The constraint solving process involves an interplay between satisfying structural requirements and the induced numeric constraints. Second, supporting invariants are found implicitly. This choice avoids the full cost of invariant generation. Our numeric constraint solver exploits the implicit nature of the supporting invariants, using a feasibility check to exclude sets of irrelevant assertions and invariants. In a real sense, the ranking conditions guide the search for supporting invariants.

Acknowledgments. We thank the reviewers for their insightful comments.

References

1. Codish, M., Genaim, S., Bruynooghe, M., Gallagher, J., and Vanhoof, W. One lop at a time. In *WST* (2003).
2. Collins, G. E. Quantifier elimination for real closed fields by cylindrical algebraic decomposition. In *GI Conf. Automata Theory and Formal Languages* (1975), pp. 515–532.
3. Colón, M. A., Sankaranarayanan, S., and Sipma, H. B. Linear invariant generation using non-linear constraint solving. In *CAV* (2003), pp. 420–433.
4. Colón, M. A., and Sipma, H. B. Synthesis of linear ranking functions. In *TACAS* (2001), pp. 67–81.
5. Colón, M. A., and Sipma, H. B. Practical methods for proving program termination. In *CAV* (2002), pp. 442–454.
6. Dershowitz, N., Lindenstrauss, N., Sagiv, Y., and Serebrenik, A. A general framework for automatic termination analysis of logic programs. *Applicable Algebra in Engineering, Communication and Computing 12* (2001), 117–156.
7. Karr, M. Affine relationships among variables of a program. *Acta Inf. 6* (1976).
8. Katz, S. M., and Manna, Z. A closer look at termination. *Acta Informatica 5*, 4 (1975), 333–352.
9. Lee, C. S., Jones, N. D., and Ben-Amram, A. M. The size-change principle for program termination. In *POPL* (2001), pp. 81–92.
10. Manna, Z. *Mathematical Theory of Computation.* McGraw-Hill, 1974.
11. Manna, Z., Browne, A., Sipma, H. B., and Uribe, T. E. Visual abstractions for temporal verification. In *Algebraic Methodology and Software Technology* (1998), pp. 28–41.
12. Necula, G. C., McPeak, S., Rahul, S. P., and Weimer, W. CIL: Intermediate language and tools for analysis and transformation of C programs. In *Proceedings of Conf. on Compiler Construction* (2002).
13. *Netlib Repository*, 2004. (`http://www.netlib.org`).
14. Podelski, A., and Rybalchenko, A. A complete method for the synthesis of linear ranking functions. In *VMCAI* (2004), pp. 239–251.
15. Podelski, A., and Rybalchenko, A. Transition invariants. In *LICS* (2004), pp. 32–41.
16. Sankaranarayanan, S., Sipma, H. B., and Manna, Z. Constraint-based linear-relations analysis. In *SAS* (2004), pp. 53–68.
17. Sankaranarayanan, S., Sipma, H. B., and Manna, Z. Scalable analysis of linear systems using mathematical programming. In *VMCAI* (2005), pp. 25–41.
18. Schrijver, A. *Theory of Linear and Integer Programming.* Wiley, 1986.

19. Sipma, H. B., Uribe, T. E., and Manna, Z. Deductive model checking. In *CAV* (1996), pp. 209–219.
20. *SourceForge*, 2004. (http://sourceforge.net).
21. Tarski, A. *A Decision Method for Elementary Algebra and Geometry*, 2 ed. University of California Press, Berkeley, CA, 1951.

Reasoning About Threads Communicating via Locks

Vineet Kahlon, Franjo Ivančić, and Aarti Gupta

NEC Labs America, 4 Independence Way, Suite 200,
Princeton, NJ 08536, USA
{kahlon, ivancic, agupta}@nec-labs.com

Abstract. We propose a new technique for the static analysis of concurrent programs comprised of multiple threads. In general, the problem is known to be undecidable even for programs with only two threads but where the threads communicate using CCS-style pairwise rendezvous [11]. However, in practice, a large fraction of concurrent programs can either be directly modeled as threads communicating solely using locks or can be reduced to such systems either by applying standard abstract interpretation techniques or by exploiting separation of control from data. For such a framework, we show that for the commonly occurring case of threads with nested access to locks, the problem is efficiently decidable. Our technique involves reducing the analysis of a concurrent program with multiple threads to individually analyzing augmented versions of the given threads. This not only yields decidability but also avoids construction of the state space of the concurrent program at hand and thus bypasses the state explosion problem making our technique scalable. We go on to show that for programs with threads that have non-nested access to locks, the static analysis problem for programs with even two threads becomes undecidable even for reachability, thus sharpening the result of [11]. As a case study, we consider the Daisy file system [1] which is a benchmark for analyzing the efficacy of different methodologies for debugging concurrent programs and provide results for the detection of several bugs.

1 Introduction

Multi-threading is a standard way of enhancing performance by exploiting parallelism among the different components of a computer system. As a result the use of concurrent multi-threaded programs is becoming pervasive. Examples include operating systems, databases and embedded systems. This necessitates the development of new methodologies to debug such systems especially since existing techniques for debugging sequential programs are inadequate in handling concurrent programs. The key reason for that is the presence of many possible interleavings among the local operations of individual threads giving rise to subtle unintended behaviors. This makes multi-threaded software behaviorally complex and hard to analyze thus requiring the use of formal methods for their validation.

One of the most widely used techniques in the validation of sequential programs is dataflow analysis [12] which can essentially be looked upon as a combination of abstract interpretation and model checking [13]. Here, abstract interpretation is used to get a finite representation of the control part of the program while recursion is modeled using a stack. Pushdown systems (PDSs) provide a natural framework to model such

K. Etessami and S.K. Rajamani (Eds.): CAV 2005, LNCS 3576, pp. 505–518, 2005.

abstractly interpreted structures. A PDS has a finite control part corresponding to the valuation of the variables of the program and a stack which provides a means to model recursion. Dataflow analysis then exploits the fact that the model checking problem for PDSs is decidable for very expressive classes of properties - both linear and branching time (cf. [2, 16]).

Following data-flow analysis for sequential programs, we model a multi-threaded program as a system comprised of multiple pushdown systems interacting with each other using a communication mechanism like a shared variable or a synchronization primitive[1]. While for a single PDS the model checking problem is efficiently decidable for very expressive logics, it was shown in [11] that even simple properties like reachability become undecidable even for systems with only two threads but where the threads communicate using CCS-style pairwise rendezvous.

However, in a large fraction of real-world concurrent software used, for example, in file systems, databases or device drivers, the key issue is to resolve conflicts between different threads competing for access to shared resources. Conflicts are typically resolved using locks which allow mutually exclusive access to a shared resource. Before a thread can have access to a shared resource it has to acquire the lock associated with that resource which is released after executing all the intended operations. For such software, the interaction between concurrently executing threads is very limited making them loosely coupled. For instance, in a standard file system the control flow in the implementation of the various file operations is usually independent of the data being written to or read from a file. Consequently such programs can either be directly modeled as systems comprised of PDSs communicating via locks or can be reduced to such systems either by applying standard abstract interpretation techniques or by exploiting separation of control and data. Therefore, in this paper, we consider the model checking problem for PDSs interacting using locks.

Absence of conflicts and deadlock freedom are among the most crucial properties that need to be checked for multi-threaded programs, particularly because checking for these is usually a pre-cursor for verifying more complex properties. Typical conflicts include, for example, data races where two or more threads try to access a shared memory location with at least one of the accesses being a write operation. This and most other commonly occurring conflicts (can be formulated to) occur pairwise among threads. With this in mind, given a concurrent program comprised of the n threads T_1,...,T_n, we consider correctness properties of the following forms:

- Liveness (Single-indexed Properties): $\mathsf{E}h(i)$ and $\mathsf{A}h(i)$, where $h(i)$ is an LTL\X formula (built using F "eventually," U "until," G "always," but without X "next-time") interpreted over the local control states of the PDS representing thread T_i, and E (for some computation starting at the initial global configuration) and A (for all computations starting at the initial global configuration) are the usual path quantifiers.
- Safety (Double-indexed Properties): $\bigwedge_{i \neq j} \mathsf{EF}(a_i \wedge b_j)$, where a_i and b_j are local control states of PDSs T_i and T_j, respectively.
- Deadlock Freedom.

[1] Henceforth we shall use the terms thread and PDS interchangeably.

For single-indexed properties, we show that the model checking problem is efficiently decidable. Towards that end, given a correctness property $\mathsf{E}h(i)$ over the local states of thread T_i, we show how to reduce reasoning in an exact, i.e., sound and complete, fashion about a system with n threads to a system comprised of just the thread T_i. This reduces the problem of model checking a single-indexed LTL\X formula for a system with n threads to model checking a single thread (PDS), which by [2] is known to be efficiently decidable.

The model checking problem for double-indexed properties is more interesting. As for single-indexed properties, we show that we can reduce the model checking problem for $\mathsf{E}h(i,j)$ for a system with n threads to the system comprised of just the two threads T_i and T_j. However, unlike the single index case, this still does not yield decidability of the associated model checking problem. We show that, in general, the problem of model checking remains undecidable even for pairwise reachability, viz., properties of the form $\mathsf{EF}(a_i \wedge b_j)$, where a_i and b_j are local control states of thread T_i and T_j, even for programs with only two threads.

However, most real-world concurrent programs use locks in a nested fashion, viz., each thread can only release the lock that it acquired last and that has not yet been released. Indeed, practical programming guidelines used by software developers often require that locks be used in a nested fashion. In fact, in Java and C# locking is syntactically guaranteed to be nested. In this case, we show that we can reduce reasoning about pairwise reachability of a given two-threaded program to individually model checking augmented versions of each of the threads, which by [2] is efficiently decidable. The augmentation involves storing for each control location of a thread the history of locks that were acquired or released in order to get to that location. We show that storing this history information guarantees a sound and complete reduction. Furthermore, it avoids construction of the state space of the system at hand thereby bypassing the state explosion problem thus making our technique scalable to large programs. Thus we have given an efficient technique for reasoning about threads communicating via locks which can be combined synergistically with existing methodologies.

As a case study, we have applied our technique to check race conditions in the Daisy file system [1] and shown the existence of several bugs. Proofs of the results presented in the paper have been omitted for the sake of brevity and can be found in the full version which is available upon request.

2 System Model

In this paper, we consider multi-threaded programs wherein threads communicate using locks. We model each thread using the trace flow graph framework (cf. [4]). Here each procedure of a thread is modeled as a flow graph, each node of which represents a control point of the procedure. The edges of the flow graph are annotated with statements that could either be assignments, calls to other procedures of the same thread or the acquire and release of locks when the thread needs to access shared resources. Recursion and mutual procedure calls are allowed. So that the flow graph of a program has a finite number of nodes, abstract interpretation techniques are often used in order to get a finite representation of the (potentially infinitely many) control states of the original thread. This typically introduces non-determinism which is explicitly allowed. Each thread can then be modeled as a system of flow graphs representing its procedures.

The resulting framework of finite state flow graphs with recursion can be naturally modeled as a *pushdown system (PDS)*. A PDS has a finite control part corresponding to the valuation of the local variables of the procedure it represents and a stack which provides a means to model recursion.

Formally, a PDS is a five-tuple $\mathcal{P} = (P, Act, \Gamma, c_0, \Delta)$, where P is a finite set of *control locations*, *Act* is a finite set of *actions*, Γ is a finite *stack alphabet*, and $\Delta \subseteq (P \times \Gamma) \times Act \times (P \times \Gamma^*)$ is a finite set of *transition rules*. If $((p, \gamma), a, (p', w)) \in \Delta$ then we write $\langle p, \gamma \rangle \overset{a}{\hookrightarrow} \langle p', w \rangle$. A *configuration* of $\mathcal{P}$ is a pair $\langle p, w \rangle$, where $p \in P$ denotes the control location and $w \in \Gamma^*$ the *stack content*. We call c_0 the *initial configuration* of $\mathcal{P}$. The set of all configurations of $\mathcal{P}$ is denoted by $\mathcal{C}$. For each action a, we define a relation $\overset{a}{\rightarrow} \subseteq \mathcal{C} \times \mathcal{C}$ as follows: if $\langle q, \gamma \rangle \overset{a}{\hookrightarrow} \langle q', w \rangle$, then $\langle q, \gamma v \rangle \overset{a}{\rightarrow} \langle q', wv \rangle$ for every $v \in \Gamma^*$.

We model multi-threaded programs using PDSs communicating using locks. For a concurrent program comprised of threads T_1,...,T_n, a lock l is a globally shared variable taking on values from the set $\{1, ..., n, \bot\}$. The value of l can be modified by a thread using the operations *acquire*(l) and *release*(l). A thread can acquire a lock l only if its value is currently $\bot$, viz., none of the other threads currently has possession of it. Once l has been acquired by thread T_i, its value is set to i and it remains so until T_i releases it by executing *release*(l) thereby resetting its value to $\bot$. Locks are not pre-emptible, viz., a thread cannot be forced to give up any lock acquired by it.

Formally, we model a concurrent program with n threads and m locks $\mathsf{l}_1, ..., \mathsf{l}_m$ as a tuple of the form $\mathcal{CP} = (T_1, ..., T_n, L_1, ..., L_m)$, where T_1,...,T_n are pushdown systems (representing threads) with the same set *Act* of non-*acquire* and non-*release* actions, and for each i, $L_i \subseteq \{\bot, 1, ..., n\}$ is the possible set of values that lock l_i can be assigned to. A global configuration of $\mathcal{CP}$ is a tuple $c = (t_1, ..., t_n, l_1, ..., l_m)$ where $t_1, ..., t_n$ are, respectively, the configurations of threads $T_1, ..., T_n$ and $l_1, ..., l_m$ the values of the locks. If no thread holds the lock in configuration c, then $l_i = \bot$, else l_i is the index of the thread currently holding the lock. The initial global configuration of $\mathcal{CP}$ is $(c_1, ..., c_n, \underbrace{\bot, ..., \bot}_{m})$, where c_i is the initial configuration of thread T_i. Thus all locks are *free* to start with. We extend the relation $\overset{a}{\longrightarrow}$ to pairs of global configurations as follows: Let $c = (c_1, ..., c_n, l_1, ..., l_m)$ and $c' = (c'_1, ..., c'_n, l'_1, ..., l'_m)$ be global configurations. Then

- $c \overset{a}{\longrightarrow} c'$ if there exists $1 \leq i \leq n$ such that $c_i \overset{a}{\longrightarrow} c'_i$, and for all $1 \leq j \leq n$ such that $i \neq j$, $c_j = c'_j$, and for all $1 \leq k \leq m$, $l_k = l'_k$.
- $c \overset{acquire(\mathsf{l}_i)}{\longrightarrow} c'$ if there exists $1 \leq j \leq n$ such that $c_j \overset{acquire(\mathsf{l}_i)}{\longrightarrow} c'_j$, and $l_i = \bot$, and $l'_i = j$, and for all $1 \leq k \leq n$ such that $k \neq j$, $c_k = c'_k$, and for all $1 \leq p \leq m$ such that $p \neq i$, $l_p = l'_p$.

- $c \xrightarrow{release(\mathsf{l}_i)} c'$ if there exists $1 \leq j \leq n$ such that $c_j \xrightarrow{release(\mathsf{l}_i)} c'_j$, and $l_i = j$, and $l'_i = \perp$, and for all $1 \leq k \leq n$ such that $k \neq j$, $c_k = c'_k$, and for all $1 \leq p \leq m$ such that $p \neq i$, $l_p = l'_p$.

A sequence $x = x_1, x_2, ...$ of global configurations of $\mathcal{CP}$ is a *computation* if x_1 is the initial global configuration of $\mathcal{CP}$ and for each i, $x_i \xrightarrow{a} x_{i+1}$, where either $a \in Act$ or for some $1 \leq j \leq m$, $a = release(\mathsf{l}_j)$ or $a = acquire(\mathsf{l}_j)$. Given a thread T_i and a reachable global configuration $c = (c_1, ..., c_n, l_1, ..., l_m)$ of $\mathcal{CP}$ we use *Lock-Set*(T_i, c) to denote the set of indices of locks held by T_i in c, viz., the set $\{j \mid l_j = i\}$.

Nested versus Non-nested Lock Access. We say that a concurrent program accesses locks in a nested fashion if and only if along each computation of the program a thread can only release the last lock that it acquired along that computation and that has not yet been released. For example in the figure below, the thread comprised of procedures `foo_nested` and `bar` accesses locks `a,b,` and `c` in a nested fashion whereas the thread comprised of procedures `foo_not_nested` and `bar` does not. This is because calling `bar` from `foo_non_nested` releases lock `b` before lock `a` even though lock `a` was the last one to be acquired.

Global Locks: `a,b,c`

```
foo_nested() {          bar(){                foo_non_nested(){
   acquire(a);             release(b);           acquire(b);
   acquire(b);             release(a);           acquire(a);
   bar();                  acquire(c);           bar();
   release(c);                                   release(c);
}                       }                     }
```

3 Many to Few

Let $\mathcal{CP}$ be a concurrent program comprised of n threads $T_1, ..., T_n$ and let f be a correctness property either of the form $\mathsf{E}_{\mathsf{fin}} h(i,j)$ or of the form $\mathsf{A}_{\mathsf{fin}} h(i,j)$, where $h(i,j)$ is an LTL\X formula with atomic propositions over the control states of threads T_i and T_j and $\mathsf{E}_{\mathsf{fin}}$ and $\mathsf{A}_{\mathsf{fin}}$ quantify solely over finite computation paths. Note that since $\mathsf{A}_{\mathsf{fin}}$ and $\mathsf{E}_{\mathsf{fin}}$ are dual path quantifiers it suffices to only consider the case where f is of the form $\mathsf{E}_{\mathsf{fin}} h(i,j)$. We show that in order to model check $\mathcal{CP}$ for f it suffices to model check the program $\mathcal{CP}(i,j)$ comprised solely of the threads T_i and T_j. We emphasize that this result does not require the given concurrent program to have nested locks. Formally, we show the following.

Proposition 1 (Double-Indexed Reduction Result). *Given a concurrent program $\mathcal{CP}$ comprised of n threads $T_1, ..., T_n$, $\mathcal{CP} \models \mathsf{E}_{\mathsf{fin}} h(i,j)$ iff $\mathcal{CP}(i,j) \models \mathsf{E}_{\mathsf{fin}} h(i,j)$, where $\mathcal{CP}(i,j)$ is the concurrent program comprised solely of the threads T_i and T_j.*

Proposition 2 (Single-Indexed Reduction Result). *Given a concurrent program $\mathcal{CP}$ comprised of n threads $T_1, ..., T_n$, $\mathcal{CP} \models \mathsf{E}_{\mathsf{fin}} h(i)$ iff $\mathcal{CP}(i) \models \mathsf{E}_{\mathsf{fin}} h(i)$, where $\mathcal{CP}(i)$ is the program comprised solely of the thread T_i.*

Similar results holds for properties of the form $\mathsf{E}_{\mathsf{inf}} h(i,j)$, where $\mathsf{E}_{\mathsf{inf}}$ quantifies solely over infinite computations.

4 Liveness Properties

Using proposition 2, we can reduce the model checking problem for a single-indexed LTL\X formula f for a system with n threads to a system comprised solely of the single thread whose control states are being tracked by f. Thus the problem now reduces to model checking a pushdown system for LTL\X properties which is known to be decidable in polynomial time in size of the control part of the pushdown system [2]. We thus have the following.

Theorem 3 *The model checking problem for single-indexed LTL\X properties for a system with n threads is decidable in polynomial time in the size of the PDS representing the thread being tracked by the property.*

5 Safety Properties

Even though proposition 2 allows us to reduce reasoning about double-indexed LTL\X properties from a system with n threads to one with 2 threads, it still does not yield decidability. This is because although the model checking of LTL\X is decidable for a single pushdown system, it becomes undecidable even for simple reachability and even for systems with only two PDSs communicating via pairwise rendezvous [11]. The proof of undecidability rests on the fact that synchronization using pairwise rendezvous couples the two PDSs tightly enough to allow construction of a system that accepts the intersection of the two given context free languages (CFLs) the non-emptiness of which is undecidable.

We show that if we allow PDSs with non-nested lock access then the coupling, though seemingly weaker than pairwise rendezvous, is still strong enough to build a system accepting the intersection of the CFLs corresponding to the given PDSs thus yielding undecidability for even pairwise reachability. This is discouraging from a practical standpoint. However we exploit the observation that in most real-world concurrent programs locks are accessed by threads in a nested fashion. In fact, in certain programming languages like Java and C#, locks are syntactically guaranteed to be nested. In that case, we can reduce the model checking of LTL\X properties in a sound and complete fashion for a concurrent program comprised of two threads to individually model checking augmented versions of the thread for LTL\X properties, which by [2] is efficiently decidable. Then combining this with the reduction result of the previous section, we get that the model checking problem of doubly-indexed LTL\X formulas is efficiently decidable for concurrent programs with nested locks.

5.1 Decidability of Pairwise Reachability for Nested Lock Programs

We motivate our technique with the help of a simple concurrent program $\mathcal{CP}$ shown below comprised of thread one with procedures `thread_one` and `acq_rel_c`, and thread two with procedures `thread_two` and `acq_rel_b`.

Suppose that we are interested in deciding whether $\mathsf{EF}(c4 \wedge g4)$ holds. The key idea is to reduce this to checking $\mathsf{EF}c4$ and $\mathsf{EF}g4$ individually on (modifications of) the two threads. Then given computations x and y leading to $c4$ and $g4$, respectively, we merge them to construct a computation z of $\mathcal{CP}$ leading to a global configuration with threads one and two in local control states $c4$ and $g4$, respectively. Consider, for example, the computations x: `c1,c2,d1,d2,c3,c4` and y: `g1,g2,g3,h1,h2,g4` of threads one and two, respectively. Note that at control location `g4`, thread 2 holds locks `c` and `d`. Also, along computation y once thread two acquires lock `c` at control location `g1`, it does not release it and so we have to make sure that before we let it execute `g1` along z, all operations that acquire and release lock `c` along x should already have been executed. Thus in our case `g1` must be scheduled to fire only after `d2` (and hence `c1, c2` and `d1`) have already been executed. Similarly, operation `c3` of thread one must be executed after `h2` has already been fired along z. Thus one possible computation z of $\mathcal{CP}$ with the desired properties is z: `c1, c2, d1, d2, g1, g2, g3, h1, h2, g4, c3, c4`.

```
thread_one(){            acq_rel_c(){              thread_two(){
  c1: acquire(a) ;         d1: acquire(c) ;          g1: acquire(c) ;
  c2: acq_rel_c() ;        d2: release(c) ;          g2: acquire(d) ;
  c3: acquire(b) ;       }                           g3: acq_rel_b() ;
  c4: release(b) ;       acq_rel_b(){                g4: release(d) ;
  c5: release(a) ;         h1: acquire(b) ;        }
}                          h2 release(b) ;
                         }
```

Note that if we replace the function call at control location `g3` of thread two by `acq_rel_a()` which first acquires and then releases lock `a`, then there is no way to reconcile the two local computations x and y to get a global computation leading to a configuration with threads one and two, respectively, at control locations `c4` and `g4`, even though they are reachable in their respective individual threads. This is because in this case `h2` (and hence `g1, g2, g3` and `h1`) should be executed before `c1` (and hence `c2, d1, d2, c3` and `c4`). Again, as before, `g1` can be fired only after `d2` (and hence `c1, c2` and `d1`). From the above observations we get that `g1` must be fired after `h2` along z. But that violates the local ordering of the transitions fired along y wherein `g1` was fired before `h2`. This proves the claim made above.

In general when testing for reachability of control states c and c' of two different threads it suffices to test whether there exist paths x and y in the individual threads leading to states c and c' holding lock sets L and L' which can be acquired in a compatible fashion. Compatibility ensures that we do not get a scenario as above where there exist locks $a \in L$ and $a' \in L'$ such that a transition acquiring a' was fired after acquiring a for the last time along x and a transition acquiring a was fired after acquiring a' for the last time along y, else we can't reconcile x and y. The above discussion is formalized below in Theorem 5. Before proceeding further, we need the following definition.

Definition 4 (Acquisition History). *Let x be a global computation of a concurrent program $\mathcal{CP}$ leading to global configuration c. Then for thread T_i and lock l_j of $\mathcal{CP}$ such that $j \in$ Lock-Set(T_i, c), we define $AH(T_i, l_j, x)$ to be the set of indices of locks that were acquired (and possibly released) by T_i after the last acquisition of l_j by T_i along x.*

Theorem 5 (Decomposition Result). *Let $\mathcal{CP}$ be a concurrent program comprised of the two threads T_1 and T_2 with nested locks. Then for control states a_1 and b_2 of T_1 and T_2, respectively, $\mathcal{CP} \models \mathsf{EF}(a_1 \wedge b_2)$ iff there are computations x and y of the individual threads T_1 and T_2, respectively, leading to configurations s with T_1 in control state a_1 and t with T_2 in control state b_2 such that*

- Lock-Set$(T_1, s) \cap$ Lock-Set$(T_2, t) = \emptyset$.
- *there do not exist locks $l \in$ Lock-Set(T_1, s) and $l' \in$ Lock-Set(T_2, t) with $l' \in AH(T_1, l, x)$ and $l \in AH(T_2, l', y)$.*

To make use of the above result we augment the given threads to keep track of the acquisition histories. Given a thread $\mathcal{P} = (P, Act, \Gamma, c_0, \Delta)$ of concurrent program $\mathcal{CP}$ having the set of locks L of cardinality m, we construct the augmented thread $\mathcal{P}_A = (P_A, Act, \Gamma, d_0, \Delta_A)$, where $P_A = P \times 2^L \times (2^L)^m$ and $\Delta_A \subseteq (P_A \times \Gamma) \times (P_A \times \Gamma^*)$. The augmented PDA is used to track the set of locks and acquisition histories of thread T along local computations of T. Let x be a computation of $\mathcal{CP}$ leading to global configuration s. Each control location of the augmented PDA is of the form $(a, Locks, AH_1, ..., AH_m)$, where a denotes the current control state of T in s, $Locks$ the set of locks currently held by T and for $1 \leq j \leq m$, if $l_j \in Locks$, then AH_j is the set $AH(T, l_j, x)$ else it is the empty set. The initial configuration d_0 is the $(m+2)$-tuple $(c_0, \emptyset, \emptyset, ..., \emptyset)$. The transition relation Δ_A is defined as follows:

$\langle q, Locks, AH_1, ..., AH_m, \gamma\rangle \overset{a}{\hookrightarrow} \langle q', Locks', AH'_1, ..., AH'_m, w\rangle \in \Delta_A$ iff

- a is not a lock operation, $\langle q, \gamma\rangle \overset{a}{\hookrightarrow} \langle q', w\rangle \in \Delta$, $Locks = Locks'$ and for $1 \leq j \leq m$, $AH_j = AH'_j$.
- a is the action $acquire(l_k)$, $Locks' = Locks \cup \{k\}$, $q \overset{acquire(l_k)}{\longrightarrow} q'$, $\gamma = w$ and for $1 \leq p \leq m$, if $p \in Locks$ then $AH'_p = AH_p \cup \{k\}$ and $AH'_p = AH_p$ otherwise.
- a is the action $release(l_k)$, $Lock' = Locks \backslash \{k\}$, $q \overset{release(l_k)}{\longrightarrow} q'$, $\gamma = w$, $AH'_k = \emptyset$ and for $1 \leq p \leq m$ such that $p \neq k$, $AH'_p = AH_p$.

Proposition 6. *Given a concurrent program $\mathcal{CP}$ comprised of threads T and T', the model checking problem for pairwise reachability, viz., formulas of the form $\mathsf{EF}(a_1 \wedge b_2)$ is decidable.*

Implementation Issues. Given a concurrent program, to implement our technique we introduce for each lock `l` two extra global variables defined as follows:

1. `possession_l`: to track whether `l` is currently in the possession of a thread
2. `history_l`: to track the acquisition history of `l`.

To begin with, `possession_l` is initialized to *false* and `history_l` to the emptyset. Then each statement of the form `acquire(lk)` in the original code is replaced by the following statements:

```
acquire(lk) ;
possession_lk := true ;
for each lock l
    if (possession_l = true)
        history_l := history_l ∪ {lk} ;
```

Similarly, each statement of the form `release(lk)` is replaced with the following sequence of statements:

```
release(lk) ;
possession_lk := false ;
history_lk := emptyset ;
```

Optimizations. The above naive implementation keeps the acquisition history for each lock of the concurrent program and tests for all possible disjoint pairs L and L' of lock sets and all possible compatible acquisition histories at two given error control locations a_i and b_j, say. In the worst case this is exponential in the number of locks. However by exploiting program analysis techniques one can severely cut down on the number of such lock sets and acquisition histories that need to be tested for each control location of the given program as discussed below.

Combining Lock Analysis with Program Analysis. Using static analysis on the control flow graph of a given thread we can get a conservative estimate of the set of locks that could possibly have been acquired by a thread with its program counter at a given control location c. This gives us a superset L_c of the set of locks that could possibly have been acquired at control location c and also the possible acquisition histories. Thus in performing the reachability analysis, $\mathsf{EF}(a_i \wedge b_j)$, we only need to consider sets L and L' of locks such that $L \cap L' = \emptyset$, $L \subseteq L_{a_i}$ and $L' \subseteq L_{b_j}$. This can exponentially cut down on the lock sets and acquisition histories that need be explored as, in practice, the nesting depth of locks is usually one and so the cardinality of L_c will usually be one.

Combining Lock Analysis with Program Slicing. By theorem 5, for a control location c of thread T we need to track histories of only those locks that are in possession of T at c instead of every lock as was done in the naive implementation. Furthermore for a lock l in possession of T at c we can ignore all lock operations performed by T before l was acquired for the last time by T before reaching c as these don't affect the acquisition history of l. Such statements can thus be deleted using program slicing techniques.

6 Deadlockability

In our framework, since synchronization among threads is carried out using locks, the only way a deadlock can occur is if there is a reachable global state s with a dependency cycle of the form $T_{i_1} \rightarrow T_{i_2} \rightarrow \ldots \rightarrow T_{i_p} \rightarrow T_{i_1}$, where $T_{i_{k-1}} \rightarrow T_{i_k}$ if the program counter of $T_{i_{k-1}}$ is currently at an acquire operation for a lock that is currently held by T_{i_k}. Thus to decide whether any thread in the given program $\mathcal{CP}$ is deadlockable, for each thread T_i of $\mathcal{CP}$ we first construct the set of reachable configurations of the corresponding augmented thread $(T_i)_A$ (defined above) where the control location is such that an acquire operation can be executed from it. Denote the set of such configurations by Acq_i. We then construct a directed graph $D_{\mathcal{CP}}$ whose nodes are elements of the set $\bigcup_i Acq_i$ and there is a directed edge from configuration $\mathbf{a} = (a, L, AH_1, \ldots, AH_m)$ to $\mathbf{a}' = (a', L', AH'_1, \ldots, AH'_m)$ iff there exist $i \neq i'$ such that (i) $\mathbf{a} \in Acq_i$, $\mathbf{a}' \in Acq_{i'}$, and (ii) a and a' both correspond to acquire operations, say, $acquire(l)$ and $acquire(l')$, respectively, and (iii) thread $T_{i'}$ currently holds lock l required by thread T_i, viz., $l \in L'$. Then the given current program is deadlockable iff there exists a cycle $\mathbf{c}_1 \to ... \to \mathbf{c}_p \to \mathbf{c}_1$ in $D_{\mathcal{CP}}$ such that every pair of configurations $\mathbf{c}_j = (c_j, L_j, AH_{j1}, ..., AH_{jm})$ and $\mathbf{c}_{j'} = (c_{j'}, L_{j'}, AH_{j'1}, ..., AH_{j'm})$ is consistent, viz., $L_j \cap L_{j'} = \emptyset$ and there do not exist locks $l_r \in L_j$ and $l_{r'} \in L_{j'}$ such that $l_{r'} \in AH_{jr}$ and $l_r \in AH_{j'r'}$. By theorem 5, consistency ensures that the global state encompassing the cycle is a reachable state of $\mathcal{CP}$. Note that again we have bypassed the state explosion problem by not constructing the state space of the system at hand. Furthermore using the optimizations discussed in the previous section, we can severely cut down on the possible lock sets and acquisition histories that we need to track for each acquire location in each thread. This ensures that the size of $D_{\mathcal{CP}}$ remains tractable.

7 Undecidability for Programs with Non-nested Locks

In this section, we show that for concurrent programs comprised of two threads T_1 and T_2 communicating via locks (not necessarily nested), the model checking problem for *pairwise reachability*, viz., properties of the form $\mathsf{EF}(a_1 \wedge b_2)$, where a_1 and b_2 are control states of T_1 and T_2, respectively, is undecidable.

Given a concurrent program $\mathcal{CP}$ comprised of two threads T_1 and T_2 communicating via pairwise rendezvous, we construct a new concurrent program $\mathcal{CP}'$ comprised of threads T_1 and T_2 by (weakly) simulating pairwise rendezvous using non-nested locks such that the set of control states of T_1 and T_2 are supersets of the sets of control states of T_1 and T_2, respectively, and for control states a_1 and b_2 of T_1 and T_2, respectively, $\mathcal{CP} \models \mathsf{EF}(a_1 \wedge b_2)$ iff $\mathcal{CP}' \models \mathsf{EF}(a_1 \wedge b_2)$. This reduces the decision problem for pairwise reachability for threads communicating via pairwise rendezvous to threads communicating via locks. But since pairwise reachability for threads communicating via pairwise rendezvous is undecidable, our result follows.

Simulating Pairwise Rendezvous using Locks. We now present the key idea behind the simulation. We show how to simulate a given pair $a \xrightarrow{m!} b$ and $c \xrightarrow{m?} d$ of send and receive pairwise rendezvous transitions, respectively. Recall that for this rendezvous to be executed, both the send and receive transitions must be simultaneously enabled, else neither transition can fire. Corresponding to the labels $m!$ and $m?$, we first introduce the new locks $l_{m!}$, $l_{m?}$ and l_m.

Cons ider now the send transition $tr : a \xrightarrow{m!} b$ of thread T_1, say. Our construction ensures that before T_1 starts mimicking tr in local state a it already has possession of lock $l_{m?}$. Then T_1 simulates T_1 via the following sequence of transitions: $a \xrightarrow{acquire(l_m)} a_1 \xrightarrow{release(l_{m?})} a_2 \xrightarrow{acquire(l_{m!})} a_3 \xrightarrow{release(l_m)} b \xrightarrow{acquire(l_{m?})} b_1 \xrightarrow{release(l_{m!})} b_2$. Similarly we assume that T_2 has possession of $l_{m!}$ before it starts mimicking $tr' : c \xrightarrow{m?} d$. Then T_2 simulates tr' by firing the following sequence of transitions: $c \xrightarrow{acquire(l_{m?})} c_1 \xrightarrow{release(l_{m!})} c_2 \xrightarrow{acquire(l_m)} c_3 \xrightarrow{release(l_{m?})} d \xrightarrow{acquire(l_{m!})} d_1 \xrightarrow{release(l_m)} d_2$.

The reason for letting thread T_1 acquire $l_{m?}$ at the outset is to prevent thread T_2 from firing transition $c \xrightarrow{m?} d$ without synchronizing with $tr : a \xrightarrow{m!} d$. To initiate execution of the pairwise rendezvous involving tr, thread T_1 releases lock $l_{m?}$ and only when lock $l_{m?}$ is released can T_2 pick it up in order to execute the matching receive transition labeled with $m?$. But before T_1 releases $l_{m?}$ it acquires l_m. Note that this trick involving *chaining* wherein before releasing a lock a thread is forced to pick up another lock gives us the ability to introduce a relative ordering on the firing of local transitions of T_1 and T_2 which in turn allows us to simulate (in a weak sense) the firing of the pairwise rendezvous comprised of tr and tr'. It can be seen that due to chaining, the local transitions in the two sequences defined above can only be interleaved in the following order: $a \xrightarrow{acquire(l_m)} a_1$, $a_1 \xrightarrow{release(l_{m?})} a_2$, $c \xrightarrow{acquire(l_{m?})} c_1$, $c_1 \xrightarrow{release(l_{m!})} c_2$, $a_2 \xrightarrow{acquire(l_{m!})} a_3$ $a_3 \xrightarrow{release(l_m)} b$, $c_2 \xrightarrow{acquire(l_m)} c_3$, $c_3 \xrightarrow{release(l_{m?})} d$, $b \xrightarrow{acquire(l_{m?})} b_1$, $b_1 \xrightarrow{release(l_{m!})} b_2$, $d \xrightarrow{acquire(l_{m!})} d_1$, $d_1 \xrightarrow{release(l_m)} d_2$.

It is important to note that the use of overlapping locks is essential in implementing chaining thereby forcing a pre-determined order of firing of the local transitions which cannot be accomplished using nested locks alone. Since the model checking problem for pairwise reachability is known to be undecidable for threads communicating using pairwise rendezvous [11] and since we can, by the above result, simulate pairwise rendezvous using locks in a way so as to preserve pairwise reachability, we have the following undecidability result.

Theorem 8. *The model checking problem for pairwise reachability is undecidable for concurrent programs comprised of two threads communicating using locks.*

8 The Daisy Case Study

We have used our technique to find bugs in the Daisy file system which is a benchmark for analyzing the efficacy of different methodologies for verifying concurrent programs [1]. Daisy is a 1KLOC Java implementation of a toy file system where each file is allocated a unique inode that stores the file parameters and a unique block which stores data. An interesting feature of Daisy is that it has fine grained locking in that access to each file, inode or block is guarded by a dedicated lock. Moreover, the acquire and release of each of these locks is guarded by a 'token' lock. Thus control locations in the program might possibly have multiple open locks and furthermore the acquire and release of a given lock can occur in different procedures.

We have incorporated our lock analysis technique into F-Soft [8] which is a framework for model checking sequential software. We have implemented the decision procedure for pairwise reachability and used it to detect race conditions in the Daisy file system. Towards that end we check that for all n, any n-threaded Daisy program does not have a given race condition. Since a race condition can be expressed as pairwise reachability, using Proposition 1, we see that it suffices to check a 2-thread instance. Currently F-Soft only accepts programs written in C and so we first manually translated the Daisy code which is written in Java into C. Furthermore, to reduce the model sizes, we truncated the sizes of the data structures modeling the disk, inodes, blocks, file names, etc., which were not relevant to the race conditions we checked, resulting in a sound and complete *small-domain* reduction. We emphasize that beyond redefining the constants limiting these sizes no code restructuring was carried out on the translated C code.

Given a race condition to be verified, we use a fully automated procedure to generate two augmented thread representation (Control Flow Graphs (CFG)) on which the verification is carried out individually. A race condition occurs if and only if the labels in both the modified threads are reachable. Using this fully automated procedure, we have shown the existence of the following race conditions also noted by other researchers (cf. [1]):

1. Daisy maintains an allocation area where for each block in the file system a bit is assigned 0 or 1 accordingly as the block has been allocated to a file or not. But each disk operation reads/writes an entire byte. Two threads accessing two different files might access two different blocks. However since bytes are not guarded by locks in order to set their allocation bits these two different threads may access the same byte in the allocation block containing the allocation bit for each of these locks thus setting up a race condition. For the data race described above, the statistics are as follows. The pre-processing phase which includes slicing, range analysis, using static analysis to find the possible set of open locks at the control state corresponding to the error label and then incorporating the acquisition history statements in the CFGs corresponding to the threads for only these locks took 77 secs[2] for both the threads. The two model checking runs took 5.3 and 21.67 secs and the error labels corresponding to the race condition were reached at depths 75 and 333, respectively in the two threads using SAT-based BMC in F-Soft.

2. In Daisy reading/writing a particular byte on the disk is broken down into two operations: a seek operation that mimics the positioning of the head and a read/write operation that transfers the actual data. Due to this separation between seeking and data transfer a race condition may occur. For example, reading two disk locations, say n and m, we must make sure that $seek(n)$ is followed by $read(n)$ without $seek(m)$ or $read(m)$ scheduled in between. Here the pre-processing phase took about the same time as above. The model checking runs on the two threads took 15 and 35 secs.

9 Conclusion and Related Work

In this paper, we have considered the static analysis of concurrent multi-threaded programs wherein the threads communicate via locks. We have shown that for single index LTL\X properties the problem is efficiently decidable. On the other hand, for double index LTL\X properties, the problem can be shown to be undecidable even for reachability and for systems with only two threads. However, for the practically important case where the locks are nested we get efficient decidability for pairwise reachability. We have implemented our technique in a prototype software verification platform and our preliminary results on the Daisy benchmark are encouraging.

There has been interesting prior work on extending data flow analysis to handle concurrent programs. In [3], the authors attempt to generalize the decision procedures given

[2] Machine Specifications: Intel Pentium4 3.20GHz CPU, 2MB RAM.

in [2] to handle pushdown systems communicating via CCS-style pairwise rendezvous. However since even reachability is undecidable for such a framework the procedures are not guaranteed to terminate in general but only for certain special cases, some of which the authors identify. However their practical utility is not clear. The key idea in identifying the above cases was to restrict the interaction among the threads so as to bypass the undecidability barrier. A natural way to accomplish that which was formulated in [10] is to explore the state spaces of the concurrent program for a bounded number of context switches among the threads.

A commonly used approach to cut down on the number of interleavings when reasoning about concurrent systems is to exploit syntactic independence among the local operations of different components of the system. In [9] this idea is exploited using the concept of transactions, wherein executing a transaction is equivalent to atomically executing a sequence of operations of each thread that do not involve communication with other threads and thus their execution does not interfere in the operation of other threads. The advantage of this technique is that it works well provided one can statically decide whether two given operations from two different threads are independent, a problem which is, in general, hard. The disadvantage is that although this technique can potentially cut down on the number of interleavings to be explored, it still does not completely address the core issue of state explosion. The use of partial order techniques ([6, 5, 14, 15]) also exploits syntactic independence of transitions to cut down on the number of interleavings to be explored and although extremely useful, suffers from the same drawback as above.

Another technique that has been adapted from concurrent protocol verification is the use of compositional reasoning wherein one tries to reduce reasoning about the correctness of a system comprised of many concurrently executing components to reasoning about each individual components. In [7] an assume-guarantee style reasoning is used to abstract out the environment of each thread in a purely automatic fashion for system where the threads are loosely coupled. A drawback is that the technique is not complete for reachability and thus is not guaranteed to find all errors. Furthermore, error trace recovery is hard because abstracting the environment causes a lot of information to be lost and thus it may not be possible to construct a concrete error trace purely from the environment assumptions.

We, on the other hand, have identified a practically important case of threads communicating using locks and shown how to reason efficiently about a rich class of properties. We address the state explosion problem by reducing reasoning about indexed $\mathrm{LTL}\setminus\mathrm{X}$ properties and deadlockability to reasoning about individual threads. Our methods are exact, i.e., both sound and complete, and cater to automatic error trace recovery. A key advantage of our method is that by avoiding construction of the state space of the system at hand we bypass the state explosion problem, thus guaranteeing scalability of our approach. Most multi-threaded programs use shared data structures that are guarded by locks to communicate. A potential drawback of our method is that it works only for threads that communicate purely using locks. However we believe that a very large fraction of concurrent software is loosely coupled and even where richer communication mechanisms are used, the interaction between the threads is not very subtle and can often, by using standard abstract interpretation techniques, be modeled as threads communicating solely using locks. Furthermore, even if it not possible to abstract out the shared data structures, by considering only communication via the locks we over-approximate the set of behaviors of the given program. Our technique can then be used to generate warnings for potential data race violations. This is advantageous as model checking a single thread is more tractable than model checking an entire multi-threaded program. Once these potential data race violations have been isolated, more general but less tractable techniques like model checking using partial order reductions can be deployed to further refine the analysis by focusing precisely on these violations. Our technique can therefore be looked upon as a first line of attack in combating state explosion in the context of multi-threaded software providing an exact and efficient procedure for verifying an important class of multi-threaded software.

References

1. Joint CAV/ISSTA Special Event on Specification, Verification, and Testing of Concurrent Software. In *http://research.microsoft.com/ qadeer/cav-issta.htm*.
2. Ahmed Bouajjani, Javier Esparza, and Oded Maler. Reachability Analysis of Pushdown Automata: Application to Model-Checking. In *CONCUR*, LNCS 1243, pages 135–150, 1997.
3. Ahmed Bouajjani, Javier Esparza, and Tayssir Touili. A generic approach to the static analysis of concurrent programs with procedures. In *IJFCS*, volume 14(4), pages 551–, 2003.
4. M. B. Dwyer and L. A. Clarke. Data flow analysis for verifying properties of concurrent programs. In *ACM SIGSOFT*, pages 62–75, 1994.
5. P. Godefroid. Model Checking for Programming Languages using Verisoft. In *POPL*, pages 174–186, 1997.
6. P. Godefroid and P. Wolper. Using Partial Orders for Efficient Verification of deadlock-freedom and safety properties. In *Formal Methods in Systems Design*, pages 149–164, 1993.
7. T. Henzinger, R. Jhala, R. Mazumdar, and S. Qadeer. Thread-Modular Abstraction Refinement. In *CAV*, LNCS 2725, pages 262–274, 2003.
8. F. Ivančić, Z. Yang, M. Ganai, A. Gupta, and P. Ashar. Efficient SAT-based Bounded Model Checking for Software Verification. In *Symposium on Leveraging Applications of Formal Methods*, 2004.
9. S. Qadeer, S. K. Rajamani, and J. Rehof. Summarizing procedures in concurrent programs. In *POPL*, pages 245–255, 2004.
10. S. Qadeer and J. Rehof. Context-Bounded Model Checking of Concurrent Software. In *TACAS*, 2005.
11. G. Ramalingam. Context-sensitive synchronization-sensitive analysis is undecidable. In *ACM Trans. Program. Lang. Syst.*, volume 22(2), pages 416–430, 2000.
12. T. W. Reps, S. Horwitz, and S. Sagiv. Precise Interprocedural Dataflow Analysis via Graph Reachability. In *POPL*, pages 49–61, 1985.
13. D. A. Schmidt and B. Steffen. Program Analysis as Model Checking of Abstract Interpretations. In *Static Analysis, 5th International Symposium,*, LNCS 1503, pages 351–380, 1998.
14. S. D. Stoller. Model-Checking Multi-Threaded Distributed Java Programs. In *STTT*, volume 4(1), pages 71–91, 2002.
15. W. Visser, K. Havelund, G. P. Brat, S. Park, and F. Lerda. Model Checking Programs. In *Automated Software Engineering*, volume 10(2), pages 203–232, 2003.
16. I. Walukeiwicz. Model Checking CTL Properties of Pushdown Systems. In *FSTTCS*, LNCS 1974, pages 127–138, 2000.

Abstraction Refinement via Inductive Learning

Alexey Loginov[1], Thomas Reps[1], and Mooly Sagiv[2]

[1] Comp. Sci. Dept., University of Wisconsin
{alexey, reps}@cs.wisc.edu
[2] School of Comp. Sci., Tel-Aviv University
msagiv@post.tau.ac.il

Abstract. This paper concerns how to automatically create abstractions for program analysis. We show that inductive learning, the goal of which is to identify general rules from a set of observed instances, provides new leverage on the problem. An advantage of an approach based on inductive learning is that it does not require the use of a theorem prover.

1 Introduction

We present an approach to automatically creating abstractions for use in program analysis. As in some previous work [12, 4, 13, 18, 5, 2, 8], the approach involves the successive refinement of the abstraction in use. Unlike previous work, the work presented in this paper is aimed at programs that manipulate pointers and heap-allocated data structures. However, while we demonstrate our approach on shape-analysis problems, the approach is applicable in any program-analysis setting that uses first-order logic.

The paper presents an abstraction-refinement method for use in static analyses based on 3-valued logic [21], where the semantics of statements and the query of interest are expressed using logical formulas. In this setting, a memory configuration is modeled by a *logical structure*; an individual of the structure's universe either models a single memory element or, in the case of a *summary individual*, it models a collection of memory elements. Summary individuals are used to ensure that abstract descriptors have an *a priori* bounded size, which guarantees that a fixed-point is always reached. However, the constraint of working with limited-size descriptors implies a loss of information about the store. Intuitively, certain properties of concrete individuals are lost due to abstraction, which groups together multiple individuals into summary individuals: a property can be true for some concrete individuals of the group, but false for other individuals. The TVLA system is a tool for creating such analyses [1].

With the method proposed in this paper, refinement is performed by introducing new *instrumentation relations* (defined via logical formulas over core relations, which capture the basic properties of memory configurations). Instrumentation relations record auxiliary information in a logical structure, thus providing a mechanism to fine-tune an abstraction: an instrumentation relation captures a property that an individual memory cell may or may not possess. In general, the introduction of additional instrumentation relations refines an abstraction into one that is prepared to track finer distinctions among stores. The choice of instrumentation relations is crucial to the precision, as well as the cost, of the analysis. Until now, TVLA users have been faced with the task of identifying an instrumentation-relation set that gives them a definite answer to the query, but does not make the cost prohibitive. This was arguably the key remaining challenge in the TVLA user-model. The contributions of this work can be summarized as follows:

K. Etessami and S.K. Rajamani (Eds.): CAV 2005, LNCS 3576, pp. 519–533, 2005.

- It establishes a new connection between program analysis and machine learning by showing that *inductive logic programming* (ILP) [19, 17, 14] is relevant to the problem of creating abstractions. We use ILP for learning new instrumentation relations that preserve information that would otherwise be lost due to abstraction.
- The method has been implemented as an extension of TVLA. In this system, all of the user-level obligations for which TVLA has been criticized in the past have been addressed. The input required to specify a program analysis consists of: (i) a transition system, (ii) a query (a formula that identifies acceptable outputs), and (iii) a characterization of the program's valid inputs.
- We present experimental evidence of the value of the approach. We tested the method on sortedness, stability, and antistability queries for a set of programs that perform destructive list manipulation, as well as on partial-correctness queries for two binary-search-tree programs. The method succeeds in all cases tested.

Inductive learning concerns identifying general rules from a set of observed instances—in our case, from relationships observed in a logical structure. An advantage of an approach based on inductive learning is that it does not require the use of a theorem prover. This is particularly beneficial in our setting because our logic is undecidable.

The paper is organized as follows: §2 introduces terminology and notation. Readers familiar with TVLA can skip to §2.2, which briefly summarizes ILP. §3 illustrates our goals on the problem of verifying the partial correctness of a sorting routine. §4 describes the techniques used for learning abstractions. (Further details can be found in [16].) §5 presents experimental results. §6 discusses related work.

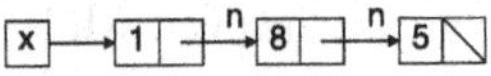

Fig. 1. A possible store for a linked list

2 Background

2.1 Stores as Logical Structures and Their Abstractions

Our work extends the program-analysis framework of [21]. In that approach, concrete memory configurations (i.e., *stores*) are encoded as logical structures in terms of a fixed collection of *core relations*, $\mathcal{C}$. Core relations are part of the underlying semantics of the language to be analyzed. For instance, Tab. 1 gives the definition of a C linked-list datatype, and lists the relations that would be used to represent the stores manipulated by programs that use type `List`, such as the store in Fig. 1. 2-valued logical structures then represent memory configurations: the individuals are the set of memory cells; in this example, unary relations represent pointer variables and binary relation n represents the n-field of a `List` cell. The `data` field is modeled indirectly, via the binary relation *dle* (which stands for "`data` less-than-or-equal-to") listed in Tab. 1. Fig. 2 shows 2-valued structure S_2, which represents the store of Fig. 1 (relations t_n, $r_{n,x}$, and c_n will be explained below).

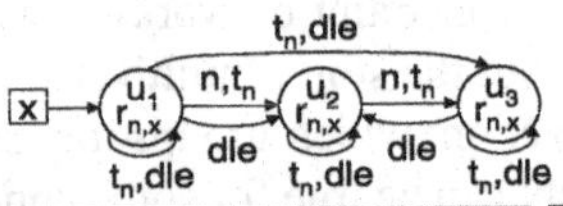

	x	$r_{n,x}$	c_n
u_1	1	1	0
u_2	0	1	0
u_3	0	1	0

n	u_1	u_2	u_3
u_1	0	1	0
u_2	0	0	1
u_3	0	0	0

t_n	u_1	u_2	u_3
u_1	1	1	1
u_2	0	1	1
u_3	0	0	1

dle	u_1	u_2	u_3
u_1	1	1	1
u_2	0	1	0
u_3	0	1	1

Fig. 2. A logical structure S_2 that represents the store shown in Fig. 1 in graphical and tabular forms

Table 1. (a) Declaration of a linked-list datatype in C. (b) Core relations used for representing the stores manipulated by programs that use type `List`

(a)

```
typedef struct node {
  struct node *n;
  int data;
} *List;
```

(b)

Relation	Intended Meaning
$eq(v_1, v_2)$	Do v_1 and v_2 denote the same memory cell?
$q(v)$	Does pointer variable `q` point to memory cell v?
$n(v_1, v_2)$	Does the `n` field of v_1 point to v_2?
$dle(v_1, v_2)$	Is the `data` field of v_1 less than or equal to that of v_2?

Let $\mathcal{R} = \{eq, p_1, \ldots, p_n\}$ be a finite vocabulary of relation symbols, where $\mathcal{R}_k$ denotes the set of relation symbols of arity k (and $eq \in \mathcal{R}_2$). A *2-valued logical structure* S over $\mathcal{R}$ is a set of *individuals* U^S, along with an *interpretation* that maps each relation symbol p of arity k to a truth-valued function: $p^S\colon (U^S)^k \to \{0, 1\}$, where eq^S is the equality relation on individuals. The set of 2-valued structures is denoted by $\mathcal{S}_2[\mathcal{R}]$.

In 3-valued logic, a third truth value—1/2—is introduced to denote uncertainty. For $l_1, l_2 \in \{0, 1/2, 1\}$, the *information order* is defined as follows: $l_1 \sqsubseteq l_2$ iff $l_1 = l_2$ or $l_2 = 1/2$. A *3-valued logical structure* S is defined like a 2-valued logical structure, except that the values in relations can be $\{0, 1/2, 1\}$. An individual for which $eq^S(u, u) = 1/2$ is called a *summary individual*. A summary individual abstracts one or more fragments of a data structure, and can represent more than one concrete memory cell. The set of 3-valued structures is denoted by $\mathcal{S}_3[\mathcal{R}]$.

Concrete and Abstract Semantics. A concrete operational semantics is defined by specifying a structure transformer for each kind of edge e that can appear in a transition system. A structure transformer is specified by providing *relation-update formulas* for the core relations.[1] These formulas define how the core relations of a 2-valued logical structure S that arises at the source of e are transformed by e to create a 2-valued logical structure S' at the target of e. Edge e may optionally have a *precondition formula*, which filters out structures that should not follow the transition along e.

However, sets of 2-valued structures do not yield a suitable abstract domain; for instance, when the language being modeled supports allocation from the heap, the set of individuals that may appear in a structure is unbounded, and thus there is no a priori upper bound on the number of 2-valued structures that may arise during the analysis.

To ensure termination, we abstract sets of 2-valued structures using 3-valued structures. A set of stores is then represented by a (finite) set of 3-valued logical structures. The abstraction is defined using an equivalence relation on individuals: each individual of a 2-valued logical structure (representing a concrete memory cell) is mapped to an individual of a 3-valued logical structure according to the vector of values that the concrete individual has for a user-chosen collection of unary abstraction relations:

Definition (Canonical Abstraction). Let $S \in \mathcal{S}_2$, and let $\mathcal{A} \subseteq \mathcal{R}_1$ be some chosen subset of the unary relation symbols. The relations in $\mathcal{A}$ are called *abstraction relations*; they define the following equivalence relation $\simeq_{\mathcal{A}}$ on U^S:

$$u_1 \simeq_{\mathcal{A}} u_2 \iff \text{for all } p \in \mathcal{A}, p^S(u_1) = p^S(u_2),$$

[1] Formulas are first-order formulas with transitive closure: a *formula* over the vocabulary $\mathcal{R}$ is defined as follows (where $p^*(v_1, v_2)$ stands for the reflexive transitive closure of $p(v_1, v_2)$):

$$\begin{array}{ll} p \in \mathcal{R}, & \varphi ::= \mathbf{0} \mid \mathbf{1} \mid p(v_1, \ldots, v_k) \mid (\neg\varphi_1) \mid (v_1 = v_2) \\ \varphi \in \textit{Formulas}, & \quad \mid (\varphi_1 \wedge \varphi_2) \mid (\varphi_1 \vee \varphi_2) \mid (\varphi_1 \to \varphi_2) \mid (\varphi_1 \leftrightarrow \varphi_2) \\ v \in \textit{Variables} & \quad \mid (\exists v\colon \varphi_1) \mid (\forall v\colon \varphi_1) \mid p^*(v_1, v_2) \end{array}$$

and the surjective function $f_{\mathcal{A}} : U^S \to U^S/\simeq_{\mathcal{A}}$, such that $f_{\mathcal{A}}(u) = [u]_{\simeq_{\mathcal{A}}}$, which maps an individual to its equivalence class. The *canonical abstraction* of S with respect to $\mathcal{A}$ (denoted by $f_{\mathcal{A}}(S)$) performs the join (in the information order) of predicate values, thereby introducing $1/2$'s. □

If all unary relations are abstraction relations ($\mathcal{A} = \mathcal{R}_1$), the canonical abstraction of 2-valued logical structure S_2 is S_3, shown in Fig. 3, with $f_{\mathcal{A}}(u_1) = u_1$ and $f_{\mathcal{A}}(u_2) = f_{\mathcal{A}}(u_3) = u_{23}$. S_3 represents all lists with two or more elements, in which the first element's `data` value is lower than the `data` values in the rest of the list. The following graphical notation is used for depicting 3-valued logical structures:

- Individuals are represented by circles containing their names and (non-0) values for unary relations. Summary individuals are represented by double circles.
- A unary relation p corresponding to a pointer-valued program variable is represented by a solid arrow from p to the individual u for which $p(u) = 1$, and by the absence of a p-arrow to each node u' for which $p(u') = 0$. (If $p = 0$ for all individuals, the relation name p is not shown.)
- A binary relation q is represented by a solid arrow labeled q between each pair of individuals u_i and u_j for which $q(u_i, u_j) = 1$, and by the absence of a q-arrow between pairs u'_i and u'_j for which $q(u'_i, u'_j) = 0$.
- Relations with value $1/2$ are represented by dotted arrows.

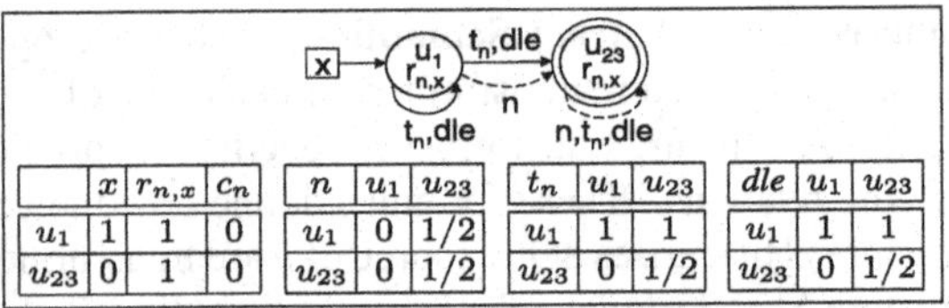

	x	$r_{n,x}$	c_n
u_1	1	1	0
u_{23}	0	1	0

n	u_1	u_{23}
u_1	0	1/2
u_{23}	0	1/2

t_n	u_1	u_{23}
u_1	1	1
u_{23}	0	1/2

dle	u_1	u_{23}
u_1	1	1
u_{23}	0	1/2

Fig. 3. A 3-valued structure S_3 that is the canonical abstraction of structure S_2

Canonical abstraction ensures that each 3-valued structure is no larger than some fixed size, known *a priori*. Moreover, the meaning of a given formula in the concrete domain ($\wp(\mathcal{S}_2)$) is consistent with its meaning in the abstract domain ($\wp(\mathcal{S}_3)$), although the formula's value in an abstract structure $f_{\mathcal{A}}(S)$ may be less precise than its value in the concrete structure S.

Abstract interpretation collects a set of 3-valued structures at each program point. It can be implemented as an iterative procedure that finds the least fixed point of a certain collection of equations on variables that take their values in $\wp(\mathcal{S}_3)$ [21].

Table 2. Defining formulas of some commonly used instrumentation relations. There is a separate reachability relation $r_{n,x}$ for every program variable x

p	**Intended Meaning**	ψ_p
$t_n(v_1, v_2)$	Is v_2 reachable from v_1 along n fields?	$n^*(v_1, v_2)$
$r_{n,x}(v)$	Is v reachable from pointer variable x along n fields?	$\exists v_1 : x(v_1) \wedge t_n(v_1, v)$
$c_n(v)$	Is v on a directed cycle of n fields?	$\exists v_1 : n(v_1, v) \wedge t_n(v, v_1)$

Instrumentation Relations. The abstraction function on which an analysis is based, and hence the precision of the analysis defined, can be tuned by (i) choosing to equip structures with additional *instrumentation relations* to record derived properties, and (ii) varying which of the unary core and unary instrumentation relations are used as the set of abstraction relations. The set of instrumentation relations is denoted by $\mathcal{I}$. Each relation symbol $p \in \mathcal{I}_k \subseteq \mathcal{R}_k$ is defined by an *instrumentation-relation definition formula* $\psi_p(v_1, \ldots, v_k)$. Instrumentation relation symbols may appear in the defining formulas of other instrumentation relations as long as there are no circular dependences.

The introduction of unary instrumentation relations that are used as abstraction relations provides a way to control which concrete individuals are merged together, and thereby control the amount of information lost by abstraction. Tab. 2 lists some instrumentation relations that are important for the analysis of programs that use type `List`.

2.2 Inductive Logic Programming (ILP)

Given a logical structure, the goal of an ILP algorithm is to learn a logical relation (defined in terms of the logical structure's other relations) that agrees with the classification of input examples. ILP algorithms produce the answer in the form of a logic program. (Non-recursive) logic programs correspond to a subset of first-order logic.[2] A logic program can be thought of as a disjunction over the program rules, with each rule corresponding to a conjunction of literals. Variables not appearing in the head of a rule are implicitly existentially quantified.

Definition (ILP). Given a set of positive example tuples E^+, a set of negative example tuples E^-, and a logical structure, the goal of ILP is to find a formula ψ_E such that all $e \in E^+$ are satisfied (or *covered*) by ψ_E and no $e \in E^-$ is satisfied by ψ_E. □

For example, consider learning a unary formula that holds for linked-list elements that are pointed to by the n fields of more than one element (as used in [11,3]). We let $E^+ = \{u_3, u_5\}$ and $E^- = \{u_1, u_4\}$ in the 2-valued structure of Fig. 4. The formula $\psi_{isShared}(v) \stackrel{\text{def}}{=} \exists\, v_1, v_2 : n(v_1, v) \wedge n(v_2, v) \wedge \neg eq(v_1, v_2)$ meets the objective, as it covers all positive and no negative example tuples.

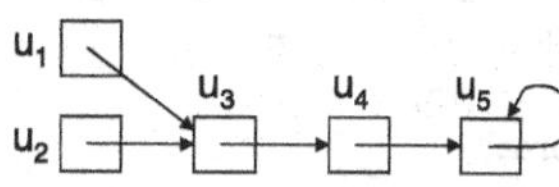

Fig. 4. A linked list with shared elements

Fig. 5 presents the ILP algorithm used by systems such as FOIL [19], modified to construct the answer as a first-order logic formula in disjunctive normal form. This algorithm is capable of learning the formula $\psi_{isShared}(v)$ (by performing one iteration of the outer loop and three iterations of the inner loop to successively choose literals $n(v_1, v)$, $n(v_2, v)$, and

```
Input: Target relation E(v1,...,vk),
       Structure S ∈ S3[R],
       Set of tuples Pos, Set of tuples Neg
ψE := 0
while (Pos ≠ ∅)
   NewDisjunct := 1
   NewNeg := Neg
   while (NewNeg ≠ ∅)
      Cand := candidate literals using R
      Best := L ∈ Cand with max Gain(L, NewDisjunct)
      NewDisjunct := NewDisjunct ∧ L
      NewNeg := subset of NewNeg satisfying L
   ∃-quantify NewDisjunct variables ∉ {v1,...,vk}
   ψE := ψE ∨ NewDisjunct
   Pos := subset of Pos not satisfying NewDisjunct
```

Fig. 5. Pseudo-code for FOIL

---

[2] ILP algorithms are capable of producing recursive programs, which correspond to first-order logic plus a least-fixpoint operator (which is more general than transitive closure).

$\neg eq(v_1, v_2)$). It is a sequential covering algorithm parameterized by the function *Gain*, which characterizes the usefulness of adding a particular literal (generally, in some heuristic fashion). The algorithm creates a new disjunct as long as there are positive examples that are not covered by existing disjuncts. The disjunct is extended by conjoining a new literal until it covers no negative examples. Each literal uses a relation symbol from the vocabulary of structure S; valid arguments to a literal are the variables of target relation E, as well as new variables, as long as at least one of the arguments is a variable already used in the current disjunct. In FOIL, one literal is chosen using a heuristic value based on the information gain (see line [7]). FOIL uses information gain to find the literal that differentiates best between positive and negative examples.

3 Example: Verifying Sortedness

Given the static-analysis algorithm defined in §2.1, to demonstrate the partial correctness of a procedure, the user must supply the following program-specific information:

- The procedure's control-flow graph.
- A *data-structure constructor* (DSC): a code fragment that non-deterministically constructs all valid inputs.
- A query; i.e., a formula that identifies the intended outputs.

The analysis algorithm is run on the DSC concatenated with the procedure's control-flow graph; the query is then evaluated on the structures that are generated at exit.

Consider the problem of establishing that `InsertSort` shown in Fig. 6 is partially correct. This is an assertion that compares the state of a store at the end of a procedure with its state at the start. In particular, a correct sorting routine must perform a permutation of the input list, i.e. all list elements reachable from variable x at the start of the routine must be reachable from x at the end. We can express the permutation property as follows:

```
void InsertSort(List x){
  List r, pr, rn, l, pl;
  r = x;
  pr = NULL;
  while (r != NULL) {
    l = x;
    rn = r->n;
    pl = NULL;
    while (l != r) {
      if (l->data > r->data){
        pr->n = rn;
        r->n = l;
        if (pl == NULL) x = r;
        else pl->n = r;
        r = pr;
        break;
      }
      pl = l;
      l = l->n;
    }
    pr = r;
    r = rn;
  }
}
```

Fig. 6. A stable version of insertion sort

$$\forall v : r^0_{n,x}(v) \leftrightarrow r_{n,x}(v), \tag{1}$$

where $r^0_{n,x}$ denotes the reachability relation for x at the beginning of `InsertSort`. If Formula (1) holds, then the elements reachable from x after `InsertSort` executes are exactly the same as those reachable at the beginning, and consequently the procedure performs a permutation of list x. In general, for each relation p, we have such a *history relation* p^0.

Fig. 7 shows the three structures that characterize the valid inputs to `InsertSort` (they represent the set of stores in which program variable x points to an acyclic linked list). To verify that `InsertSort` produces a *sorted* permutation of the input list, we would check to see whether, for all of the structures that arise at the procedure's exit node, the following formula evaluates to 1:

$$\forall v_1 : r_{n,x}(v_1) \rightarrow (\forall v_2 : n(v_1, v_2) \rightarrow dle(v_1, v_2)). \tag{2}$$

If it does, then the nodes reachable from x must be in non-decreasing order.

Abstract interpretation collects 3-valued structure S_3 shown in Fig. 3 at line [24]. Note that Formula (2) evaluates to $1/2$ on S_3. While the first list element is guaranteed to be in correct order with respect to the remaining elements, there is no guarantee that all list nodes represented by the summary node are in correct order. In particular, because S_3 represents S_2, shown in Fig. 2, the analysis admits the possibility that the (correct) implementation of insertion sort of Fig. 6 can produce the store shown in Fig. 1. Thus, the abstraction that we used was not fine-grained enough to establish the partial correctness of `InsertSort`. In fact, the abstraction is not fine-grained enough to separate the set of sorted lists from the lists not in sorted order.

In [15], Lev-Ami et al. used TVLA to establish the partial correctness of `InsertSort`. The key step was the introduction of instrumentation relation $inOrder_{dle,n}(v)$, which holds for nodes whose `data`-components are less than or equal to those of their n-successors; $inOrder_{dle,n}(v)$ was defined by:

$$inOrder_{dle,n}(v) \stackrel{\text{def}}{=} \forall v_1 : n(v, v_1) \rightarrow dle(v, v_1). \tag{3}$$

The sortedness property was then stated as follows (cf. Formula (2)):

$$\forall v : r_{n,x}(v) \rightarrow inOrder_{dle,n}(v). \tag{4}$$

After the introduction of relation $inOrder_{dle,n}$, the 3-valued structures that are collected by abstract interpretation at the end of `InsertSort` describe all stores in which variable x points to an acyclic, *sorted* linked list. In all of these structures, Formulas (4) and (1) evaluate to 1. Consequently, `InsertSort` is guaranteed to work correctly on all valid inputs.

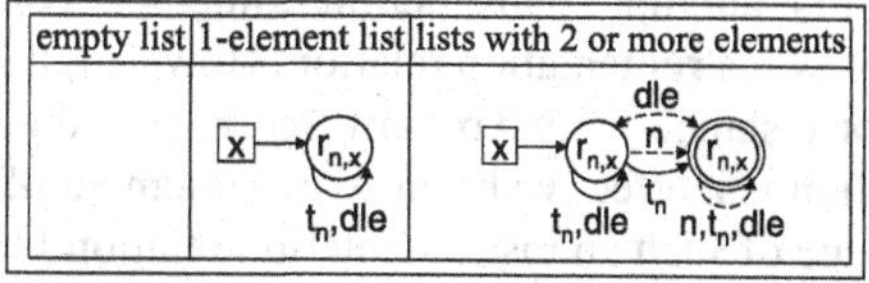

Fig. 7. The structures that describe possible inputs to `InsertSort`

4 Learning an Abstraction

In [15], instrumentation relation $inOrder_{dle,n}$ was defined explicitly (by the TVLA user). Heretofore, there have really been two burdens placed on the TVLA user:

(i) he must have insight into the behavior of the program, and
(ii) he must translate this insight into appropriate instrumentation relations.

The goal of this paper is to automate the identification of appropriate instrumentation relations, such as $inOrder_{dle,n}$. For `InsertSort`, the goal is to obtain definite answers when evaluating Formula (2) on the structures collected by abstract interpretation at line [24] of Fig. 6. Fig. 8 gives pseudo-code for our method, the steps of which can be explained as follows:

```
Input: a transition system,
       a data-structure constructor,
       a query $\varphi$ (a closed formula)
[1] Construct abstract input
[2] do
[3]   Perform abstract interpretation
[4]   Let $S_1, \ldots, S_k$ be the set of
       3-valued structures at exit
[5]   if for all $S_i$, $[\![\varphi]\!]_3^{S_i}([]) \neq 1/2$ break
[6]   Find formulas $\psi_{p_1}, \ldots, \psi_{p_k}$ for new
       instrumentation rels $p_1, \ldots, p_k$
[7]   Refine the actions that define
       the transition system
[8]   Refine the abstract input
[9] while(true)
```

Fig. 8. Pseudo-code for iterative abstraction refinement

- (Line [1]; [16, §4.3]) Use a data-structure constructor to compute the abstract input structures that represent all valid inputs to the program.
- Perform an abstract interpretation to collect a set of structures at each program point, and evaluate the query on the structures at exit. If a definite answer is obtained on all structures, terminate. Otherwise, perform abstraction refinement.
- (Line [6]; §4.1 and §4.2) Find defining formulas for new instrumentation relations.
- (Line [7]) Replace all occurrences of these formulas in the query and in the definitions of other instrumentation relations with the use of the corresponding new instrumentation relation symbols, and apply finite differencing [20] to generate refined relation-update formulas for the transition system.
- (Line [8]; [16, §4.3]) Obtain the most precise possible values for the newly introduced instrumentation relations in abstract structures that define the valid inputs to the program. This is achieved by "reconstructing" the valid inputs by performing abstract interpretation of the data-structure constructor.

A first attempt at abstraction refinement could be the introduction of the query itself as a new instrumentation relation. However, this usually does not lead to a definite answer. For instance, with `InsertSort`, introducing the query as a new instrumentation relation is ineffective because no statement of the program has the effect of changing the value of such an instrumentation relation from $1/2$ to 1.

In contrast, when unary instrumentation relation $inOrder_{dle,n}$ is present, there are several statements of the program where abstract interpretation results in new definite entries for $inOrder_{dle,n}$. For instance, because of the comparison in line [10] of Fig. 6, the insertion in lines [12]–[14] of the node pointed to by `r` (say u) before the node pointed to by `l` results in a new definite entry $inOrder_{dle,n}(u)$.

An algorithm to generate new instrumentation relations should take into account the sources of imprecision. §4.1 describes subformula-based refinement; §4.2 describes ILP-based refinement. At present, we employ subformula-based refinement first, because the cost of this strategy is reasonable (see §5) and the strategy is often successful. When subformula-based refinement can no longer refine the abstraction, we turn to ILP.

Because a query has finitely many subformulas and we currently limit ourselves to one round of ILP-based refinement, the number of abstraction-refinement steps is finite. Because, additionally, each run of the analysis explores a bounded number of 3-valued structures, the algorithm is guaranteed to terminate.

4.1 Subformula-Based Refinement

When the query φ evaluates to $1/2$ on a structure S collected at the exit node, we invoke function *instrum*, a recursive-descent procedure to generate defining formulas for new instrumentation relations based on the subformulas of φ responsible for the imprecision. The details of function *instrum* are given in [16, §4.1].

Example. As we saw in §3, abstract interpretation collects 3-valued structure S_3 of Fig. 3 at the exit node of `InsertSort`. The sortedness query (Formula (2)) evaluates to $1/2$ on S_3, triggering a call to *instrum* with Formula (2) and structure S_3, as arguments. Column 2 of Tab. 3 shows the instrumentation relations that are created as a result of the call. Note that $sorted_3$ is defined exactly as $inOrder_{dle,n}$, which was the key insight for the results of [15]. □

Table 3. Instrumentation relations created by subformula-based refinement

p	ψ_p (after call to *instrum*)	ψ_p (final version)
$sorted_1()$	$\forall v_1 : r_{n,x}(v_1) \rightarrow (\forall v_2 : n(v_1, v_2) \rightarrow dle(v_1, v_2))$	$\forall v_1 : sorted_2(v_1)$
$sorted_2(v_1)$	$r_{n,x}(v_1) \rightarrow (\forall v_2 : n(v_1, v_2) \rightarrow dle(v_1, v_2))$	$r_{n,x}(v_1) \rightarrow sorted_3(v_1)$
$sorted_3(v_1)$	$\forall v_2 : n(v_1, v_2) \rightarrow dle(v_1, v_2)$	$\forall v_2 : sorted_4(v_1, v_2)$
$sorted_4(v_1, v_2)$	$n(v_1, v_2) \rightarrow dle(v_1, v_2)$	$n(v_1, v_2) \rightarrow dle(v_1, v_2)$

The actions that define the program's transition relation need to be modified to gain precision improvements from storing and maintaining the new instrumentation relations. To accomplish this, refinement of the program's actions (line [7] in Fig. 8) replaces all occurrences of the defining formulas for the new instrumentation relations in the query and in the definitions of other instrumentation relations with the use of the corresponding new instrumentation-relation symbols.

Example. For `InsertSort`, the use of Formula (2) in the query is replaced with the use of the stored value $sorted_1()$. Then the definitions of all instrumentation relations are scanned for occurrences of $\psi_{sorted_1}, \ldots, \psi_{sorted_4}$. These occurrences are replaced with the names of the four relations. In this case, only the new relations' definitions are changed, yielding the definitions given in Column 3 of Tab. 3.

In all of the structures collected at the exit node of `InsertSort` by the second run of abstract interpretation, $sorted_1() = 1$. The permutation property also holds on all of the structures. These two facts establish the partial correctness of `InsertSort`. This process required one iteration of abstraction refinement, used the basic version of the specification (the vocabulary consisted of the relations of Tabs. 1 and 2, together with the corresponding history relations), and needed no user intervention. □

4.2 ILP-Based Refinement

Shortcomings of Subformula-Based Refinement. To illustrate a weakness in subformula-based refinement, we introduce the stability property. The stability property usually arises in the context of sorting procedures, but actually applies to list-manipulating programs in general: the stability query (Formula (5)) asserts that the relative order of elements with equal `data`-components remains the same.[3]

$$\forall v_1, v_2 : (dle(v_1, v_2) \wedge dle(v_2, v_1) \wedge t_n^0(v_1, v_2)) \rightarrow t_n(v_1, v_2) \qquad (5)$$

Procedure `InsertSort` consists of two nested loops (see Fig. 6). The outer loop traverses the list, setting pointer variable `r` to point to list nodes. For each iteration of the outer loop, the inner loop finds the correct place to insert `r`'s target, by traversing the list from the start using pointer variable `l`; `r`'s target is inserted before `l`'s target when `l->data > r->data`. Because `InsertSort` satisfies the invariant that all list nodes that appear in the list before `r`'s target are already in the correct order, the `data`-component of `r`'s target is less than the `data`-component of *all* nodes ahead of which `r`'s target is moved. Thus, `InsertSort` preserves the original order of elements with equal `data`-components, and `InsertSort` is a stable routine.

However, subformula-based refinement is not capable of establishing the stability of `InsertSort`. By considering only subformulas of the query (in this case, Formula (5)) as candidate instrumentation relations, the strategy is unable to introduce instrumentation relations that maintain information about the *transitive* successors with which a list node has the correct relative order.

Learning Instrumentation Relations. Fig. 9 shows the structure S_9, which arises during abstract interpretation just before line [6] of Fig. 6, together with a tabular version of relations t_n and *dle*. (We omit reachability relations from the figure for clarity.) After the assignment `l = x;`, nodes u_2 and u_3 have identical vectors of values for the unary abstraction relations. The subsequent application of canonical abstraction produces structure S_{10}, shown in Fig. 10. Bold entries of tables in Fig. 9 indicate definite values that are transformed into 1/2 in S_{10}. Structure S_9 satisfies the sortedness invariant discussed above: every node among $u_1, ..., u_4$ has the *dle* relationship with all nodes appearing later in the list, except `r`'s target, u_5. However, a piece of this information is lost in structure S_{10}: $dle(u_{23}, u_{23}) = 1/2$, indicating that some nodes represented by summary node u_{23} might not be in sorted order with respect to their successors. We will refer to such abstraction steps as *information-loss points*.

An abstract structure transformer may temporarily create a structure S_1 that is not in the image of canonical abstraction [21]. The subsequent application of canonical abstraction transforms S_1 into structure S_2 by grouping a set U_1 of two or more individuals of S_1 into a single summary individual of S_2. The loss of precision is due to one or both of the following circumstances:

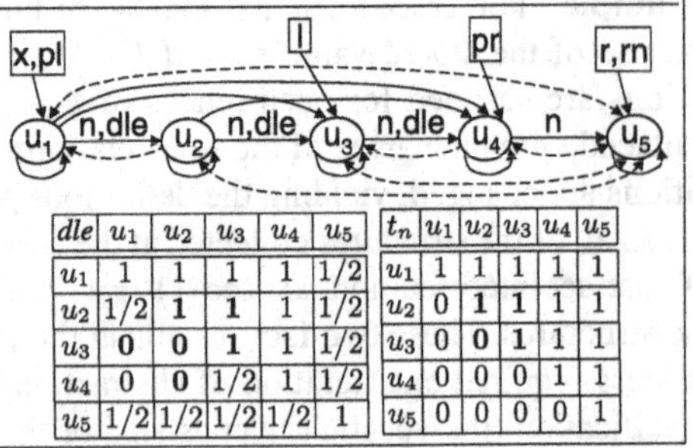

dle	u_1	u_2	u_3	u_4	u_5
u_1	1	1	1	1	1/2
u_2	1/2	**1**	**1**	1	1/2
u_3	**0**	**0**	**1**	1	1/2
u_4	0	**0**	1/2	1	1/2
u_5	1/2	1/2	1/2	1/2	1

t_n	u_1	u_2	u_3	u_4	u_5
u_1	1	1	1	1	1
u_2	0	**1**	**1**	1	1
u_3	0	**0**	**1**	1	1
u_4	0	0	0	1	1
u_5	0	0	0	0	1

Fig. 9. Structure S_9, which arises just before line [6] of Fig. 6. Unlabeled edges between nodes represent the *dle* relation

[3] A related property, antistability, asserts that the order of elements with equal `data`-components is reversed: $\forall v_1, v_2 : (dle(v_1, v_2) \wedge dle(v_2, v_1) \wedge t_n^0(v_1, v_2)) \rightarrow t_n(v_2, v_1)$ Our test suite also includes program `InsertSort_AS`, which is identical to `InsertSort` except that it uses $\geq$ instead of $>$ in line [10] of Fig. 6 (i.e., when looking for the correct place to insert the current node). This implementation of insertion sort is antistable.

- One of the individuals in U_1 possesses a property that another individual does not possess; thus, the property for the summary individual is $1/2$.
- Individuals in U_1 have a property in common, which cannot be recomputed precisely in S_2.

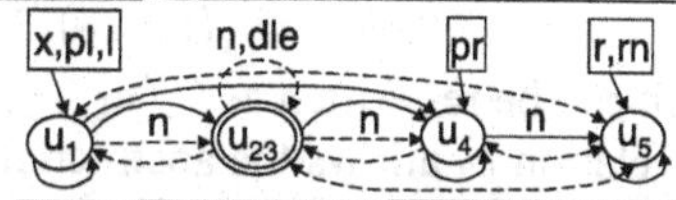

In both cases, the solution lies in the introduction of new instrumentation relations. In the former case, it is necessary to introduce a unary abstraction relation to keep the individuals of U_1 that possess the property from being grouped with those that do not. In the latter case, it is sufficient to introduce a non-abstraction relation of appropriate arity that captures the common property of individuals in U_1. The algorithm described in §2.2 can be used to learn formulas for the following three kinds of relations:[4]

dle	u_1	u_{23}	u_4	u_5
u_1	1	1	1	1/2
u_{23}	**1/2**	**1/2**	1	1/2
u_4	0	**1/2**	1	1/2
u_5	1/2	1/2	1/2	1

t_n	u_1	u_{23}	u_4	u_5
u_1	1	1	1	1
u_{23}	0	**1/2**	1	1
u_4	0	0	1	1
u_5	0	0	0	1

Fig. 10. Structure S_{10}, corresponding to the transformation of S_9 by the statement on line [6] of Fig. 6. Unlabeled edges between nodes represent the *dle* relation

Type I: Unary relation r_1 with $E^+ = \{u\}$ for one $u \in U_1$, and $E^- = U_1 - \{u\}$.
Type II: Unary relation r_2 with $E^+ = U_1$.
Type III: Binary relation r_3 with $E^+ = U_1 \times U_1$.

Type I relations are intended to prevent the grouping of individuals with different properties, while Types II and III are intended to capture the common properties of individuals in U_1. (Type III relations can be generalized to higher-arity relations.)

For the logical structure that serves as input to ILP, we pass the structure S_1 identified at an information-loss point. We restrict the algorithm to use only non-history relations of the structure that lose definite entries as a result of abstraction (e.g., t_n and *dle* in the above example). Definite entries of those relations are then used to learn formulas that evaluate to 1 for every positive example and to 0 for every negative example.

We modified the algorithm of §2.2 to learn multiple formulas in one invocation of the algorithm. Our motivation is not to find a single instrumentation relation that explains something about the structure, but rather to find all instrumentation relations that help the analysis establish the property of interest. Whenever we find multiple literals of the same quality (see line [7] of Fig. 5), we extend distinct copies of the current disjunct using each of the literals, and then we extend distinct copies of the current formula using the resulting disjuncts.

This variant of ILP is able to learn a useful binary formula using structure S_9 of Fig. 9. The set of individuals of S_9 that are grouped by the abstraction is $U = \{u_2, u_3\}$, so the input set of positive examples is $\{(u_2, u_2), (u_2, u_3), (u_3, u_2), (u_3, u_3)\}$. The set of relations that lose definite values due to abstraction includes t_n and *dle*. Literal $dle(v_1, v_2)$ covers three of the four examples because it holds for bindings $(v_1, v_2) \mapsto (u_2, u_2)$, $(v_1, v_2) \mapsto (u_2, u_3)$, and $(v_1, v_2) \mapsto (u_3, u_3)$. The algorithm picks that literal

4 These are what are needed for our analysis framework, which uses abstractions that generalize predicate-abstraction domains. A fourth use of ILP provides a new technique for predicate abstraction itself: ILP can be used to identify nullary relations that differentiate a positive-example structure S from the other structures arising at a program point. The steps of ILP go beyond merely forming Boolean combinations of existing relations; they involve the creation of new relations by introducing quantifiers during the learning process.

and, because there are no negative examples, $dle(v_1, v_2)$ becomes the first disjunct. Literal $\neg t_n(v_1, v_2)$ covers the remaining positive example, (u_3, u_2), and the algorithm returns the formula

$$\psi_{r_3}(v_1, v_2) \stackrel{\text{def}}{=} dle(v_1, v_2) \vee \neg t_n(v_1, v_2), \tag{6}$$

which can be re-written as $t_n(v_1, v_2) \rightarrow dle(v_1, v_2)$.

Relation r_3 allows the abstraction to maintain information about the transitive successors with which a list node has the correct relative order. In particular, although $dle(u_{23}, u_{23})$ is $1/2$ in S_{10}, $r_3(u_{23}, u_{23})$ is 1, which allows establishing the fact that all list nodes appearing prior to `r`'s target are in sorted order.

Other formulas, such as $dle(v_1, v_2) \vee t_n(v_2, v_1)$, are also learned using ILP (cf. Fig. 12). Not all of them are useful to the verification process, but introducing extra instrumentation relations cannot harm the analysis, aside from increasing its cost.

5 Experimental Evaluation

We extended TVLA to perform iterative abstraction refinement, and applied it to three queries and five programs (see Fig. 11). Besides `InsertSort`, the test programs included sorting procedures `BubbleSort` and `InsertSort_AS`, list-merging procedure `Merge`, and *in-situ* list-reversal procedure `Reverse`.

At present, we employ subformula-based refinement first. During each iteration of subformula-based refinement, we save logical structures at information-loss points. Upon the failure of subformula-based refinement, we invoke the ILP algorithm described in §4.2. To lower the cost of the analysis we prune the returned set of formulas. For example, we currently remove formulas defined in terms of a single relation symbol; such formulas are usually tautologies (e.g., $dle(v_1, v_2) \vee dle(v_2, v_1)$). We then define new instrumentation relations, and use these relations to refine the abstraction by performing the steps of lines [7] and [8] of Fig. 8. Our implementation can learn relations of all types described in §4.2: unary, binary, as well as nullary. However, due to the present cost of maintaining many unary instrumentation relations in TVLA, in the experiments reported here we only learn binary formulas (i.e., of Type III). Moreover, we define new instrumentation relations using only learned formulas of a simple form (currently, those with two atomic subformulas). We are in the process of extending our techniques for pruning useless instrumentation relations. This should make it practical for us to use all types of relations that can be learned by ILP for refining the abstraction.

Test Program	*sorted*	*stable*	*antistable*
BubbleSort	1	1	1/2
InsertSort	1	1	1/2
InsertSort_AS	1	1/2	1
Merge	1/2	1	1/2
Reverse	1/2	1/2	1

Fig. 11. Results from applying iterative abstraction refinement to the verification of properties of programs that manipulate linked lists

Example. When attempting to verify the stability of `InsertSort`, ILP creates nine formulas including Formula (6). The subsequent run of the analysis successfully verifies the stability of `InsertSort`. □

Fig. 11 shows that the method was able to generate the right instrumentation relations for TVLA to establish all properties that we expect to hold. Namely, TVLA succeeds in demonstrating that all three sorting routines produce sorted lists, that `BubbleSort`, `InsertSort`, and `Merge` are stable routines, and that `InsertSort_AS` and `Reverse` are antistable routines.

Indefinite answers are indicated by $1/2$ entries. *It is important to understand that all of the occurrences of* $1/2$ *in Fig. 11 are the most precise correct answers*. For instance, the result of applying `Reverse` to an unsorted list is usually an unsorted list; however, in the case that the input list happens to be in non-increasing order, `Reverse` produces a sorted list. Consequently, the most precise answer to the query is $1/2$, not 0.

Test Program	*sorted* # instrum rels total/ILP	*stable* # instrum rels total/ILP	*antistable* # instrum rels total/ILP
BubbleSort	31/0	32/0	41/9
InsertSort	39/0	49/9	43/3
InsertSort_AS	39/0	43/3	40/0
Merge	30/3	28/0	31/3
Reverse	26/3	27/3	24/0

Fig. 12. The numbers of instrumentation relations (total and learned by ILP) used during the last iteration of abstraction refinement

Fig. 12 shows the numbers of instrumentation relations used during the last iteration of abstraction refinement. The number of ILP-learned relations used by the analysis is small relative to the total number of instrumentation relations.

Fig. 13 gives execution times that were collected on a 3GHz Linux PC. The longest-running analysis, which verifies that `InsertSort` is stable, takes 8.5 minutes. Seven of the analyses take under a minute. The rest take between 70 seconds and 6 minutes. The total time for the 15 tests is 35 minutes. These numbers are very close to how long it takes to verify the sortedness queries when the user carefully chooses the right instrumentation relations [15].[5] The maximum amount of memory used by the analyses varied from just under 2 MB to 32 MB.[6]

The cost of the invocations of the ILP algorithm when attempting to verify the antistability of `BubbleSort` was 25 seconds (total, for 133 information-loss points). For all other benchmarks, the ILP cost was less than ten seconds.

Three additional experiments tested the applicability of our method to other queries and data structures. In the first experiment, subformula-based refinement successfully verified that the *in-situ* list-reversal procedure `Reverse` indeed produces a list that is the reversal of the input list. The query that expresses this property is $\forall v_1, v_2 : n(v_1, v_2) \leftrightarrow n^0(v_2, v_1)$. This experiment took only 5 seconds and used less than 2 MB of memory. The second and third experiments involved two programs that manipulate binary-search trees. `InsertBST` inserts a new node into a binary-search tree, and `DeleteBST` deletes a node from a binary-search tree. For both programs, subformula-based refinement successfully verified the query that the nodes of the tree pointed to by variable `t` remain in sorted order at the end of the programs:

$$\forall v_1\colon r_t(v_1) \rightarrow (\forall v_2\colon (\mathit{left}(v_1, v_2) \rightarrow \mathit{dle}(v_2, v_1)) \wedge (\mathit{right}(v_1, v_2) \rightarrow \mathit{dle}(v_1, v_2))) \quad (7)$$

The initial specifications for the analyses included only three standard instrumentation relations, similar to those listed in Tab. 2. Relation $r_t(v_1)$ from Formula (7), for example, distinguishes nodes in the (sub)tree pointed to by `t`. The `InsertBST` experiment took 30 seconds and used less than 3 MB of memory, while the `DeleteBST` experiment took approximately 10 minutes and used 37 MB of memory.

[5] Sortedness is the only query in our set to which TVLA has been applied before this work.

[6] TVLA is written in Java. Here we report the maximum of total memory minus free memory, as returned by Runtime.

6 Related Work

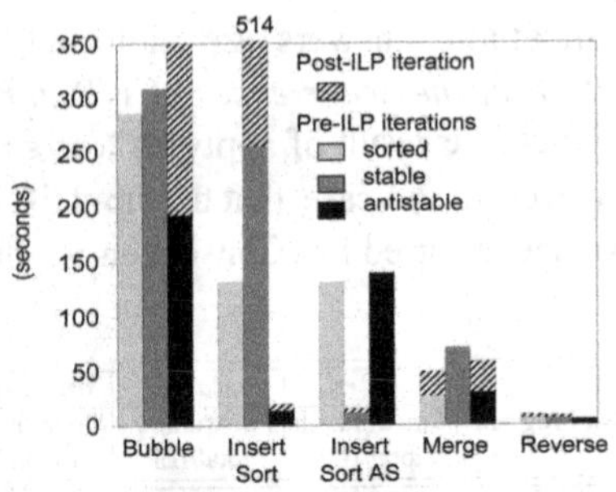

Fig. 13. Execution times. For each program, the three bars represent the sorted, stable, and antistable queries. In cases where subformula-based refinement failed, the upper portion of the bars shows the cost of the last iteration of the analysis (on both the DSC and the program) together with the ILP cost

The work reported here is similar in spirit to counterexample-guided abstraction refinement [12, 4, 13, 18, 5, 2, 8, 6]. A key difference between this work and prior work in the model-checking community is the abstract domain: prior work has used abstract domains that are fixed, finite, Cartesian products of Boolean values (i.e., predicate-abstraction domains), and hence the only relations introduced are nullary relations. Our work applies to a richer class of abstractions—3-valued structures—that generalize predicate-abstraction domains. The abstraction-refinement algorithm described in this paper can introduce unary, binary, ternary, etc. relations, in addition to nullary relations. While we demonstrated our approach using shape-analysis queries, this approach is applicable in any setting in which first-order logic is used to describe program states.

A second distinguishing feature of our work is that the method is driven not by counterexample traces, but instead by imprecise results of evaluating a query (in the case of subformula-based refinement) and by loss of information during abstraction steps (in the case of ILP-based refinement). There do not currently exist theorem provers for first-order logic extended with transitive closure capable of identifying infeasible error traces [9]; hence we needed to develop techniques different from those used in SLAM, BLAST, etc. SLAM identifies the shortest prefix of a spurious counterexample trace that cannot be extended to a feasible path; in general, however, the first information-loss point occurs before the end of the prefix. Information-loss-guided refinement can identify the earliest points at which information is lost due to abstraction, as well as what new instrumentation relations need to be added to the abstraction at those points. A potential advantage of counterexample-guided refinement over information-loss-guided refinement is that the former is goal-driven. Information-loss-guided refinement can discover many relationships that do not help in establishing the query. To alleviate this problem, we restricted the ILP algorithm to only use relations that occur in the query.

Abstraction-refinement techniques from the abstract-interpretation community are capable of refining domains that are not based on predicate abstraction. In [10], for example, a polyhedra-based domain is dynamically refined. Our work is based on a different abstract domain, and led us to develop some new approaches to abstraction refinement, based on machine learning.

In the abstract-interpretation community, a strong (albeit often unattainable) form of abstraction refinement has been identified in which the goal is to make abstract interpretation complete (a.k.a. "optimal") [7]. In our case, the goal is to extend the abstraction just enough to be able to answer the query, rather than to make the abstraction optimal.

References

1. TVLA system. http://www.cs.tau.ac.il/ tvla/.
2. T. Ball and S. Rajamani. Automatically validating temporal safety properties of interfaces. In *SPIN*, pages 103–122, 2001.
3. D.R. Chase, M. Wegman, and F. Zadeck. Analysis of pointers and structures. In *PLDI*, pages 296–310, 1990.
4. E.M. Clarke, O. Grumberg, S. Jha, Y. Lu, and H. Veith. Counterexample-guided abstraction refinement. In *CAV*, pages 154–169, 2000.
5. S. Das and D. Dill. Counter-example based predicate discovery in predicate abstraction. In *FMCAD*, pages 19–32, 2002.
6. C. Flanagan. Software model checking via iterative abstraction refinement of constraint logic queries. In *CP+CV*, 2004.
7. R. Giacobazzi, F. Ranzato, and F. Scozzari. Making abstract interpretations complete. *J. ACM*, 47(2):361–416, 2000.
8. T. Henzinger, R. Jhala, R. Majumdar, and K. McMillan. Abstractions from proofs. In *POPL*, pages 232–244, 2004.
9. N. Immerman, A. Rabinovich, T. Reps, M. Sagiv, and G. Yorsh. The boundary between decidability and undecidability for transitive closure logics. In *CSL*, pages 160–174, 2004.
10. B. Jeannet, N. Halbwachs, and P. Raymond. Dynamic partitioning in analyses of numerical properties. In *SAS*, pages 39–50, 1999.
11. N. Jones and S. Muchnick. Flow analysis and optimization of Lisp-like structures. In *Program Flow Analysis: Theory and Applications*, pages 102–131. Prentice-Hall, 1981.
12. R. Kurshan. *Computer-aided Verification of Coordinating Processes*. Princeton University Press, 1994.
13. Y. Lakhnech, S. Bensalem, S. Berezin, and S. Owre. Incremental verification by abstraction. In *TACAS*, pages 98–112, 2001.
14. N. Lavrač and S. Džeroski. *Inductive Logic Programming: Techniques and Applications*. Ellis Horwood, 1994.
15. T. Lev-Ami, T. Reps, M. Sagiv, and R. Wilhelm. Putting static analysis to work for verification: A case study. In *ISSTA*, pages 26–38, 2000.
16. A. Loginov, T. Reps, and M. Sagiv. Learning abstractions for verifying data-structure properties. report TR-1519, Comp. Sci. Dept., Univ. of Wisconsin, January 2005. Available at "http://www.cs.wisc.edu/wpis/papers/tr1519.ps".
17. S. Muggleton. Inductive logic programming. *New Generation Comp.*, 8(4):295–317, 1991.
18. C. Pasareanu, M. Dwyer, and W. Visser. Finding feasible counter-examples when model checking Java programs. In *TACAS*, pages 284–298, 2001.
19. J.R. Quinlan. Learning logical definitions from relations. *Mach. Learn.*, 5:239–266, 1990.
20. T. Reps, M. Sagiv, and A. Loginov. Finite differencing of logical formulas with applications to program analysis. In *ESOP*, pages 380–398, 2003.
21. M. Sagiv, T. Reps, and R. Wilhelm. Parametric shape analysis via 3-valued logic. *TOPLAS*, 24(3):217–298, 2002.

Automated Assume-Guarantee Reasoning for Simulation Conformance

Sagar Chaki, Edmund Clarke, Nishant Sinha, and Prasanna Thati

chaki@sei.cmu.edu, {emc, nishants, thati}@cs.cmu.edu

Abstract. We address the issue of efficiently automating assume-guarantee reasoning for simulation conformance between finite state systems and specifications. We focus on a non-circular assume-guarantee proof rule, and show that there is a weakest assumption that can be represented canonically by a deterministic tree automata (DTA). We then present an algorithm L^T that learns this DTA automatically in an incremental fashion, in time that is polynomial in the number of states in the equivalent minimal DTA. The algorithm assumes a teacher that can answer membership and candidate queries pertaining to the language of the unknown DTA. We show how the teacher can be implemented using a model checker. We have implemented this framework in the COMFORT toolkit and we report encouraging results (over an order of magnitude improvement in memory consumption) on non-trivial benchmarks.

1 Introduction

Formal verification is an important tool in the hands of software practitioners for ascertaining correctness of safety critical software systems. However, scaling formal techniques like model checking [11] to concurrent software of industrial complexity remains an open challenge. The primary hurdle is the state-space explosion problem whereby the number of reachable states of a concurrent system increases exponentially with the number of components.

Two paradigms hold the key to alleviating state-space explosion – abstraction [10, 9] and compositional reasoning [23, 8]. Both of these techniques have been extensively studied by the formal verification community and there have been significant breakthroughs from time to time. One of the most important advancements in the domain of compositional analysis is the concept of assume-guarantee [23] (AG) reasoning. The essential idea here is to model-check each component independently by making an assumption about its environment, and then discharge the assumption on the collection of the rest of the components. A variety of AG proof-rules are known, of which we will concern ourselves with the following non-circular rule called **AG-NC**:

$$\frac{M_1 \parallel M_A \preccurlyeq S \qquad\qquad M_2 \preccurlyeq M_A}{M_1 \parallel M_2 \preccurlyeq S}$$

where $M_1 \parallel M_2$ is the concurrent system to be verified, S is the specification, and $\preccurlyeq$ an appropriate notion of conformance between the system and the specification. **AG-NC** is known to be sound and complete for a number of conformance notions, including

K. Etessami and S.K. Rajamani (Eds.): CAV 2005, LNCS 3576, pp. 534–547, 2005.

trace containment and simulation. The rule essentially states that if there is an *assumption* M_A that satisfies the two premises, then the system conforms to the specification. However, the main drawback here from a practical point of view is that, in general, the assumption M_A has to be constructed manually. This requirement of manual effort has been a major hindrance towards wider applicability of AG-style reasoning on realistic systems.

An important development in this context is the recent use of automata-theoretic learning algorithms by Cobleigh et al. [12] to automate AG reasoning for *trace* containment, when both the system and the specification are finite state machines. Briefly, the idea is to automatically learn an assumption M_A that can be used to discharge **AG-NC**. The specific learning algorithm that is employed is Angluin's L^* [2], which learns finite state machines up to trace equivalence. Empirical evidence [12] indeed suggests that, often in practice, this learning based approach automatically constructs simple (small in size) assumptions that can be used to discharge **AG-NC**.

In this article, we apply the learning paradigm to automate AG-reasoning for *simulation* conformance between finite systems and specifications. We first show that there is a weakest assumption M_W for **AG-NC** such that $M_1 \parallel M_2 \preccurlyeq S$ if and only if $M_2 \preccurlyeq M_W$. Further, M_W is regular in that the set of trees it can simulate can be accepted by a tree automata. Although one can compute M_W and use it to check if $M_2 \preccurlyeq M_W$, doing so would be computationally as expensive as directly checking if $M_1 \parallel M_2 \preccurlyeq S$. We therefore learn the weakest assumption in an *incremental* fashion, and use the successive approximations that are learnt to try and discharge **AG-NC**. If at any stage an approximation is successfully used, then we are done. Otherwise, we extract a counterexample from the premise of **AG-NC** that has failed, and use it to further improve the current approximation.

To realize the above approach, we need an algorithm that learns the weakest assumption up to simulation equivalence. As mentioned above the weakest assumption corresponds to a regular tree language. We present an algorithm L^T that learns the minimal deterministic tree automata (DTA) for this assumption in an incremental fashion. Although a similar learning algorithm for tree languages has been proposed earlier [14], L^T was developed by us independently and has a much better worst-case complexity than the previous algorithm. The algorithm L^T may be of independent interest besides the specific application we consider in this paper. It assumes that an unknown regular tree language U is presented by a *minimally adequate teacher* (teacher for short) that can answer membership queries about U, and that can also test conjectures about U and provide counterexamples to wrong conjectures. The algorithm L^T learns the minimal DTA for U in time polynomial in the number of states in the minimal DTA.

We will show how the teacher can be efficiently implemented in a model checker, i.e., how the membership and candidate queries can be answered without paying the price of explicitly composing M_1 and M_2. Further, we show how while processing the candidate queries, the teacher can try to discharge **AG-NC** with the proposed candidate. We have empirical evidence supporting our claim that **AG-NC** can often be discharged with a coarse approximation (candidate), well before the weakest assumption is learnt. We have implemented the proposed framework in the ComFoRT [7] toolkit and experimented with realistic examples. Specifically, we have experimented with a set of benchmarks constructed from the OPENSSL source code and the SSL specification. The experimental results indicate memory savings by over an order of magnitude compared to a non-AG based approach.

Related Work. A number of applications of machine learning techniques to verification problems have been proposed in the recent past. These include automatic synthesis of interface specifications for application programs [1], automatically learning the set of reachable states in regular model checking [20], *black-box-testing* [22] and its subsequent extension to *adaptive model-checking* [19] to learn an accurate finite state model of an unknown system starting from an approximate one, and learning likely program invariants based on observed values in sample executions [15].

The work we present in this paper closely parallels the approach proposed by Cobleigh et al. [12], where they automate assume-guarantee reasoning for finite state concurrent systems in a trace-containment setting. They show the existence of a weakest environment assumption for an LTS and *automatically* learn successive approximations to it using Angluin's L^* algorithm [2, 24]. Our contribution is to apply this general paradigm to a branching time setting. Further, the L^T algorithm that we present may be of independent interest. L^T may be viewed as a branching time analogue of L^* where the minimally adequate teacher must be capable of answering queries on trees and tree automata (as opposed to traces and finite state machines in L^*). Finally, Rivest et al. [24] proposed an improvement to Angluin's L^* that substantially improves its complexity; our L^T has the same spirit as this improved version of L^*.

Language *identification in the limit* paradigm was introduced by Gold [17]. This forms the basis of *active* algorithms which learn in an online fashion by querying an oracle (teacher); both L^* and L^T fall in this category. Gold also proposed another paradigm, namely *identification from given data*, for learning from a fixed training sample set [18]. The training set consists of a set of positive and negative samples from the unknown language and must be a *characteristic* [18] set of the language. Algorithms have been proposed in this setting for learning word languages [21], tree languages [16, 4] and stochastic tree languages [5]. Unlike the algorithms in [16, 4] which learn tree languages offline from a training set, L^T learns actively by querying a teacher. An anonymous reviewer pointed us to a recently proposed active algorithm for learning tree languages [14], which is closely related to L^T. However, L^T has a better worst-case complexity of $O(n^3)$ as compared to $O(n^5)$ of the previous algorithm. Finally, we note that learning from derivation trees was investigated initially in the context of context-free grammars [25] and forms the basis of several inference algorithms for tree languages [16, 4, 14] including ours.

2 Preliminaries

Definition 1 (Labeled Transition System). *A labeled transition system (LTS) is a 4-tuple* $(S, Init, \Sigma, T)$ *where (i)* S *is a finite set of states, (ii)* $Init \subseteq S$ *is the set of initial states, (iii)* Σ *is a finite alphabet, and (iv)* $T \subseteq S \times \Sigma \times S$ *is the transition relation. We write* $s \xrightarrow{\alpha} s'$ *as a shorthand for* $(s, \alpha, s') \in T$.

Definition 2 (Simulation). *Let $M_1 = (S_1, Init_1, \Sigma_1, T_1)$ and $M_2 = (S_2, Init_2, \Sigma_2, T_2)$ be LTSs such that $\Sigma_1 = \Sigma_2 = \Sigma$ say. A relation $\mathcal{R} \subseteq S_1 \times S_2$ is said to be a simulation relation if:*

$$\forall s_1, s_1' \in S_1 \centerdot \forall a \in \Sigma \centerdot \forall s_2 \in S_2 \centerdot s_1 \mathcal{R} s_2 \wedge s_1 \xrightarrow{a} s_1' \Rightarrow \exists s_2' \in S_2 \centerdot s_2 \xrightarrow{a} s_2' \wedge s_1' \mathcal{R} s_2'$$

We say M_1 is simulated by M_2, and denote this by $M_1 \preccurlyeq M_2$, if there is a simulation relation $\mathcal{R}$ such that $\forall s_1 \in I_1 \centerdot \exists s_2 \in I_2 \centerdot s_1 \mathcal{R} s_2$. We say M_1 and M_2 are simulation equivalent if $M_1 \preccurlyeq M_2$ and $M_2 \preccurlyeq M_1$.

Definition 3 (Tree). *Let λ denote the empty tree and Σ be an alphabet. The set of trees over Σ is defined by the grammar: $T := \lambda \mid \Sigma \bullet T \mid T + T$. The set of all trees over the alphabet Σ is denote by Σ^T, and we let t range over it.*

Definition 4 (Context). *The set of contexts over an alphabet Σ can be defined by the grammar: $C := \square \mid \Sigma \bullet C \mid C + T \mid T + C$. We let c range over the set of contexts.*

A context is like a tree except that it has exactly one hole denoted by $\square$ at one of its nodes. When we plug in a tree t in a context c, we essentially replace the single $\square$ in c by t. The resulting tree is denoted by $c[t]$. A tree t can naturally be seen as an LTS. Specifically, the states of the LTS are the nodes of t, the only initial state is the root node of t, and there is a labeled transition from node t_1 to t_2 labeled with α if $t_1 = \alpha \bullet t_2$ or $t_1 = \alpha \bullet t_2 + t_3$ or $t_1 = t_2 + \alpha \bullet t_3$.

Definition 5 (Tree Language of an LTS). *An LTS M induces a tree language, which is denoted by $\mathcal{T}(M)$ and is defined as: $\mathcal{T}(M) = \{t \mid t \preccurlyeq M\}$. In other words, the tree language of an LTS contains all the trees that can be simulated by the LTS.*

For example, the language of M (Figure 1(a)) contains the trees λ, $\alpha \bullet \lambda$, $\alpha \bullet (\lambda + \lambda)$, $\alpha \bullet \lambda + \beta \bullet \lambda$, $\beta \bullet \lambda + \beta \bullet \lambda$ and so on. The notion of tree languages of LTSs and simulation between LTSs are fundamentally connected. Specifically, it follows from the definition of simulation between LTSs that for any two LTSs M_1 and M_2, the following holds:

$$M_1 \preccurlyeq M_2 \iff \mathcal{T}(M_1) \subseteq \mathcal{T}(M_2) \tag{1}$$

Definition 6 (Tree Automaton). *A (bottom-up) tree automaton (TA) is a 6-tuple $A = (S, Init, \Sigma, \delta, \otimes, F)$ where: (i) S is a set of states, (ii) $Init \subseteq S$ is a set of initial states, (iii) Σ is an alphabet, (iv) $\delta \subseteq S \times \Sigma \times S$ is a forward transition relation, (v) $\otimes \subseteq S \times S \times S$ is a cross transition relation, and (vi) $F \subseteq S$ is a set of accepting states.*

Tree automata accept trees and can be viewed as two-dimensional extensions of finite automata. Since trees can be extended either forward (via the $\bullet$ operator) and across (via the $+$ operator), a TA must have transitions defined when either of these two kinds of extensions of its input tree are encountered. This is achieved via the forward and cross transitions respectively. The automaton starts at each leaf of the input tree at some initial state, and then runs bottom-up in accordance with its forward and cross transition relations. The forward transition is applied when a tree of the form $\alpha \bullet T$ is

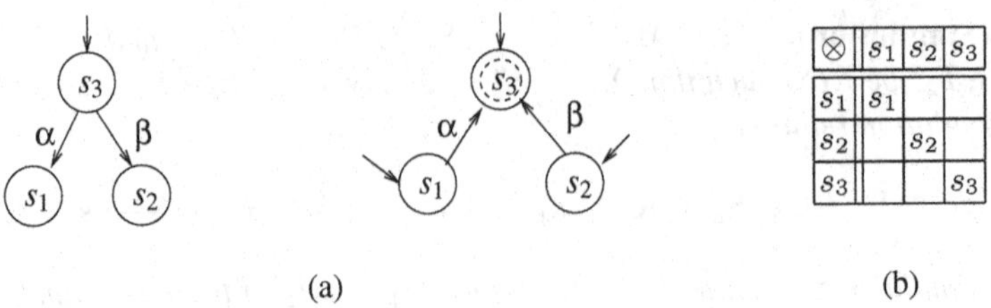

⊗	s_1	s_2	s_3
s_1	s_1		
s_2		s_2	
s_3			s_3

Fig. 1. (a-left) an LTS M with initial state s_3; (a-right) forward transitions of a tree automaton A accepting $\mathcal{T}(M)$; all states are initial; (b) table showing cross transition relation $\otimes$ of A. Note that some table entries are absent since the relation $\otimes$ is not total

encountered. The cross transition is applied when a tree of the form $T_1 + T_2$ is found. The tree is accepted if the run ends at the root of the tree in some accepting state of A.

Before we formally define the notions of runs and acceptance, we introduce a few notational conventions. We may sometimes write $s \xrightarrow{\alpha} s'$ or $s' \in \delta(s, \alpha)$ as a shorthand for $(s, \alpha, s') \in \delta$, and $s_1 \otimes s_2 \longrightarrow s$ as a shorthand for $(s_1, s_2, s) \in \otimes$. Similarly, for sets of states S_1, S_2, we use the following shorthand notations:

$$\delta(S_1, \alpha) = \{s' \mid \exists s \in S_1 \centerdot s \xrightarrow{\alpha} s'\}$$
$$S_1 \otimes S_2 = \{s \mid \exists s_1 \in S_1 \centerdot \exists s_2 \in S_2 \centerdot (s_1, s_2, s) \in \otimes\}$$

Definition 7 (Run/Acceptance). *Let $A = (S, Init, \Sigma, \delta, \otimes, F)$ be a TA. The run of A is a function $r : \Sigma^{\mathcal{T}} \rightarrow 2^S$ from trees to sets of states of A that satisfies the following conditions: (i) $r(\lambda) = Init$, (ii) $r(\alpha \bullet t) = \delta(r(t), \alpha)$, and (iii) $r(t_1 + t_2) = r(t_1) \otimes r(t_2)$. A tree T is accepted by A iff $r(T) \cap F \neq \emptyset$. The set of trees accepted by A is known as the language of A and is denoted by $\mathcal{L}(A)$.*

A *deterministic* tree automaton (DTA) is one which has a single initial state and where the forward and cross transition relations are *functions* $\delta : S \times \Sigma \rightarrow S$ and $\otimes : S \times S \rightarrow S$ respectively. If $A = (S, Init, \Sigma, \delta, \otimes, F)$ is a DTA then $Init$ refers to the single initial state, and $\delta(s, \alpha)$ and $s_1 \otimes s_2$ refer to the unique state s' such that $s \xrightarrow{\alpha} s'$ and $s_1 \otimes s_2 \longrightarrow s'$ respectively. Note that if A is deterministic then for every tree t the set $r(t)$ is a singleton, i.e., the run of A on any tree t ends at a unique state of A. Further, we recall [13] the following facts about tree-automata. The set of languages recognized by TA (referred to as *regular tree languages* henceforth) is closed under union, intersection and complementation. For every TA A there is a DTA A' such that $\mathcal{L}(A) = \mathcal{L}(A')$. Given any regular tree language L there is always a *unique* (up to isomorphism) *smallest* DTA A such that $\mathcal{L}(A) = L$.

The following lemma, which is easy to prove, asserts that for any LTS M, the set $\mathcal{T}(M)$ is a regular tree language. Thus, using (1), the simulation problem between LTSs can also be viewed as the language containment problem between tree automata.

Lemma 1. *For any LTS M there is a TA A such that $\mathcal{L}(A) = \mathcal{T}(M)$.*

For example, for the LTS M and TA A as shown in Figure 1, we have $\mathcal{L}(A) = \mathcal{T}(M)$. We now provide the standard notion of parallel composition between LTSs, where components synchronize on shared actions and proceed asynchronously on local actions.

Definition 8 (Parallel Composition of LTSs). *Given LTSs $M_1 = (S_1, Init_1, \Sigma_1, T_1)$ and $M_2 = (S_2, Init_2, \Sigma_2, T_2)$, their parallel composition $M_1 \parallel M_2$ is an LTS $M = (S, Init, \Sigma, T)$ where $S = S_1 \times S_2$, $Init = Init_1 \times Init_2$, $\Sigma = \Sigma_1 \cup \Sigma_2$, and the transition relation T is defined as follows: $((s_1, s_2), \alpha, (s_1', s_2')) \in T$ iff for $i \in \{1, 2\}$ the following holds:*

$$(\alpha \in \Sigma_i) \wedge (s_i, \alpha, s_i') \in T_i \bigvee (\alpha \notin \Sigma_i) \wedge (s_i = s_i')$$

Working with different alphabets for each component would needlessly complicate the exposition in Section 4. For this reason, without loss of generality, we make the simplifying assumption that $\Sigma_1 = \Sigma_2$. This is justified because we can construct LTSs M_1' and M_2', each with the same alphabet $\Sigma = \Sigma_1 \cup \Sigma_2$ such that $M_1' \parallel M_2'$ is simulation equivalent (in fact bisimilar) to $M_1 \parallel M_2$. Specifically, $M_1' = (S_1, Init_1, \Sigma, T_1')$ and $M_2' = (S_2, Init_2, \Sigma, T_2')$ where

$$T_1' = T_1 \cup \{(s, \alpha, s) \mid s \in S_1 \text{ and } \alpha \in \Sigma_2 \setminus \Sigma_1\}$$
$$T_2' = T_2 \cup \{(s, \alpha, s) \mid s \in S_2 \text{ and } \alpha \in \Sigma_1 \setminus \Sigma_2\}$$

Finally, the reader can check that if M_1 and M_2 are LTSs with the same alphabet then $\mathcal{T}(M_1 \parallel M_2) = \mathcal{T}(M_1) \cap \mathcal{T}(M_2)$.

3 Learning Minimal DTA

We now present the algorithm L^T that learns the minimal DTA for an unknown regular language U. It is assumed that the alphabet Σ of U is fixed, and that the language U is presented by a minimally adequate teacher that answers two kinds of queries:

1. *Membership.* Given a tree t, is t an element of U, i.e., $t \in U$?
2. *Candidate.* Given a DTA A does A accept U, i.e., $\mathcal{L}(A) = U$? If $\mathcal{L}(A) = U$ the teacher returns TRUE, else it returns FALSE along with a counterexample tree CE that is in the symmetric difference of $\mathcal{L}(A)$ and U.

We will use the following notation. Given any sets of trees S_1, S_2 and an alphabet Σ we denote by $\Sigma \bullet S_1$ the set of trees $\Sigma \bullet S_1 = \{\alpha \bullet t \mid \alpha \in \Sigma \wedge t \in S_1\}$, and by $S_1 + S_2$ the set $S_1 + S_2 = \{t_1 + t_2 \mid t_1 \in S_1 \wedge t_2 \in S_2\}$, and by $\widehat{\mathcal{S}}$ the set $\mathcal{S} \cup (\Sigma \bullet \mathcal{S}) \cup (\mathcal{S} + \mathcal{S})$.

Observation Table: The algorithm L^T maintains an observation table $\tau = (\mathcal{S}, \mathcal{E}, \mathcal{R})$ where (i) $\mathcal{S}$ is a set of trees such that $\lambda \in \mathcal{S}$, (ii) $\mathcal{E}$ is a set of contexts such that $\Box \in \mathcal{E}$, and (iii) $\mathcal{R}$ is a function from $\widehat{\mathcal{S}} \times \mathcal{E}$ to $\{0, 1\}$ that is defined as follows: $\mathcal{R}(t, c) = 1$ if $c[t] \in U$ and 0 otherwise. Note that given $\mathcal{S}$ and $\mathcal{E}$ we can compute $\mathcal{R}$ using membership queries. The information in the table is eventually used to construct a candidate DTA A_τ. Intuitively, the elements of $\mathcal{S}$ will serve as states of A_τ, and the contexts in $\mathcal{E}$ will play the role of *experiments* that distinguish the states in $\mathcal{S}$. Henceforth, the term experiment will essentially mean a context. The function $\mathcal{R}$ and the elements in $\widehat{\mathcal{S}} \setminus \mathcal{S}$ will be used to construct the forward and cross transitions between the states.

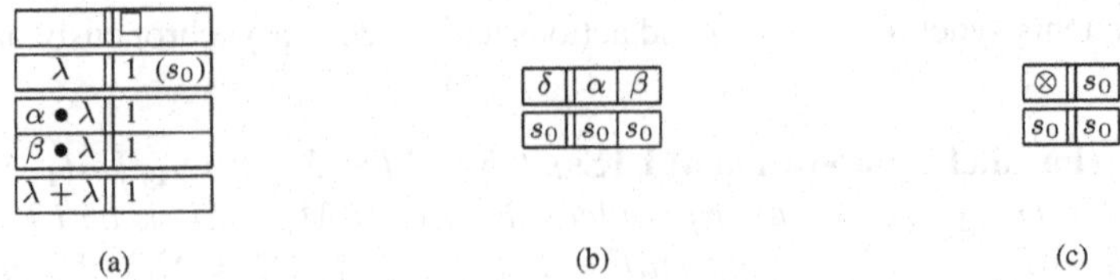

Fig. 2. (a) A well-formed and closed observation table $\mathcal{T}$; (b) forward transition relation of the candidate $A^1_{\mathcal{T}}$ constructed from $\mathcal{T}$; (c) cross transition relation of $A^1_{\mathcal{T}}$

For any tree $t \in \widehat{\mathcal{S}}$, we denote by $Row(t)$ the function from the set of experiments $\mathcal{E}$ to $\{0, 1\}$ defined as: $\forall c \in \mathcal{E} \,.\, Row(t)(c) = \mathcal{R}(t, c)$.

Definition 9 (Well-formed). *An observation table $(\mathcal{S}, \mathcal{E}, \mathcal{R})$ is said to be well-formed if: $\forall t, t' \in \mathcal{S} \,.\, t \neq t' \Rightarrow Row(t) \neq Row(t')$. From the definition of $Row(t)$ above, this boils down to: $\forall t, t' \in \mathcal{S} \,.\, t \neq t' \Rightarrow \exists c \in \mathcal{E} \,.\, \mathcal{R}(t, c) \neq \mathcal{R}(t', c)$.*

In other words, any two different row entries of a well-formed observation table must be distinguishable by at least one experiment in $\mathcal{E}$. The following crucial lemma imposes an upper-bound on the size of any well-formed observation table corresponding to a given regular tree language U.

Lemma 2. *Let $(\mathcal{S}, \mathcal{E}, \mathcal{R})$ be any well-formed observation table for a regular tree language U. Then $|\mathcal{S}| \leq n$, where n is the number of states of the smallest DTA which accepts U. In other words, the number of rows in any well-formed observation table for U cannot exceed the number of states in the smallest DTA that accepts U.*

Proof. The proof is by contradiction. Let A be the smallest DTA accepting U and let $(\mathcal{S}, \mathcal{E}, \mathcal{R})$ be a well-formed observation table such that $|\mathcal{S}| > n$. Then there are two distinct trees t_1 and t_2 in $\mathcal{S}$ such that the runs of A on both t_1 and t_2 end on the same state of A. Then for any context c, the runs of A on $c[t_1]$ and $c[t_2]$ both end on the same state. But on the other hand, since the observation table is well-formed, there exists an experiment $c \in \mathcal{E}$ such that $\mathcal{R}(t_1, c) \neq \mathcal{R}(t_2, c)$, which implies that the runs of A on $c[t_1]$ and $c[t_2]$ end on different states of A. Contradiction. □

Definition 10 (Closed). *An observation table $(\mathcal{S}, \mathcal{E}, \mathcal{R})$ is said to be closed if*

$$\forall t \in \widehat{\mathcal{S}} \setminus \mathcal{S} \,.\, \exists t' \in \mathcal{S} \,.\, Row(t') = Row(t)$$

Note that, given any well-formed observation table $(\mathcal{S}, \mathcal{E}, \mathcal{R})$, one can always construct a well-formed and closed observation table $(\mathcal{S}', \mathcal{E}, \mathcal{R}')$ such that $\mathcal{S} \subseteq \mathcal{S}'$. Specifically, we repeatedly try to find an element t in $\widehat{\mathcal{S}} \setminus \mathcal{S}$ such that $\forall t' \in \mathcal{S} \,.\, Row(t') \neq Row(t)$. If no such t can be found then the table is already closed and we stop. Otherwise, we add t to $\mathcal{S}$ and repeat the process. Note that, the table always stays well-formed. Then by Lemma 2, the size of $\mathcal{S}$ cannot exceed the number of states of the smallest DTA that accepts U. Hence this process always terminates.

Figure 2a shows a well-formed and closed table with $\mathcal{S} = \{\lambda\}$, $\mathcal{E} = \{\square\}$, $\Sigma = \{\alpha, \beta\}$, and for the regular tree language defined by the TA in Figure 1. Note that $Row(t) = Row(\lambda)$ for every $t \in \{\alpha \bullet \lambda, \beta \bullet \lambda, \lambda + \lambda\}$, and hence the table is closed.

Conjecture Construction: From a well-formed and closed observation table $\tau = (\mathcal{S}, \mathcal{E}, \mathcal{R})$, the learner constructs a candidate DTA $A_\tau = (S, Init, \Sigma, \delta, \otimes, F)$ where (i) $S = \mathcal{S}$, (ii) $Init = \lambda$, (iii) $F = \{t \in \mathcal{S} \mid \mathcal{R}(t, \Box) = 1\}$, (iv) $\delta(t, \alpha) := t'$ such that $Row(t') = Row(\alpha \bullet t)$, and (v) $t_1 \otimes t_2 := t'$ such that $Row(t') = Row(t_1 + t_2)$. Note that in (iv) and (v) above there is guaranteed to be a unique such t' since τ is closed and well-formed, hence A_τ is well-defined.

Consider again the closed table in Figure 2a. The learner extracts a conjecture A_τ from it with a single state s_0, which is both initial and final. Figures 2b and 2c show the forward and cross transitions of A_τ.

The Learning Algorithm: The algorithm L^T is iterative and always maintains a well-formed observation table $\tau = (\mathcal{S}, \mathcal{E}, \mathcal{R})$. Initially, $\mathcal{S} = \{\lambda\}$ and $\mathcal{E} = \{\Box\}$. In each iteration, L^T proceeds as follows:

1. Make τ closed as described previously.
2. Construct a conjecture DTA A_τ from τ, and make a candidate query with A_τ. If A_τ is a correct conjecture, then L^T terminates with A_τ as the answer. Otherwise, let CE be the counterexample returned by the teacher.
3. Extract a context c from CE, add it to $\mathcal{E}$, and proceed with the next iteration from step 1. The newly added c is such that when we make τ closed in the next iteration, the size of $\mathcal{S}$ is guaranteed to increase.

Extracting an Experiment From CE: Let r be the run function of the failed candidate A_τ. For any tree t, let $\tau(t) = r(t)$, i.e., $\tau(t)$ is the state at which the run of A_τ on t ends. Note that since states of A_τ are elements in $\mathcal{S}$, $\tau(t)$ is itself a tree. The unknown language U induces a natural equivalence relation $\approx$ on the set of trees as follows: $t_1 \approx t_2$ iff $t_1 \in U \iff t_2 \in U$.

The procedure **ExpGen** for extracting a new experiment from the counterexample is iterative. It maintains a context c and a tree t that satisfy the following condition: **(INV)** $c[t] \not\approx c[\tau(t)]$. Initially $c = \Box$ and $t = CE$. Note that this satisfies **INV** because $CE \in U \iff CE \notin \mathcal{L}(A_\tau)$. In each iteration, **ExpGen** either generates an appropriate experiment or updates c and t such that **INV** is maintained and the size of t strictly decreases. Note that t cannot become λ since at that point **INV** can no longer be maintained; this is because if $t = \lambda$ then $\tau(t) = \lambda$ and therefore $c[t] \approx c[\tau(t)]$, which would contradict **INV**. Hence, **ExpGen** must terminate at some stage by generating an appropriate experiment. Now, there are two possible cases:

Case 1: ($t = \alpha \bullet t'$). Let $c' = c[\alpha \bullet \Box]$. We consider two sub-cases. Suppose that $c[\tau(t)] \approx c'[\tau(t')]$. From **INV** we know that $c[t] \not\approx c[\tau(t)]$. Hence $c'[\tau(t')] \not\approx c[t] \approx c'[t']$. Hence, **ExpGen** proceeds to the next iteration with $c = c'$ and $t = t'$. Note that **INV** is preserved and the size of t strictly decreases.

Otherwise, suppose that $c[\tau(t)] \not\approx c'[\tau(t')]$. In this case, **ExpGen** terminates by adding the experiment c to $\mathcal{E}$. Note that A_τ has the transition $\tau(t') \xrightarrow{\alpha} \tau(t)$, i.e., $Row(\tau(t)) = Row(\alpha \bullet \tau(t'))$. But now, since $c[\tau(t)] \not\approx c'[\tau(t')] \approx c[\alpha \bullet \tau(t')]$, the

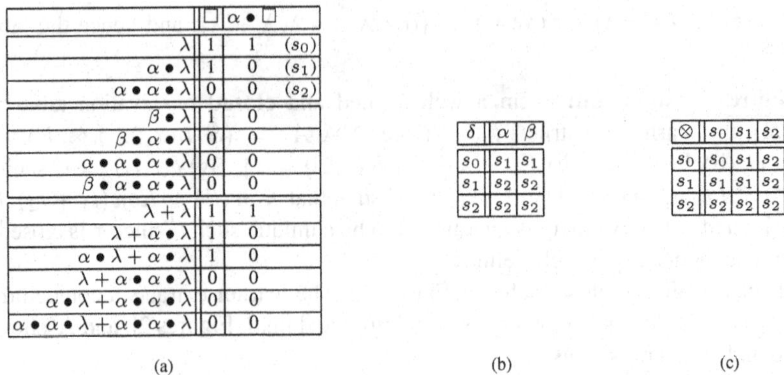

	$\square$	$\alpha \bullet \square$	
λ	1	1	(s_0)
$\alpha \bullet \lambda$	1	0	(s_1)
$\alpha \bullet \alpha \bullet \lambda$	0	0	(s_2)
$\beta \bullet \lambda$	1	0	
$\beta \bullet \alpha \bullet \lambda$	0	0	
$\alpha \bullet \alpha \bullet \alpha \bullet \lambda$	0	0	
$\beta \bullet \alpha \bullet \alpha \bullet \lambda$	0	0	
$\lambda + \lambda$	1	1	
$\lambda + \alpha \bullet \lambda$	1	0	
$\alpha \bullet \lambda + \alpha \bullet \lambda$	1	0	
$\lambda + \alpha \bullet \alpha \bullet \lambda$	0	0	
$\alpha \bullet \lambda + \alpha \bullet \alpha \bullet \lambda$	0	0	
$\alpha \bullet \alpha \bullet \lambda + \alpha \bullet \alpha \bullet \lambda$	0	0	

(a)

δ	α	β
s_0	s_1	s_1
s_1	s_2	s_2
s_2	s_2	s_2

(b)

$\otimes$	s_0	s_1	s_2
s_0	s_0	s_1	s_2
s_1	s_1	s_1	s_2
s_2	s_2	s_2	s_2

(c)

Fig. 3. (a) observation table τ and (b) transitions for the second conjecture A^2_τ

experiment c is guaranteed to distinguish between $\tau(t)$ and $\alpha \bullet \tau(t')$. Therefore, the size of $\mathcal{S}$ is guaranteed to increase when we attempt to close τ in the next iteration.

Case 2: ($t = t_1 + t_2$). There are two sub-cases. Suppose that $c[\tau(t)] \not\approx c[\tau(t_1) + \tau(t_2)]$. In this case, **ExpGen** terminates by adding the experiment c to $\mathcal{E}$. The experiment c is guaranteed to distinguish between $\tau(t)$ and $\tau(t_1) + \tau(t_2)$ and therefore strictly increase the size of $\mathcal{S}$ when we attempt to close τ in the next iteration.

Otherwise, suppose that $c[\tau(t)] \approx c[\tau(t_1) + \tau(t_2)]$. We again consider two sub-cases. Suppose that $c[\tau(t_1) + \tau(t_2)] \not\approx c[\tau(t_1) + t_2]$. In this case, **ExpGen** proceeds to the next iteration with $c = c[\tau(t_1) + \square]$ and $t = t_2$. Note that **INV** is preserved and the size of t strictly decreases.

Otherwise, we have $c[\tau(t_1) + t_2] \approx c[\tau(t_1) + \tau(t_2)] \approx c[\tau(t)]$, and by **INV** we know that $c[\tau(t)] \not\approx c[t] \approx c[t_1 + t_2]$. Hence, it must be the case that $c[\tau(t_1) + t_2] \not\approx c[t_1 + t_2]$. In this case, **ExpGen** proceeds to the next iteration with $c = c[\square + t_2]$ and $t = t_1$. Note that, once again **INV** is preserved and the size of t strictly decreases. This completes the argument for all cases.

Example 1. We show how L^T learns the minimal DTA corresponding to the language U of TA A of Figure 1. L^T starts with an observation table τ with $\mathcal{S} = \{\lambda\}$ and $\mathcal{E} = \{\square\}$. The table is then made closed by asking membership queries, first for λ and then for its (forward and cross) extensions $\{\alpha \bullet \lambda, \beta \bullet \lambda, \lambda + \lambda\}$. The resulting closed table τ_1 is shown in Figure 2a. L^T then extracts a candidate A^1_τ from τ_1, which is shown in Figure 2b.

When the conjecture A^1_τ is presented to the teacher, it checks if $\mathcal{L}(A^1_\tau) = U$. In our case, it detects otherwise and returns a counterexample CE from the symmetric difference of $\mathcal{L}(A^1_\tau)$ and U. For the purpose of illustration, let us assume CE to be $\alpha \bullet \beta \bullet \lambda$. Note that $CE \in \mathcal{L}(A^1_\tau) \setminus U$. The algorithm **ExpGen** extracts the context $\alpha \bullet \square$ from CE and adds it to the set of experiments $\mathcal{E}$. L^T now asks membership queries corresponding to the new experiment and checks if the new table τ is closed. It finds that $Row(\alpha \bullet \lambda) \neq Row(t)$ for all $t \in \mathcal{S}$, and hence it moves $\alpha \bullet \lambda$ from $\widehat{\mathcal{S}} \setminus \mathcal{S}$ to $\mathcal{S}$ in order to make τ closed. Again, membership queries for all possible forward and cross extensions of $\alpha \bullet \lambda$ are asked. This process is repeated till τ becomes closed. Figure 3a shows the final closed τ. As an optimization, we omit rows for the trees t_1+t_2 whenever there is already a row for $t_2 + t_1$; we know that the rows for both these trees will have the same markings. The corresponding conjecture A^2_τ contains three states s_0, s_1 and s_2 and its forward and cross transitions are shown in Figure 3b and Figure 3c. s_0 is the initial state and both s_0 and s_1 are final states. The candidate query with A^2_τ returns TRUE since $\mathcal{L}(A^2_\tau) = U$, and L^T terminates with A^2_τ as the output.

Correctness and Complexity:

Theorem 1. *Algorithm L^T terminates and outputs the minimal DTA that accepts the unknown regular language U.*

Proof. Termination is guaranteed by the facts that each iteration of L^T terminates, and in each iteration $|\mathcal{S}|$ must strictly increase, and, by Lemma 2, $|\mathcal{S}|$ cannot exceed the number of states of the smallest DTA that accepts U. Further, since L^T terminates only after a correct conjecture, if the DTA A_τ is its output then $\mathcal{L}(A_\tau) = U$. Finally, since the number of states in A_τ equals $|\mathcal{S}|$, by Lemma 2 it also follows that A_τ is the minimal DTA for U. □

To keep the space consumption of L^T within polynomial bounds, the trees and contexts in $\widehat{\mathcal{S}}$ and $\mathcal{E}$ are kept in a DAG form, where common subtrees between different elements in $\widehat{\mathcal{S}}$ and $\mathcal{E}$ are shared. Without this optimization, the space consumption can be exponential in the worst case. The other point to note is that the time taken by L^T depends on the counterexamples returned by the teacher; this is because the teacher can return counterexamples of any size in response to a failed candidate query.

To analyze the complexity of L^T, we make the following standard assumption: every query to the teacher, whether a membership query or a candidate query, takes unit time and space. Further, since the alphabet Σ of the unknown language U is fixed, we assume that the size of Σ is a constant. Then the following theorem summarizes the complexity of L^T.

Theorem 2. *The algorithm L^T takes $O(mn + n^3)$ time and space where n is the number of states in the minimal DTA for the unknown language U and m is the size of the largest counterexample returned by the teacher.*

Proof. By Lemma 2, we have $|\mathcal{S}| \leq n$. Then the number of rows in the table, which is $|\widehat{\mathcal{S}}| = |\mathcal{S} \cup (\Sigma \bullet \mathcal{S}) \cup (\mathcal{S} + \mathcal{S})|$, is of $O(n^2)$. Further, recall that every time a new experiment is added to $\mathcal{E}$, $|\mathcal{S}|$ increases by one. Hence the number of table columns $|\mathcal{E}| \leq n$, and the number of table entries $|\widehat{\mathcal{S}}||\mathcal{E}|$ is of $O(n^3)$.

The trees and contexts in $\widehat{\mathcal{S}}$ and $\mathcal{E}$ are kept in a DAG form, where common subtrees between different elements in $\widehat{\mathcal{S}}$ and $\mathcal{E}$ are shared in order to keep the space consumption within polynomial bounds. Specifically, recall that whenever a tree t is moved from $\widehat{\mathcal{S}} \setminus \mathcal{S}$ to $\mathcal{S}$, all trees of the form $\alpha \bullet t$ for each $\alpha \in \Sigma$ and $t + t'$ for each $t' \in \mathcal{S}$ (which are $O(|\mathcal{S}|)$ in number) are to be added to $\widehat{\mathcal{S}}$. Adding the tree $\alpha \bullet t$ to $\widehat{\mathcal{S}}$ only needs constant space since t is already in $\widehat{\mathcal{S}}$ and hence is shared in the DAG representation. Similarly adding a tree of form $t + t'$ takes only constant space, since both t and t' are already in

$\widehat{\mathcal{S}}$. Thus, each time $\mathcal{S}$ is expanded, a total of $O(|\mathcal{S}|)$ space is required to add all the new trees to $\widehat{\mathcal{S}}$. Since at most n trees can be added $\mathcal{S}$ in all, it follows that the total space consumed by elements in $\widehat{\mathcal{S}}$ is $O(n^2)$.

Now, we compute the total space consumed by the contexts in $\mathcal{E}$. Note that the teacher can return counterexamples of arbitrary size in response to a wrong conjecture. Suppose m is the size of the largest counterexample. Observe that an experiment is extracted from CE (procedure **ExpGen**) essentially by replacing some of the subtrees of CE with trees in $\mathcal{S}$, and exactly one subtree of CE with $\square$. But, since in the DAG form, common subtrees are shared between trees and contexts in $\mathcal{S}$ and $\mathcal{E}$, none of the above replacements consume any extra space. Hence, the size of the experiment extracted from CE is utmost the size of CE. Since there are at most n contexts in $\mathcal{E}$, the total space consumed by contexts in $\mathcal{E}$ is $O(mn)$. Putting together all observations so far, we get that the total space consumed by L^T is $O(mn + n^3)$.

Now, we compute the time consumed by L^T. It takes $O(n^3)$ membership queries to fill in the $O(n^3)$ table entries. Since each query is assumed to take $O(1)$ time, this takes a total of $O(n^3)$ time. The time taken to extract an experiment from a counterexample CE is linear on the size of CE. This is because procedure **ExpGen** involves making a constant number of membership queries for each node of CE (branch conditions in lines 3, 6, and 8) as CE is processed in a top down fashion. Thus, the time taken to extract an experiment from CE is at most $O(m)$. Since there can be at most n wrong conjectures, the total time spent on processing counterexamples is $O(mn)$. Putting these observations together we conclude that L^T takes $O(mn+n^3)$ time. We thus have the following theorem.

4 Automating Assume-Guarantee for Simulation

For M_1, M_2 and M_S, suppose we are to check if $M_1 \parallel M_2 \preccurlyeq M_S$. Recall from Section 2 that $M_1 \parallel M_2 \preccurlyeq M_S$ if and only if $\mathcal{T}(M_1 \parallel M_2) \subseteq \mathcal{T}(M_S)$, and $\mathcal{T}(M_1 \parallel M_2) = \mathcal{T}(M_1) \cap \mathcal{T}(M_2)$. Therefore, the verification problem is equivalent to checking if $\mathcal{T}(M_1) \cap \mathcal{T}(M_2) \subseteq \mathcal{T}(M_S)$. Now, define $\mathcal{T}_{max} = \overline{\mathcal{T}(M_1) \cap \overline{\mathcal{T}(M_S)}}$. Then

$$\mathcal{T}(M_1) \cap \mathcal{T}(M_2) \subseteq \mathcal{T}(M_S) \iff \mathcal{T}(M_2) \subseteq \mathcal{T}_{max}$$

Thus, $\mathcal{T}_{max}$ represents the maximal environment under which M_1 satisfies M_S, and

$$M_1 \parallel M_2 \preccurlyeq M_S \Leftrightarrow \mathcal{T}(M_2) \subseteq \mathcal{T}_{max}$$

Checking $\mathcal{T}(M_2) \subseteq \mathcal{T}_{max}$ is as expensive as directly checking $M_1 \parallel M_2 \preccurlyeq M_S$ since it involves both M_1 and M_2. In the following, we show how the L^T algorithm can be used for a more efficient solution.

Since regular tree languages are closed under intersection and complementation, $\mathcal{T}_{max}$ is a regular tree language. We therefore use the L^T algorithm to learn the canonical DTA for $\mathcal{T}_{max}$ in an incremental fashion. The key idea is that when a candidate query is made by L^T, the teacher checks if the **AG-NC** proof rule can be discharged by using the proposed candidate as the assumption. Empirical evidence (see Section 5) suggests that this often succeeds well before $\mathcal{T}_{max}$ is learnt, leading to substantial savings in time and memory consumption.

We now elaborate on how the teacher assumed by L^T is implemented. Specifically, the membership and candidate queries of L^T are processed as follows.

Membership Query. For a given tree t we are to check if $t \in \mathcal{T}_{max}$. This is equivalent to checking if $t \notin \mathcal{T}(M_1)$ or $t \in \mathcal{T}(M_S)$. In our implementation, both $\mathcal{T}(M_1)$ and $\mathcal{T}(M_S)$ are maintained as tree automata, and the above check amounts to membership queries on these automata.

Candidate Query. Given a DTA D we are to check if $\mathcal{L}(D) = \mathcal{T}_{max}$. We proceed in three steps as follows.

1. Check if **(C1)** $\mathcal{L}(D) \subseteq \mathcal{T}_{max} = \overline{\mathcal{T}(M_1) \cap \overline{\mathcal{L}(M_S)}}$. This is implemented using the complementation, intersection and emptyness checking operations on tree automata. If **C1** holds, then we proceed to step 2. Otherwise, we return some $t \in \mathcal{T}_{max} \setminus \mathcal{L}(D)$ as a counterexample to the candidate query D.
2. Check if **(C2)** $\mathcal{T}(M_2) \subseteq \mathcal{L}(D)$. If this is true, then **(C1)** and **(C2)** together imply that $\mathcal{T}(M_2) \subseteq \mathcal{T}_{max}$, and thus our overall verification procedure terminates concluding that $M_1 \parallel M_2 \preccurlyeq M_S$. Note that even though the procedure terminates $\mathcal{L}(D)$ may not be equal to $\mathcal{T}_{max}$. On the other hand, if **(C2)** does not hold, we proceed to step 3 with some $t \in \mathcal{T}(M_2) \setminus \mathcal{L}(D)$.
3. Check if $t \in \mathcal{T}_{max}$, which is handled as in the membership query above. If this is true, then it follows that $t \in \mathcal{T}_{max} \setminus \mathcal{L}(D)$, and hence we return t as a counterexample to the candidate query D. Otherwise, if $t \notin \mathcal{T}_{max}$ then $\mathcal{T}(M_2) \not\subseteq \mathcal{T}_{max}$, and therefore we conclude that $M_1 \parallel M_2 \not\preccurlyeq M_S$.

Thus, the procedure for processing the candidate query can either answer the query or terminate the entire verification procedure with a positive or negative outcome. Further, the reader may note that M_1 and M_2 are never considered together in any of the above steps. For instance, the candidate D is used instead of M_1 in step 1, and instead of M_2 in step 2. Since D is typically very small in size, we achieve significant savings in time and memory consumption, as reported in Section 5.

5 Experimental Results

Our primary target has been the analysis of concurrent message-passing C programs. Specifically, we have experimented with a set of benchmarks derived from the OpenSSL-0.9.6c source code. We analyzed the source code that implements the critical handshake that occurs when an SSL server and client establish a secure communication channel between them. The server and client source code contained roughly 2500 LOC each. Since these programs have an infinite state space, we constructed finite conservative labeled transition system (LTS) models from them using various abstraction techniques [6][1]. The abstraction process was carried out component-wise.

[1] Spurious counterexamples arising due to abstraction are handled by iterative counterexample guided abstraction refinement.

Name		Direct		AG		Gain			
	Result	T_1	M_1	T_2	M_2	M_1/M_2	$\|A\|$	MQ	CQ
SSL-1	*Invalid*	*	2146	**325**	**207**	10.4	8	265	3
SSL-2	*Valid*	*	2080	**309**	**163**	12.8	8	279	3
SSL-3	*Valid*	*	2077	**309**	**163**	12.7	8	279	3
SSL-4	*Valid*	*	2076	**976**	**167**	12.4	16	770	4
SSL-5	*Valid*	*	2075	**969**	**167**	12.4	16	767	4
SSL-6	*Invalid*	*	2074	**3009**	**234**	8.9	24	1514	5
SSL-7	*Invalid*	*	2075	**3059**	**234**	8.9	24	1514	5
SSL-8	*Invalid*	*	2072	**3048**	**234**	8.9	24	1514	5

Fig. 4. Experimental results. Result = specification valid/invalid; T_1 and T_2 are times in seconds; M_1 and M_2 are memory in mega bytes; $|A|$ is the assumption size that sufficed to prove/disprove specification; MQ is the number of membership queries; CQ is the number of candidate queries. A * indicates out of memory (2 GB limit). Best figures are in bold

We designed a set of eight LTS specifications on the basis of the SSL documentation. We verified these specifications on a system composed of one server (M_1) and one client (M_2) using both the brute-force composition ($M_1 \parallel M_2$), and our proposed automated AG approach. All experiments were carried out on a 1800+ XP AMD machine with 3 GB of RAM running RedHat 9.0. Our results are summarized in Figure 4. The learning based approach shows superior performance in all cases in terms of **memory** consumption (up to a **factor of 12.8**). An important reason behind such improvement is that the sizes of the (automatically learnt) assumptions that suffice to prove or disprove the specification (shown in column labeled $|A|$) are much smaller than the size of the second (client) component (3136 states).

6 Conclusion

We have presented an automated AG-style framework for checking simulation conformance between LTSs. Our approach uses a learning algorithm L^T to incrementally construct the weakest assumption that can discharge the premises of a non-circular AG proof rule. The learning algorithm requires a minimally adequate teacher that is implemented in our framework via a model checker. We have implemented this framework in the COMFORT [7] toolkit and experimented with a set of benchmarks based on the OPENSSL source code and the SSL specification. Our experiments indicate that in practice, extremely small assumptions often suffice to discharge the AG premises. This can lead to orders of magnitude improvement in the memory and time required for verification. Extending learning-based AG proof frameworks to other kinds of conformances, such as LTL model checking and deadlock detection, and to other AG-proof rules [3] remains an important direction for future investigation.

Acknowledgement. We thank the CAV 2005 referees for their invaluable comments and suggestions. The first author is also grateful to Corina Păsăreanu and Dimitra Giannakopoulou for informative discussions on assume-guarantee and learning.

References

1. R. Alur, P. Cerný, P. Madhusudan, and W. Nam. Synthesis of interface specifications for java classes. In *POPL*, pages 98–109, 2005.
2. D. Angluin. Learning regular sets from queries and counterexamples. *Information and Computation*, 75(2):87–106, 1987.
3. H. Barringer, D. Giannakopoulou, and C.S Pasareanu. Proof rules for automated compositional verification. In *Proc. of the 2nd Workshop on SAVCBS*, 2003.
4. M. Bernard and C. de la Higuera. Gift: Grammatical inference for terms. In *International Conference on Inductive Logic Programming*, 1999.
5. R. C. Carrasco, J. Oncina, and J. Calera-Rubio. Stochastic inference of regular tree languages. In *Proc. of ICGI*, pages 187–198. Springer-Verlag, 1998.
6. S. Chaki, E. Clarke, A. Groce, J. Ouaknine, O. Strichman, and K. Yorav. Efficient verification of sequential and concurrent C programs. *FMSD*, 25(2–3), 2004.
7. S. Chaki, J. Ivers, N. Sharygina, and K. Wallnau. The ComFoRT Reasoning Framework. In *Proc. of CAV*, 2005. to appear.
8. E. Clarke, D. Long, and K. McMillan. Compositional model checking. In *LICS*, 1989.
9. E. M. Clarke, O. Grumberg, S. Jha, Y. Lu, and H. Veith. Counterexample-guided abstraction refinement. In *Proc. of CAV*, 2000.
10. E. M. Clarke, O. Grumberg, and D. E. Long. Model checking and abstraction. *ACM Transactions on Programming Languages and System (TOPLAS)*, 16(5):1512–1542, 1994.
11. E. M. Clarke, O. Grumberg, and D. Peled. *Model Checking*. MIT Press, 2000.
12. J. M. Cobleigh, D. Giannakopoulou, and C. S. Păsăreanu. Learning assumptions for compositional verification. In *Proceedings of TACAS '03*.
13. H. Comon, M. Dauchet, R. Gilleron, F. Jacquemard, D. Lugiez, S. Tison, and M. Tommasi. *Tree Automata Techniques and Applications*, chapter 1. 2002. available at http://www.grappa.univ-lille3.fr/tata.
14. F. Drewes and J. Hogberg. Learning a regular tree language. In *LNCS 2710, pp. 279–291, Proc. Developments in Language Theory (DLT) '03*.
15. M.D. Ernst, J. Cockrell, W.G. Griswold, and D. Notkin. Dynamically discovering likely program invariants to support program evolution. In *Proc. of ICSE*, 1999.
16. P. Garca and J. Oncina. Inference of recognizable tree sets. Technical Report II/47/1993, Dept. de Sistemas Informticos y Computacin, Universidad Politcnica de Valencia, 1993.
17. E. M. Gold. Language identification in the limit. *Information and Control*, 10(5), 1967.
18. E. M. Gold. Complexity of automaton identification from given data. *Information and Control*, 37(3):302–320, June 1978.
19. A. Groce, D. Peled, and M. Yannakakis. Adaptive model checking. In *Tools and Algorithms for Construction and Analysis of Systems*, pages 357–370, 2002.
20. P. Habermehl and T. Vojnar. Regular model checking using inference of regular languages. In *Proc. of INFINITY'04*, 2004.
21. P. Oncina, J.; Garca. Identifying regular languages in polynomial time. World Scientific Publishing, 1992. Advances in Structural and Syntactic Pattern Recognition,.
22. D. Peled, M.Y. Vardi, and M. Yannakakis. Black box checking. In *FORTE/PSTV*, 1999.
23. A. Pnueli. In transition from global to modular temporal reasoning about programs. *Logics and models of concurrent systems*, pages 123–144, 1985.
24. R. L. Rivest and R. E. Schapire. Inference of finite automata using homing sequences. In *Information and Computation*, volume 103(2), pages 299–347, 1993.
25. Y. Sakakibara. Learning context-free grammars from structural data in polynomial time. *Theoretical Computer Science (TCS)*, 76(2-3):223–242, 1990.

Symbolic Compositional Verification by Learning Assumptions*

Rajeev Alur[1], P. Madhusudan[2], and Wonhong Nam[1]

[1] University of Pennsylvania
[2] University of Illinois at Urbana-Champaign
alur@cis.upenn.edu, madhu@cs.uiuc.edu, wnam@cis.upenn.edu

Abstract. The verification problem for a system consisting of components can be decomposed into simpler subproblems for the components using assume-guarantee reasoning. However, such compositional reasoning requires user guidance to identify appropriate assumptions for components. In this paper, we propose an automated solution for discovering assumptions based on the L^* algorithm for active learning of regular languages. We present a symbolic implementation of the learning algorithm, and incorporate it in the model checker NuSMV. Our experiments demonstrate significant savings in the computational requirements of symbolic model checking.

1 Introduction

In spite of impressive progress in heuristics for searching the reachable state-space of system models, scalability still remains a challenge. Compositional verification techniques address this challenge by a "divide and conquer" strategy aimed at exploiting the modular structure naturally present in system designs. One such prominent technique is the *assume-guarantee* rule: to verify that a state property φ is an invariant of a system M composed of two modules M_1 and M_2, it suffices to find an abstract module A such that (1) the composition of M_1 and A satisfies the invariant φ, and (2) the module M_2 is a refinement of A. Here, A can be viewed as an assumption on the environment of M_1 for it to satisfy the property φ. If we can find such an assumption A that is significantly smaller than M_2, then we can verify the requirements (1) and (2) using automated search techniques without having to explore M. In this paper, we propose an approach to find the desired assumption A automatically in the context of symbolic state-space exploration.

If M_1 communicates with M_2 via a set X of common boolean variables, then the assumption A can be viewed as a language over the alphabet 2^X. We compute this assumption using the L^* algorithm for learning a regular language using membership and equivalence queries [6, 21]. The learning-based approach

* This research was partially supported by ARO grant DAAD19-01-1-0473, and NSF grants ITR/SY 0121431 and CCR0306382.

K. Etessami and S.K. Rajamani (Eds.): CAV 2005, LNCS 3576, pp. 548–562, 2005.

produces a *minimal* DFA, and the number of queries is only polynomial in the size of the output automaton. The membership query is to test whether a given sequence σ over the communication variables belongs to the desired assumption. We implement this as a symbolic invariant verification query that checks whether the module M_1 composed with the sequence σ satisfies φ [16]. For an equivalence query, given a current conjecture assumption A, we first test whether M_1 composed with A satisfies φ using symbolic state-space exploration. If not, the counter-example provided by the model checker is used by the learning algorithm to revise A. Otherwise, we test if M_2 refines A, which is feasible since A is represented as a DFA. If the refinement test succeeds, we can conclude that M satisfies the invariant, otherwise the model checker gives a sequence σ allowed by M_2, but ruled out by A. We then check if the module M_1 stays safe when executed according to σ: if so, σ is used as a counter-example by the learning algorithm to adjust A, and otherwise, σ is a witness to the fact that the original model M does not satisfy φ.

While the standard L^* algorithm is designed to learn a particular language, and the desired assumption A belongs to a class of languages containing all languages that satisfy the two requirements of the assume-guarantee rule, we show that the above strategy works correctly. The learning-based approach to automatic generation of assumptions is appealing as it builds the assumption incrementally guided by the model-checking queries, and if it encounters an assumption that has a small representation as a minimal DFA, the algorithm will stop and use it to prove the property. In our context, the size of the alphabet itself grows exponentially with the number of communication variables. Consequently, we propose a symbolic implementation of the L^* algorithm where the required data structures for representing membership information and the assumption automaton are maintained compactly using ordered BDDs [9] for processing the communication variables.

For evaluating the proposed approach, we modified the state-of-the-art symbolic model checker NuSMV [10]. In Section 5, we report on a few examples where the original models contain around 100 variables, and the computational requirements of NuSMV are significant. The only manual step in the current prototype involves specifying the syntactic decomposition of the model M into modules M_1 and M_2. While the proposed compositional approach does not always lead to improvement (this can happen when no "good" assumption exists for the chosen decomposition into modules M_1 and M_2), dramatic gains are observed in some cases reducing either the required time or memory by one or two orders of magnitude, or converting infeasible problems into feasible ones.

Finally, it is worth pointing out that, while our prototype uses BDD-based state-space exploration, the approach can easily be adopted to permit other model checking strategies such as SAT-based model checking [8, 18] and counter-example guided abstraction refinement [15, 11].

Related Work. Compositional reasoning using assume-guarantee rules has a long history in the formal verification literature [22, 13, 1, 4, 17, 14, 19]. While such reasoning is supported by some tools (e.g. MOCHA [5]), the challenging task of finding the appropriate assumptions is typically left to the user and only a few attempts have been made to automate the assumption generation (in [3], the authors present some heuristics for automatically constructing assumptions using game-theoretic techniques).

Our work is inspired by the recent series of papers by the researchers at NASA Ames on compositional verification using learning [12, 7]. Compared to these papers, we believe that our work makes three contributions. First, we present a symbolic implementation of the learning algorithm, and this is essential since the alphabet is exponential in the number of communication variables. Second, we address and explain explicitly how the L^* algorithm designed to learn an unknown, but fixed, language is adapted to learn *some* assumption from a class of correct assumption languages. Finally, we demonstrate the benefits of the method by incorporating it in a state-of-the-art publicly available symbolic model checker.

It is worth noting that recently the L^* algorithm has found applications in formal verification besides automating assume-guarantee reasoning: our software verification project JIST uses predicate abstraction and learning to synthesize (dynamic) interfaces for Java classes [2]; [23] uses learning to compute the set of reachable states for verifying infinite-state systems; while [20] uses learning for *black box checking*, that is, verifying properties of partially specified implementations.

2 Symbolic Modules

In this section, we formalize the notion of a symbolic module, the notion of composition of modules and explain the assume-guarantee rule we use in this paper.

Symbolic Modules. In the following, for any set of variables X, we will denote the set of primed variables of X as $X' = \{x' \mid x \in X\}$. A predicate φ over X is a boolean formula over X, and for a valuation s for variables in X, we write $\varphi(s)$ to mean that s satisfies the formula φ.

A *symbolic module* is a tuple $M(X, X^I, X^O, \mathit{Init}, T)$ with the following components:

- X is a finite set of boolean *variables* controlled by the module,
- X^I is a finite set of boolean *input variables* that the module reads from its environment; X^I is disjoint from X,
- $X^O \subseteq X$ is a finite set of boolean *output variables* that are observable to the environment of M,
- $\mathit{Init}(X)$ is an *initial state predicate* over X,
- $T(X, X^I, X')$ is a *transition predicate* over $X \cup X^I \cup X'$ where X' represents the variables encoding the successor state.

Let $X^{IO} = X^I \cup X^O$ denote the set of communication variables. A *state* s of M is a valuation of the variables in X; i.e. $s : X \rightarrow \{\mathit{true}, \mathit{false}\}$. Let S denote the set of all states of M. An *input state* s^I is a valuation of the input variables X^I and an *output state* s^O is a valuation of X^O. Let S^I and S^O denote the set of input states and output states, respectively. Also, $S^{IO} = S^I \times S^O$. For a state s over a set X of variables, let $s[Y]$, where $Y \subseteq X$ denote the valuation over Y obtained by restricting s to Y.

The semantics of a module is defined in terms of the set of runs it exhibits. A *run* of M is a sequence $s_0, s_1, \cdots$, where each s_i is a state over $X \cup X^I$, such that $Init(s_0[X])$ holds, and for every $i \geq 0$, $T(s_i[X], s_i[X^I], s'_{i+1}[X'])$ holds (where $s'_{i+1}(x') = s_{i+1}(x)$, for every $x \in X$). For a module $M(X, X^I, X^O, Init, T)$ and a *safety property* $\varphi(X^{IO})$, which is a boolean formula over X^{IO}, we define $M \models \varphi$ if, for every *run* $s_0, s_1, \cdots$, for every $i \geq 0$, $\varphi(s_i)$ holds. Given a *run* $s_0, s_1, \cdots$ of M, the *trace* of M is a sequence $s_0[X^{IO}], s_1[X^{IO}], \cdots$ of input and output states. Let us denote the set of all the traces of M as $L(M)$. Given two modules $M_1 = (X_1, X^I, X^O, Init_1, T_1)$ and $M_2 = (X_2, X^I, X^O, Init_2, T_2)$ that have the same input and output variables, we say M_1 is a *refinement* of M_2, denoted $M_1 \sqsubseteq M_2$, if $L(M_1) \subseteq L(M_2)$.

Composition of Modules. The synchronous composition operator $\|$ is a commutative and associative operator that composes modules. Given two modules $M_1 = (X_1, X_1^I, X_1^O, Init_1, T_1)$ and $M_2 = (X_2, X_2^I, X_2^O, Init_2, T_2)$, with $X_1 \cap X_2 = \emptyset$, $M_1 \| M_2 = (X, X^I, X^O, Init, T)$ is a module where:

- $X = X_1 \cup X_2$, $X^I = (X_1^I \cup X_2^I) \setminus (X_1^O \uplus X_2^O)$, $X^O = X_1^O \uplus X_2^O$,
- $Init(X) = Init_1(X_1) \wedge Init_2(X_2)$,
- $T(X, X^I, X') = T_1(X_1, X_1^I, X_1') \wedge T_2(X_2, X_2^I, X_2')$.

We can now define the model-checking problem we consider in this paper:

> Given modules $M_1 = (X_1, X_1^I, X_1^O, Init_1, T_1)$ and $M_2 = (X_2, X_2^I, X_2^O, Init_2, T_2)$, with $X_1 \cap X_2 = \emptyset$, $X_1^I = X_2^O$ and $X_1^O = X_2^I$ (let $X^{IO} = X_1^{IO} = X_2^{IO}$), and a safety property $\varphi(X^{IO})$, does $(M_1 \| M_2) \models \varphi$?

Note that we are assuming that the safety property φ is a predicate over the common communication variables X^{IO}. This is not a restriction: to check a property that refers to private variables of the modules, we can simply declare them to be outputs.

Assume-Guarantee Rule. We use the following assume-guarantee rule to prove that a safety property φ holds for a module $M = M_1 \| M_2$. In the rule below, A is a module that has the same input and output variables as M_2:

$$\frac{\begin{array}{c} M_1 \| A \models \varphi \\ M_2 \sqsubseteq A \end{array}}{M_1 \| M_2 \models \varphi}$$

The rule above says that if there exists (some) module A such that the composition of M_1 and A is safe (i.e. satisfies the property φ) and M_2 refines A, then $M_1 \| M_2$ satisfies φ. We can view such an A as an *adequate assumption* between M_1 and M_2: it is an abstraction of M_2 (possibly admitting more behaviors than

M_2) that is a strong enough assumption for M_1 to make in order to satisfy φ. Our aim is to construct such an assumption A to show that $M_1 \| M_2$ satisfies φ. This rule is sound and complete [19].

3 Assumption Generation via Computational Learning

Given a symbolic module $M = M_1 \| M_2$ consisting of two sub-modules and a safety property φ, our aim is to verify that M satisfies φ by finding an A that satisfies the premises of the assume-guarantee rule explained in Section 2. Let us fix a pair of such modules $M_1 = (X_1, X_1^I, X_1^O, Init_1, T_1)$ and $M_2 = (X_2, X_2^I, X_2^O, Init_2, T_2)$ for the rest of this section.

Let L_1 be the set of *all* traces $\rho = s_0, s_1, \cdots$, where each $s_i \in S^{IO}$, such that either $\rho \notin L(M_1)$ or $\varphi(s_i)$ holds for all $i \geq 0$. Thus, L_1 is the largest language for M_1's environment that can keep M_1 safe. Note that the languages of the candidates for A that satisfy the first premise of the proof rule is precisely the set of all subsets of L_1.

Let L_2 be the set of traces of M_2, that is, $L(M_2)$. The languages of candidates for A that satisfy the second premise of the proof rule is precisely the set of all supersets of L_2. Since M_1 and M_2 are finite, it is easy to see that L_1 and L_2 are in fact regular languages. Let B_1 be the module corresponding to the minimum state DFA accepting L_1.

The problem of finding A satisfying both proof premises hence reduces to checking for a language which is a superset of L_2 and a subset of L_1. To discover such an assumption A, our strategy is to construct A using a *learning algorithm for regular languages*, called the L^* algorithm. The L^* algorithm is an algorithm for a learner trying to learn a *fixed* unknown regular language U through membership queries and equivalence queries. Membership queries ask whether a given string is in U. An equivalence query asks whether a given language $L(C)$ (presented as a DFA C) equals U; if so, the teacher answers 'yes' and the learner has learnt the language, and if not, the teacher provides a counter-example which is a string that is in the symmetric difference of $L(C)$ and U.

We adapt the L^* algorithm to learn *some* language from a *range* of languages, namely to learn a language that is a superset of L_2 and a subset of L_1. We do not, of course, construct L_1 or L_2 explicitly, but instead answer queries using model-checking queries performed on M_1 and M_2 respectively.

Given an equivalence query with conjecture $L(C)$, the test for equivalence can be split into two— checking the *subset* query $L(C) \subseteq U$ and checking the *superset* query $L(C) \supseteq U$. To check the subset query, we check if $L(C) \subseteq L_1$, and to check the superset query we check whether $L(C) \supseteq L_2$. If these two tests pass, then we declare that the learner has indeed learnt the language as the conjecture is an adequate assumption.

The membership query is more ambiguous to handle. When the learner asks whether a word w is in U, if w is not in L_1, then we can clearly answer in the negative, and if w is in L_2 then we can answer in the affirmative. However, if

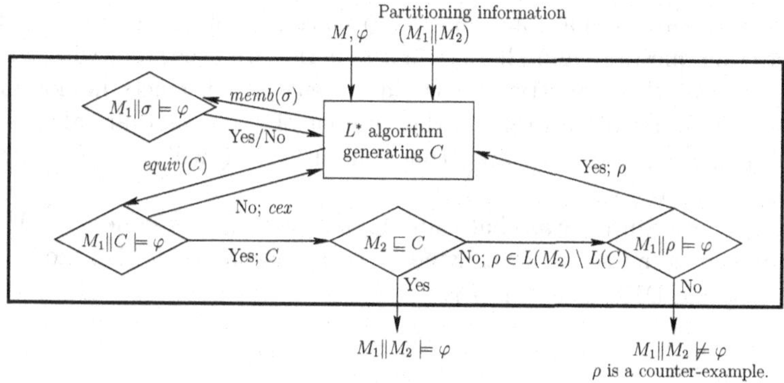

Fig. 1. Overview of compositional verification by learning assumptions

w is in L_1 but not in L_2, then answering either positively or negatively can rule out certain candidates for A.

In this paper, the strategy we have chosen is to always answer membership queries with respect to L_1. It is possible to explore alternative strategies that involve L_2 also.

Figure 1 illustrates the high-level overview of our compositional verification procedure. Membership queries are answered by checking safety with respect to M_1. To answer the equivalence query, we first check the subset query (by a safety check with respect to M_1); if the query fails, we return the counterexample found to L^*. If the subset query passes, then we check for the superset query by checking refinement with respect to M_2. If this superset query also passes, then we declare M satisfies φ since C satisfies both premises of the proof rule. Otherwise, we check if the counter-example trace ρ (which is a behavior of M_2 but not in $L(C)$) keeps M_1 safe. If it does not, we conclude that $M_1 \| M_2$ does not satisfy φ; otherwise, we give ρ back to the L^* algorithm as a counter-example to the superset query.

One of the nice properties of the L^* algorithm is that it takes time polynomial in the size of the minimal automaton accepting the learnt language (and polynomial in the lengths of the counter-examples provided by the teacher). Let us now estimate bounds on the size of the automaton constructed by our algorithm, and simultaneously show that our procedure always terminates. Note that all membership queries and all counter-examples provided by the teacher in our algorithm are consistent with respect to L_1 (membership and subset queries are resolved using L_1 and counter-examples to superset queries, though derived using M_2, are checked for consistency with L_1 before it is passed to the learner).

Now, if $M_1 \| M_2$ does indeed satisfy φ, then L_2 is a subset of L_1 and hence B_1 is an adequate assumption that witnesses the fact that $M_1 \| M_2$ satisfies φ. If $M_1 \| M_2$ does not satisfy φ, then L_2 is not a subset of L_1. Again B_1 is an adequate automaton which if learnt will show that $M_1 \| M_2$ does not satisfy φ (since this assumption when checked with M_2, will result in a run ρ which is exhibited by M_2 but not in L_1, and hence not safe with respect to M_1).

Hence B_1 is an adequate automaton to learn in both cases to answer the model-checking question, and all answers to queries are consistent with B_1. The L^* algorithm has the property that the automata it constructs monotonically grow with each iteration in terms of the number of states, and are always minimal. Consequently, we are assured that our procedure will not construct any automaton larger than B_1.

Hence our procedure always halts and reports correctly whether $M_1 \| M_2$ satisfies φ, and in doing so, it never generates any assumption with more states than the minimal DFA accepting L_1.

4 Symbolic Implementation of L^* Algorithm

4.1 L^* Algorithm

The L^* algorithm learns an unknown regular language and generates a minimal DFA that accepts the regular language. This algorithm was introduced by Angluin [6], but we use an improved version by Rivest and Schapire [21]. The algorithm infers the structure of the DFA by asking a teacher, who knows the unknown language, membership and equivalence queries.

Figure 2 illustrates the improved version of L^* algorithm [21]. Let U be the unknown regular language and Σ be its alphabet. At any given time, the L^* algorithm has, in order to construct a conjecture machine, information about a finite collection of strings over Σ, classified either as members or non-members of U. This information is maintained in an *observation table* (R, E, G) where R and E are sets of strings over Σ, and G is a function from $(R \cup R{\cdot}\Sigma) \cdot E$ to $\{0, 1\}$. More precisely, R is a set of representative strings for states in the DFA such that each representative string $r_q \in R$ for a state q leads from the initial state (uniquely) to the state q, and E is a set of experiment suffix strings that are used

```
R := {ε}; E := {ε};
foreach (a ∈ Σ) { G[ε, ε] := member(ε·ε); G[ε·a, ε] := member(ε·a·ε); }
repeat:
    while ((r_new := closed(R, E, G)) ≠ null) {
        add(R, r_new);
        foreach (a ∈ Σ), (e ∈ E) { G[r_new·a, e] := member(r_new·a·e); }
    }
    C := makeConjectureMachine(R, E, G);
    if ((cex := equivalent(C)) = null) then return C;
    else {
        e_new := findSuffix(cex);
        add(E, e_new);
        foreach (r ∈ R), (a ∈ Σ) {
            G[r, e_new] := member(r·e_new); G[r·a, e_new] := member(r·a·e_new);
    } }
```

Fig. 2. L^* algorithm

to distinguish states (for any two states of the automaton being built, there is a string in E which is accepted from one and rejected from the other). G maps strings σ in $(R \cup R{\cdot}\Sigma) \cdot E$ to 1 if σ is in U, and to 0 otherwise. Initially, R and E are set to $\{\varepsilon\}$, and G is initialized using membership queries for every string in $(R \cup R{\cdot}\Sigma) \cdot E$ (line 2). In line 4, it checks whether the observation table is *closed.* The function *closed(R, E, G)* returns *null* (meaning true) if for every $r \in R$ and $a \in \Sigma$, there exists $r' \in R$ such that $G[r \cdot a, e] = G[r', e]$ for every $e \in E$; otherwise, it returns $r{\cdot}a$ such that there is no r' satisfying the above condition. If the table is not closed, each such $r \cdot a$ (e.g., r_{new} is $r \cdot a$ in line 5) is simply added to R. The algorithm again updates G with regard to $r{\cdot}a$ (line 6). Once the table is closed, it constructs a conjecture DFA $C = (Q, q_0, F, \delta)$ as follows (line 8): $Q = R$, $q_0 = \varepsilon$, $F = \{r \in R \mid G[r, \varepsilon] = 1\}$, and for every $r \in R$ and $a \in \Sigma$, $\delta(r, a) = r'$ such that $G[r \cdot a, e] = G[r', e]$ for every $e \in E$. Finally, if the answer for the equivalence query is 'yes', it returns the current conjecture machine C; otherwise, a counter-example $cex \in ((L(C) \setminus U) \cup (U \setminus L(C))$ is provided by the teacher. The algorithm analyzes the counter-example cex in order to find the longest suffix e_{new} of cex that witnesses a difference between U and $L(C)$ (line 14). Intuitively, the current conjecture machine has guessed wrong since this point. Adding e_{new} to E reflects the difference in the next conjecture by splitting states in C. It then updates G with respect to e_{new}.

The L^* algorithm is guaranteed to construct a minimal DFA for the unknown regular language using only $O(|\Sigma|n^2 + n \log m)$ membership queries and at most $n - 1$ equivalence queries, where n is the number of states in the final DFA and m is the length of the longest counter-example provided by the teacher for equivalence queries.

As we discussed in Section 3, we use the L^* algorithm to identify $A(X_A, X_A^I, X_A^O, Init_A, T_A)$ satisfying the premises of the proof rule, where $X_A^{IO} = X^{IO}$. A is hence a language over the alphabet S^{IO}, and the L^* algorithm can learn A in time polynomial in the size of A (and the counter-examples). However, when we apply the L^* algorithm to analyze a large module (especially when the number of input and output variables is large), the large alphabet size poses many problems: (1) the constructed DFA has too many edges when represented explicitly, (2) the size of the observation table, which is polynomial in Σ and the size of the conjectured automaton, gets very large, and (3) the number of membership queries needed to fill each entry in the observation table also increases. To resolve these problems, we present a symbolic implementation of the L^* algorithm.

4.2 Symbolic Implementation

For describing our symbolic implementation for the L^* algorithm, we first explain the essential data structures the algorithm needs, and then present our implicit data structures corresponding to them. The L^* algorithm uses the following data structures:

- `string R[int]`: each `R[i]` is a representative string for i-th state q_i in the conjecture DFA.

- `string E[int]`: each `E[i]` is i-th experiment string.
- `boolean G1[int][int]`: each `G1[i][j]` is the result of the membership query for `R[i]`·`E[j]`.
- `boolean G2[int][int][int]`: each `G2[i][j][k]` is the result of the membership query for `R[i]`$\cdot a_j \cdot$`E[k]` where a_j is the j-th alphabet symbol in Σ.

Note that G of the observation table is split into two arrays, `G1` and `G2`, where `G1` is an array for a function from $R \cdot E$ to $\{0, 1\}$ and `G2` is for a function from $R \cdot \Sigma \cdot E$ to $\{0, 1\}$. The L^* algorithm initializes the data structures as following: `R[0]=E[0]=`ε, `G1[0][0]=`$member(\varepsilon \cdot \varepsilon)$, and `G2[0][i][0]=`$member(\varepsilon \cdot a_i \cdot \varepsilon)$ (for every $a_i \in \Sigma$). Once it introduces a new state or a new experiment, it adds to `R[]` or `E[]` and updates `G1` and `G2` by membership queries. These arrays also encode the edges of the conjecture machine: there is an edge from state q_i to q_j on a_k when `G2[i][k][l]=G1[j][l]` for every `l`.

For symbolic implementation, we do not wish to construct `G2` in order to construct conjecture DFAs by explicit membership queries since $|\Sigma|$ is too large. While the explicit L^* algorithm asks for each state r, alphabet symbol a and experiment e, if $r \cdot a \cdot e$ is a member, we compute, given a state r and a *boolean vector* v, the set of alphabet symbols a such that for every $j \leq |v|$, $member(r \cdot a \cdot e_j) = v[j]$. For this, we have the following data structures:

- `int nQ`: the number of states in the current DFA.
- `int nE`: the number of experiment strings.
- `BDD R[int]`: each `R[i]` ($0 \leq$ `i` $<$ `nQ`) is a BDD over X_1 to represent the set of states of the module M_1 that are reachable from an initial state of M_1 by the representative string r_i of the i-th state q_i: $postImage(Init_1(X_1), r_i)$.
- `BDD E[int]`: each `E[i]` ($0 \leq$ `i` $<$ `nE`) is a BDD over X_1 to capture a set of states of M_1 from which some state violating φ is reachable by the i-th experiment string e_i: $preImage(\neg\varphi(X_1), e_i)$.
- `booleanVector G1[int]`: Each `G1[i]` ($0 \leq$ `i` $<$ `nQ`) is the *boolean vector* for the state q_i, where the length of each boolean vector always equals to `nE`. Note that as `nE` is increased, the length of each boolean vector is also increased. For $i \neq j$, `G1[i]` $\neq$ `G1[j]`. Each element `G1[i][j]` of `G1[i]` ($0 \leq$ `j` $<$ `nE`) represents whether $r_i \cdot e_j$ is a member where r_i is a representative string for `R[i]` and e_j is an experiment string for `E[j]`: whether `R[i]` and `E[j]` have empty intersection.
- `booleanVector Cd[int]`: every iteration of the L^* algorithm splits some states of the current conjecture DFA by a new experiment string. More precisely, the new experiment splits every state into two *state candidates*, and among them, only reachable ones are constructed as states of the next conjecture DFA. The `Cd[]` vector describes all these state candidates and each element is the boolean vector of each candidate. $|$`Cd`$| = 2\cdot$`nQ`.

Given $M = M_1 \| M_2$ and φ, we initialize the data structures as follows. `R[0]` is the BDD for $Init_1(X_1)$ and `E[0]` is the BDD for $\neg\varphi$ since the corresponding representative and experiment string are ε, and `G1[0][0] = 1` since we assume that every initial state satisfies φ. In addition, we have the following functions that manipulate the above data structures for implementing the L^* algorithm implicitly (Figure 3 illustrates the pseudo-code for the important ones.):

- `BDD edges(int, booleanVector)`: this function, given an integer `i` and a boolean vector `v` ($0 \le$ `i` $<$ `nQ`, $|$`v`$| =$ `nE`), returns a BDD over X^{IO} representing the set of alphabet symbols by which there is an edge from state q_i to a state that has `v` as its boolean vector.
- `void addR(int, BDD, booleanVector)`: when we introduce a new state (whose predecessor state is q_i, the BDD representing edges from q_i is `b` and the boolean vector is `v`), `addR(i, b, v)` updates `R, G1` and `nQ`.
- `void addE(BDD[])`: given a new experiment string represented as an array of BDDs (where each BDD of the array encodes the corresponding state in the experiment string), this function updates `E, G1` and `nE`. It also constructs a new set `Cd[]` of state candidates for the next iteration.
- `boolean isInR(booleanVector)`: given a boolean vector `v`, `isInR(v)` checks whether `v` $=$ `G1[i]` for some `i`.
- `BDD[] findSuffix(BDD[])`: given a counter-example `cex` (from equivalence queries) represented by a BDD array, `findSuffix(cex)` returns a BDD array representing the longest suffix that witnesses the difference between the conjecture DFA and A.

While the L^* algorithm constructs a conjecture machine by computing `G2` and comparing between `G1` and `G2`, we directly make a symbolic conjecture DFA $C(X_C, X^{IO}, Init_C, F_C, T_C)$ with the following components:

- X_C is a set of boolean variables representing states in C ($|X_C| = \lceil \log_2 \texttt{nQ} \rceil$). Valuations of the variables can be encoded from its index for `R`.
- X^{IO} is a set of boolean variables defining its alphabet, which comes from M_1 and M_2.
- $Init_C(X_C)$ is an initial state predicate over X_C. $Init_C(X_C)$ is encoded from the index of the state q_0: $Init_C(X_C) = \bigwedge_{x \in X_C} (x \equiv 0)$.
- $F_C(X_C)$ is a predicate for accepting states. It is encoded from the indices of the states q_i such that `G1[`i`][0]`$=1$.
- $T_C(X_C, X^{IO}, X'_C)$ is a transition predicate over $X_C \cup X^{IO} \cup X'_C$; that is, if $T_C(i, a, j) = true$, then the DFA has an edge from state q_i to q_j labeled by a. To get this predicate, we compute a set of edges from every state q_i to every state candidate with boolean vector v by calling `edges(i, v)`.

This symbolic DFA $C(X_C, X^{IO}, Init_C, F_C, T_C)$ can be easily converted to a symbolic module $M_C(X_C, X^I, X^O, Init_C, T_C)$. Now, we can construct a symbolic conjecture DFA C using implicit membership queries by `edges()`. In addition, we have the following functions for equivalence queries:

- `BDD[] subsetQ(SymbolicDFA)`: our subset query is to check whether all strings *allowed by* C make M_1 stay in states satisfying φ. Hence, given a symbolic DFA $C(X_C, X^{IO}, Init_C, F_C, T_C)$, we check $M_1 \| M_C \models (F_C \rightarrow \varphi)$ by reachability checking, where M_C is a symbolic module converted from C. If so, it returns *null*; otherwise, it returns a BDD array as a counter-example.

```
BDD edges(int i, booleanVector v){
  BDD eds := true; // eds is a BDD over X^IO.
  foreach (0 ≤ j < nE){ // In the below, X_1^L = X_1 \ X^IO.
    if (v[j]) then eds := eds ∧ ¬(∃X_1^L, X_1'. R[i](X_1)∧T_1(X_1, X_1^I, X_1')∧E[j](X_1'));
    else eds := eds ∧ (∃X_1^L, X_1'. R[i](X_1) ∧ T_1(X_1, X_1^I, X_1') ∧ E[j](X_1'));
  }
  return eds;
}
void addR(int i, BDD b, booleanVector v){
  BDD io := pickOneState(b); // io is a BDD representing one alphabet symbol.
  R[nQ] := (∃X_1, X_1^I. R[i](X_1) ∧ io ∧ T_1(X_1, X_1^I, X_1'))[X_1' → X_1];
  G1[nQ++] := v;
}
void addE(BDD[] bs){
  BDD b := φ; // b is a BDD over X_1.
  for (j := length(bs); j > 0; j--) { b := ∃X_1^I, X_1'. b(X_1') ∧ bs[j] ∧ T_1(X_1, X_1^I, X_1'); }
  E[nE] := ¬b;
  foreach (0 ≤ i < nQ) {
    if ((R[i] ∧ E[nE]) = false) then G1[i][nE] := 1;
    else G1[i][nE] := 0;
    foreach (0 ≤ j < nE) { Cd[2i][j] := G1[i][j]; Cd[2i + 1][j] := G1[i][j]; }
    Cd[2i][nE] := 0;  Cd[2i + 1][nE] := 1;
  }
  nE++;
}
```

Fig. 3. Symbolic implementation of observation table

- `BDD[] supersetQ(SymbolicDFA)`: it checks that $M_2 \sqsubseteq C$. The return value is similar with `subsetQ()`. Since C is again a (symbolic) DFA, we can simply implement it by symbolic reachability computation for the product of M_2 and M_C. If it reaches the non-accepting state of C, the sequence reaching the non-accepting state is a witness showing $M_2 \not\sqsubseteq C$.
- `boolean safeM1(BDD [])`: given a string σ represented by a BDD array, it executes M_1 according to σ. If the execution reaches a state violating φ, it returns *false*; otherwise, returns *true*.

Figure 4 illustrates our symbolic compositional verification (SCV) algorithm. We initialize `nQ, nE, R, E, G1, Cd` and C in lines 1–3. We then compute a set of edges (a BDD) from every source state q_i to every state candidate with boolean vector `Cd[j]`. Once we reach a new state, we update `R, nQ` and `G1` by `addR()` (line 9). This step makes the conjecture machine closed. If we have a non-empty edge set by `edges()`, then we update the conjecture C (line 10). After constructing a conjecture DFA, we ask an equivalence query as discussed in Section 3 (lines 12–15). If we cannot conclude true nor false from the query, we are provided a counter-example from the teacher and get a new experiment string from the counter-example. `E, nE, Cd` and `G1` are then updated based on

```
boolean SCV(M1, M2, φ)
    nQ := 1; nE := 1; R[0] := Init1(X1); E[0] := ¬φ;
    G1[0][0] := 1; Cd[0] := 0; Cd[1] := 1;
    C := initializeC();
    repeat:
        foreach (0 ≤ i < nQ) {
            foreach (0 ≤ j < 2·nQ) {
                eds := edges(i, Cd[j]);
                if (eds ≠ false) then {
                    if (¬isInR(Cd[j])) then addR(i, eds, Cd[j]);
                    C := updateC(i, eds, indexofR(Cd[j]));
        }}}
        if ((cex := subsetQ(C)) = null) then {
            if ((cex := supersetQ(C) = null) then return true;
            else if (¬safeM1(cex)) then return false;
        }
        addE(findSuffix(cex));
```

Fig. 4. Symbolic compositional verification algorithm

the new experiment string. We implement this algorithm with the BDD package in a symbolic model checker NuSMV.

5 Experiments

We first explain an artificial example (called '`simple`') to illustrate our method and then report results on '`simple`' and four examples from the NuSMV package.

Example: Simple. Module M_1 has a variable x (initially set to 0 and updated by the rule $x' := y$ in each round where y is an input variable) and a dummy array that does not affect x at all. Module M_2 has a variable y (initially set to 0 and is never updated) and also a dummy array that does not affect y at all. For $M_1 \| M_2$, we want to check that x is always 0. Both dummy arrays are from an example *swap* known to be hard for BDD encoding [18]. Our tool explores M_1 and M_2 separately with a two-state assumption (which allows only $y = 0$), while ordinary model checkers will search whole state space of $M_1 \| M_2$.

For some examples from the NuSMV package, we slightly modified them because our tool does not support the full syntax of the NuSMV language. The primary selection criterion was to include examples for which NuSMV takes a long time or fails to complete. All experiments were performed on a Sun-Blade-1000 workstation using 1GB memory and SunOS 5.9. The results for the examples are shown in Table 1. We compare our symbolic compositional verification tool (SCV) with the invariant checking (with early termination) of NuSMV 2.2.2. The table has the number of variables in total, in M_1, in M_2 and the number of input/output variables between the modules, execution time in seconds, the

Table 1. Experimental results

example name	spec	tot var	M_1 var	M_2 var	IO var	SCV time	SCV peak BDD	SCV assumption states	NuSMV time	NuSMV peak BDD
simple1		69	36	33	4	19.2	607,068	2	269	3,993,976
simple2	true	78	41	37	5	106	828,842	2	4032	32,934,972
simple3		86	45	41	5	754	3,668,980	2	–	–
simple4		94	49	45	5	4601	12,450,004	2	–	–
guidance1	false	135	24	111	23	124	686,784	20	–	–
guidance2	true	122	24	98	22	196	1,052,660	2	–	–
guidance3	true	122	58	64	46	357	619,332	2	–	–
barrel1	false					20.3	345,436	3	1201	28,118,286
barrel2	true	60	30	30	10	23.4	472,164	4	4886	36,521,170
barrel3	true					–	–	too many	–	–
msi1		45	26	19	25	2.1	289,226	2	157	1,554,462
msi2	true	57	26	31	25	37.0	619,332	2	3324	16,183,370
msi3		70	26	44	26	1183	6,991,502	2	–	–
robot1	false	92	8	84	12	1271	4,169,760	11	654	2,729,762
robot2	true	92	22	70	12	1604	2,804,368	42	1039	1,117,046

peak BDD size and the number of states in the assumption we learn (for SCV). Entries denoted '–' mean that a tool did not complete within 2 hours.

The results of `simple` are also shown in Table 1. For `simple1` through `simple4`, we just increased the size of dummy arrays from 8 to 11, and checked the same specification. As we expected, SCV generated a 2-state assumption and performed significantly better than NuSMV.

The second example, `guidance`, is a model of a space shuttle digital autopilot. We added redundant variables to M_1 and M_2 and did not use a given variable ordering information as both tools finished fast with the original model and the ordering. The specifications were picked from the given pool: `guidance1`, `guidance2`, `guidance3` have the same models but have different specifications. For `guidance1`, our tool found a counter-example with an assumption having 20 states (If this assumption had been explicitly constructed, the 23 I/O variables would have caused way too many edges to store explicitly).

The third set, `barrel`, is an example for bounded model checking and no variable ordering works well for BDD-based tools. `barrel1` has an invariant derived from the original, but `barrel2` and `barrel3` have our own ones. `barrel1`, `barrel2` and `barrel3` have the same model scaled-up from the original, but with different initial predicates.

The fourth set, `msi`, is a MSI cache protocol model and shows how the tools scale on a real example. We scaled-up the original model with 3 nodes: `msi1` has 3 nodes, `msi2` has 4 nodes and `msi3` has 5 nodes. They have the same specification that is related to only two nodes, and we fixed the same component M_1 in all of them. As the number of nodes grew, NuSMV required much more time and the BDD sizes grew more quickly than in our tool.

`robot1` and `robot2` are robotics controller models and we again added redundant variables to M_1 and M_2, as in the case of `guidance` example. Even though SCV took more time, this example shows that SCV can be applied to models for which non-trivial assumptions are needed. More details about the examples are available at `http://www.cis.upenn.edu/~wnam/cav05/`.

References

1. M. Abadi and L. Lamport. Conjoining specifications. *ACM TOPLAS*, 17:507–534, 1995.
2. R. Alur, P. Cerny, P. Madhusudan, and W. Nam. Synthesis of interface specifications for Java classes. In *Proc. 32nd ACM POPL*, pages 98–109, 2005.
3. R. Alur, L. de Alfaro, T.A. Henzinger, and F. Mang. Automating modular verification. In *CONCUR'99: Concurrency Theory*, LNCS 1664, pages 82–97, 1999.
4. R. Alur and T.A. Henzinger. Reactive modules. *Formal Methods in System Design*, 15(1):7–48, 1999. A preliminary version appears in *Proc. 11th LICS, 1996.*
5. R. Alur, T.A. Henzinger, F. Mang, S. Qadeer, S. Rajamani, and S. Tasiran. MOCHA: Modularity in model checking. In *10th CAV*, pages 516–520, 1998.
6. D. Angluin. Learning regular sets from queries and counterexamples. *Information and Computation*, 75:87–106, 1987.
7. H. Barringer, C.S. Pasareanu, and D. Giannakopolou. Proof rules for automated compositional verification through learning. In *Proc. 2nd SVCBS*, 2003.
8. A. Biere, A. Cimatti, E. Clarke, and Y. Zhu. Symbolic model checking without BDDs. In *Proc. 5th TACAS*, pages 193–207, 1999.
9. R.E. Bryant. Graph-based algorithms for boolean-function manipulation. *IEEE Transactions on Computers*, C-35(8):677–691, 1986.
10. A. Cimatti, E. Clarke, E. Giunchiglia, F. Giunchiglia, M. Pistore, M. Roveri, R. Sebastiani, and A. Tacchella. NuSMV Version 2: An OpenSource Tool for Symbolic Model Checking. In *Proc. CAV 2002*, LNCS 2404, pages 359–364, 2002.
11. E. Clarke, O. Grumberg, S. Jha, Y. Lu, and H. Veith. Counterexample-guided abstraction refinement. In *Computer Aided Verification*, pages 154–169, 2000.
12. J.M. Cobleigh, D. Giannakopoulou, and C.S. Pasareanu. Learning assumptions for compositional verification. In *Proc. 9th TACAS*, LNCS 2619, pages 331–346, 2003.
13. O. Grümberg and D.E. Long. Model checking and modular verification. *ACM Transactions on Programming Languages and Systems*, 16(3):843–871, 1994.
14. T.A. Henzinger, S. Qadeer, and S. Rajamani. You assume, we guarantee: Methodology and case studies. In *Proc. CAV 98*, LNCS 1427, pages 521–525, 1998.
15. R.P. Kurshan. *Computer-aided Verification of Coordinating Processes: the automata-theoretic approach.* Princeton University Press, 1994.
16. K.L. McMillan. *Symbolic model checking.* Kluwer Academic Publishers, 1993.
17. K.L. McMillan. A compositional rule for hardware design refinement. In *CAV 97: Computer-Aided Verification*, LNCS 1254, pages 24–35, 1997.
18. K.L. McMillan. Applying SAT methods in unbounded symbolic model checking. In *Proc. 14th Computer Aided Verification*, LNCS 2404, pages 250–264, 2002.
19. K.S. Namjoshi and R.J. Trefler. On the completeness of compositional reasoning. In *CAV 2000: Computer-Aided Verification*, LNCS 1855, pages 139–153, 2000.
20. D. Peled, M.Y. Vardi and M. Yannakakis. Black box checking. *Journal of Automata, Languages and Combinatorics*, 7(2): 225-246, 2002.

21. R.L. Rivest and R.E. Schapire. Inference of finite automata using homing sequences. *Information and Computation*, 103(2):299–347, 1993.
22. E.W. Stark. A proof technique for rely-guarantee properties. In *FST & TCS 85*, LNCS 206, pages 369–391, 1985.
23. A. Vardhan, K. Sen, M. Viswanathan, and G. Agha. Actively learning to verify safety properties for FIFO automata. In *Proc. 24th FSTTCS*, pages 494–505, 2004.

Author Index

Lecture Notes in Computer Science

For information about Vols. 1–3472

please contact your bookseller or Springer

Vol. 3576: K. Etessami, S.K. Rajamani (Eds.), Computer Aided Verification. XV, 564 pages. 2005.

Vol. 3574: C. Boyd, J.M. González Nieto (Eds.), Information Security and Privacy. XIII, 586 pages. 2005.

Vol. 3573: S. Etalle (Ed.), Logic Based Program Synthesis and Transformation. VIII, 279 pages. 2005.

Vol. 3572: C. De Felice, A. Restivo (Eds.), Developments in Language Theory. XI, 409 pages. 2005.

Vol. 3570: A. S. Patrick, M. Yung (Eds.), Financial Cryptography and Data Security. XII, 376 pages. 2005.

Vol. 3569: F. Bacchus, T. Walsh (Eds.), Theory and Applications of Satisfiability Testing. XII, 492 pages. 2005.

Vol. 3567: M. Jackson, D. Nelson, S. Stirk (Eds.), Database: Enterprise, Skills and Innovation. XII, 185 pages. 2005.

Vol. 3565: G.E. Christensen, M. Sonka (Eds.), Information Processing in Medical Imaging. XXI, 777 pages. 2005.

Vol. 3562: J. Mira, J.R. Álvarez (Eds.), Artificial Intelligence and Knowledge Engineering Applications: A Bioinspired Approach, Part II. XXIV, 636 pages. 2005.

Vol. 3561: J. Mira, J.R. Álvarez (Eds.), Mechanisms, Symbols, and Models Underlying Cognition, Part I. XXIV, 532 pages. 2005.

Vol. 3560: V.K. Prasanna, S. Iyengar, P.G. Spirakis, M. Welsh (Eds.), Distributed Computing in Sensor Systems. XV, 423 pages. 2005.

Vol. 3559: P. Auer, R. Meir (Eds.), Learning Theory. XI, 692 pages. 2005. (Subseries LNAI).

Vol. 3557: H. Gilbert, H. Handschuh (Eds.), Fast Software Encryption. XI, 443 pages. 2005.

Vol. 3556: H. Baumeister, M. Marchesi, M. Holcombe (Eds.), Extreme Programming and Agile Processes in Software Engineering. XIV, 332 pages. 2005.

Vol. 3555: T. Vardanega, A. Wellings (Eds.), Reliable Software Technology - Ada-Europe 2005. XV, 273 pages. 2005.

Vol. 3553: T.D. Hämäläinen, A.D. Pimentel, J. Takala, S. Vassiliadis (Eds.), Embedded Computer Systems: Architectures, Modeling, and Simulation. XV, 476 pages. 2005.

Vol. 3552: H. de Meer, N. Bhatti (Eds.), Quality of Service - IWQoS 2005. XV, 400 pages. 2005.

Vol. 3551: T. Härder, W. Lehner (Eds.), Data Management in a Connected World. XIX, 371 pages. 2005.

Vol. 3548: K. Julisch, C. Kruegel (Eds.), Intrusion and Malware Detection and Vulnerability Assessment. X, 241 pages. 2005.

Vol. 3547: F. Bomarius, S. Komi-Sirviö (Eds.), Product Focused Software Process Improvement. XIII, 588 pages. 2005.

Vol. 3543: L. Kutvonen, N. Alonistioti (Eds.), Distributed Applications and Interoperable Systems. XI, 235 pages. 2005.

Vol. 3541: N.C. Oza, R. Polikar, J. Kittler, F. Roli (Eds.), Multiple Classifier Systems. XII, 430 pages. 2005.

Vol. 3540: H. Kalviainen, J. Parkkinen, A. Kaarna (Eds.), Image Analysis. XXII, 1270 pages. 2005.

Vol. 3537: A. Apostolico, M. Crochemore, K. Park (Eds.), Combinatorial Pattern Matching. XI, 444 pages. 2005.

Vol. 3536: G. Ciardo, P. Darondeau (Eds.), Applications and Theory of Petri Nets 2005. XI, 470 pages. 2005.

Vol. 3535: M. Steffen, G. Zavattaro (Eds.), Formal Methods for Open Object-Based Distributed Systems. X, 323 pages. 2005.

Vol. 3533: M. Ali, F. Esposito (Eds.), Innovations in Applied Artificial Intelligence. XX, 858 pages. 2005. (Subseries LNAI).

Vol. 3532: A. Gómez-Pérez, J. Euzenat (Eds.), The Semantic Web: Research and Applications. XV, 728 pages. 2005.

Vol. 3531: J. Ioannidis, A. Keromytis, M. Yung (Eds.), Applied Cryptography and Network Security. XI, 530 pages. 2005.

Vol. 3530: A. Prinz, R. Reed, J. Reed (Eds.), SDL 2005: Model Driven. XI, 361 pages. 2005.

Vol. 3528: P.S. Szczepaniak, J. Kacprzyk, A. Niewiadomski (Eds.), Advances in Web Intelligence. XVII, 513 pages. 2005. (Subseries LNAI).

Vol. 3527: R. Morrison, F. Oquendo (Eds.), Software Architecture. XII, 263 pages. 2005.

Vol. 3526: S.B. Cooper, B. Löwe, L. Torenvliet (Eds.), New Computational Paradigms. XVII, 574 pages. 2005.

Vol. 3525: A.E. Abdallah, C.B. Jones, J.W. Sanders (Eds.), Communicating Sequential Processes. XIV, 321 pages. 2005.

Vol. 3524: R. Barták, M. Milano (Eds.), Integration of AI and OR Techniques in Constraint Programming for Combinatorial Optimization Problems. XI, 320 pages. 2005.

Vol. 3523: J.S. Marques, N. Pérez de la Blanca, P. Pina (Eds.), Pattern Recognition and Image Analysis, Part II. XXVI, 733 pages. 2005.

Vol. 3522: J.S. Marques, N. Pérez de la Blanca, P. Pina (Eds.), Pattern Recognition and Image Analysis, Part I. XXVI, 703 pages. 2005.

Vol. 3521: N. Megiddo, Y. Xu, B. Zhu (Eds.), Algorithmic Applications in Management. XIII, 484 pages. 2005.

Vol. 3520: O. Pastor, J. Falcão e Cunha (Eds.), Advanced Information Systems Engineering. XVI, 584 pages. 2005.

Vol. 3519: H. Li, P. J. Olver, G. Sommer (Eds.), Computer Algebra and Geometric Algebra with Applications. IX, 449 pages. 2005.

Vol. 3518: T.B. Ho, D. Cheung, H. Liu (Eds.), Advances in Knowledge Discovery and Data Mining. XXI, 864 pages. 2005. (Subseries LNAI).

Vol. 3517: H.S. Baird, D.P. Lopresti (Eds.), Human Interactive Proofs. IX, 143 pages. 2005.

Vol. 3516: V.S. Sunderam, G.D.v. Albada, P.M.A. Sloot, J.J. Dongarra (Eds.), Computational Science – ICCS 2005, Part III. LXIII, 1143 pages. 2005.

Vol. 3515: V.S. Sunderam, G.D.v. Albada, P.M.A. Sloot, J.J. Dongarra (Eds.), Computational Science – ICCS 2005, Part II. LXIII, 1101 pages. 2005.

Vol. 3514: V.S. Sunderam, G.D.v. Albada, P.M.A. Sloot, J.J. Dongarra (Eds.), Computational Science – ICCS 2005, Part I. LXIII, 1089 pages. 2005.

Vol. 3513: A. Montoyo, R. Muñoz, E. Métais (Eds.), Natural Language Processing and Information Systems. XII, 408 pages. 2005.

Vol. 3512: J. Cabestany, A. Prieto, F. Sandoval (Eds.), Computational Intelligence and Bioinspired Systems. XXV, 1260 pages. 2005.

Vol. 3510: T. Braun, G. Carle, Y. Koucheryavy, V. Tsaoussidis (Eds.), Wired/Wireless Internet Communications. XIV, 366 pages. 2005.

Vol. 3509: M. Jünger, V. Kaibel (Eds.), Integer Programming and Combinatorial Optimization. XI, 484 pages. 2005.

Vol. 3508: P. Bresciani, P. Giorgini, B. Henderson-Sellers, G. Low, M. Winikoff (Eds.), Agent-Oriented Information Systems II. X, 227 pages. 2005. (Subseries LNAI).

Vol. 3507: F. Crestani, I. Ruthven (Eds.), Information Context: Nature, Impact, and Role. XIII, 253 pages. 2005.

Vol. 3506: C. Park, S. Chee (Eds.), Information Security and Cryptology – ICISC 2004. XIV, 490 pages. 2005.

Vol. 3505: V. Gorodetsky, J. Liu, V. A. Skormin (Eds.), Autonomous Intelligent Systems: Agents and Data Mining. XIII, 303 pages. 2005. (Subseries LNAI).

Vol. 3504: A.F. Frangi, P.I. Radeva, A. Santos, M. Hernandez (Eds.), Functional Imaging and Modeling of the Heart. XV, 489 pages. 2005.

Vol. 3503: S.E. Nikoletseas (Ed.), Experimental and Efficient Algorithms. XV, 624 pages. 2005.

Vol. 3502: F. Khendek, R. Dssouli (Eds.), Testing of Communicating Systems. X, 381 pages. 2005.

Vol. 3501: B. Kégl, G. Lapalme (Eds.), Advances in Artificial Intelligence. XV, 458 pages. 2005. (Subseries LNAI).

Vol. 3500: S. Miyano, J. Mesirov, S. Kasif, S. Istrail, P. Pevzner, M. Waterman (Eds.), Research in Computational Molecular Biology. XVII, 632 pages. 2005. (Subseries LNBI).

Vol. 3499: A. Pelc, M. Raynal (Eds.), Structural Information and Communication Complexity. X, 323 pages. 2005.

Vol. 3498: J. Wang, X. Liao, Z. Yi (Eds.), Advances in Neural Networks – ISNN 2005, Part III. XLIX, 1077 pages. 2005.

Vol. 3497: J. Wang, X. Liao, Z. Yi (Eds.), Advances in Neural Networks – ISNN 2005, Part II. XLIX, 947 pages. 2005.

Vol. 3496: J. Wang, X. Liao, Z. Yi (Eds.), Advances in Neural Networks – ISNN 2005, Part II. L, 1055 pages. 2005.

Vol. 3495: P. Kantor, G. Muresan, F. Roberts, D.D. Zeng, F.-Y. Wang, H. Chen, R.C. Merkle (Eds.), Intelligence and Security Informatics. XVIII, 674 pages. 2005.

Vol. 3494: R. Cramer (Ed.), Advances in Cryptology – EUROCRYPT 2005. XIV, 576 pages. 2005.

Vol. 3493: N. Fuhr, M. Lalmas, S. Malik, Z. Szlávik (Eds.), Advances in XML Information Retrieval. XI, 438 pages. 2005.

Vol. 3492: P. Blache, E. Stabler, J. Busquets, R. Moot (Eds.), Logical Aspects of Computational Linguistics. X, 363 pages. 2005. (Subseries LNAI).

Vol. 3489: G.T. Heineman, I. Crnkovic, H.W. Schmidt, J.A. Stafford, C. Szyperski, K. Wallnau (Eds.), Component-Based Software Engineering. XI, 358 pages. 2005.

Vol. 3488: M.-S. Hacid, N.V. Murray, Z.W. Raś, S. Tsumoto (Eds.), Foundations of Intelligent Systems. XIII, 700 pages. 2005. (Subseries LNAI).

Vol. 3486: T. Helleseth, D. Sarwate, H.-Y. Song, K. Yang (Eds.), Sequences and Their Applications - SETA 2004. XII, 451 pages. 2005.

Vol. 3483: O. Gervasi, M.L. Gavrilova, V. Kumar, A. Laganà, H.P. Lee, Y. Mun, D. Taniar, C.J.K. Tan (Eds.), Computational Science and Its Applications – ICCSA 2005, Part IV. LXV, 1362 pages. 2005.

Vol. 3482: O. Gervasi, M.L. Gavrilova, V. Kumar, A. Laganà, H.P. Lee, Y. Mun, D. Taniar, C.J.K. Tan (Eds.), Computational Science and Its Applications – ICCSA 2005, Part III. LXV, 1340 pages. 2005.

Vol. 3481: O. Gervasi, M.L. Gavrilova, V. Kumar, A. Laganà, H.P. Lee, Y. Mun, D. Taniar, C.J.K. Tan (Eds.), Computational Science and Its Applications – ICCSA 2005, Part II. LXV, 1316 pages. 2005.

Vol. 3480: O. Gervasi, M.L. Gavrilova, V. Kumar, A. Laganà, H.P. Lee, Y. Mun, D. Taniar, C.J.K. Tan (Eds.), Computational Science and Its Applications – ICCSA 2005, Part I. LXV, 1234 pages. 2005.

Vol. 3479: T. Strang, C. Linnhoff-Popien (Eds.), Location- and Context-Awareness. XII, 378 pages. 2005.

Vol. 3478: C. Jermann, A. Neumaier, D. Sam (Eds.), Global Optimization and Constraint Satisfaction. XIII, 193 pages. 2005.

Vol. 3477: P. Herrmann, V. Issarny, S. Shiu (Eds.), Trust Management. XII, 426 pages. 2005.

Vol. 3476: J. Leite, A. Omicini, P. Torroni, P. Yolum (Eds.), Declarative Agent Languages and Technologies II. XII, 289 pages. 2005. (Subseries LNAI).

Vol. 3475: N. Guelfi (Ed.), Rapid Integration of Software Engineering Techniques. X, 145 pages. 2005.

Vol. 3474: C. Grelck, F. Huch, G.J. Michaelson, P. Trinder (Eds.), Implementation and Application of Functional Languages. X, 227 pages. 2005.